The Ḥusainī Revolution of Islām

By the same author

- The Essence of Islam

About the Author

Professor Saiyed Jafar Reza, Born on December 1, 1939 at Utraon close to Allahabad, Professor Saiyed Jafar Reza is an internationally known scholar, thinker and litterateur. His father late Saiyed Khairat Hasan was a freedom fighter, scholar and writer. Reza has not only continued the family tradition of scholarship, but also broadened and enriched it. He did his Ph.D. in two different disciplines at the University of Allahabad, plus D. Litt. at ihe University of Kashmir, Srinagar.

Reza is the brilliant product of the University of Allahabad, Where he started his academic career in 1965 After a short stay at the University of Kashmir (1980-83) as a reader, he returned to the University of Allahabad where he served as a Prem Chand Chair Professor until his retirement in 2000.

Reza has more than four dozen books to his credit. His literary work is path breaking and his verse is personal discovery and vision of life. He looks at all religions from spiritual perspectives and hence his views on Islam are different from others.

Reza is an academic of great repute an educational administrator of wide experience and above all a true human being full of love and compassion.

The Ḥusainī Revolution of Islām

SAIYED JAFAR REZA
M.A., Ph.D., D.Phil., D.Litt.

CONCEPT PUBLISHING COMPANY PVT. LTD.
NEW DELHI-110059

ISBN-13: 978-93-5125-217-7

First Published 2016

Published and Printed by

Concept
Since 1974

Concept Publishing Company Pvt. Ltd.
Regd. Office:
A/15-16, Commercial Block, Mohan Garden,
New Delhi-110059 (INDIA)
Phones : 25351460, 25351794, *Fax* : 091-11-25357109
Email : publishing@conceptpub.com
Website: www.conceptpub.com

Editorial Office:
H-13, Bali Nagar, New Delhi-110 015, India.

Cataloging in Publication Data—DK Courtesy: D.K. Agencies (P) Ltd. <docinfo@dkagencies.com>

Reza, Saiyed Jafar, 1939- **author.**
The Ḥusainī revolution of Islām / Saiyed Jafar Reza (M.A., Ph.D., D.Phil., D. Litt.).
pages cm
Includes bibliographical references and index.
ISBN 9789351252177

1. ʻAlī ibn al-Ḥusayn, -680. 2. Imams (Shiites)—Biography. 3. Karbalā, Battle of, Karbalā, Iraq, 680. 4. Islamic Empire—History—661-750. I. Title.
BP193.13.A3R49 2016 DDC 297.64 23

To all the activists of Truth and Justice,

"And say not those who are slain in the path of God that they are dead; Nay, *(they are)* living, but ye perceive not."

(*Qur'an* : 2/154)

Lord Jesus saith unto his disciples : "The harvest truly is plenteous, but the labourers are few; Pay ye therefore the Lord of the harvest, that he will send forth labourers into his harvest."

(*Matthew* : 9/37-38)

Preface

You would have many times witnessed a unique mourning procession, people with bare foot, beating their chest and head, various standards in hand, a replica of coffin on their shoulders, a horse dressed with warlike apparels, slow-paced, walking in the mourning procession and the mourners producing heart rending sound "Ḥusain, Imām Ḥusain, Ḥusain!" A question would have arisen in your mind. What are all these? Who was this Ḥusain, as chanting his name in their lips tears roll down from their eyes? You would have observed there also, thousands of people with funeral bier and everyone wants to extend his shoulder and get his blessings. Of course, there is stampede pull and push injuries, but there is no quarrel at all, only the attempt to extend one's own shoulder! Probably this may be the feeling that some atrocity was on a particular person that even his funeral rituals could not take place and his dead body was left unattended. Even then you would have also observed thousands of people are proceeding in the procession. Some people are displaying their skills and talents with swords, spears and attacking with axes on each other, but, there is no disturbance, people are moving with silence. There are also procession of camels, horses and other animals. Perhaps this is the procession on somebody's death reminding some war.

Drinking water cells are arranged on many places on the way, in memories of thirst of the great martyr. Hindu-Muslim-Christian-Sikh and all other people are craving to quench his thirst. The drinking water taken is beckoning :

> Brothers! come, if craving to quench thirst,
> Here is, Ḥusain's beneficent overflowing river.

Yes Sir, your guess is correct. This is the famous mourning

procession of Imām Ḥusain, who became a martyr with his supporters and family for the cause and survival of humanity; fighting in a battle against injustice in hunger and thirst. This battle which he fought for justice is called the Ḥusainī Revolution in modern terminology.

It is essential for the apt knowledge of the Ḥusainī Revolution that one may know that background in which such distintegration spread in side Islām that there was danger even for the existence of Islām.

The very objective of the Ḥusainī Revolution was to re-establish Islām eradicating the entire distortions. The person and Hero of the Ḥusainī Revolution Imām Ḥusain, who was none other than the real grandson of Prophet Muḥammad, became immortal with his supporters and family members to safeguard the very humanity fighting the war of justice against injustice and evils in a state of hunger and thirst. A detailed discussion would follow on this subject in the ensuing pages.

Islām is not just a way of worship. It is also not the name of performing rituals. Every human activity, if performed in accordance with Divine Will, is virtue and the defiance of His Will is vice. The man who is subject to Divine sovereignty is neither entitled to Heaven nor Hell, he creates his own heaven or Hell in this world and hereafter by his own free will. Islām is another name for the crusade to safeguard human rights. But instead of being a single one time campaign, Islām, like other great religions of the world, has waged a perpetual struggle to secure truth and justice, but does not only accept some of their campaigns. For example in the Indian perspective it gives credit to the positive human values in Jainism, Buddhism, Hinduism and in the non-Indian perspective it accepts the best of Judaism, Christianity etc.

The reason for the advent of Islām from 'Arab country, of course, the mere advent from somewhere, never mean to confine it to the place of origin only. There may be a special context for its advent from 'Arabia as it exhibits a beautiful instance of cultural ups and down. At the initial state, there is Mesopotomia, from where the universe had got, received civilization and culture and the later period was that, wherein there was a loss of most of the human-values. During the same period, the founder of Islām was born, who saved the 'Arabs from their distress. The beacon of Islām was not confined to 'Arabs alone. Not even confined alone to Muslims. Islām beacons to all human beings of the universe. It would be appropriate to study the following verses of the holy Qur'an on religious mindedness, because it is clear from them what does the holy Qur'an say:

> "Verily ! those believe *(in that)* which is revealed unto thee *(O' Our Apostle Muḥammad)* and those who are Jews and Christians and Sābeans—whosoever believeth in God and the Last Day *(of Judgement)* and does right – surely their reward is with their Lord, and there shall be no fear come upon them neither shall they grieve." (*Qur'an* : 2/62)

For the Ḥusainī Revolution, which has re-established Islām and obtained Inernational reputation, and which requires the availability of high standard hooks, encourging situation is not visualized, because during the eighty nine years of reign of Umāyyites, their malicious attititude had ruined the Islāmic fabric, specially for *Ahlu'l-Bayt* or *'Itrat* (Household or Progeny of the Prophet Muḥammad) in particular against Imām 'Alī and his followers, although the adoration and love of the *Ahlu'l-Bayt* has been made obligatory on every Muslim, as enjoined by the holy Qur'an. In these verses quoted below, the *Ahlu'l-Bayt* have been praised collectively.[1] The Qur'an says :

> "Say thou (*O' Our Apostle Muḥammad*): I demand not of you any recompense for it (*the toils of the apostleship*) save the love of (*my*) relatives." (*Qur'an* : 42/23)

The holy Prophet was under the Divine Command and also best he knew 'Ali and the wishes of *Ummah* chosen. So for 'Alī-Ibn-Abū Ṭālib, the Prophet's words were :

> "Thou art to me what Aaron was to Moses."[2]

Thus every Muslim concludes his daily five time *Namāż* with the *Salām* (Salutation) declaring his solidarity with the holy prophet and his pious progeny :

> "O' Lord ! bestow mercy on our Divine-leader and Commander Muḥammad and his pious progeny as Thou hast bestowed mercy on Abraham and his pious progeny, Verily, Thou art the Most Praiseworthy, the Most exalted, and O' Lord shower Your blessing on Muḥammad and his holy progeny as Thou hast showered blessing on Abraham and his holy progeny, Verily, Thou art the Most Praiseworthy and the Most Exalted."[3]

The salutation of the Shi'īs is much the same in which they too invoke God's blessing for the holy Prophet Muḥammad and his holy progeny.

But in total contrast of the Islāmic faith, Umāyyites made it mandatory to curse and abuse Imām 'Alī, Progeny of the Prophet Muḥammad in every Friday Sermon at every Masjid in their entire empire during their eighty nine years reign. Imagine, if the largest empire of the world of the time, reigning in todays' about thirty three countries of the world, (see Figure 1) with all its might has been bent upon to constantly spread malicious information and incur character assassination. Would any good be safe. But today picture is reversed, because of the fact that the Ḥusainī Revolution has turned the table.

Nevertheless in hostile cicumstances to expect from any historian to report objectively correct information, when most of the writers of the period were stipendiaries of the the empire. So what they wrote, all was not good. Some of them were influenced by *Nāṣibīs*, (People against the Progeny of the Prophet Muḥammad), who have not left any stone unturned in creating illusions and confusions. Regarding Ibn Kathīr (d. 1372 AD), whose scholastic learning is admired, renowned scholar Ziyā Aḥmad Badāyūnī says:

> "He was influenced by *Nāṣibīs* Tradition showering praise on Amīr Mu'āwiya and Yażīd and finds faults in the *Ḥadīth* (Tradition, the words of the holy Prophet, Muḥammad), regarding *Ahlu'l-Bayt*, which is evident from his famous book *al-Bidāyah w'an-Nihāyah.*"[4]

In support of his views about the Progeny of the Prophet Muḥammad, he has written that 'Abu'l Khair Qażwīnī (d. 1193 AD) believed Yażīd as *Imām* (next pivot of Islām, after *Rasūl.*) and *Mujtahid* (competent religious scholar).[5] Similarly, Shaykh 'Abu'l Mughīth Ḥanbalī (d.1187 AD) wrote a book in the praise of Yażid entitled *Fazāil Yażīd-bin-Mu'āwiya.* Ibn-Kathīr praise him for his work, saying, he was a pure Ḥanbalī. [6] Qāzī Abū Bakr-bin-'Arabī (Not to be confused with great Ṣūfī Ibn-'Arabī) has crossed all the limits asserting that Imām Ḥusain was killed by the sword of his grandfather (holy Prophet Muḥammad).[7]

Shaykh Ibn-Taymiyya (d. 1328 AD)'s prejudice and narrow outlook is known to everyone. Famous scholar 'Abu'l 'Olā Maudūdī (d. 1979 AD) says :

> "All are aware of Imām Ibn-Taymiyya, if he feels in a person even a smell of being the followers of Imām 'Alī, he never allows him".[8]

He was against the admonishment of evils of Yażīd. Almost all historians have discussed regarding the arrest of family members of Imām Ḥusain in Damascus (Syria). In an attempt of dishonouring them, he denied the atrocities in the jail and dismissed inmemberable witnesses in his unsuccessful attempt of saving Yażīd, Ibn-Taymiyya asserted that the family members Imām Ḥusain were not arrested and brought to Syria at all ! Patting on back of his dear disciple Ibn-Jaużī (d. 1201 AD), Ibn-Taymiyya said that he and 'Abu'l Mughīth both would be in Heaven together.[9]

Ibn-ul-Rabi'ya Sulaymān (d. 1236 AD) enumerated the achievements of three Caliphs (Abū Bakr, 'Omar and 'Othmān) in his history, but not at all discussed regarding the fourth Caliph 'Alī.[10] Famous historian Ibn-Khaldūn, Abū Żayd 'Abdu'r-Raḥmān (d. 1405 AD) started the description of great Battle of Karbala, but not written the incidents of Karbala. After the discussion of incident regarding Imām Ḥusain's Peace-Ambassador Muslim-bin-'Aqīl for Kufa left three leaves of the book blank.[11] Because, if he discusses about the great Battle of Karbala, then he would have to write against his favourite people.

Abū Ja'far Muḥammad Jarīr Ṭabarī (d.923 AD) has been considered to be a reliable historian by all catergories. I have also given the maximum referrences, but some dangerous virus influenced by Nāṣibī Tradition are seen in his book, which have been condemmed by scholars after sharply criticizing it. For example : He has written that the peace proposal of Imām Ḥusain suggesting his going to Damascus (Syria), was with the intension of :

> "To give his hand in the hands of Yażīd".[12]

It means Imām Ḥusain was agreeable to accept Yażīd as true Caliph. It is in total contradiction of all the facts. Renowned scholar Ziyā Aḥmad Badāyūnī has discussed in details on this issue and has condemmed with strong words after criticizing on the basis of seven points. His conclusion is:

> "We can say with confidence that this portion has been added by Nāṣibīs, the objective being to diminish the high

> conduct and noble mission of Ḥusain. These missleading words do not fit in the Islāmic standard hisory, therefore, are not reliable."[13]

Almost the same condition prevails in other historians, such as al-Wāqadī (d. 802 AD), Ibn S'ad, Abū-'Abdu'llāh Muḥammad (d. 844 AD), Ibn-Qutaybā (d. 889 AD), al-Yaqūbī (d. 897 AD), Ibn Athīr, 'Iżżu'd-Din, 'Abu'l Ḥasan (d. 1232 AD), 'Abu'l Fidā, 'Imādu'd-Dīn, Ismā'īl (d. 1331 AD), al-Žahabī (d.1347 AD), Ḥusain Dayār Bakrī, (d. 1558 AD), *as*-Suyūtı, Jalālu'd-Dīn (d. 1505 AD), Abū Ḥanīfā Dīnāwarī (d.1558 AD), al-Balāžurī, Aḥmad-bin-Yaḥyā (d. 893 AD), Ibn Ḥajar, al-Haythamī, al-Makkī (d.1565 AD), Damīrī, Kamālu'd-Dīn Muḥammad (d. 1405 AD) etc.

Therefore, we should not be contended by seeing the big names of Muslim historians and if at all there is any information regarding the family members of the Prophet of Islām, discussions and presented hypotheses in the books should be taken only after absolute analysis.

The famous statement of Urdu translator of *Jām'au's-Ṣaḥīḥul-Bukhārī,* Mirżā Ḥairat Dehlawī (d. 1928 AD) has astonished the world. How dare a person to tell such a big lie! His view is that there was no Battle of Karbala at all. Imām-Ḥusain went away to Rome.

It is clear that hypotheses influenced by Nāṣibī Tradition are being presented. If anybody dares enough say the truth then he would loose his life. Imām Nasā'ī, 'Abdu'r-Rahmān (d. 915 AD) who is regarded as one of the author of the *Ṣaḥiḥu'l-Sittah* (six authentic collections) on which Muslims believe and who is one of the six greatest personalities of a school of Muslim theology, whose words are considered true and most authentic :

> "When authored his book *al-Khaṣayṣ Murtazwī* on the virtues of Ḥazarat 'Alī, desired to read it out at the Jam'a-Mosque of Damascus (Syria). As the Nāṣibī attitude had commonly spread among the mass, because of the influence of Umayyites' kingdom, Imām Nasā'ī with a view of reform presented his work. People asked him about the virtues of Amīr Mu'āwiya. He told the audience, if Mu'āwiya could be pardoned would be enough and narated the superiority of Ḥazarat 'Alī... At this people beated Imām Nasā'ī to the extent that he became a martyr on this score."[14]

Nāṣibī Tradition has no *locus stande* in the Islāmic society.[15] Islām is the religion of tolerance, harmony and peaceful coexistence.

Extremist tendency of Nāṣibīs in Islām has borne the worst consequences when the fascism in the form of terrorism has found its ways into human instinct and manifested itself in different fashions. They may be terned as 'enemies of Islām.' As Nāṣibīs denied the award of God for *Muwaddatu'l-Qurba,* love of the relatives of holy Prophet (*Qur'an* : 42/23) incumbent upon every Muslim. So, in view of Shāh 'Abdu'l Ażīż Muḥaddith Dehlawī (d.1824 AD) viewed Nāṣibīs in the category of dogs and pigs, the most hated impure by nature, rather worst than :

"Nāṣibīs are worst than dogs and pigs."[16]

Imām Ḥusain's eldest son Imām Żainu'l-Ābidīn was present at the great Battle of Karbala, but could not participate in *Jihād* being seriously indisposed of. He and other family members, say the family of holy Prophet Muḥammad, were made prisoners tied in string from Karbala to Kufā and Damascus.

They are eye witnesses of brute mass massacre and tyranny in the way and in the courts. On the return to Medina, they told the visitors about Imām Ḥusain's mission and the incidents. These became most authentic source for future writers.

The event of Karbala had the deepest and most painful impact on Imām Żainu'l-Ābidīn. He had made the propagation of the message of Karbala, the exclusive goal of his life. He institutionalized the message of the martyrdom of Karbala which in course of time became the guiding force in the name of *Ażādārī* or *Tāżiādārī* (commemoration ceremony) and became the inseparable part of Islāmic religious life, especially for Shi'īs.

Besides, the eye witnesses of the family members of Imām Ḥusain, the next reliable sources are *Maqtal* (pl. *Maqātil*), recorded facts of the martyrdom of Imām Ḥusain. Firstly written in 'Arabic, then in Persian languages. It has proved to be source for the histotian from time to time.

Among the valuable witnesses of the great Battle of Karbala 'Oqbā-bin-Sam'ān is very important. who was in the sevice of Ḥazarat Rabāb, wife of Imām Ḥusain. Similarly, Zaḥḥāk-bin-'Obaydu'llāh Mashriqī had also survived. Both are eye witnesses of all incidents. 'Allāmmah Saiyed Mujtabā Ḥasan Kāmānpurī (d. 1974 AD) has published translations of both accounts of the great incidences in their *Maqātil* along with his valuable prefaces. These books are considered very authentic source of the great Battle of Karbala. *Maqtal* of Ḥamīd-bin-Muslim is also impotant to know the enemy side version, as he was clerk in the Yażīd army.

One of the Imām 'Alī's companions, Aṣbāgh-bin-Nabātā Mujāshaī's *Maqtal-i-Karbal,* is also based on information collected from contemporary sources.

Famous author of eighth century, Abū-Mikhnaf,[17] Lūt-bin-Yaḥyā Aždī (d. 774 AD) has given detailed account of the incidents in his Maqtal, which has been profoundly quoted by famous historian Jarīr Ṭabarī (d. 922 AD) as a reliable source. His other work *Kitāb al-Mukhtār-bin-'Obaidā* is also extremely valuable to understand the series of happenings after the great Battle of Karbala. Of the same century Abū-Aḥmad Baṣarī authored four books, *Žikru'l Ḥusain, Maqtalu'l Ḥusain, Akhbāru'l Tawwābīn and Akhbāru'l Mukhtār* and Abū-Isḥāq Ibrāhīm Nahāwandī his *Maqtalu'l Ḥusain.*

In nineth century, the Maqātil of Abū-'Abdu'llāh Muḥammad-bin-'Omarū Wāqdī Madanī (d. 822 AD), al-Khwārizmī, Muḥammad-bin-Mūsā (d..850 AD), and Ibrāhīm-bin-Muḥammad Saqafī Kūfī (d. 895 AD), authored three books, *Maqtalu'l Ḥusain, al-Tawwābīn* and *Akhbāru'l Yažīd.*

Al-Khawārižmī, Abū Jā'far Muḥammad-bin-Mūsā (d. 850 AD) was the greatest mathematician and astronomer of his time, who introduced *Hindsah* (numerals) and concept of algebra into European mathematics. He had prepared a horoscope describing the position of stars and planets on 10 October, 680 at the time of assassination of Imām Ḥusain. No scholar has paid attention towards his findings, although so many secret matters could be understood with its help, such as appearance of black and thick storms arising in the canals and so many facts, after the assassination of Imām Ḥusain. For the first time various facts of astronomy and astrology have been discussed in this humble book.

Shaykh Ṣadūq, Ibn-Bābūya, Abū Ja'far Muḥammad al-Qummī (d. 991 AD) has been considered great religious scholar, source of authority and reference point for emulation. His book *Maqtal u'l Ḥusain* is very authentic document with special significance. It contains the incidents told by infallible *Ithna-'Ash'arī* (Twelver) Imāms, which are unquestionable source of authenticity. This book is also important for making available *Žiyārat Nāḥiyā,* an edict for well-being, sanctioned by Imām Mahdī Ākhiru'ž-Žamān. It included the names of the martyrs and their killers, which is the primary source for later writings. The *Maqātil* of Abū-'Abdu'llāh Muḥammad-bin-Žakariyā Baṣarī (d. 910 AD), 'Abdu'l 'Ažiž-bin-Yaḥyā (d. 943 AD) are also important.

Al-Mufīd, Ibn-al-Ma'allim, Shaykh Abū-'Abdu'llāh Muḥammad (d. 1022 AD)'s *al-Irshād* and *al-Majlisī,* Muḥammad Bāqir (d. 1699 AD)'s voluminous *Biḥāru'l Anwār* are also considered as the primary sources. But most famous primary source book are Ibn-Ṭāūs, 'Alī-bin-Mūsā-bin-J'āfar-bin-Muḥammad (d. 1265 AD)'s *al-Lahūf 'Alā Qatlu'l Ṭafūf* alias *Asūf.* Many other Maqātil may also be mentioned, but with a view to avoid protractedness, a number of them could not be mentioned. Among some very valuable works have been included in the Bibliography of this book. Morever, 'Allāmah Majtabā Ḥasan Kāmānpurī has pulished a number of Maqātil as extracts from reputed historian. Unfortunately some are not found originally, but they have been referred by scholars.

Renowned scholar and writer, Saiyedu'l 'Ulmā 'Alī Naqī Naqavī (d. 1988 AD) has written about fifty books regarding Battle of Karbala and from among them *Shuhada-i-Karbala, Mujāhida-i-Karbala,* and *Shahīd-i-Insāniyat* are essential works. Of them *Shahīd-i-Insāniyat* is very popular for various reasons.

The Ḥusainī Revolution in the span of last forteen centuries has captured the mind and heart of people irrespective of caste, creed and religious faith. In order to establish the truth of Islāmic cause and the devotion to it, against the pseudo Islāmic power, Imām Ḥusain along with the members of his family and his companions and all had laid their lives and attained martyrdom. Imām Ḥusain, for this glorious martyrdom, is popularly known as *Saiyed-ush-Shuhadah* (Doyen of Martyrs). His revolutionary martyrdom, his courage, steadfastness, perseverance and sacrifice for a noble cause left deep impression on the world-history. To keep mourning for these victims of the oppressive rulers, and keep their deeds alive is the unforgettable goal of the life of every human being.

The impact of the Ḥusainī Revolution is very extensive, so much on life sciences, culture, literature, arts etc. Its message is a symbol of the highest human ideals. Each and every year throughout the world, the incidents of Karbala are commemorated. The dedicated common-mass listens to the scholarly lectures hours together on various aspects of the incidents. Sometimes, being immersed emotionally, or to make one's own lectures much effective and at times due to ignorance such things are uttered, which are not real, but just imaginary. For this, time-to-time attempt is made to make the orators to confine to actual descriptions only. There is, of course, enough tragedy in the Karbala incident that real description will do. In the words of 'Allāmmah Kāmānpurī :

> "Few tears have more value which turnout on the actual incidents, than rain of tears from false incidents, ignorance of

the objectives, being unfamiliar with Karbala incidents and detachment of Imām Ḥusain."[18]

This is a universal call that there should be the exact description of the Battle of Karbala and thereafter. 'Āyatu'llāh Murtazā Muṭaharī (d. 1979 AD)'s *Taḥrīfāt-i-Wāqyāt-i-Karbala* is a book in this direction. He has spelled out how wrong and misleading facts are being spread. Along with the incidents there are, of course, mistakes regarding the names of many individuals. Different names are available in so many books and their pronunciation is also different one.

This humble book elaborates many of the issues raised above. After an intensive research the exact description has been made of the incident of Karbala in this book. The names of individuals also have been written with proper pronunciation as far as possible. On one side there is a problem of spelling. There are so many 'Arabic words which have many synonyms. There is a minute difference in the sound and pronunciation of all words. I have used internationally accepted principle of having the words as pronounced in its original form. For further simplification, a few deviations have also been allowed in some cases of 'Arabic phonetics. The complications of special diacritical marks of vowels and diphthongs have also been avoided in case of Urdu, Persian, Sanskrit and other phonetics. So, many names may be unaquainted on account of difference in pronunciation. Such as : 'Omar-S'ad (Amar-S'ad), Khiwallā (Khūlī), Ḥarmallā (Ḥuramalā), Ḥiṣṣīn (Haīsn), Nomayr (Namīr) etc.

Writing only the correct incidents is a very extensive work. It is hoped that other scholars would go ahead with this research work in future. So, many literary creations take place in a year, even then in a few matters, there is difficulty in understanding the sequence of incidents on many places to a person of analytical point of view because sometimes and somewhere this prime incident of the Islāmic history cannot be put up on the norms of the conditions of history, which has its own singular glory. There should be a conformity in the time, place and period of the sequence of incidents. But sorry, due attention was not paid on this aspect in which illusion arises in many dates concerning with the sequence of incidents. There are so many historical and geographical problems as after the assassination of Imām Ḥusain his captive family members were taken *via* which routes, where and how long were stayed, when liberated, from which date, when reached, what is the distance between one place to another and how much time it took. These solutions are required. Environmental problems related to Karbala, Damascus etc., temperature and on the way problem and different basic documents of researchers.

The author of these lines has attempted to search solution of all the problems concerning above discussed historical, geographical and environmental matters. At present sufficient materials are available on the Ḥusainī Revolution through enormous powerful technogical, technical and communication media. Though most of them are based on translation and little attention has been given towards research, no attention to astrological store of knowledge. We have taken advantage as per our capacity and specified the sequence of incident and dates. For fulfilling this great and difficult task help was available from so many scholars, researchers and specialists and, therefore, the author of these lines is grateful to them. Writing all their names may not be possible, even then gratitude has been expressed at due places to a few important persons.

There are so many such families of followers and disciples, as are motivated and encourraged by the progeny of the holy Prophet Muḥammad, Fāṭimah aż-Żahrah and Imām 'Alī and their children and descendants and especially by the great event of Karbala. Living or dying every action has had been dedicated only to them, with the amazing ideal: *live like 'Alī and die like Ḥusain.* My family also is one among them. I have heard of the *Ḥusainī elegies* since my mother's lullaby. Nurished, nurtured and brought up in a noble and faithful atmosphere, the great Karbala event has been my study's primary part. My first published book *Tanwīr-i-Gham* (1954) containing my first poetry and prose writings has the subject matter of Karbala. As a post-graduate student (1958) a compilation entitled *Tanwīr-i-Majālis* carrying the ideal discourses on the prescribed problems rejoindering Karbala from the prestigious 'Ulmā was published by me, with the objective that functions organised over Karbala event should not be confined to homage paying functions only, but a social awareness may also be developed through them, which was and is the aim of the Ḥusainī Revolution. Also, tolerance should be inculcated in the society, there should not be such words, which may hurt others.

I have spent my life in the universities studying and teaching language and literature, the universal facts and values of life, as revealed in the socio-cultural context of India. So, my approach of understanding religions in general and the Ḥusainī Revolution in particular, cannot be like that of a professional orator. My specialization has been *Marthiya* (elegical epic). For doctoral degree my book has been related to Karbala's event and have published some other research work on it. I had been supervisor for so many researchers on the subject and some of them have also been published. Although, during the last more than fourteen hundred years innumerable literature has been written on Karbala's subject. Still it appears that nothing worth while has been done so far. Of course, the feeling of discontentment was the reason, why the present book has come into existence!

My humble endeavour is to introduce the Ḥusainī Revolution and to get its due place in the history of the religions of the world. The eradication of rumours spread about Islām could also be possible through the knowledge of the Ḥusainī Revolution. Apart from the facilities of study, besides Introduction, Bibliography and Index, this book is divided into nine chapters, based on the following topics :

In the first chapter an introduction of 'Arabian life prior to Islām, in which the Islāmic Revolutionary background was developed, is given. An attempt at analysis of the permanency of previous religions and greatness of Islām has been made and its specific qualities have been highlighted, which were helpful for human society through Islām.

In the second chapter, through hypothesis have been discussed the political system of Islām which was subsequently changed and entangled within the clutches of Imperialism within Islāmic system of governance. The loss of Islāmic values and the re-establishment of the evils of 'Arabian society, prior to Islām have been analysed.

In the third chapter, Imām Ḥusain's great contributions have been discussed, which has been also rubricated on his name itself. Re-establishment of the Islāmic values and Almighty's administrative machinery have been analysed in detail.

In the fourth chapter the incidents of Imām Ḥusain's outset from Medina, starting prior to *Ḥajj* in Mecca, assassination of Ḥusain's peace-envoy Muslim-bin-Aqīl in Kufa, blocking the way of Imām Ḥusain by the Yażīdī Army, arrival in Karbala etc., have been put up in an analytical review.

In the fifth chapter, the peace-attempts of Imām Ḥusain after the arrival at Karbala have been discussed. Details of the Yażīdī Army's structure, its number, Imām Ḥusain's peace-attempt, sealing the Furat by the Yażīdī Army for banning water to Imām Ḥusain and his followers. Sudden attack by the Yażīdī Army, have been narrated, the last night of Karbala, the Revolution of great sacrifice of Imām Ḥusain and his followers have been analysed.

The subject-matter of the sixth chapter is the detailed description of the wonderful courage and sacrifice of Imām Ḥusain and his family and associates, pondering over how they battled for the security of truth against injustice, after starving three consecutive days and various inhuman behaviours of the Yażīdī Army, the battle was lost and won.

In the seventh chapter the atrocity and cruelty of Yażīdīs on Imām Ḥusain's family and followers have been described after the great martyrdom of Imām Ḥusain and his supporters. How Yażīdī Army misbehaved with the ladies after arresting them, how they were taken to Kufa from Karbala and from Kufa to Damascus. They were imprisoned for about a year and then Imām Ḥusain's family returned to Medina. Other incidents also have been discussed along with Karbala tragedy.

In the eighth chapter the life of Imām Ḥusain and his supporters has been presented, so that, it may be clearly evident, who were all the great personalities, who joined this great sacrifice and what is their greatness, status and glory in Islām.

The achievements of the Ḥusainī Revolution and its influence have been explained in the nineth chapter. The religious duty and maintenance, the rights of Imāms etc. have been explained.

In spite of my unwillingness repetition is found in a few places. Such is in an indispensable condition, but I have made it precise as far as possible. The learned readers may forgive me and kindly put up with me and I shall be grateful. I would feel happy and rewarded, if this book is helpful and useful in understanding and convincing various stages of Islāmic awakening.

In preparing a book of this nature, I am burdended with debt of authors of a large number of books, their libraries, and various websites available on particular aspects of the subject and have utilized them to my humble capacity. I have also relied upon the assistance of many people without whose help, I would have failed to convey my message. I am thankful to them all. But I shall be failing in my duty, if I do not acknowledge indebtedness to my esteemed friends Prof. R.P. Misra, Maj. M. Z. Ḥasan, Dr. 'Abida Ḥasan and Dr. Muḥammad Ḥasan Možaffarī, who very kindly took pains in collection of material, going through my manuscript and making most valuable suggestions.

I shall be highly grateful, if I could get any suggestion from you.

Saiyed Jafar Reza

'Shabistan'
786, Shahganj, Allahabad, U.P.-211003
Mīlādu'l Ḥusain 1435
June 2, 2014
drsjreza@gmail.com

Notes and References

1. Anwāru't-Tanżīl, p. 387, al-Kashshāf 'an Ḥaqāyiqu'l-Tanżīl, Vol. 3, p. 67, Mufātīḥu'l-Ghayb al-Mushtahir bi'l Tafsīru'l-Kabīr, Vol. 7, p. 406, Arjaḥu'l-Maṭālib, p. 337, Yanābia'u'l-Muwaddah, p. 86.
2. Jām'au'ṣ-Ṣaḥīḥ al-Muslim, Vol. 1, Tr. 2262.
3. Qaul-i-Sadīd, p. 27.
4. *Ibid.*
5. al-Bidāyah w'an-Nihāyah, Vol. 9, p. 13.
6. al-Bidāyah w'an-Nihāyah, Vol. 12, p. 328.
7. Qaul-i-Sadīd, p. 57.
8. Khilāfat-o Mulūkiyat, p. 289.
9. al-Muntaẓim- fī-Tārīkhu'l-Ummam, p. 73.
10. ath-Thaqāfatu'l-Islāmia, vol. 2, p. 310.
11. *Kitābu'l-'Ibar's famous Urdu translator Aḥmad Ḥusain 'Othmānī, has admitted the fact and completed the remaining portion himself.* Vide Tarjumah-i-Tarikh-i-Ibn Khaldūn, vol 5, p. 69, Allahabad, 1899-1930. – Author.
12. Tārīkhu'r-Rusūl wa'l-Mulūk, vol. 6, p. 235.
13. Qaul-i-Sadīd, pp. 48-51.
14. Qaul-i-Sadīd, p. 26.
15. Minhāju's-Sunnau'n-Nabawiyyā, p. 290.
16. Tuḥfā-i-Ithnā-'Asharīya, p. 8.
17. The basic text of this valuable book is missing, but the favourit pupil of Abū-Mikhnaf, Ḥishām Kalbī (d. 819 AD) traced the book, of which four copies are preserved and available at Goth (sl.no. 1836), Berlin (Spencer collection no. 159-60), Lydein (sl. 792) and St. Peterburg (sl. 78).
18. Tanwīr-i-Majālis, p. 6.

Contents

Transliteration

The internationally accepted principle of having the words as pronounced in its original form has been followed. With a view to further simplification, a few deviations have been allowed in some cases of 'Arabic phonetics'. Similarly, the complications of special diacritical marks of vowels and diphthongs have also been avoided in case of Urdu, Persian, Sanskrit and other phonetics. While transliterating it into English, same system has also been followed in the words of identical sounds, especially in 'Arabic for non-Arabic' readers. It is at providing authentic material to the readers. However, some words and names commonly occurring in the book carry no transliteration marks, because the readers are better familiar to the name of geographical places mentioned in Atlas, such as Mecca, Medina, Damascus etc. instead of Makkah, Madīnah, Dami<u>sh</u>q, <u>Sh</u>ām etc. But the places of indigenous nature have been mentioned with diacritical marks, such as Tan'īm, Ṣaffāḥ, <u>Th</u>a'labiyah,'Ažību'l Hijānāt, Qaṣru'l Banī Maqātil etc. for making the readers familier to the original form.

The following table is intended to assist them:

ا अ	=	a	آ आ	=	ā
أ ए	=	ē	ا इ	=	i
إ ई	=	ī	ء	=	'
ا उ	=	u	و ऊ	=	ū
ب ब	=	b	بھ भ	=	bh
پ प	=	p	پھ फ	=	ph
ت त	=	t	تھ थ	=	th
ٹ ट	=	ṭ	تھ B	=	ṫh
ث	=	<u>th</u>	ج ज	=	j
جھ झ	=	jh	چ छ	=	<u>ch</u>

چھ छ	=	ch	ح	=	ḥ
خ	=	kh	د द	=	d
دھ ध	=	dh	ڈ ड	=	ḍ
ڈھ ढ	=	ḍh	ذ	=	ž
ر र	=	r	ڑ ड़	=	ṛ
ڑھ ढ़	=	ṛh	ز	=	ż
ژ	=	żh	س स	=	s
ش श	=	sh	ص	=	ṣ
ض	=	z	ط	=	ṭ
ظ	=	ẓ	ع	=	ʻ
غ	=	gh	ف	=	f
ق	=	q	ك क	=	k
کھ ख	=	kh	گ ग	=	g
گھ घ	=	gh	ل ल	=	l
م म	=	m	ن न	=	n
ه/ة ह	=	h	و व	=	w
ي य	=	t	ے ऐ	=	y

The following alphabets, set of symbols or characters used to represent some specific sounds of ʻArabic language, which have also been adopted in Persian, Urdu and some other languages:

ء(*ḥamżah*): penultimate letter of ا (alif).
ث (*thē*): pronounced with a lisp like *th* in *thin.*
ح(*ḥē*): strong aspirate, stressed guttural *h.*
خ(*khē*): guttural sound, as in German *machen.*
ذ (*žāl*): close to soft *th* in *father*.
ز (*żē*): close to *z* in *zebra.*
ژ (*żhē*): close to *sion, television.*
ص (*ṣād*): strong articulated *s.*
ض (*zād*): stressed, explosive *z.*
ط (*toē*): strong palatal sound, strong articulated *t.*
ظ (*ẓoē*): strong palatal sound, articulated *z.*
ع(*ʻēn*): guttural sound close to *a.*
غ(*ghēn*): gargling sound similar to French *r.*
ف (*fā*): close to soft *f* in *first.*
ق (*qāf*): *k* sound at back of throat, close to *qua.*

Glossary

With a view to convey the import of the technical terminology to the reader, it has been explained right at the place where it is used for the first time and given its English equivalents. However, with a view to avoid repetition in explaining the same technical terminology again and again at various places, a brief glossary is given here for the readers' convenience:

'Abbāsites (*'Abbāsī*): Descendants of 'Abbās-bin-'Abdu'l-Muṭṭalib, uncle of the Prophet Muḥammad. This family seized the Caliphate for 507 years (750-1257).

'Adl: Divine Justice, one of the Principles of Islām.

Ahlu'l-Bayt or *'Itrat:* Household or Progeny of the Prophet Muḥammad.

Ahlu'l-Kitāb: The people of the revealed Books. Some have restricted it to Jews and Christians, but others include Zoroastrians, Hindus and all the claimants of the Divine Book.

Ahlu'r-Ra'i: Those who follow their own opinion in the absence of a clear instruction of God in Qur'an or Sunnat.

Ahlu'r-Ra'i-w'al-Qiyās: Those who follow hypothetical assumptions and opinion in religion.

Ākhirat: Last Judgement, one of the three most important Pivots of Islāmic faith, mainly four components; *Ma'd* (Resurrection), *Barżakh* (Purgatory), *'Adālat* (Judgement) and *Nijāt* (Salvation).

Amr-bil-Ma'rūf: Enjoining of God, things permitted in Islam.

Amīn: The truthful person, trustee to God.

Amīr: Commander, chief, leader.

Amīru'l-Mominīn: The leader of the faithful, the term used for the Caliph.

Angra Mainyu or *Ahriman:* Destructive Spirit, as believed by Zoroastrians.

Anṣār: Helpers, the residents of Yathrib who were ready to sacrifice anything to their brothers-in-faith.

'Aql: wisdom,

'Aqlī: Intellectual.

Asās (or *Asāsu'l-Imāmah*): Founder of the Imamate. Ismā'īlīs regard 'Alī-Ibn-Abū Ṭālib to be the bedrock of the Muslim Ummah, with Universal Soul, more than just an Imām.

Asurās: Demons.

'Ażādārī or *Tā'żiādārī*: Commemoration ceremony, which in course of time became guiding force to institutionalise the message of the martyrdom of Karbala and became the inseparable part of Islāmic religious life, especially for Shi'īs.

'Ażān : Formal Call to Prayer.

Bada: Change in intention.

B'adu'l-Ijtihād: Closing of the door of the *Ijtihād*, completely and permamently by *al-Ghażāli*.

Barżakh: Isthmus or purgatory. Interval period between Death and Resurrection, as per Islāmic theology.

Bātini'īn: Secretistics, sub-sect of Ismā'īlīs.

Bay'at: Oath of Allegiance.

Baytu'l-Māl: State Exchequer.

Bid'ah: Unlawful innovation in Islām.

Bin (or *Ibn*): Son of.

Bint: Daughter of.

Burhān: Demonstration, evidence of fact as universally observed and confirmed.

Dā'ī: Claimant, missionary, emissary; Nāyab-Imām in the Ismā'īlīs.

Dā'īsm has three steps – In the first step is *Makāsir*, the second is *Māžūn,* and the third is *Dā'ī.*

Dā'īu'l-Muṭlaq: In absolute charge in Ismā'īlīs.

Dāru'l-Ḥarb: An unjust and untrue ruling order, propounded the principle of establishing a justice-predominant state, Shāh Wali'ullāh declared the contemporary India to be a *Dāru'l-Ḥarb* for which he campaigned the principle of *Fakku'l-Nizām* (the end of each wornout system), organised a powerfully armed struggle by the name of *Jihād.*

Dauru's-Sitar: Veiled or covered period of Ismā'īlīs. Imamate in which the Shi'īs were exposed to calamities perpetrated on them by the 'Abbāsite Caliphs.

Dā'wat: Feast; propagation, extension programme.

Dā'wat-al-žul-'Ashīra: Feast of the Family.

Devas: Gods.

Diyat: Wehrgeld, the price which any homicide pays to the family of the victim, if they so consented.

Durūd-wa'l-Salām: God's blessing.

'Eīdu'l-Mīlādu'l-Nabī: Celebrating the birth anniversary of the Prophet Muḥammad.

Faqīh (pl. *Fuqahā*): Expert in the *Fiqh*, theologist of Islām. Shi'īs prefer to say him *Mujtahid.*

Faraiz ad-Dīn: Religious Obligations. Shi'īs call it *Furū'ad-Dīn* (Branches of Religion) and Sunnī term as *Arkān ad-Dīn* (Pillars of Religion). These are, actually, compulsory duties for each and every Muslim, such as *Ṣalāt* or *Namāż* (the Prayer), *Ṣaum* or *Rożah* (the Fasting), *Ḥajj* (the Pilgrimage) and *Žakāt* (the Poor-Rate), *Khumus* (fifth part of wealth sacrifice and *Jihād* (struggle).

Fāsid-al-'Aqīdah: Perverted in belief.

Fāsiq: Sinful.

Fatwā: Edict.

Fidaī' (pl. *Fidaī'n*): Devotee, who willingly hazards his life. A rank of the extremist militant of al-Bāṭiniyya or Ta'līmiyya order of the Ismā'īlīs which remained steadfast ready to kill or die like inevitable death.

Fiqh: Islāmic jurisprudence, elucidation and application of the *Sharī'a*.

Firqah (pl. *Firaq*): Sects, differences.

Ghadīru'l-Khumm: It is known for general announcement of the Prophet regarding 'Alī to be his successor. Shi'īs' celebrate in the commemoration of this event every year on 18th Žilḥajjah AH.

Ghulāt (sing. *Ghālīn*): One who exaggerates in religious matters, follower of the *Ghuluww* or *Ghalīyya*, holding such heretical doctrines, which put them outside the pale of Islām.

Ḥādī: Spiritual Guide.

Ḥadīth: Tradition, the words of the holy Prophet, Muḥammad. *Hadīths* are classified into four categories – *Ṣaḥīḥ* (correct), *Ḥasan* (fine), *Muwaththaq* (proved authentic), and *Za'īf* (weak).

Ḥadīthu'l-Qudsī: Heaven Traditions, the holy Traditions in the words of Gabriel.

Ḥadīthu'th-Thaqalayn: Tradition of Immense Gravity. Because, it has deal with 'two things of immense gravity', *viz. Qur'an* and *Ahlu'l-Bayt.*

Ḥāfiẓ : Literally means, a guardian or a protector, but actually he is considerd the Preserver of the Qur'an, who knows by heart each and every word of the Qur'an.

Ḥajaru'l-Aswad: Black Stone, believed by Muslims to have come from Heaven.

Ḥajj: Pilgrimmage to Ka'ba (Mecca) in the Islamic modes of worship, is an obligation which has to be fulfilled once in the lifetime.

Ḥaqqu'l-Allāh: Religious Obligations regarding God Himself.

Ḥaqqu'l-'Ibād: Religious Obligations regarding the servants of God, i.e the Society.

Ḥaram: Mosque and sacred well Zemzem, located inside and in the central courtyard is Ka'ba, the holiest shrine of Islām.

Hāshimites : The most respected clan of Quraysh, in which Prophet Muḥammad was born.

Ḥijrā: The base year of Muslim calendar in which Prophet Muḥammad emigrated from Mecca to Medina in 622 AD, called AH.

Ḥikma: Wisdom, considered to be the aim of Islāmic Philopophy.

Ḥikmat-i-Ilāhī: Divine Wisdom or of Islāmic Philosophy, Theosophy.

Hindsah : Numerals.

Ḥizān : Imbalance of a breast, to be polluted.

Ḥujjat: Proof of God, High position's title in the hierarchy of Islāmic society.

Ḥukamā (sing. *Ḥakīm*): Philosophers, who are divided into two categories – *Masha'īyūn* (Peripatic Philosophers) who believe that the Wisdom may be achieved through intellectual efforts and rational process. *Ishrāqīyūn* (Illuminationist Philosophers) who consider that the true Wisdom could only be achieved under the spiritual discipline, the cleanig the soul from all defilements and acquisition of the virtues.

Ḥulūl: Incarnation.

Hurqālya or *Huvarqālya:* Intermediary world, between the physical world and the spiritual world. Every human being in the physical world has two bodies, one in physical shape and the other in the *Hurqālya.*

Ijmā': To agree or to resolve – According to Shi'īs, it is possible only by the consensus of all the clergies. Shi'īs principles like *Qiyās* (Analogical Reasoning), *Istiḥsān* (Lenient Interpretation) and *Masāelu'l-Mursala* (Expedient Issues) do not help reach an authentic judgement, so, it is not wise to act upon them. But according to Sunn'īs, the above three principlees are the constituent elements of *Ijmā'.* Similar is the case with *Taqlīd* (emulation) and *Ijtihād.*

Ijtihād: Exertion; the process of innovative exegesis to arrive at judgement on points of religious law using reason and principles of jurisprudence.

Ikhtiyār: Free-will, the human being is responsible for his actions.

Ilḥād: Heresy.

'Ilmu'l-Ghayb: Knowledge of Unseen.

'Ilmu'l-Ḥadīth: Science of Tradition in Islāmic academics.

'Ilmu'l-Kalām: Science of Religious Polemics.

'Ilmu'r-Rijāl: Science of Testing and Sorting the True *Ḥadīths* from the false ones and ascertaining the narrator's validity and credibility through the study of their biographies and other sources.

Imām: Head, leader or guide, other pivot of Islām, after *Rasūl.*

Imāmu'l-Ākhiru'ż-Żamān: The Divine Guide of the last period, whose Imamate will persist now for every age to come until the Last Day, who will appear in the time preceding the Dooms Day.

Imāmu'l-Maktūm: Undisclosed Imām, a chain of Ismā'īlī Imamate.

Imāmu'l-Muntaẓar: Awaited Imām, Imām Mahdī.

Imāmat: Imamate.

Imāmu'ż-Żamāna: Contemporary Imām of the period.

Irādah: Will.

'Irfān: Spiritual Wisdom.

'Iṣmat: Sinlessness and Infallibility.

Istiḥsān: Lenient Interpretation of the Sharī'a.

Ithna-Ash'arī: Twelver Shi'īs.

Jabr: Predeterminism, the human being is bound to do as he is predestined, he has no choice.

al-Jafr: the Divination.

Jāhilīyah: Age of Ignorance. A period of 500 years before the advent of Islām in the history of Arabian peninsula.

al-Jāmi'a: The Compilation.

Jidāl: Dialectics, in which the fact is reached through the scientific debate.

Jihād: Struggle, to strive hard in the path of God.

Jiziyah: Tax for newly converted Muslims.

Kāfir: Infidel, apostat.

Kalām: Dogmatics, Speculative Theology.

Kalamatu'sh-Shahadah or *Kalamah:* Profession of Faith. It is read or recited in two different forms among the Shi'īs and Sunn'īs. For Sunn'īs it is quite simple – *Lā Ilāh Ill'allāh Muḥammadu'r Rasūla'llāh.* (There is no good but God, Muḥammad His Prophet.) But Shi'īs add their faith in the Imamate and read or recite as – *Lā Ilāh Ill'allāh Muḥammadu'r Rasūla'llāh 'Alīyan Ḥujjatu'llāh.* (There is no good but God, Muḥammad His Prophet, 'Alī is Argument of God.)

Khayr: Good.

Khārijī (pl. *Khawārij*): A sect driven out of Islām.

Khālwah: Spiritual retreat.

Khilāfat: Vicegerency, succession of the Prophet after his death.

Khilāfatu'r-Rāshida: Rightly Guided Caliphate. First-four Caliphates of Abū Bakr, 'Omar, 'Othmān and 'Alī.

Khula': Dismissal, the rights of wife to get separated from her husband, lent within the limits set by God.

Khumus: 1/5 of the annual tax on net profit.

Kisf: Fragment of heaven falling down.

Kufr: Blasphemy.

L'anat : Curse.

al-Mahdī: Rightly Guided One. The last saviour of the Divine and Justice on tha earth. He has a large number of other titles, all indicative of specific qualifications – *Ṣāḥib-aż-Żamān* (the Lord of the Age), *Ṣāḥib-al-Amr* (the Lord of Command), *Al-Qā'im* (He who will arise) and the *Baqīyyātu'llāh* (the Remnant of God) etc. The doctrine of the *Ghayāba* (Occultation) and *Rij'ā* (Return) maintains that Twelfth Imām 'Abu'l Qāsim Muḥammad, al-Mahdī has not died, but has been concealed by God, that is what he is called *Imāmu'l-Ghayāb* (Hidden Imām).

Manṣūṣ-mina'llāh: Divinely Ordained and Appointed Exclusively by God.

*Maqtal (*pl.*Maqātil):* Recorded facts of the martyrdom of Imām Ḥusain.

Marjau't-Taqlīd: Reference Point for Emulation; Source of Authority; Great Religious Scholar, who through his learning and probity is qualified to be followed in all points of religious practice and law and whose teachings should be observed by all Shi'īs.

Marsiya (Marthiya): Elegy, in commemoration on the martyrdom of Imām Ḥusain and his companions.

Meḥrāb: Central place, specifically provided in to lead the congregation-prayers.

Mimbar : Rosturm, which is used for the Sermons.

Mishkāt : Lady of Light; *Qur'an* (24/35) appellation of Fāṭimah aż-Żahrah, the daughter of the holy Prophet Muḥammad.

Mufiī : Religious Jurist.

Mūmin (pl. *Mūminīn*): Believer, the person perfect in Islām.

Muḥaddith (pl. *Muḥaddithīn*): Expert of *Ḥadīth*.

Muhājirīn (sing. *Muhājir*) : Emigrants, who had foresaken their birth-place the ties of kith and kin and every tie of home for the sake of Islām.

Mujtahid (pl. *Mujtahidīn*): Competent Religious Scholar having permission to practice.

Muṣḥafu'l Fāṭimah: Book of Fāṭimah aż-Żahrah.

Mushrik (pl. *Mushrikīn*): Polytheist.

Mulāḥedah (sing. *Mulḥid*): Heretics in religious matters.

Mulūkiyat: Imperialism.

Munāfiqūn (sing. *Munāfiq*): Hypocrites, who actually did not believe in Islām, but mingled with Muslims, Outwardly Muslim, Inwardly Dangerous Enemies of Islām, while remaining within Islām, they had played foul with it.

Nabī (pl. *Anbiya*) or *Rasūl* (pl. *Rusūl*): Prophet, Messenger or Apostle of God. (Christians use the word *Apostle* for one of the disciples of Jesus.)

Nahī-'anil-Munkir: Prevention and Obliteration from Bad.

Naqlī: Transmitted.

Naṣṣ: Authority of God, Specific Designation, used in relation to designation of 'Alī by the Prophet or any Imām by his predecessor. The process is sometimes may be in the *Mithāq* or *'Ahd* (convenant).

Nāṣibī : People against the Progeny of the holy Prophet Muḥammad. They have not left any stone unturned in creating illusions and confusions in Islām.

Nātiq: Vocal. Ismā'īlīs emphasize the circle of seven Grand-Prophets, who brings the revelation of truth. They are – Adam, Noah, Abraham, Moses, Jesus Christ, Muḥammad and Ismā'īl.

Navroze: Iranī festival.

Qadr: Fate, Self-determination.

Qiyāmah: Catastrophe.

Qazā: Divine Decree.

Qāzī: Judge in Islāmic legal court.

Qārī: Reciter of the Word of God.

Qur'an: Word of God.

Rāfizī (pl. *Rawāfiz*): Dissenter and swindler, a pure abusive term often used by some Sunn'īs for Shi'īs.

Rāsikhūn-fil-'Ilm: Firmly established in knowledge.

Rāwī: Narrator, the one who had directly heard the words of the holy Prophet Muḥammad.

Risālat: Prophethood, the second unanimous pivot of Islām, embassy, messenger which stands for that Embassy which God employs to communicate with mankind and sends some infallible human being to act as the representative of the Divine Kingdom in human world.

Rūḥ: Spirit.

Sabath Day: Saturday, special day for Jews.

Ṣabr: To deconstruct self-confidence and strength of willpower.

Ṣādiq: Absolutely truthful person.

Ṣaḥābah: Prophet's Companions.

Ṣaḥifa: The Book.

Saiyed (pl. *Sādāt*): Venerable, Descendant of the Progeny of the holy Prophet Muḥammad, in the family-tree of his daughter Fāṭimah aż-Żahrah (*the Lady of Light*), but due to political reasons the 'Arab world in general now use the word *Saiyed* as an equivalent of *Mr.*

Saiyed-ush-Shuhadah : The Doyen of the Martyrs. This appellation was firstly used for the Prophet's uncle, Ḥamżah-bin-'Abdu'l-Mṭṭalib. After the event of

Karbala, this appellation became the part of the name of the Prophet's grandson Imām Ḥusain.

Ṣalāt or *Namāż*: the Prayer, the foremost pivot of the Religious Obligations of Islām, which occupies the central place in the elements of an appellation for Islāmic practices to draw closer to the Almighty. It has seven components – *Ażān* (formal call), *Aqāmat* (staying), *Qayām* (standing), *Rukū'* (the bowing position), *Sajdā* (placing forehead on the ground in prostration), *Tashahhud* (bearing witness), and *Salām* (salutation).

Pesh-Imām (who leads congrational prayer), *Mu'ażżin* (who calls for prayer).

Ṣāmit: Silent, Ismāilias emphasize the circle of seven Grand-Imāms. They are: Shīth, Sām, Ishmail, Aroan, Shamūn, 'Alī and Muḥammad-bin-Ismā'īl.

Ṣaum or *Roża:* Fasting is observed daily during the holy month of Ramazān for special blessing of the Almighty.

Shafā't: To seek the mediation and intercession of the Prophet.

Shahādah: Profession of Faith.

Shar: Evil.

Shari'a: Sacred Law of Islām, the Divine Jurisprudence.

Sharīkatu'l Ḥusain : The Associate of Imām Ḥusain, famous appellation of Żainab-bin-Imām 'Alī, the daughter of Fāṭimah aż-Żahrah, *Lady of Light*, the daughter of the holy Prophet Muḥammad.

Shi'a or *Shi'ī:* Friend and follower, from the earliest time to the present, the theologian have used, this word for the followers of Imām 'Alī.

Shi'atu'l-'Alī: Followers of Imām 'Alī.

Shirku'l-Akbar: The greatest sin.

Silsilahu'ż-Żahab: Golden Chain. The spiritual chain of *Ṣūfīs* starting from Imām 'Alī to Imām ar-Reza. One of its main branches gave rise to the branch of Khwāja Ma'rūf Karkhī which in turn gave rise to many other branches like Saqṭiyya, Junaidīyya, Qādarīyya, Chishtīyya etc.

Spenta Mainyu or *Yażdān:* Beneficent Spirit, as believed by Zoroastrians.

Ṣūfī: Muslim Mystic. Other terms associated with *Ṣūfīs* are: *Walī* (Divine Saint), *Ṣaleḥ* (Perfectly virtuous person), *Pīrī* (mystic patronage), *Murīdī* (disciplehood of a mystic), *Mujāwirī* (to be attendant of a shrine), *'Urs* (annual festival on the shrines), *Qull* and *Fātiḥa* (recitation of Qur'anic verses for the benefit of the dead), *Chādar* (sheet of cloth spreading on the grave of a saint) etc.

Sultān: Monarch, addressed as *Zille-Ilāhī* (Shadow of God) and *Zille-Subḥanī* (Shadow of Glory).

Sunnī or *Ahlu'l-Sunnat-wa'l-Jamā't:* The people of tradition and group. This naming makes it clear that in this sect, it is essential to have faith in the life-pattern of the holy Prophet, and the collective model of the companion of the Prophet in general and *Khilāfatu'r-Rāshidūn* in particular. The majority of Muslims belong to *Sunnī* community.

Sūra: Chapter of Qur'an.

Tabarrah: To be detatched emotionally from the enemies of the Prophet and his pious Progeny. A few enthusiastic Shi'īs feel no wrong in openly condemning and using abusives terms for the enemies of the Prophet and his pious family, but the large majority of Shi'īs is against this.

Tafsīr: Commentary or exegesis of whole or part of Qur'an.

Tafwīz: Hand-over of power.

Talāq: Divorce, the rights of husband to get separated from his wife, lent within the limits set by God.

Tanāsukh: Transmigration of soul.

Taqiyyah: Self-protection, Concealment of Faith, when it causes life to be threatened.

Tasbīḥ: Reciting glorification of God on the beads of rosary.

Ṭawāf : Circumambulating,walking on all the four sides of holy Ka'bah.

Tawalla: To be in love with the Prophet and his pious progeny. The difficulty arises with extremes, holding doctrines that the persons loved are so heretical as to put those holding them outside Islām.

Tawḥīd: Divine Unity, the first and foremost unanimous pivot of Islām.

Al-Ṭayyār : The Flying Man, a title bestowed by the holy Prophet upon Jā'far-Ibn-Abī Ṭālib, the brother of Imām 'Alī, because he lost his both hands in the *Jihād*.

Thaqīfa Banīu's-Sa'da: Portico of Sa'da clan, where Abū Bakr was chosen as first Caliph.

Ṭolaqā' : Captives of the Battle of Badr, who were released, due to mercy by the Prophet, and Yażīd's ancestors were among them.

'Ulama (sing. *'Ālim*): learned persons, scholars, erudites – the religious class.

Ulul-Amr-Minkum: Best in knowledge and character to merit a commanding position in the Muslim nation.

'Ulūmu'l-'Aqliyah: Intellectual Sciences.

Umayyites: Descendants of Umayya-bin-'Abdu'sh-Shams. 'Abdu'sh-Shams was brother of Prophet Muḥammad's grandfather 'Abdu'l Manāf. This family seized the Caliphate for 89 years (661-750).

Ummah: Islāmic Commonwealth.

Ummu'l-Mūminīn: Mother of Believers, the title used for the wife of the Prophet.

Uṣūlu'd-Dīn: Principles of Islām.

Uṣūlu'l-Fiqh: Principles of the Islāmic Jurisprudence.

Walī: Religious guardian, helper or defender, a title used for Imām or Sūfī saint.

Waḥy: Revelation from God.

Wikāla: Agency.

Wilāyatu'l-Faqīh: Guardianship of the Expert Theologist of Islām. A concept that government belongs by right to those who are most learned in Islāmic Jurisprudence.

Żakāt: Poor-Rate, which is 2.5 per cent annual tax on the capital or total assets to be distributed amongst the poors.

Ẓan: Strong Presumption.

Żanādiqa: Followers of the Ancient Religion of Persia, i.e., Zoarastiams.

Ẓawāhiru'd-Dīn: Literal and Textual Explanations of Islām.

Żiyārat Nāḥiyā : An Ediction for well-being, sanctioned by Imām Mahdī Ākhiru'ż-Żamān.

Chapter One

Islāmic Religious Perspective

With a view to form acquaintance with the scenario of Islāmic religious perspective, it is imperative to impress on the mind the distinguishing features of Islām. It is not merely a system of worship, but a philosophy of life. It gives reasons and a set purpose for living. Furthermore, it defines the best ways to secure progress and happiness. This is done by elevating the spiritual side and satisfying the material needs of people.

Islām considers man as a vicegerent of God on earth. This status is a fine one, but it is also critical for the requirements must be satisfied. Thus, he is in an envied position, and consequently his acts and behaviour are expected to conform to the high level, he is occupying. The Islāmic concepts and laws are inseparable parts of the Islāmic ideology. They are the practical expression of Islām in society and life in general. These concepts and laws are essentially concerned with harmonizing people's relationships among themselves, with other beings, and above all with the Creator.

The basic of Islāmic outlook to this life is that of an introductory course. This worldly life is viewed as a prelude to another eternal life. Therefore, this world is a preparatory stage for people in order to attain the spiritual level, which permits them to enter Paradise. The other side of the picture is the horror of Hell for people who misuse the powers at their disposal. Hence, success and failure are not measured with this worldly or materialistic supremacy. The Islāmic measure differs from materialistic standard by accounting for the life hereafter. The satisfaction of God is the sublime aim, which surpasses all other inclinations and wishes. This is by no account neglecting materialistic supremacy, but putting it in its rightful place. It is with the satisfaction of God that Muslims seek materialistic supremacy.

The knowledge of the Ḥusainī Revolution is linked with the knowledge of Islām. The Ḥusainī Revolution's various stages, which has committed a powerful signature on the universal religious history. It was not the revolution, in terms of social and political sciences, which aims major, sudden and hence typically violent alteration in government. The Ḥusainī Revolution's inherent ability was to help a society realize its potential. The Ḥusainī Revolution was the right of the society to defend itself against abusive tyrants, creating a fresh order that reflected the needs of the people. It was the means of accomplishing freedom to people.

The revolutionary perspective inheres the principle of optimism against deadlock. There is a symptom of movement and knowledge of Almighty, against impediments and ignorance, which has provided time weighing context to various and so many stages of human-life. As the impediments and ignorance have made a loss of the movement and youthful energy of life, therefore, there was a dire need of such a revolution, naturally, which could stop the destruction arisen through the elements of human-impediments, between Almighty and creation; because the Religious Revolution can be the only medium, which can establish diversity and adjustment, cohesiveness in place of the unanimity of movement in rudiment. The nature of the stoppage of movement and process is based on inactivity, whereas, on the contrary the resolution is the basic and fundamental element of active nature.

The impediment of movement is considered to be in the form of say, uniformity and archaeology, whereas the movement of progress makes a journey in an open atmosphere. When the impediment movement reaches its climax, then disarmament becomes indispensable. Then one Abraham, takes birth destroys the symbols of those passive traditions, rigidity and superstitions. So a change, a conversion is visible in all the spheres of human-life.

A desire of change produces vibration by itself, on which most of the rules of development of creation are based upon. To this extent the physiology has discovered special creative and similar groups of nerves and joints in human body, which prompt man to proceed and go ahead finding out most beautiful things, under whose action-reaction human individual desires, feelings, trends and attitudes arise but in a society a symbol of change is based on explicit elements and not on internal, but it can be said that on a few occasions even storm and rainfall may be helpful in the impediment of progress.

Background of the Islāmic Revolution

The Islāmic Revolution has established the safety and security of human-rights as high values and the Ḥusainī Revolution has achieved its unique importance and specialities of surmounting and surpasing all the revolutions for ever.

The Islāmic Revolution was the victory over darkness, enlightening the glittering sun-shine atmosphere in the Western world, which has been called as a movement of the West by George Fredrick Hegel (1831). Bertrend Russel (1872) has made a measured description of this universal influence that the basis and source of cultural and mental progress was not only Europe, but also when Europe was under the great grip of evil slumber, the progressive culture of Islām that become a Lighthouse from India to Spain.

This is the wonderful side of Islāmic Revolution that it originated from 'Arab peninsula, whose major portion (about 2,330,000 km), dryland, severe summer make their population agog for rains, the people used to be continuously nomadic in nature. Very few people were in the towns whose occupation was agriculture and business. They were of lazy, fighting and egoistic nature.

Arabia, a peninsular region, together with the offshore islands, is located in South-west Asia. It is surrounded by the Red Sea in the west and south-west, the Gulf of 'Aden in the south, the Arabian Sea in south and south-east, Gulf of Arabia in the north-east. Its area is about 1,000,000 square miles (2,590,000 square km.). Arabia is a basin-shaped plateau, which is separated from the sea on three sides by mountains. The interior of the plateau is marked by succession of sandy desert region. None of the mountain regions is high. The wall of the mountains of the peninsula are very dry, usually with less than 4 inches (100 mm) of rain fall annually, except for a few eastern areas under the influence of Indian Ocean monsoon and far-off western coastal areas, which benefit from the mountain rain barriers.

Each desert group was believed to be connected through commom ancestor. Not all inhabitants of Arabia were nomads. Scattered over most of the country were oases, kown as Ya<u>th</u>rib, now Medina. Having small settlements without oasis or agriculture, Mecca became by far the most important.

Mecca, which was, at the time, a city of great importance, both for its associations and position. Situated in a low-lying valley stretching from the north to south and west bordered by a range of hills and at the east high granite rocks, in which Holy Ka'bah is in the centre. Its public hall opens on the platform of the temple. The city presented an unusual appearance of prosperity and strength, recognized for religious sanctity, besides being a trade-centre.

Mecca was a cultural and business centre, which obtained religious importance and honour due to the presence of Holy Ka'bah. Because of the fact, Holy Ka'bah was founded by the forefather of the 'Arabs, Prophet Ibrāhīm (Abraham) and his son Prophet Ism'āil (Ishmael), originally, in a passage of time, the children of Ism'āil, had in consequence of Babylonian attack, passed into the hands of Jurhumites, who were the combination of secular and religious power, whose chiefs assumed the title of *Malik*, the king. In the third century overwhelmed by Qaḥetānite tribe, who, issuing from Yemen, took possesion of Mecca and the southern part of Ḥijāż. In the mean time, the descendants of Prophet Ism'āil, who had suffered so terribly at the hands Babylonians, gradually regained their former strength. 'Adnān, was consided the ancestor of prophet Ism'āil, from whom the Qurayshite proudly trace their genealogical tree, flourished about a century BC. 'Adnān married the daughter of the chief of Jurhummite tribe and settled at Mecca and his son M'ad became the real progenitor of all the descendants of Prophet Ism'āil inhabiting in Ḥijāż, Najd, Fihr, who had the surname Quraysh, and the descendants of M'ad, flourished in the third century, had the great honour of being the ancestor of Prophet Muḥammad.

In the ancient time, 'Arabians believed in Monotheism, but after many generations, they started idol worship, leaving Abraham's doctrine, but even then there remained some believers of the Traditions and the doctrine of Ibrahīm. Such as, considering Holy Ka'bah as most august place, the rites and rituals of *Ḥajj,* like *Ṭawāf* (making a circumambulation of holy Ka'bah), performing *Ḥajj*, stopping in *'Arafāt* and *Mużdalifah,* sacrificing animals etc. On every point of these performances the people were constantly conscious of the Greatness of God and their humbleness in presence of His Supremacy. Though, so many superstitions were added in the very basis of Abraham's doctrine which got themselves converted and changed, Arabians considered four months – first, seventh, eleventh and twelfth month, i.e. *Muḥarram, Rajab, Żīqādah, Żilḥijjah* repectively of their calendar, as very great sacred months, when it was forbidden to engage in war or shed human blood in anger – 'a sort of Gods truce.' They shunned battles-quarrels and war in these months. They postponed some other protected deeds too.

Idol-worship started in such a manner that whenever the 'Arabians' would visit other countries in connection with their trade and business with others, they used to keep a stone of Mecca with them, as a symbol of its greatness and holiness. Wherever they would go, they used to worship the stone of Mecca, brought by them, and also make a circumambulation (*Ṭawāf*), as if they are worshipping in holy Ka'bah itself. Wherever they observed any beautiful stones, they started worshipping the same. Ibn Isḥāq, Muḥammad-bin-Isḥāq-bin-Yasār (768 AD) has written[1] that a person 'Omaru-bin-Lahi went to Syria in connection with his business. He observed idol worship there. People told him that the idols were most helpful in resolving human hardship. He borrowing an idol from them, brought it to Mecca and established in Holy Ka'bah and encouraged the people to worship it. That was the same idol, which is called *Hubal*. It was engraved in the shape of a person in a red cornelian. In Ka'bah, it was planted in its underground, in which the stairs and the other articles were preserved. Near the *Hubal* seven arrows were also placed, under whose blessing the Arabians started meditation and also performing *'Aqīqah* (shaving of head of a newly born child), *Khatnah* (circumcision), marriage and funeral rites etc. There was a belief that the idols *Asāf'* (male) and *Na'ilah* (female) of Arabian Jurham clan, being guilty of copulation in the Holy Ka'bah were cursed into stones. There was a space in between these idols, where animals were sacrificed. The statues of Prophet Ibrāhīm (Abraham) and his son Prophet Ismā'īl (Ishmael) were also installed there. In a row 360 idols were established, as a separate deity for everyday. The Sun was the most Venerable God. The Moon had three goddesses, namely *Al-Lāt* (light), *Al-Manāt* (dark) and *Al-'Ozzā* (light plus dark combined) which were called *Binātu-'l Ilah* (daughters of Almighty). *Al-Lāt* was situated at Ṭā'if and *Al-Manāt* was the name of a hill, which was at the highway between Mecca and Syria. At some distance from Mecca, a tree *Nakhalah* was worshipped, considering it as *Al-'Ozzā*. Each and every Arabian clan had a separate deity and its idols and it is not possible here to produce a detailed account. Penis-worship was also done. Besides, mountains, trees and animals and their favourites, some othet idols were also worshipped, particularly, among the animals, deers, horses and camels were most popular. On the presumption of Arabians being idol worshippers, Pandit Aditya Chaturvedi has tried to establish that they, prior to Islām, were the followers of Vedic religion, but without producing any proof in support of his own statement.[2]

On the basis of above discussion, it would not be appropriated to guess that all 'Arabian people were not familiar with Almighty God. Though short in numbers, there were followers of Abraham's doctrine and the path against Idol-worship. Often they were captured by local Traditionalists, but they demonstrated amicable religious tolerance.

Among them were the *Sābeans* (worshippers of stars), aware and familiar with the concept of Almighty God of Greek and Christians and were also against the then prevalent illicit copulation and were hopeful of the arrival of any Aspostle-Prophet and would often want deliverance from that bad conditions and distress to them.[3]

In a study of the social and cultural life of 'Arabians prior to Islām, it is indispensable to bear in mind the specialities of the southern and northern regions of 'Arab peninsula. Qaḥetān was the name of their legator, the person from whom was derived inheritance of the peoples of southern area (Yemen), has two big branches, *Kahlān* and *Ḥamīr*. Kahlānis were living in wards or parts of a town in different parts of southern region, which were called *Mukhellāf*. There would be a leader of each ward, called *Qīl* (pl. *Aqeyāl*). Every *Qīl* was independent in his own conduct and activities and was ruler of his state without any interference. There was no mutual connection among the various *Aqeyāl*. They were used to quarrel among themselves. The mighty one used to loot and murder the weak one. After a long period, states were established among themselves. The three most famous and largest states-*cum*-empires were the Minaean, the Sabaean (the Bibical *Sheba* and Qu'ranic *Sabā*), and the Himyarite (called Homeritae by Roman), all of which were known throughout the ancient Mediterranean world; their periods of ascendancy overlap somewhat, extending from roughly 1200 BC to 525 AD. In contrast of southern Yemenī Kahlāns, northern 'Adnānīs of Ḥejāż, Tahāmah, Najd etc., were much undeveloped. Kahlānites lived in built houses and were cvilized people and most of 'Adnāninite were mere nomadic and wanderers, but its clan Quraysh lived in built houses. In the 6th century Quraysh—the noble and holy house of the confederation of the Ḥijāż controlling the sacred enclave (*Ḥaram*) of Mecca—contrived a chain of agreements with the northern and southern tribes that opened the highways of 'Arabia to commerce, under Quraysh aegis, caravans moved freely from the southern Yemen coast to Mecca and thence northward to Byzatium or eastward to Iraq.

The procedure for benediction, prayer, even demigods and deities of southern Yemenite Kahlāns were different in all manners from the northern 'Adnānīs of Ḥijāż. Both considered their language superior and greater on the basis of phonetics, but in due course both accepted the standards of Quraysh's language and phonetics. Among the 'Adnānī clans *Rabi'ah* and *Muzar* were considered mostly mighty and effective. For a period of two hunderd years prior to Islām. There had been ferocious enmity between them and they fought blood thitrsty wars against each other. Thousands of people were massacred and families perished, generations ended, but the battles could not be ended. These wars used to occur on some very ridiculous issues. For example: a female camel, namely *Sarab* became cause for the murder and destruction of two branches Bakar and Taghalab of Rabi'ah clan. In the same way a war continued for forty years between two branches of Muzar clan, Žabyān and 'Abas. The reason was just a quarrel in a horse-race. These wars were the root-cause for the loss of lives, damages of wealth and properties and loss of peace of mind and happiness, which had became parts of their daily life. But the fighters of Arabian clans supposed it necessary for their prestige and honour. 'Arab poets recited highly emotional poems exaggerating hatred in the name of honour.

The daily routine of lives of 'Arabian clans included war, looting, murdering etc. and they were proud of it. Having false notion of an egoistic self-respect and self-prestige, they had no peaceful co-existence in their life. They considered themselves superior to all other human beings of the world, called themselves *'Arab*, (perfect in language) and all other human being *'Ajam* (dumb people). Regionalism was the basis of their abnormal ego and self-styled superiortity. There were two features of 'Arabian lives—excessive descriptions of war, destructive events and allowing the fire of hatred and revenge to burn for ever in their minds, crushing their own live for their false ego. Secondly, to be frenzy drunkard, black-beetle gambler and habitual in all sorts of voluptuous actions. Young girls in the bars and dance-parties, called *Qīnāṭ*, were freely available for the addicts of liquor. An example of it in their history was Sumayyah, mother of Żiyād, Yażīdī Chief's father at the Battle of Karbala. The married women were also free to joviality and sex with other men. Therefore, the founder of Islām ordered the ladies, especially Umayyites', warned Hindahh[4], the mother of Amīr Mu'āwiyah-bin-Abū Sufyyān and all the men that no one should indulge in illicit coition, who embraces Islām!

There was no regard for ladies in the society and no share in the property. Man could keep any number of women as wives and slave coubnines for sexual use. The owner could also use the slave coubnines for earning money by making them prostitutes. The slavery was at its peak and it was a must for them to obey the commands of their masters, howsoever, it would be the most unjustifiable. Free carnal intercourse was quite common in the women. Some of the clans murdered innocent child girls in the name of maintaing family honour.[5]

Fairs and concourse of people for religious or commercial purposes were quite popular in 'Arabian social life and were specially held in the months of festivals, especially in the month of Žīqādah and all the enmity and tribal vendetta was supposed to lie buried for the time. These fairs were held at Majannah, near Marr-uẓ-Ẓuhrān, not far from Mecca, and at Žu'l-Majāž, at the foot of Mount of 'Arafāt, is a dwelling colony near Mecca. The most glorious 'Okāẓ, which was the great national affair. People flowed from all parts of Arabian peninsula and even more distant lands of the world for trade and commerce. 'Okāẓ was a highly valuable fair, which was started from 540 AD and was prevalent even after Islām. It came to an end in 746 AD due to looting-murdering by *Khārjīs*. There were both constructive and destructive side of this fair. There were organised meetings of artists, poets and litterateurs for mutual coordination and trade development. Prostitution, gambling and other unethical activities, were also allowed as a new fashion. It was negative and destructive side. All the 'Arabians used to assemble in these fairs. In making a circuit of it was, as if they are worshipping in holy Ka'bah itself. Ladies and gents used to make a circuit of nakedly holy K'aba. To please the deities, circum animals as well as human life sacrifices were also done.

There was a wonderful influence of ghosts and goblins in the life of 'Arabians. They would seek prosperity and help from the deities and offer gifts prior to journey and after return from travel and they would even hug the idols! 'Arabs had a special passion for *Kāhin* (fore-teller) and *'Arrāf* (past-teller) also. They used to consult them on important issues and they, in their view, have captured the genies and demons, who work for them as slaves. In 'Arabic language *Żajar* means the sound for making the animals affraid and birds to fritter away. 'Arabs used to practice augury also out of it. They considered it good, if the birds fly to the right side having seen fling with stone and considered it bad, and if they fly to the left. Various types of superstitions were prevalent in them.

During this period, besides Greeks and Christians, there was also a group among 'Arabs, who believed in the Unity of God, worship only one *Ilah*. They were no Greeks and Christians. They did not observe idol-worship and they never allowed any credulity in their life. They never consumed meat of animals after offering to deities. Jews inhabited in Yemen, Yathrib (Medīnā) and Khaybar. Some Christian clans were settled at Ḥīrah, who were called al-'Abad and also some branches of *Rabi'ah* clan, Ghasān Quza'ah, Christen's densely populated area was Najrān in Yemen.

The objective of presenting the above background is to clarify this fact that how unetthical elements in course of time, entering into the religion, defiled the very soul of religion. The Qur'an has clarified:

"Verily those who deny God and His apostles and desire that they differentiate between God and His apostles and say 'we believe in some and we deny some', intend they to take between (*this and*) that a (*midway*)". (*Qur'an*: 4/ 150)

"These are they the infields truly, and We have prepared for the infields a disgraceful torment." (*Qur'an*: 4/ 151)

The process of religious destruction has taken place regarding it prior to Islām and after the Islāmic Revolution. The only reason was the religious pollution that one after another. They firmly believed that a saviour would come from God, who would establish pure and chaste conduct, save the religion from getting polluted. But, on each occation, the religion was polluted afterwards. To this extent that there was an the Islāmic Revolution which enlightened the brightness of pure and chaste conduct removing the dirt of pollution.

The Holy Prophet Muḥammad

The propounder of the Islāmic Revolution, the last of the series of the Prophets of God, Muḥammad (in full: *Abu'l Qāsim* Muḥammad, son of 'Abdu'llāh, son of 'Abdu'l-Muṭṭalib, son of Hāshim, son of 'Abdu'l-Munāf, son of Qossay) was born on the Friday, 17th Rabi' I, in the First year of the Era of the Elephant, or the 20th August, 570 AD in Mecca and passed away while praying to God in the noon of Monday, on the 28th Ṣafar 11 AH, or the 25th May, 632 AD in Medina and buried at the place of his death.[6] The cause of his death is said to be slow poisoning given to him at the battle of Khaybar in the year 629 AD.[7]

Qossay (d. 480 AD), a descendant of Fihr was known as the 'Master of Mecca', and gradually of the entire Hijāz. He made various rules for proper governance of the people and introduced tax system. He rebuilt the Ka'bah, the sacred shrine and also erected a palace, the *Daru'n-Nadwā* (the Council Hall), where the transactions of public business were performed. He arranged food and water for the pilgrims who came from different parts of the 'Arabia to worship at Ka'bah. He was succeeded by his eldest son 'Adbu'd-Dār, but upon his death a dispute broke out among his grandsons and the sons of his brother 'Abdu'l-Munāf dividing various clans, their allies and neighbours themselves on either side. The dispute was settled in dividing the position of profit and prestige among themselves: *Sikāya* (the custody of the sacred wells of Zemzem) and *Rifāda* (the administration of poor-rates) were entrusted to 'Abdu'-ash-Shams son of 'Abdu'l-Munāf, whilst the *Ḥijāba* (the guardianship of the keys of the Ka'bah), *Nadwā* (the presidency of the assembly), *Diyat* (the civil and criminal magistracy), *Sifārah* (legation), *Khaymmuh* (the guardianship of council chamber), *Liwa* (the custody of the standard), *Khāżina* (the administration of public finance and *Ażlam* (the guardianship of the dividing arrow through which they believed to get the judgement of god/goddess remained in the hands of the family of 'Adbu'd-Dār.

'Abdu'l-Munāf had during his lifetime designated his eldest son 'Abdu'-ash-Shams as his successor and he succeeded him without any dispute. 'Abdu'-ash-Shams, who was comparatively a poor man, transferred the authority to his brother Hāshim son of 'Abdu'l-Munāf. A man of great status as well as riches among the Quraysh. Umayya a Roman slave boy, who was the personal servant of 'Abdu'-ash-Shams.[8] After the death of his master, Umayya's family seriously disputed the succession and transfer of the authority to Hāshim by his brother 'Abdu'-ash-Shams and claimed to be the real descendants of 'Abdu'-ash-Shams. This so-called successor of 'Abdu'-ash-Shams, Umayya, is the founder of Umayyite clan.

Despite such unequal, unjust and unscrupulous distribution, the celebrated son of 'Abdu'l-Munāf, Hāshim (d. 510 AD), the founder of Hāshimite clan, rose on the basis of personal character and had been most revered in masses for providing food to the strangers, who congregated during pilgrimages in Mecca. He also founded the custom of sending Quraysh twice in caravans, one in winter to Yemen and other in summer to Syria and so he was called *Father of Commerce*. Hāshim was succeeded by his brother Muṭṭalib (d. 520 AD), surnamed *al-Fāiz* (the Generous), who was again succeeded by his nephew Shayba son of Hāshim, better known as 'Abdu'l-Muṭṭalib. Unfortunately, the envious and malignant Umayyites could not digest the rise of Hāshimites and became their blood thirsty rivals. In these hostile circumstances, when an orphan of Hāshimites, Muḥammad raised the issues relating to justice and equality, the Umayyites felt every position of profit and prestige going out of their hands and so opposed them tooth and nail.

Muḥammad was born after the death of his father 'Abdu'llāh and so was at first under the care of his paternal grandfather, 'Abdu'l-Muṭṭalib, who gave the infant to a wet nurse Ḥalīmā from a nomadic tribe for a better climate for health and spent some time in the desert life. At six Muḥammad lost his mother, Āmina of Żuhrā clan and at eight his grandfather, so, he was taken under the care of his uncle and the new head of the Hāshimite clan, Abū Ṭālib and his wife Fāṭimah daughter of Asad, who bestowed their love and affection, upon him as a result of which Muḥammad also regarded them as his own parents and grew up in their house. Fāṭimah used to feed him, bathe and dress him like her own child. Abū Ṭālib never allowed him to be away from his eyes and even after his reaching the age of adolescence used to keep him in his company on journeys in the Caravans. Muḥammad also responded in the same fashion and when his cousin 'Alī son of Fāṭimah and Abū Ṭālib was born, he took him under his care and he was like a son unto him.

Around year 595 AD, when Muḥammad was accompanying his uncle Abū Ṭālib in a journey, a rich lady Khadījah of Asad clan requested him to take charge of merchandise which resulted in a very high profit. Greatly impressed by his honesty and skill, she proposed marriage. She was forty and he was twenty five. Muḥammad sought permission of his uncle Abū Ṭālib, who not only consented, but also performed the matrimonial rites, and awarded the couple the status of husband and wife. The marriage has been a turning point in the life of Muḥammad. As per the then 'Arab custom, posthumous did not inherit, so, the orphan Muḥammad had no share in the properties of his father or grandfather, but the marriage with Khadījah brought sufficient capital to promote mercantile activities on the scale commensurating with his high abilities. Khadījah has been the most notable figure and an exemplar among the womanhood of Islām. She and her daughter Fāṭimah, *the Lady of Light* occupy a distinguished position in the estimation of Islām. Khadījah bore Muḥammad four children, i.e. three sons – Qāsim, on whose basis he is called *Abu'l Qāsim* (father of Qāsim), Ibrāhīm and 'Abdu'llāh *alias* Ṭayyab and Ṭāhir. All the sons died in infancy and the only daughter Fāṭimah servived. Some add names of more daughters, Ruqqayya, Żaynab and Umm Kulthūm, who were daughters of Khadījah from her first husband, other scholars say they were daughters of Hāla, sister of Khadījah and brought up by her. It is notable that while the Prophet Muḥammad has said so many good words for Fāṭimah, but nothing about these ladies. Fāṭimah aż-Żahrah, *the Lady of Light* was married to Imām 'Alī, who had two sons Ḥasan and Ḥusain and two daughters Żaynab and Umm Kulthūm, who are the most distinguished figures in the history of Islām.

Seen in the socio-religious context of the then 'Arabia, the significance of the prevailing polytheistic religion was that the gods were ascribed power of vendetta or revenge against enemies and the era of their idolatry has been called the *Jāhiliyah* (Age of Ignorance). The most notable point in the present context had been their 'terrorism' and then the specifically 'Arabian character of the ties of blood and family *esprit de corps* afforded protection against partisan and injustice, but other clans, especially strangers were, exposed to all types of oppression. They were robbed, not only of their goods and chattels, but also their daughters and wives. In this atmosphere of lawlessness and crimes, when the institutions of the *Diyat* (the civil and criminal majesty, and also the *wehrgeld*, the price which a murderer pays to the family of victim, if they so consented) and the *Sifārah* (the legation) had totally collapsed in the hands of Umayyites and their men. At the hint of an energetic youth of 25, Muḥammad, the descendants of al-Hāshim and al-Muṭṭalib and some members of Żuhra and Taym clans, bound themselves by a solemn oath to defend each and every human being, irrespective of the caste, creed and region, whether stranger, free or slave from any wrong or injustice to which he might be subjected in Meccan territories and he shall obtain redress for him from the oppressors. It was composed mainly of four persons – Fazl, Fāzal, Muffazzal and Fuzayl, collectively *Fuzūl* (plural of above), so this chivalrous league was named *Ḥilfu'l-Fuzūl* (League of *Fuzūl*). It was founded by Muḥammad in 595 AD, shortly after his marriage and, which continued up to half a century.[9]

Muḥammad's scrupulous refinement, austerity of conduct and behaviour, gentle disposition, strict purity in life, ever readiness to help the downtrodden, the poor and the deprived of basics of life and his commitment towards them had kindled hope in their life and earned for him the appellation of *al-Amīn* (the Trustee).[10] The people kept their valuables with him, having full faith in his trusteeship. In 605 AD when Muḥammad was thirty-five, the Quraysh decided to reconstruct Ka'bah, but in the course of work a dispute arose among them on the issue as to which clan would get the privilege of placing *Ḥajaru'l-Aswad* (the sacred Black Stone) to its right place. The dispute seemed likely to lead to a big bloodshed. Muḥammad was unanimously chosen as the judge and his judgement happily settled the dispute to the satisfaction of all concerned.[11] Till the age of forty, Muḥammad had gained a widespread reputation for wisdom and trustworthiness. He never worshipped idols which was a common religious practice in Mecca. However, occasionally, he resorted to *Khalwah* (spiritual retreat) in which he prayed and discoursed secretly with God.

About 610 AD, at the age of forty in the cave of *Ḥira* (the Tihamah mountain region, near Mecca), when Muḥammad was in spiritual retreat, God chose him as Prophet with a mission of propagating His religion. The first and foremost message conveyed to holy Prophet Muḥammad is a categorical imperative for all mankind in every part of the globe for all times to come:

> "Read thou (*O' our Prophet Muḥammad!*). In the name of the Lord Who created (*Everything in the Universe*). He created man from a clot. Recite (*thou O' Our Prophet Muḥammad*!). And thy Lord is the Most Honourable! (*He*) Who taught (*to write*) with Pen. (*He*) taught man what he knew not!" (*Qur'an*: 96/1-5)

It is most amazing that in a society which was totally illiterate and only 17-18 persons were in a position to somehow read and write in the entire Arabian peninsula, such an order of God emphasized that Islām is the religion of 'reading' and 'reciting'. The Pen is the most powerful tool of knowledge, ignorance and illiteracy has no place in Islām.[12]

After the first revelation from God, the Prophet returned to his house and told his wife Khadījah what had occurred. She and 'Alī declared their acceptance of the faith. Then, the Prophet invited the people of his clan to a party, which has been named by the historians as *Da'watu'l-Žul-'Ashīra* (Feast of the Families). The holy Prophet told them that God has chosen him to declare himself Prophet with a mission of propagating His religion. He also promised whosoever extend his helping hand would be his natural successor. He had to face distressing and painful reactions. 'Alī promised his humble assistance and the Prophet nominated him his vicegerent. The famous historian Abū Ja'far Muḥammad Jarīr Ṭabarī has recorded the event. Thus:

> "The Prophet of God said, 'O clan of 'Abdu'l-Muṭṭalib, I know not if any 'Arab before me has brought to you a gift better than this in which there is all good for this world as well as for the world hereinafter. God has commanded me to call upon you to come to this gift. Whoever among you offers to share my burden will become my brother, my will-bearer and my successor among you. After this invitation, all held a silence. No one supported the call of the Prophet, except 'Alī who got up and said to the Prophet, although I am the youngest in this gathering, my eyes are the smallest, my belly is bigger, my shin is thinner, but 'O Prophet of God I am ready to assist you and share your burden.' The Prophet, held 'Alī by his shoulder and announced: 'He is my brother, bearer of my will, and my

> successor among you. You' listen to his words and obey his commands."[13]

Necessity forced him henceforth to preach the Message of God secretly among the people close to him, which enabled some men and women to choose the path of those upon whom God had bestowed His favours. They were his beloved servant, and former slave Żayd, his uncle Abū Ṭālib and his old friend Abū Bakr, etc. Some dispute Abū Ṭālib's faith in Islām, but it is also evident from the poetry composed by him in the praise of the Prophet that Abu Ṭālib was the follower of Islām. Morever, he was sole protector of Prophet Muḥammad during the period of insurgency, his wife Fāṭimah daughter of Asad nourished the Prophet like her own son.

At the end of third year God commanded the Prophet:

> "O thou (*O' Our Prophet Muḥammad!*) covered under thy mantle! Arise (*thou*) and warn (*mankind*)." (*Qur'an*: 74/1-2)

Whereupon, Prophet Muḥammad began to throw his heart and soul into his preaching in public. He told them in burning words which stirred the hearts of the listeners to abandon their evil ways and abominations. He explained to them the nature's tremendous laws of day and night, the problems of life and death, the growth and decay and how the creations manifest the power of their Creator and attest to the sovereignty of God. And also that all human beings are equal, exceptions and gradation could only be made on the basis of sanctity in his life. He asked them not to discriminate on the basis of caste, creed, wealth, manpower etc. The Meccan took these messages most horribly and Muḥammad instead of being called the most trusted, honest and the man of wisdom, was declared a wizard, a poet and even insane. Quraysh with all possible hatred and hostility at their command began mocking and insulting him and persecuting the poor newcomers to Islām, who were mostly the humble folk unable to defend themselves. On the advise of Prophet Muḥammad in 615 AD most of them migrated to Abyssinia, a Christian country, from there also the Meccan tried to get Muslims expelled out but the king did not agree to their request.[14]

Meccan were sad that despite the emigration of some persons and the cruel persecutions of newcomers, the Muslims were growing in number day by day. Failed in their attempts, Meccan proposed a compromise to the Prophet, offering to accept his religion, if he would so modify it as to make room for their gods and intercessor with God and they would regard him as their king, promising him wealth, power and best of the fair sex. The Prophet replied them using metaphorical language, that if they were to put the sun in the palm of his right hand and the moon in the palm of his left hand, he would not forsake obeying the Unique God or refrain from performing His mission.[15]

The unsuccessful Meccan went to his uncle Abū Ṭālib offering him best of their young men in place of Muḥammad with all that he desired, if he allowed them to kill Muḥammad. Abū Ṭālib refused and condemned them.[16] In about 616 AD Umayyite clan-chief Abū Sufyyān, his brothers-in-law 'Utbah and Shībah, Saham clan chief Abū Jahl and other Meccan clan chiefs caused a document drawn to the effect that none of their clan would have any interaction, sale or purchase and completely boycott the Hāshimite clan, because it was protecting Muḥammad. The document was deposited in Ka'bah.[17] The Prophet and his uncle Abū Ṭālib, along with other members of Hāshimite clan took refuge in the *Sh'obu'l-Abū Ṭālib* (the mountain pass of Abū Ṭālib) for three years, during which none had any dealing or transaction with them and the Hāshimite did not dare leave their place of refuge. After three years the social boycott lost momentum, not only because of harm it did to their economic interest, but also because the 'Arabs deeply believed and respected the kind of wisdom and knowledge that Muḥammad clearly had. Some of them grew weary of the boycott of old friends and neighbours and managed to have the document reconsidered and when it was brought from the Ka'bah, it was found that all the writings have been eaten by the white ants, except *Bismika-Allāh-Hummah* (thy name, O God). Astounded by the happenings they lifted the ban.[18]

The Prophet was again free to go about the city but the opposition to his Preaching was made more strong. The Prophet Muḥammad went to the city of Ṭā'if, but his mission was not taken there kindly and he returned wounded.[19] But God was kind enough that a group of twelve men, in the summer of 621 AD, during annual pilgrimage season came to Mecca from Yathrib, more than two hundred miles away, met the Prophet Muḥammad of whom they had already heard, gladly embraced Islām and returned to their native place.[20]

Islām was growing and expanding from day by day, the Meccans continued inflicting all kinds of pressure and torture, striking and beating, insulting, ridiculing and defaming Muslims and also the Prophet Muḥammad. This scenario turned worse when Prophets wife Khadījah, and uncle Abū Ṭālib, who stood like a rock in his protection died in about 619 AD and another uncle Abū Lahab, who joined with his arch enemy clan Umayyites, because of his wife who was of that clan, succeeded as the head of Hāshimite clan. He was only Hāshimite who bitterly opposed and made it his business to torment the Prophet Muḥammad and his wife picked thorn bushes and strew them in the sand, where she knew that the Prophet was sure to walk barefoot. In the whole Qur'an his case is the only one, among the opponents of the Prophet, who are denounced by name. All the five verses denouncing Abū Lahab (*Father of Flame*) read as under:

> "May perish both hands of Abū Lahab. Shall avail him not his wealth nor what he earneth. Soon shall he burn in flaming fire. And his wife, the bearer of firewood, Upon her neck shall be halter of twisted rope." (*Qur'an:* 111/1-5)

The only consideration which had prevented Quraysh from killing Prophet Muḥammad was the fear of the blood-vengeance of Hāshimites to which clan his family belonged but now the head of the clan was himself after his head. The Prophet waited for God's command, which came at length in the night appointed for his murder by Quraysh. It was July 16, 622 AD. The slayers surrounded the house from all sides. The Prophet gave his cloak to 'Alī, bidding him to lie down on the bed, so that, the slayer looking in night would think their target was there, and he left the house along with Abū Bakr for Yathrib. After travelling for many days by unfrequented paths reached a suburb of Yathrib, where the people of the city used to go every morning, watching till the heat drove them to shelter. It was a Jew who saw him first and called out Muslims in a derisive tone that he whom they were waiting had at last arrived. It was forenoon of the Friday, September 24, 622 AD, when the Prophet reached Yathrib safely, thus, became famous as *Medina'ur-Rasūl* (the city of Rasūl) and *Medina'ul-Munawwara* (the illuminated or par excellence city). Imām 'Alī, who was left in Mecca for returning the valuables of some Meccans, which they had kept in the trust of Prophet Muḥammad, after the completion of job, emigrated from Mecca, with the family of the Prophet, women and children on foot hiding themselves in the day time and travelling only at night, lest they should fall into the hands of Meccans, reached Medina some months later. Most of other Muslims residing in Mecca, who had been in a position to emigrate had already sold their properties and shifted to Medina.

Emigration was not just a historical event, it was transfer of a primitive tribe from one place to another, affecting the life. But it had deep philosophical and social implications too, which can be seen in all the twenty-seven civilizations, we know. The emigration had resulted in the development of the civilizations and a primitive tribe became civilized and gave rise to a higher culture. The other most important implication was geographical in nature. Medina was different from rocky, inflexible and barren Mecca. Medina was an oasis where date palms and cereals grew and agriculture had already been developed by the inhabitants, which changed the psyche of the immigrants of Mecca.

The Prophet was given a piece of land to build a house for him and later a mosque also. It was a free gift from two orphan brothers. Prophet Muḥammad affectionately agreed to receive the payment of the value. The construction was simplest with walls of brick and earth and the roofs of palm leave. A portion of the mosque was also allowed for residential purpose for those who had no shelter of their own. The Prophet used to preach and pray standing on the bare ground or leaning against a palm tree and the Muslim devotees heard him bent in unison with the soul-stirring words.

The purity and nobleness of Prophet Muḥammad and his earnestness and fiery enthusiasm for the Truth he preached brought various persons, tribes and clans of the Yathrib and surrounding areas, rallying round the standard of Islām and formed the nucleus of Islāmic commonwealth. The Hāshimites of Medina, later named as *Anṣār* (the Helpers) were ready to scarifice anything to their brothers-in-faith, and those who had forsaken their birth-place the ties of kith and kin and every tie of home for the sake of Islām, were later named as *Muhājirīn* (Emigrants). In order to unite the helpers and the emigrants into closer bonds, the Prophet established brotherhood between them in practical shape, as a result of which they found themselves together in sorrow and happiness and also distributed their properties equally with their brothers-in-faith. The Jews, who may be said to be the third party, had close business relations with the Qurayshite Meccans, extended half-hearted welcome, to the holy Prophet Muḥammad, they were, however, inclined to look with favour on the preaching of Islām on the basis of their faith in the promised Messiah. Now, the greatness of the Prophet Muḥammad can be seen from the fact, that he granted a charter to the people, which is most relevant even today. It reveals his real greatness not in his own age, but all ages to come, as no one of that age could even dream to pull down the existing fabrics of the society and take the task of reconstructing a State, a commonwealth and introducing a society based on universal humanity.

Ibn Hishām has carefully preserved in his biography of the holy Prophet Muḥammad the document, which reads as under:

"In the name of the most merciful, compassionate God."

Commenced the first charter of the freedom of conscience:

> "Given by Muḥammad, the Prophet, to the Believers whether Qurayshite of Yathrib, and all individuals of whatever origin who have made common cause with them, all these shall constitute one nation."

Further, puts certain norms for payment of the *Diyat* (the wehrgeld price, which any homicide pays to the family of the victim, if they so consented) by different clans, and fixing some important duties of Muslims among themselves, the Charter proceeds, thus:

> "The state of peace and war shall be common to all Muslims, no one among them shall have the right of concluding peace with, or declaring war against, the enemies of his co-religionist. The Jews who attach themselves to our commonwealth shall be protected from all insults and vexations, they shall have equal rights with our own people to our assistance and good offices: the Jews of various branches of 'Auf, Najjār, Ḥārith, Jashm, Thalāba, Ans and others domiciled in the Yathrib, shall form with the Muslims of composite nation; they shall practice their religion as free as Muslims; the *clients* (the protected) and allies of the Jews shall enjoy the same security and freedom; the guilty shall be pursued and punished; the Jews shall join the Muslims in defending Yathrib (Medina) against all enemies; the interior of Yathrib shall be a sacred place for all who accept this Charter; the *clients* and allies of Muslims and Jews shall be as respected as the patrons; all true Muslims shall hold in abhorrence every man guilty of crime, injustice, or disorder: no one shall uphold the culpable, though he was his nearest Kin."

Further, there are some provisions of internal administration of the state and it concludes with:

> "All future disputes between those who accepted this Charter shall be referred to The Prophet of God."[21]

It was about April 627 AD, The Prophet sanctioned a Charter, to the monks of the monastery of St. Catherine (near Mount Sinai) and to all Christians, which may be mentioned as one of the noblest monuments of enlightened tolerance, which secured to Christians privileges and immunities, which they could not possess even under the sovereigns of their own creed. This Charter, unique in nature, declared:

> "That any Muslim violating and abusing what was therein ordered, should be regarded as a violator of God's testament, a transgressor of His commandments, and a slighter of His faith."

The Prophet along with his followers monitored the strict adherence of the Charter to the effect that, it was:

> "To protect Christians, to defend their Churches, the residences of their priests and to guard them from all injuries. They were not to be unfairly taxed, no bishop was to be driven out of his bishopric, no Christian was to be forced to reject his religion; no monk was to be expelled from his monastery, no pilgrim was to be detained from his pilgrimage. Nor were the Christian Churches to be pulled down for the sake of building mosques or homes for the Muslims. Christian women married to Muslims were to enjoy their own religion and not to be subjected to compulsion or annoyance of any kind on that account. If Christian should stand in need of assistance for the repair of their Churches or monasteries, or any other matter pertaining to their religion, the Muslims were to assist them. This was not to be considered as taking part in their religion, but as merely rendering the assistance to their need, and complying with the ordinances of the Prophet, which were made in their favour by the authority of God and this Prophet. Should the Muslims be engaged in hostilities with outside Christians, no Christian resident among Muslims should be treated with contempt on account of his creed. Any Muslim so treating a Christian should be accounted recalcitrant to the Prophet...... etc."[22]

Needless to emphasize that if the Charters cited above could be reciprocated by Jews and Christians to the Muslims and the *vice versa*, it would immediately result in global peace and harmony. These are guidelines for every religion of the world. It was because of this generous attitude of Prophet Muḥammad that the religion of Islām spread so rapidly. Various scholars, representing different religious clans and creed came to the holy Prophet to discuss various aspects of religion and society. Prophet received them with great honour and affection, usually took off his shoulders the mantle and spread it on the earth for the guests and discussed the issue. The kindness of the Prophet even for the enemies soon converted them into most devoted followers.

The Meccan infidels were burning with revenge. They made formidable preparation to pounce upon Muslims and succeeded in obtaining the help and assistance of other tribes and clans including Jews of the Ḥejāż, who had desisted from the Charter cited above. They were unrestrained in their harassment of the Muslims with the help of *Munāfiqūn* (the hypocrites, who actually did not believe in Islām, but mingled with Muslims) created hardship everyday until finally the matter led to war.

There were altogether over eighty major and minor battles, in most of which Muslims had been victorious, amongst them Badr (624 AD), Uḥud (625 AD), <u>Kh</u>andaq (627 AD), <u>Kh</u>aybar (629 AD) and Ḥunayn (630 AD) were the battles, in which the Prophet Muḥammad personally participated. If we look at the topology of these wars, all of which have been fought in close vicinity of Medina, it becomes crystal clear that the war were imposed on Muslims and they fought in self-defence. In these wars less than two hundred Muslims and more than a thousand infidels were killed. Mostly, Muslims' victory was through the efforts of Imām 'Alī, who was the only person, who never turned away from the battles. Most of the stalwarts of enemies, especially Umayyites, were killed by Imām 'Alī, which resulted in personal enmity of Umayyites towards him and his descendants.

Kind hearted holy Prophet Muḥammad was grieved to see the war captives corded, when produced before him for final verdict, amongst them was his uncle 'Abbās. The merciful Prophet ordered the release of the war captives after paying a meagre sum as a token fine. There was no compulsion for being converted to Islām. Similarly, a tormenting event had happened, when a poor Bedouin was brought by the Quray<u>sh</u> as a captive to Mecca! Muḥammad had recognized her with tears of joy, she was none else than his caretaker mother, Ḥalīmah of Sa'd clan, during his early infancy. He obtained her from Quray<u>sh</u> after some payment and made an ample provision for the rest of her life. The Prophet himself paid for release of his uncle 'Abbās, whose descendants established 'Abbāsite Caliphate and ruled for about five centuries and vexed every type of oppression, tyranny and finally assassinated. But it was most torturous for the Prophet in the battle of Uḥud to see the barbarously mutilated body of his brave uncle Ḥamża, slain in the yaw battle. The wife of Abū Sufyyān, Hindah, had shown the greatest ferocity in the savage vengeance, tearing out the heart of holy Prophet's uncle, Ḥamżah-bin-'Abdu'l-Mṭṭalib, and making bracelets and necklaces of the ears and noses of the slain Ḥamżah. The holy Prophet was profoundly sad and wept bitterly like an ordinary human being.

But in total contrast to his enemies, this Man, Muḥammad above all human beings, when victoriously entered Mecca, where he was hunted out of his place of birth and had been stoned out at various places, pardoned, each and every person, including Abū Sufyyān and declared general amnesty, natural equality and brotherhood of mankind. Mecca regained its past glory, the most holy city of Islām, *Mecca al-Muaẓẓamah* (the revered Mecca), centres upon *al-Ḥaram* Mosque and sacred well Žemžem, located inside and in the central courtyard is Ka'bah, the holiest shrine of Islām. Mecca is the city where *Ḥajj* pilgrimage is performed.

Now, the mission of the Prophet Muḥammad was achieved and people steeped in barbarism, utter darkness, degrading and sanguinary superstition have been inspired to believe in one, solo God of truth and love. At a time when the hosts of Arabian peninsula came flocking to join the faith of Islām, the prophet felt that his task was accomplished, the holy Prophet Muḥammad received the message of God:

> "When cometh the help of God and the Victory, And thou seest people entering the religion of God in multitudes, Celebrate then the praises of thy Lord, and seek thou His protection (*for*) verily He is Oft-Turning (*merciful*)!" (*Qur'an*: 110/1-3)

In the light of the above Qur'anic verses, the farewell pilgrimage of Mecca could be visualized. On 23rd February, 632 AD, the Prophet Muḥammad left Medina with an immense, concourse of Muslims, whose numbers are estimated to be from ninety thousands to one lac forty thousands. This pilgrimage had been called by historians and scholars as *Ḥajjatu'l-Balāghah* (the Great *Ḥajj*) or *Ḥajjatu'l-Islām* (the *Ḥajj* of Islām) and more popularly *Ḥajjatu'l-Wada'a* (the pilgrimage of farewell). Before completing the rites of the pilgrimage, the holy Prophet addressed the assembled multitude from the top of the *Jabal al-'Arafāt* on 8th Žilḥajjih, the 7th March, 632 AD, in such words which shall ever live in the hearts of all generations of Muslims:

> "Ye people! listen to my words, for I know not whether another year will be vouchsafed to me after this year to find myself amongst you at this place....
>
> "Your lives and property are sacred and inviolable amongst one another until ye appear before the Lord, as this day and this month is sacred for all; and (*remember*) ye shall have to appear before your Lord, who shall demand from you an account of all actions ....
>
> "Henceforth the vengeance of blood practised in the days of paganism (*Jàhilyah*) is prohibited; and all blood-feud abolished ...
>
> "Ye people! listen to my words and understand the same. Know that *all Muslims are brothers unto one another*. Ye are one brotherhood. Nothing which belongs to another is lawful unto his brother, unless freely given out of good-will. Guard yourselves from committing injustice...
>
> "Let him that is present tell it unto him that is absent. Haply he that shall be told may remember better than he who hath heard it...."[23]

After each sentence the holy Prophet Muḥammad stopped and his words were repeated in a stentorian voice by the Muslims present, so that made clear that whatever was said was heard by the entire assembled host. This practice was again repeated while returning from the pilgrimage, the Prophet halted at a place called *Khumm* and convened an assembly of the people accompanying him and made a long sermon to the huge gathering and then raised Imām 'Alī aloft with his arms and made this vital announcement. The following is the account given in Ibn Ḥanbal, a Sunnī collection of *Ḥadīths*:

> "We were with the Apostle of God in his journey and we stopped at *Ghadīru'l-Khumm*. We performed the obligatory prayer together and a place was swept for the Apostle under two trees and he performed the mid-day prayer. And then took 'Alī by the hand and said to people: 'Do you not acknowledge that I have a greater claim on each of the believers than they have on themselves?' And they replied: 'Yes!' and he took 'Alī's hand and said: 'Of whomsoever I am Lord (*Mawlā*), then this 'Alī is

> also his Lord. O God! Be Thou the supporter of whoever supports 'Alī and be the enemy of whoever oppose him.'
>
> And 'Omar met him ('Alī) after this and said to him: 'Congratulations, 'O son of Abū Ṭālib! Now, morning and evening (i.e. for ever) you are master of every believing man and woman."[24]

This wishing of Caliph 'Omar has been mentioned by many historians. Many Arab poets said *Qaṣīdāhs* by way of congratulating Imām 'Alī and celebrating the occasion of the announcement of his *wilāyah*. The couplets of the famous Arabic poet Ḥassān-bin-Thābit became very popular. And thus, made announcement of his *Khalīfāh* in favour of Imām 'Alī.[25] In the past too, Imām 'Alī was nominated as his Vicegerent on the occasion of *Da'watu'l-Žul-'Ashīra*. This was second occasion. Since, the succession of the Prophet is the deciding factor between Shi'īs and Sunnīs, it has already been dealt with in detail at the appropriate place in the preceding pages. But it should be clearly borne in mind that the Imām 'Alī's nomination as the Vicegerent was not based on the personal liking but on the criterion of merit and excellence.

With respect to being the best of Companions of the Prophet, every Shi'īs and the majority of Sunnīs, specially the *Ṣūfīs*, regard Imām 'Alī to be the best after the Prophet Muḥammad. Books are replete with Traditions in the appreciation of the various aspects Imām 'Alī's excellences. In founding the Caliphate, all the four Caliphs, from a practical consideration, were the highly placed companions of the Prophet, who were also respectable for their being in close relationship with the Prophet. But, of them all, Imām 'Alī's was of the highest order in knowledge, valour, moral nobility and the superiority of clan. He had to his merit an additional edge, because all the participants of the Battle of Badr (624 AD) were regarded to be distinguished, and he was the victor of Badr and, therefore, the most distinguished.

The conduct of the holy Prophet Muḥammad was, however, directly against any kind of the nepotism, he never allowed the family relations and personal liking to be the criterion of merit and excellence. An objective observation would show that the Prophet Muḥammad always kept his relations on back foot from available benefits and rewards and put them forward in times of danger and material loss. When her daughter Fāṭimah who was dearer to him than his life, came to request for a maid-servant to assist in the hard labour of grinding mill, the Prophet sent her away by telling her, how to mutter on the string of leads, the greatness, praise and glory of God, and told her to say 34 times *Allāhu'-Akbar* (God is Great), 33 times *Alḥamdū'-Lillāh* (Praise is due to God) and 33 times *Subḥān-Allāh* (God is all perfection). This specific muttering, on the string of beads is known as *Tasbīḥu'l-Fāṭimah* (Rosary of Fāṭimah), which is practiced even today after the daily prayers.

In the Battle of Badr in 623, the arch-opponents of Islām, 'Atbah, Walīd and Shībah, respectively the maternal-grandfather, the maternal-uncle and the brother of Mu'āwiyah-bin-Abū Sufyyān and also Ibn Rabī'h, the renowned merciless warrior of his time, all under leadership of the Quraysh clan, challenged the Muslims to fight and there were among the Muslims the men who could be sent to combat them, but the Prophet sent the closest of his relations, namely 'Alī his cousin, Ḥamżah and 'Obaydah, his uncles, who smashed their vanity and made them lick the dust. 'Alī and Ḥamżah returned victorious, while 'Obaydah was severely wounded.

The backbone of Islāmic economic system is *Żakāt*, the payment of which is mandatory for every Muslim, accordingly a portion of every one's capital enjoined by the law of poor-due gets distributed among the needy Muslims, and would remain ever in practice, the only exception in this law of poor-due is that it has been made *Ḥarām* (unlawful) for Fāṭimah aż-Żahrah, the beloved daughter of Prophet Muḥammad, and her family, the descendants. It means that the Prophet's own family cannot get any share out of the poor-due fund. This was made so, lest Islām should become a property of inheritance, and the people of Prophet's genealogy should not get used to earn their living without due labour. The Prophet used to prefer for his family, devotion to God, purity of self, sacrifice, and a life of contentment in moderation, and he consistently used to pray God:

> "O Lord, the livelihood of the people of my family be just in keeping with their needs."[26]

The last year of the life of the Prophet Muḥammad was spent in Medina, where he settled the organization of provinces and tribal communities, which had embraced Islām and had become the part of Islāmic federation. He visited the sick, followed each and every bier that came accross him, participated in a slave's dinner, mended his own clothes, milked his goats and met the people and told them about high Traditions. His physical health and strength rapidly failed.

The holy Prophet Muḥammad in his last days called for pen and paper which was refused, is famous as the *Wāqiyau'l-Qirṭās-wa'l-*

Qalam (Episode of Pen and Paper). Imām al-Bukhārī, Abū 'Abdu'llāh Muḥammad-bin-Ismā'īl (d. 870 AD), the most trusted Sunnī Traditionist, has given the account of it:

> "When the Prophet's illness became serious, he said: 'Bring me writing materials that I may write for you something, after which you will not be led into error.
>
> 'Omar said: 'The illness has overwhelmed the holy Prophet. We have the Book of God and that is enough for us.'
>
> 'Then the people differed about this and spoke many words. And he (the Prophet) said: 'Leave me! There ought not be quarrelling in my presence.'
>
> And Ibn 'Abbās went out saying: The greatest of all calamities is what intervened between the Apostle and his writing."[27]

At the age of 63, while praying God earnestly in whisper, the spirit of this great Man took flight to the blessed compansionship of the High. After the departure of the Prophet, 'Alī was neither present nor was asked to participate in the election in which Abū Bakr was made the first Caliph. How Imām 'Alī could do so. Should anyone expire in a family, its members are used to be with the funeral rites of the deceased and never leave him to settle the matter of election along with the aspirants of Caliphate. Although the responsibility of the funeral rites of the departed Prophet was equally obligatory on all Muslims, but the most trusted and closest companions of Prophet were too keen for the issue of election to heed their moral and human obligation to attend the funeral rites of the Prophet. These were the companions who had defied the command of the Prophet to join the army under commandership of Usāmah-bin-Żayd and had argued with prophet a few days before his death.[28] It was only after the issue of the Caliphate was *willy nilly* settled in *Saqīfau'l-Banīu's-Sa'da* (Terrace of Sa'da clan) that they thought of joining the last rites of the Prophet. Having come after two days, they disputed as to where should be the place of burial of the Prophet. As a result of all these the Prophet could be buried only after two days of his death.[29] 'Alī, 'Abbās and others performed the funeral rites of the Prophet Muḥammad.[30]

The holy Prophet Muḥammad was extremely simple in his dress, belongings, habits and mode of life. Often, went without a meal, some dates and water were the source of nourishment. For several months no fire could be lighted in his house for scantiness of means. God had given him the key to the treasures of this world, but he never used it for him or his family. He had the mind of the Teacher, with the highest intellectualism, progressive ideals, innovative and most modern thought. Fourteen centuries have passed after him but the time has developed his concept of life, human relationship, equity, peace and love for all. The holy Qur'an denotes the essence of his personality:

> "And that man hath only for which he maketh effort."
>
> (*Qur'an* 53/39)

Fāṭimah aż-Żahrah, the Lady of Light

According to the Chapter XXIV, *An-Nūr* (the Light) of the holy Qur'an Fāṭimah aż-Żahrah is symbolic of tree and fruits, the analogy of the *Kalamahu'sh-Shahādah* (profession of faith). It has been said to be like a blessed tree, which refers to the chosen genealogy of the Prophet Ibrāhīm in whose progeny were numerous Prophets, including Mūsā (Moses), 'Īsā (Jesus) and Muḥammad. In the same chapter in the verse of the *An-Nūr,* the word *Mishkāt* (the Chandelier) stands for Fāṭimah aż-Żahrah and *Miṣbāḥ* (the Lamp) stands for Ḥasan and Ḥusain.[31] A description of this has to be made in the following pages, so, they are collectively called *Panjtan*, means five grand persons of Islām, namely Prophets of God, Muḥammad, her beloved daughter, Fāṭimah aż-Żahrah, *the Lady of Light,* Imām 'Alī, the successor of the holy Prophet Muḥammad and sons Imām Ḥasan and Imām Ḥusain, both are popularly called Ḥasnayn. However, some of the Traditions of the Prophet may be mentioned hereunder:

> "Fāṭimah is the Head of the womenfolk of the Paradise."[32]
>
> "Fāṭimah is a piece of myself and one he who pained her."[33], pained me[34]and who pained me, pained God and who pained God, his place shall be Hell."[35]

"*Ummu'l-Mūminīn* 'Ā'ishah said, I found no one superior to Fāṭimah, except her father, the Prophet."[36]

The Lady of the Light, Fāṭimah aż-Żahrah (in full: *Khātūnu'l-Jannah* Fāṭimah aż-Żahrah, daughter of *Ummu'l-Mūminīn* Khadījah daughter of Khawaled of Asad clan and the holy Prophet *Abu'l Qāsim* Muḥammad, was born on the Friday, the 20th Jamādī II, in the 45th year of the Era of the Elephant[37], or 614 AD in Mecca. Expired while praying God in the noon of Wednesday, 3rd Jamādī II, 11 AH or 26th August, 632 AD in Medina and buried in al-Bāqī' cemetery, ignoring her last wish to be buried by the side of his father the holy Prophet Muḥammad.

'Arabs are known for their pride, pugnacity, peculiar sense of honour, and the wonderful force and patience for vindictiveness. Their horrible custom was burying alive the female children, which was most prevalent in the tribes of Quraysh and Kindah along with many other notions of antiquity, observed, on altar of sacrificing the children to their gods. Islām prohibited all inhuman practices and imposed severe punishments, brushed aside all the complexes in a single stroke in the famous declaration of the Prophet: Paradise is at the foot of the mother.

Islām enforced it as one of the essential teachings, the respect of the womenfolk. It was a routine practice by the Prophet Muḥammad to come daily in morning at the doors of his daughter and calling out aloud: O' Lord! bestow Mercy on my *Ahlu'l-Bayt.* Whenever his daughter Fāṭimah called upon him, the Prophet Muḥammad would stand up in her respect, kiss her forehead and offer his seat to her.[38] Every Muslim, male or female, in their love and reverence for all the pure, true or/and the noblest ideal of human imagination in a holy women, proclaimed her the Lady of Paradise, the representative of womenfolk and the *Lady of Light* for she was the embodiment of all divine elements in womanhood.

Daughter of the Great Lady, the sole companion, helper and the first wife of the Prophet Muḥammad, *Ummu'l-Mūminīn* Khadījah when Fāṭimah married Imām 'Alī, the Prophet's cousin on Friday, 25th May, 624 AD, she was only 9 years old. Their sons Ḥasan and Ḥusain are the grandsons of the Prophet. A third son Muḥsin died in infancy. Żaynab and Umm Kulthūm were the other daughters. Though the married life of 'Alī and Fāṭimah was of a short period of eight years; Fāṭimah died due to unbearable shocks after the demise of her father within six months. But during the said period the couple presented exemplary ideals of uninterrupted sunshine of faithfulness and blessedness.

In the early years of Islām women continued to occupy an exalted position. Fāṭimah was tall, slender, and endowed with great beauty, for which she was called *aż-Żahrah*, the beautiful. She was a brilliant, accomplished and virtuous lady. Her sermons and aphorisms were the index to her strength of character and nobility of mind. She was noted for her learning, her virtues and strength of character. Fāṭimah was a lady covered with the orbits of *ar-Rāsikhūn-fi'l-'Ilm.* She was a good commentator and interpreter of the holy Qur'an. She was expert in Islāmic *Sharī'a.* The womenfolk used to take her guidance in various issues facing them. It is notable that during the lifetime of the Prophet,

Fāṭimah avoided involvement in political affairs but after the demise of her father, the Prophet Muḥammad, she had a sharp clash with the first Caliph Abū Bakr and whenever she took part in the crucial discussions regarding the succession of the Prophet, her eloquent reasoning and presentation of facts, made her opponents speechless. It was her intellectual heritage and training that her daughter Żaynab shielded her youthful nephew 'Alī, mostly known as Imām Żainu'l-Ābidīn from Umayyites after the butchery of Karbala. Fāṭimah's maid-servant Fizzah, to whom she had distributed the household work in the ideal way that she would be completely free to take rest on every alternate day and Fāṭimah would do all the household work in her place.

Imām 'Alī-ibn-Abī Ṭālib

The first and grand Imām of the series of the twelve Imāms and Fourth in the order of Caliphate, the emeritus and the excellent soul in knowledge and virtue, next to the holy Prophet Muḥammad, his cousin and son-in-law, *Abu'l Ḥasan*, 'Alī son of Hāshimite parents, Fāṭimah-bint-Asad and Abī Ṭālib. He was born on the 13th Rajab, in the Era of the Elephent 30, or in 600 AD within the four walls of Ka'bah the revered house of God in Mecca. Martyred while leading the prayer of God and left after two days for Heavens on Tuesday, 21st Ramazān, 40 AH or 28th January, 661 AD in the mosque of Kufa and buried at Najaf (Iraq).

Imām 'Alī 's father, Abū Ṭālib was the chief of Hāshimite clan and was real brother of 'Abdu'llāh, father of the holy Prophet Muḥammad, who were sons of 'Abdu'l-Muṭṭalib and Fāṭimah daughter of 'Omaro of the Makhżumī clan. Prophet Muḥammad regarded Abū Ṭālib and his wife Fāṭimah, daughter of Asad, father and mother of 'Alī, as his own parents and under whose care in their house he grew up from his tender age, and when the members of the Qurayshite had united to oppose the holy Prophet Muḥammad and frustrate his mission, then Abū Ṭālib himself and along with his family had stood like a iron wall to all challenges and faced all distress to protect the Prophet and support and facilitate his mission.

When Imām 'Alī was born, Prophet Muḥammad took his cousin under his care and he was like a son unto him. He used to live with him, used to sleep with him and feed, wash and dress him and even carried him on outings, whenever went out, so naturally Imām 'Alī was brought up right from his childhood to his youth under the guardianship of the Prophet Muḥammad.

Imām 'Alī was ten years old when the revelation of God was announced by the holy Prophet Muḥammad, he had inducted Islām in constant exposure with the Prophet Muḥammad. From the very beginning he was Muslim and remained his lifelong devoted follower and also risked his life by sleeping in the bed of the Prophet Muḥammad, when enemies has gathered to assassinate the Prophet. The holy Prophet Muḥammad could emigrate to Medīnā in 622 AD. 'Alī left Mecca, only after he returned all the properties of merchants of Mecca to their respective owners that they had entrusted to the *Amīn* (truthful) Muḥammad.

Imām 'Alī displayed rare courage in battles, became renowned as warrior during Islām's struggle for survival, often leading the Islāmic army. He was also one of the Prophet's scribes and chosen to lead several important missions. When the hostile Meccans fully demoralized finally surrendered to Islām without any fighting or battle, it was Imām 'Alī who smashed the pagan idols in the Ka'bah, the foremost shrine in Mecca.

A man of great amiable look and kindness, soft gray eyes, ruddy complexion, medium height, with a flowing beard, extremely strong, inclined to the stoutness, 'Alī was 21, when the Prophet Muḥammad married him to his only daughter Fāṭimah aż-Żahrah in the year 631 AD. Out of this unique wedlock of the infallible couples, were born Ḥasan and Ḥusain, that the progeny of the holy Prophet Muḥammad, the *Saiyeds* descend. A third son Muḥsin who died in infancy and two daughters Żaynab and Umm-Kul<u>th</u>ūm survived.

Imām 'Alī is revered by the <u>Sh</u>i'īs as the only true successor of the holy Prophet Muḥammad, because he was unequivocally twice nominated as his successor first on the occasion of the *Da'watu'l-Žul-'A<u>sh</u>īra*[39] and also while he was returning from his 'farewell pilgrimage to Mecca.'[40] Most of the Sunnīs believe that the nomination was for spiritual succession and not for all matters. So, a conflict arose resulting into the split in Islām as <u>Sh</u>i'īs and Sunnīs. It is the attachment to Imām 'Alī that the <u>Sh</u>i'īs are popularly referred to as *<u>Sh</u>i'ianu'l-'Alī* (the Followers of Imām 'Alī).

Imām 'Alī became the Fourth Caliph of *<u>Kh</u>ilāfatu'r-Rā<u>sh</u>idah*, after twenty four years of the death of the Prophet Muḥammad and was martyred after four and half years of his Caliphate. Imām 'Alī was invited by the Muslims to accept the Caliphate after the murder of the third Caliph 'O<u>th</u>mān, which he accepted very reluctantly after long hesitation and faced great difficulties due mostly to the corrupt state of affairs, when he had succession. Imām 'Alī was ranked as Caliph on

23rd day of June, 655 AD, at a general meeting held at Medina in the Prophet's mosque where nearly all Muslims pledged allegiance at the hand of Imām 'Alī.[41]

Soon after the accession to the Caliphate, Imām 'Alī based his rule on the Islāmic ideals of justice and equality, which was a blow to the interest of the Quraysh aristocracy, which, had highly grown due to various conquests. Umayyite clan was by birth the adversary to the Hāshimites clan to which belonged the Prophet Muḥammad and Imām 'Alī. Umayyites were highly apprehensive of Imām 'Alī having been chosen as the successor of the Prophet. All the wealth taken and used in personal pleasures and luxury in the ruling period of Caliph 'Othmān, was under threat to be checked and confiscated, so, the future looked dark. So, Mu'āwiyah-bin-Abū Sufyyān made a huge army by bringing together Umayyites and the pseudo-Muslims and occupied some areas by setting up a battle front against Imām 'Alī.[42] But some of them mounted difficulties and unrest against him and forced him to fight against the rebellion which resulted in the battles of Jamal, Siffin, Nahrwan etc.

They organised several battles against the Caliph and were defeated. The first rebellion was led by the daughter of the first Caliph and widow of the Prophet, *Ummu'l-Mūminīn* 'Ā'isha, known as battle of *Jamal* (camel). Second rebellion was led by Mu'āwiyah-bin-Abū Sufyyān, a kinsman of 'Othmān was on the verge of being crushed by the army of Imām 'Alī, but he was forced to accept arbitration of a friend. Again Imām 'Alī was forced to war by *Khawārijīs* (Seceders). They were killed but one of them struck with a poisoned sword on Imām 'Alī, while he was praying in the Mosque of Kufa, which resulted in his death after two days.

Chivalrous, humane, and forbearing, Imām 'Alī was a ruler who had come before his time, whose forbearance and magnanimity were misunderstood, and his humanity and love of truth was twisted by the enemies of Islām to their own advantage. But the accounts of his valorous deeds are still remembered and recited with enthusiasm among the people. Ever ready to succour the weak and to redress the wrongs of the injured, though facing heaviest odds, during the short span of the reign for four years as Caliph, he worked for the uplift of the masses, consolidation of the state, creation of a Central Bureau and re-introduction of Islāmic governance. He made it possible by turning various divisions of public service departments into Public Finance, Army, Central Secretariat, Judiciary, Provincial Offices etc.

There is the consensus among all Muslims about his highest status in knowledge, devotion, purity, holiness, spiritual attitude and multi-dimensional nobility. It is noteworthy that while the Muslim militia under the reign of Caliphate was busy in the extension of territorial limits of the kingdom, Imām 'Alī's endeavour was to give an intellectual turn to the newly developed energy of the people. Imām 'Alī and alumnus-cousin 'Abdullāh-bin-'Abbās delivered weekly lectures on philosophy and logic, history, traditions, rhetoric and law, whilst others dealt with other subjects, in the public mosque at Medina. Thus, it formed the nucleus of the intellectual movement which displayed itself in such great force in later times.[43]

In creating a Central Bureau, he intended the training of the crude Arabs for becoming educated and cultured persons – 'Abdu'r-Raḥmān Sulmī for training them for the correct recitation of the holy Qur'an, Burayr-bin-Khuzayr Hamadānī for training Qāri's as per rules of recitation of Qur'an. 'Abdu'l-Asswad Dawelī for teaching 'Arabic language, grammar and syntax, 'Omar-bin-Salmah for 'Arabic prose, 'Obaydah-bin-Ṣāmit for poetry and logic, Kumayl-bin-Żiyad for teaching Mathematics, Engineering and Astronomy, 'Abdu'llāh-bin-'Abbās for making the principles of rhetoric and administration. For himself he retained philosophy of religion, ethics, exegesis of the Qur'an and the Traditions of the Prophet.

Talking of the merits of Imām 'Alī, 'Abdu'llāh-bin-'Abbās said that Imām 'Alī had four such distinctions in which no one else could be his equal. Firstly, he was the first in 'Arabs and non-'Arabs to say prayer along with the Prophet of Islām. Secondly, he was the commander of army in all the battles fought in the lifetime of the Prophet Muḥammad. Thirdly, when other companions of the Prophet Muḥammad would flee for life and leave the Prophet Muḥammad behind, he would remain steadfast and guard the Prophet with utmost courage and faithful valour. Fourthly, he remained by the Prophet Muḥammad at his death-bed and after his death, he performed his funeral rites and set his body in the grave.

Likewise the statement of Imām Muḥammad-bin-Idrīs ash-Shāfi'ī (d. 819 AD) in praise of Imām 'Alī is well-known, he says:

> "What words can I use in praise of the man who had combined in him three such merits with three opportunities which no mortal can combine in his person. Extreme charity with extreme poverty, highest valour with highest wisdom and marvellous work-efficiency with unbound knowledge."[44]

Imām 'Alī was the paragon of all virtues bearing an ideal human personality. A lot can be said in his praise. All that this humble author can say is that God had put together all divine attributes to be manifest in him at the highest level. In the single life of Imām 'Alī, the Almighty compressed an exhaustive experience and achievement of a thousand lives. Every experience was without a parallel in its originality, novelty and relevance. Each act he performed and word he uttered was an outlet for a ceaseless variety of new chapters of thought and ideas.

Imām 'Alī's socio-political discourses, religious sermons, important letters and thought-provoking sayings have been collected and compiled by revered scholar ash-Sharīf ar-Razī (d. 1015 AD) in a book entitled *Nahju'l-Balāghah* (the Road of Eloquence) which is well known in 'Arabic literature and so in the commentary by 'Abī al-Ḥadīd (d. 1258 AD).

Imām Ḥasan-bin-Imām 'Alī

The second in the order of Imām ate, Imām Ḥasan was the eldest son of Imām 'Alī and Fāṭimah aż-Żahrah, the daughter of holy Prophet Muḥammad, popularly called son of holy Prophet and *Saiyed* (the (Venerable Leader) as he was the progeny of the holy Prophet Muḥammad. He was born in the night of Friday, 15th Ramazān, 03 AH, or Febraury 28, 625 AD in Medina. Martyred by poison on Thursday, 28th Ṣafar, 50 AH, March 27, 670 AD in Medina and buried in al-Bāqi cemetery next to his mother, Fāṭimah aż-Żahrah.

Ḥasan in Hebrew *Shabbar*, meaning to embellish, was the son of Aaron and the holy Prophet Muḥammad had already declared: "O' Imām 'Alī, art thou not content that thou art to me what Aaron was to Moses"[45], so, he named him Ḥasan and when second child of Imām 'Alī was born, he named him Ḥusain, after *Shabbīr*, second son of Aaron, meaning small Ḥasan.

They were brought up by the holy Prophet Muḥammad in his own household. The early years of the two brothers were spent in close and consistent touch with the holy Prophet Muḥammad right unto the end of his life. There could be no doubt that he had greatest fondness for Ḥasnain, the holy Prophet used to caress and kiss them, not only because of blood-relations, but faithful Muslims believe, it was in response to the will of God. The Prophet Muḥammad, as given in the Qur'an, does not even speak except as willed by God:

> "It (*the wording*) is naught, but a revelation revealed (*unto him*)." (*Qur'an* 53/3-4)

So whatever, the holy Prophet Muḥammad said or did about Ḥasnain was in keeping with the will of God. He had been widely quoted as saying:

> "Ḥasan is *Saiyed* (chief), who will bring peace among two in fighting groups of Muslims."[46]
> "Ḥasan and Ḥusain are chief of the youth of paradise."[47]
> "He who has loved Ḥasan and Ḥusain, loved me and he who has hated them has hated me."[48]

It was in keeping with the will of God, for instance when on the eve of Eīd, the two children desired to wear new clothes, as Muslims believe, the *Janitor of Paradise* (a distinguished Angel) descended from Heaven with new clothes for Ḥasnain priding himself to be their tailor. While preparing to go to the mosque, the children told the Prophet Muḥammad that other children were going on camel; they didn't have a camel and how could they go to the mosque. The holy Prophet Muḥammad, then, put them on his shoulders and said "I am your camel". "But there is the nose-string with their camels", said the children. The Prophet Muḥammad asked them to hold his hair locks into their hands. Then the children told him, "The camels make camel-cry but our does not do so." Then the Prophet Muḥammad made the sound of camel-cry with his mouth. Some of the revered companions of the Prophet offered to take at least one of the two children on their shoulder, but the Prophet declined. One companion said to the children, "What a fine carriage!" "Nay, say what a fine rider", asserted the holy Prophet.[49]

On another occasion the Prophet was making sermon in the mosque when Ḥasnain appeared in the mosque. Rushing to their grandfather, their feet got tangled in the floor-sheet. The Prophet Muḥammad interrupted his sermon, climbed down the pulpit went to the children, raised them up in his lap, went back to the pulpit, started sermon while keeping them in his lap.[50] There are numerous episodes of this nature whereby the holy Prophet Muḥammad tells his Companions to realize the love and significance that Ḥasnain have in the eyes of God and the Prophet. Then he enjoins his companions to love Ḥasnain and note his significance and statements of the Traditions in praise of Ḥasnain and their value in Islām. The revered companions were witness, but of no avail after the death of the Prophet Muḥammad.

Imām Ḥasan was thirty-seven years old when Imām 'Alī, the fourth *Rāshdūn* Caliph was assassinated at Kūfah in 661 AD. He was chosen as fifth *Rāshdūn* Caliph in succession to his father 'Alī a few days later without any dissent, except from Syrians under Mu'āwiyah-bin-Abū Sufyyān, whose secret agents spread false propaganda and liberal bribes, the army melt away and rebelled against Imām Ḥasan, and a part of it went over to the Syrians. His own tent was plundered, he himself was wounded. In this situation what Ḥasan decided was the only realistic course of action to avoid senseless bloodshed.

Imām Ḥasan was outstanding in generosity, tolerance, morality and non-violence. But by that time political power had become the arbitrator of leadership in Islām rather than religious merit or precedence. Mu'āwiyah-bin-Abū Sufyyān knew well that mere seizer of power and military victory would not be justified, until Imām Ḥasan was regarded as Caliph.

Mu'āwiyah proposed to Imām Ḥasan, if he could agree handing over the Caliphate to him, he would be happy to offer generous terms such as general amnesty for Shi'īs, abolishing regular cursing against Imām 'Alī in the most abusive words from the official pulpits, large financial settlement and the Caliphate shall revert to Imām Ḥasan (in case of his death to Imām Ḥusain) on the death of Mu'āwiyah-bin-Abū Sufyyān.

Be it borne in mind that since the martyrdom of Imām 'Alī in 661 AD until that time, two principles of establishing divine polity had assumed the forms of a religious faith among the Muslims. One, the principle of selecting the Caliph by the vote of allegiance; and two, the principle of Imām ate in which the Imām is divinely appointed in the same way as a Prophet is appointed. However, in both of these systems no one stands as candidate but he is accorded the leadership of Muslims. Imām Ḥasan was the head of the Muslim nation by both of these principles. In order to forestall the fragmentation among Muslims, after the death of Mu'āwiyah-bin-Abū Sufyyān.

Imām Ḥasan handed over the rulership to Mu'āwiyah, within a few months of his succession to Caliphate on Tuesday, 29th July, 661 AD through a written treaty on the condition that after him he would hand it over to the younger brother Imām Ḥusain who was already the Imām next to Imām Ḥasan. Had the terms of the treaty been observed both principles would have come together and under the leadership of Imām Ḥusain, the Divine polity as guided by the holy Qur'an would have been established. Mu'āwiyah crushed the paper of treaty under his feet saying that all he meant by the treaty was to secure the power and rule the masses; he had no obligation to fulfil the terms of the treaty. Imām Ḥasan on the other hand, kept living by the terms of the treaty, yet Mu'āwiyah got him poisoned.[51]

It was Mu'āwiyah who transformed Islāmic polity into dynastic polity and made his son Yażīd-bin-Mu'āwiyah-bin-Abū Sufyyān his successor. After this, the Islāmic order of the rulership came to an end and the dictatorial imperialism was adopted in the name of Islām.

Imām Ḥusain-bin-Imām 'Alī

The third in the order of Imām ate, Imām Ḥusain, the *Saiyed-ush-Shuhadah* (the Doyen of Martyrs) was the younger brother of Imām Ḥasan, the second son of Imām 'Alī and Fāṭimah aż-Żahrah, the daughter of holy Prophet Muḥammad, popularly called the son of holy Prophet Muḥammad and through his offspring the progeny of the Prophet Muḥammad.

He was born in the fourth year of Prophet's emigration on Thursday, the 3rd of Sha'bān 4 AH or 10th January, 626 AD at Medina. The holy Prophet Muḥammad took him on his lap, said *Ażān* into his right ear and *Aqāmat* into his left ear, and put his tongue into the mouth of the child to suckle, which served as the first food of Imām Ḥusain. He was martyred at Karbala on 10th Muḥarram, 61 AH or 10th October, 680 AD.

No one else could share these genealogical distinctions with Imām Ḥusain, save his real elder brother Imām Ḥasan. Being one of the prominent members of the *Ahlu'l-Bayt*, he is entitled for all Qur'anic verses and Prophets' Traditions addressed to *Ahlu'l-Bayt* in glorifying their ranks and status over and above all Muslims. Imām Ḥusain was 10 months 17 days younger than his elder brother Imām Ḥasan. As stated earlier, the two brothers were so similar in piety and purity of nature and conduct that they were also collectively called by a single name Ḥasnain.

In order to establish the truth of Islāmic cause and the devotion to it, against the pseudo Islāmic power, he came along with the members of his family and his companions and all laid down their lives and attained martyrdom. Imām Ḥusain, for this glorious martyrdom, is popularly known as *Saiyed ush-Shuhadah* (Leader of Martyrs). His revolutionary martyrdom, his courage, steadfastness, perseverance and sacrifice for a noble cause left deep impression on the world history. To keep mourning for these victims of the oppressive rulership, and keep their deeds alive is the unforgettable goal of the life of a Muslim.

Imām Ḥusain was still a small child of six years and six months when the Prophet died (May 25, 632 AD) and he was deprived of the shelter and warmth he enjoyed in the life of the Prophet. Then after only 3 months and 6 days, his mother Fāṭimah aż-Żahrah too died on 26th August, 632 AD. These two deaths, one after the other, were not just deaths, but the severest blow to Muslims in general and to Ḥasnain, the young children in particular. A shocking event as it was, the first Caliph Abū Bakr was in deep agony and he repented his failure not to have asked the Prophet Muḥammad about various problems arising after his death. He would also repent his failure not to concede to the Prophet's daughter Fāṭimah aż-Żahrah, when she came over to his court with her claim to her property bequeathed to her in his own writing by her father.[52]

Events encountered in childhood left deep impressions on the tender minds of children, which got all the more deepened in course of time. The extraordinary brain of Imām Ḥusain was not only storing these events in his mind but also reflecting on the consequences and dimensions of these events. His eyes had witnessed the painful scene when his reverend mother Fāṭimah aż-Żahrah, who apart from being the most affectionate daughter of the Prophet Muḥammad, was herself the noblest of all ladies in her spiritual purity and piety and for whose glorious character were revealed many verses of the Qur'an and the Prophet had eulogized her in his Traditions, and whose respect was so lofty in his eyes that whenever she would appear before him, he would stand up in her honour. Imām Ḥusain witnessed that the same Fāṭimah aż-Żahrah appeared as a plaintiff and her appeal was turned down. After her death, this hostile attitude towards the Prophet's progeny subsided a little in the middle of the regime of the second Caliph 'Omar (634-44 AD).

Thereafter, came a period when the situation became so bad that every tom, dick and harry of Umayyite clan became the ruling Lords over the Muslim nation. In the regime of the third Caliph 'O<u>th</u>mān (644-56 AD), numerous remarkable events took place; like the monopoly of the ruling power by one Umayyite clan, revolt of the masses against it, murder of Caliph 'O<u>th</u>mān and the eventual come back of the Caliphate to Imām 'Alī, which could not be tolerated by Umayyite clan who went on fighting one battle after another against Imām 'Alī, widening network of conspiracy, monopolization of power by Mu'āwiyah-bin-Abū Sufyyān under the nose of the rightly-guided Caliphs, regular cursing against Caliph-*cum*-Imām 'Alī in the most abusive words from the official pulpits and in the very midst of these hostile conditions, while leading the morning prayer on the 19th day of the venerable month of the Ramazān, Imām 'Alī was attacked resulting in his martyrdom three days later on 28th January, 661 AD.

Imām 'Alī was confidentially buried at the dead hour of night in Najaf in an atmosphere charged with gloom. The reason of keeping secret the place of his burial, was that if it was discovered, his body would have been exhumed and made the object of severe revenge in accordance with the practice of the brutal Arabs of pre-Islāmic era against their enemies.[53]

Imām Ḥusain had lived under the holy shelter and care of his father Imām 'Alī for about thirty years, in getting the light of knowledge and nobility of conduct from his father, the erudite like Imām 'Alī, learned-theologist, interpreter of the Qur'an, equitable, generous, expert in Divine polity and social science and matchless in manhood and valour. If a man of his excellence, enlightens and grooms a person, then what less can be thought of the able recipient of knowledge from him. If a careful observation is made of Ḥusain's conduct, every step in his life would seem as if it were Imām 'Alī in action.

If the greatest tragedy of Islāmic history, namely Karbala (10th October, 680), in which Imām Ḥusain sacrificed his family, relatives and friends is thoughtfully studied, it will make it clear beyond doubt that in this battle, his message was that of peace and harmony among the people and security for all. The principles of setting apart the truth from falsehood, is not confined only to Islām, it is universally accepted by all human beings, who proclaim to follow a Divine Faith; be they Christian, Jews, Hindu, Buddhist, Sikh or of any other religion or faith. Imām Ḥusain's message is to make truth distinct from non-truth using the doctrine of your faith.

Imām Ḥusain added: Do try to realize what is humanly expected of you? While living in the society, do undertake to execute your social responsibilities. Do respect the ways of developing human culture. Never go back to corruption, once you have come out of it. Do have courage to oppose the factors which tend to make hell of this earth through exploitation. Put them to an end, even if you have to part with your life. If you sacrifice this mortal life for an immortal cause you will attain immortality and enter the Divine realm of everlasting grace, as indicated in the Qur'an:

> "And say not those who are slain in the path of God that they are dead; Nay (*they are*) living, but ye perceive not."
>
> (*Qur'an* 2/154)

The Principles of Islām

Islām is an 'Arabic word derived from the root word *Silm*, from which other words like *salām, muslīm, muslimīn* etc. are derived. The holy Qur'an sheds light on various aspects of its meaning by using the word *Islām* in many connotations. In the sense of peace, concord and harmony, indicating that accepting Islām would demand to live in harmony with yourself and to be at peace with all other members of the society without creating any interference in the process of social order. Some verses of the holy Qur'an may be seen:

> "And if they lean to peace, then leaneth thou too to it and trust in God." (*Qur'an*: 8/61)
>
> "When you are greeted with a greeting, then greet ye with a better (*than it*) or return it." (*Qur'an*: 4/86)
>
> "And God calleth (*you*) to the abode of peace." (*Qur'an*: 10/25)
>
> "And if anyone from the idolaters seeketh protection from thee, grant thou protection to him till he hears the Word of God, then convey him to his place of safety; this is because they are the people who know not." (*Qur'an*: 9/6)
>
> "(*The angels saying unto them:*) Enter ye therein in Peace, Secure." (*Qur'an*: 15/46)
>
> "Those who spend (*in alms*) alike in prosperity and straitness, and who restrain (*their*) anger and forgive (*the faults of*) men; for God loveth those who do good (*to others*)." (*Qur'an*: 3/133)
>
> "(*The angels*) while receiving them will say: Peace be on you; Enter ye the Garden, for what ye were doing." (*Qur'an*: 16/32)

The Divine Unity is the foremost pivot of Islāmic faith, one and unique, no partner, no equal, etymologically, the name *God* may be probably, a contraction of the 'Arabic word *al-Ilāh* (the god), which can he traced back to the earliest Semitic writings where the words *Il* or *El* (with the same meaning as the god or God) have been used. *El* has been synonym to *Yahwah* in the Old Testament. But *God* is most standard 'Arabic word for god or God, which also being used by 'Arabic speeking Christians for God. Qur'an's surah *at-Tawḥīd* (The Unity) takes name from its subject and reveals the nature of God in such a way that it has been called the essence of the Qur'an:

> "Say He, God, is ONE (alone), God, the Needless, He begetteth not, nor He Begotten. And there is none like unto Him." (*Qur'an*: 112/1-4)
>
> " God is the Lord of the Worlds." (*Qur'an*: 1/2)

'Adl (Justice) is other pivot of Islāmic faith, which is most powerful positive attribute of God. The Just is considered as the Divine Nature. God would never act in unjust manner, because of the fact that He is of Just Nature. Unjust action shall violate His own Nature, which is impossible and shall never happen. Whatever God's will, shall be just and based on Divine Justice.

> "And We sent thee not (*O' Our Aspotle Muḥammad !*), but Mercy unto (all) the worlds." (*Qur'an*: 21/ 107)

The Islām is the custodian and nurturer of ancient healthy values. It develops its entire constructive and progressive values. Islām is not a name of any new religion, but it is the last camp of development succession of ancient religions. In this way it cannot be the claimant of offering any new religion or life-style, the number of ancient religious founders is said to be one lac twenty four thousand. The Qur'an says:

> "Verily, We sent thee with truth, as a bearer of glad tidings and a warner: and there is not a people, but a warner hath gone among them." (*Qur'an*: 35/24)

Says other verse also:

> "And for every people (*was sent*) an apostle; and when came their apostle, the matter between them was decided with equity and they shall not (*in the least*) be done (*any*) injustice." (*Qur'an*: 10/ 47)

Qur'an has clarified the situation of the Islāmic Revolution:

> "This day have I perfected for you, your religion and have completed My favour on you." (*Qur'an*: 5/ 3)

Islām represents a later development of the religious faculty of mankind and recognizes the true concern of man's cognizance of a Supreme Power with his sense of benefaction, which leads him to pour out the overflowing sentiments in literal words of love and gratitude or his repentance and solicitation to God. The *Qur'an* says:

> "So when you have your Devotion, then laud God as you lauded your fathers, rather a greater lauding." (*Qur'an:* 2/200)

This is the guideline for the human beings. God never wished that the human beings should only *laud Himself*, as *the most Compassionate, the Merciful.* But *laud Himself rather a greater lauding*, of course, after the lauding of their fathers, which is the logical conclusion. Because, if the fathers were not lauded, it cannot be referred to follow suit. It is the core of Islāmic philosophy that Islām has given equal weightage to the obligations towards God Himself and also towards His creations in the Universe, especially human beings, which is a distinguished aspect of the Theology of Islām.

The Religious Obligations of human beings regarding their fellow beings and the cosmos have been termed as *Ḥaqqu'l-'Ibād* (the Religious Obligations regarding the servants of God), i.e. Obligations regarding the Society. It has been specifically laid down that if an Obligation to a person remains, it could only be pardoned by the person concerned. God has relinquished His power to pardon such remains! It shall be discussed in details in the forthcoming chapter entitled 'The Universal Life-Order'.

The other part of the Religious Obligations towards God is termed as *Ḥaqqu'-llāh* (the Religious Obligations regarding God Himself) shall be dealt with here. For the believers, these religious obligations are as important as breathing. It has been significant and universal aspect of religion, whether of the primitive people or of modern philosophical thinkers of the religion. It distinguishes the phenomenon of religion from the phenomenon of aesthetic feelings. Though the historians of religion, psychologists and anthropologists debate various theories and forms of the religious obligations, the core aspects remain whatever their inspirations reveal otherwise.

> "Say He is God ! God, the eternally Besought of all ! He begetteth not nor He is Begotten. And there is none comparable unto Him." (*Qur'an*: 112/1-4)
>
> "God, Lord of the Worlds." (*Qur'an*:1/1)
>
> "Verily the earth is God's, granteth He as heritage unto whomsoever He pleaseth among His servants." (*Qur'an*: 7/128)

"The King of people ! The God of people !" (*Qur'an*: 114/2-3)

"His is the Kingdom of the heavens and the earth; and unto God *(alone)* are returned *(all)* affairs." (*Qur'an*: 57/5),

"That is God, your Lord, the Creator of everything; there is no god but He; why then are ye turned away ?" (*Qur'an*: 39/62)

"Nothing whatsoever *(is there)* like the like Him." (*Qur'an*: 42/11)

"And hath not taken He (*unto Himself*) any son, and there is not any partner, in the kingdom." (*Qur'an*: 25/2)

After accepting the above responsibility the Qur'an passes orders:

"O' ye who believe ! Believe in God, and His Apostle and the Book which He hath sent down unto His Apostle *(Muḥammad)* and the Book which He hath sent down before *(him)*; and whoever denieth God, and His Angels, and His Books, and His Apostles and the Last Day *(of judgement)* hath indeed stayed off, far away *(from the right path)*." (*Qur'an*: 4/136)

On this basis Prophet or Aspostle is the Ruler appointed by God. As a messenger of God Prophet discharges his duties as per the command of God. He has no right to have either any Amendment or change of his own. To this extent that he never tells as per his desire. The Qur'an says:

"It *(the wording)* is naught but a revelation *(unto him)*."
(*Qur'an*: 53/4)

No body can compel his own religion on any other person.

"No compulsion be in religion." (*Qur'an*: 2/256)

"And work not confusion in the earth after fair ordering thereof." (*Qur'an*: 7/85)

Disturbance and strive is forbidden in the land:

"And strive in the land, spreading mischief *(therein)*, is only that they be slain or crucified or their hands and their feet should be cut off, from opposite sides, or be banished from land." (*Qur'an*: 5/33)

Follow the commitment:

> "And fulfil ye the promise; Verily (every) promise shall be questioned about." (*Qur'an*: 17/34)

Remember the help of anyone throughout your life.

> "Is the recompense for good aught, but good."
> (*Qur'an*: 55/60)

The revenge of any evil can be only to the extent of evil done and if pardoned, it is the best:

> "And the recompense for an evil shall be an ill-return like unto it, but (if) one pardoneth and ameneth, his reward is incumbent on God; Verily, He loveth not the unjust." (*Qur'an*: 42/40)

It is the responsibility of the Ruler and Power side that be firm at the command of Justice:

> "Those, if We establish them in the earth, will establish prayer and pay the poor-rate and enjoin good and forbid evil; and unto God *(alone)* is the sequel of *(all)* affairs." (*Qur'an*: 22/41)

Islām has presented before the universe the principles of Heavenly Ruled system:

> "There is no judgement but God's" (*Qur'an*: 12/40)

Risālat (Prophethood) is the basic pivot of Islām, literally meaning embassy, messengership and popularly known as Prophethood, which stands for that Embassy which God employs to communicate with mankind and sends some infallible human being to act as the representative of the Divine Kingdom in the human world. The Prophet is enjoined to put before mankind the Divine Law, and direct them to follow the same. It becomes most important subject of enthralling interest when studied in the context of continuity of religious progress of mankind.

Qur'an has clarified that no cruel can be made the Head of Heavenly kingdom:

> "And remember when his Lord tried Abraham with certain words then he fulfilled them, He said, 'Verily I make thee Imām for mankind', *(Abraham)* said, 'And of my offspring'? He said, 'My covenant reacheth not the unjust." (*Qur'an*: 2/124)

Regarding the Heavenly Kingdom also explanation has been given. Such a state when there are no frontiers of State, the whole universe is within the state frontiers, when there is no frontier then there would be no question of any restriction. There would be no need for any army for the security of these frontiers. No state would attack the frontiers of other states for widening of its frontiers. All people can freely move anywhere and would be benefited with the knowledge of one another. They can make use of one another's materials, can make trade and can give and take. People will not become enemies in the name of nation. There would be happiness and peace on all sides and prosperity would flourish. Humanity would proceed ahead on the path of progress. Police would discharge its duties not only for administration but also for the establishment of happiness and peace. With this, administrative integration would be established in between the individual and the state. Neither the state could make anyone helpless and embarrassed being uncontrollable, nor any person getting more freedom and be uncontrollable and become an enemy of social order. Providing original rights to a person and giving priority to the Rules of Heavenly state, safety and security can be provided without any unnecessary interference. It is mandatory to provide absolute co-operation from the Heavenly state for the betterment and welfare of the society on the basis of morality.

God's Representative Aspostle or Prophet would fulfil and maintain the practical aspects of Heavenly state. Afterwards his heir, who would be highly reliable among the common-people and uncomparable and par excellent in his purity and sanctity of His own character and conduct. But he would not aspire and anticipate any post by himself. Heavenly orders are:

> "That abode in the hereafter, We assign it for those who intend not to exult themselves in the earth, nor *(to make)* mischief *(therein)*; and the end is *(best)* for the pious ones."
>
> (*Qur'an*: 28/83)

Just as Prophets are chosen by God himself, the holy Prophet would select his successor. The Qur'an has clarified his jurisdiction:

> "O' ye who believe ! obey God and obey the Apostle and those vested with authority from among you; and then if ye qurrel about anything refer it to God and the Apostle, if ye believe in God and in the Last day *(of judgement)*; This is the best and fairest way of ending *(dispute)*." (*Qur'an*: 4/59)

This administrative set-up is quite difference from usually prevalent theocracy. There is, of course, similarity, equality and certainty in this with the prevalent religious set-up till the limit of accepting the supremacy of the Almighty, but a separate philosophy has been exhibited in providing a practical image to that. According to this philosophy in spite of accepting any special category of religious great personalities as managing centre of Supremacy, in the place of fulfilling the materialistic gain and objective, in these polities we have to accept the supremacy of the moral authority. The external form of this sovereignty should be absolutely based on truth, peace, nobility, mercy, justice and benevolence. No group should be deprived of essential commodities in his Nation, and every person has birth-right on them.

An attempt has been made in the above lines to clarify what is the fundamental and basic message of Islāmic state. Certainly, an independent Islāmic state can assume existence in that condition and situation, when that being absolutely independent surrenders itself before the Almighty and the sovereignty may be surrendered under it for the welfare of the common people.

That would be such a state, as would be free from all the clutches of Regional, Linguistic and Communal boundaries. Wherever they may live all human beings of the whole universe can accept these principles and without any difference and siding offer equal rights to all human beings. Wherever a state is established on the basis of these principles in the world that would be the Islāmic State whatever may be its name and the Administrators whether they are white or black or yellow, belonging to Europe, Asia or America. This type of Divine sovereignty would establish International Relationship.

Equality and Unity

Islām has given the message of Equality and Unity to all the people of the whole universe erasing the racial, provincial and regional narrow-mindedness. The Qur'an has clarified its base:

> "O' ye people ! Verily We have created you of a male and a female, and made you nations and tribes, that ye may recognize each other." (*Qur'an*: 49/13)

All the people of the whole universe are the children of one parents—mother-father, then all humans are equally respectable. The practical and mental abilities (power) of all human beings are the same: (God) The beneficent Taught He the Qur'an:

> "(*God*) The Beneficent, Taught He the Qur'an, He created man, He taught him expression, The sun and the moon follow the (*prescribed*) timings, And the herbs and trees do obeisance (*unto Him*), And the Heaven, He did raise it high, and placed the scale (within reach), So, that ye may not transgress the scale, And maintain ye the measure with justice and do not cut short in the scale, And the earth, He has made it for (*His*) (*living*) creatures, Therein is fruit and palms having sheathed clusters, And corn with (*its*) leaves and stalks and with sweet-smelling herbs, Which then of the bounties of your Lord will ye two *(men and jinn)* belie ?" (*Qur'an*: 55/1-13)
>
> "And granted We unto them of Our mercy, and assigned unto them a lofty tongue of truthfulness." (*Qur'an*: 19/50)
>
> "And the variety of your languages and your complexions; verily in this are signs for the learned (ones)." (*Qur'an*: 30/22)
>
> "And We sent not any apostle but with the language of people that he might clearly explain *(Our commandment)* unto them." (*Qur'an*: 14/4)

Justice for All

Justice is included in the original principle of the religion Islām. Justice is not only a medium of behaviour only in the Eternal Legislation of Human Life, but also is a symbol of enigmas of God:

> "God will exalt (*you in*) in ranks (*unto him*), those who believe among you, and those who have been given knowledge; and God is All-Aware of whatsoever ye do." (*Qur'an*: 58/11)

The Qur'an is fundamental frame of the Kingdom-Establishment which is equal for every person. Islām passes orders equally for all the rights from the lowest category to even the Head of the state. Nobody can get any priority outside the orders, which God has given to his Prophet in the Qur'an to proclaim this:

> "And if only those who are unjust could see (*what they will realize*) when they behold the torment, that unto God belongeth all power and verily God is severe in punishing." (*Qur'an*: 2/165)

The Prophet has discussed in the charters to treat equally all the people: Whatever has gone before yourself with past is washed out because those people used to admonish the criminals of lower category and people of higher category were left free unpunished. It is vowed on that by God in whose hands is the life of Muḥammad:

> "If at all the very daughter of Muḥammad had stolen then I would have cut her hand."[54]

Law has been recognised as supreme in Islām. There are Divine statements regarding Prophets:

> "And for every people (*was sent*) a Prophet; and when came their Prophet, the matter between them was decided with equity and they shall not (*in the least*) be done (*any*) injustice." (*Qur'an*: 10/47)

The Basis of being honest and sincere to the Religion of people also has been recognised as Law:

> "Verily God doeth not any injustice to people but men to their own selves do injustice." (*Qur'an*: 10/44)

Happy and Peaceful Life

The Islāmic Revolution has ended the frontier line between spiritualism, religion and physical life. Spiritualism and religion are the necessary parts of material life. One is the complement of the other. Man is a social animal, he should not be without a society. The directive principle of this social life is:

> "In the name of God, the Beneficent, the Merciful. (*all*) Praise is (*only*) God's, the Lord of the worlds. The Beneficent,

the Merciful. Master of the Day of Judgement. Thee (*alone*) worship we and of Thee (*only*) we seek help. Guide us (*O' Lord*) on the Right path. The path of those upon whom thou hast bestowed Thy bounties, not (*the path*) of those inflicted with Thy wrath, nor (*of those*) gone astray." (*Qur'an*: 1/1-7)

Good people, whoever likes, has given their identity also which follows:

"And the servants of the Beneficient (God) are they who walk on earth humbly; and when address them the ignorant; say they *Salam* (Peace)". (*Qur'an*: 25/63)

Economic and Social Order

The Islāmic Economic Order is for the continuous flowing of money and wealth. Therefore, Hoarding of food commodities in view of selling at a higher price in future is prohibited. Islām gives a special stress and emphasis on the relationship among one-another for the sake of building up of society—free from exploitation. It is a blessing to free a person from any financial constraint by offering him a loan, but at the same time there is also a prohibition of any pressure in receiving back that loan. If his financial situation does not improve, advice has been given to pardon him;

"And if *(any debtor)* be in strained circumstances, then let there be respite until *(he is in)* ease; and if ye forego it *(even the capital) (as charity)* it is better for you if ye only knew."
(*Qur'an*: 2/280)

In the same sequence, Gold-movement is the backbone of Economic system. There is a clear order of the Qur'an:

"And those who hoard up gold and silver and spend it not in God's way; announce thou unto them a painful chastisement." (*Qur'an*: 9/34)

Further, it is said:

"And do not swallow your property among yourselve by wrongfulmeans, neither seek to gain access thereby to the authorities that ye may swallow up aportion of the property of men wrongfully while ye know." (*Qur'an*: 2/188)

Islām has given orders for the mutual co-operation between men and women ensuring their rights. After the marriage they have a small unit or portion:

> "And of His signs is that He created for you from yourselves mates that ye may dwell (*inclined*) up to them, and caused between you love and compassion: Verily in this are signs for a people who reflect." (*Qur'an*: 30/21)

Again at another place:

> "Then marry those who seem good to you, two, or three or four and if ye fear that ye shall not deal justly (*with so many*) then (*marry*) one only." (*Qur'an*: 4/3)
>
> "And approach ye not adultery, Verily, it is a shameful act, and evil way (*opening to many other evils*)." (*Qur'an*:17/32)

The Divine Constitution

There is the Divine Legislation of the Divine State, which is in a written form. Its only name is the Qur'an, Its orders and Prophet's Traditions, which have been established on the basis of this Law, it is a must to follow it. No other new or old Legislation contrary to Divine Legislation and its word and spirit can be propounded:

> "And verily thy Lord well-knoweth what do enshroud their breast and what they declare. Nothing is there hidden in the heavens and the earth, but it is in the manifest Book." (*Qur'an*: 27/74-75)
>
> "And perfect is the word of thy Lord in truth and justice; There is none who can change His words and He is the All-Hearing and All-Knowing." (*Qur'an*: 6/115)

Islām and Other Religions

Fairly liberal disposition of Islām towards other religions has a special relevance in the contemporary perspective. The common tendency of the believers of almost each religion is to be faithfully bound and committed only to their respective scriptures, religious founders and religious ideologies. Their liberal attitude towards other religions, at best, is confined to have only a sense of respect for other faiths. To go beyond that is not desirable. But the spirit and ideal of other religions is to have equal reverence for all religions. Islām has picked up this sentiment and broad-based it on reasonable grounds and has emphasized to have regards for all the older religions.

It is necessary to refer here the verses of the holy Qur'an already mentioned above regarding identification of Islām that besides the three cardinal belief of Divine Unity, Divine Prophethood and the Divine Resurrections and Day of Final Judgement, every Muslim must believe in the continuity of previous religions and all possible respect to their religious leader, already quoted in these pages that the person who has accepted Islām has to have faith in all the holy Prophets preceding the last Prophet Muḥammad and the Books revealed before the last Book, the Qur'an with equal weight and sincerity for all of them.

We all know that the continuity of religious progress amongst the human beings has been the source of awakening of human minds, which resulted in recognition of an Universal Soul say God regarding pervading and guiding all existence. Some of men, chosen by God as *Messengers of Heavens* were proclaimed as His Prophets. To know about the religious morality of Islām, it would be fitting to study the following verses of the Qur'an so as to learn what the Qur'an has to say about the kinships of Islām with other religions, *vide* Chapter II, *al-Baqarah* (The Cow), the verse:

> "Lo ! those who believe (*in that which is revealed unto thee, Muḥammad*) and those who are Jews, and Christians and Sābeans – whoever believeth in God and the Last Day and doeth right – surely their reward is with their Lord and there shall be no fear come upon them neither shall they grieve." (*Qur'an*: 2/62)

At another place the holy Qur'an clearly upholds the same spirit; almost identical to above verse:

> "Lo ! those who believe, and those who are Jews, and Sābeans, and Christians – whosoever believeth in God and the Last Day and doeth right – there shall be no fear come upon them neither shall they grieve." (*Qur'an*: 5/69)

In both these verses, one very significant fact is noteworthy. In the former verse *Sābeans* has come after Christians while in the latter *Sābeans* occurs before Christians. In another place in the Qur'an, it has been said:

> "Lo! Those who believe (*this Revelation*), and those who are Jews and Sābeans and Christians, and the Magians and the idolaters – Lo! God will decide between them on the Day of Resurrection. Lo! God is Witness over all things." (*Qur'an* 22/17)

In this verse *Sābeans* have been mentioned before the Christians and *Magians* (Zoroastrians) which indicates their significance as a religious cult or group. In the above verses of the Qur'an, five religious-groups have been mentioned. Muslims have been addressed as *People in Faith*, (Muslims), *Magians* (fire worshippers, Aryans of Iran, Zoroastrians) and *Sābeans* (stars worshippers, Aryans of India, Hindus), Jews and Christians have been directly addressed.

The other highly influential group of the Āryans is well spread from central Asia to east Asia who may have been addressed as *Sābeans* but their existence is not clear. Historians differ, but the tenth century historian Qāzī Sa'd Undulusī has maintained that *Sābeans* are Hindus, his view is shared by Abu'l Fatḥ Muḥammad S̲hahristanī, the twelfth century scholar, and by T̲hanau'llāh Pānīpatī, a nineteenth century scholar. According to Abu'l Kalām Āżād, Hindus are the religious group better and distinct from both *Sābeans* and the fire-worshippers or *Magians*.[55]

All the five religious groups mentioned above have been given recognition as religions in their own right and have been mentioned together with Islām. As such no one of these religious groups have been dismissed as devoid of Truth, nor the followers of these religions condemned as corrupt or damned. They have been bracketed with Muslims with the proviso that whoever among them will have sincere faith in God and the Day of Judgement and be righteous will get reward and grace from their Lord and no fear shall be upon them nor shall they grieve.

At another point the variance in religions, has been dealt in the Qur'an in an unusual way and the difference of religion has been given a purpose of trial so that the difference may initiate a spirit of striving and excelling each other in attaining virtues and goodness, while the goal of all is to realize God Who will show the truth of the matters in which they were disputing? God would have made them into a community of one religion, but He did not choose to unify them by compulsion because a forced unification would have deprived them of exercising their own free will, their reasons and intuition to compete each other in discovering the Truth, The Qur'an says:

> "For each We have appointed a divine law and trace out way. Had God willed He could have made you one community? But that He may try you by that which He hath given you. (*He hath made you as ye are*). So, vie one with another in good work. Unto God ye will all return, and He will then inform you of that wherein ye differ." (*Qur'an*: 5/48)

Accordingly, only respect for all religions is not sufficient but respecting and protecting their places of worship is also obligatory. The Qur'an has clearly pointed it out:

> "Had God not checked one set of people by means of another, there would surely have been pulled down monasteries, churches, synagogue and mosques, in which the name of God is commemorated in abundant measure. God will certainly aid those who aid His (*cause*)." (*Qur'an*: 22/40)

By ignorance some people hold that Islām calls its followers to be believers and the followers of other faith to be *Kāfir* or unbelievers. This attitude is entirely wrong. You may find that some Muslim sects who claim themselves to be pure Muslims keep passing *Fatwā* (edict) for other Muslim sects to be *Kāfir*. Refer to history and you will find sects, engaged in *Jihād* against others treating them *Kāfir*. The battle of Karbala (10th October, 680) leading to the martyrdom of Imām Ḥusain, is the most prominent of such *Jihāds*. Who does not know that the Umayyite king Yażīd-bin-Mu'āwiya was not a Hindu or the follower of any other religion other than Islām. He proclaimed to be a Muslim, who forced the holy Prophet Muḥammad's grandson Imām Ḥusain to submit to his infidelity. Imām Ḥusain refused to yield to him, and became a martyr along with his children and companions. In commemoration of this tragic event, processions are taken out every year on the occasion of Muḥarram as a mark of protest against the *Muslim Kāfirs*.

Famous scholar, as Suyūtī, Jalālu'd-Dīn (d. 1505) has quoted the following verse of Qur'an as a sufficient proof for a corrupt Muslim to be a real *Kāfir*:

"And God will protect thee from (*the mischief*) of men; Verilly God guideth not infidel people." (*Qur'an*: 5/67)

With regard to other religions, the Qur'an has presented a fairly high standard of equity that all human beings are absolutely free to observe their own religions. No individual or group has the right to impose his religion on others by force:

"Let there be no compulsion in religion." (*Qur'an*: 2/256)

In the Islāmic terminology, the people of other faiths may be divided as the *People of the Books* and others. Jews and Christians are accepted as the *People of the Books*. Zoroastrian and Hindus are also regarded as *People of the Books*, by majority of Islāmic scholars. Others who have not been considered as the *People of the Books*, their religions and its leaders are also equally regarded.

Notes and References

1. Sīratu'n-Nabī, p. 3.
2. Vedic Part of Pre-Islāmic Arabic p. 123.
3. The Spirit of Islām, p. 51.
4. Tārīkhu'l-Fakhrī, p. 167.
5. Sīratu'n-Nabī, pp 116-127.
6. *There is difference of opinion regarding the actual dates of birth and death. Sunnīs are not unanimous on the dates of birth and death and say 3rd or 9th or 12th of Rabi' I as date of birth and say 2nd or 12th of Rabi' I, as date of death. Some also dispute the names of month as Muḥarram, Ṣafar, Rajab or Ramazān. But majority of them believe and observe 12th of Rabi' I as the Birth Anniversary of the holy Prophet. However, Shi'īs believe and observe 17th of Rabi' I in the First year of the Era of the Elephant, or the 20th August, 570 as true date of birth and 28th Ṣafar 11 AH, or 25th May, 632 as date of death. Since these dates believed and observed by Shi'īs are based on family Traditions, they have more creditability, hence mentioned here. The family sources better know the family affairs !*—Author
   Ḥayātu'l-Muḥammad, pp. 120-1, *Sīratu'n-Nabī*: Shiblī vol. 1, p. 34; *Kanżu'l-Ansāb*, p. 29, *The Spirit of Islām*, p. 7.
7. 'Aqā'idu'sh-Shaykh Ṣadūq, p. 88 (Urdu tr. *Hadiyā-i-Jā'fariyā*, Muḥammad 'Aejāz Ḥasan, Delhi, 1928.
8. Jām'ans-Saḥīḥ al Muslim Vol. II, p. 251, Tradition No. 2431; Kanżu'l-Ansāb, p. 26; Yake AżShākh-i-thamarbār, p. 27.

9. aṭ-Ṭabaqātu'l-Kabīr, Vol. 1, p. 82.
10. Sīrat Rasūlu'llāh, Vol. 1, p. 115, aṭ-Ṭabaqātu'l-Kabīr, Vol. 1, p. 76.
11. aṭ-Ṭabaqātu'l-Kabīr, vol. 1, p. 93, Sīrat Rasūlu'llāh, Vol. 1, p. 124.
12. Mutālia'i-Qur'an, p. 645.
13. Tārīkhu'r-Rusūl wa'l-Mulūk, Vol. 1, p. 89 similar Traditions in al-Musnad: Aḥmad, Vol. 1, pp. 11, 159, al-Mustadraku's-Saḥiḥayn, Vol. 3, p. 32; Labābu't-Tāwīl fī Mā'nī-at-Tanzīl 5/106; Kanżu'l-Ummah-fī-Sunnatu'l-Aqwāl-w'al-Alfāz, Vol. 6, pp. 396-97; al-Mukhtaṣar fī Akhbāru'l-Bashar, Vol. 1, p. 116; Tārīkhu'l-Khulafa, p. 65.
14. Tārīkh-i-Islām, p. 83.
15. Sīrat Rasūlu'llāh, Vol. 1, p. 89.
16. aṭ-Ṭabaqātu'l-Kabīr, Vol. 1, p. 134.
17. aṭ-Ṭabaqātu'l-Kabīr, Vol. 1, pp. 139-40.
18. aṭ-Ṭabaqātu'l-Kabīr, Vol. 1, p. 140.
19. aṭ-Ṭabaqātu'l-Kabīr, Vol. 1, p. 142.
20. aṭ-Ṭabaqātu'l-Kabīr, Vol. 1, p. 146.
21. Sīrat Rasūlu'llāh, pp. 341-43.
22. al-Kāmil fī't-Tārīkh, Vol. 2, p. 143; Tārīkhu'r-Rusūl wa'l-Mulūk, Vol. 3, p. 72.
23. Sīrat Rasūlu'llāh, p. 966; al-Kāmil fī't-Tārīkh, vol. II, p. 230.
24. al-Musnad: Aḥmad, vol. 4, p. 281, similar Traditions in the same book, vol. 1, pp. 84, 118, 119, 331, vol. 4, pp. 367, 370, 372, vol. 5, pp. 347, 366, 419; as-Sunan: Ibn Māja, vol. 1, p. 43.
25. Madārijul-Nabūwat, p. 182.
26. Jām'au'ṣ-Ṣaḥīḥul-Bukhārī, Vol. 3, p. 298 (Tr. 1376).
27. Jām'au'ṣ-Ṣaḥīḥul-Bukhārī, Chapter 40, Vol. 1, p. 41.
28. Tārīkhu'r-Rusūl wa'l-Mulūk, Vol. 3, p. 188; al-Kāmil fī't-Tārīkh, Vol. 2, p. 120; Madārijul-Nabūwat, Vol. 2, p. 488.
29. Hayātu'l-Muḥammad, p. 54.
30. Sīratu'n-Nabī, Vol. 2, p. 814.
31. Tarjima-i-Kalām-i-Ilāhī, pp.565-66; Aḥqāqu'l-Ḥaqq, p.17; Arjaḥu'l-Maṭālib, p. 96.
32. Jām'au'ṣ-Ṣaḥīḥul-Bukhārī, Vol. 2, p. 258; Muwaddatu'l-Qurba, p. 101.
33. Jām'au'ṣ-Ṣaḥīḥul-Bukhārī, Vol. 2, p. 258 (Tr. 947); Jām'au'ṣ-Ṣaḥīḥ al-Muslim, Vol. 2, p. 238 (Tr. 2349).
34. Yanābia'u'l-Muwaddah, p. 276.
35. Yanābia'u'l-Muwaddah, p. 277.
36. Bihāru'l-Anwār, Vol. 3, p. 14.
37. Yanābia'u'l-Muwaddah, p. 275.
38. Tārīkhu'r-Rusūl wa'l-Mulūk, Vol. 2, p. 217.
39. A Short History of the Saracens, p. 47.
40. ar-Risālah, p. 35.
41. Sīrat Rasūlu'llāh, p. 897
42. Jām'au'ṣ-Ṣaḥīḥul-Bukhārī, Vol. 2, Tradition No. 927.
43. as-Sunan: Ibn Māja, Vol. I, p. 44.

44. as-Sunan: Ibn Māja, Vol. I, p. 51.
45. Jām'au'ṣ-Ṣaḥīḥu'l-Mishkātu 'l-Maṣābīḥ, Vol. 3, p. 260, Tr. 5910.
46. Jām'au'ṣ-Ṣaḥīḥul-Bukhārī, vol. 2, Tr. 927.
47. as-Sunan: Ibn Māja, vol. I, p. 44.
48. as-Sunan: Ibn Māja, vol. I, p. 51.
49. Jām'au'ṣ-Ṣaḥīḥu'l-Mishkātu 'l-Maṣābīḥ, vol. 3, p. 260, Tr. 5910.
50. Jām'au'ṣ-Ṣaḥīḥu'l-Mishkātu 'l-Maṣābīḥ Vol. 3, p. 260 Tr. 5876.
51. *Khwāja Ḥasan Niẓāmī states that this was the first murder historically well established and undisputed of which Mu'āwiyah-bin-Abū Sufyyān was guilty and no ancient or historical and legal analysis can deliver Mu'āwiyah of this guilt.* Muḥarram Nama, p. 174.
52. Tārīkhu'r-Rusūl wa'l-Mulūk, vol. 2, pp. 254-57.
53. al-Kāmil fī't-Tārīkh, Vol. 3, p. 156; al-Mukhtaṣar fī Akhbāru'l-Bashar, vol. 1, p. 181.
54. Jām'au'ṣ-Ṣaḥīḥu'l-Bukhārī, vol. 3, p. 357 Tradition no. 1688.
55. Jām'au'sh-Shawāhid fī'l Dakhūl Ghayr-Muslim fī'l-Masjid, p. 55.

Chapter: Two

Clutches of the Imperialism

Islām in a very strong word has had declared that all human beings irrespective of caste, creed, colour and country, men or women are equal with each other. While demolishing the 'Arabian centuries old the Age of Ignorance way of life based on inequality and communalism and also conferred legal rights:

> "O' mankind! Lo! We have created you male and female, and have made you nations and tribes that ye may know one another. Lo! The noblest of you, in the sight of God, is the best in conduct." (*Qur'an*: 49/13)

The holy Prophet Muḥammad laboured quietly to wean the people from the worship of idols. But the Quraysh had vested interests in the old worship. The holy Prophet met great trouble and sorrow, facing so many extremely wanton injuries, oppression, distress and other painful problems, almost for three years during the social boycott by Meccans, they even did not let him go outside his house. He was not allowed to earn the livelihood, resulting in the worst condition for want of food for children and elders of his family. Any sensible person would tremble to ponder over the plight of children and elders of his family. Anyhow when the problems were over and the Prophet began to preach Islām, stones were thrown at him. He would fall down being unconscious, family members would take him home to treat medically, apply medicine and find out ways and means.

When he would be cured, preach the people: *Qūlū lā illāh illalāh fa tuf lehū* (Say He is God, the One! God, the eternally Besought of all.)

To torture him, thorns were spread in his way, sometimes a blanket trasseled around the neck and pulled to extend the pupil of eyes vomit.

Often putting the bones of animals on his neck and inflicting other various atrocities on him.

Even then some people were coverted into Islām. If the Meccan catch hold of any Muslim on the way, they would insist him to abuse Muḥammad, if they refused, they would be serverly punished. Tying would his legs and hands, he would be kept on hot-hot pyre and beat him. Various historians have recorded the fury of the events. Had the Prophet taken revenge after Mecca victory, it would have been justifiable. Islām permits to take revenge to that extent there was atrocity towards it, but, if pardoned, this conduct would be more pleasant to God. This order is for all.

The Qur'an has conferred the title of *Raḥmatu'l 'Ālamīn* (*Qur'an* 21/107). *The Merciful for the Whole Universe* to Ḥazarat Muḥammad, *Rasūl Allāh* (Prophet of God). When he entered Mecca in April 628, as a conqueror, the persons, who had disgraced humanity by inflicting cruel outrages upon inoffensive men and women, and even upon the lifeless dead, were now completely at his mercy. He, who was once a fugitive and persecuted, in the hour of triumph every evil suffered forgotten and pardoned all his old persecuters, relentless and ruthless, a general amnesty was extended to all and declared that whoever gets asylum even in his foe Umayyites Abū Sufyyān's house would also be in peace and safety.

The Liberated Captive Umayyites

Ṭulaqa (liberated captives) is a terminology used by scholars for the Umayyites, who were enemies of Islām and its development and spread. Prophet pardoned them after being shamelessly defeated by Muslims. They half heartedly embraced Islām, but could not endure it. Among the members of these families include noxious and wicked, Abū Sufyyān, his son Mu'āwiyah, Walīd-bin-'Oqbah, Marwān-bin-Ḥakam and 'Abdu'llāh-bin-Sa'd-bin-Abī Saraḥ, who came around Muslims, later the turncoat converted to his old faith.[1]

As far as the question of religious belief of *Ṭulaqā'h* is concerned, Imām 'Alī in his sermon has clarified that these people had adopted Islām as a veil to conceal their infidelity, being helpless wore the turban of Islām. Therefore, whenever a chance was available to them, they never used to hesitate to express their perfidious faith.[2]

Shāh Walīu'llāh Muḥaddis Dehalavī (d. 1762 AD) has written a *Ḥadīth* (Tradition) of the Prophet that they were not to be treated at par with other Muslims.[3]

If looked, at the historical perspective then *Ṭulaqa*, the liberated captives, whose competent representation was made by Amīr Mu'āwiyah (d. 681 AD) and his father Abū Sufyyān, even after coming into the periphery of Islām, could not rise from their narrow communal and tribal bias. When Abū Bakr became Caliph I (632-34 AD), Umayyites' turbulent Abū Sufyyān, came and asked Imām 'Alī-Ibn-Abī Ṭālib that how a man of lower ebb of all in Quraysh clan became the Caliph ? If you could be ready to get up, I would fill plaintiff indeed ! Imām 'Alī replied that your matters are based on enmity towards Islām and nothing else.[4]

Regarding Caliph II 'Omar (634-44 AD) who made Mu'āwiyah the Governor of Damascus (Syria) for the first time, Ibn Khaldūn, Abū Żayd 'Abdu'r-Raḥmān (d. 1406 AD) has written:

> "(Caliph II) 'Omar Fārūq's observation cleared the actual position of Mu'āwiyah and expressed his hatred towards his functioning."[5]

Abu'l 'Olā Maudūdī (d. 1979 AD) has also expressed the same views:

> "Caliph 'Omar during his last stage of life had felt the danger of tribal traditions over shadowing the Islāmic principles (which could not absolutely be erased in spite of the Islāmic movement's abnormal revolution) may rope up and as a result troubles within Islām may shoot up." [6]

Abū Sufyyān

The accession of 'Othmān as the Caliph III was as good as the monopolization of Umayyite clan on the Islāmic kingdom. The mischievous character of Umayyite clan Abū Sufyyān became old. Deprived of inner vision, now he had lost also his outer eyesight. Walking with a stick he came down to congratulate 'Othmān on his Caliphate and explained to him:

> "I am witness to the fact that there is no such things as Hell and Paradise and no such thing as *Qiyāmah* (Catastrophe) that is going to happen; all is humbug of the Hāshimite to deceive the world. Now, that the crown has come your way, play it like a ball."[7]

So, many true Traditions are also available for admonishing through the Prophet. For example, we may refer just an event, which has been discussed by so many historians in their books:

> "Caliph II 'Omar's son 'Abdu'llāh used to describe that the Prophet, while arising from a valley, saw first Abū Sufyyān, who was riding on a donkey and Mu'āwiyah and his elder brother Yażīd-bin-Abū Sufyyān were bawling forward and backward. When the holy Prophet caught sight of him, then he said—Oh God ! Be *L'anat* (Curs) on all these three !"[8]

The Caliph I Abū Bakr's son Muḥammad has recalled in his letter addressed to Mu'āwiyah and Imām Ḥasan in his letter taking a vow on Mu'āwiyah has also on an occasion, mentioned about this event[9].

Amīr Mu'āwiyah

Most reverend Ṣūfī saint Khwājah Ḥasan Baṣarī (d. 721 AD) in a sermon has said regarding Amīr Mu'āwiyah:

> "Four deeds of Mu'āwiyah are such that even one among them would become enough proof that he was on the path of those inflicted with the charge having gone astray:
>
> Firstly, his war against Imām 'Alī and taking over the Islāmic reign.
>
> Secondly, making his son Yażīd as his successor Caliph, whose bad character and prostitution was known to him and was clear on all Muslims.
>
> Thirdly, although he was familiar with the Tradition of the Prophet that the child is his, whose bed he was born and stone for others, Mu'āwiyah included Żiyād-bin-Abīh[10] in his genealogy, and
>
> Fourthly, murdering renowned *Ṣaḥābī* (pl. *Ṣaḥābah*) (Prophet's Companion) Ḥujr-bin-'Adī and his associates without any guilt."[11]

Imām Nasā'ī, 'Abdu'r-Raḥmān, (d. 915 AD), who had obtained glory on the basis of his being a writer among the *Ṣaḥīḥu'l-Sittah* (six authentic collections), Ziyā Aḥamad Badāyūnī has written, citing the references of Muḥammad-bin-Isḥāq Iṣfahānī and Ḥāfiẓ Abu'l Ḥasan Warqaṭnī that when he authored his famous book *al-Khaṣayṣ Murtazwī,* some people asked about the good qualities of Amīr Mu'āwiyah, his reply was:

> "Where is good quality in Mu'āwiyah? I am not at all familiar with any of his good quality." [12]

Ṭulqa'h not accepted Islām whole Heartedly

Prior to Islām, clan phenomena was the symbol of communal prestige in 'Arabian peninsula, for which they used to fight and die. Islām derecognised communal hatred and made people feel one-another as brother, which is called *Ukhūwat* (fraternity). In *Ṭulqa'h* many people especially Umaiyyite's elders, who had not accepted Islām whole heartedly, due to their communal hatred, were masking conspiracies to put an end to it. They had more hatred towards Hāshimites, because, in the same clan the holy Prophet Muḥammad was born. Afterwards Hāshimites obtained regards from whole Arabian society.

Umayyites were burning in the fire of emulation to see that Hāshimites, despite not having power and wealth like them, had secured respects and regards in social life. They scared other Quraysh clans, who were rich business class that Hāshimites in the name of Islām would snatch their wealth and distribute among Muslims. They were successful in creating a joint army, with Commander-in-Chief Abū Sufyyān, his son Mu'āwiyah as next to Command. They faught several unsuccessful battles, But there was more happiness than sorrow on this score that Abū Sufyyān and his son Mu'āwiyah became the Leader of entire Quraysh clans without any dispute. If Islāmic power was defeated, their kingdom would be established in the whole 'Arabian peninsula. Nature laughed at their evil design and were smashed till 644 AD in which their elders and veterans were killed mostly by Imām 'Alī. Defeated at all fronts, in frustration they bowed downed at the feets of the Prophet Muḥammad, and prayed for mercy, who showered mercy like anything and with all grace condoned them. There was a dominant role of Imām 'Alī in Islām's victory and the defeat of its enemies. Therefore, now the entire hatred and enmity shifted to Imām 'Alī. Mu'āwiyah emerged as staunch enemy against 'Alī.

Secondly, 'Arabian society was hesitant to include Umayyites into Quraysh clans, because of the facts that their legator Umayya was not the heir of Quraysh leader 'Abd Shams. Umayya was a Roman slave, who due to some reasons became the heir of 'Abd Shams. To this extent that

Umayya became the leader and the very name of clan called *Banī Umayya* (Umayyites) is on his name.

Arabian society had been extremely proud of its legator, maintain the genealogical tree, a list of important predecessors and keeps safely its lineage. Umayyites obtained the ruling power, as if, it would have erased as a black mark to be the heir of the slave. It became possible after attaining power. Umayyites asserted to be called the heir of 'Abd Shams, thus, of the Quraysh clan. But the actual situation at that time was adverse. Prophet's senior Associate and Arab's famous poet Ḥassān-bin-Thābit, in his verse has exposed the genealogy to be of a slave heredity. His verse is put-up in the context of Prophet's wife 'Ā'ishah, poet Ḥassān says:

> "In the Hāshimites the basis of greatness remains with the child of Makthūm's daughter (Arabians most reverend clan, in which Prophet's grandmother was). Oh ! Abū Sufyyān, your grandfather was a slave."[13]

Amīr Mu'āwiyah called the oldest man of his time and asked in his darbar regarding Amīr Umayya. The old man replied that he was a short and blind man, evil was evident from his face. He used to pull his master's vehicle. Mu'āwiyah angrily asked about the Hāshim. He said, very strong, tall and handsome person. Mu'āwiyah could not overcome his passion, asked. Have you seen Muḥammad too? Who Muḥammad? asked the old man. Mu'āwiyah said, the prophet ! The old man wrathfully said, Shame ! you pronounce his *Kalamah* (testimony of faith) and address his name with out the respect." [14]

Amīr Mu'āwiyah in his vicious ambition for changing the Islāmic governance into monarchy of the Age of Ignorance uplifted 'Arab communality with the attractive slogan of '*Arabian Prestige,* which was against the established norms prescribed by the holy Qur'an, encouraging black history becoming Islām's opponent attitude. Actually speaking it was a movement based on 'Arabian Chauvinism.

To understand the outcome of this pseudo 'Arabian Prestige, the famous event of Ghassān's last king Jiballah-binu'l-Eham assumed Islām after getting defeated by Muslims in the Battle of Yarmūq (634 AD). Once while making a circuit of holy Ka'bah his royal cloak hit a poor Bedouin's leg. Being angry Jiballah slapped at his neck. Bedouin's fellow begged juctice before Caliph 'Omar. He enquired Jiballah. His reply was, the Bedouin has disregarded him. If not been at the holy place, he would have killed him. Caliph 'Omar ordered Jiballah should beg for pardon or undergo punishment. Jiballah replied that he was a king and that man was an ordinary Bedouin. Caliph 'Omar's reply was, that Islām has destroyed the difference between a king and a pauper. He asked excuse for a night and ran away hiding, again he converted into Christianity, declaring he could not remain in a religion, where the glory earned by the forefathers could not be safe. This religion, you see, destroys even the glory made by predecessors.[15]

The same was the mental attitude of the custodians of the glory of 'Arabian Prestige, but they could not dare renounce Islām openly. Their Islām was a situation of helplessness, because on sacrificing Islām, power and worldly happiness both would be going away from their hands.

'Arabian Communal Prestige

Amīr Mu'āwiyah wanted to establish monarch on the basis of prior to Islām venemous ruling set-up prevailed, the *Jāhiliyah,* Age of Ignorance, prior to the Islāmic ruling system and he did his best and left no stone unturned, did all his efforts. The term used by the historians the 'Arabian Nationalism was nothing other than attempt to convert Islām itself into their own ancient Traditions, in the name of 'Arabian Prestige.

The message of Islām has had been peace, harmony and brotherhood. The holy Qur'an has repeatedly laid emphasis on unity and warm heartedness amongst the people in general and Muslims in particular. The Qur'an has made clear that the persons of different sects should be even treated as Muslims. The Qur'an has made it rather clear that those who create divisions have nothing to do with Islām, *vide* the verse:

> "As for those who divide their religion and break up into sects, thou hast no part in them in the least." (*Qur'an*: 6/159)

Then in another place the Qur'an orders to proceed on straight path and keep away from all those paths, which create divisions:

> "And hold fast all together, by the cable, which God (*Stretch, out for you*) and be not divided among yourselves." (*Qur'an*: 3/103)

To save from these scattering, the holy Prophet Muḥammad had provided the directive principle underlying the *Hadīthu'th-Thaqalayn* which has already been discussed in the previous pages.

"As for those who divide their religion and break up into sects, thou hast no part in them in the least." (*Qur'an*: 6/159)

But Amīr Mu'āwiyah fighting against Imām 'Alī, who was Caliph declared by all Muslims whole-heartedly with their full consent, divided Muslims. As a result many cults were formed in Muslims. Since then factionalism gained momentum. Islām was being divided into so many factions. Islām has seventy three cults as such. If a real calculation is made, then the figures may reach in thousands. In view of the limitation of this book only a few facts have been presented.

On account of Amīr Mu'āwiyah's personal conduct and his continuous negligence of the Islāmic religious norms, there was a terrific dissatisfaction towards him among many senior companions of the holy Prophet. They continued to warn Mu'āwiyah on various issues. Miqdām-bin-Ma'dī objected to Mu'āwiyah for wearing golden ornaments and sitting on the skin of wild animals and wearing their skins. Abū Ayūb Anṣārī visited Syria, and observed that all the toilets were constructed facing the direction of Ka'bah. He turned his face seeking pardon from God?[16] The hatred of Muslims had developed to this extent that when Mu'āwiyah went to Mecca on *Ḥajj* pilgrimage, and at dawn passed along the side of famous Ṣaḥābī Sa'd-bin-Abī Waqāṣ. Mu'āwiyah saluted, but there was no response from Sa'd. Mu'āwiyah told his friends, he is Sa'd, Propeht's Ṣaḥābī. His routine is not to talk to anybody till sun-rise. Sa'd got this information and said, there is no truth in Mu'āwiyah's words, of course. By God, I do not wish to talk to him.[17]

The reaction of 'Arabian Prestige, gave birth *to Sha'ubī Movement* (National Movement), sponsored by Īrānī-Muslims which got encouragement against Umayyite. Khurāsān (Īrān) became the centre of the movement. Hatred developed against 'Arabs among Īrānīs, which was used against Umayyite caliphate by the opponents extended help to 'Abbāsīs in overthrowing with this hope that the revolution would emerge with its attempts, Umayyite Caliphate and establishing 'Abbāsite Caliphate in course of time.

Any detailed objective study of 'Arabian communal prestige, nurtured by Amīr Mu'āwiyah is not possible here, due to paucity of space. However, a few events only can be discussed. On account of Amīr Mu'āwiyah's reactional behaviour, situation went on assuming negative form continuously. Difference between 'Arabs and non-'Arab peoples arose to a burning point. Non-'Arab peoples felt that the Islāmic victory journey has indeed made them slaves of 'Arabs and even after accepting Islām could not be equal to them. In the governance they had been denied their due share. Even while appointing *Qāzī* (Judge), *Muftī* (Jurist), *Pesh-Imām* (Leader of Prayer), *Mu'ażżin* (Caller of Prayer) etc. It was essential to be an 'Arab by birth. No non-'Arab was entitled to get any respectful post.[18]

In Iraq seal was engraved on Nabatī's hands for their identity and in Basra converted new Muslims were driven away from the town.[19]

Sayīd-bin-Żubayr was a distinguished scholar of his time. None other in the Islāmic world was parallel to him, but he was non-'Arab. When he was made *Qāzī* of Kūfah, the society was gripped in narrow-mindedness and there was severe opposition on his appointment. So, he was replaced by a 'Arab, Abū Mūsā 'Ash'ari's son Abū Burdah, but he was not a competent person, therefore, was advised not to take any decision without consulting Sayīd-bin-Żubayr.[20]

The narrow-mindedness went to the limit that no other person except an 'Arab was permitted to lead the congregational prayer. If there was no 'Arabian present, the dead body of a person was to be buried with out a funeral prayer.[21]

If any person wanted to marry such a young girl, who was not an 'Arab, he should not consult the girl's father, but the 'Arab custodian under whom the girl's father lived.[22]

A term *Ḥizān* (imbalance of a breast, to be polluted) was prevalent among 'Arabs, for those whose wife is not an 'Arab. His child was not entitled for inheritance, which a child of an 'Arabian wife was. Under the sacred law of Islām provision for inheritance are similar to ancestry of an 'Arab wife. As per Islāmic Tradition the rights of both are equal. A person of Sulaym clan gave his daughter in marriage to a non-'Arab. Medina's Administrator made separation between that husband and wife and the other native Muslim was whipped, who arranged the marriage of his daughter. Then the other native Muslim was dishonoured by tonsuring his head, beard and eye-brows.[23]

Such type of narrowness was not only prevalent between 'Arab and the other native Muslim, but also even among 'Arabs a severe tribal difference of opinion developed. There was nutural enmity between 'Adnānī and Kayḥṭānī, Yemenī and Muzārī, Āzud and Tāmin, Kalb and Qaiys were immersed in the *Jāhiliyah* (Age of Ignorance). Old quarrels became alive. The ruling group also was in tribal conflict. Against a tribe another tribe was used. The then Administrator in their own jurisdiction encouraged their own tribe, *ex parte* and did injustice towards other tribes.

Prior to Islām special emphasis was given on revenge in the *Jāhiliyah.* In the name of revenge different types of atrocities were allowed. Islām has given permission for revenge only to the extent, to which atrocity was done, but if person can be accorded pardon, it would be the best.

It was the tragic event in the history of Islām that in the Battle of Oḥod (March 625 AD) while protecting Prophet Muḥammad, his uncle Ḥamżah became a martyr. Amīr Mu'āwiyah's mother Hindah rent the dead body of the martyr Ḥamżah, splited his chest and chewed and tore his nose, ears etc., and made a human neckless and put on. For the reason the very name Hindah is affixed as *Jigar-Khwārah* (heart-chewer) in the history. The holy Prophet was very sad on the event and he ordered that Hindah should not came before him.[24]

Islām has ordered to treat with respect the dead bodies of opponents in the war. Amīr Mu'āwiyah again made prevalent the very savage practice of taking revenge from the dead bodies by cutting off and sending the head to the other place etc. First of all, the head which was chopped off, after his becoming martyr in the war was that of Prophet's very dear companion 'Ammār-bin-Yāsir's was presented before Mu'āwiyah as a gift.[25]

In the same way at the orders of Amīr Mu'āwiyah Prophet's compamion 'Omarū'l Ḥamaq Khiżarajjī's head was kept at the tip of spear and rotated on all the four sides, and then it was put in the lap of his wife.[26]

Umayyites had lost their image and prestige in Quraysh clans due to their psyche of hatred and debauchery, they were considered incendiary, wicked and mischief makers and punished in the summits of Quraysh from time to time. Lastly, on the complaint of some local Jews for loot and murder, a jury of Quraysh, headed by Caliph 'Omar's grandfather Nafīl-bin-Abdu'l 'Ożā punished Amīr Mu'āwiyah's grandfather Ḥarab-bin Umayyah to pay the Jews hundred golden eyes camels, as compensation and also exiled all Umayyites from the orbits of Ḥejāż, so, they took asylum in Damascus.[27]

Umayyites had an occasion of flourishing during the reign Caliph III 'Othmān-bin-'Affān (644-56 AD) when they had secured uncontrolled power over the then biggest Empire of the time. Amīr Mu'āwiyah emerged among them as one of the most influential power point. Caliph 'Othmān appointed him Governor for an area from Ela to Rome border and from Algeria to sea-shore. In this region presently five states are established, namely Syria, Lebenon, UAE, Palistine and Israel.[28] Almost the same composite square miles are prevalent even now, which was available during the Governorship of Amīr Mu'āwiyah, who reigned like a monarch during the whole twelve years period of Caliph 'Othmān.

Ultimately Amīr Mu'āwiyah made a strong root there, to such an extent that caliphate head office was dependent on him and it was at his mercy and sympathy. Its bad effects were thrust on Imām 'Alī, when he assumed the office, as Caliph IV after the murder of Caliph III 'Othmān in the year 656 AD.[29]

In the verse of the Qur'an, it has been pointed out as to what is the nature of rulership:

> "He is God, than whom there is no other God, the sovereign Lord, the Holy One, Peace, the Keeper of Faith, the Guardian, the Majestic, the Compeller, the Superb, Glorified be God from all that they ascribe as partner (*unto Him*)". (*Qur'an*: 59/23)

This is the principle of the Divine Unity in Islām, after which come the principles related with the Prophethood and the Imām ate, which are cardinal pivots of Islām. Islām regards the Creator, the only Ruler without any partner. Entire Universe is subject to His sole-rulership. The Prophet is the liaison to Him who carries out his commands. The Prophet has no right or power to add or alter the Divine commands. The command of Supreme Lord has to remain in execution till the end of the world, and the chain of the Divine Prophets has terminated in Muḥammad-Ibn-'Abdu'llāh, the last Prophet. The protection, execution and establishment of the Divine Order on earth has to be looked after by the Divinely guided successors of the Prophet called Imāms or the infallible leaders. This principle makes it necessary for an Imām to be present in every age till the Divine mission is fulfilled and justice established on earth:

> "And everything have We confined into a Manifesting Imām (*Guide*)." (*Qur'an*: 36/12)

Therefore, the aim of Imām 'Alī was to safeguard Islām's diplomatic power (rule), which was in danger from the advent of Islām, venemous rule-system and he did his best public efforts Amīr Mu'āwiyah opposed him at each and every stage.

Caliph II 'Omar estimating the situation after him, said, I swear, you won't make Imām 'Alī Caliph, because of the fact that if you make him Caliph, even if you are unhappy he won't leave you a hindrance in establishing the path of Justice.[30] In the same way regarding accession of 'Othmān-bin-'Affān as Caliph, he said, if I make 'Othmān as my heir, he would carry Abī Muī'ṭ tribals heredity, he would make the Umayyite clan ride on the shoulders of Muslims and Muslims will rebel and kill 'Othmān, I swear.[31]

Umayyite 'Othmān-bin-'Affān became Caliph III and during his ten years reign, he showered all benefits upon his clan. Caliph 'Othmān used the *Baytu'l-Māl* (State Exchequer) as his personal property. The bounty earned from the conquest of various countries were distributed amongst the Umayyites in preference to others. Some of the cases of beneficiaries from State Exchequer, without any justification, were of the family and clan of the Caliph 'Othmān mentioned as under.[32]

(i) The *Fidak*, the personal property of the Prophet Muḥammad for which his daughter Fāṭimah aż-Żahrah had made claim before the Caliph I Abū Bakr and was refused and had been made the part of the State Exchequer was given by Caliph III 'Othmān to his son-in-law Marwān in addition to a sum of five lakhs from the State Exchequer.

(ii) When Caliph 'Othmān married his next daughter to Ḥārith-bin-Ḥakam, brother of Marwān, he was given one lakh as dowry from the State Exchequer.

(iii) Marwān's father Ḥakam was also gifted one lakh from the State Exchequer.

(iv) Noxious Abū Sufyyān was awarded two lakhs from the State Exchequer.

(v) Walid son of 'Uqbah, half-brother of the Caliph 'Othmān, who was declared transgressor by the Qur'an, was offered one lakh from the State Exchequer.

(vi) 'Abdu'llāh-bin-Khālid was given the sum of four lakhs from the State Exchequer, etc.

These are some of the cases where awardees were from Umayyite clan and close relations of the Caliph 'Othmān. Here, no speciousness of language could help in conniving the corruption and nepotism, which has been vehemently criticized and condemned by the famous scholars, like Ibn Ḥajar Ḥaythmī al-Makkī, Badru'd-Dīn 'Aynī, Ibn Qudāmah, Abu'l 'Olā Maudūdī[33] etc.

The weakness of Caliph 'Othman and wickedness of his favourite created great ferment among the people. By 650 AD rebellion had broken out. The rebels besieged 'Othmān in his house and after several days of desultory fighting, he was killed. The forecast of the Caliph II 'Omar was cent per cent true.

Imām 'Alī became the Fourth Caliph of *Khilāfatu'r-Rāshidah*, after twenty four years of the death of the Prophet Muḥammad and was martyred after four and half years of his Caliphate. Imām 'Alī was invited by the Muslims to accept the Caliphate after the murder of the third Caliph 'Othmān, which he accepted very reluctantly after long hesitation and faced great difficulties due mostly to the corrupt state of affairs, when acceded it. Imām 'Alī was ranked as Caliph on 23rd day of June, 655 AD, at a general meeting held at Medina in the Prophet's mosque where nearly all Muslims pledged allegiance at the hand of Imām 'Alī.[34]

Soon after the accession to the Caliphate, Imām 'Alī based his rule on the Islāmic ideals of justice and equality, which was a blow to the interest of the Quraysh aristocracy, which, had highly grown rich and powerful due to various conquests. Umayyite clan was by birth the adversary to the Hāshimites clan to which belonged the Prophet Muḥammad and Imām 'Alī. Umayyites were highly apprehensive of Imām 'Alī having been chosen as the successor of the Prophet. All the wealth taken and used in personal pleasures and luxury in the ruling period of Caliph 'Othmān, was threatened to be checked and confiscated, so, their future looked dark. So, Mu'āwiyah-bin-Abū Sufyyān made a huge army by bringing together Umayyites and the pseudo-Muslims and occupied some areas by setting up a battle front against Imām 'Alī.[35] But some of them mounted difficulties and unrest against him and forced him to fight against the rebellion which resulted in the battles of Jamal, Siffīn, Nahrwān etc. Again, Caliph 'Omar's forecast appeared cent per cent true.

War Against Imām 'Alī

If we analyse this psyche of pseudo hallucination of hatred, which was riding over Amīr Mu'āwiyah, it was vicious celebral dysrhythmic for him that he could not become *Khalīfah* (Vicegerency of the Prophet), which resulted into retardation to the extent that started nurturing the very ambition to be considered himself as the Prophet of Islām. That is why in a full *darbar* when he was addressed, *As-Salām Alayek, Yā Rasūl Allāh* (Salute to you, Oh ! Prophet of God), neither he had any objection, nor any of his courtiers objected, whereas all Muslims are aware that the last Muḥammad is the last and final Prophet of God. To say any other person Prophet of God would be out of the ambit of Islām.[36] In his enthusiasm and lust of posing himself as prophet he tried his best to shift the Prophet's *Minbar* (Pulpit, sitting on it Prophet used to address) from

Medina to Damascus, but could not succeed due to some Divine obstacle.[37]

The flame of hatred spread to this extent that though there was no complaint against Imām 'Alī, Mu'āwiyah started abusing him with bad words regularly in his sermon after the prayer everyday, which continued till the end of Umayyites regime in 750 AD. This naked exhibition of hatred betrayed the original colour of Mu'āwiyah, because it had never been tolerable to hear abuses in any decent society. It was not before and prevalent then, anywhere to tarnish the image of Imām 'Alī and also to spread elsewhere the network of bad pubicity against him.

Amīr Mu'āwiyah blew the clarion call of war against Imām 'Alī, Caliph of the time for establishing his own monarchical state, even though he was Governor under the Caliph. In spite of being familiar with the clear Tradition of the Islāmic Prophet, regarding fighting a war against the Islāmic Rule and Caliph II 'Omar's son 'Abdu'llāh having described the Tradition of Prophet thus:

> "The Prophet of Islām has said—who used weapon over us, he was not from among us."[38]

That means, he or she is no more Muslim. There is another Tradition also of the same directive. *Ummu'l Mūminīn* (Believer's Mother, i.e. Prophet's wife) 'A'ishah, the daughter of Caliph I Abū Bakr said that Prophet told her:

> "Who ever would fight against 'Alī, he is an infidel and would go to Hell."[39]
>
> "Keep 'Alī-Ibn-Abī Ṭālib as a friend because God too keeps him as a friend."[40]

There are so many Traditions of the holy Prophet in praise of Imām 'Alī, wherein he had claims of being his successor. There is a discussion quoted in *Jām'au'ṣ-Ṣaḥīḥul-Bukhārī,* in which Prophet said while addressing Imām 'Alī:

> "Don't you feel delighted with the honour that you are just like Hārūn (Aaron) as he was with Mūsā (Moses). But only this difference that there would be no Prophet after myself."[41]

There may be so may reasons of the enmity of Amīr Mu'āwiyah with Imām 'Alī, but two of them may be:

First and foremost was, after Imām 'Alī, becoming fourth Caliph of the Islāmic Empire, Mu'āwiyah's vicious desire to establish his monarchical empire shattered into pieces.

Secondly, Imām 'Alī's close association with the Islāmic Prophet. During the life-time of Prophet whatsover wars held for the uplift of Islām, Imām 'Alī was cosidered hero. So, many family members of Amīr Mu'āwiyah became victims in the hands of Imām 'Alī, who were fighting against Islām, like his maternal grandfather 'Aqbah, two maternal uncles, his brother and many other close relatives and elders of Umayyite clan.

All good people has have the opinion that while fighting with Imām 'Alī, Amīr Mu'āwiyah was on unjust path. This is the statement of famous Islāmic scholar Ḥāfiẓ Ibn Ḥajar, Shihābu'ddīn Aḥmad-bin-'Alī, 'Asqalānī (d. 1448 AD):

> "It is clear from 'Ammār's killing that Imām 'Alī is on true path and Amīr Mu'āwiyah is a rebel."[42]

So, many other renowned scholars like Ibn 'Abdu'l-Barr (d.1070 AD)[43], Ibn Kathīr, 'Imādu'd-Dīn Ismā'il-bin-'Omar (d.1373 AD)[44], Abu'l 'Olā Maudūdī (d.)[45] have also expressed the same views.

The fact of consideration is that Caliph III 'Othmān was in captivity of enemies for twenty one days, who refused to give food and water. Imām 'Alī for the safety of the Caliph 'Othmān kept his sons Imām Ḥasan and Imām Ḥusain, who were alert as watch men at his gate whole night and day and arranged for his food and water also. Caliph 'Othmān was killed and Imām 'Alī was angry with his sons. They said that the rebels entered from the backyard of his house cutting the roof, we were watching at the gate. Caliph 'Othmān's dead body was buried only after three days, but Amīr Mu'āwiyah never turned up to help Caliph 'Othmān, any time during twenty one days of his captivity and never bothered about his final ritual also. But afterwards, raised banner of revolt against Caliph III, 'Othmān's murder for getting political mileage out of it at that time. Maulana Abu'l 'Olā Maudūdī along with context of aṭ-Ṭabarī, Ibn Jarīr Abū Ja'far[46], Ibn Athīr, 'Izz ad-Dīn Abu'l Ḥasan,[47] and Ibn Kathīr[48] expressed his reaction in severe terms, In the words of Maulana Abu'l 'Olā Maudūdī (d. 1979 AD):

> "It is clear that there was tribal arrangement of *Jāhiliyah* (Age of Ignorance), Pre-Islāmic period, that taking for the revenge of killing of any dead person anyhow and anywhere

and using any method to fulfil one's own desire. Now, it was a legal state, wherein a formal law was with the heir of dead, who were alive, as prevalent for every claim. Taking the claim of heir themselves, if Imām 'Alī was not a bonafied Caliph, then what was the justification to demand of him that criminals might be found out and punished. Was he any tribal leader, who without legal power can catch hold of anybody and punish?—(Amīr Mu'āwiyah) an administrator of Syria to take revenge of Caliph 'Othmān emerged, refused to comply with Central Rule, utilised for this purpose the power of the governorship and there was no demand, to file a suit and punish the murderers to be handed over. So, that he himself could murder him. All these denote the prior to Islām, *Jāhiliyah* period, instead of the period of Islāmic regime."[49]

"Hatching conspiracy against legal Caliph Imām 'Alī, Amīr Mu'āwiyah did all possible attempts in the name of avenging Caliph 'Othmān's murder by anti-propaganda, arousing the feelings of people. His clothes full of blood and his wife's cut off fingers were displayed in a public place to evoke public sympathy and arose their feelings."[50]

"Mu'āwiyah wanted to take revenge of the murder of Caliph 'Othmān in an illegal manner and not through the proper means or law. Otherwise it is clear that the very fact of Caliph 'Othmān, being murdered was sufficient to make the people angrry and to arouse their feelings, there was no need to exhibit his clothes smeared with blood and his wife's cut off fingers."[51]

"In such a situation, it was imperative for the existing Caliph to take action against the rebellions and revolting Governor. If at all Imām 'Alī had made any delay in passing the rule of suspension of Mu'āwiyah, it would have been a severe mistake from his activities it became clear even at the beginning itself, where Mu'āwiyah was standing. There would be curtain on his motives for a long time, then it would have been a false curtain, which would have been very severe."[52]

In the view of famous scholar Syed Abu'l Ḥasan 'Alī Ḥasanī Nadawī:

"Caliph 'Alī's policies and his state structure and his official machinery was roaming on the pivot which was the essence of Islām, its soul, its principles, its values and specimens of political wisdom and sacrifice. It could not be sacrificed for the sake of short time diplomacy. The Prophet's reign and *Khilāfatu'r-Rāshidah* (Rightly Guided Caliphate) is the dynasty to be recognised as an ideal one. Caliph should be the example of Islāmic ideals, good conduct and being the ruler and leader of Muslim Ummah should be an example. He should not be merely the ruler and leader of Muslims, therefore, he had to be fully prepared for the situation made alive and prevalent and that side by side may obtain other diplomatic priorities and administrative preferances on problems, whatever may be the value to be paid for it. Therefore, to keep alive the objective, he had to pay a heavy price, which he paid cheerfully and his inner conscience was contented with it."[53]

The Distortion of Islāmic Norms

The main cause of distortion of Islāmic Norms was the closure of the Islāmic system of governance. Whatever ruling authority was appointed by Amīr Mu'āwiyah, was on the basis monarchy just against the Islāmic state principle. He established monarchy system of governance in the place of Divine System of Governance, propounded by Islām. In monarchy each and every of those matters surface, which are against Divine Governance. Instead of God's command, emperor's command prevails.

Such a ruling-system came into existence, which was not answerable to anyone. Neither the fear of God, nor shame from the Prophet, nor care for the Qur'an, and not at all any fear from the public, that would be reviewing good and bad and might tell some thing ill could deter them. Such a mad independence came, wherein there was no rule-regulation, morality, whatever you like and in what form you may desire. There was nothing like law, discipline, traditions, no control on anything and everything, all were away from goodness.

Amīr Mu'āwiyah had appointed eunuchs for his own personal service,[54] who eanred a position as *Khwājahsarā* (chief of household) at the courts of later Muslim kings. The eunuchs were also used as a medium of immoral and unnatural sex-relationship. Besides eunuchs Amīr Mu'āwiyah's assembly had one hundred *Qīnạts* (call-girls) for singers and dancers were also employed, who used to entertain spectators and listeners, exhibiting their arts and skills in the open assembly from time to time.[55]

In brief it would be enough to say that during that period there was an absolute refusal to accept any thing Godly. Out of so many subjects an attempt will be made to invite attention towards only a few facts. In their basis so many facts would be clear by themselves, without telling anything about them or not. The learned and mature readers would realise it themselves.

How monarchy crushed the Islāmic Principles under its feet, will be discussed further. Amīr Mu'āwiyah and his companions were proud of the establishment of monarchic ruling system in the place of this Divine Governance. Amīr Mu'āwiyah's Administrator, who afterwards became Caliph Marwān-bin-Ḥakam used to say proudly that now Prophet's statehood has, already been demolished.[56] Although Prophet's clear orders are available at present:

> "Whoever reveals such a matter in against, whoever is not at the root, his matter is condemnable, worth ill-telling." [57]

Killing of Resource Persons

Prophet Muḥammad's *Ahl'l-Bayt* or *'Itrat* (Household or Progeny) and close *Ṣaḥābah* (Prophet's Companions) were the only the then present resource persons, who could prevent Amīr Mu'āwiyah's vicious ambition for changing the Islāmic governance into *Jāhiliyah-cum*-monarchy. They sincerely fulfilled their obligation, as a result of which an uncomparable task of editing the Islāmic *Sharī'a* (Sacred Law) could be possible. They have collected a good storage of various sources of knowledge, science, literature, doctrine etc. based on the Qur'an and the Traditions of the Prophet, which had not at all any glimps of influence of *Jāhiliyah-cum*-monarchy. Prophet's *Ahl'l-Bayt* and true and close *Ṣaḥābah* were very highly regarded and respected for their very pure life-style, ideal conduct and prestige. The holy Prophet Muḥammad was the main source for them, therefore, they were considered to be final in all respects. They were the main challenge for Amīr Mu'āwiyah. They could not be defeated by arguments. A conspiracy of putting an end to their life was hatched. Amīr Mu'āwiyah arranged for the murder of thousands of *Ṣaḥābah* or they became Martyrs by fighting on the path of God, against Amīr Mu'āwiyah, a few of whom alone can be discussed here –

Imām Ḥasan-bin-Imām 'Alī

Mu'āwiyah made the eldest grandson of the Prophet, Imām Ḥasan martyred by poison, despite a signed Agreement of Peace with him. All historians are unanimous in one voice of his killing by Mu'āwiyah. We have also discussed its details at other places in the present book.

Muḥammad-bin-Abū Bakr

Caliph I Abū Bakr's son Muḥammad was martyred. After murdering him, his dead body was kept inside the hide of a donkey and burnt. [58]

Mālik-bin-Ashtar

He was martyred by giving him poison.[59] There is a Tradition of the Prophet in this regard that 'Ammār would be killed by those, who would revolt against Islām. So, when in the Battle of Ṣiffīn (656-57 AD) Amīr Mu'āwiyah's army murdered him, a civil-war started in his army that they are not on the path of God. Amīr Mu'āwiyah gave a false argument that 'Alī arranged for his murder, not myself, because 'Alī neither brought 'Ammār to battlefield, nor he became martyred![60]

Historians have recorded that since the advent of Islām, it was only his head, which was hung at the tip of a sword.[61] It was inhuman practice in the *Jāhiliyah* age to cut the head of dead soldier and his body to be trampled under the foots of horses, which had been totally banned by Islām.[62] Amīr Mu'āwiyah got cut the head of 'Ammār and the trampling under the foots of horses was done with the body of Prophet's grandson Imām Ḥusain, *Saiyed-ush-Shuhadah* by Mu'āwiyah's son Yażīd's army after the Battle of Karbala.

Khawājah Ovays Qarnī

Famous Ṣūfī saint, Khawājah Ovays Qarnī in whose praise there are so many Traditions of the Prophet,[63] Mu'āwiyah made him also a martyr in the Battle of Ṣiffīn.[64]

'Omarū'l Ḥamaq Khiżarajjī

He was such a great personality, the holy Prophet himself arranged to send his greetings to him, therefore, he was very highly regarded and respected in the Muslim society. He was arrested and nine times whipped forcefully and his body was wounded with many gashes. Being an old man, he could not bear the very first whipping and was dead. His body was chopped with holes and his head was hung at the point of a sword and his body was thrown into the lap of his wife.[65]

'Abdu'r Raḥmān-bin-Ḥasan

He raised his voice against injustice and Mu'āwiyah buried him alive.[66]

Ṣayfī-bin-Faṣīl Shaybānī

He was a very popular companion of the holy Prophet. When Mu'āwiyah, as a routine, used abusive words for Imām 'Alī in his *darbar* openly, Shaybānī could not tolerate. He was beaten to the extent that he could not get up from the floor. Afterwards, he was murdered.[67]

Ḥujr-bin-'Adī Kindī and His Associates

The martyrs, who were murdered for the sake of truth along with Ḥujr-bin-'Adī Kindī were Sharīk-bin-Shaddād, Zayfī-bin-Fuzayl, Qabīsah-bin-Zabī'ah, Muharaz-bin-Shahāb, Karām-bin-Jabān and 'Abdu'r-Raḥmān-bin-Ḥasan. Some other *Ṣaḥābah* were also imprisoned along with Ḥujr-bin-'Adī, but they were later released on an effective influence and initiative of Umayyites favourites. But Ḥujr-bin-'Adī with his five associates were murdered by sword and 'Abdu'r-Raḥmān-bin-Ḥasan was buried alive at the orders of Mu'āwiyah.[68]

These events made the entire Islāmic world grief-sticken. Prophet's wife, *Ummu'l Mūminīn* 'Ā'ishah, was very sad and when Mu'āwiyah went to meet her, he was admonished with serious words by her.[69] When Mu'āwiyah's Khurāsān Governor Rabi'a-bin-Żiyād'l Ḥarithī heard this bad event, he shouted—if at all there is any balance of blessing with me, O' God ! take me from this world.[70]

Besides being an august companion of the Prophet, Ḥujr-bin-'Adī had a very high reputation of candour, chastity and angelic life style, so, everyone who heard about his killing was taken aback and openly condemned this act of Amīr Mu'āwiyah, which has been discussed by various historians, including, even those said to be supporters of the Umayyites.[71]

Ummu'l Mūminīn 'Ā'ishah

Ummu'l Mūminīn 'Ā'ishah also became a victim of conspiracy of Amīr Mu'āwiyah and she was murdered. She was the Prophet's beloved wife and also the daughter of the Caliph I Abū Bakr. In all the wives, she was a *Bakr* (maiden), that is why the Caliph I was called Abū Bakr (Father of the Maiden). Otherwise, his name was 'Abdu'llāh. Thousand of the

Prophet's Tradition have been received thro' her. She was brilliant in her scholastic achievements. But she was not in good terms with Imām 'Alī. According to famous historian aṭ-Ṭabarī, Ibn Jarīr Abū Ja'far (d. 923 AD):

> "It was the nature of 'Ā'ishah that as far as possible, she never discussed about 'Alī in a positive manner."[72]

When 'Alī became Caliph IV, she could not accept it, but fought Battle of Jamal (656 AD) against Imām 'Alī. She herself came to the battlefield, but could not win in the battle. Her nephew Żubayr was murdered by his own friends. Imām 'Alī sent back her to Medina in a respectful and decent manner. Clearly, she was the supporter of opponents of Imām 'Alī, and thus supported Amīr Mu'āwiyah against Imām 'Alī. But when Amīr Mu'āwiyah murdered her brother Muḥammad-bin-Abū Bakr and kept the dead-body inside the hide of donkey and burnt it, she could not tolerate, she prayed to God for malediction of Mu'āwiyah. As, she had never openly opposed Mu'āwiyah, generally, she was considered to be a supporters of him, but later on, she vehemently criticised. Mu'āwiyah also exhibited respect to her only to show the public and also helped her financially from time to time. This easy going relationship was being maintained by both of them. In the same way she recommended for the release of Ḥujr-bin-'Adī Kindī, discussed already in the above lines. When Mu'āwiyah went to meet her, she raised strong objection—Mu'āwiyah, while murdering Ḥujr you were not afraid of God.[73] Mu'āwiyah replied—Please leave me and Ḥujr, it will be seen.[74]

Ummu'l Mūminīn 'Ā'ishah's criticism was unbearable to Mu'āwiyah. When he came to Medina to enquire people and also for justifying his attempt of making Yażīd Caliph, after him. Mu'āwiyah sat on the rosturm of Prophet and began to take *Bay't* (Oath of Allegiance) from the Muslims. 'Ā'ishah could not relish it at all. She took the task severely in bitter terms to Mu'āwiyah and orderd him—Be calm what are you doing? Has any previous Caliph has done like this? Had any Caliph made his son as his sucessor? Mu'āwiyah replied, No! Then who gave you this right? Amīr Mu'āwiyah came down from the rosturm and went away being ashamed. Medina Administrator and Mu'āwiyah's cousin, Marwān-bin-Ḥakam misbehaved with 'Ā'ishah's brother 'Abdu'r-Raḥmān son of the Caliph I Abū Bakr and the Caliph II 'Omar's son 'Abdu'llāh and abused them with bad words, then 'Ā'ishah herself went to Amīr Mu'āwiyah and shouted at him—It is not at all good; you have already murdered one of my brothers (Muḥammad-bin-Abū Bakr) and you have burnt his dead body also. Today coming to Medina you are making my another brother sad and threatening Prophet's son (Imām Ḥusain), 'Abdu'llāh-bin-'Omar and 'Abdu'llāh-bin-Żubayr. You are among those people on whom Prophet sympathized and pitied after Mecca's victory and librated you and your family members. Your behaviour is not correct.

Uncontrolled and irriting arguments by 'Ā'ishah could not get any response. *Ummu'l Mūminīn* 'Ā'ishah wanted to convince Mu'āwiyah on the basis of arguments. Then the same happen which the erratic attitude does in such a situation. Renowned scholar-historian Ibn Khaldūn, Abū Żayd 'Abdu'r-Raḥmān has written that Amīr Mu'āwiyah's confidant Governor of Medina, Marwān-bin-Ḥakam invited in the pretext of a feast in his house and already digging a deep pit, placed knives, spears, swords etc. A blanket was spread above. *Ummu'l Mūminīn* 'Ā'ishah came she was seated there herslf. As soon as she sat, she fell down. She was aged lady and physically weak, such wounds she could not survive afterwards.[75]

Ibn Qutaybah (d. 889 AD), Ibn 'Abd Ribbo, Abū 'Omar, Aḥmad-bin-Muḥammad, Imām Mālik etc. have mentioned that *Ummu'l Mūminīn* 'Ā'ishah, when her last time came, people asked, whether she might be buried near the Prophet. Her reply was that after his death my some acts are such, which were not proper. Please burry me along with his other wive. Therefore, she was buried in al-Bāqī cemetery (Medina).[76]

Depravity in Sources and Contexts

The Holy Qur'an is the fundamental source of the religion of Islām. Its each and every *Ayat* reveals the Divine Wisdom or Philosophy of Islām. The principles, canons, rules and laws laid down in the holy Qur'an are the bedrock of the Islāmic Jurisprudence. It is in their elucidation and elaboration that the secret of Islām lies. In its present written form, it is accepted as the earthly reproduction of an uncreated and eternal heavenly original. As the Qur'an refers:

"And everything have We recorded in a book." (*Qur'an*: 78/29)

It is regarded by its believers as the true words of God, as revealed to the holy Prophet Muḥammad. None can have the power of amending or changing it. This power was not available to even the holy Prophet of

Islām, Muḥammad. Hence no amendment would be acceptable to Muslims.

The other source of reference is *Ḥadīth* (Traditions, the words of the holy Prophet Muḥammad) in which some people from time to time have mixed their own words, as suited to their designs. To collect the authentic *Ḥadīth* (Tradition) there developed a branch of study called *'Ilmu'l-Ḥadīth* (Science of Tradition) in the Islāmic academics. This branch was greatly expanded, each Tradition was explored with regard to its source, who was its *Rāwī* (Narrator), what was his family background? From whom did he learn it? Who had directly heard it from the holy Prophet? In the chain of these narrators, (from the one who had directly heard it from the holy Prophet) what is to be checked is the validity of each narrator, whether or not he is false or fake on any ground. If a single link is proved fake or false, the Tradition is rendered weak.

Amīr Mu'āwiyah's knew it well that his vicious ambition for changing the Islāmic governance into monarchy of the Age of Ignorance could not be achieved unless, he did not acquire the support of *Ṣaḥābah (*singl. *Ṣaḥābī*: Prophet's Companion) who are the *Rāwī* (Narrator) of the Tradition. If none can amend or change the Qur'an, its words and spirit would reintrepreted suitably to his design. It could only be possible, if learned scholars and authors could be hired. With their help and guidance favourable new Tradition might be coined and existing ones might be reinterpreted in a suitable design. The verses of the Qur'an, regarding various events connected or in praise of *Ahl'l-Bayt* (or *'Itrat:* Household or Progeny of the Prophet Muḥammad) were elucidated and interpreted in favour of Umayyites by the solitary and greedy pseudo scholars and writers and also persons among the so called Companions. They were purchased on any amount and condition. As a result a market of sale and purchase of conscience, honour and honesty was established.

Under the strict orders of Amīr Mu'āwiyah, the exchequer was opened for purchase of scholars and writers and the Prophet's Companions. Those not prepared to be sold, were injured or murdered. As a result a pile of fraudulent secret Tradition accumulated. The greatest damage was spoiling and assassination of the very character of the holy Prophet. Traditions were prepared and they are used even at present by the foes of Islām, as authentic source, Muslims remain mere helpless spectators. Amīr Mu'āwiyah gave a special emphasis on the propaganda and publicity of these false sources and contexts in books prepared for the purpose. He insisted to establish their reliability and making the minds of youngsters, including in their text-books and schools curriculum. Piosonous propaganda were made against the Progeny of the Prophet Muḥammad. In every *Namāż* (Prayer) especially Friday Prayer abusing, criticising and cursing Imām 'Alī were made regular part of the ritual. These atrocities continued to exist for ninety years during the entire reign of Umayyites (661-750), leaving just about two years in the middle. 'Allāmah Shiblī Nu'amānī (d. 1914 AD) also has agreed with it:

> "Editing of the Prophet's Tradition was done during the period of Umayyites, who ruled for the whole ninty years from Sindh to Central Asia and up to Unduls, they in Friday Prayer openly cursed and scolded Imām 'Alī and the other members of the family of Prophet. Hundreds and thousands of Traditions in praise of Amīr Mu'āwiyah were fabricated."[77]

The insulting and object statements minted by Amīr Mu'āwiyah are active even at present in some form or the other. It is incredible that those false lines being very familiar in the situations are going on presenting these false Traditions coined during Amīr Mu'āwiyah reign, as a Tradition of the holy Prophet. If we analyse and criticised on the basis of original and Reality of Traditions, there would be no suspicion and doubt in their being fake and fabricated. For example, please see the very popular Tradition of the holy Prophet:

> "All my Companions are full of Justice. All will be in the Paradise. None will go to Hell."[78]

Who are Companions, there is also a Tadition for that:

> "Those Muslims who were with the holy Prophet or saw him, they are all his Companions."[79]

If we look at these Traditions surfacially, they are all in praise of Companions of holy Prophet and as all the Muslims give more regards to the Companions who have secured prestige on the basis of their saintliness, religious faith and sincerity and good conduct. They have been the medium between *Sharī'a* (Islāmic Sacred Law) and Muslims and they, the saintly great people, who make the Islāmic Sacred Law reach up to the common Muslims. Making their prestige like an armour, in very sweet words put forward such rules which are not at all justifiable in anyway and at any cost.

After Divine Unity, Islāmic second foremost pivot is Justice *('Adl)*. Justice with all. Is it justifiable that all the people of a particular era, how much they could have committed bad deeds, are pardonable, and people of other eras receive their fruits on the basis of their acts. To believe that everyone, who has seen the holy Prophet in person would be exempted for his bad deeds, did not tally with the spirit of Islām. The Qur'an says:

> "And this is the path of the Lord, a Straight path, indeed have We made clear the sign for the people take heed." (*Qur'an*: 6/126)

Again says:

> "They should speak not save he whom Beneficent God giveth leave, who spoke (only) the truth." (*Qur'an*: 78/38)

During the life-time of the holy Prophet, there are so many events wherein the people of the period, in spite of being Muslims, went on doing conspiracies against the holy Prophet and Islām, which had been admonished by the Qur'an and the Prophet and they have condemned them. Chapter LXIII of Holy Qur'an has been named as Al-*Munāfiqūn* (The Hypocrites), which reveals that the hidden rancour of hypocrisy is more dangerous and more harmful than any open hostility for in whichever society it may exist, its causes, disruption in it which undoubtedly is dangerous not only to the social health of the people, but also to its very existence. These hypocrites were also the people of the period. Are they all justified? Study may be undertaken for more knowledge in this subject.[80]

See some more stounding Traditions, which have been attributed to holy Prophet:

> "Fire will not touch that Muslim, who saw me or saw those who saw me."[81]

Here not only the Companions of the holy Prophet, but the successive generations all false and fradulent Muslims, received their own for their acts. Not only Amīr Mu'āwiyah, his atrocious son Yażīd and all his fellows, will be saved from Hell, because all among them saw Prophet or saw those who saw Prophet. There was no solace from all these, unless there was a stamp affixed taking the name of Amīr

Mu'āwiyah, to the effect, all his bad deeds are pardonable. Therefore, a Tradition came into existence:

> "Ibn Abī Malīkā says that Mu'āwiyah did something unprecedented in the night prayer and a slave of Ibn 'Abbās was sitting at that time, he came to his master and told him about the event. Ibn-'Abbās said, don't say anything against, Mu'āwiyah has sat near the Prophet."[82]

Monarchy tried to establish forcefully its legs on the Islāmic soil for being ploughed for monarchy. 'Amīr Mu'āwiyah considered his officials more and above the Law. His clear orders were:

> "There is no provision of *Sharī'a* (Sacred Law of Islām, the Divine Jurisprudence) to take any action against my official staff."[83]

This statement is just opposite to the Islāmic code:

> "Whenever the holy Prophet appointed any person to any job, he issued strict intstuctions to him—Escape from the cry of a tyranny, there is no curtain between him and God."[84]

To sustain Amīr Mu'āwiyah's view point, some more Traditions were coined. Only a few may be mentioned here:

> "Every contemporary Caliph is exempted from being questioned for his deed at the Day of Judgement. He would not be prosecuted by the Lord."[85]

This bashful statement was countersigned by forty the then senior most *'Ulmā*[86] (sing. *'Ālim*, learned persons, scholars, erudite—the religious class).

To declare Yażīd-bin-Mu'āwiyah', aboded in paradise, a Tradition was coined that the first attack on Constantinople by sea-side was during the reign of Amīr Mu'āwiyah, that is prior to four decades of the death of the holy Prophet. A blatant lie was propagated that the holy Prophet himself had said in praise of the soldiers of first attack on Constantinople by sea-side:

> "I see the soldiers of *Ummah* (Islāmic Commonwealth), who will travel for *Jihād* (struggle, to strive hard in the path of God) and seated in the ships like, an emperor on his seat and all of them are aboded in paradise."[87]

This false Tradition was coined for the reason that Amīr Mu'āwiyah's son and heir and Karbala's chief criminal Yażīd was brought into the safe custody of the Tradition, on the so-called ground that Yażīd was also, as per his father's orders, in those soldiers of God, who were travelling and seated in the ship just as an emperor and thus he was aboded in Paradise! Now Yażīd may redicule Islām, as he desired, all may do bad deeds as he did, Paradise of course his paternal property definitely will be available! Can such kind of Traditions considered as correct!

The memory of every lier always fails ! Famous historian aṭ-Ṭabarī, Ibn Jarīr Abū Jā'far (d. 923 AD) has exposed the reality of this Tradition that in the first attack of Constantinople by sea-side Yażīd did not participate in 49 AH/670 AD. Yażīd participated in seventh attack (677 AD). Hence, the said Tradition is totally false.[88]

It is noteworthy the cleverness of recognising imperialism in Islām that Prophet was cheerful seeing 'an emperor (Yażīd) on his seat', as per the above fake Tradition, the imperialism becomes the Islāmic style of governance.

Another fake Tradition is also mentioned, it was a matter of pleasure for the holy Prophet, that Amīr Mu'āwiyah established imperialism. The narrater of such a false Tradition, none else than Mu'āwiyah himself. He said:

> "Prophet told me, Oh! Mu'āwiyah, when you become the emperor, behave good."[89]

These types of so many false Taditions coined by his own mint are available regarding Amīr Mu'āwiyah.[90]

To prove the existence of imperialism in Islām, so many such Traditions were coined, so that it could be said that Islām has no objection to monarchism. But the change of mode of governance was a natural phenomena and it was established as per prediction of the Prophet:

> "After my demise, the Caliphate would exist for thirty years then there would be imperialism."[91]

There are so many such fake Traditions, wherein there is a discussion of attacks on different countries, which continued till hundreds of years after the death of Prophet.[92] To this extent that there was an attack on India also as per a verse and statement of Prophet wherein he said:

"Muslims would do *Jihād* in Hindustān."[93]

The reason for such high-handedness with the Prophet is very simple. For the guilty persons and their favourite monorchs' bad deeds may be covered under the benevolence of Islām, the Religion, even if the form of Islām itself is altered as a result.

The confirmation of above mentioned Traditions' falsehood has been objectively analysed by Imām as-Suyūtī, Jalālu'd-Dīn. He has proved beyond doubts that false statements, cannot be cosidered as Traditions of the holy Prophet. Imām as-Suyūtī, collecting these fraudulent statements in his famous book *Lawālīu'l Maṣnū'ah* (Artifitial Jewelleries) has condemned after in tense analysis on the basis of the authentic Traditions. But what to do with this floating from a few channels of writers and scholars making these statements as base even at present vehenently argumenting.

Closure of Judiciary

Prior to Amīr Mu'āwiyah, during *Khilāfatu'r-Rāshidah,* Caliphs never considered their own individuality above the *Sharī'ā*, the Divine Jurisprudence. They behaved as ordinary citizens. Qāzī's appointment was made by them, because of their capacity of being head of the state. But after appointment Qāzīs were totally free to give decision in accordance with the provisions of the Islāmic sacred laws. Imām 'Alī, during his period as Caliph IV, saw a person selling his lost armour in the market. Using the rights of the Caliph, he did not snatched his armour, but presented his case before the Qāzī. Imām 'Alī could not present any witness on his side. Therefore, Qāzī passed his verdict against him.[94] In another event Imām 'Alī appeared before the court of famous Qāzī Sharīḥ to present his case. Qāzī Sharīḥ got up to welcome him. Imām 'Alī said, This is your first injustice ![95]

During the reign of Amīr Mu'āwiyah the official interference in judiciary went to such an extent that the Governors took up for themselves the posts of Qāzīs and their status. During the period of Caliphs, the right to justice was available to anybody other than Caliph.

The Caliphs were answerable to any person. In some cases they asked very embarrassing questions, which were also replied to the satisfaction of the plaintiff. [96]

Amīr Mu'āwiyah for his narrow diplomatic reasons and personal gains, could not allow the judiciary to remain independent. It resulted in the loss of faith in the judiciary. Even the enlightened and chaste persons refused to accept the post of Qāzī. Their integrity had gone to so low level, if any of pure *'Ulmā*, or learned scholars could be persuaded for the post, the people became suspicious against person concerned. The '*Ulmā* who have already occupied the chair of Qāzī, were looked at doubtfully by the people. When judiciary was closed, evil and injustice prevailed like anything, as:

> If you take stock of the situation of contemporary so-called Islāmic society, headed by Amīr Mu'āwiyah, it would be seen clear that such society was extending its horizon, which had nothing-to-do with Islām. Rulers themselves were inmersed in the worst possible crimes. Kufic Administrator Walīd-bin-'Oqbah was such a terrible drunkard that all time he used to be in a deranged state of mind. Once at *Fajr* (dawn's prayer) he read out four *Rikats* (bendings) instead of two. When people objected to it, he said, I may read more ![97]

Marwān and his father Ḥakam both were so terrific criminals that the holy Prophet sent out them from Medina, keeping the same *status quo* Caliph I Abū Bakr and the Caliph II 'Omar did not permit them to enter Medina, but at the time of Amīr Mu'āwiyah's reign Marwān was the prime officer.[98] During the reign of Amīr Mu'āwiyah the concept of society nurtured by him was different from Islāmic society. People freely used to go to prostitutes' house and enjoyed the whole night.[99]

Incredulous Strategy

Amīr Mu'āwiyah after succeeding his ambition for changing the Islāmic governance into monarchy, the strategy to the closure of Divine Governance, it was necessary to uproot the sacred legislations, which form the basis of Divine Governance. Therefore, attempts were made to destroy the cardinal faith, which have complete unanimity in three principles related to God, Prophethood and Resurrection and Last Judgement. The Islāmic religious obligations emerge from its basic principles and belief in

Divine Unity. Amongst all religious obligations *Ṣalāt* or *Namāż* (the Prayer) is the foremost pivot of Islām.

1. Prayer

Namāż (Prayer) is highly ensured duty for every Muslim. Its negligence spread so rapidly that *Ṣaḥābah* were crying and expressed their anguish and grief. It is in the prestigious sacred books of the Traditions like *Jām'au'ṣ-Ṣaḥīḥu'l-Bukhārī* and *Jām'au'ṣ-Ṣaḥīḥu'l-Muslim* that the famous Companion Abū-Dardā used to say that I do not see any portion of Islām in these people, except this that they are steadfast in *Namāż* (Prayer).[100]

Imām Mālik said, their Islām was limited just to offer *Ażān* (Call for Prayer). They were not performing Prayer in its prescribed manner, as the holy Prophet used to perform, but they changed that also.[101]

A very famous event has been told by historians reveals that Amīr Mu'āwiyah while going to Ṣiffīn War against Imām 'Alī performed *Jum'ā Namāż* (Friday's Prayer) on Wednesday![102]

Similarly, in a situation of negligence 'Abdu'llāh son of Caliph 'Omar was seen shouting at the delay of Friday's Prayer, then he was replied—I think the head where your both eyes are fixed should be wounded.[103]

Once Friday's speech prolonged to such an extent that *'Aṣr Namāż* (Afternoon's Prayer) time was also over, then somebody objected to it and said that you shall be answerable to God. He was told, you spoke the truth, but such a true person's place is not there, where you are standing, the place of such person should be Paradise. So, the bodyguard was instructed thro' winking at him. He murdered the person and arranged for his departure to the Heaven.[104]

Such types of other events have also been mentioned by various historians, which are not given here for paucity of space.[105]

2. The Wealth Sacrifice

Żakāt (Poor-Rate) and *Khumus* (Fifth Part of Wealth Sacrifice) are separately numbered, but because of their similar nature and objective we have preferred to discuss them jointly as the obligations of the Faith. Poor-Rate is 2.5 per cent annual tax on the capital or total assets for the poor, and Fifth Part of Wealth Sacrifice is the 1/5 of the annual tax on net profit.

In the holy Qur'an Poor-Rate has been mentioned frequently side by side with mandatory Prayer, so, here as well, the Poor-Rate is being taken up just after the brief introduction of the Prayer. Poor-Rate was obligatory on the foregoing communities and is also mandatory on the Muslim community, Jesus Christ in his praise to God says in the Qur'an:

> "And He hath made me blessed wherever I be and He hath enjoined on me prayer and poor-rate so long as I live!" (*Qur'an*: 19/31)

Further, in the forthcoming verse of the same chapter, the Qur'an enumerates the people whom *Żakāt* should be paid:

> "And giveth his wealth out of love for Him to the kindred and the orphans and the poor and the wayfarer and the needy and for those in the bondage; And established prayer and payeth the poor-rate." (*Qur'an*: 2/177)

It is quite clear from the above mentioned verses that both *Żakāt* and *Khumus* form the right of the poor, parentless, orphans etc. But in Khumuz, a part is special for Prophet and his family-members, which is not available in *Żakāt,* because *Żakāt* is just poor-rate and poor-rate is forbidden for the members of the family of the holy Prophet. Amīr Mu'āwiyah converted and changed the norms of *Żakāt* and *Firṭa,* which could not be approved by learned Muslims. Prophet's famous *Ṣaḥābah* registered their disapproval against the orders of Amīr Mu'āwiyah. Abū Sa'īd Khużrī forcefully said this that he would not accept the changes of rules of Mu'āwiyah through out his life. Ibn-Żubayr also expressed the same feeling and declared it, as a similar action, if a person after adhereing *Īmān* (honesty) again becomes dishonest.[106] But Mu'āwiyah never cared about the objections and continued to deposit the amount of *Khumus* in the State Exchequer, which was actually his personal and private exchequer.[107]

3. State Exchequer

There was no *Baytu'l-Māl* (State Exchequer) during the life period of the holy Prophet. Whatever thing coming from anywhere, used to be distributed among the people as per rules at the same moment. One evening two renowned Companions, Abūżar Ghaffārī and 'Othmān (later Caliph III) went to meet the holy Prophet, saw that he was very much worried, no body conversed with him. Both people returned with heavy heart. Again they went in the morning and observed the Prophet in a cheerful mood. They asked him, why was he upset the last evening that he did not even converse with us. The holy Prophet replied, that the last evening some materials were given to him and he could not immediately distribute them. He was worried, if he was not alive in the night, then he would have been resposible to the people for the reason he could not discharge his duty. That day at the dawn he has distributed every thing; then there was no problem at all.

Imām 'Alī kept alive the very Tradition of distributing wealth. Whenever any material was received in the State Exchequor, he used to distribute it immediately among the people as per rules. Then the place where the material was kept used to be washed off and in the same place thanks giving prayer would he performed.

In Mu'āwiyah's monarchy, the Islāmic State Exchequer became the personal treasury and unlawful and forceful recovery was made from the people. Amīr Mu'āwiyah's men were free for looting and usurping any sum from the people. The Governor of Iraq, Khālid collected one crore gold-coins, as a gift from the people on the occasion of annual Irani festival Navroze and usurped.[108] Another administrator Ḥakam-bin-'Omarū unlawfully recovered enormous wealth by looting the people. He was ordered to deposit the amount in the State Exchequer, but he refused on the ground that all others were doing the same. He becme terror in the region and died in harness.[109] In the same way so many instances are available for usurping public wealth-money for personal gains by men of authority.

During the reign of Amīr Mu'āwiyah the State Exchequer was fully availed for his personal luxury and of his family. His officers were openly leading highly luxurious life and the poor becoming poorer and poorer. It is rather difficult to estimate how much amount of the State Exchequer had became their personal wealth. However, 'Omar-bin-'Abdu'l 'Ażīż (d. 720 AD) of the same family, who was by nature honest, when assumed Caliphate, inspected his princely cash, gold and other asset and also officers unauthorised wealth. He observed that he himself had obtained 40,000 gold coins left unused from his predecessors and issued orders to distribute everything among the poor. Umayyite officers refused to distribute their wealth, rather, killed the Caliph.[110]

4. Anti-Islāmic Economy

In the year 650 AD, when Amīr Mu'āwiyah was the Administrator of

Damascus (Syria), his unlawful personal money, gold and silver have grown enermously. Most reverend Companion Abūżar Ghaffārī, on whom holy Prophet has said, if there are ten stages of honesty, then Abūżar Ghaffārī has obtained nine out of ten. He had warned Mu'āwiyah for his unlawful deposits of gold and cited a verse from the Qur'an:

> "And those who hoard up gold and silver and spent it not in God's way, announce thou unto them a painful chastisement." (*Qur'an*: 9/34)

Similarly, famous Companion Abū Darda objected for wrong weighing the item and told that he has heard from the holy Prophet, it is prohibited in Islām. Amīr Mu'āwiyah replied, that in his opinion, there was nothing wrong in it. Abū Darda said, I am telling you the orders of the holy Prophet and you are telling your opinion. May God remove me from this place. I will not remain on this soil where you are the ruler.[111] In the same manner there was an event between another Companion 'Abādah-bin-Ṣāmit and Amīr Mu'āwiyah. 'Abādah told the Traditions of the holy Prophet regarding the sale and purchase of gold. Mu'āwiyah replied, I do not find anything bad in my practice.[112]

5. Intoxication

Consuming intoxicats or its business is totally prohibited in Islām. But instances against it are easily available during the reign of Amīr Mu'āwiyah. At a time when Mu'āwiyah was monarch of Muslim empire, the aged *Ṣaḥābī* 'Abdu'r-Raḥmān-bin-Sahl Aṇsārī visited Damascus (Syria). He saw so many containers with liquor were carried by camels. 'Abdu'r-Raḥmān Anṣārī went ahead and made holes with his spear on the containers on the camels. The owners slaves wanted to stop him, but could not succeed. The slaves sent the message to Mu'āwiyah. He replied, Leave it, the very brain of this old man has become corrupt. 'Abdu'r-Raḥmān Aṇsārī said, My brain has not gone corrupt. I have just told what the holy Prophet has told all the Muslims. Islām has forbidden intoxication. Liquor should not enter in our body or in our utensils.[113]

6. Inheritance

The Sacred Law of Islām, the Divine Jurisprudence has special provision for inheritance. The Qur'an has determined its various aspects. Amīr Mu'āwiyah ridiculed the Divine Jurisprudence for his personal gains. For instance, he usurped the property of Ḥaṭṭāṭ-bin-Żayd after death on a filthy ground that the decease was his 'Brother-in-Faith'. There were a series of reactions agaist this event among the Muslims to the extent that the famous 'Arabic poet Farażdaq wrote a poem admonishing him.[114] In the same way Amīr Mu'āwiyah dared to change the Sacred Law of Islām regarding provisions for inheritance of non-Muslims. As per the Divine Jurisprudence, no Muslim can become the heir of any non-Muslim and no Non-Muslim can become the heir of any Muslim. Amīr Mu'āwiyah changed the Sacred Law of Islām to the effect that a Muslim may become heir of non-Muslim person, so that when he dies, his wealth-estates etc. can be captured.[115]

7. The Wehrgeld

Diyat (Wehrgeld) is the civil and criminal majesty, the price which any homicide pays to the family of the victim, if they so consent. This Islāmic law aims to end the retaliation and come to a peaceful negociation between to waring parties. It provided safety to all human being irrespective caste, creed and religion. Peace to all is the basic principle of Islām. The wehrgeld is a fine paid for murder, wounding or maiming; blood money; compensation for man-slaughtered. Amīr Mu'āwiyah ordered only half of the wehrgeld be paid to the family of the victim, the balance half he used to be taken away.[116]

8. Illicit Sexuality

Sex is no taboo in Islām, if within the prescribed limits of the Divine Jurisprudence. Provision has also been made for severe punishments on violating prescribed limits. The Qur'an warned:

> "And approach ye not adultery. Verily, it is a shameful act, and evil way (*opening to many other evils*)." (*Qur'an*: 17/32)

Death-punishment can also be awarded, because adultery destroys social life. Amīr Mu'āwiyah had no objection to the adultery and prostitution. Żiyād-bin-Abīh's case also is of this type; whom made a part of his own genealogy with political objectives. Famous Ṣūfī saint Khwājah Ḥasan Baṣarī has included Amīr Mu'āwiyah in those stern and heinous crimes, which have been discussed at the appropriate place in the previous pages. *Ummu'l Mūminīn* Umm Ḥabībah, Mu'āwiyah's sister did not consider Żiyād-bin-Abīh as her brother and she used to put *purdah* (curtain) before him.[117]

9. Murder, Destruction and Terrorism

The word *Islām* is derived from the 'Arabic root word *Silm,* which means peace concored and harmony to all human beings. Its message is:

> "He who slayeth anyone (*man*), without (*that being for*) murder, or for mischief in the land, (*It shall be*) as though he hath slain mankind as a whole; and he who saveth it (*a human life*), shall be as though he hath saved mankind as a whole."
>
> (*Qur'an*: 5/32)

Whereas, *Jāhiliyah*, age of ignorance, encourages to stick on power through murder, destruction and terrorism. Such a life-style has been an ideal for Amīr Mu'āwiyah. If anybody's inner soul is so powerful that he could not hesitate from telling Truth, then he should be ready for murder, arrest or whipping. Those people who were not getting back from Truth, were punished severely, so that, the entire society might be terrorised and dare not enough collect strength against the reign of Amīr Mu'āwiyah. When his Baṣrah Administrator 'Abdu'llāh-bin-'Omarū Ghīlān was being checked on injustice, his hands were cut off ![118]

Historians have mentioned regarding Mu'āwiyah's right hand Administrator Żiyād-bin-Abīh whether anybody had done any mistake or not, if he has decided then the person concerned would be certainly punished. If Żiyād-bin-Abīh has decided no punishment, then whatever big crime he had committed, he would not be punished. There was no limit to his terrorism. Among innocent people anybody could be arrested any time any where and without any inquiry could be punished, both physically and mentally. Murdering any person was very easy for him. He passed orders, if any body was found in midnight any where, then the person would be killed. Once in a night a rural 'Arab was arrested and brough to Żiyād-bin-Abīh. The poor man said in his safety that he did not belong to the place. He had gone there from his village just on that day, he was not aware of the orders, otherwise, would not have gone in the night. Żiyād said, By God, you are telling truth and you are not guilty, but your murder is in public interest. So, he was killed immediately.[119]

Samerah-bin-Junadab, succeeded Żiyād-bin-Abīh as the Administrator. His atrocities surpassed even the Żiyād. Once he arranged for the killing of eight thousand people in six month's period. A contemporary, Abū Sawwar Addī's statement is that Samerah killed forty seven people from his community in a day, who all were devoted Muslims and noble *Ḥuffāẓ* (sl. *Ḥāfiẓ* means, a person having learnt the whole Qur'an by heart). Once Samara with his army went outside the town, a person of Asad clan had gone in the near by street for any need. One of the mounted soldiers made him wounded with his spear as soon as he saw him, he fell on the ground and began to struggle for his safety. Samara passed thro' the street and saw the dead body, and said, people should remember, whenever our convoy passes at that side, they should escape from our spear.[120]

Muslim 'Ijlī told another terrorist event. A devotee Muslim paid *Żakāt* (poor-rate) to Samerah in person and went to the mosque for prayer. As he was praying, a soldier chopped of his head. In the way that his head fell on one side and body wriggled on the other side.[121]

10. Corruption and Bribery

Amīr Mu'āwiyah never cared for good or bad for achieving his target. He adopted corrupt means and paid bribe to purchase people for unlawful jobs. He used to be cheerful on achieving evil targets. The situation has gone so bad that the people suggested him ill to get his favour, its worst example was famous *Ṣaḥābī* Mughīrah-bin-Sho'abah, who suggested Mu'āwiyah for Yażīd's nomination as the caliph of the Islāmic kingdom. Mu'āwiyah had deputed him to prepare public opinion in his favour. Mughīrah sent his son Mūsā with a group of some people to convey their willingness for the proposal. When they came to Mu'āwiyah's assembly, he became over joyed over the achievement and asked Mūsā, at what cost your father purchased those people. He replied that at three thousand Dirahams. Mu'āwiyah said then their Islām, was so cheap ![122]

In the same manner when the influence of Khalid-bin-Valid's son 'Abdu'r- Raḥamān increased in Syria, Amīr Mu'āwiyah became worried that people might not make 'Abdu'r-Raḥmān as Caliph. He bribed the killer Ibn 'Asal and got him poisoned. Mu'āwiyah awarded him a high job for his crime.[123]

It is well established fact that Mu'āwiyah committed the crime of giving poison to Imām Ḥasan. This is the worst deed of Amīr Mu'āwiyah, who had bribed J'ādah-bint-'Ash'ath with a cash of one Lakh Dirahams and a promise to marry her with Yażīd.[124] Other historian also recorded the same fact.[125]

The Hereditary Monarchy

The Hereditary Monarchy nurtured by Amīr Mu'āwiyah advancing from his ruling period, and through the regimes of Umayyites (661-750 AD) and 'Abbāsites (750-1257 AD), till the present has become a part of rulling set-up. It has so many sides, whose appropriate study is not possible within the periphery of this book. There is no need to go in detail of it even here. The curious readers may refer to my other book, *Islāmic State* vs. *Muslim State.*[126] Here, we will limit our discussion unto Amīr Mu'āwiyah and his son Yażīd's ruling period (661-83 AD). There are so many things during this period, which became the reason for making the Islām's foundation and base a loof and devoid of dirt accumulated, which continued to destroy Islām.

A brief introduction has already been done about the Islāmic system of governance in the previous chapter. Islām has presented such a universal system of governance, in which an individual discharging fully his duties and responsibilities and without any pressure leads his life. The Islāmic system of governance's central point is the establishment of Divine ruling-power. The Islāmic state used to establish a type of democratic state accepting Almighty as the Ruler in accordance with His prescribed norms. The holy Prophet presented it through his successful following during his life-time. *Rāshdīn-Khulafā* (Rightly Guided Caliphate) made the same ruling-system as their own base after him. Imām 'Alī, after becoming Caliph IV practised the basic original standards established by the holy Prophet, leading his life as an ordinary man, sitting on a mat. The message was very clear, the luxury, pomp or show would not be allowed any more.

'Amīr Mu'āwiyah, as one of the governors, under the Islāmic Caliphate, had made his assembly, as if he was Qaiysar-Kisarā of Iran or a Roman Emperor. Amīr Mu'āwiyah was captured by his vicious ambition of becoming the Islāmic Prophet or at least his successor. He completely ignored their ways and system and, in its place laid foundation for monarchy on the lines of Roman Emperors, in which in the place of Almighty's sovereingnity and governance, it was in favour of monarch's personal taste.

In the basis of Islām's revolutionary social-system, there cannot be any misunderstanding in accepting monarchy naturally advantageous and good set-up, but if in ground facts situation is analysed, it seems the Islāmic revolution has been gripped with severe counter-revolution. In this open exploitation of monarchy and uncontrolled mono-dictatorship as major set-up has been changed, which sometimes covers Islām over it for its own personal gain and never worries for it also. At present, monarchy and uncontrolled dictatorship ruling-system, which has brought with it cursed terrorism, treachery, murder, destruction etc. is really deplorable. What a strange and tragic situation that Islām whose name and deed are blessings and peace, may be addressed with the name of terrorism. We should analyse that what such events happened in the Islāmic history, as the concept of Divine governance was converted into monarchy and anarchy. It should also be considered, what should be done for stopping counter-movement and towards which value Muslims should return and by which mediums the effects of this counter-movement could be stopped first this disease should be identified that both condition and direction of monarchy made its entry into Islām.

Monarchy, anarchy and faschism are complimentary to each other. In a state of personal pomp and show, misconduct and injustice, high handedness in governance and misuse of resources without any check or answerable situation, a statutory government cannot be established. The Judiciary has to decide as per the whims and fancies of ruling power. The chief officers of government are outside the periphery of Islāmic body. Not only in their personal life, but also the administration and set-up of governance, the essence of Islām must be reflected. Laws and Legislations have always been the reflection of legal formation and commencement its implementation.

Obtaining authority over Islāmic state, Amīr Mu'āwiyah propounded monarchy in the Islāmic stateship. In due course Monarchy became a synonym of the Islāmic state. He used to present an adverse situation of Islāmic state. First of all Imām Ḥusain challenged this same political system and explained his un-Islāmic sides. It would be appropriate to discuss this pseudo Islāmic state, which was the first step of monarchy actually, its concerned problems, the following points of which are worth contemplation:

1. Islām's Divine stateship was propounded into monarchy. The anti-Islāmic defeated elements, which had cleverly surrendered, were lying on earth. Not dead, but closing eyes, pretending sleeping, casually woke up. Monarchy assumed the form of the pseudo-worship of God. Previously, *Kufr* (Infidelity) was widely apparent. It was easy to struggle against ingratitudes. Now, they had covered their face by a curtain, say Islām. Those infidels had been worshippers of so many gods and godesses, there was pomp and show in their belief of God, but beside it, there was regard of truth, justice and promise. They were unlikely to accept Muḥammad, as the Prophet of God, but always regarded him as a highly truthful and

honest person, to the extent that they kept their valuable things in his custody. In fact, they were Traditionalist of the Age of Ignorance, prior to Islām.

If a call was given for fighting against the enemies of Islām, all religious minded persons would be united. Lakhs of people would be ready to sacrifice their lives taking their lives on plams of their hands. No Muslim would support openly any Islāmic enemy. But, if any occasion comes to fight against pseudo Muslims, not only anti-religious, but also religious minded persons would object to it, rather would charge from opposite side. This is the same out of the few, Imām 'Alī, had to struggle, fight against this pseudo Islām. It was the glory of his great personality that even his enemies could not put their finger at his great sincere religious conduct and character.

2. In monarchy, the ruler secures the supreme position. Islām had proclaimed only the Almighty the supreme Ruler, whose orders are implemented through his nominated Aspostle, Prophet or his vicegerent. In monarchy, the emperer obtain the position of God. The audacity and the persistence of calling him directly Allāh, they could not do, but called *Ẓillu'l-Allāh* or *Ẓillu'l-Subḥānī*, which means: the shadow of God.

Amīr Mu'āwiyah had been proudly telling about himself, *Anā-Awwalu'l Mulūk* (I am the first emperor). Others also soluted him telling: *Ya Ahlu'l Mulūk* (Oh, the king).[127] As is the proverb: *As is the king, so are the subjects*. When emperorship prevailed, the Devilish system of governance was demolished. However, a few people were able to remain aloof from this pseuedo Islām. Whoever opposed, the administration took severe suppressive actions against them.

3. Monarchy, for the sake of expantion of its geographical horizons, attacks other countries. Amīr Mu'āwiyah's armies attacked the countries and looted wealth and properties. All these monarchical attacks were in the name of propagating Islām, due to which Islām had a bad name that it was spread forcefully with the sword. The reality is, all the monarchical attacks were with the view of amassing wealth. As per monarchy, the name of power is truth and weakness only is false, the mighty person suppress their weak people. The weak people suppress their weaker people! This order will go on like anything: to this extent, that the most weak people would become slaves. Slaves' wealth-property, respect-prestige, religion and everything would be usurped, by the master. The palaces become colourful parade with the slaves and their mothers, sisters and daughters become automatatically slaves. The ruler wants to expand his power in new areas and the chain of attacks on foreign

countries continue to fulfil his desires. An ordinary Muslim feels Islām is being spread to other countries!

4. Monarchy, closed down all the recognised institutions of Islām for estabishing its own rights firmly. The recognised Islāmic institutions were: Prophet's *Ahlu'l-Bayt* (people of the house) *Ṣaḥābah* (companions) and their supporters, the main among them was Imām 'Alī. Therefore, different types of rumours against him among the common people, were spread, attempts were made to make the common people distant from him. One of the staunch enemies and Amīr Mu'āwiyah's cousin, Marwān-bin-Ḥakam was asked by someone, why he was telling bad words against Imām 'Alī. He replid—Our power cannot continue to remain without it.[128]

5. Monarchy utilised all sorts of means apt and in-apt for fulfilling its own objectives. Islām has given special attention to the sacredness of means for fulfilling the objectives of life. But in Monarchy, there is no place for the sanctity of materials and means. Whatever atrocities, forces, greed, bribe etc. may be helpful for fulfilling its objectives, were utilised without any hesitation. Religion was auctioned for meagre amount of money and people were sold, were going on purchased. The very event of the purchase of honesty for some cash amount is available in history, among which there is an event that four people Ḥaṭṭāṭ Mujā'shī, Jāriya-bin-Quddāmah, Aḥnaf-bin-Qaiys, and Jaun-bin-Qatādah, came to Mu'āwiyah to get their remuneration. Mu'āwiyah offered one Lakh Diraham (gold coins) to every person. But offered only seventy thousand Diraham to Ḥaṭṭāṭ. Ḥaṭṭāṭ counted money, asked the reason. Mu'āwiyah replied, I have purchased their Islām from these people. Ḥaṭṭāṭ said, O.K. Then please purchase my Islām also.[129] The very occupation, of purchasing and selling honesty had been so advanced, that it became a general evil and weakness. It would be good not to make further discussion on it.

6. It is not possible here to proceed further with all provisions of monarchy. Amīr Mu'āwiyah was the supporter of personal ruling on the basis of which the pseudo power-system was prevalent prior to Islām. He established monarchy-system of rule and then converted it into hereditary monarchy.

Appropriate discussion of Ḥasan-Mu'āwiyah Treaty would be in the ensuing chapter, but it is necessary to tell here that in this treaty Amīr Mu'āwiyah was bound by a clause to the effect that he would not have any right to nominate any Caliph after him. After his death, the Caliph's post would be returned to Imām Ḥasan, and if he also dies, then Imām Ḥusain would be the Caliph. But Amīr Mu'āwiyah did not abide the treaty converted the Divine Statehood propounded by the Islāmic Sacred Laws into his personal kingdom, along with violating the other clauses of Ḥasan-Mu'āwiyah Treaty. Converted his own personal kingdom into hereditary monarchy. How all these happened and through which conspiracy, it would be appropriate to know precisely in that regard.

Amīr Mu'āwiyah used to say in supporting his side: "We, of course, were immersed in the world and remained in it rolling down."[130] In continuation of amassing the pleasures of worldly life, he began to make planning of making his notorious and disgraceful son Yażīd, as the Caliph after himself. Caliph, was regarded as the heir of the holy Prophet, being supremo of both religion and state. The ideally high conduct and behaviour of Islām used to be established with his conduct and behaviour. But Yażīd-bin-Mu'āwiyah was a man of the meanest habits in his conduct and behaviour. It is not possible to imagine a person inferior to himself. It would be introduced in the ensuing lines.

The proposal of appointing Yażīd as heir was from his Kūfah's Administrator Mughīrah-bin-Sho'abah. Mu'āwiyah was angry at him on some matter. He wanted to remove him from the post. Mughīrah got news, rushed to Damascus and met Yażīd and said, most of the Companions of the Prophet have already died, none of Quraysh clan better than he would be available. I do not understand why he (Yażīd) not being declared as the next Caliph. Yażīd told the matter to his father. This was already in his mind. Mu'āwiyah called Mughīrah immediately and discussed about it. Mughīrah put up the same proposal before him. Mu'āwiyah was aware that Muslims would not accept Yażīd as their Caliph. Mughīrah argued, I would manage Kufa people and Żiyād-bin-Abīh would manage Baṣra people. Mu'āwiyah wrote to Baṣrah's Administrator Żiyād about the proposal of Mughīrah regarding this matter. Żiyād went to Damascus and convinced Mu'āwiyah that it was not an appropriate time for it.

After the death (672 AD) of Żiyād, Amīr Mu'āwiyah made faster his attempt of making Yażīd as his successor and sent one lakh Diraham to late Caliph II 'Omar's son, 'Abdu'llāh, for Yażīd's *Bay'at* (Oath of Allegiance) and tried to pursuade him. 'Abdu'llāh refused to accept the money and said, if this wealth has been sent, with this objective then, my Islām would be very cheap for me. But Mu'āwiyah did not stop, he wrote to Medina's Administrator Marwān-bin-Ḥakam for making public opinion in favour of Yażīd as his heir. People could not be ready. Afterwards, showering money on people, Mu'āwiyah started convincing people. Mu'āwiyah himself travelled Syria, Iraq and a few other regions for taking support for Yażīd and was going on distributing gold-bags.

Obtaining consent of Medina people was the most difficult problem. Amīr Mu'āwiyah's plunder developed to this extent that he came to Medina to obtain *Bay'at* for making Yażīd as Caliph. He met Imām Ḥusain at outscurt of the town itself. He descended on the daucity of Imām Ḥusain. Famous historian Ibn Athīr, 'Iżżu'd-Din, Abu'l Ḥasan 'Ali-bin-Muḥammad (d. 1233 AD) has described his talk as follows:

> "When Mu'āwiyah came near Medina first of all, met Imām Ḥusain. Seeing him Mu'āwiyah said, Neither happiness nor greetings for you. Your are a goat for sacrifice, whose blood is emotional. God's promise, this blood would certainly be made fallen. Imām Ḥusain replied please be calm, I should not be addressed like this. Mu'āwiyah said, Your are worth the worst words than these."[131]

Mu'āwiyah returned the empty handed in his objective and could not obtain support from the citizens of Medina. But after the death of Amīr Mu'āwiyah's (May 680 AD) on the basis of his attitude the events are the subject-matter of this book, and that would be enlightened in the ensuing chapter. But telling this much is necessary that the way by which Amīr Mu'āwiyah made Yażīd as Caliph, breaking the Ḥasan-Mu'āwiyah-Treaty, Mu'āwiyah and his son Yażīd both are guilty for their misdeeds. However, Amīr Mu'āwiyah is also answerable and responsible for making his son Yażīd as Caliph.

Yażīd-bin-Mu'āwiyah

Yażīd-bin-Mu'āwiyah's period of reign is limited to about three years (680-83 AD), but on account of his own anti-Islāmic activities his period is considered as extremely dark, the worst and most notorious. During this period Islāmic disintegration was highly visible. During the twenty years of Mu'āwiyah's reign (640-60 AD) slowly and steadily the Islāmic Divine principles and its image being tarnished the venoumous set-up prior to Islām, *Jāhiliyah* (the age of ignorance) was being established. The gradual study from the Yażīd's reign prior to him cannot make us reach any conclusion. It can be inferred only from the scenario of the reign of Amīr Mu'āwiyah. A precise introduction has already been given in the previous pages of the disturbed situation. Only this much of remnant was left in the destruction of the source soul of Islāmic principles that people had no connection at all with Islām in their practical works, the same *status quo* continued. It would be appropriate that a discussion may be had regarding his family background, nature and behaviour, which normally is not discussed.

Yażīd was the eldest son of Mu'āwiyah. Al-Damīrī, Shaykh Kamālu'd-Dīn, Muḥammad-bin-Īsā (d. 1405 AD) has given details of the parentage of Yażīd.[132] His mother's name was Mysūn, who was a roving nomadic girl. Mu'āwiyah got her lifted from her tribal clan and made sexual relation with her. She was unhappy with him. One day she was singing alone. The verses of the poem were such as—I love a person of my clan, who was lean and dirty, but better than this misbehaved rogue. Mu'āwiyah himself heared her song. He bcame very angry and sent her back to the people of her clan 'lean and dirty'. After two years, (in 642 AD) she gave birth of a male child. Mu'āwiyah was not having any issue till then, claimed the child his son and grabed the child from his mother. Yażīd's mother Mysūn struggled to get back her child, but in vein.

Birth of the child after separation of two years put questions, but no source would be available. Who could identify and separate so many pinches of mixed flour wheat of the bag of a begger, which belonged to whom ! Had been today, a DNA test could decide the fatherhood of Yażīd, now only God knows whether Yażīd was the son of Mu'āwiyah or of that 'lean and bad' man.

Not only Yażīd but the fatherhood of Mu'āwiyah also was disputed, because his mother Hindah, Abū Sufyyān's wife was also having physical contact with other people also, which has been discussed in the previous pages.

Conduct and Behaviour

Yażīd was brought up in the king's palace of Damascus. All the materials and means for luxurious life were available. He was immersed in it. *Qīnạts* (call-girls) singing-dancing, sexual contact with concubines and free-sex and allied bad activities, which are prohibited in Islām, were part and parcel of Yażīd's life. He was characterless right from his boyhood. There was no restriction at all. By the period of youth, he was fully engrossed in all sorts of sexual and luxurious life without any restriction. All prohibited bad activities which are ban in every civil society, were part and parcel of his life. All the twenty four hours he was drinking liquor. He was bringing up a monkey, which he called 'Abū Qaiys'. He made it to sit on the throne. In horse-race he used to present monkey.[133] He used to enjoy and promote sex, liquor, lustful activities and discuss so many mean activities. It was not only the atmosphere of king's palace, but also of the whole city of Damascus. To achieve the climax of lustful pleasures, he had crossed all the limits of shame. Famous historian Ibn S'ad, Abū 'Abdu'llāh Muḥammad (d. 844 AD) and Allāmah Jalālu'd-Dīn Suyūṭī (d. 1505 AD) have quoted the statement of 'Abdu'llāh-bin-Ḥanzalah as under:

> "By God, there would be a showering of stones, but for our opposition. He was such a person, who not only enjoyed the maid slaves, already enjoyed by his father, but also his own daughters and sisters."[134]

The same types of events have also been recorded by Ibn Ḥajar, al-Haythamī, al-Makkī, (d. 1566 AD):

> "Yażīd was not at all worried about the prescribed limits of Islām and used to enjoy his own step-mothers."[135]

When Amīr Mu'āwiyah sent him with the objective of improving his image among the people by exhibiting noble life-style, Yażīd could never give up his very dirty life in Medina, taking liquor night and day, against the very sentiments of Muslim.[136] Ibn Khaldūn, Abū Żayd 'Abdu'r-Raḥmān (d. 1406 AD) has written about Yażīd with the statement of Żiyād-bin-Abīh, the most confidant person of Amīr Mu'āwiyah:

> "In Yażīd, there are characterlessness, lack of manners, ungratefulness and a number of other disqualifications."[137]

Every Muslim considers Yażīd as wretched and all Muslim '*Ulmā* and Ṣūfī saints are unananimously among themselve to consider fifth kick for him. Most of them also pronounce *La'nct* (Curse) on Yażīd, but Maulānā Abu'l 'Olā Maudūdī (d. 1979 AD) has his reservation of pronouncing *La'nat* on him, because it may open door of pronouncing *La'nat* on other *Ṣaḥābah.*[138] What a mocking argument that accepting that Yażīd and his father's activities were such, on the basis of which, the *prima facia* is proved against Yażīd and his father to curse them, but he did not want to punish his father. So, his son also may be left. As if, no principle, only as per convenience.

But other '*Ulmā* and Ṣūfī saints had never endorse the above view point. Imām Aḥmad-bin-Ḥanbal (d. 855 AD) was asked by his son 'Abdu'llāh, What would be the order to curse Yażīd? Imām Ḥanbal replied, Why don't we curse such a person who has been cursed by Allāh and to certify his views, he cited a verse of the Qur'an: [139]

> "Every time they will intend to go forth from it, from the very anguish, back shall they be turned into it: and (*it will be said unto them*) '(Taste ye the torment of the burning (*fire*)." (*Qur'an*: 22/22)

Famous scholar Ibn Kat<u>h</u>īr, Abu'l Fidā has cited a *Ḥadī<u>th</u>* of the holy Prophet:

> "Rasūla'llāh said whoever perpetuates injustice and frightens the residents of Medina, the curse of God, His Angels and all people is on such a person."[140]

Someone ridiculed famous Ṣūfī-saint <u>Kh</u>wājah Ḥasan Baṣrī (d. 728 AD), Why don't you fight against Damascus rulers, then <u>Kh</u>wājah being provoked said, God may curse and destroy them![141]

Once someone wanted to know from famous Ṣufī-saint <u>Kh</u>wājah Muḥammad A<u>sh</u>raf Jahangīr Ṣamnānī (d. 1405 AD) the justification of pronouncing *La'nat* on Yażīd. <u>Kh</u>wājah Ṣamnānī replied, Yes, I pronounce *La'nat* on Yażīd, and quoted the verse of the Qur'an:[142]

> "Verily those who annoy God and His Apostle (*Muḥammad*), God, hath cursed them in this world and the hereafter, and He hath prepared for them a chastisement disgraceful." (*Qur'an*: 33/57)

Besides, 'Allāmah Ibna'l Jawżī, 'Abdu'r-Raḥmān-bin-'Alī Muntaẓam (d. 1200 AD), Qāzī Abū Mu'ālī, 'Allāmah Jalālu'd-Dīn Suyūṭī (d. 1505 AD) etc consider it correct comments. Somebody mentioned Yażīd as *Amīr-ul-Mūminīn* (leader of the faithful, the term used for the Caliphs) in the court of Umayyite Caliph 'Omar-bin-'Abdu'l 'Ażīż (717-20 AD). He became very angry and ordered punishment of twenty whipping for his.[143]

Enmity towards Prophet and His Progeny

Love and devotion towards the Prophet and his progeny is the essence of Islām. Numerous *Ḥadī<u>th</u>* are available in this regard. Some of them have been mentioned in present book at the proper places. Its importance could be contemplated from the fact that five time daily *Namāż* is compulsory for every Muslim and *Namāż* always conclude with the *Salām* (salutation) to the Prophet and his progeny:

> "O Lord! bestow mercy on our Divine-leader and Commander Muḥammad and his pious progeny as Thou hast bestowed mercy on Abraham and his pious progeny, Verily, Thou art the Most Praiseworthy, the Most exalted, and O' Lord shower Your blessing on Muḥammad and his holy progeny as Thou hast showered blessing on Abraham and his holy progeny, Verily, Thou art the Most Praiseworthy and the Most Exalted."

It has been inconceivable *Munāfiqat* (hypocracy) of Abū Sufyyān, Mu'āwiyah and Yażīd and their followers that they practically behaving criminally like enemies and five times daily *Namāż* conclude with the salutation to the Prophet, declaring:

> "O Lord! bestow mercy on our Divine-leader and Commander Muḥammad and his pious progeny."

These were hypocrites, who actually did not believe in Islām, mingled with Muslim's, outwardly Muslim, inwardly dangerous enemies of Islām. While remaining with Islām, they started playing foul with it, showering abuses on Imām 'Alī as soon as they got up from bed. They never considered any importance for the Divine-leader and Commander Muḥammad and his pious progeny. Yażīd used to speak openly against God, Prophet and Day of Last Judgement. Yażīd had no faith in Islām. In an intoxicating mood he had said in his various poems. To mention here a few:

> "Oh, beauty, my love, narrate to me and tell me in a louder voice, tell singing, I do not relish stealthy talk and act. Tell me that old tale of Abū Sufyyān, his achievements in Uḥad, where he destroyed enemy's (Muslims) houses.
>
> Yes, along with this tale, give me the brother, liquor that liquor which has been prepared with their special grapes of Damascus.
>
> When we give attention towards ancient system, it appears, drinking has always been in accordance with religion and saint.
>
> I die, oh my darling, my love, you marry any other person and don't hope to meet after this separation.
>
> Whatever stories would have been heard in this regard of other life, all of them are old tales, which keeps a person in illusion. It is decided that I would meet Muḥammad.
>
> Immersing in such an intoxication of liquor, whose influence would have gone into my bones.

He says in another place:

> Whatever Aḥmad has done, if I do not take revenge from the child of Aḥmad, I would not have been the hairy Juna, the bad.
>
> Once addressing a crowd, he said, You speak or not I have finished repaying my loan.

He says Islām as impracticable:

> "If drinking liquor is a sin in Aḥmad's view, then drink joining the people of Christ."[144]

Only a few examples are given. The other illustrations are given at the appropriate places. On the basis of these examples the aim is to make clear that regarding a person expressing this type of views what Islāmic Divine codes say. Qāzī: Thināu'llāh 'Othmanī Pānīpatī (d. 1810 AD) clearly said quoting the Qur'an ragarding such a person that Yažīd has gone beyond the periphery of Islām and he was *Kāfir* (infidel, apostate).[145] 'Allāmah Maḥmūd-bin-'Abdu'llāh Ālūsī (d. 1853 AD) also quoting the Qur'an proclaimed that Yažīd is a *Kāfir.* Mullā Mubīn Firangīmahalī (d.1810 AD) also declared on the basis of satirical talks of Yažīd that Yažīd is a foe and traitor of Islām.[146]

Four Unpardonable Crimes and Sins

The Islāmic history cannot present any other example than that of Yažīd-bin-Mu'āwiyah, as an unpardonable sinner. There are indelible sins and crimes of Yažīd according to religion, morality and society. These cannot be counted. The very existence of Yažīd is synonymous to sins and crimes. He is an embodiment of sins and crimes. Such a person, all the has no quality of human being even in world history, no other such person can be found out.

Yažīd occupied the throne after the death of his father Mu'āwiyah-bin-Abū Sufyyān (30 March, 680 AD). During his little period of the reign, he committed innumerable crimes. It is not possible to count them at all. Just four formidable crimes among them are being discussed in the ensuing lines.

The First Crime

The first and most condemmed crime of Yažīd-bin-Mu'āwiyah has been to murder the entire family of the holy Prophet in Karbala. As a result of the Battle of Karbala, developed the Ḥusainī Revolution, which is the subject-matter of the present book; A detailed discussion has been made on its different aspects. A unique feature of the martyrdom of Imām Ḥusain has been pointed out by Shāh 'Abdu'l Ażīż Muḥaddith Dehlawī (d. 1824 AD) that God has awarded all sorts of the highest prestige to his beloved Prophet Muḥammad, which have ever been awarded to any of the Prophets and Apostles. But the prestige of martyrdom was awarded through His beloved Prophet Muḥammad's beloved grandsons, Ḥasan and Ḥusain. As the martyrdom is possible in two ways in the struggling in the path of God, Firstly being secretly poisoned, which Imām Ḥasan obtained while struggling on the path of God. Secondly, the martyrdom could be obtained openly by struggling with his sword and being killed. This meritorious martyrdom has been obtained by Imām Ḥusain, who was assassinated along with his companions and family members, while struggling on the path of God. In this way assassination of Imām Ḥasan and Imām Ḥusain amounts to killing of God's beloved Prophet Muḥammad.[147]

The Second Crime

The second crime of Yażīd was the attack on Medina. Medina had been loved by the holy Prophet. So, many *Ḥadīths* of the holy Prophet are available in praise of Medina. Prophet has said in a *Ḥadīth*:

> "Whoever does any evil with Medina God will throw him in hell and use like a glass melting in a fire."[148]

But Yażīd didn't care anything. He made all sorts of evils against Medina and destroyed the entire town. He not only ordered the army to attack the Medina, but the army was given full liberty to do any sort of atrocities, in whatever manner it wanted. A very high terrific situation arose. The army after destroying the town, looting the wealth, did coercive sexual intercourse by force with ladies and young girls of the houses. It resulted into thousands of illegal children. In the Islāmic history this event has been said as *Ḥarrah.* An eminent scholar *Shaykhu'l Ḥadīth* Muḥammad Żakaiyā has given the account of the event:

> "The army that Yażīd had sent to Medina comprised 15,000 infantry. For three days they shed blood freely, 1,000 women were raped and 700 named Quraysh and Anṣār were killed.

10,000 chldren were made slaves. Muslim-bin-'Uqbah forced people to give allegiance to Yażīd in such a manner that people were enslaved and Yażīd could sell them as he pleased. No *Ṣaḥābah*, who were (with the Prophet) at *Ḥudaybiyah* were spared."[149]

The Third Crime

The third crime of Yażīd was the attack on Mecca after Medina. The holy Ka'bah is situated in Mecca only, both cities are now in Saudi Arabia. The importance of Mecca could be understood by the fact that five times daily *Namāż,* compulsory for every Muslim, could only be performed, if his face is towards the holy Ka'bah. Without the circumabulating of the holy Ka'bah, a Muslim cannot complete his *Ḥajj* pilgrimage. In Islām Ka'bah is Divinely protected piece of land, even a leaf cannot be plucked in its area. At the orders of Yażīd, an attack was made on Ka'bah. Stones were hurled upon Ka'bah through the catapults. As a result the very wall of Ka'bah was shattered. Fire-balls were also thrown, which burnt the curtains and screens of Ka'bah.[150]

The Fourth Crime

The pen of this humble author feels shame in writing the fourth crime of Yażīd, because it is concerned with one of the reverend wife of the holy Prophet. The Qur'an has ordained that every wife of the Prophet is the mother of all Muslims. Accordingly, every wife of the Prophet is addressed with title *Ummu'l Mūminīn* (mother of believing Muslims). In the eyes of Yażīd, what was the position of his own mothers, sisters etc., has already been discussed in the previous pages. His temerity advanced to this extent that he flung insult at Islām and all Muslims. As mentioned by Shaykh Abdu'l Ḥaq Muḥaddith Dehlawī (d. 1642 AD) he had proposed marriage with *Ummu'l Mūminīn* 'Ā'ishah.[151]

This shameful event had been of that time, when Yażīd was the prince of Damascus and was shattering, the fame of Islām in maintaining the power of his father Amīr Mu'āwiyah.[152]

Mu'āwiyah-bin-Yażīd

Mu'āwiyah-bin-Yażīd (Mu'āwiyah II) has been fully five fingers' slap on the face of Amīr Mu'āwiyah, and the hereditary imperialism. This five fingers' slap on the face of Amīr Mu'āwiyah emerged as a symbol against injustice! It is the fact, if any injustice is entrusted to the Almighty. He would certainly take revenge of it. To quote from the words of God:

> "We vengeance upon those who were guilty; and was incumbent on Us the succor of the believers." (*Qur'an*: 30/ 47)

It is the wonderful form of his revenge that he starts it, from the very house of that atrocious person. He digraces him before all those, who may be witness of the event. He makes the person to fall down every now and then, at the feet of the person, who was dishonoured. God had these few through Mu'āwiyah II.

Mu'āwiyah II was born on 28th March, 661 AD, and was regarded as the eldest son of Yażīd, with other five brothers and many sisters. In the same year his grandfather Amīr Mu'āwiyah had an opportunity to become a Caliph. He said so delightfully that now it is decided that the hereditary Empire would be in my family. I myself, afterward my son and there after my grandson! But God had arranged something else. The Mu'āwiyah II was just 13 years, when Mu'āwiyah passed away.

At the time of expiry of Yażīd (November 683 AD) the age of Mu'āwiyah II was 22 years and in his behaviour, he was like an experienced scholar. Power was entrusted to him, as being the Caliph designate. He clarified the reality of his hereditary monarchy. Renowned historian Ibn Ḥajar, al-Haythamī, al-Makkī (1566 AD) has mentioned that after Yażīd's death, when Mu'āwiyah II (Yażīd's son) was made to be Caliph, he stated the following in his inaugural address with regard to his father and grandfather (Mu'āwiyah I) as under:

> "Caliphate is from God. My grandfather faught for the Caliphate against a person, who was more entitled to it, that was (Imām) 'Alī. He (Mu'āwiyah I) did activities that you all are aware of, and he is suffering in his grave for that. Then my father Yażīd became the Caliph, even though he was not deserving of the Caliphate. He fought the grandson of the Prophet (Ḥusain) and is suffering in the grave on account of his sins."

Mu'āwiyah-bin-Yażīd then proceeded to cry:

> "It is a terrible thing that we are fully aware of Yażīd's bad deeds; he slaughtered the family of the Prophet, he deemed

> alcohol legitimate by Divine Laws, and set fire to the Ka'bah."[153]

Well, how could Umayyites bear with such constructive and peaceful words. Since Mu'āwiyah II has no children, therefore, remainder went to the other branch of *Umayyite clan*: In this way Amīr Mu'āwiyah's hereditary monarchy, become a symbol of his defeat, which was going on provoking Umayyites.

Entangling within the clutches of Imperialism in the Islāmic system of governance, is actually a tale of injustice, cruelty, exploitation and barbarism, instead of justice, truth, compassion, tenderness and affability, which are standards of Islām. It would be noteworthy to referesh that the Islāmic Prophet had offered general pardon to his foes after Mecca victory of January 630 AD. They were offered a chance of leading a life of self-prestige, self-respect, peace and happiness. It was optimistic to hope that there would be no atmosphere of misunderstanding and hatred and jealousy; but on the contrary these foes of Islām exceeded all the limits of atrocities on the family of the holy Prophet. Admonishing the same Abu'l 'Olā Maudūdī (d. 1979 AD) has observed:

> "Islām, of course, is at a very high pedestal, if at all there was a bit gleam of humanity, then he (Amīr Mu'āwiyah-bin-Abū Sufyyān) would have thought of that after Mecca victory what obligation the Prophet of Islām has offered towards their (Umayyite) family-prestige and how their goverment behaved with the grandson of the Prophet."[154]

Notes and References

1. Khilāfat-o-Mulūkiyat, p. 100.
2. Nahju'l-Balāghah.
3. Iżālatu'l-Khulafā, vol. 1, p. 396.
4. Tārīkhu'r-Rusūl wa'l-Mulūk vol. 2, p. 449; Kanżu'l-'Ummāl-fī-Sunnau'l-Aqwāl-w'al-Alfāẓ vol. 5, tr. 2374; al-Isti'āb fi Mā'rifatu'l-Aṣḥāb, vol. 2, p. 689.
5. Kitābu'l-'Ibar, vol. 4, p. 257.
6. Khilāfat-o-Mulūkiyat, p. 91.
7. al-Kāmil fī't-Tārīkh, Vol. 3, p. 46; al-Isti'āb fi Mā'rifatu'l-Aṣḥāb, vol. 4, pp. 76-77.
8. Tārīkhu'r-Rusūl wa'l-Mulūk, vol. 11, p. 357.
9. Nafas-i-Rasūl, vol. 4 (3), pp. 287-88.

10. *The Tradition of the holy Prophet referred by Khwājah Ḥasan Baṣarī stands as under:*
"Abū Ḥuraira says that the holy Prophet has said that the baby belongs to the woman who gave birth and stone for others."
(Jām'au'ṣ-Ṣaḥīḥu'l –Bukhārī, vol. 3, p. 363, tr. 1718)
Because of his disputed parenty, the historians have mentioned his name in three fashions—Żiyād-bin-Abīh (Żiyād son of his father) as his unknown parenty, Żiyād-bin-'Obayd (Żiyād son of 'Obayd), as her mother Sumayyah was the wife of 'Obayd. To avoid any controversy the historians called him Żiyād-bin-Sumayyah. Beside being strong warrior and administer, Żiyād had an shameful genealogy and wanted an honourable solution. 'Amīr Mu'āwiyah hatched a story, "Sometime, Abū Sufyyān visited Abū Maryam and after eating and driking asked him to bring a harlot. Abū Maryam brought Sumayyah and introduced him to join Abū Sufyyān. She agreed to do so." Accodingly, Mu'āwiyah declared and accepted Żiyād, as a son of his father Abū Sufyyān and also called him as Żiyād-bin-Abū Sufyyān. Żiyād has been very notorious figure in the Islāmic history and was a symbol of terror and murders. He was made Governor of Kūfā by 'Amīr Mu'āwiyah. Later on his son 'Obaydu'llāh was made Governor of Kūfā by 'Amīr Mu'āwiyah's son Yażīd, who administerd the Battle of Karbala under his orders. For more details may be seen— K.A. Fāriq's Żiyād-bin-Abīh – Author.
11. Tārīkhu'r-Rusūl wa'l-Mulūk, vol. 4, p. 166.
12. Qaul-i-Sadīd, p. 26.
13. Jām'au'ṣ-Ṣaḥīḥ al-Muslim, vol. 2, p. 250 (Tradition no. 2431).
14. Usadu'l Ghābah fī Muā'rifu'l Ṣaḥābah, vol. 6, p. 189; al-Mua'rramīn, p. 78.
15. Kitābu'l-Aghānī, vol. 14, p. 4; ath-Thaqāfatu 'l-Islāmia, vol. 1, p. 83.
16. Dirāsatu'l Labīb, p. 139.
17. Tārīkhu'r-Rusūl wa'l-Mulūk, vol. 5, p. 66.
18. Wafiyyātu'l-'Ayān wa anbā'aż-Żamān, vol. 2, p. 115.
19. al-'Iqdu'l Farīd, vol. 3, pp. 416-17.
20. Wafiyyātu'l-'Ayān wa anbā'aż-Żamān, vol. 2, p. 115.
21. al-'Iqdu'l Farīd, vol. 3, p. 413.
22. 'Ayānu'l Akhbār, vol. 2, p. 61.
23. Khilāfat-o-Mulūkiyat, p. 159.
24. Kitābu'l-'Ibar, vol. 3, pp. 93-96.
25. Khilāfat-o-Mulūkiyat, p. 165.
26. aṭ-Ṭabaqātu'l-Kabīr, vol. 6, p. 25; al-Isti'āb fi Mā'rifatu'l-Aṣḥāb, vol. 2, p. 440; al-Bidāyah w'an-Nihāyah, vol. 8, p. 48; aṭ-Tahżību'l Tahżīb, vol. 8, p. 24.
27. al-Kāmil fī't-Tārīkh, vol. 4, p. 6; Tārīkh-i-A'imah, p. 85; Islām-Nāmah, p. 266
28. aṭ-Ṭabaqātu'l-Kabīr, vol. 7, p. 406; al-Isti'āb fi Mā'rifatu'l-Aṣḥāb, vol. 1, p. 253.

29. Khilāfat-o-Mulūkiyat, p. 106.
30. Kanżu'l-'Ummāl-fī-Sunnau'l-Aqwāl-w'al-Alfāẓ, vol. 3, p. 158, tr. no. 2447.
31. al-Isti'āb fi Mā'rifatu'l-Aṣḥāb, vol. 2, p. 467.
32. Khilāfat-o-Mulūkiyat, p. 99.
33. Khilāfat-o-Mulūkiyat, pp. 96-107.
34. Tārīkhu'r-Rusūl wa'l-Mulūk, vol. 3. (iii) p. 37.
35. Tārīkhu'r-Rusūl wa'l-Mulūk, vol. 3. (ii) p. 239.
36. Tārīkhu'r-Rusūl wa'l-Mulūk, vol. 1, p. 151; Usadu'l Ghābah fī Muā'rifu'l Ṣaḥābah, vol. 6, p. 184.
37. Tārīkh-i-Aḥmadī, p. 234.
38. Jām'au'ṣ-Ṣaḥīḥul-Bukhārī, vol. 3, p. 425, Tr. No. 1949.
39. Muwaddatu'l-Qurbā pt. 3, p. 39.
40. Muwaddatu'l-Qurbā pt.3, p. 44.
41. Jām'au'ṣ-Ṣaḥīḥul-Bukhārī vol. 2, p. 402, Tr. no. 1532; al-Murtaza, p. 85.
42. Tahżību'l-Tahżīb vol. 7, p. 41
43. al-Isti'āb fi Mā'rifatu'l-Aṣḥāb, vol. 2, p. 424,
44. al-Bidāyah w'an-Nihāyah, vol.7, p. 241,
45. Khilāfat-o-Mulūkiyat, pp. 128-30.
46. Tārīkhu'r-Rusūl wa'l-Mulūk, vol. 4, pp. 3-4.
47. al-Kāmil fī't-Tārīkh, vol. 3, p. 148.
48. al-Bidāyah w'an-Nihāyah, vol. 7, pp. 257-58.
49. Khilāfat-o-Mulūkiyat, p. 116.
50. aṭ-Ṭabaqātu'l-Kabīr, vol. 3, pp. 224-25.
51. Khilāfat-o-Mulūkiyat, p. 123.
52. Khilāfat-o-Mulūkiyat, p. 125.
53. al-Murtazā, p. 313.
54. A Short History of the Saracens, p. 67.
55. Urdu Dāerah-i-Mu'ārif-i-Islām, vol. 15, p. 555.
56. al-Bidāyah w'an-Nihāyah, vol. 8, p. 135.
57. Jām'au'ṣ-Ṣaḥīḥu't-Tirmiżī, vol. 1 49, tr. 132/1.
58. al-Isti'āb fi Mā'rifatu'l-Aṣḥāb, vol. 1, p. 235; Tārīkhu'r-Rusūl wa'l-Mulūk, vol. 4, p. 79; al-Kāmil fī't-Tārīkh vol. 3, p. 180.
59. Murūju'ž – Žahab-wa'l-M'adinu'l-Jauhar, vol. 3, p. 420; al-Kāmil fī't-Tārīkh vol. 3, p. 179; aṭ-Ṭabaqātu'l-Kabīr, vol. 6, p. 213.
60. Kitābu'l-'Ibar, vol. 4, p. 317.
61. Khilāfat-o-Mulūkiyat, p. 165.
62. al-Musnad: Aḥmad, tr. nos. 6538-6929 .
63. Jām'au'ṣ-Ṣaḥīḥu'l –Muslim, vol. 2, p. 262 tr. nos. 2527-29.
64. Tārīkhu'r-Rusūl wa'l-Mulūk, vol. 6, p. 148.
65. Khilāfat-o-Mulūkiyat, p. 165.
66. al-Kāmil fī't-Tārīkh, vol. 3, p. 245; al-Bidāyah w'an-Nihāyah, vol. 8, p. 52.
67. Tārīkhu'r-Rusūl wa'l-Mulūk, vol. 6, p. 149.
68. al-Kāmil fī't-Tārīkh, vol. 3, pp. 245-49; al-Bidāyah w'an-Nihāyah, vol. 8, p. 52; Tārīkhu'r-Rusūl wa'l-Mulūk, vol. 6, p. 155; Murūju'ž-Žahab-wa'l-

M'adinu'l Jauhar, vol. 3, p. 12; aṭ-Ṭabaqātu'l-Kabīr, vol. 6, p. 217; Kitābu'l-'Ibar, vol. 4, pp. 24-31; Khilāfat-o-Mulūkiyat, p. 165.
69. Khilāfat-o-Mulūkiyat, p. 153.
70. al-Isti'āb fi Mā'rifatu'l-Aṣḥāb, vol. 1, p. 135; Tārīkhu'r-Rusūl wa'l-Mulūk, vol. 4, p. 208.
71. Kanżu'l-'Ummāl-fī-Sunnau'l-Aqwāl-w'al-Alfāẓ, vol. 3, p. 88; al-Isti'āb fi Mā'rifatu'l-Aṣḥāb, vol. 1, p. 97.
72. Tārīkhu'r-Rusūl wa'l-Mulūk, vol. 1, p. 516.
73. Khilāfat-o-Mulūkiyat, p. 153.
74. Shahīd-i-Insāniyat, p. 140.
75. Kitābu'l-'Ibar, vol. 5, p. 59.
76. Kitābu'l-M'ārif, p. 59; al-'Iqdu'l Farīd, vol. 2, p. 223.
77. Sīratu'n-Nabī:Shiblī, vol. 1, pp. 21-254.
78. al-Iṣābah fī Tamayyażu'ṣ-Ṣaḥābah, pp. 9-10.
79. Jām'au'ṣ-Ṣaḥīḥu'l –Bukhārī, vol. 2, p. 233.
80. Naẓariya-i-'Adālat-i-Ṣaḥābah, pp. 19-114.
81. Jām'au'ṣ-Ṣaḥīḥu'l-Mishkātu'l-Maṣābīḥ, vol. 2, p. 223, tr. no. 5757/6.
82. Jām'au'ṣ-Ṣaḥīḥu'l –Bukhārī, vol. 2, p. 257, tr. no. 944.
83. al-Kāmil fī't-Tārīkh, vol. 3, p. 248; al-Bidāyah w'an-Nihāyah, vol. 8, p. 71.
84. Jām'au'ṣ-Ṣaḥīḥu'l –Bukhārī, vol. 2, p. 89.
85. Tārīkhu'l-Khulafah, p. 263.
86. Tārīkhu'l-Khulafah, p. 263.
87. Jām'au'ṣ-Ṣaḥīḥu'l –Bukhārī, vol. 2, p. 218.
88. Tārīkhu'r-Rusūl wa'l-Mulūk, vol. 1!, p. 1.
89. Iżālatu'l-Khulafā, vol. 1, p. 569.
90. Tārīkhu'l-Khulafah, pp. 201-13.
91. Jām'au'ṣ-Ṣaḥīḥu'l-Muslim, vol. 3, tr. 1552.
92. Kitābu'l-Jihād, vol. 2, pp. 64-65; Jām'au'ṣ-Ṣaḥīḥu'l-Muslim, vol. 2, trs. nos. 1008, 1388-89, vol. 3, tr. 1552, vol. 4, trs. nos. 2225, 2901; al-Musnad:Aḥmad vol. 5, p. 241.
93. as-Sunan: *Nasā'ī*, vol. 2, p. 64.
94. as-Sunanu'l Kubrā, vol. 1, p. 136.
95. Wafiyyātu'l-'Ayān wa anbā'aż-Żamān, vol. 2, p. 168.
96. Ḥusnu'l-Muḥāzara fī Akhbār Miùr wa'l-Qāhirah, vol. 2, p. 88.
97. al-Bidāyah w'an-Nihāyah, vol. 7, p. 155; al-Isti'āb fi Mā'rifatu'l-Aṣḥāb, vol. 2, p. 604.
98. al-Iṣābah fī Tamayyażu'ṣ-Ṣaḥābah, vol. 1, pp. 344-45.
99. The Social Stucture of Islām, p. 67.
100. Jām'au'ṣ-Ṣaḥīḥu'l-Bukhārī, vol. 1, pp. 91, 96; Jām'au'ṣ-Ṣaḥīḥu'l-Muslim, vol. 1, p. 77.
101. Jām'au'ṣ-Ṣaḥīḥu'l-Bukhārī, vol. 1, pp. 65, 77.
102. Islām-Nāmah, p. 273.
103. al-Isti'āb fi Mā'rifatu'l-Aṣḥāb, vol. 1, p. 369.
104. al-Kāmil fī' t-Tārīkh, vol. 4, pp. 104-41; al-'Iqdu'l Farīd, vol. 1, p. 62.

105. aṭ-Ṭabaqātu'l-Kabīr, vol. 4, p. 184.
106. Dirāsatu'l Labīb, p. 77.
107. Tārīkhu'r-Rusūl wa'l-Mulūk, vol. 4, p. 187; al-Bidāyah w'an-Nihāyah, vol. 8, p. 29; al-Isti'āb fi Mā'rifatu'l-Aṣḥāb, vol. 1, p. 118; aṭ-Ṭabaqātu'l-Kabīr, vol. 7, pp. 28-29.
108. Kitābu'l Wuzrā, p. 11.
109. Tārīkhu'r-Rusūl wa'l-Mulūk, vol. 6, pp. 140-41.
110. al-Bidāyah w'an-Nihāyah, vol. 9, pp. 200-208.
111. as-Sunan: Ibn Māja, vol. 1, p. 7.
112. *Ibid.*
113. al-Iṣābah fī Tamayyażu'ṣ-Ṣaḥābah, vol. 2, p. 401.
114. Usadu'l Ghābah fī Muā'rifu'l Ṣaḥābah, vol. 1, p. 379.
115. al-Bidāyah w'an-Nihāyah, vol. 8, p. 139, vol. 9, p. 232.
116. *Ibid.*
117. al-Isti'āb fi Mā'rifatu'l-Aṣḥāb, vol. 1, p. 196; Kitābu'l-'Ibar, vol. 3, pp. 7-8.
118. Khilāfat-o-Mulūkiyat, p. 163.
119. Tārīkhu'r-Rusūl wa'l-Mulūk, vol. 6, p. 126.
120. Tārīkhu'r-Rusūl wa'l-Mulūk, vol. 6, p. 132.
121. Tārīkhu'r-Rusūl wa'l-Mulūk, vol. 6, p. 164.
122. al-Kāmil fī't-Tārīkh, vol. 3, p. 249; al-Bidāyah w'an-Nihāyah, vol. 8, p. 79; Kitābu'l-'Ibar, vol. 3, pp. 15-16;
123. Tārīkhu'r-Rusūl wa'l-Mulūk, vol. 5, pp. 128-29.
124. Muḥarram Nāmah, p. 174.
125. al-Irshād fī Ma'rifat Ḥujjāj Allāh 'Alā 'Ibād, p. 197.
126. Islāmī Rājya Banām Muslim Rājya (Hindī), Lokbhārtī Prakāshan, Allahabad.
127. al-Bidāyah w'an-Nihāyah, vol. 8, p. 135.
128. aṣ-Ṣawa 'qu'l-Muḥriqah fi'r-radd 'alā ahli'l Rafz wa'l Zanadiqah, p. 33.
129. Tārīkhu'r-Rusūl wa'l-Mulūk, vol. 6, p. 135; al-Isti'āb fi Mā'rifatu'l-Aṣḥāb, vol. 1, p. 154; Usadu'l Ghābah fī Muā'rifu'l Ṣaḥābah, vol. 1, p. 379.
130. Tārīkhu'r-Rusūl wa'l-Mulūk, vol. 6, p. 186.
131. al-Kāmil fī' t-Tārīkh, vol. 3, p. 454.
132. Ḥayātu'l Ḥaywan, vol. 2, p. 207.
133. al-Bidāyah w'an-Nihāyah, vol. 8, p. 1169.
134. aṭ-Ṭabaqātu'l-Kabīr, vol. 5, p. 66; Tārīkhu'l-Khulafah, p. 146
135. aṣ-Ṣawa 'qu'l-Muḥriqah fi'r-radd 'alā ahli'l Rafz wa'l Zanadiqah, p. 135.
136. al-Kāmil fī' t-Tārīkh, p. 135.
137. Kitābu'l-'Ibar, vol. 4, p. 38.
138. Khilāfat-o-Mulūkiyat, p. 17.
139. al-Bidāyah w'an-Ṇihāyah, vol. 8, p. 223.
140. al-Bidāyah w'an-Nihāyah, vol. 8, p. 1147.
141. al-Kāmil fī' t-Tārīkh, vol. 4, p. 135.
142. Laṭā'fu'l-Ashari (Mss).
143. Tahžību'l Tahžīb, vol. 11, p. 36.

144. Shahīd-i-Insāniyat, p. 174.
145. Tafsīru'l-Maẓharī ,vol. 26, p. 66.
146. Wasīyatu'n Nijāt vol. 2, p. 207
147. Sirru'l Shahādatain, pp. 33-35.
148. Jām'au'ṣ-Ṣaḥīḥu'l –Bukhārī, vol. 1, p. 421, tr. 1731; Khilāfat-o-Mulūkiyat, p. 170.
149. al-Khanāru'l Masālik, vol. 3, p. 450.
150. Tārīkhu'r-Rusūl wa'l-Mulūk, vol. 4, p. 283.
151. Madāriju'l-Nabūwat, vol. 1, p. 145.
152. Tārīkh-i-A'imah, p. 193.
153. aṣ-Ṣawa 'qu'l Muḥriqah fi'r-radd 'alā ahli'l Rafz wa'l Zanadiqah, p. 134.
154. *Khilāfat-o-Mulūkiyat*, p. 169.

Chapter: Three

The Islāmic Resurrection

The Islāmic revolutionary fundamental principles and dimensions based on new life perspective to the human being and also its polluted and distorted form presented by the foes of Islām, in the garb of Islām, has already been discussed in previous two chapters. Keeping in view the curiosity of knowing further the events, the wish of learned readers has been, indeed, our objective to put-up in details the sequence of incidents. It would not be sufficient just to describe the incidents only; it has to be clearly anyalised along with the proper description. It is the same process which has been adopted previously, would be continued in the ensuing pages. Readers may be aware of some facts, situations, its background, but not necessarily could be in knowledge of multi-dimensions of the great the Ḥusainī Revolution. There are so many such shades, if discussed, unless be incomplete and illusionary or they may feel that nothing has been contemplated fully. That is why, we felt that it would be absolutely indispensable that prior to detailed discussions; we may first discuss this essential subjects, then describe the incidents, so that, all the learned readers would identify the foes of Islām, who had mingled in Muslims and were claiming themselves as the followers of Islām, though, they wanted to throw away, uproot Islām with their efforts. Against these elements under the great leadership of Imām Ḥusain, a successful struggle commenced to establish Islām on its own true and real roots. It has coverted as a matcheless sacrifice.

The indispensable subject which we have covered as most highly valuable is Ḥasan-Mu'āwiyah-Treaty which is the compliment of the Ḥusainī Revolution. Without the knowledge of the Ḥasan-Mu'āwiyah-Treaty, the Ḥusainī Revolution could not be understood. Without knowing the basis of the decision of Imām Ḥusain against the then biggest ruling power of the world, how could it be possible to understand the Battle of Karbala, which had the support of right minded people, although many people among them could not include themselves physically in the Battle of Karbala. Imām Ḥusain's attempt was not a personal affair, or it was never for any personal benefits. It was an attempt to re-establish the Divine-Power. Why was the full force on the attainment of *Bay'at*, the oath of allegiance in favour of Yażīd? Why Imām Ḥusain challenged the paternal-monarchism? Whether *War of Justice* had become inavitable, or it could be avoided etc. There are so many problems, an attempt has been made for its solutions in the ensuing pages and also to clarify the propriety of Imām Ḥusain's *Jihād*, with which the learned readers should be acqainted with.

The Ḥasan-Mu'āwiyah Treaty

The Ḥusainī Revolution was not an incident that took place just suddenly, but it was the result of continuity of the great awakening which was being led equally prior to Imām Ḥusain, by his father Imām 'Alī and brother Imām Ḥasan. Imām 'Alī had been Caliph for a very short period of four and half years. While leading *Namāż*, the prayer, in the mosque of Kufa, there was a murderous attack and he passed away after three days. One may imagine up to what extent lawlessness was prevailing that the Caliph was not safe and in the presence of large number of Muslims, while perfoming his duty to lead the foremost pivot of the Religious Obligations of Islām he was attacked. After the death of Imām 'Alī, the same day all Muslims accepted his eldest son Imām Ḥasan as Caliph. This is an event took place on Friday, 21st *Ramzān*, 40 AH (28th January, 661 AD) With a view to establishing peace and harmony and imposing stoppage to regular killings by Amīr Mu'āwiyah. Imām Ḥasan signed a peace agreement with the waring Amīr Mu'āwiyah. This historical compromise between Imām Ḥasan and Amīr Mu'āwiyah is famous with the name of the Ḥasan-Mu'āwiyah-Treaty. It would be appropriate to know various facts for having true picture in this regard.

Firstly, it is essential to understand the necessity of the Ḥasan-Mu'āwiyah-Treaty and its background. After the passing away of Imām 'Alī, when there was grief sticken atmosphere in the family, the Damascus's trouble shooters had started their attempts of creating uncertainty and imbalance in the Islāmic State. So, many spies were caught in Kufa and Baṣra.[1] Keeping in view the seriousness of the alarming situation, Imām Ḥasan himself wrote a letter to Mu'āwiyah:

> "You have started creating trouble. You have sent people to create mischief and confusion in my state and spread your spies here and there. It appears that you want to fight. If it is so, be ready, this goal is not far off and I have information that you uttered satirical and highly objectionable words at the death of my father. It is never an act of any intelligent person. Death is universally, common to all living beings. Today we had to endure with this incident, it would happen to you tomorrow and it is true that we do not consider our dead dear one as dead. It is like that one goes from one house to another one and has a sound sleep."[2]

But circumstances have already changed to this extent that even so many followers of Imām Ḥusain tied up to the Assembly of Amīr Mu'āwiyah.

When Imām 'Alī had became Caliph IV, those people also accompanied him, who were previously with all the three Caliphs (Abū Bakr, 'Omar and 'Othman), also declared to be his followers. Actually speaking they were not his true followers. Imām 'Alī's followers were not with them. But they were ordinary people, who were good and gentle, religious minded as well as going behind the Caliph for enjoying the ruling power. Somehow with some reasons, of course, they had come along with Imām 'Alī, but mentally they were somewhere else. They were shirkers similar to languid bullocks, which lie down, when cultivator would wish to yoke them for the field, then whatever efforts the plowgher takes, they never get up. Imām 'Alī was unhappy and worried with these people. His various serious remarks may be seen in *Nahju'l-Balāghah*, which are brimming with sadness and pain. While addressing them at various occasions, Imām 'Alī said:

> "You have broken my heart and filled my chest with sadness and grief."[3]
>
> "It would have been better, if Mu'āwiyah could exchange my people with his people, just as gold coins are exchanged with silver coins. That is, he would take ten of you and give one from his."[4]
>
> "What a sad thing that they are organised on the path of unjust and you are not co-operating on the path of Truth."[5]
>
> "They are committed towards the orders of their own ruler, who disobeys the Almighty and you do not agree with you Imām, who is in compliances with God."[6]

The same were the comrades and commanders, who had been given to Imām Ḥasan from the past, on becoming Caliph after Imām 'Alī. It is clear up to what limit anything could be relied upon them.

Whatever may be the prevailing circumstances, Imām Ḥasan was very much acquainted with his duties as the Imām of the time, the Almighty has expressed in this regard:

> "Those, if We establish them in the earth, will establish prayer and pay the poor-rate". (*Qur'an*: 22/41)

Of course, Imām Ḥasan had to maintain his responsibility. Therefore, only two options were remaining before him. Come to perform war of justice to safeguard the Islāmic principle against Amīr Mu'āwiyah. Or, to compromise on the basis of Islāmic principles of enjoining the good and forbidding the evils (*Qur'an*: 41/22). In between the same Amīr Mu'āwiyah attacked Iraq Imām Ḥasan also started arranging self-defence. Imām Ḥasan deputed for fact finding job, Ḥujr-bin-'Adī Kindī, the holy Prophet's one of the most trusted companion, so that, people may be apprised of the situation. Ḥujr informed him regarding the lack of enthusiasm of the people. Yes, the people of the sect driven out of Islām, *Khārijī* (pl. *Khawārij*), were prepared to extend their co-operation, because of being harsh enemies of Mu'āwiyah, wanted war against Mu'āwiyah on any account at any cost.

Imām Ḥasan also deputed an army of twenty thousand soldiers under the command of Qaiys-bin-Sa'd-bin-'Ibādah. Alas! Mu'āwiyah's trouble shooters spread a rumour that Qaiys-bin-Sa'd was killed. It worsened the situation to this extent that where Imām Ḥasan was living was sieged. The place where he was seated was pulled down.[7] Imām Ḥasan mounted on a horse and Rabī'ā and Ḥamadān clans ran for help and chased trouble-shooters who ran away. Imām Ḥasan went towards Madāyan, where there was an attack on hiding. After standing for medical treatment in Madāyan for sufficient time, Imām Ḥasan was taking rest and he received a messege from Amīr Mu'āwiyah that he was ready to compromise with Imām Ḥasan on any conditions. Also wrote a letter to his men in the Army of Imām Ḥasan to do needful. These traiters assured Amīr Mu'āwiyah that they would arrest and hand over Imām Ḥasan to him or they would kill him.[8]

The Qur'an has clarified the rules of compromise, its basis and its operation. It would be better to be understood the norms for the compromise:

> "And fulfil ye your covenant with Me, I shall fulfil My covenant with you." (*Qur'an*: 2/40)
>
> "When ye have covenanted, and break ye not the oath." (*Qur'an*: 16/ 91)
>
> "And fulfil ye promise; Verily *(every)* promise shall be questioned about." (*Qur'an*: 17 /34)

In Islāmic terminology a traitor, an ungrateful one has been called *Munāfiq* who actually does not believe in Islām, inwardly a dangerous enemy, while showing himself as Muslim, playing foul with it. The Qur'an says:

> "The *Munāfiqūn* (Hypocrites) are certainly the liars." (*Qur'an*: 63/1)

The Caliph II 'Omar's son 'Abdu'llāh has described a verse of the Islāmic Prophet quoted in his statement to the effect; wherever there would be four things, it would be a pure hypocrite and wherever there would be one of four things, it would be becuase of hostility, they should be avoided. Other things are:

(i) when they are made trustee, steal the thing,
(ii) while conversing utters lie,
(iii) when make promises acts agaist it, and
(iv) when fights uses abusive words.[9]

Imām Ḥasan maintained his responsibility of the Islāmic principles against Amīr Mu'āwiyah. He had two options; Either to compromise on the basis of Islāmic principle or to keep him aloofe and allow further deterioration of Islāmic norms. Imām Ḥasan took firm decision in the interest of Islām, enjoining the good and forbidding the evils (*Qur'an*: 41/22), in accordance with the forecast of the holy Prophet, when he said:

> "My son (Ḥasan) is an *Imām* (leader) and I hope Allāh may cause a compromise between the two groups of Muslims through his medium."[10]

An incident has been mentioned by the scholars and also a verse of the holy Prophet as under:

> "Ḥasan-bin-'Alī was on the shoulders of the holy Prophet and he used to say, Oh, Allāh, I keep him as a friend. You also keep him as a friend."[11]

Imām Ḥasan before giving any reply to Amīr Mu'āwiyah on the proposal of compromise collecting his companions addressed in detail and said:

> "Mu'āwiyah has called on me regarding such a trivial thing, wherein there has been neither justice nor any honour. Now, please tell me, what is your opinion? If you want to save your life on every occasion, with a heavy heart I may accept the proposal of compromise, and if you are prepared to sacrifice your life on the Almighty's path, then I am also ready to offer everything on the path of the Almighty and leave the results to the wish of God. In a chorus vioce all said, 'Please give us life."[12]

Now, there remained only one option that in compliance with the Tradition of the holy Prophet of Islām, exhibiting very foresightedness, like *Ḥudaiybiyah-Compromise*, a treaty may be made with Amīr Mu'āwiyah and in the same way Imām Ḥasan also did, which is famous as Ḥasan-Mu'āwiyah-Treatry in the Islāmic history: The conditions of this agreement have been discussed in different way in various books. However, all agree on following important conditions: [13]

1. That Mu'āwiyah would be following the Qur'an and the life of Islāmic Prophet and his words and the working-precedance of *Rāshdīn-Khulafā* (Caliph I Abū Bakr, Caliph II 'Omar, Caliph III 'Othmān and Caliph IV Imām 'Alī). Famous historian Ibn Athīr, 'Izz a'd-Dīn Abu'l Ḥasan (d. 1233 AD) has clarified that Mu'āwiyah on basis of his personal conduct was debared from using the title *Amīru'l-Mominīn* (the leader of the faithful Muslims), the term used for the Caliph. He may be addressed saying only 'Amīr'. Abū Bakr Muḥammad Khażīmah used to say that Mu'āwiyah was prohibited in this way from the position of Imām or Caliph.[14]
2. That Mu'āwiyah would not have any right to nominate any other person as Caliph after him. After his death, the Caliphate would be returned to Imām Ḥasan and if he also dies, then Imām Ḥusain would become Caliph.

3. That safety, peace and protection of life would be provided to all the citizens of Iraq, Ḥijāż and Yemen.
4. That wherever the *Shi'atu'l-'Alī* (Followers of Imām 'Alī) live, their life, wealth and family and their faith would be protected.
5. That Mu'āwiyah would not attempt to make any harm to any one of the family members of Imām Ḥasan, his brother Imām Ḥusain and others from the family of the holy Prophet. No attempt to take away their life, neither secretly nor openly. None of them would be threatened, made afraid or terrorized.
6. That whatever abuse or bad words used by Amīr Mu'āwiyah and his people against Imām 'Alī in Jām'a-Masjid and sermon after *Namāż* would be stopped. A few have written that Mu'āwiyah refused to accept the last condition, then it was decided that at least on those occasions when Imām Ḥasan would be present, such a deed would not be done.

This Agreement is of Ḥijrī year 41, month Rabī'au'l-Avval or Jamadīu'l-Avval (June or July, 661 AD). It may be pointed out that whenever any Agreement is singned, there would be certain points of dispute for which actuals have to be agreed with by both the parties, otherwise there could be no compromise at all. These realities could be of two types—either the point of dispute has already occurred or there are strong possibilities of reoccurring of the same. The issues of argument of Ḥasan-Mu'āwiyah compromise were—Amīr Mu'āwiyah would maintain the Administrative codes and comducts of the Divine Laws of Islām practiced earlier by *Rāshdīn-Khulafā*. This clause speeks itself that Mu'āwiyah was not following the codes of Islām, and would follow them thereafter. In the same way there were also other disputed issues, as, Amīr Mu'āwiyah would not nominate any Caliph after him. That the practice of nominating a person to the post of Caliph would be stopped. During the reign of Amīr Mu'āwiyah the citizens of Syria, Iraq, Ḥijāj and Yemen were facing hardship for want of safety, peace and protection, would be saved everywhere. Imām 'Alī's followers who were being punished by Mu'āwiyah, their life, wealth, family members all would be saved and secured. Mu'āwiyah would then do no harm or kill the members of families of the Islāmic Prophet, Imām 'Alī, Imām Ḥasan, Imām Ḥusain, neither secrectly nor openly. Nor any of them would be harassed, threatened or terrorised at any place. If any dispute arises, would be resolved on the terms of Ḥasan-Mu'āwiyah Treaty. The aim of presenting again all the conditions here, is that terroristic historical atmosphere may be introduced in which Imām Ḥasan, Imām 'Alī's associates and followers were threatened and terrorised.

Ḥasan-Mu'āwiyah-Treatry was not an ordinary political document. There are so many historical, social, moral, religious, phenonemena, in which nets of conspiracies were spread. The religious minded people were threatened, and terrorised. The main-source of all these was Amīr Mu'āwiyah, which were tied up under the above Treatry. Secondly, that after signing of Ḥasan-Mu'āwiyah-Treatry, he himself automatically became the witness of all facts mentioned in the text of the Treatry. In other words, this is the accepted document of Amīr Mu'āwiyah in which he himself cannot deny the registered facts. Umayyite brought historians, whose cleverness of speech would workout, who are experts in writing contrary to the Truth. It takes of atmosphere of that period has been protected in this historical document. Thirdly, the Qur'an's orders: No option remained besides agreement in the compliance of accepting Divine orders and not agreeing with the prohibited ones, but not complimentary Qur'an's Advices and Prophet's verses are quoted above. Foresighted Divine wisdom of Imām Ḥasan passed the message of happiness, peace through this historical document.

Imām Ḥasan's unparallel political wisdom of Ḥasan-Mu'āwiyah-Treaty is the preface of the Ḥusainī Revolution, which is absolutely in accordance with the Divine orders. Qur'an's versions have been quoted in the above mentioned lines that, if agreement proposal comes from any direction, then it should not be discorded, but it should be accepted.

The policy of sacrificing the post of Caliph reflects Imām Ḥasan intense foresightedness, on the basic issues, which he wanted to resolve for ever; the problem of appointment of the Islāmic Caliph and accepting the Imām of the time as the real Caliph. This principle was signed by both parties that after the death of Amīr Mu'āwiyah the Caliphate would be returned to Imām Ḥasan and after him Imām Ḥusain would be Imām-*cum*-Caliph, both positions would be combined and then Imām Ḥusain would nominate his successor. In this way the misunderstanding and enmity among Muslims might be put to an end for ever.

For this high noble purpose, Imām Ḥasan sacrificed his own personal benefits. He presented such a matchless example of sacrifice which is going on in writing even at present among the supporters of Muslim unity for consideration. This Ḥasan-Mu'āwiyah-Treaty was violated, as a result of which misunderstanding developed between the two groups of Muslims instead of unity and this *status quo* prevails till today, then its entire responsibility rests only on the Amīr Mu'āwiyah.

The following condition is clear if Ḥasan-Mu'āwiyah-Treaty is analysed. As, the first condition was that Amīr Mu'āwiyah would maintain the administrative principles of Islāmic Divine codes and conduct established previously, but who would say the adherence of Islāmic codes and conduct, the very Islāmic itself remained maintained. A detailed discussion has already been done in the previous chapter.

The second condition was that there would be no right to Amīr Mu'āwiyah to nominate anybody to the post of Caliph after him. But he appointed his son Yażīd as his heir neglecting it. It was also discussed in detail in the previous chapter.

The third condition was that during the reign of Amīr Mu'āwiyah peace would be provided to the people of Syria, Iraq, Ḥijāż and Yemen. But during the reign of Amīr Mu'āwiyah not only in Syria, Iraq, Ḥijāż and Yemen, but also in the whole of Islāmic State harassment and injustice were at their peak. In Iraq, Żiyād-bin-Abīh was the administrator of Iraq, it has been written in his regard that he used to murder people before inquiring itself even if he had commited any crime.[15] Afterwards Samrah-bin-Junadab became his successor. His atrocities were more than that of *Żiyād*, once in six months time he murdered eight thousand men, women and children. Samrah was doing all these things as per the orders of Amīr Mu'āwiyah. When Mu'āwiyah dismissed him from the post, he said, May God, destroy Mu'āwiyah, had I done this much of service to God, Mu'āwiyah would not have given so much problems.[16]

The fourth condition was that wherever the associates of Imām 'Alī and his Followers would be their life, honour and property would be saved and secured and would stop the punishments against them. During the reign of Amīr Mu'āwiyah atrocities on the associates and the followers of Imām 'Alī were in an extraordinary way, among which the least was his that his head was removed from his body. His properties etc. were usurped and any of Mu'āwiyah's supporters were made to settle in their place.[17] The Shi'atu'l-'Alī of Kufa and Baṣra were put in a barren land called Qansarīn of Syria, exiling them from their mother land. Innumerable innocent persons were arrested and put in jail for long periods, without any hearing and given different types of punishments. It has been discussed by so many historians.[18] Those Shiā's were also not small in number, who were murdered without having done any crime. Their number is in thousands whose discussion is available in the books of history.

The fifth condition was that during the reign of Amīr Mu'āwiyah no attempt would be done either to do any harm or to kill any body of holy Prophet's family members and they would not be harassed by threatening fearing terrorising Amīr Mu'āwiyah threw away this condition also in the wind. He attempted in all respects to harm the members of the family of Prophet, he threatened them, made them afraid of and by giving pioson to Imām Ḥasan, Mu'āwiyah made him a martyr.[19]

The sixth condition was that Amīr Mu'āwiyah would stop usage of bad words and abuses against Imām 'Alī. It is also prohibited in any religious society, civilization and morality; Islām has prohibited abuses and bad words especially. The Qur'an orders:

> "And abuse ye not." (*Qur'an*: 6/109)

There is also a famous Tradition of the holy Prophet:

> "Who ever abused 'Alī, he abused me and whoever abused me, he abused Allāh."[20]

Renowned scholar Abu'l 'Olā Maudūdī had condemned in severe words the use of abuses by Mu'āwiyah and his associates against Imām 'Alī:

> "One more condemnable incident took place during the reign of Amīr Mu'āwiyah that he himself and his associates, all administrators were showering abuses and bad words against Imām 'Alī. To this extent that in the *Masjidu'l Nabwī* (Prophet's Mosque) on the Prophet's *Membar* (the rosturm, used for the sermons) and in front of Prophet's holy mausoleum abuses were made against his most dear relative and the family members of Imām 'Alī and his nearest relatives used to hear them. It was against the codes of justice to abuse a person after his death; especially it is the very worst deed on the basis of justice and morality."[21]

There are various similarities and equalities between Ḥasan-Mu'āwiyah-Treaty and Ḥudaiybia-Treaty of the holy Prophet of Islām. At the outset Ḥudaiybia-Treaty was also surrounded by distresses and difficulties and objections, but it got the title of *Manifest Victory* (*Qur'an*: 48/1) afterwards. In the same way, the compromise done by Imām Ḥasan also has come out successful as the touch-stone of history, there is an abnormal role in clearing the difference between the real Islām and pseudo-Islām. Imām Ḥusain was adhering with pleasure of Imām Ḥasan in all situations. In the context of this Treaty he always praised the political wisdom of Imām Ḥasan. After the withdrwal of the post of

Caliph, Imām Ḥasan returned to Medina of the holy Prophet, leaving the capital Kufa, Imām Ḥusain also came down to Medina along with him. Both the respective brothers were following cent-per-cent each and every paragraph of Ḥasan-Mu'āwiyah-Treaty through out their life very politely and peacefully.

It was indispensable for both the sides to adhere to Treaty between Imām Ḥasan and Amīr Mu'āwiyah after its successful completion, but Amīr Mu'āwiyah declared in his speech of Friday prayer in a mosque near Kufa after a little time itself:

> "My aim in battling was not this that you people perform *Namāż*, keep fasting for *Rozā*, do *Ḥajj* or pay *Żakāt*. You may go on doing these things as you were doing in the past. My aim has been just to establish my ruling power over you people. That phase has been over after this Treaty with Ḥasan. I know well that despite of being concurred you people hate me. With all distaste and displeasure I am successful in my aim. As far as those conditions of the Treaty, which I had with Ḥasan, they are under my feet, fulfilling them or not is in my hands."

In the madness of ruling power, Amīr Mu'āwiyah proceeded ahead to this extent that he said bad words and abuses against Imām 'Alī and Imām Ḥasan in the presence of Imām Ḥasan and Imām Ḥusain. Imām Ḥusain stood up to reply, but Imām Ḥasan made him sit down and he himself gave a befitting reply in a gentle manner that Mu'āwiyah could not speak further and became stunned.[22]

In these circumstances the followers of Imām Ḥasan started to be impatient and worried and sad. They would tell insisting that when Mu'āwiyah had been wilfully rejecting the Ḥasan-Mu'āwiyah-Treaty, why don't you react to in the same way. Whatever Imām Ḥasan was visualising with his inner sight, others had no glimpse of it at all. His suffocation increased in such a way that the people started opposing Imām Ḥasan. A follower 'Alī-bin-Muḥammad Hamadanī went to Medina to meet Imām Ḥasan along with other associates. They saluted, *as-Salām Alyakum Ya Mużallinu'l Muminīn* (Salute to you, you the misguider of religious minded people!). Neither any anger nor distress, Imām Ḥasan convinced them, I have not misguided the relegious minded people, I am the guardian of his respects, I have saved them from the destruction of the terrific war. Were there any war, then the situation was such that one day the emperorship of Mu'āwiyah would be established.[23]

On the other side, Amīr Mu'āwiyah started spreading untrue and baseless propaganda about Imām Ḥasan and Imām Ḥusain through the then his mass media. He attempted character assassination of Imām Ḥasan by making issue of polygamy against him, but when challenged, Mu'āwiyah could not say that Imām Ḥasan had more than four wives at a time, including one J'adah-bint-Ash'ath, who was planted by him to poison Imām Ḥasan, which she did. Failed to prove his allegation of polygamy, he propagated that Imām Ḥasan used to marry and divorce.

It was spread regarding Imām Ḥusain that was very angry and proud. He was against Ḥasan-Mu'āwiyah-Treaty. On that basis he had tried to create misunderstanding with Imām Ḥasan also. How much Imām Ḥusain was peaceful and courageous, matured, Karbala is its best proof. Its detailed discussion would follow in the ensuing chapters with the Ḥasan-Mu'āwiyah-Treaty through him and also of Imām Ḥasan, that Imām Ḥusain was completety contented. Imām Ḥasan did this Treaty for the defence and benefits of Imām Ḥusain and the later was also fully aware of it. There how can the very question of enmity arise. The very sincere life of Imām Ḥusain towards Imām Ḥasan proves that he always extended his full support and regard to his brother and the Imām of that period. As long as Imām Ḥasan was in Kufa, Imām Ḥusain also lived along with him and when Imām Ḥasan came to Medina leaving Kufa, Imām Ḥusain accompanied him to Medina and lived safeguarding him through out his life.

The Ḥasanī Agreement and the Ḥusainī Revolution

If observed really the Ḥasanī Agreemnts and the Ḥusainī Revolution are the two sucessful attempts of same objective. Both are the complements of each other. At the first stage, the Ḥusainī Revolution also becomes a part of the Ḥasanī Agreement movement in a natural manner. But, its inducement, encouragement and its influence became more evident. The Ḥusainī movement had been based on the principle of Islāmic awakening against the ignorance. If observed, the Battle of Karbala has been the most important factor against injustice, atrocities and inequalities, which took the form of storms. There was a renaissance of Islām due to wonderful sacrifice of Imām Ḥusain and his companious. The Ḥusainī movement became the Ḥusainī Revolution getting developed.

The Ḥusainī Revolution, the great incident of human history has been dedicated to Imām Ḥusain, the grandson of Islāmic Prophet, the hero of the Battle of Karbala, who had designed the introduction of eternity of life with the sacred blood of himself and his family members and companions. He had changed the very direction and movement of the Islāmic history, descended the curtain of personal rulership in the name of Islāmic Divine governance, drew a line of demarcation limit in between real Islām and pseudo-Islām. Presenting an unparallel sacrifice, he had established the power of Divine Rule. His Divine forecasting came true. Imām Ḥusain's victory has proved the Qur'anic term *Fatḥu'l Mubīn* (Manifest Victory) with its clarifications and explanations:

> "Verily we caused Victory for thee a manifest Victory". (*Qur'an*: 48/1)

This Manifest Victory has not been obtained by attacking in war, but in the name of great the Ḥusainī Revolution whose slogan was:

> *Lā Ilāh Ill'allāh Muḥammadu'r Rasūl'allāh.*
> (There is no god but God, Muḥammad His Prophet).

Therefore, just the assumption of the post of Caliph by Yažīd-bin-Mu'āwiyah was not only the forceful violation on the Islāmic governance system, but it was problem of leadership of *Muslim Ummah.* It was not a matter of establishing or not establishing any political state, but it was a problem of implementing the orders based on the Qur'an in Islām, the religion. A ray of light emerging in this terrific darkness, which covers the entire horizon is being spread. It enlightens the visible world with its own light. The name of that light is Ḥusain-bin-'Alī.

Imām Ḥusain had intelligently analysed the situations of frequently changing, forms of Islām after the expiry of his own grandfather Islāmic Prophet (8 June, 632 AD). It was clear before him that with the saying and doing of Yažīd leave the heights of Islām, even the normal morality was blown into air. Due to his bad conduct and character Yažīd was standing naked and hollow with his entire environment. His audacity went to the extent that wherever his father was unsuccessful, he was adament on those deeds. His father returned from Medina being unsuccessful and ashamed without obtaining *Bay'at* from Imām Ḥusain. But Yažīd passed orders in favour of his own administrator Walīd-bin-'Otbah in Medina to take the *Bay'at* from Imām Ḥusain, otherwise cut his head and send the head to Damascus. Now, the situation had come; if Imām Ḥusain accepts *Bay'at,* it would be as if on the grave of Islām was offered *Fātiḥā* (to pray for dead). If refuse the demand of *Bay'at*, then accept to become a martyr and if he continue the *status quo* by any diplomatic dicussions, the unbridled so called 'Ulmā' (scholars) of Umayyite would allow him to remain as *status quo*? They would never. Such baseless rumours would be spread that Islām would become a toy of a child. Imām Ḥusain took a concrete decision contemplated and thought over since so many years. He shall again make Islām sacred and holy by removing all falses dirty, misguidings, ignorance and darkness and injustice and change them. Certainly, it would be indispensable to sacrifice even our own life, then I would accept it. For the safety and security and defence of Islām, all sorts of sacrifices and sufferings are acceptable to me. I would give priority to a respectable death over an irrespectable life. Imām Ḥusain prepared his war-policy with full wisdom and determination on the basis of his own divine and highly valuable foresightedness.

Struggle with the Great Muslim Empire

It becomes clear with the perusal of political map[24] of the Muslim Empire in the year 680 AD (Figure 1), that it was mostly wide and mighty empire, the then biggest super power of the world, evident from its own geographical limits. All the trifling low mean kingdoms were afraid of and terrorised. In such a situation when no other power was to challenge this highly wide empire, Imām Ḥusain took a vow of struggling and directing against un-Islāmic conduct and behaviour by so called the Muslim Empire. His objective was to establish Truth and Justice, struggling against the cruelties and atrocities and exploitations of the ruling class of that period in the context of entire human-relationships.

The glory of mighty Muslim Empire can be estimated with the fact that it was very wide with the frontiers, consisting of currently 33 countries, mostly in full and a few in partial:

(1) Saudi Arabia, (2) Oman, (3) Yemen, (4) United Arab Emirates, (5) Qatar, (6) Kuwait, (7) Iraq, (8) Jordan, (9) Israel, (10) Palestine, (11) Lebanon, (12) Bahrain, (13) Syria, (14) Iran, (15) Turkey, (16) Gorgia, (17) Armenia, (18) Azarbaijan, (19) Albania, (20) Turkmenistan, (21) Uzbekistan, (22) Kazakhstan, (23) Kyrgyzstan, (24) Tajikstan, (25) Afghanistan, (26) Pakistan, (27) Egypt, (28) Libya, (29) Tunisia, (30) Algeria, (31) Morocco, (32) Spain and (33) Potrugal (see Fig. 1).

There was no existence of such a widely spread Muslim Empire during the life-time of the holy Prophet of Islām. After himself when extending of geographical limits started, other countries were attacked by sending the armies and making them the part of Muslim Empire and appointing Viceroys in those countries, who were ruling as per orders and instructions of the Caliph. The progeny of the Prophet Muḥammad neither participated in the victory of various countries nor any viceroy was appointed among them. It is clear from this that the family members of Prophet did not agree with the strategies of contemporary rulers of Muslim Empire. In all the conquered countries a routine and orderly propaganda was continued to be done against the family-members of the holy Prophet. Therefore, after conquering various countries most of those people who became Muslims were either ignorant of the family-members of Prophet or illusioned and confused and misguided by their anti-publicities. Amīr Mu'āwiyah had not left any stone unturned in doing harms and harassments to the family members of the holy Prophet. It has already been discussed in the previous pages.

Although the circumstances were risky and dangerous and Imām Ḥusain's decisions were wise and strong and full of intelligence yet mostly his dear and near ones advised to escape, but his successful leadership had preserved the great incident as the Battle of Karbala in the history of humanity in the name of the Ḥusainī Revolution. The time had proved and certified his foresightedness.

Supportive Basis of Ḥusainī Decision

There are so many phases of supportive bases of important and foresighted decisions of Imām Ḥusain. The foremost duties of any *Imām* have been declared as under:

> "Enjoin ye upon the people righteousness and ye forget yourselves." (*Qur'an*: 2/44)
>
> "And believer men and the believer women, they are guardian to one to other, they enjoin good and forbid evil." (*Qur'an*: 9/71)

Morever:

> "And fight them on until there is no more persecution and religion be only for God, but if they cease, then there should be no hostility save against the aggressors." (*Qur'an*: 2/193)

There are clear Traditions of the holy Prophet that it is the responsibility of each and every person to raise vioce against evils:

> "To say things of justice before the most atrocious and cruel Ruler has been the best of *Jihād*."[25]

Then said:

> "When people meet the atrocious and cruel and not catch hold of his hands, then there is no wonder that they would become the part of the anger of God."[26]

There is a special Tradition of the holy Prophet regarding Imām Ḥusain, described by Anas-bin-Ḥārth, one of the beloved associates of the Prophet. Anas says:

> "I saw that tho baby Ḥusain was in the laps of his grandfather Prophet Muḥammad, whom he was loving frequently and said at a time that his this son would be murdered on that soil, whose name is Karbala, asked to see, if anyone of them were present at that time, it was a must for him to help him."[27]

On the basis of this Tradition Anas-bin-Ḥārth himself and the other all present associates participated in *Jihād* and became martyrs along with Imām Ḥusain.

Imām Ḥusain had frequently clarified his own objectives along with the authenticity of *Ḥadīth* and Qur'an what was the basis of his struggle. A discussion is available in the history that prior to giving up his life Imām 'Alī had given his own will to his son and heir Imām Ḥasan and said that it might be given to Imām Ḥusain after him. An extract of the will:

> "Go on sacrificing your wealth and life as *Jihād* in the way of God. Enjoin upon the people righteousness and forget yourselves. Accept the recognised orders and reject the prohibited ones and never overlook it. God may forbid the establishment of rule of wicked and bad people."[28]

Besides the above mentioned religious moral and daily responsibility, the personal commitment of Imām Ḥusain was also towards those religious honest persons, whom he had been giving continuous assurances that he would bless at the appropriate time. So, many groups of religious-minded persons were living, who did not raise their voice being afraid of the death-punishment, which was a normal thing. People were buried alive. The limbs of people were cut, tongues were pulled out to terrorise. They were dishonoured in different ways. These religious conscious groups of people were having lighted the lamp of hope, *Light-House,* in their mind that Imām has promised that he would eradicate all our difficulties and miseries at an appropriate time. Imām's promise is always true and real. Certainly, it would be fulfilled. How could Imām Ḥusain break this belief that it is indispensable to be being blessed. It would be apt that for refreshing the memory of readers those incidents may be discussed. A brief reference of which has already been given in the previous chapter, but in the context of the promise of Imām Ḥusain it would be appropriate to have that knowledge.

Imām Ḥusain had given the first assurance of blessings at the appropriate time, at the time, when Amīr Mu'āwiyah in the presence of Imām Ḥasan and Imām Ḥusain, had began abusing in bad words Imām 'Alī and Imām Ḥasan, after the Ḥasan-Mu'āwiyah-Treatry. With this Imām Ḥusain's followers also being impatient and sorrowful began to ask with insistence, why he did not give befitting replies to Mu'āwiyah.[29] In this order 'Alī-bin-Muḥammad Hamadānī went to Medina to meet Imām Ḥasan. At that time, Musaiyyab-bin-Nakhbah, 'Abdu'llāh Tayamī and Sirāj Khith'amī also were present. Hamadānī replied to Imām Ḥasan replied courageously, but he remained dissatisfied. All of them went to Imām Ḥusain, informed about their talk with Imām Ḥasan and submitted that Imām Ḥasan has signed the Agreement with the Mu'āwiyah and so he would not act against it. Mu'āwiyah's atrocities were unbearable, they would not tolerate any more cruelties. They would raise their voice against injustice. They requested to rise and lead them. Imām Ḥusain, who had been by nature peaceful and calm made their angry followers calm and peaceful with his beautiful arguments, telling that Imām Ḥasan was on the path of Truth, his decision should be adhered. It established for ever that one Imām is not a rival of another Imām. He is his complementary providing continuity to his Traditions. Imām Ḥusain said to them. It was a must for them that everyone of them should be sitting in his house calm, till Mu'āwiyah is 'alive'. In other words that Ḥasan-Mu'āwiyah-Treatry is 'alive' legally only till the death of Amīr Mu'āwiyah.[30] Afterwards, we would raise voices independantly against the injustice.

The highly honoured companion of the holy Prophet, Imām Ḥujr-bin-'Adī Kindī and his associates Sharīk-bin-Shaddād, Zayfī-bin-Fuzayl, Qabīsah-bin-Zabī'ah, Muharaz-bin-Shahāb, Karām-bin-Jabān, 'Abdu'r-Raḥmān-bin-Ḥassān were killed on charge that they refused the order of Amīr Mu'āwiyah to use bad words and abuse against Imām 'Alī. On their being murdered, there was a severe reaction in the entire Islāmic world. This event has already been discussed in the previous chapter. Imām Ḥusain was also very much offended with this incident. The followers insisted Imām Ḥusain to raise his voice taking advantage of prevailing discontent in the atmosphere. Imām Ḥusain gave them the message of peace and said that time was not ripe to raise their voice. Here is implied also a promise that we would raise voices when time comes.[31]

Targetting the dead body of Imām Ḥasan arrows were showered by Umayyites, resulting serious damage to the shround. All those present there were boiling in anger; to do something. The family members of the holy Prophet also could not tolerate it, swords were taken out of sheath. What would have happened to Imām Ḥusain seeing the arrows on the dead body of his brother is just beyond imagination. But even in that terrific moment Imām Ḥusain maintained control, all those present, especially the family members of the Prophet were made calm by persuation. The same was the reply time has not come yet to raise our voice. After this incident the followers Iraq, especially, were deeply moved and they wrote to Imām Ḥusain that they were prepared to put an end to bondage with Mu'āwiyah and they were ready to attack them. Imām Ḥusain replied in negative that an Agreement had already been reached between them and Mu'āwiyah. It was not appropriate for him to break it. Undoubtedly, some action might be taken after the death of Mu'āwiyah.[32]

The false assumption arose by ignoring the correct-context of Ḥasan-Mu'āwiyah-Treaty. *Saiyedu'l-Ulmā* 'Alī Naqī Naqavī (d. 1988 AD) has analysed various aspects of the Agreement:

> "The supportive bases on which Imām Ḥusain resolved for the battle of justice among themselves, the eradication of that false assumptions being spread after the Ḥasan-Mu'āwiyah-Treatry, had also become essential. Since then Imām's struggle regarding Islāmic states came to an end by itself, because making the agreement by himself, he had entrusted it to the other side."[33]

Renowned scholar al-Majlisī, Muḥammad Bāqir (d. 1699 AD) has cleared the positions of both the parties after Ḥasan-Mu'āwiyah-Treaty as under:

> "Whatever Agreemnt Imām Ḥasan had made, it is a reality, of course, that Imām was not empowered for the title *Amīru'l-Mominīn*, (the ruler of the true Muslims), the term used for the Caliph. In this way Mu'āwiyah was allowed to use the title of

Amīr (ruler) only. Hence, prohibited from the both posts of Imām or Caliph of Muslim."[34]

Rising for the Divine Governance

What Imām Ḥusain wanted was to improve the deplorable condition of the Muslim Ummah and to correct the perverseness of the society by means of effective rising. He had endeavoured to re-establish Divine Governance in the grand Islāmic Empire of the time. It had been most neglected point of study for centuries. Though *'Ālamu'l Hudā* Saiyed Murtazā Mūsāwī (d. 1044 AD) had stated that Imām Ḥusain would have never proceeded to Kufa, unless he was assured of success in establishing again Divine Governance.[35] But most of scholars could not pay heed to this view point, until Imām Khomeinī (d. 1989 AD) turned the table, taking the arguments to its logical conclusion, raised the slogan *Kull Arzin Karbala Kull Yaumin 'Āshūrah* (All the earth is Karbala All the days are martyrdom day) and successfully founded Islāmic Republic of Iran as per guidelines of the Ḥusainī Revolution. He has clarified in his statement:

> "Imām Ḥusain had came out for the cause of establishing Divine Governance and it is a matter of glory. Those who think otherwise, should know that they are wrong. The governance must be in the hands of persons like him."[36]

Whether we use the word *Imām* (head, leader or guide) or *Khālīfah* (successor) or *Maulā* (as in the *Ḥadīth*—'Alī is Maulā of whomever I am Maulā); Its meaning in the terminology of religion is the man who rules the Muslim Ummah in the capacity of the successor of the holy Prophet. His decisions are according to the Holy Qur'an. He should be just—*Al-Qaymu bil Qist.* He should follow the true faith or make others follow the true faith. He should dedicate himself to God. Only that person whose object is only to seek the pleasure of God is fit for Imām ate. The phrase *'Alā Żātu'llāh* also carries the same meaning as *Fī Sabīli'llāh.* Every act which is for the benefit and welfare of the Ummah is considered to be in the path of God. The path of God is not limited to offering Prayers, Fasting and performing *Ḥajj*. Whatever step is taken for the welfare and advancement of the Muslim Ummah and whatever action brings the Muslims of the world nearer to their Islāmic objects and helps them in becoming a power befitting the followers of the Holy Qur'an is the path of God and following that path is dedicating oneself to God.

In a technically defined manner by Imām Ḥusain the special Islāmic terminology of re-establishment of Divine Governance is 'the enjoining good and forbidding evil', which has been already explained several times. Analysis of circumstances explains and clarifies earlier also, it appeared indispensable to battle against corruption and injustice. Had Yażīd not insisted and forced Imām Ḥusain for his *Bay'at* (Oath of Allegiance) or had Kufan people not invited him, even in that situation Imām Ḥusain would have led the Islāmic Revolution and had certainly insisted for enjoining good and forbidding evil. The demand by Yażīd for his *Bay'at* or Kufan people's invitation could not be the basic reason and result of the Ḥusainī Revolution, but they could be its supporting elements, say cause of action. The reason is quite clear, if Imām Ḥusain had not refused the *Bay'at,* then he would had no reason for refusing the prohibiting evils and enjoining the good ones. He would have been free for leading his life on the basis of his own independence, but the situation was just against, apposite to it.

Till the arrival of Imām Ḥusain in the scene to formulate the establishment of Divine Governance, there had already been two forms of religious belief in Muslims—

Firstly, *Khilāfat* (Caliphate) in which the Mulsims were accepting the election of Caliph by its *Bay'at* (Vote) putting his hand to Caliph's hand.

Secondly, *Imāmat* (Imāmate) in which the selection of leadership of Islāmic State is considered in the same way just like the selection of Prophet is done by the God. In both the procedures no individual used to become the condidate, but he is provided the leadership of Muslims.

Imām Ḥusain was the chief of Islāmic States on the basis of both the principles. On the basis of Ḥasan-Mu'āwiyah-Treaty Imām Ḥusain was officially Caliph of Islāmic States after the death of Imām Ḥasan and then Amīr Mu'āwiyah. He was already holding the position of Imām. In this manner, there could be a union of both the principles and with the leadership of Imām Ḥusain, the Divine Governance would be re-establish on the basis of its Qur'anic orders.

For the first, when Imām Ḥusain was asked by Medina's Governor, Walīd-bin-'Oqbah, and Marwān-bin-Ḥakam had objected and asked to get *Bay'at* from him immediately. Ibn Ṭāūs, Saiyed Razīu'd-Dīn, Abu'l Qāsim (d.1266 AD), has written some facts relevant to our discussion:

> "When morning of 27th of Rajab came (5th May, 680 AD) Imām Ḥusain went out of his house to find out what the political

conditions were and how the people had reacted to the death of Mu'āwiyah-bin-Abū Sufyyān, the succession of Yażīd-bin-Mu'āwiyah and the demand of Walīd-bin-'Otbah that Imām Ḥusain should swear allegiance to Yażīd. In the street he met Marwān-bin-Ḥakam. He said, 'O Abā 'Abdu'llāh! I tender you a sincere advice. If you agree to what I say it will be good'. His manner of speech was strangely presumptuous. Imām Ḥusain said, 'What is your advice? Let me hear it.' That impudent man said, 'O' Ḥusain-ibn-'Alī ! I, Marwān-bin-Ḥakam order you to swear allegiance to Yażīd-bin-Mu'āwiyah, to acknowledge his Caliphate, Imām ate and leadership and to accept him as the Head of the Ummah, for, in my opinion, therein lies the goodness of your religion as well as your world. If you do not swear allegiance to Yażīd-bin-Mu'āwiyah, your faith as well as your world will be ruined. Imām Ḥusain said, "We are from God and we have to return to Him."[37]

"We are from God and we have to return to Him" is the famous holy verse. (*Qur'an*: 2/156)

It is usually read, when a calamity befalls a person. I think the great tragedy on account of which Imām Ḥusain recited *We are from God* was the intellectual deviation of the Muslims. They had gone astray to such an extent that Marwān said that the faith and the world of Imām Ḥusain could remain safe only if he swore allegiance to Yażīd-bin-Mu'āwiya. We are from God throws more light on the causes of his rising and the Ḥusainī Revolution.

If ponder over, the mission of Imām Ḥusain-bin-'Alī, *Saiyed-ush-Shuhadah* (Doyen of the Martyrs) and demand of the rising and movement was not limited to teach the people of Iraq or 'Arabian peninsula the religious rules and laws, for the matter was different and important in many ways. The task of teaching the religious rules and laws could very well be performed by the clergy and preachers of the city. However, the task which Imām Ḥusain wanted to perform was extremely high. The problem which was before him was much more important than any ritual. The condition of the Islāmic government and the condition of the Muslim Ummah had become so deplorable that it could not be corrected the perverseness of the society would not be set right unless through an effective rising by a personality like Imām Ḥusain. His views were highly clear, when he said:

> "If matters have really taken such a turn that a person like Yażīd-bin-Mu'āwiya has become the leader of the Ummah and the chief of the Muslims of the world, in other words their *Imām*, then good bye should be said to such an Islām for I have heard my grandfather, the holy Prophet of God, saying that Caliphate is unlawful for the family of Abū Sufyyān, because they are not fit to become the chiefs of the Muslims and to rule over them."

With a view of objective study of the points 'causes and reasons', which compelled to rise against the then socalled Muslim Empire. The first question would be—If there was any person better than Imām Ḥusain, to come and stage a rising and lead the revolution ? His uncle 'Abdu'llāh-bin-'Abbās-bin-'Abdu'l-Maṭṭalib did not enjoy that position. His younger brother Muḥammad-bin-Ḥanafiyyah, too, did not enjoy that position. Ḥabīb-bin-Maẓāhir Asadī was a companion of the holy Prophet, but even he could not perform the task, which could be performed by Imām Ḥusain. Similar was the case with Muslim-bin-'Ausajah Asadī and Ḥānī-bin-'Orwah. Imām Ḥusain's cousin Muslim-bin-'Aqīl-bin-Abī Ṭālib and his own beloved brother Abu'l-Faẓl'il-'Abbās-bin-Imām 'Alī were persons who could lay down their lives for the achievement of the object of the rising, but even they could not become its central figure. Only the personality of Ḥusain-bin-I 'Alī-bin-Abī Ṭālib was the central figure of this revolution.

Imām Ḥusain while addressing the then Yażīdī Commander, Ḥurr-bin-Yażīd-Riyāḥī and his soldiers at the Jabalu'l Żī-Ḥasam[38] during his journey, delivered a speech wherein he stated the reasons for his rising:

> "Don't you see that truth is not being followed and falsehood is not being refrained from?"[39]

And when the condition of the Muslim Ummah becomes like this. Rising becomes obligatory for a responsible personality like Imām Ḥusain. He said:

> "Don't you see yourself? Why do you ask me as to why I don't swear allegiance to Yażīd-bin-Mu'āwiyah and why I do not accept this Islāmic government and why I do not acknowledge Yażīd son of Mu'āwiyah-bin-Abū Sufyyān as the leader and Head of the Muslim Ummah? In short it is not necessary to ask me this question. Why don't you see the

present condition of the Ummah yourselves? Don't you see yourselves that truth is not being followed? It does not mean that the people have begun telling lies or while in their homes they resort to excessive backbiting. Such sins have always been committed by the people. But don't you see how much the Islāmic leadership has deviated from Truth and Justice, and oppression and lending support to the oppressors have become its business.

We, the members of the holy Prophet's household and his heirs, are more entitled to be your rulers and your leaders and guardians in the matter of your faith and your world. We are more rightful than the pretenders who wrongly claim this office and who have no concern with it. They are those who treat you cruelly and oppress you."[40]

Again while on the way to Karbala, at Bayzah, a halting place between Ḥijāż and Iraq, Imām Ḥusain delivered a sermon before his own companions as well as those of then Yażīdī Commander, Ḥurr-bin-Yażīd-Riyāḥī and his soldiers. He told the Tradition of holy Prophet that any person who sees a cruel ruler or leader who treats as lawful the things made unlawful by God, violates the covenant made with God and opposes the Tradition of the holy Prophet and keeps silent and does not move, his end will be like that of the same tyrant ruler (in the Hell).[41]

"I (Ḥusain-Ibn-Imām 'Alī-Ibn-Abī Ṭālib) am observing in the Government of Yażīd-bin-Mu'āwiyah the Muslim (who observes these conditions) who does not endeavour to change the conditions by means of his words and deeds, does not rise against the cruel ruler, does not take any practical step against him or does not oppose him at least with his tongue, it is incumbent upon God by Himself to send that Muslim to the place, where he sends the cruel ruler, and to mete out identical treatment to both of them."[42]

"Now (in 61 AH/680 AD) the Muslim Ummah is also faced with the same situation. You can see that these people (Yażīd-bin-Mu'āwiyah and his agents) have become permanently subservient to Satan and have ceased to obey God. They are committing heinous acts openly and have suspended the penal laws. If a merchant or an ordinary man commits a crime they punish him according to the Islāmic penal laws, but if their

> favourites and those who work in their interest commit one hundred crimes they are not administered even one lash."[43]

The above statement of Imām Ḥusain that any perfect believer in Islām cannot accept Yażīd-bin-Mu'āwiyah to be the successors of the holy Prophet and the guardian of the Qur'an.

It has been explained in the previous chapters that in the life-time Imām Ḥusain, the concept of Divine Governance has been converted into imperialism and Islāmic State had loosened its form in corrupt 'Arabian communalisation. Therefore, it had become inevitable that a line of limit should be drawn between real Islām and pseudo-Islām. Imām Ḥusain brightend the line of limit with the sacred blood of his ownself, relatives and companions. Or one side of it was darkness of corruption, lawlessness and lack of ideal. There was an attempt of obtaining forcefully rights and Ruling powers, there was narow-mindedness and communalism born from tribal rivalaries, by usurping the rights of Islāmic civil society. There was a mentality of securing more and more personal gains. On the other side there are messages of Islām. The norm of the Governance was to be converted as advocated and propounded by the Qur'an, so that, every individual might obtain equal opportunity and justice. Instead of personal gains in anyway on the basis of Divine Law, all might obtain benefits. It's biggest advantage was to give greatness to humanity; and the inducement, encouragement of God's obediance in the life. Imām Ḥusain perfomed *Namāż* in the midst of swords, spears and arrows attacks; explained the meaningfulness of relations between independents and the Almighty.

Imām Ḥusain's last *Namāż* on the earth of Karbala rouses the mind even today towards the Almighty. In the same base, there came emerging the basics of Islāmic point of view criticizing again the objectives of Imām Ḥusain. On account of this the same the Ḥusainī Revolution secures the apex revolution on status in human history the influence of which is not limited to Muslims only but extended and widened to all human beings.

In Imām Ḥusain's life-time the situations had became indispensable for the Islāmic Revolution and there was no other person than himself. He was competent enough to lead the Islāmic Revolution, because if at all any thing should get-up against the down fall of human values and corruptions such a leadership was a must, nobody could raise finger at his great personality. There was no possibility at all of any kind of blame on his personality.

Imām Ḥusain is the basic reference of Islāmic religious belief, from which every Muslim earns his profits and gains as per his own capability and capacity. Besides Qur'an verses and Testaments, Whatever is in praise of the family members of Prophet and Imāms it would be approprate her to discuss a few verses of the Qur'an regarding which all the scholars agree unanimously that these cover Imām Ḥusain:

> "And fight (endeavour) ye in (the way of) God as it behoveth you to fight (endeavour) for Him He hath chosen you and hath laid not upon you any hardship in religion." (*Qur'an*: 22/ 78)

Accoding to Caliph II 'Omar the following verse has been regarding Imām Ḥusain[44]:

> "So wept not on them the heavens and the earth nor were they respited." (*Qur'an*: 44/29)

Many historians have written that Imām 'Alī wept while passing from Karbala during the course of pilgrimage.[45] And this verse also, for which scholars have said this is related to Imām Ḥusain:[46]

> " I may do good which pleaseth Thee." (*Qur'an*: 46/15)

Imām Ḥusain was a rose of the garden of the holy Prophet Muḥammad. There was nobody equal to the Islāmic Prophet in the relationship his own family. During his babyhood itself the Islāmic Prophet had conferred on him the title: *'Saiyed-us-Shababu'l Jannah'* (Lord of Young Inhabitants of the Heavens). On another occasion again the Prophet proclaimed:

> "Ḥusain is from me and I am from Ḥusain."[47]

After Imām Ḥusain becoming a martyr there was no in existence superior to Imām Ḥusain in the world of Islām. There was also no person equal to him. Imām Ḥusain judged the situations with great tolerance, patience and understanding. He observed how Amīr Mu'āwiyah undertook his policy of suppression and atrocites during his twenty years reign especially during the final decade, with which the atmosphere of Islāmic world had been terrorised. At each and every place within the territories of his kingdom, including Mecca-Medina, Imām 'Alī was abused in each and every mosque in Jum'a sermon.

The Islāmic Religious Treasury was spent for personal gains. Religious personalities had become slaves of the Rulers. Prophet's teachings were broken and twisted and false and fraudulant Traditions were imposed. Whatever praises were in the Traditions, especially in praise of Imām 'Alī, changing them, removing the names of Imām 'Alī and other households of the Prophet, their enemy's names were replaced, so that, those Traditions would not be in praise of Imām 'Alī or household of the Prophet, they might be in praise of others. The very form and shape of Islām itself was changed, all the prohibited became acceptable and all permitted were made prohibited. The reigning atmosphere was so hard and strong that it seemed impossible to raise any voice against it. It was Imām Ḥusain who made the impossible as possible. Had Imām Ḥusain made himself aloof, neutral in such a hard time, the very original colour and form and shape of Islāmic history itself would have been something different. Who could be more familiar with the statements of the holy Prophet, than Imām Ḥusain, that a person who remains just a dumb and deaf spectator by his own deeds and behaviour in polluted circumstances, who is not attempting to change the very circumstances does not oppose and agitate does not exhibit dislike for wrong, then as per the Divine Laws, his place would belong to cruel atrocious bad elements and thieves. Therefore, Imām Ḥusain had explained and clarified to accept the recognised orders and to derecognise the prohibited ones on every occasion during his struggle. With this the various stages of the Ḥusainī Revolution's reasons and causes and objectives and aims can be understood.

With the refusal of *Bay'at* Imām Ḥusain clarified the fundamental ideals and objectives at the primary stage itself of the Ḥusainī Revolution, Kufa people wrote in numerable letters to Imām Ḥusain for getting his support and approval. There were also diplomatic reasons for writing these letters. As Amīr Mu'āwiyah did a great loss of the human lives of Kufa people, so, they wanted to take revenge for it. There were two types of people among them—Firstly, those who wanted to be united according to the principles of Islām, that is enjoining good and prohibiting bad. They were the great people. Secondly, their counterparts, who were pure opportunists, greedy of wealth and property. The first type of people who were strict in their words, most of them became martyr along with Imām Ḥusain. The other type of people betrayed Imām Ḥusain and fought against him at the Battle of Karbala. Imām Ḥusain was well acquainted with the greedy people and was fully aware of the circumstances too. He was aware that if these people were united with the same ideals, followed their own promises, did not make any trouble, even in that situation on their strength only cent-per-cent success could not be achieved. Maxium 50 per cent of success only could be hopeful, because Yażīd Army was before it, with more than 50 per cent possibilities. Therefore, Imām Ḥusain had to ascertain the limit of support of these people. Sending Muslim-bin-'Aqīl his Peace-Envoy to Kufa got clarified all the situation. It was clear that Imām Ḥusain was well familiar with the history. He was competent to take such a decision which was the symbol of ever-lasting results. It was even then clear that the beckons of support of Kufa people had no place in the bases of the Ḥusainī Revolution. For reaching the basic points of this Islāmic Revolution, understanding of the revolution at all the stages of the Battle of Karbala and Imām Ḥusain is a must.

Bay'at: The Basic Point of Struggle

Imām Ḥusain was performing his own social and religious duties without entangling in any conflict and leading his peaceful life in Medina. No idea what happened casually that he considered it must to struggle against un-Islāmic Governance, then questions arise naturally in the minds of every thoughtful reader. If this question is analysed, it would clarif the reason that as soon as Yażīd occupy the throne of Caliph, Imām Ḥusain was forced to accept his *Bay'at.* Therefore, it should be understood clearly what is the basic point of *Bay'at* or struggle between Imām Ḥusain and Yażīd.

Bay'at is derived from the 'Arabic word *Bay* which means purchaser or trader. The other word of this order is *Ushtara* which means purchasing. Both are the words of Qur'an. It says:

> "Therefore rejoice ye in the bargain that ye have transacted; and that, it is the great achievement." (*Qur'an*: 9/111)

In the same verse *Ushtara* is also a word the Qur'an says:

> "Verily God hath purchased from the faithful their selves and their properties, for theirs *(in return)* be the Garden (*of Paradise*)." (*Qur'an*: 9/111)

Here, the situation is the total surrender towards God. To surrender one's inner mind in compliance of God.

The other situation of *Bay'at* is to surrender before the Prophet of God. This is a type of taking a vow, whose best example is *Bay'atu'r Rizwān,* which happened on the occasion of Mecca Victory (630 AD). This *Bay'at* was done on the hands of the holy Prophet. Muslims came one by one and repeated the resolution of being strong during Mecca Victory. This also has the testimony of Qur'an:

> "And they shall set before the Lord in ranks."
>
> (*Qur'an*: 18/48)

The other situation of *Bay'at* was to abtain a vote in the preliminary selection process of all the four Caliphs. A quite different situation was used as an appellant by Amīr Mu'āwiyah, which has already been discussed in the last pages. During his caliphate *Bay'at* was taken accepting the Qur'an and the Prophet as witness, but Yażīd's *Bay'at* was taken on the condition that he would be his property, not a human being, but an article to be sold anywhere any time. Today we have movement against the tendencies of man being treated as a thing. The root of this tendency is found in Yażīd's *Bay'at.* Yażīd had the authority to buy or sell his honour, his property and family members were to be surrendered to Yażīd's wishes like slaves. In Medina, a person, Ibn 'Abdu'llāh Asvad was ready to perform Yażīd's *Bay'at* on the oath for Prophet and Qur'an, as per the prior Tradition. He was murdered as he refused to be a slave of Yażīd.[48]

The demand of *Bay'at* for Yażīd was virtually a demand from Imām Ḥusain to surrender accepting to be a slave of him. Imām Ḥusain had to accept the compliance and be a blind follower of Yażīd. This would be the meaning of being a follower that accepted the conduct and behaviour of Yażīd as ideal and to follow in accordance with them. Qur'an has defined the compliance in these terms that comply God, Prophet and qualīfied persons:

> "Ye who believe ! obey God and obey the Apostle and those vested with authority among you." (*Qur'an*: 4/59)

In defining the 'vested with authority'(*Ulu'l-Amr)* there are so may views among Muslims. But there is no difference of opinion in this matter that the meaning of compliance is not just becoming of a citizen king, but he should be accepted as Divine Power and head of the State, who by Tradition is appointed as the successor of the holy Prophet. His each and every saying and doing reflects the Islām in its original form.

The thing is that the wary Imām Ḥusain was within the periphery the orders of Islāmic Divine Laws, because the Qur'an itself had established arguments/counterarguments for this in the above verse (*Qur'an*: 4/59). Regarding following God and His Prophet there is no difference of opinion among the different sects of Islām, but for the condition 'vested with authority' mentioned in the Qur'an, a few person's opinion is that there could be even ordinary people, but those who ruling upon any great person can occupy the post only in accordance with Divine orders, for them the addressing *Ulu'l-Amr* could only be for the twelve Imāms. Being aloof from the minute points of this problem there is no person in the Islāmic sects, who consider Yażīd-bin-Mu'āwiyah as *Ulu'l-Amr*. Therefore, there can be no argument on the basis of Islāmic Divine Laws in doing revolt against him. It is to contemplate on that period when Imām Ḥusain fought against Yażīd most of the holy Companions of the holy of Islāmic Prophet of Islām were alive, his next generation also had come, who are called *Tāba'īn*, but no body asked the question of legality of *Jihād* of Imām Ḥusain. None said any word against it. Therefore, the *Jihād* against Yażīd by Imām Ḥusain has been considered justified on the basis of Islāmic Divine Laws. It was undisputed and fully justified.

Divine Power *Vs.* Hereditary Monarchy

Opposing the conversion of Divine Ruling Power into Hereditary Monarchy, not only the Hāshimite, but also all religiously conscious Muslims were in a very difficult and sorrowful situation. The struggle also had already started even before Imām Ḥusain, so that Islām could be saved from increasing corruption and deterioration of human values.[49] If attentively looked into after the Caliph II 'Omar (644 AD), it is clearly visible. For an example, insisting on exiling the holy Prophet's most favourite companion Abūżar Ghaffārīs into the desert, murder of a number of other renowned Companions which has already been mentioned in the previous pages. So, many distinguised persons have already sacrificed their life and properties in protecting Islām; but, the martyrdom of Imām Ḥusain, his family-members and their companions has a special significance in this order, because battle for the defence of religion is a must, the Qur'an's directive is:

> "Unless ye go forth, He will chastise you with a painful chastisement." (*Qur'an*: 9/39)

Therefore, if at all anyone does not come out to prove religion in the path of God after getting this order his conduct and the responsibility of his deeds would be on himself. No one else would be responsible.

The other persons, who were asked to do *Bay'at* for Yażīd, besides Imām Ḥusain were—Muḥammad-bin-Ḥanafia, 'Abdu'llāh-bin-Żubayr and 'Abdu'llāh-bin-'Omar, but the main focus was to obtain *Bay'at* from Imām Ḥusain. Muḥammad-bin-Ḥanafia was such a brother of Imām Ḥusain, whose mothers were different. While leaving Medina Imām Ḥusain had made him his working successor. After the refusal of Imām Ḥusain, he was not asked for *Bay'at* and under any circumstance and conditions he did not do any *Bay'at* of Yażīd. 'Abdu'llāh-bin-Żubayr was one of the biggest enemy of *Ahlu'l-Bayt* (people of the house of the Prophet). He did not read *Durūd-wa'l-Salām* (God's blessing), in the *Namāż* till forty Jum'ā prayers, because *Ahlu'l-Bayt* are inclusive in *Durūd-wa'l-Salām.*[50] He used to be very angry hearing the names of Imām 'Alī and his family members and would begin to tremble and babble out.[51] He was an open enemy, but he established his own kingdom taking advantage of Imām Ḥusain becoming a martyr.[52] The third dignity was 'Abdu'llāh-bin-'Omar, whose position was entangled. He was among the enemies of Imām 'Alī to the extent that when Muslims unanimously chosen Imām 'Alī as their fourth Caliph, those few people who remained aloof in accepting Imām 'Alī as Caliph, 'Abdu'llāh-bin-'Omar was also among them. He was the supporter of Amīr Mu'āwiyah and was such among supporters of Yażīd that after Imām Ḥusain's martyrdom when all the people of Medina left Yażīd, he stressed on being united accepting Yażīd as Caliph, collecting his own family members and relatives. It was to this extent that he threatened, if any person against his permission would break his connection from the *Bay'at* of Yażīd, then he would also become aloof.[53] On the other side is Imām Ḥusain, who sacrificed everything on the path of God for the defence of humanity that Imām Ḥusain became *Saiyed-ush-Shuhadah,* an appellation for him.

With reference to the establishment of monarchy by Amīr Mu'āwiyah already discussed in the previous chapter, a study and analysis of those possibilities may be done, one the basic of which Imām Ḥusain did not accept the *Bay'at* of Yażīd, so many important stages may come before us, as:

1. Would Islām recognise Hereditary Monarchy ? Whereas Islām negates monarchism. The right of governance rests only with God. There are so many verses which have already been discussed at the appropriate placces. In the situation of the *Bay'at* of Yażīd, these verses would be negated.

2. As soon as the establishment of the Hereditary Monarchy takes place, the Islāmic governing system would be dissolved automatically, because the right of taking any decision rests with Empire, wheras as per Islām its entire rights rests with God.
3. No sooner did the Monarchy, formed than there ended the religious and spiritual situation of Islām. It would become in accordance with the needs of the Monarchy, at the situation of its *Bay'at* Imām Ḥusain would have to accept. The Qur'an says:

> "*(Or)* shall We treat those who believe and do good deeds like the mischief-makers in earth? Or shall We treat the pious ones like the wicked ones?" (*Qur'an*: 38/28)

4. Islām represents the continuity of all previous religions. All religions follow the Divine Laws. But as soon as the Hereditary Monarchy would be accepted, its Rules of Power would be recognised. Only on this account of Monarchy Islām had been charged being spread by the force of sword. Qur'an orders:

> "And obey not the bidding of extravagant. Those who mischief in the earth; and amend not." (*Qur'an*: 26/151-152)

5. In accepting Yażīd's *Bay'at* not only the matchless deeds of Islāmic Prophet would have become spoiled, but also Imām 'Alī, Imām Ḥasan and other religious personalities achievements would have been over. With its unhealthy commencement, the great deeds of one lac twenty four thousand Aspostles and Prophets would be destroyed, who have been sent by the Almighty to establish the society on the path of justice. The Qur'an says:

> "And verily sent We apostles before thee, of them there are those whom We have mentioned unto thee." (*Qur'an*: 40/78)

6. Yażīd's conduct was bringing with injustice and corruption. He was inferior even to the ordinery people. The stage of his inferiority cannot be even emagined. Had Imām Ḥusain did

Bay'at with him, then the same would have become Islāmic ideal behaviour. The words like Justice, Truth, Honesty, Compassion etc. would have become meaningless.

7. The ensuing history could have raised questions to Imām Ḥusain, why did he not stop destroying of Islām by the hands of Yażīd in spite of his knowing everything. Imām Ḥusain did not give any chance of audacity and to be adamant to the historian, but sacrificing his own and his associates life, saved Islām from getting destroyed.

Eradication of an Illusion

An illusion has become common in the mind of people, firstly, that the great Battle of Karbala has become so vital and important, because of being lead by the son (Imām Ḥusain, grandson) of the holy Prophet Muḥammad himself. Secondly, there was old genealogical enmity between Hāshimites, the clan in which Prophet Muḥammad and his grandson Imām Ḥusain were born and Umayyites, in which Abū Sufyyān, his son Mu'āwiyah and grandson Yażīd were born. Both the tribes were fighting constantly and up to Karbala. Let us thrash out the issues:

Firstly, the role of hereditary relationship. On the basis of mere relationship no one ever could get any favour from the holy Prophet, hence, it has no place in Islām. It has been the strenth of moral character, which was always recognised. Abū Ṭālib and Abū Lahab both were real uncles and their wives real aunts of the holy Prophet. Abū Ṭālib and his wife Fāṭimah-bint-Asad both have highest reverend status in the history of Islām, whereas the Divine verses have cursed Abū Lahab and his wife by name:

> "May perish both the hands of Abū Lahab, may perish (*he himself*). Shall avail him not his wealth nor what he earneth. Soon shall he burn in the flaming firewood, And his wife, bearer of firewood, Upon her neck shall be a halter of twisted rope." (*Qur'an*: 111 /1-5)

Ummu'l Mūminīn Umm Ḥabībah was the august wife of the holy Prophet Muḥammad. She was the daughter of Abū Sufyyān, so his son Mu'āwiyah was her brother and his son Yażīd was her real nephew and as such also nephew of the Prophet Muḥammad. Yażīdī Army's

Commandor-in-Chief, 'Omar-bin-Sa'd, was also nephew of the holy Prophet's mother Ḥazrat Āminah.

After knowing about so called many close relatives of the holy Prophet, who faught against Imām Ḥusain, the mere being his grandson of the holy Prophet, could not only be cause of his impotance. No doubt Imām Ḥusain was the proud son of the holy Prophet, but he has been important in the history of the world on the basis of his vision and far reaching impact on the humanity in general and Muslims in particular. On account of the experience which Imām Ḥusain had regarding the government of Umayyites and the people of that time and keeping in view the treatment which these people had meted out to his father, the Commander of the Faithful Imām 'Alī, and his brother Imām Ḥasan, he took the right decision at right time. What Imām Ḥusain wanted to do was to improve the deplorable condition of the Muslim Ummah and to correct the perverseness of the society by means of an effective rising.

The Second point of contention that the old genealogical enmity between Hāshimites and Umayyites was in the base of the Battle of Karbala. Its notion has been coined with the aim of reducing the glory of Karbala's great struggle, some writers and historians have also tried to creat an illusion that 'Arabian tribal hatred was its reason. Main cause, behind the context of tribal hatred was also reducing the intensity of crime of Yażīd and his associates. At the first stage, Umayyite's paid historians spread this sort of illusion. Then in view of the Tradition of tribal hatred of 'Arabs, the writers also cooperated in spreading it. There is no doubt that tribal hatred was a part of normal life of 'Arabs. Prior to Islām tribal hatred was common in the entire 'Arabian peninsula. Even on very small dispute tribes used to wage war against each other. Generations after generations the families, their heirs and supporters were in the habit of becoming flames in the War. Their ladies would motivate men in the battlefield, the tribal poets used to make sky hemisphere in praise of warriors. Islām applied break and check forcefully over the past bad customs and manners, hateful deeds, abhorrent attitudes etc. Islām had closed down all the source of inducement and enthusiasm and encouragement among tribal people. But Umayyite's those people who could not accept Islām by heart and encouraged the continuance of bad things of *Jāhiliyah* (Age of Ignorance), after being defeated hiding themselves in the garb of Islām. They themselves indulged in the tribal cursed life, and when they secured the rights of ruling power, their tribal hatred started exhibiting itself in clear way and forms.

Umayyite's tribal hatred has been very clear, which has already been discussed in the previous chapters but viewing the attempts of Hās͟himites on the basis of tribal hatred is too much farfetched notion. If, for the sake of argument, it may be accepted that the hatred of Umayyites towards Hās͟himites was on the basis of their clan concept or tribal hatred, then its order could not stop limited only to Imām Ḥusain. The vehement charges would be on Islāmic Prophet himself that he had fought against Abū Sufyyān only on account of their clan concept or tribal hatred. Undoubtedly one who believes like this, would go out of the orbits of Islām. It is not also historically true. Quraysh clan's fundamental enmity was with Islām, therefore, to stop the continuous expansion and extention of Islām they were prepared to accept the holy Prophet as their emperor. But the condition was that he should give up the cause of Islām. Leave their gods *status quo*.[54]

Before four generations of the holy Prophet and since generations before of Imām Ḥusain, Umayya, founder of Umayyite clan, his hereditary son had certainly struggled and fought regarding the rights of heredity with the holy Prophet's grandfather Hās͟him (510 AD), the founder of Hās͟himite clan. Since then the heir of Umayya, maintained their enmity and hatred towards the social regards, religious honesty and popularity of Hās͟himites. They used to make harms to them from time to time. But nowhere a mention or discussion of any type of deeds based on hostility from Hās͟himites is available. The pages of history are the cruelties and atrocities of Umayyites' chief Abū Sufyyān towards the holy Prophet. To this extent that the Prophet had to exile himself helplessly from his motherland Mecca.

All his injustices, cruelties, atrocities anti-Islām activities on one side, but when the holy Prophet of Islām became victorious over Mecca, if there were even a slight tribal hatred in his mind, he could have taken revenge from his enemies. He could have destroyed them completely. But the Prophet gave the message and advice to all the people to remain calm and maintain happiness and peace at the time of his entry into Mecca, rather he pordoned all the wicked people for their bad deeds. He showered compassion and sympathy upon Abū Sufyyān himself and proclaimed—whoever would take asylem in Abū Sufyyān's house, he too would be pandoned.

The same was the conduct and behaviour of Imām Ḥusain. When Yażīdi's army stopped his way near Karbala for the first time. Yażīdi's army was tired, and thirsty and hungry and it was in a very sorry state of affairs and most of the soldiers would have died themselves, if had they continued some more time. Though some people advised Imām

Ḥusain to let the enemy's soldiers and others die of their own, but Imām Ḥusain made available all the food materials and water with him to the Army of Yażīd. Can anybody have had courage of having imposed the charge of tribal hatred on any Hāshimites after this incident!

A student of the Islāmic History comes across this fact curiously that those persons who fought with holy Prophet against his religious cause before their children were fighting even now. At that time Abū Sufyyān was waging the war against Islām now this time the very grandson of Abū Sufyyān, Yażīd was waging the war against Islām and against Imām Ḥusain the grandson of Islāmic Prophet.

Abū Sufyyān's anti-Islāmic believes that there are no such things as Hell and Paradise and Catastrophe; all is humbug of the Hāshimite to deceive the world.[55]

Yażīd had also exhibited his pride repeating the same anti-Islāmic views that Hāshimite had played a game for obtaining ruling powers. There was neither any revelation came nor the birth of any Prophet.[56]

It is clear from these both statements that neither Abū Sufyyān absorbed Islām as a religion nor Yażīd himself had any faith in Islām. Therefore, it is quite clear and proved beyond any doubts that he just came and stood for fighting against Imām Ḥusain and he had no connection at all with Islām. The war was indeed in between Islām and enemies of Islām.

There is also similarty between Yażīd's war against Islām and the anti-Islām war of his predecessors. At this time also all the tribal people united, who wanted to remain unjust. Certainly, there were few such people among them who were not well familiar with the *Shari'a*: Sacred Laws of Islām, the Divine Jurisprudence.

They joined the Yażīdī Army for various reasons or would have come under pressure and suppression. On the contrary the people who were with Imām Ḥusain, everyone was a staunch supporter of Islām. They were fully aware of and completely understood all the possibilities. There was no pressure at all because in spite of frequent warning of Imām Ḥusain that Yażīd's Army was blood thirsty, they have no enmity with them. They could go, nobody would tell them anything, if they were ashamed of going alone catch hold of the people. A single person of Ḥusainī Army could not be ready to leave him. A detailed discussion would come at the appropriate places.

War Strategy of Imām Ḥusain

1. Highly Planned Procedure

All the plannings and schemes of Imām Ḥusain were carried out on the basis of his own ideas and thoughts and opinions. Imām Ḥusain himself had taken all his decisions. For example, the departing from Medina, travelling along with ladies and children, was against the suggession of his highly reliable brother Muḥammad Ḥanafia. Imām Ḥusain did not need his advice. Thousands of people expressed their willingness to co-operate in Mecca, but Imām Ḥusain did not accept their offer. On the other hand he sought co-operation from some Basra people and wrote letters himself. Though not relying on the letters of Kufa people, sent his own brother-in-law Muslim-bin-'Aqīl, as Peace-Envoy. On one side rejecting the support of majority of soldiers and on the other side calling a few most revered personalities to join him in path of justice and writing letters to them by himself etc. All these decisions of Imām Ḥusain could not be understood at that time. But his foresightedness became clear in due course. At present no historian would dare enough say against correct and appropriate decisions of Imām Ḥusain, because his decisions are quite correct at the touch-stone of time.

2. No Army Power

The result of achieving Victory through the medium of Army, and various wars, i.e. Jamal (656 AD), Ṣiffīn (657-58 AD), Nahrwān (658 AD) etc. were putup, good and bad, all types of people, all were available in heavy majority of soldiers in the armies. Can an army be of a few persons, but all of them being of a very high standard in their character, conduct behaviours etc. sometimes appearing almost equal to Imāms, of complete sanctity and holiness. None of them having any black mark at all in their character and behaviour. The selection of this Army would be made in such a way that the representatives of all categories, classes, grades, communities, sex and age would be included. The people of the family of the holy Prophet would be available, and also the very old companions of Prophet would be there.

The holy Prophet's next generation and his next generation's youth would be there. Young men and young women would be available there. Even some babies and small boy also would be there. There would be such small corps as could be brought to battlefield. Imām Ḥusain rejected the prevalent army systems and traditions. There was also no need of different types of weapons etc. When there would be no big army, then there would be no necessity of collecting heavy amount of food materials. Just a small quantity of food-stuff would do for quenching the thirst and hunger of the few soldiers. These soldiers, the good people in all respects would not come to the war front for any food or weapons etc., but their objective would be re-establishing Islām. Therefore, if it was necessary, the weapons would be of different type, whose names would be the purity of conduct, character and behaviour, piety, holiness and the firmness towards religion, their pure soul would only then be satisfied.

3. No War in Medina or Mecca

If the war happened in Medina or its vicinty, not only its peace would be spoiled, but its glory and prestige would also be tarnished. After sacrificing their own life, there could not be any recognition of the objectives of the Ḥusainī Revolution. This great sacrifice would be suppressed and nipped in the bud. For example what did not happen after the murder of the Caliph III 'U<u>th</u>mān and afterwards? His wife was attacked with deadly weapons. The dead body could not be burried continuously for three days. Leave Islām, it is against even an ordinary human conduct that after the expiry of somebody, his rituals are not allowed to be done.

Comparatively, Mecca could have been more useful and better place. *Ḥajj* time was approaching near. There were more possibilites of informing the people about objectives of rising for Truth and Justice. But at the same time, Imām Ḥusain did not wish to become the base of the prophecy of the Prophet in which he had predicted that the sanctity of Ka'bah would be shattered by a 'sheep' (say a man). Imām Ḥusain could not become that person. Therefore, the war of justice against Yażīd could not be held in Mecca or its vicinty. But for informing people about the objectives of the Ḥusainī Revolution, it was necessary to go to Mecca. Imām Ḥusain resolved, if situation and circumstances were normal, then he would abide by his last *Ḥajj* also.

4. Search for Appropriate Place

There was no appropriate place before Imām Ḥusain duly safe and protected. It was a complicated problem to choose the place, which Imām Ḥusain could prefer for his Revolution's head quarters. Among those the foremost was Mecca, which by itself was a peaceful spot, but Imām Ḥusain could not get an asylum and he had to leave Mecca. The other could be Kufa, towards which he naturally could have kept the eyes. Kufa was the capital of Imām 'Alī. In Kufa there had been population of his faithful followers. But during the reign of Amīr Mu'āwiyah Kufa's Governor Żiyād-bin-Abīh picked out faithful followers of Imām 'Alī one by one and murdered them. Even then, a few people remained there. The third place could be Basra. As compared to Kufa, Basra was safer. Therefore, Imām Ḥusain also sent some letters to Basra people. But the fate had determined already Karbala as the appropriate place for Imām Ḥusain performing his duties, the same remained his destination. It would be discussed in detail in the ensuing chapters.

5. The Battle-Policy

If Ḥusainī *Jihād*'s War-Strategy and his highly planned procedure with the past and the then prevalent in 'Arabian peninsula or the todays' war strategy or procedure, in their types of war strategy, so many differences and changes are visible and marked, like:

(1) Only well trained soldiers were allowed to fight in the war in those days. In the entire Islāmic world these four were considered as the best warriors—Imām Ḥusain himself and his three brothers, Muḥammad Ḥanafiah, Muslim-bin-'Aqīl and 'Abbās-bin-'Alī. Imām Ḥusain brought with him 'Abbās undoubtedly, but left Muḥammad Hanafiah as his representative in Medina. Muslim was sent alone to Kufa, where he was made a martyr. No doubt Imām Ḥusain kept 'Abbās with him; but did not accord permission to him to fight openly till the end.

(2) Three things were necessary in those days for the preparation of the War—Army, Weapons and Foodstuff. If we analyse the preparations of war by Imām Ḥusain, then we come to know that he had neither organised the Army, nor arranged for the Weapons nor accumulated foodstuff. But on the contarary, it was observed that while starting from Mecca, thousands of people gathered together to accompany Imām Ḥusain, but Imām Ḥusain made all of them returned. He did not take them along with him. He kept the number of his soldiers at the bare minimum. But a few distinguished people, who could not be with him for some reasons, were called by him through letters. It is clear from this that Imām Ḥusain did not want to fight with ordinary soldiers, but wanted to come to the battle field with a few special distinguished people, observing them it might

become clear that Imām Ḥusain was not fighting for obtaining Worldly Powers, but for protecting Truth and Justice. He came to the war front with distinguished persons, a few among those people were the distinguished Companions of the Prophet of Islām, a few, the friends of Imām 'Alī. These were so many scholars, saints and reverend persons.

No information at all is available of collecting weapons. It seems that whatever would be the weapons with which Imām Ḥusain wanted to fight in the war, there was no need of prevalant weapons. He used good conduct, integrity, sagacity, knowledge, religious duty etc., as weapons. He raised weapons of good conduct against corruption of integrity, against disbelief of sagacity, against lust and luxury, against dishonour to God of meditation and prayer, against ignorance of knowledge, against injustice by justice and against dutylessness by duty-fulness and he fought only on this basis.

There was no possibility of foodstuff being collected. But history is the witness that whatever foodstuff was available with Imām Ḥusain, he gave away as a hospitable gesture to Yażīdī soldiers, who were very hungry, but the Yażīdī Army as a revenge gave him only this that water was stopped for three days to Imām Ḥusain and his companions. Ḥusainī soldiers got only thirst and hunger as food-materials.

(3) In those days fighting used to take palce in a war between two soldiers. The holy Prophets Tradition was that in a war they used to keep their family-members and relatives in the forefront. They only would reply to the challenge and risk their life, Companions of the Islāmic Prophet would be behind him for offering any assistance and help and they would also follow their own war duty with more sincerity. Therefore, in no war objection could ever be raised that the family-members and relatives of the Prophet escaped and the Companions were murdered. Who ever went to the battlefield, was aware that death was his fortune. He had to sacrifice own life. Who would offer his life and when, was a different matter. The holy associates of Imām Ḥusain and Prophet's family-members might become martyrs. They showed it by their doing that on their being alive there could be no impact or problem to anyone of the family-members of the holy Prophet. The situation was quite clear, whoever live for a longer time would face miseries and sadness for a longer time, the sadness of loosing

companions, the agony of hunger, thirst, physical and mental tortures etc. Therefore, Imām Ḥusain also offered them a chance to become martyrs earlier, so that, there would be an end to their difficulties and miseries at the earliest. Imām Ḥusain came to the war-front at the last, he continued to face the miseries of all types, he was going on fighting a new war each and every time; fighting for the dead body of his relatives, friends, family-members, elders, youngsters, babies etc, after their expiry. After fighting 72 battles, the sadness, loosing their companions in hunger, thirst mental and physical tortures and above all this worry that what would happen to the surviving ladies, babies etc. after him; whether he would get strain or not from this time of sadness and if at all it would be available, then when.

6. The Perspective of Ḥusainī *Jihād*

It is essential to pay attention to the following facts to be acquainted with the perspective of Ḥusainī *Jihād*:

(1) There are so many levels or standards of *Jihād*. Firstly, towards one's own inner soul, which may be developed on pure and spiritual bases. To struggle to established justice in the community and society. In the same manner there can be so many standards, in which undertaking *Jihād* may be inevitable. But no place for violence. There is clear of order of the Qur'an:

> "No compulsion be in religion." (*Qur'an*: 2/256)

But, if unruly elements oppose, then the Qur'an says:

> "Sedition and persecution is worse than killing." (*Qur'an*: 2/191)

Then not only the permission for the use of force for suppression of mutiny or opposition, but also murdering itself is justifiable. The Qur'an orders:

> "And fight them on until there is no more persecution and religion be only for God, but if they cease, then there should be no hostility save against the aggressors." (*Qur'an* 2/193)

Ḥusainī *Jihād* was established on the basis the orders of the Qur'an.

Before coming to Karbala, Imām Ḥusain had been engaged in *Jihād* for the uplift of the people, society and the entire humanity. While presenting his life it would be discussed at the appropriate place. Here struggle for the suppression of opposition towards people, society and humanity would be discussed.

(2) It becomes clear when the Islāmic history is perused that two types of *Jihād* took place in Islām. One, *Jihād* during the life-time of the holy Prophet, whose objective was to defend Islām from the attacks of its enemies and to maintain the newly formed Islāmic State.[57] The total number of these types of battles in 66, out of which in 28 wars the holy Prophet himself participated, which are called *Ghaẓwah* in Islāmic terminology. In the remaining 38 battles Islāmic Prophet did not participate which are called *Siryah*. These wars were held for counter defence. The enemies attacked and the Muslims fought to defend. However, in the battles held after the holy Prophet their situation was different. Their objective was the expansion of Islāmic Empire.

Imām Ḥusain's *Jihād* also can be kept in the chain of Islāmic Prophet's wars. Its aim was also to safeguard Islām. The difference is just this much that the holy Prophet had to fight with those *Kāfirs* (Infidels, apostate) who were out of the periphery of Islām. Imām Ḥusain had to fight with psedo-Muslims who called themselves as Muslims, but they were inferior even than the *Kāfirs* by their conduct and behaviour.

(3) The soldiers, along with Imām Ḥusain performed *Jihād*, were representing various categories, regions and communities. All of them were dignified and absolutely pious that no body could raise finger at them on any account. Imām Ḥusain was himself the specimen of the holy Prophet, the appearance of 'Abbās 'Alī, on looking 'Alī Akbar the appearance of the holy Prophet would come before one's own eyes, Companions of the holy Prophet, Followers of Imām 'Alī, so many Scholars, Saints and reverend persons; and all were high warriors.

Notes and References

1. al-Irshād fī Ma'rifat Ḥujjāj Allāh 'Alā 'Ibād, p. 192.
2. Shahīd-i-Insāniyat, p. 112.
3. Nahju'l-Balāghah, vol. 1, p. 78; al-Akhbāru'ṭ Ṭawāl, p. 214.
4. Nahju'l-Balāghah, vol. 1, p. 205; al-Irshād fī Ma'rifat Ḥujjāj Allāh 'Alā 'Ibād, p.164.
5. Nahju'l-Balāghah, vol. 1, p. 72; al-Irshād fī Ma'rifat Ḥujjāj Allāh 'Alā 'Ibād, p. 148.

6. Nahju'l-Balāghah, vol. 1, p. 205; al-Irshād fī Ma'rifat Ḥujjāj Allāh 'Alā'Ibād, p. 164.
7. Tārīkhu'r-Rusūl wa'l-Mulūk, vol. 6, p. 92.
8. Jām'au'ṣ-Ṣaḥīḥu'l –Bukhārī, vol. 2, p. 71; al-Irshād fī Ma'rifat Ḥujjāj Allāh 'Alā 'Ibād, p. 195.
9. Jām'au'ṣ-Ṣaḥīḥu'l-Bukhārī, vol. 1, p. 69.
10. Jām'au'ṣ-Ṣaḥīḥu'l –Bukhārī, vol. 2, p. 255 tr. no. 927.
11. Jām'au'ṣ-Ṣaḥīḥu'l –Bukhārī, vol. 2, p. 255, tr. no. 930.
12. Usadu'l Ghābah fī Muā'rifu'l Ṣaḥābah, vol. 2, p. 13.
13. Tārīkhu'r-Rusūl wa'l-Mulūk, vol. 6, p. 97; aṣ-Ṣawa 'qu'l-Muḥriqah fī'r-radd 'alā Ahlı'l Rafz wa'l Zanadiqah, p. 81; Bihāru'l-Anwār, vol. 10, pp. 237-39.
14. Bihāru'l-Anwār, vol. 10, p. 237.
15. Tārīkhu'r-Rusūl wa'l-Mulūk, vol. 6, p. 126.
16. Tārīkhu'r-Rusūl wa'l-Mulūk, vol. 6, p. 164.
17. Tārīkhu'r-Rusūl wa'l-Mulūk, vol. 3, p. 240.
18. al-Bidāyah w'an-Nihāyah, vol. 8, p. 52; Usadu'l Ghābah fī Muā'rifu'l Ṣaḥābah, vol. 1, p. 846, at-Tārīkh: al-Yā'qūbī, vol. 2, p. 200.
19. Muḥarram Nāmah, p. 174.
20. Muwaddatu'l-Qurbā, p. 37.
21. Khilāfat-o-Mulūkiyat, p. 162.
22. al-Irshād fī Ma'rifat Ḥujjāj Allāh 'Alā 'Ibād, p. 196.
23. al-Akhbāru'ṭ Ṭawāl, p. 222.
24. An Historical Atlas of Islām, Leiden, 1991.
25. as-Sunan: Abū Dāwūd tr. no. 17; Jām'au'ṣ-Ṣaḥīḥu't-Tirmiżī tr. no. 12.
26. as-Sunan: Abū Dāwūd tr. no. 17; Jām'au'ṣ-Ṣaḥīḥu't-Tirmiżī tr. no. 12.
27. al-Iṣābah fī Tamayyażu'ṣ-Ṣaḥābah, vol. 1, p. 68; Usadu'l Ghābah fī Muā'rifu'l Ṣaḥābah, vol. 1, p. 123; Kanżu'l-'Ummāl-fī-Sunnau'l-Aqwāl-w'al-Alfāẓ, vol. 6, p. 223; Żakhayiru'l-'Uqbā, p. 146.
28. Shahīd-i-Insāniyat, p. 110.
29. al-Irshād fī Ma'rifat Ḥujjāj Allāh 'Alā 'Ibād, p. 196.
30. al-Akhbāru'ṭ Ṭawāl, p. 222.
31. Tārīkhu'r-Rusūl wa'l-Mulūk, vol. 6, pp. 143-48.
32. al-Irshād fī Ma'rifat Ḥujjāj Allāh 'Alā 'Ibād, p. 206; Bihāru'l-Anwār, vol. 1/2, p. 144.
33. Shahīd-i-Insāniyat, p. 218.
34. Bihāru'l-Anwār, vol. 10, p. 237.
35. Shahīd-i-Fāteḥ, p. 169.
36. Ṣahīfah-i-Nūr, vol. 20, p. 190.
37. Luhūf 'Alā Qatlu'l Ṭafūf.
38. *There is some difference of opinion about the pronunciation of the name and probably the pronunciation adopted by me is more acceptable.*

    –Author
39. Tārīkhu'r-Rusūl wa'l-Mulūk, vol. 6, p. 228.

40. al-Irshād fī Ma'rifat Ḥujjāj Allāh 'Alā 'Ibād, pp 235-36; Tārīkhu'r-Rusūl wa'l-Mulūk, vol. 6, p. 228.
41. al-Irshād fī Ma'rifat Ḥujjāj Allāh 'Alā'Ibād, p. 236; Tārīkhu'r-Rusūl wa'l-Mulūk, vol. 6, p. 229.
42. Tārīkhu'r-Rusūl wa'l-Mulūk, vol. 6, p. 228.
43. Tārīkhu'r-Rusūl wa'l-Mulūk, vol. 6, p. 228.
44. al-Durru'l-Manthūr fī'l-Tafsīr bi'l Māthūr, vol. 4, p. 371.
45. Tarjima-i-Kalām-i-Ilāhī, p. 792.
46. Tarjima-i-Kalām-i-Ilāhī, p. 804.
47. Muwaddatu'l-Qurbā, p. 113.
48. al-Akhbāru'ṭ Ṭawāl, p. 261.
49. For detailed study of the issue the other works may be useful such as—Qaul-i-Sadīd: Ziyā Aḥamd Badāyūnī, Falsafa-i-Shahādat-i-Ḥusain: Saiyed Ṭāhiru'l Qādirī, Shahīd-i-Karbala Aur Yażīd: Muḥammad Ṭaiyab, Imām-i-Pāk Aur Yażīd-i-Palīd: Muḥammad Shafī'a, Shahādat-i-Ḥusain and *Khilāfat-o-Mulūkiyat:* Abu'l 'Olā Maudūdī etc.
50. *al-Naṣāehu'l Kāfiyah*, p. 93.
51. *Sharhu 'l Nahju'l-Balāghah,* vol. 1, p. 360.
52. *A Short History of the Saracens,* p. 89.
53. *Jām'au'ṣ-Ṣaḥīḥu'l –Bukhārī*, vol. 3, p. 434, tr. 1985.
54. Sīrat Rasūlu'llāh: Ibn Hishām, vol. 1, p. 89.
55. al-Kāmil fī't-Tārīkh, Vol. 3, p. 46; al-Isti'āb fi Mā'rifatu'l-Aṣḥāb, vol. 4, pp. 76-77.
56. al-Akhbāru'ṭ Ṭawāl, p. 258
57. Islām-Nāmah, p. 82.

Chapter: Four

Medina to Karbala

For knowing the Ḥusainī Revolution, the role and sequence of some 'Arabian towns is indispensable, they are Mecca, Kufa and Karbala. Damascus has also its own impotence, which would be discussed at the appropriate place. The present chapter deals with the discussion of Medina at the out-set, which is the birth-place of Imām Ḥusain. From there Imām Ḥusain started his journey to Mecca, a very sacred land, Godly, safe belt of the earth. But the enemies had conspired to murder Imām Ḥusain in Mecca itself, which failed due to strategical planning of Imām Ḥusain, as he made departure from Mecca before his known schedule. The incidents of Medina and Mecca were faced by Imām Ḥusain himself. Imām could not go to Kufa, but he had sent his younger brother-in-law Muslim-bin-'Aqīl as his peace-envoy, who was murdered there along with his supporters. Appropriate discussion has been made in the present chapter regarding the departure of Imām Ḥusain from Mecca, his travel between Mecca and Karbala, the arrival of Imām Ḥusain at Karbala. In a way, the present chapter presents a detailed background of the Battle of Karbala.

In the present chapter, a few facts have been put up as a result of intense research, objective and neutral study, I feel that with the detailed study, new paths of research will emerge in future from my humble submissions. There are so many aspects of geographical, historical, political, archaeological and religious importance, which are still to be explored. My humble submission is limited to the following materials and information:

1. Political Map of the most wide and powerful Muslim Empire of the world at that time (680 AD) against whom Imām Ḥusain fought in the Battle of Karbala[1] (Figure 1)

2. The Map of the Routs of the Journey:
   (i) Imām Ḥusain's Journey from Medina to Karbala *via* Mecca.
   (ii) The rout from Karbala to Damascus *via* Kufa, through which the Captives of the family of the holy Prophet passed, after the martyrdom of Imām Ḥusain.
   (iii) The rout from Damascus to Medina *via* Karbala, through which the family of the holy Prophet passed, after being freed from the prison. (Figure 2)
3. The Battle of Karbala: An Imaginative Painting. (Figure 3).
4. The holy Tomb of Imām Ḥusain at Karbala (Iraq) (Figure 4).
5. Distance from one place to another of the above discussed places. How much time the travel took. The usual travel time of that time. At what place Imām Ḥusain travelled. At what place Yażīd army travelled, while taking the Captives of the family of the holy Prophet and what was the distance while returning from Medina.
6. Those Halting Places from where Imām Ḥusain passed or encamped and the places through which the Captives of holy family passed.[2]
7. The Speed of Journey has been calculated by this hunble author on the basis of various travel accounts of ancient 'Arabian peninsula. Such as; At what speed the messenger brought the information of the expiry of Amīr Mu'āwiyah came to Medina or at what speed the messenger went back and at what speed he went from Kufa to Damascus and came back.
8. Prescription of Dates—a few dates are decided and prevalent, there is no confusion about them, but there are so many such dates that either there is no information about them or there are confusion in them. After due research, this Author has submitted the specification of correct dates and also Christian era dates thereof.

Medina, the Motherland

Imām Ḥusain was peaceful at home with the soil of his mother and Medina, its water, greenery, beautiful, date trees all in pure atmosphere. Here the inhabitant feels peace, purity, sacredness, and holiness. Presently known as *Madīnatu'n Nabī*, (Town of the Prophet), it is an important town of 'Arabian peninsula. This town was free from all

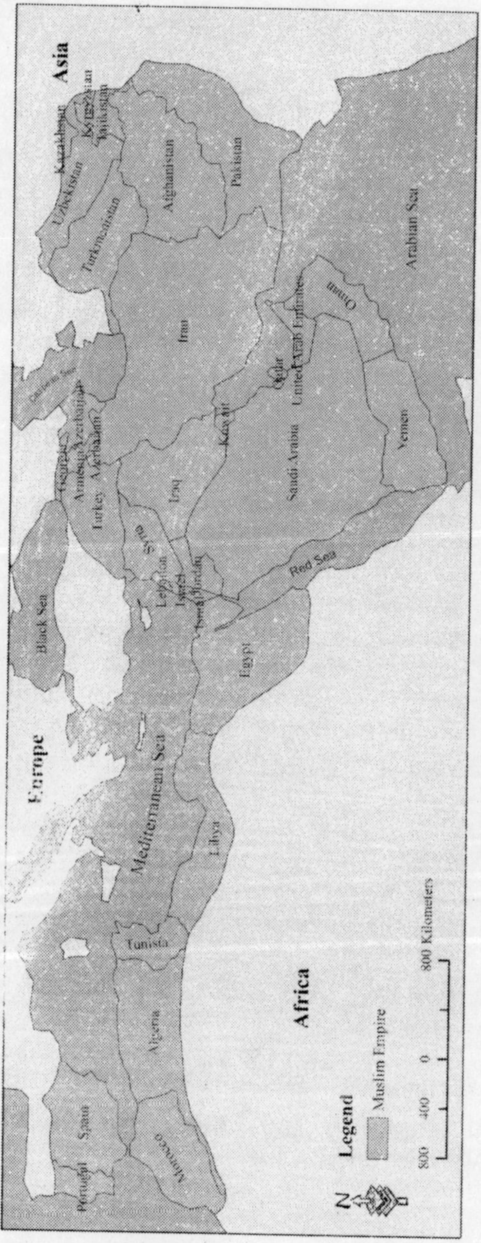

Fig. 1: The Muslim Empire in 680 AD

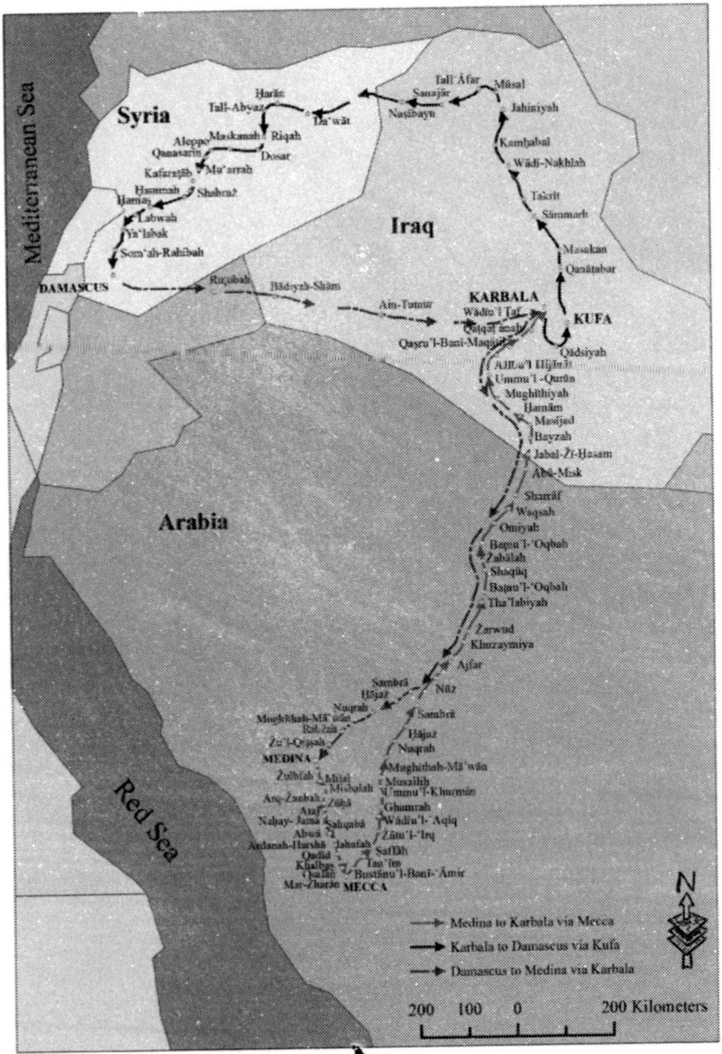

Fig. 2: Routes of the Journey

Courtesy: Prof. Harikesh N. Misra, Ex-Head, Department of Geography, University of Allahabad (India)

Fig. 3: Battle of Karbala

Courtesy: Ms. Javedan Reza, Senior Research Fellow, Department of Visual Art, University of Allahabad (India).

Fig. 4: The Tomb of Imām Ḥusain

sorts of pollution. Previously known as Yat̲h̲rib, when the Prophet migrated here in 622 AD the Yat̲h̲rib became *Madīnatu'r Rasūl* (Town of the Prophet). It has been considered the second holy pilgrim centre after Mecca. The holy Prophet has built with his own hands a mosque, which is famous with the name of *Masjidu'n-Nabavī* (Aspostle's Mosque). There are so many Traditions of the holy Prophet of Islām in praise of Medina. Only 27 verses among them are mentioned in *Jām'au'ṣ-Ṣaḥīḥu'l-Buk̲h̲ārī* itself.[3] The holy Prophet himself has explained the specialities of Medina in them. Like, from a particular place of Medina to a particular place, its respect is like *Ḥaram* (Ka'bah). It is a peaceful place. No harm can be made to anyone, after reaching there. It is absolutely protected. If you observe deers grazing in Medina, don't provoke them, never, never. If a person harms Medina people, will be dissolved in Hell just like salt in water etc. Remains of the predecessors of Imām Ḥusain are in Medina. There are graves of his grandfather, the holy Prophet Muḥammad, mother Fāṭimah Żahrā and elder brother Imām Ḥasan. Imām Ḥusain used to go to these graves daily, recite the holy Qur'an, spend some time, to get mental and spiritual peace. The heart wishes to have its own grave here, mingle with the soil. But having his responsibility as the Imām, the religious leader, has to fulfil his duties. God has already prescribed his foremost duty:

> "Those, if We establish them in the earth, will establish prayer and pay the poor-rate and enjoin good and forbid evil; and up to God (*alone*) is the sequel of (*all*) affairs." (*Qur'an*: 22/41)

It was a must. War was indespensable for that. Imām Ḥusain did not want to spoil the sanctity of Medina. Even an ordinary student of history is familiar well with it, that there would be an attack certainly on the sanctity of Medina. How the enemies of Islām could allow the people of Medina to lead a peaceful life. It is only Medina the last place of asylum of Islām. For destroying it Yażīd's grandfather Abū Sufyyān was attacking frequently why not his grandson Yażīd would smash it totally. But Imām Ḥusain would not take upon himself the blame of desecration and destruction of Medina. Therefore, with a heavy heart would leave Medina for good. Whatever sorrows he had to bear, his heart might be full of problems and difficulties still he would remain outside Medina, would strive hard till his last breath to establish the religion of Islām – enjoin the good and forbid evil.

In fact Imām Ḥusain assessed the condition of the Islāmic society at the time, and came to the conclusion that the Muslims had deviated so much that their reformation and the removal of the dangerous social evils were not possible without such a rising and such a sacred movement. Imām Ḥusain was feeling that the religion of Islām and the Muslim Ummah could not survive without a rising for the Truth and Justice. It was, therefore, inevitable for him to invite the attention of the Muslim Ummah to the disgraceful state of affairs of that time, and save the Muslims for ever from the danger of death and extinction, might keep alive the sacred movement, which existed since the time prior to Imām Ḥusain, and might pave the path for such sacred movements in future.

The time for such a rising for Islām has come. Amīr Mu'āwiyah expired on 22 Rajab, 60 AH / 30 March, 680 AD.[4] With his disturbed deluged eyes, he expected his son Yażīd would be near his death bed. But his heir Yażīd was away from Damascus, fully engrossed in luxurious life and entertainments. Amīr Mu'āwiyah told his officers Zaḥāk-bin-Qays Faḥrī and Muslim-bin-'Oqbah that whenever Yażīd would come, to tell him, his will that it was his order that he should behave kindly with the people of Medina. Whoever went from there to Damascus, should be honoured and those, who belong to high class and elders, who were away from there, should also be taken care of. Syrian people should be helpful with strength of their eyes and ears. They may not be allowed to remain outside for a long times. So, that the life of those places may not have influence upon them. He also asked to tell him after that Mu'āwiyah was afraid just with four person against him. Firstly, Ḥusain-bin-'Alī, secondly, 'Abdu'llāh-bin-'Omar, thirdly, 'Abdu'r-Raḥmān-bin-Abū Bakr and forthly, 'Abdu'llāh-bin-Żubayr.[5]

Amīr Mu'āwiyah had also made separate instructions regarding these four persons—Ibn-'Omar would accept your ruling power in the end. Ḥusain-Ibn-'Alī is a person of simple and straight farward nature. But Iraq people would provoke him, certainly, against you. Therefore, even if Ḥusain-Ibn-'Alī attacks and if Yażīd wins, then pardon him. They have bigger right and he is the heir of *Rasūl Allāh.* However, Ibn-Abū Bakr has no wisdom of his own, what ever his friends say, he would do the same. If he has any courage, he is coward like women. Yes, whoever attacks you, like a lion and does fraud like a fox and whenever occasion comes, certainly, would do, he is Ibn-Żubayr. Therefore, if he does like that, then you be with him and cut his hands and legs.[6]

Every student of history knows that 'Abdu'r-Raḥmān-bin-Abū Bakr already died seven years before in 53 AH (610 AD).[7] It clears that till then Mu'āwiyah's connection had brocken with the family of Caliph I

Abū Bakr to the extent that he was not aware of the death of 'Abdu'r-Raḥmān-bin-Abū Bakr, even after a lapse of seven years.

Mu'āwiyah, literally means fox, which is synonym of cheat, clever and selfish. It is not necessary for a name always to reflect its qualities, but exceptions make the formula. Our learned readers are fully aware of his inherent qualities. As a clever politician he wished to give a line of action to his son Yażīd. No doubt if Yażīd had followed the instructions of his father, possibly the Battle of Karbala could not have happened and Yażīd could be saved from present accursed position in the Islāmic history.

As soon as Yażīd got the message of the death of his father, he rushed to Damascus for occupying the throne. He was informed of the will of his father, Amīr Mu'āwiyah. He was a completely spoiled wicked youth, drenched intoxicated, voluptuous, busy with sexual activities day and night. Yażīd took the will of his father in a reverse spirit. His experienced father has given the tips how to deal with impotant persons. Yażīd viewed, those persons as his enemies, who should not be allowed to live for a moment. They were the persons who made his father sad, certainly, He would take revenge from them. Proud of strength, arrogance of ruling power of very wide kingdom, surrounded by flames of ignorance, blank in polity, Yażīd made his aim that somehow all these people should be made under his control. He immediately passed orders to his cousin-brother and Medina's Governor Walīd-bin-'Otbah:

> "Insist upon Ḥusain-bin-'Alī, 'Abdu'llāh-bin-'Omar and 'Abdu'llāh-bin-Żubayr to do *Bay'at* (Oath of Allegiance) and don't give even a fraction of time for *Bay'at*."[8]

Medina's Governor Walīd-bin-'Otbah got the orders of Yażīd, became frightened, because, he was aware of its terrific results. He consulted Marwān-bin-Ḥakam, the man, who along with his father Ḥakam was exiled for their mischievous deeds from Medina by the holy Prophet and Caliph I and Caliph II 'Omar had continued their exile. Marwān was a dead enemy of Prophet and his family. He advised that he should not delay in implementing the orders of Yażīd, immediately contact Ḥusain and get *Bay'at* from him. Walīd-bin-'Otbah send his messenger to Imām Ḥusain, who was praying in the *Masjidu'n-Nabvī* at that time. This incident happened on 26 Rajab, 60 AH / 2 May, 680 AD.[9]

Imām Ḥusain silently set out to Governor's palace from Mosque. The family members residing at Medina got the information and ran with their weapons to save him and appealed, not go alone and told that they would also go along with him. Imām Ḥusain's reply was, not to be impatient. His going alone would be better. When the request of family members increased, he convinced them, that it was good for them to accompany, but they must stop out side the Governor's palace. If need arrise for him, he would call them. Imām Ḥusain went before the Governor, who informed about the death of Amīr Mu'āwiyah. Imām Ḥusain expressed the usual formalities prevalent at anybody's death, the Verse to be read on this occasion:

> "Verily we are God's and verily unto Him shall we return."
> (*Qur'an*: 2/156)

Imām Ḥusain recited the above verse and behaved very decently. The Governor Walīd put up the order of Yaẓīd before him. Imām Ḥusain replied that it could not be advantageous to him making his *Bay'at* stealthily and asked to put up his proposal before all in the *Masjidu'n-Nabvī*. Imām Ḥusain would also placc his views. Walīd said that it was a good proposal, again come at that time and he would place the proposal of Yaẓīd's *Bay'at* before all. Marwān-bin-Ḥakam objected and warned, 'O Walīd ! with what a bad mind you are puting the order of Yaẓīd, if Ḥusain could be missed from your hand just now, you would never be able to get Yaẓīd's *Bay'at* from him. It would be appropriate either Ḥusain does the *Bay'at* of Yaẓīd now, or cut his head and send it to Damascus. No sooner did he say this, Imām Ḥusain absolutely warned him, saying, how can he dare cut his head. As his voice raised all his family members entered in side the palace and took Imām Ḥusain with them safely.

Till then there was only a demand of *Bay'at* of Yaẓīd, there was no order of cutting and sending his head to Damascus, but Yaẓīd in his an other order to Medina's Governor was clear:

> "Along with the reply of your letter Ḥusain-bin-'Alī's head may be send."[10]

Before this sever order could be implemented, and Walīd could show courage, Imām Ḥusain had already left Medina before obtaining the letter itself.[11] Among other four names mentioned by Amīr Mu'āwiyah in his dying will, as discussed above, 'Abdu'r-Raḥmān-bin-Abū Bakr had already died. The case of 'Abdu'llāh-bin-'Omar has been quite complicated one. Two types of informations are available regarding him. Firstly, he did the *Bay'at* of Yaẓīd forthwith. Secondly, he evaded at that time and said that he was with him, and requested take the *Bay'at* from others. After the Battle of Karbala, he immediately did Yażīd's *Bay'at*. 'Abdu'llāh-bin-Żubayr exhibited cleverness. When Medina's Governor Walīd called him, he disappeared and escaped to Mecca in the night, hoping Mecca would be favourable for becoming Caliph there.

Imām Ḥusain remained in Medina for all the three nights even after that incident. How painfully his time would have been passed, it is beyond the limits of imagination.[12] He did not have the mind of leaving Medina, but in Medina, peace could be available only by sacrificing his own principles and ideals. If he did *Jihād* staying in Medina, it would effect the peace and happiness of Medina. Keeping in view the safety of Medina, the holy Prophet waged all the wars only outside Medina. He could not break this Tradition, therefore, he had to come outside Medina. To emerge from the hardships of this mental journey, Imām Ḥusain used to spend most of his time in the prayer at the holy grave of the holy Prophet. He would be engaged in the Prayer and reciting the Qur'an. In Medina he spent his last night at the graves of his mother Fāṭimah aż-Żahrah and his brother Imām Ḥasan.[13]

Prior to declaring his ultimate decision Imām Ḥusain consulted his younger brother Muḥammad-bin-Ḥanafiyah.[14] His opinion was that he should proceed towards holy Mecca. If Meccan people did not behave well, then go to Yemen, where in a large number of his and *Ahlu'l-Bayt's* followers live. If the situation there too, was not conducive, then to any hilly area and go on moving from one town to the other town. Imām Ḥusain felt his suggestion as appropriate. Afterwards, making Muḥammad-bin-Ḥanafiyah his working representative, left him in Medina and along with offered him a written will also, where in Imām Ḥusain has clearly discussed in clear words his objectives:

> "My aim is to bring reform in Muslims. I may send the message to follow the prescribed norms, to enjoin good commitment to enjoin good and forbid evils Whoever accept my message, making his life as ideal as my grandfather Prophet's and my father 'Alī's life, God would reward them and whoever redicule, I would be contented, until God does not pass the orders on the truth myself and himselves and God's order is sole and final. 'O brother! This is my work and except God, no body can offer any sort of opportunity and same only repeating."[15]

Muḥammad-bin-Ḥanafiyah further suggested that Imām Ḥusain

might go out of Medina along with a few select family members and not with ladies and children. They may be left in Medina itself, he would take care of them. Imām Ḥusain did not agree with this proposal. Imām Ḥusain was aware that whatever would happen in future, concrete proof would be required for that. If the ladies and children were not along with him, then there would be nobody, to present the facts in detail of the events. Ruling group's paid historians would write, whatever come to their mind, following the whims and fancies of the rulers. Nobody would be there to catch hold of their hands. Condemnable versions of distorted facts produced by them, with their connivance would be available as powerful authentic proof. The scholars and well-wishers were the problems of that time before Muḥammad-bin-Ḥanafiyah, but Imām Ḥusain was successfully visualising the very far off situations. Today there is no need to tell how much foreseeing, objective and practical was the decision of Imām Ḥusain.

After this Imām Ḥusain met his grandmother *Ummu'l Mūminīn* Umm Salmah, wife of the holy Prophet. He apprised her of his views. This is the belief that the holy Prophet had already informed her of the Battle of Karbala and offered the soil of the place also, wherein Imām Ḥusain was to be martyred, and told, when Imām Ḥusain would be assasinated, the very soil would become red in colour. It is said that as per the prophecy of the holy Prophet the said soil became red after Imām Ḥusain's martyrdom.[16] It is a matter of religious recognition and belief. These type of matters are available in all religions.

Departure from Medina

After consultations about various aspects Imām Ḥusain set out of Medina on the 28th Rajab, 60 AH/ 4th May, 680 AD.[17] To accompany him in the very difficult and important travel, Imām Ḥusain took his clan Hāshimites' some very important and selected persons along with him, in which babies, children, youths, ladies and elders were included. The speciality was, he took all the people of the lineage of Abū Ṭālib, (his grandfather and Imām 'Alī's father) in which Imām Ḥusain's two sisters Żainab and Umm Kulthūm were also included. All brothers, nephews and others related to them, besides a few exceptions like Muḥammad-bin-Ḥanafiyah, who was left in Medina as his representative, his aunt Umm Hānī, who was so old that she could not move. His ailing daughter Fāṭimah Ṣughrā, and to look after her. He also left Ummu'l Banīn (literally means, the mother of sons) who was proud mother of Abu'l-Faẓl'il-'Abbās-bin-Imām'Alī, the Commandor-in-Chief at the Battle of

Karbala. Her four sons had also attained martyrdom at the Battle of Karbala. It seems strange the absence of Imām Ḥusain's brother-in-law 'Abdu'llāh-bin-Ja'far. He was not in favour of the decision of Imām Ḥusain for leaving Medina and he had continued pursuation to influence his views. Imām Ḥusain had left him in Medina itself. But his wife Żainab, also known as *S̲harīkatu'l Ḥusain* (Husain's Associate) was the lady-leader of the Caravan. It is surprising to note that except the persons from the family tree of Abū Tālib, others of his clan Hās̲himites are missing. Among the people outside his clan, was Naṣar-bin-Abī Nīżar, who was very close associate to the family. In the same way, Prophet's famous Companion Abūžar G̲haffārī's servant Jaun, after the demise of his master, continued to live in his family and his son. 'Aun was along with him. Similarly, Ḥārit̲h-bin-Nibhān (Prophet's uncle Ḥamżah-bin-'Abdu'l-Maṭṭalib's servant), who after him was at the service of the holy Prophet, was with his family members and his son Sa'd. Munjiḥ-bin-Sahm, whose mother was Imām Żainu'l-Ābidīn's servant, he was with his mother. 'Oqbah-bin-Sama'n, who was Imām Ḥusain's wife Umm Rabāb's servant. Turkish servant of Imām Ḥusain, Qārib-bin-'Abdu'llāh had accompanied him naturally. It is clear from his taking along with him his family members and their related people that Imām Ḥusain was not going to conquer and subdue some particular tract of land.

The distance of Mecca from Medina is 210 miles (338 km) in between there are 14 important places:

> Medina → Žūḥabfah → Milal → Misbalah → 'Arq-Ẓanbah → Żūḥā'→ 'Araj → Naḥay-Jamal → Sahqabā → Abwā' → Kardanah-Hars̲hā → Jaḥafah → Qadīd → K̲halbaṣ → 'Osafān → Mar-Żaharān → Mecca.

It is difficult to say what are the places where Imām Ḥusain took rest, but in view of the duration of his journey of five days, the speed of the travel normally would be 210 miles in five days. It appears that the journey was comfortable, symbolizing the peaceful mental set-up of Imām Ḥusain. There was no hury for him, slowly and steadily proceeded ahead towards his target. He was travelling very peacefully with tranquillity.[18]

The Days of Asylum in Mecca

Mecca, located in the Ṣirāt Mountains 45 miles (72 km) in land from Red Sea, is the most holy city of Islām. It has been the birth place of the

Prophet Muḥammad. The holy Ka'bah is also situated here and is religious centre to which Muslims come for a pilgrimage, or *Hajj*, during their lifetime. Mecca surrounds al-Ḥaram Mosque and the sacred well Žamžam is in the precincts of the holy Ka'bah. As per Traditions, the holy Ka'bah is a replica of God's house in Heaven, built by the Prophet Ibrāhīm (*Abraham*), and his son the Prophet Ismāīl (*Ishmael*). Every Muslim steadfast in prayer five times a day faces Ka'bah.

Mecca was the place from where the holy Prophet Muḥammad began to throw his heart and soul to preaching the Truth in the public, which was vehemently opposed by Meccans Quraysh clan, under the leadership of Abū Sufyyān and his son Mu'āwiyah. Now, the history has began repeating the incidents. In place of Prophet Muḥammad was his grandson Imām Ḥusain and in his opposion was Yažīd, the son of Mu'āwiyah and grandson of Abū Sufyyān.

Amīr Mu'āwiyah and his father Abū Sufyyān had made difficult the very life of the holy Prophet of Islām, Muḥammad. Therefore, he had to emigrate from Mecca in 622 AD. Muslims became victorious over Mecca in 630 AD. Thus, Prophet Muḥammad entered the city of Mecca, which had so cruelly ill-teated him. They had lay now completely at his mercy. But in such hours of triumph their evils, which the holy Prophet Muḥammad and his family and companions had suffered, were forgotten, every injury inflicted was forgiven, he proclaimed general amnesty, pardoned all the enemies. All sorts of safety and security was assured after coming within the precincts of holy Ka'bah. The holy Ka'bah was declared a tranquil safe and peaceful place, irrespective of caste, creed and religion. Totally secured. Even a leaf cannot be plucked in the holy Ka'bah's limits. The holy Prophet of Islām declared after the victory of Mecca:

> "O' my dear people! No doubt when God made the sky and the earth and on the same day prohibited bloodshed and war in Mecca. It would remain normal as such till the day of *Qiyāmah* (Catastrophe). Any person who brings honesty on the day of deletion, there is no permission that he may do any bloodshed and uproot any greeny-plants, everybody is prohibited to do any hostility before myself and after myself."[19]

Just giving the message not to be emotional at the time of victory, the holy Prophet had dismissed Sa'd-bin-'Abādān Anṣārī, Commandor of a Unit, because he had theatend the people. [20]

Mecca was very essential place for Imām Ḥusain on personal reasons also. It was the place of birth and the land of deeds of his forefathers. Mecca was also the birth place of all of his glorious family members—his father Imām 'Alī, and his mother Fāṭimah aż-Żahrah. When the Prophet Muḥammad had migrated from Mecca to Medina[21], the other members of the family and the other oppressed Muslims of Mecca also came to Medina and settled there. But their relationship with Mecca continued to remain somehow or other. So many people of different clans were living in Mecca. The Hās̲h̲imites, the most respected clan of Qurays̲h̲, in which Prophet Muḥammad was born, and many people were in Mecca. It was natural that it was only Mecca, which was very highly useful place for Imām Ḥusain after Medina. Imām Ḥusain departed to Mecca from Medina in a very known way. He sacrificed the love of motherland and reached Mecca. Introduced the Muslims with his resolutions.

Imām Ḥusain arrived in Mecca on 3rd S̲h̲'abān 60 AH /04 July, 680 AD.[22] He stayed there in the S̲h̲o'b-'Alī his ancestral house.[23] Of course, in the towmship of the Hās̲h̲imites. The news of his arrival spread on all around very speedly. Imām Ḥusain has refused the *Bay'at* of Yażīd. Yażīd has become Caliph in an unauthorised manner after the demise of Amīr Mu'āwiyah. He was not entitled and deserving for the post of Caliph. He was pressing Imām Ḥusain for his *Bay'at*, to which Imām Ḥusain did not agree. Now, all Muslims should be united under the leadership of Imām Ḥusain, so, they could be liberated from the cluthches of corruption. People, who came to Mecca for 'Omrah, used to meet Imām Ḥusain, make known and and propagate the objectives of Imām Ḥusain among other Muslims.

Imām Ḥusain was having his daily routine in the meditation of the Almighty in Mecca, as he did in Medina. He used to spend most of his time in the prayer of God in Ka'bah, he also met people there. Muslims from various places in large numbers presented themslves to see Imām Ḥusain. They expressed their respects and faith in him. Some people suggested *Jihād* against Yażīd. Imām Ḥusain would hear them patiently and greet them. Steadily, the number of visitors increased like anything, and they would insist upon him for *Jihād* and some of them wanted *Bay'at* at the hands of Imām Ḥusain as Caliph, but he dropped their proposal after persuading them.

It has already been discussed in the above lines that 'Abdu'llāh-bin-Żubayr, had absconded from Medina as soon as there was a demand of *Bay'at* of Yażīdī by the Governor. He disappeared unnoticed from Medina, made his centre in Mecca. 'Abdu'llāh-bin-Żubayr was in constant touch with the people to accept him as Caliph, by *Bay'at* at his hands. The affair turned just opposite with the arrival of Imām Ḥusain, instead of going to 'Abdu'llāh-bin-Żubayr people were going straight to Imām Ḥusain and were establishing contact with him. Imām Ḥusain's arrival in Mecca disturbed 'Abdu'llāh-bin-Żubayr, because his dream of becoming Caliph came to an end as no one would do *Bay'at* at his hands, when Imām Ḥusain was present there.[24] Understanding the situation, he felt it would be good for him to get catch hold of his associates. Although he was a severely opposed not only against Imām Ḥusain, but also of entire *Ahlu'l-Bayt* (people of the house of the holy Prophet), to the extent that once he gave up the daily Obligatory Prayer, because he had to praise *Ahlu'l-Bayt* in it.[25] But conspiracy was sought this time that go along with Imām Ḥusain. He would be at the service of Imām Ḥusain regularly, some time he would be present continuously for two days and at times once in two days, but would exhibit his regards towards Imām Ḥusain as soon as he came.[26] 'Abdu'llāh-bin-'Omar also met Imām Ḥusain in Mecca but as a well wisher of Yażīd, his objective was to convince Imām Ḥusain for *Bay'at*. He requested Imām Ḥusain, to compromise with the present Ruler and not to bring into the mind the very thought of war with him.[27]

Imām Ḥusain stayed for about three months in Mecca. *Ramazān*, the holy month also inclusive in it. *Ramazān* is a month of soul-purification, self-accountability of one's doings, good and bad, commitment to enjoin good and forbid evils. He prepares himself in accordance with the desire of Almighty. He has a chance absolutely to train his soul. For Imām Ḥusain the month of *Ramazān* was a special opportunity to attain his objective and convey his message to every individual. Joining Imām Ḥusain in the daily Prayer was the big opportunity to pay respect to the infalliable Imām and a great honour for everyone. Imām Ḥusain used to apprise of the basic objectives of Islām to all Muslims. Its influence came to light in a very positive manner. Imām Ḥusain was not only as a person of contemporary high status, but also a pillar of Islām, his sermons assumed the form of a movement. Muslim in large numbers gathered from all sides in support of Imām Ḥusain. The time of *Ḥajj* was approaching near, Muslims were assembling in large numbers day by day in Mecca. It seemed as if *Ḥajj* has assumed this time some special significance.

Analysing the circumstances and situations, it is quite clear that people were gathering in support of Imām Ḥusain, but Imām Ḥusain's eyes were searching some other people. Basra, Yemamah, Ṭāiyaf and Yemen were such places, where from the people were expected, there would be interest and enthusiasm in them, but everywhere was complete darkness. Only in Kufa, there was a little ray of hope. Imām Ḥusain himself wrote a letter to Basra people. A letter for general people and separate letters by name to Mālik-bin-Sama', Aḥanaf-bin-Qaiys, Mundaz-bin-Jārūd, Masu'd-bin-'Omar and Qaiys-bin-Hishām.

In the mean time Kufa people also wrote letters to Imām Ḥusain. Imām Ḥusain himself closely examined the people, who were available like, Sulayman-bin-Ṣorad Khuzā'ī, Musayyab-bin-Najbah, Rafā'h-bin-Shaddād, 'Abdu'llāh-bin-Wā'l and Ḥabīb-bin-Maẓāhir Asadī. They wrote the letter to Imām Ḥusain on the basis of their religiousness, whose details would be available in the subsequent pages. Besides, from the Kufic people letters also came. From those people, worldly luxury and happiness were before whose eyes. They wanted to fill up their own bags with the help of Imām Ḥusain. About twelve thousand letters of this type were collected slowly and steadily. Imām Ḥusain could have negated the people loving luxuorious pleasures, but could not negate those people, as they had invited Imām Ḥusain to attend gathering in the name of Truth. But the way Kufic people had cheated previously, in view of that, it was rather difficult to believe them straightway. Therefore, Imām Ḥusain sent his own cousin and brother-in-law Muslim-bin-'Aqīl to Kufa as his representative and peace-envoy to know correctly about Kufic people. The details would be discussed at the appropriate place.

Imām Ḥusain was in Mecca, so, all the Muslims were assembling in Mecca for performing *Ḥajj*. After getting acquainted with the objectives of Imām Ḥusain, thousands of people expressed their desire to join this war of justice with him, but Imām Ḥusain was not willing to recruit soldiers for a big army, as has already been discussed. Imām Ḥusain suddenly gave up the idea of performing *Ḥajj*, changed it into *'Umra* on the basis of his wise decision and addressed effectively before the companions, which is safe in the history. Vide a portion of it:

> "All praises go to God. He does for us whatever he wishes for and without him there is no power in any other thing. The death is stuck with the throat of Adam's heir, such as neckless at the throat of young girl. Don't ask how much pleasure would you desire to be in front of my predecessors? That much of pleasure as Y'aqūb (*Jacob*) found in meeting with Yūsuf (*Joseph*). My place of death has already been fixed and I would go and remain there. As if I am observing my own closure that in between the desert of Karbala wolves (i.e. Yaẓīdī army) are

> cutting into pieces and filling their empty starved stomach and utensils of food. Whatever day has been already fixed for the death by Nature's pen, there would be no relief at all. The same desire in with *Ahlu'l-Bayt* wherein God's consent may be sought. We are satisfied in the representative and it would provide us the whole rewards as satisfies. Prophets relatives would not be separated from you, but all would be assembled in the Heaven for you, seeing them your eyes would be happier and the holy Prophet would fulfil his promises there. You, please, see, whoever is ready to sacrifice his life with us, and who have already become prepared to sacrifice themselves before the Almighty only then accompany us. If God permits, I shall start tomorrow early in the morning."[28]

As per his decided programme, the same day on 8th Žilḥijjah, 60 AH/9th September, 680 AD in early morning Imām Ḥusain's Caravan came out from Mecca. By chance, on the same date, his representative and peace-envoy Muslim-bin-'Aqīl had to fight in Kufa and on the second day of it, when Muslims was martyred, Imām Ḥusain was proceeding ahead in search of the peace spot.[29] Imām Ḥusain had taken decision in such a way to proceed that people could not guess where he was to go.

Why Imām Ḥusain left Mecca so suddenly remained a mystery. What emerged in the minds of the majority of Muslims was, if that time they joined hands with the grandson of the Prophet, Imām Ḥusain, they would be benefited in both ways, the worldly success in this life as well as reward in the life hereafter. They had seen after the establishment of Caliphate how their people got due and undue benefits. Though it was not true in the case of Imām 'Alī, but the circumstances had changed, Imām Ḥusain saw all and would have understood that Imām 'Alī's polity would not succeed. The people would have to be attracted only through the distribution of wealth. Now, Imām Ḥusain also would distribute his wealth with both of his hands amongst his supporters. Whosoever would help him, was to be at a great advantage. That was the matter of Imām 'Alī, this was different the enlightened era of Imām Ḥusain. But when Imām Ḥusain clarified through his powerful address that his objective was to enjoin the good and forbid the evil, and he was not going on any victorious journey, wherein there was a possibility of obtaining a wide estate, then most of the people accompanying with great enthusiasm, estimated sixty thousand, being greeted by misfortune, dejectedly separated themselves and ran away raising dust by the hoofs of their horses, left with the same speed as had joined the Caravan. When dust settled down, a few persons were standing like a rock, who later on sacrified their lives for the sake of Truth. Just those enlightened people from Mecca, who could join Imām Ḥusain, were—'Abdu'l Raḥmān-bin-'Abd Rab Anṣarī Khiżarajjī, Jinādah-bin-K'ab-bin-Ḥārith Anṣārī Khiżarajjī, and his sons 'Omarū, 'Ābis-bin-Abī Shabīb Shākirī, and his servant Shożab-bin-'Abdu'llāh, Żāhir ('Omarū'l Ḥamaq's servant), Żāhar-bin-'Omarū Aslamī Kindī, 'Ammār-bin-Ḥassān-bin-Shurayb Ṭaī and Ḥujjāj-bin-Masrūq Ja'fī. They came to Mecca from Kufa and joined Imām Ḥusain.

Imām Ḥusain's safe exit from Mecca became a challenge for Yażīdī Administration. 'Omar-bin-Ḥujjāj was the Governor of both Mecca and Medina. He was present in Mecca at that time, he sent an army under his brother Yaḥyā-bin-Sa'd for stopping of Imām Ḥusain. This army over took Imām Ḥusain's Caravan near Mecca and Ḥusainī Army could not withstand the attack, therefore, ran away hither thither. Imām Ḥusain's Caravan proceeded further.

Peace-Envoy, Muslim in Kufa

Kufa is one of the major towns of Iraq. 'Arabic *Kūfah*, means the combination of sand and pebbles, which has an indication of the character of Kufic people. Whereas, on one side good people of constructive nature were residing, in between them fraudulant people were also there. There is a valuable role of Kufic people in the Ḥusainī Revolution. It you count the number of martyrs who sacrificed for Truth along with Imām Ḥusain, then you would find most of the people were from Kufa. Kufic people were also in the forefront at the movement for taking revenge of the blood of Imām Ḥusain. But it is also true that most of the soldiers in Yażīdī Army were Kufic people. The answer of this fate can be available in the history.

The establishment of this town was made in 638 AD as military cantonment. As soon as Imām 'Alī became Caliph, Mu'āwiyah-bin-Abū Sufyyān and his men started creating disturbances, because the capital Medina was far away from there and it was difficult to keep the mutiny under control, so Imām 'Alī made Kufa the capital of Islāmic State, which was situated in the midst of the state. Imām 'Alī came to Kufa on 12th Rajab, 36 AH / 7th January, 657 AD. He stayed in an ordinary house, avoided Administer's palace, and continued to stay there itself till the end (28 January, 661 AD). In the meantime the honest followers of the Progeny of the Prophet Muḥammad also came to Kufa and settled there, coming from various places. At a time Kufa was considered to be the place of the followers of Imām 'Alī. After a period of four years six months, Imām 'Alī being martyred, Imām Ḥasan again returned to Medina leaving Kufa under Amīr Mu'āwiyah, and as per orders of Mu'āwiyah large number of followers of Progeny of the Prophet Muḥammad were killed. Their houses were destroyed. In this context, Kufa's Governor Żiyād-bin-Abīh and Samerah-bin-Junadab have already been discussed at the appropriate places. Only a few devotees of Imām 'Alī were left, the remaining people were brought up by Umayyites, who were brought from other places and made to settle.

The knowledge of real facts is possible only when the situations alone under consideration are kept in view. Its first phase was the arrival of Muslims in Kufa and a detailed discussion on the sequence of incidents afterwards has to be done, because what happend in Kufa should be understood as the deciding factor of the sequence of incidents of Karbala. Therefore, knowing its background is essential, with which so many basic questions are connected.

The arrival of Imām Ḥusain in Mecca, the refusal of the *Bay'at* of Yażīd, the assemblage of Muslims in his support etc., were the situations, making followers of Progeny of the Prophet Muḥammad very happy. People assembled in Sulayman-bin-Ṣorad Khuzā'ī's house in Kufa because he alone was the eldest *Ṣaḥābī* (Prophet's Companion), who had seen Islāmic Prophet's eyes and joined Imām 'Alī in *Jihād*. Sulayman spread the information that Imām Ḥusain refused *Bay'at* of Yażīd, came to Mecca leaving Medina. He proclaimed, We are all his and his father's supporters and followers. If you think it correct, and if you are able to be firm in your own promise, let us co-operate with him, do *Jihād* against his enemies and be prepared to sacrifice our life, join him and insist upon to come over here, by writing a letter to him. If you are afraid of your cowardice, then you are making delay being lazy in helping him. Don't cheat him, and don't put his life in risk. All the people who were present there said unanimously, when Imām Ḥusain would come, all of them would be present. They would make *Bay'at*, help and soliditary with him, would pay all honour and struggle against the enemies. Therefore, a letter was writen in favour of Imām Ḥusain on the basis of the decision, as under:

> "This letter is addressed to Imām Ḥusain from Sulayman-bin-Ṣorad Khuzā'ī, Musayyab-bin-Najbah, Rafā'h-bin-Shaddād, 'Abdu'llāh-bin-Wā'l and Ḥabīb-bin-Maẓāhir Asadī....
>
> "We never consider any other person except you as our Imām and Caliph. Reverend sir, kindly pay attention on our insistence, we are all your supporters and followers.

Please do come, so that we may be united over the Truth."[30]

'Abdu'llāh-bin-Sabī'a Hamadānī and 'Abdu'llāh-bin-Wā'l went with this letter and Imām Ḥusain received it at his Mecca residence on 10th Ramazān, 60 AH / 14th June, 680 AD.[31]

Thereafter, the activities increased, 53 requisition-letters were written in between two days. These letters were sent by hand through Qays-bin-Muṣahar Ṣaidāvī, 'Abdu'l Raḥmān-bin-'Abdu'llāh-bin-Kadan Arḥabī and 'Ammār-bin-Ḥassān-bin-Shurayb Ṭaī. With the similar letters Ḥānī-bin-Ḥānī and Sa'īd-bin-'Abdu'llāh Ḥasafī went to Imām Ḥusain.[32]

After this there was a wave in support of Imām Ḥusain in Kufa. Those people, who were in opposite groups till the previous day, joined in support of Imām Ḥusain, they had no attachment with the mission of Imām Ḥusain. They wanted to join his possibility of establishing a new Islāmic State. They wrote to Imām Ḥusain:

> "The fields are fertile, fruits are ripe in the trees and tanks are full of water. Please visit as you wish, towards such an Army, which is presently decorated for you."[33]

Its signatories were famous persons like—Shabth-bin-Raba'ī, Ghurrah-bin-Qays Aḥsami, Khazar-bin-Aljarlra, Yażīd-bin-Ḥārth Ro'm, 'Omar-bin-Ḥujjāj Żubaydī, Muḥammad-bin-'Omayr Tamīmī etc.[34] Letters of support were received continuously. The number of letters increased like anything and they were full of three gunny-bags.[35]

Their different views could be easily seen in these two types of letters. In the letter received from Sulayman-bin-Ṣorad Khuzā'ī and his followers, there was a requisition to provide religious and spiritual leadership. There was no greed of ruling power in it. But the other types of letter written by Shabth-bin-Raba'ī etc., was full of the inspiration for obtaining right in ruling power preposition. Therefore, "the fields are fertile, fruits are ripe in the trees" is nothing but an inducement to come, become the Caliph, as has been the business, pleasures enjoyed after obtaining rights over ruling powers, he was also requested to enjoy, as the companions should get their shares in the pleasures !

Imām Ḥusain was absolutely identifying these greedy corrupt rulers. In spite of obtaining letters continuously in support of him, there was a lack of confidence in Kufic people. The well-wishers of Imām Ḥusain continued to prohibit them from relying on Kufic people, cousin 'Abdu'llāh-bin-'Abbās and the younger brother Muḥammad Ḥanafiya were special among them. Imām Ḥusain objectively considered every aspect. He never depended on or expressed his faith in Kufic people. But as a reply of the argument that Mecca was safer and secured for him, he used to tell in reply that these people would never leave him alive, even if he would hid inside a ditch.[36] However, he replied to 'Abdu'llāh-bin-Żubayr that he was aware of the fact already foretold by the holy Prophet that a *ram* (literally, a sheep; symbolically, a person) would be cause of a bloodshed and on whose account there would be bloodshed, causing dishonour to holy Ka'bah. Imām Ḥusain was not prepared to be *ram* at any cost to be killed inside the Mecca, and its sanctity to be disturbed by that, he did not like to be that *ram*. Once on the whispering of Ibn-Żubayr, Imām Ḥusain clarified, e.g. God promise, he would prefer to be murdered outside the periphery of Mecca that is the limits of Mecca.[37]

It seems from the analysis of the facts that Imām Ḥusain's visit to Kufa had become indispensable. But, besides his trusted followers, it was difficult to rely upon the mass-support emerging from Kufa. Imām Ḥusain was well aware of all circumstances. It was also clear, if Imām Ḥusain resides permanently in Mecca, then he would not be allowed to remain in peace. Yażīdī army would attack Mecca, there would be a bloodshed causing the dishonour of Ka'bah. Then what option was left. It appears that Imām Ḥusain should take the decision of proceeding towards Kufa.

Imām Ḥusain did not approve directly the offer of Kufic people. He did not decide to go to Kufa immediately, but decided to send his cousin and brother-in-law-Muslim-bin-'Aqīl as his representative-*cum*-peace-envoy. He sent a letter through the last Kufic messengers, Ḥānī-bin-'Orwah and Sa'īd-bin-'Abdu'llāh Ḥasafī with the following content:

> "As per your insistence that you have no Imām, and on my arrival all of you may be united on Truth, I am sending my brother-in-law, a man of integrity, Muslim-bin-'Aqīl, so that, he could apprise me after adjudging the situation. If, his intimation comes positive, then I would come towards you in near future. It may be clear that an Imām's basic responsibility has been to see that justice is being implemented in letter and spirit of God's book, truth being followed and everyone has been devoted to the Almighty."[38]

It in clear from the letter that Muslim was neither nominated for any invasion or assignment nor for being Kufa's administrator. His term of reference was only to judge the support towards Imām Ḥusain in Kufa under intimation to Imām Ḥusain, on the basis of which Imām Ḥusain could prescribe future course of action.

Muslim-bin-'Aqīl went first to Medina from Mecca along with Kufic messengers Qays-bin-Muṣahar Ṣaidāvī and they performed Prayer therein the *Masjidu'n-Nabvī*, then he took leave from his own relatives and took two people of Qays clan, who were acquinted with the way. By chance, both of them, who had accompanied for way guidance, were held up in desert being extremely thirsty, died at a place from where the anticipated way was visible. Although Muslim and his other friends too were in the same situation, they reached his main way somehow with his moral strength and will-power and stayed at the source of water called Mazīq. He wrote a letter to Imām Ḥusain from there that my mind refuses to go to Kufa after this incident, but Imām Ḥusain advised him to proceed ahead and Muslim proceeded for Kufa.[39]

Muslim and his friends reached Kufa safely. The news of his arrival spread like anything. People assembled in a great number and in that large crowd, the letter addressed to Kufic people by Imām Ḥusain was read out. People listened very carefully. 'Ābis-bin-Abī Shabīb Shākirī stood first for speaking. He said that he did not know other matters, but he says regarding himself that if an occasion comes for a war, he won't lag behind from sacrificing his own life and his objective would be nothing, but to follow the commands of God. Ḥabīb-bin-Maẓāhir Asadī, praising Imām Ḥusain said, that his ideals in a very four words. Others also gave their speech. It was clear from the assurance of sacrificing one's life, everyone was sure about ensuing war, which was inivitable and one had to sacrifice one's life in it.

As the peace envoy Muslim was not made a Governor, so, there was no question of his staying at state-palace, Yażīdī Governor was in state-palace. Probably Sulayman-bin-Ṣorad Khuzā'ī was out of station at the time of arrival of Muslim, otherwise Muslim would have been his guest, he was very important person, on whose initiatve letter was sent to Imām Ḥusain. Therefore, Muslim had to stay at the house of Mukhtār-bin-Abī'Obaydu'llāh Thaqafī. This house existed up to twelfth Century AD, which was called *Dāru'l Musayyab*.[40]

Kufic people started taking oath of allegiance and appoximately eighteen thousand people did *Bay'at* in the name of Imām Ḥusain within a week on the hands of Muslim.[41] It cannot be said that all these people were real religious followers of Imām Ḥusain. No doubt, during Imām Ḥusain's father Imām 'Alī's Caliphate (June 655 AD to January 661 AD) Kufa was the capital of Islāmic State, where all people were said to be his followers and supporters but since the time twenty years have lapsed and people having faith in the Progeny of the Prophet Muḥammad were mercilessly continously murdered, or exiled to other places, the remaining of them were very few people who were living inside their houses fearfully. No doubt most of the people, who were propounders of movement in support of Muslim were true, good and well-wishers, but their intention was to make the atmosphere positive and Muslim was also impressed by their support. He wrote a letter to Imām Ḥusain on 12th Žīq'adah, 60 AH / 12th August, 680 AD that Kufa's circumstances were favourable and Kufic people were strong enough and determined in their decision.[42]

It would be wrong to suppose that all people in Kufa became the supporters of Imām Ḥusain. There was a majority of supporters of Umayyites in Kufa, who had done opposition. Kufa's Governor No'mān-bin Bashīr attemped to stop people from the support of Imām Ḥusain, but-Yažīd's supporters were not satisfied with that. Ibn Ṭāūs, Saiyed Razīu'd Dīn, Abu'l Qāsim (d. 1266 AD) gave their names.[43] Ibn Qutaybah, Abū Muḥammad 'Abdu'llāh-bin-Muslim al-Dīnāwarī (d. 896 AD), [44] mentioned that Yažīd's two spies Muslim-bin-Sa'īd Ḥazramī and 'Ammarah-bin-Walīd and according to aṭ-Ṭabarī, Ibn Jarīr Abū Jā'far (d. 923 AD)[45] regarding 'Abdu'llāh-bin-Muslim Bāhilī wrote a letter to Yažīd that Muslim-bin-'Aqīl had come to Kufa and Imām Ḥusain's followers have taken oath of allegiance in his name. If he wanted his hold on Kufa, he should send a capable person, because the present administrator No'mān-bin-Bashīr was a week ruler or was purposefully showing weekness. Yažīd immediately took action over the information and appointed 'Obaydu'llāh-bin-Żiyād as the Governor of Kufa in place of No'mān-bin-Bashīr. 'Obaydu'llāh, was the son of that Żiyād, whom Amīr Mu'āwiyah had made his so-called brother and a discussion of his atrocities had already been made in the previous pages. 'Obaydu'llāh proved to be more atrocious and merciless than his own father, on whose name people used to shiver out of fear.

The information of Imām Ḥusain's visit to Mecca had already spread and people were over enthusiatic day by day. People were awaiting impatiently the arrival of Imām Ḥusain. 'Obaydu'llāh-bin-Żiyād made highly confidential the action of assuming the governance of Kufa. He came near Kufa, and suddenly changed his features of identity and wore a black turben, which was an identity of being the member of the family of the holy Prophet, and tied up a towel on his face, which 'Arab soldiers wore during war. With this dress 'Obaydu'llāh-bin-Żiyād was mounting on his horse ahead and the equipped army was behind him. People supposed, Imām Ḥusain had arrived, therefore, ran for welcoming. From all sides there was call; Welcome! 'O Imām! You are Welcome!, 'O Prophet's son, Ḥusain!, 'O Muslim's life! 'Obaydu'llāh-bin-Żiyād was going on hearing these calls, recognizing those faces, who were calling. Slowly and steadily a heavy crowd assembled, people came out of their houses and began to welcome, thinking him to be Imām Ḥusain, to this extent that there was an obstacle on the way. At that time Muslim-bin-'Omarū Bāhilī, who was the father of Qutayba-bin-Muslim, famous in the Islāmic history, was with 'Obaydu'llāh-bin-Żiyād called out; Have the way, he is Amīr 'Obaydu'llāh-bin-Żiyād.[46] On hearing, there prevailed silence, and the entire crowd scattered hither and thither. When 'Obaydu'llāh reached the Governor's palace, there were not more than ten people.[47]

It would not be so difficult to guess the bent of the mind of Kufic people. 'Obaydu'llāh-bin-Żiyād identified each and every person, recognised their voice. He would certainly punish them, It was he whose father murdered innumerable people, hanged, cut of hands, legs, tongue and head of so many people. The very apprehension of his cruel and atrocious punishments made people tremable. Whatever would happen with one's self, what would happen with family people, what would happen with infant children, this and there were so many questions which made the heart heavy. With this 'Obaydu'llāh-bin-Żiyād's very fast procedures made people shiver. He gave a threatening and harsh speech in the mosque, if anybody would do any action against Damascus ruling, he would be hanged on, the fate of culprit or his area and his family members would be compelled to get out of the purview of king's services.[48] He announced such a provision that there was terror on all sides, people were afraid of going from one place to another and five or six people dare not to meet together. As a result bringing of 'greenish fertile land owners' of Kufa's left the very company of Muslim-bin-'Aqīl, who was murdered mercilessly by 'Obaydu'llāh-bin-Żiyād. However, some true Kufic associtesbecame martyrs along with Imām Ḥusain in the war of Justice. Countless people were imprisoned. After Imām Ḥusain's martyrdom, when the prisoners broke open the jails and came out, their number has been said to be forty thousand, and they were called, *Tawwābīn* (the penitents) technically.[49]

In all sides of Kufa spies were patrolling, even a small and trival matter was sent to the ruler. Imām Ḥusain's messenger of peace, Muslim-bin-'Aqīl also felt insecure and unsafe. He felt it was safe on his part to leave the house of Mukhtār-bin-Abī'Obaydu'llāh Thaqafī, because all were aware that Muslim was staying there, and Mukhtār was not available in those days in the town. Therefore, in the darkness of the night, he came down to a reliable person Ḥānī-bin-'Orwah's house. Ḥānī was the head of his clan, whenever he uses to come out his house, 12,000 armed people used to accompany him, say today's guards.[50]

At the house of Ḥānī-bin-'Orwah another friend Sharīk-bin-Aghor was also staying in as a guest, but was ailing. Sharīk was a highly distinguished person, who had beem in good terms with the ruler of the time, but by heart he was a devotee and follower of the holy Prophet and his Household, including Imām Ḥusain. He said to Muslim that 'Obaydu'llāh-bin-Żiyād had received the information of his ill-health, he would ceartainly come to meet him, when he comes, Muslim should murder him with his sword, and get again command over Kufa. After regaining health, he would keep Basra in his support. He also suggested, when 'Obaydu'llāh-bin-Żiyād would come, he would indicate the right time for his killing. He would remove his turbon, it would be indication.

As Sharīk had said 'Obaydu'llāh-bin-Żiyād came to Ḥānī's house to enquire about his health. Sharīk said, it was a high fever and as per indication to Muslim-bin-'Aqīl removed his turn bon thrice and kept but Mulism didn't move at all from his place. On 'Obaydu'llāh-bin-Żiyād's return Sharīk complained to Muslim that he had lost a golden opportunity. Muslim replied that there are two reasons for that. Firstly, the Prophet's command that a sudden attack is not acceptable. Secondly, presently he was Ḥānī-bin-'Orwah's guest. Ḥānī permission is a must for this. It was not required of him to violate the limit.[51]

Ḥānī-bin-'Orwah kept Muslim highly secured in his house in a very highly confidential manner, but circumstances cleared the early war, for which Muslim-bin-'Ausajah Asadī took promise from people for the safety of the Muslim and Abū-Thamāmah 'Omarū-bin-'Abdu'llāh Ṣāy'dī was making available the wealth and war materials. Later on both became martyrs in Karbala with Imām Ḥusain. 'Obaydu'llāh-bin-Żiyād got the information that Muslim had taken asylum in the house of Ḥānī-bin-'Orwah, he threatned Ḥānī; firstly Ḥānī refused, but after knowing the situations, he agreed to say good bye to Muslim, but refused to hand over Muslim to him. 'Obaydu'llāh-bin-Żiyād fiercely attacked him, in which old Ḥānī bathed in his own blood and then sent to jail. Ḥānī's supporters armed with large number of followers, getting the message of his being killed rushed towards Ruler's palace, but being mislead by the mythical talk of the then Qāzī Sharīḥ, people returned.[52] The then it was a difficult time for Muslim that he may stealthily remain in Ḥānī's house and Ḥānī might be murdered. If it happened so, the entire responsibility would be on Muslim's shoulders. Muslim left the house of Ḥānī and came out of it. At that time 'Obaydu'llāh-bin-Żiyād was giving a threating speach in the mosque. Some people came running and said that

Muslim had come out. 'Obaydu'llāh-bin-Żiyād ran away and entering the palace bolted inside.[53]

The conditions in which Muslim came out suddenly for a war, assuming, that all those 18,000 people, who had taken Oath of Allegiance in the name of Imām Ḥusain, would have joined Muslim, might not be expected, but 4000 people assembled, adhering to their own promise, but Muslim could not reach those people. Only 300 people were with him in the terrifying atmosphere. The supporters of Muslim were murdered mercilessly. 'Ammarah-bin-Salkhab Ażdī and 'Abdu'l 'Olā-bin-Yażīd Kalbī and their companions were arrested even before their reaching Muslim and later murdered.[54] Ḥabīb-bin-Maẓāhir Asadī, Muslim-bin-'Ausajah Asadī and Abū-Thamāmah 'Omarū-bin-'Abdu'llāh Ṣāy'dī also could not reach Muslim, afterwards somehow reached Karbala, and became martyr in the War of Justice along with Imām Ḥusain. Even then, the war of Justice went up to evening under the leadership of Muslim, of course, only thirty people remaining at that time. When Muslim came out side the mosque after the prayer of night, the remaining thirty people also left him and he was alone. There was no one even to tell him about the lanes and roads of Kufa, wondering in the darkness of the night, he reached at the house of Kindah clans' lady Ṭo'ah.

Muslim asked for water, she brought it and he quenched the thurst. Muslim continued to sit there itself even after taking water. The lady requested him to go his home. Muslim modestly told her that he was non-resident of the city, he would be grateful, if she could offer asylum for a night. She asked about him. Muslim told the truth. She was a noble lady. She gave due respects to Muslim and took him inside the house. But her greedy son to get reward informed 'Obaydu'llāh-bin-Żiyād that Muslim was staying in his house. 'Obaydu'llāh-bin-Żiyād sent a battalion of army under Muḥammad-bin-Asha'th for arresting Muslim. From the sound steps of horses Muslim understood, that the army has come for arresting him.

Muslim came out of the house. He faught and prevented the army from entering into the house of his host. Muslim's lips were cut in the encounter and the lower lip was injured and two teeth broken, even then the enemy could not arrest Muslim. The enemy army understood that it was difficult to win over him. They started throwing stones from the roof of that house and began to throw balls of fire. Their commandar Ibn-Asha'th calling him said, peace for you, please don't use your sword. No doubt, Qur'an's Command would have echoed in the mind of God fearing Muslim:

"And if they lean to peace, then leaneth thou too to it, and trust in God; Verily He is the All-Hearing, All-Knowing."
(*Qur'an*: 8/61)

Muslim asked, is it true that peace is being offered to him? Ibn-Asha'th said, Yes. Muslim rest the sword inside the armour, within a while a horse was brought, Muslim mounted on it, then the sword was removed from the waist. Yażīdī commander Ibn Asha'th, took Muslim and reached the ruling palace, went inside with permission and apprised 'Obaydu'llāh-bin-Żiyād of the situation and said that he has brought him with a promise of peace. 'Obaydu'llāh-bin-Żiyād said who he was to decide for peace to him. Ibn-Asha'th could not dare enough to say more. Muslim was produced before 'Obaydu'llāh-bin-Żiyād. Muslim was very thirsty. As there was a continuous drench of blood from his body, his thirst increased. Water was placed before him, but he could not take it, because the blood was flowing in such a way that it mingled with water. Muslim said that, water is not in his fate, please remove it. 'Obaydu'llāh-bin-Żiyād said, O' Muslim, certainly I shall kill you. Muslim asked him, allow me to make a 'Will' and observed all sides and recognised 'Omar-bin-Sa'd (Ibn-Sa'd), later on Commandor-in-Chief of Yażīdī Army at the Battle of Karbala. Muslim addressed Ibn-Sa'd. As he belonged to Quraysh clan, he would like to say something to him, if he could listen to. Then Muslim described his 'Will'. The first thing is that he has become debtor of 700 Diraham, please, pay the debt by selling his sword and apparel. Secondly, after his murder, get the body from 'Obaydu'llāh-bin-Żiyād and burry it away. Thirdly, the most impotant one that inform Imām Ḥusain, somehow, what situations Muslim had to face, so that, he may go back and not become a victim of cheating of Kufic people.

Muslim was taken to the roof of the Governor's palace, where his head was chopped off and the dead body was thrown away.[55] Muslim had fought Yażīdī army in two days battle, which commenced on Sunday, 8th Žilḥijjah, 60 AH / 9th September, 680 AD and was martyred on the next day, Monday 9th Žilḥijjah, 60 AH / 10th September, 680 AD.[56] After the killing the legs of his dead body tied with a rope was pulled away to each lane, road and market of Kufa and his head was hung at the main gate of the Governor's palace.

Such a terroristic and fearful atmosphere arose in Kufa that people stopped coming outside from their houses and everywhere there was silence and silence only. The situation was so dreadful that Ḥānī-bin-'Orwah, who had 12,000 bodyguards present at all times, when the message of his fake murder spread in Kufa, the people attacked

Governor's palace immediately, which has already been discussed in the previous lines. But, after Muslim's martyrdom, the stituation was so tense that the same Ḥānī-bin-'Orwah was brought to palace from the jail, hand-cuffed and in the chain and was calling his people for help, but no body came for his help, to this extent there was atrocity that a slave of 'Obaydu'llāh-bin-Żiyād chopped off his head frɔm his body.[57] 'Obaydu'llāh-bin-Żiyād sent both the heads of Muslim and Ḥānī with a covering letter to Yażīd in Damascus. Yażīd, in reply appreciated him and wrote that he had done the same what was expected of him. Now, in the case of Ḥusain-bin-'Alī, his sincerety was to be observed.[58]

Muslim while coming to Kufa had brought his two sons also with him. It shows that Muslim was sure of a justifiable behaviour from Kufic people. Thinking thus was natural also, because Muslim had come as a messenger of peace and not for any military action and full security is always provided to the messenger of peace in difficult circumstances too. It is a well established Tradition which has been carried out in every period, in every rule. Being with his own two babies, there would be relief in the situation of mental stress, whatever the amount of sadness in the mind might be, the plays and games of babies would have put off naturally and easily all sorts of miseries. After Muslim's killing, both the little boys were kept in Jail for about a year. One day when the gaurd of jail came to know of the little boys, he made them free from the jail in the darkness of the mid night. Both the little boys were stranded in the streets of Kufa, in the early morning hid themselves behind the trees on the river bank. A maid-servant came to the river for filling water, observed the reflection of glittering faces in the water and informed her master, who came and took the children along with her to her house, maintained them in the good respects, her husband Ḥāri<u>th</u> came home late night, he told his wife that the children of Muslim have ran away from the jail, the Administor 'Obaydu'llāh-bin-Żiyād has announced reward of two thousands for searching them. He searched them for the whole day, but of no avail. His wife had perfect faith in Islām, she was frightened hearing it and after taking oath from Ḥāri<u>th</u>, that he will not harm them, she told that both the little boys had taken asylum, in his own house. Ḥāri<u>th</u> never cared for his oath, pulled the hair of the children and tied them with a pole outside his house. He brought them to the river-bank in the early morning, children requested him to sell them in the market as slaves, if he was for a huge money, but he did not agree. Firstly, he mudered the elder brother, kept the head in a bag and threw away the body in the river the younger brother wriggled in his elder brother's blood, he mercilessly murdered the younger brother also, he also kept his head in a bag and threw away his body also in the river. Their graves are formed on the basis of their heads, bodies were not at all traceable, so could not be burried at all.[59]

Ultimately, it would be appropriate to contemplate on the charge that Imām Ḥusain has been martyred due to Kufic people who invited him and betrayed. But it is also a fact that those people, who became martyrs along with Imām Ḥusain were Kufic people, may be compared to Medina people, who saw with their own eyes that the holy Prophets grandson, Imām Ḥusain along with his family had left the motherland Medina, but the selfish men and women of holy Prophet's holy Medina, remained inside their houses. None offered participation in the War of Justice, except all the descendants of Abū Ṭālib. Abū Ṭālib who had feciliated the Prophet Muḥammad's mission and then the same role was played by his descendants. None other of the Hāshimite did any support.

Beside the fact that Kufic people invited Imām Ḥusain and betrayed him, this reality should also be kept in mind that there were two types of people in them. The extracts of those letters have already been given in the earlier pages. Those, who were pious people, the persons perfect in Islām, enjoining good and prohibiting bad as per norms of the Divine Jurisprudence. Amongst them were—Ḥabīb-bin-Maẓāhir Asadī, Sulayman-bin-Ṣorad Khuzā'ī, Musayyab-bin-Najbah, Rafā'h-bin-Shaddād, 'Abdu'llāh-bin-Wā'l, 'Abdu'llāh-bin-Sabī'a Hamadānī, Qays-bin-Muṣahar Ṣaidāvī, 'Abdu'l Raḥmān-bin-'Abdu'llāh-bin-Kadan Arḥabī, 'Ammār-bin-Ḥassān-bin-Shurayb Ṭaī, Ḥānī-bin-Ḥānī, Sa'īd-bin-'Abdu'llāh Ḥasafī etc. Among them some of them came to Karbala and attained martyrdom, some of them could not come to Karbala, but became martyr afterwards while taking revenge from the murderers of Imām Ḥusain![60] No information is available about some others. But this much is certain that none among them joined Yażīdī army, anybody joined Yażīdī army. Had being an elite, an important post would have been given to him, but there is no reference or any such name. It is clear from this that these people also became a victim or a martyr or a prisoner of the atrocities of Yażīdī Governor 'Obaydu'llāh-bin-Żiyād in Kufa.

The other category of writers of the letters to Imām Ḥusain was those who would fly off seeing the risk, who cling to the powerful people. This category of people is found at all times, was also present at that time. They invited Imām Ḥusain, but there is no reference of either their full faith in Islām or love with the Islāmic Prophet. But there is a mention of fertile fields.[61] names are safe in the history—Shabth-bin-Raba'ī, Ḥajjār-bin-Abjar, Yażīd-bin-Ḥārith, Yażīd-bin-Roy'm, 'Ażrahbin-Qays, 'Omar-bin-Hujjāj Żubaydī, and Muḥammad-bin-'Omayr Taymīmī. All these people joined Yażīdī army against Imām Ḥusain, obtained the post of importance. Other informations are also available about these people in various history books.

See the irony of fate, on 8th-9th Žilḥijjah, 60 AH / 9th-10th September, 680 AD,[62] when peace envoy Muslim-bin-'Aqīl was facing the battle of life and then killed, Imām Ḥusain was travelling towards the same Kufa. The Caravan included, his family and associates, who had come with him from Medina and a few Basra people, who had reached and followed him.[63]

Between Mecca and Karbala

Imām Ḥusain's Caravan passed through 35 places in between Mecca and Karbala, that is:

> Mecca → Bustānu'l Banī 'Āmir → Tan'īm → Ṣaffāḥ → Žātu'l-'Irq → Wādīu'l 'Aqīq → Ghamrah → Ummu'l Khurmān → Musalliḥ → Mughīthah-Mā'wān → Nuqrah → Ḥājaż → Sambrā' → Nūż → Ajfar → Khuzaymiya → Żarwud → Tha'labiyah → Bạtnu'l'Oqbah → Shaqūq → Żabālah → Bạtnu'l 'Oqbah →'Omiyah → Waqṣah → Sharrāf → Abū Misk → Jabal-Žī Ḥasam → Bayzah → Masījad → Ḥamām → Mughīthiyah → Ummu'l Qurūn →'Ažību'l Hijānāt → Qaṣru'l Banī Maqātil → Qạtqaṭ ānah → Naynwān → Karbala (Wādīu'l Ṭaf)

All the above mentioned places have various incidents of historical, cultural and religious importance. But unfortunately no reliable information is available about them. Still, a reference of a few places is available in various sources and on the basis of which we would discuss regarding the incidents concerning 14 places from among them.[64]

Imām Ḥusain travelled without any disturbance from the first place Tan'īm to the 9th spot Sheräff. On the 10th place Yażīdī army disturbed the journey at Jabal Žuḥasm and then on forced pursuance brought him to Karbala, the place of martyrdom. Let us discuss all these sixteen spots of the journey of Imām Ḥusain:

1. Tan'īm

This place is near Mecca. Imām Ḥusain met a Caravan here, which came from Yemen. He hired from them some camels on rent for his conveyance for his companions. He offered whoever wants to go to Iraq, would be paid full fare as well, as a gift, and if he wants to go back in the mid-way then he would be paid fare up to that place. Some of them accompanied him to Iraq.[65]

Two things emerged from these facts. Firstly, putting up all aspects and everything clearly during any transaction, which presents Imām Ḥusain's efficiency of approach. Secondly, it is also clear that Imām Ḥusain set out from Mecca without any prior arrangement. To this extent that there was shortage of camel or any other thing for conveyance.[66]

Tan'īm is also the place, where Imām Ḥusain's brother-in-law 'Abdu'llāh-bin-Ja'far Ṭayyār-bin-Abī Ṭālib and Mecca's Governor's brother Yaḥyā-bin-Saī'd-binu'l-'Āṣ met Imām Ḥusain. 'Abdu'llāh-bin-Ja'far Ṭayyār was in Medina during the departure of Imām Ḥusain to Mecca. He was sorry when he heard the news that Imām Ḥusain proceeded towards Iraq. He sent a letter to Imām Ḥusain through his two sons 'Aun and Muḥammad, in which he advised on his head's promise, to stop from going a head, your departure would ceased the brightness of the earth, because you are the symbol of truth and the centre of hopes of justice. Please, do not be in hurry in the travel, I am coming behind this letter. 'Aun and Muḥammad submitted the letter at Tan'īm at the feet of Imām Ḥusain. After sending a letter to Imām Ḥusain, 'Abdu'llāh-bin-Ja'far Ṭayyār met, Medina's Governor 'Omarū-bin-Saī'd-binu'l-'Āṣ and after discussion with him obtained a letter of peace for Imām Ḥusain and took along with him his brother Yaḥyā-bin-Saī'd-binu'l-'Āṣ, as a witness. He met Imām Ḥusain at the place Tan'īm. Yaḥyā-bin-Saī'd-binu'l-'Āṣ was the same person who had attacked at the time of Imām Ḥusain's departure from Mecca. Now, he was changing the policy of war changing the facial coverage along with 'Abdu'llāh-bin-Ja'far Ṭayyār. Imām Ḥusain was quite familiar with all situations. He convinced 'Abdu'llāh-bin-Ja'far Ṭayyār that any assurance of local ruling official against the desires of central ruling authority remained meaningless. Then writing a reply to Governor gave it to his brother, instead of proceeding ahead along with Imām Ḥusain, 'Abdu'llāh-bin-Ja'far Ṭayyār returned Medina, leaving his both sons 'Aun and Muḥammad to him.[67]

2. Ṣaffāḥ

Imām Ḥusain did not camp here, but he met a famous Arabic poet Faraẓdaq-bin-Ghālib at this place.[68] Faraẓdaq asked with surprise, Oh, Sir! the entire Islāmic world assembling in Mecca for perfoming *Ḥajj* and you are leaving? Imām Ḥusain removed the curtain of secrecy, so far no body knew. He replied. If I had not worked speeding, I would have been made a prisoner. It cleared that Imām Ḥusain was ready to sacrifice his life for establishing path of justice, but could not accept to become a prisoner silently. It is a valuable side of war-policy of Imām Ḥusain, because after becoming a prisoner, there would be a curtain on the objectives of the Ḥusainī Revolution. Faraždaq appraised of the situation to Imām Ḥusain after the appointment of 'Obaydu'llāh-bin-Žiyād as Administrator of Kufa. Faraždaq's words speek of his creative talent. Sir, the Kufic people's heart is with you and the swords would be with Umayyites. Imām Ḥusain appreciated his words:

> "You are true. Our destiny is in the hands of God. He does what is wished. Everyday a new wonder. If suits us, we thanks Him and pray for help. If His will is not as per our wish, then too, it is not less important that our intention should be based on truth and our character to be can did."[69]

It clarifies the most impotant philosophy of life pronounced by Imām Ḥusain that if the objective is honest and intention is pure, then there is nothing to worry; one needs not care the idle talkers.

At a nearby place called Abtah a group of supporters met Imām Ḥusain, including Żayd-bin-Thabayt̨ Qaysī and his two sons'Abdu'l Raḥmān and 'Obaydu'llāh and 'Āmir-bin-Muslim 'Abdī Baṣrī and his servants, Sālim and Shabīb-bin-'Abdu'llāh Nahashalī, who began to accompany Imām Ḥusain.[70]

3. Žatu'l 'Irq

Al-Mufīd, Ibnu 'l-Ma 'allim, Shaykh Abū 'Abdu'llāh Muḥammad (d. 1022 AD) has written after discussing the above concerned incident with his brother-in-law 'Abdu'llāh-bin-Ja'far Ṭayyār, Imām Ḥusain advanced towards Iraq very fast and took rest after reaching Žatu'l 'Iraq.[71]

4. Ḥājaz

This area is also famous as Baytu'l-Rammah. It was the place where Imām Ḥusain felt a sign of relief. He bid good bye giving a letter to Qays-bin-Muṣahar Ṣaidāvī, the bearer of five of Kufic people.[72] The content of the letter was:

> "I have received the letter of Muslim-bin-'Aqıl-bin-Abī Ṭālib regarding a favourable atmosphere at Kufa, and also that you are united in supporting me, God may reward you. I have already departed on 8th Žilḥijjah, 60 AH (9th September, 680 AD) from Mecca. Get yourself very active, as soon as you receive my letter. I am about to reach your midst even earlier."[73]

Some scholars say, the bearer of letter was 'Abdu'llāh-bin-Yaqṭar,[74] but further proceedings confirm the name of Ibn Muṣahar, who could not reach Kufa with the letter, he just reached Qādsiyah that Yažīdī Commandor Hissīn-bin-Numayr arrested him and sent him to the Governor 'Obaydu'llāh-bin-Žiyād. He said to Ibn Muṣahar that you may get life, if you talk against Imām Ḥusain and abuse him. Ibn Muṣahar agreed. The crowd assembled in the mosque to see what the very messenger of Imām Ḥusain says. Qays-bin-Muṣahar Ṣaidāvī took this opportunity to make available the objectives of Imām Ḥusain, even to the common people. At first he prayed to God, then addressed the people:

> "O' people, at present Ḥusain-bin-'Alī is the supreme in the whole world, who is the great son of Fāṭimah aż-Żahrah, the daughter of the holy Prophet. I have come to you with his message only. It is your duty to response and accept his call."[75]

Hearing the call, 'Obaydu'llāh-bin-Żiyād became mad out of anger. He ordered, throw off Ibn Muṣahar from the roof of the palace, and so his body was broken asunder into pieces.[76]

5. Żarwud

There was a source of water near this place, where Żuhayr-bin-Qayn-bin-Qays Numayrī Bajalī was camping and taking rest. Żuhayr-Qayn was from Umayyite, so considered of enemy side, but in reality he was an ardent devotee of *Ahlu'l-Bayt* and Imām Ḥusain. He was aware of Imām Ḥusain's call, but he was avoiding Imām Ḥusain, because he was newly married. He was on tour with his wife. As he wanted to avoid Imām Ḥusain at that time, he was moving far ahead. But he was incluled in the list of the person, who were chosen by Imām Ḥusain and so he sent a letter through his son 'Alī Akbar. Żuhayr-Qayn glanced it, kept on his head, then went to his wife and said to her: That the grandson of the holy Prophet had called him. He would go certainly, if she want he could divorce her and make her free. Wife replied: So, far she was his life companion when he was an ordinary person is now he had been promoted, he was separating her, was it justice? Żuhayr-Qayn clarified to his wife and came to Karbala with his wife. They lived in the vicinity of Ḥusainī camps and if bore all tyrannies, injuries and injustice, along with Ḥusainī camps.

Żuhayr-Qayn called upon other companions to join the cause of tı uth under the leadership of Imām Ḥusain, but except his cousin Salmān-bin-Muzārib-bin-Qays Numayrī Bajalī nobody was willing to accompany him. They presented themselve at the service of Imām Ḥusain.[77]

In the mean time Imām Ḥusain's close friend Ḥabīb-bin-Maẓāhir Asadī and the famous elder Burayr-bin-Khuzayr Hamadānī Junadab-bin-Ḥajīr Kindī Khūlānī, Yażīd-bin-Żiyād-bin-Mahāṣar Abu'l al-Sh'athā Kindī, Ḥabāb-bin-'Āmir-bin-Ka'b Tayamī also joined Imām Ḥusain.

From this stage itself difficulties also commenced. The two followers of Imām Ḥusain 'Abdu'llāh-bin-Salīm Asadī and Mażrī-bin-Mushma'l Asadī, who accompanied Imām Ḥusain after perfoming *Hajj* in Mecca, observed a person coming towards Kufa. Imām Ḥusain wanted informations from them, but they turned their faces, one went to the other side. Imām Ḥusain also advanced. Both the Asadī soldiers chased and also overtook him. They introduced himself, who was also belonging to the same clan. They told, Yes listen! I had been just in outskirts of Kufa, Muslim-bin-'Aqīl and Ḥānī-bin-'Orwah were murdured. I saw with my own eyes that his dead-body was being dragged, tying the legs with a rope in the market.[78] It was a heart rending information. They didn't feel appropriate to intimate immediately, joined the Caravan, with a heavy heart, which was going ahead.

6. Tha'labiah

Imām Ḥusain reached Tha'labiah in the evening and the Caravan took rest there in the night. Both 'Abdu'llāh-bin-Salīm Asadī and Mażrī-bin-Mushma'l Asadī presented themselves before Imām Ḥusain and requested permission for telling something in privacy. Imām Ḥusain said, there is no need for any secrecy. Both the soldiers said that, the person whom he saw coming from Kufa, belonged to their own clan, true and honest persons. Then they repeated the words which they had heard. It was a very sad information for Imām Ḥusain, it was not only the woeful information about a relative and honest follower, but also an indication of sudden adverse circumstances. Grieved and afflicted Imām Ḥusain repeated many times the verses of the holy Qur'an:

> "Verily we are God's and verily unto Him shall we return."
> (*Qur'an*: 2/156)

And then he became calm.[79] Both Asadī soldiers humbly suggested not to proceed ahead in those circumstances. Imām Ḥusain looked towards Martyr Muslim's family members. All of them said in a single voice that they would take revenge for the murder of Muslim or sacrifice their own life in the battle field as Muslim did. Imām Ḥusain looking at both the Asadī and said, when they would not be there, for what would he be alive. Some expressed their views that Imām Ḥusain and Muslim were not at the same pedestal. When he would reach Kufa, then people would run for his help. Imām Ḥusain did not reply, neither for nor against, remained silent. Imām Ḥusain stopped on that day. The voices of women-children crying, beating the breast continued in the camps.[80] He spent the night there, proceeded ahead taking enough water with him.

7. Żabālah

At this stage itself 'Arabic poet Ayas-bin-'A<u>th</u>al Ṭā'ī brought the letter of Yażīdī Commander, Ibn-A<u>sh</u>a'<u>th</u> to Imām Ḥusain as per *Will* of Muslim-bin-'Aqīl, informing that the circumstance and situation of Kufa had changed and requesting not to consider to visit Kufa.[81] The hearer of the letter also intimated that Qays-bin-Muṣahar Ṣaidāvī had already been murdered.[82]

Imām Ḥusain considered to explain once again his aims and objective in clear words, if anyone has joined with his mission, should know the ultimate outcome. It has its detailed description in the history, *vide* an extract:

> "O' people! I allowed you to remain with me on the hope that Iraq would be with me. But now I have received a very sad message regarding my brother Muslim, which proves that the people who had invited us have cheated us, were ungrateful. Therefore, whoever is able to bear the sword and the attacks of spears, may come with us, otherwise may go out from here itself."[83]

After hearing the address of Imām Ḥusain, those who were interested in powers separated themselves. But three people, 'Ibad-bin-Muhājir-bin-Abī Muhājir Juhanī and Mujama'-bin-Żiyād-bin-'Omarū-

Jehnī did not leave Imām Ḥusain. In this manner, only the staunch devotees of Imām Ḥusain remained with him.

8. Baṭnu'l-'Aqbah

Shaykh al-Mufīd, Ibnu'l-Ma'allim (d. 1022 AD) has written the name of this place as Baṭnu'l-'Aqbah,[84] but some say Baṭnu'l-'Aqīq.[85] At this stage, a person of 'Akarmah clan, 'Omaru-bin-Lożān met Imām Ḥusain and told that Yażīdī Army had completely covered the area in between Qādsiyah and 'Ażību'l Hijānāt. At each and every point thousands of soldiers are posted. No one from Kufa might come or go. All routs were closed. He requested not to go there, otherwise, they would attack. Imām Ḥusain blessed him and proceeded ahead, with a little changed way, so, that Ḥiṣṣīn-bin-Numayr's army, which was in Qādsiyah border, could not attack and he proceeded ahead.

9. Sharrāf

Probably, it was Ist of Muḥarram, 61 AH/1st October, 680 AD, when Imām Ḥusain's Caravan reached Sharrāf, which has two significances. Firsly, it was the place, after Tha'labiah and Żabālah, where Imām Ḥusain made special arrangement for storing water. Secondly, when Sharrāf's border was at a distance of two to three miles from Qādsiyah, a person of Imām Ḥusain's Caravan shouted *Allāhu'-Akbar* (God is Great). Imām Ḥusain retrieved, *Allāhu'-Akbar,* no doubt God is Great. But now for what ? He replied, we see the date trees, which indicates of being a village site nearby. Other colleagues said, we have not seen any tree in this area at any time. Imām Ḥusain said, Go ahead, the reality would itself come out. He said, we see the throats of horses and their sound. Imām Ḥusain asked the Caravan to proceed further.

10. Jabalu'l-Žūhasam

Some called it, as Jabalu'l-Žīhasam also. The information about date trees was found incorrect, but it was Yażīdī army which was coming to attack. Imām Ḥusain asked his men, if there was a safer place ? People said, Jabalu'l-Žūhasam (Hills of Žūhasam), if they could reach there, before Yażīdī army, then they might succeed. Imām Ḥusain liked that suggestion and turned Caravan to that direction. Enemies also wanted to proceed ahead that direction, but Imām Ḥusain reached before them and, his companions set their camps.

Impediment by the Yażīdī Army

The Yażīdī army reached Mountain of Žūhasam, when Imām Ḥusain's Caravan people had already established their camps there. The then Yażīdī Commander, Ḥurr-bin-Yażīd-Riyāḥī had come with 1000 soldiers, to make impediments on the way of Imām Ḥusain. As Imām Ḥusain had advanced without fighting with Yażīdī army at Qādsiyah post, its spies had informed the change of way of Imām Ḥusain. Yażīdī army sent a strong battalion to stop Imām Ḥusain. In the summer season, journey after the noon in the desert had been like prefering death to life. The Yażīdī army had to take much pain to reach Imām Ḥusain. There was no water on the way and all suffered like anything. If water could not be available even within a few minutes, people would have died struggling.

Imām Ḥusain was with his companions with turbon on their heads, swords on their wrist, when the enemy's army, horses breathing heavily, and soldiers to quench thrust came infront of Imām Ḥusain. Their aflicted condition was the inminence of their death, if they could not get rescue for some time, they would die themselves. War strategist may suggest, let them die terribly. Imām Ḥusain was an embodiment of compassion, he could not tolerate even his enemy to die for want of water. He ordered that all the food and water should be made available to all those people. His honest and sincere associates just waited only for the order of Imām Ḥusain. They served the humanity in its real sense. Imām Ḥusain himself was offering and under his supervision water and food was made available, utensils filled with drinking water and food materials. Not only the soldiers, but also their animals were offered water and food and made satisfied. Water was offered even to the animal at least three times.[86] A soldier of Yażīdī army, 'Alī-bin-Ṭ'ān narrates that his condition was so pitiable due to not quenching thrust, that he was unable to speak and was so disturbed that could not drink. Water was flowing on the ground. Imām Ḥusain suggested him, to make the palm of hand for drinking the water. He could not make palm of hand. Imām Ḥusain himself made palm of hand and relieved him from mortal thirst and also provided water to his horse.[87]

The then Yażīdī Commander, Ḥurr-Riyāḥī was in a fix. How to initiate stupid discussion to a noble august personality, who had just saved not only his life, but also of his entire army. His army personals were looking at him in a tense position, sitting in the shadows of date trees, holding the bridles of their horses. At the time of *Żuhr* (noon prayer), Imām Ḥusain asked Ḥujjāj-bin-Masrūq Ja'fī for *Ažān* (call for prayer) and enquired of Ḥurr-Riyāḥī, if he would like to perform prayer separately. He replied, No Sir, they would also perfom prayer under him. Both parties performed the prayer unitedly. Imām Ḥusain made a short speech before the enemy army:

> "O' people of God, I wish to clarify my position. I have not come here as per my desire. I have come in reponse of your constant request that you have no *Imām* (Head, leader or guide, the other pivot of Islām, after *Rasūl*). Of course, God may unite us on the path of Truth. If you are to keep your words, then I have come, conform wit your with, otherwise, I may return to the same place from where I have come."[88]

After listening the speech of Imām Ḥusain there continued silence and was no reply. Then Imām retired to his camp. Ḥurr-Riyāḥī also went to his camp. Both parties perfomed the 'Aṣr (afternoon) prayer unitedly too. After prayer Imām Ḥusain addressed again and explained his rights of being genuine claimant as a member of the people of the house of the holy Prophet are more entitled to the governace of Islāmic world, than those men of powers who are pressing their inappropriate claim. They have been imposing cruelty on Muslims. Further he said:

> "However, if you don't like us and do not agree to give our rights and refuse the content of your letters, which you have sent while inviting as guest and those promises, which were clear through your letters and statement of the people who brought the letters, then I would go back." [89]

Now, Ḥurr-Riyāḥī broke his silence and said, By God, that he did not know about those letters which Imām Ḥusain refer to. As per the orders of Imām, 'Oqbah-bin-Sama'n brought those bags, which were full of letters. Ḥurr-Riyāḥī said that he was not among those people, who wrote letters, he has been sent wherever Imām Ḥusain meet, not to leave his association till he produce him before 'Obaydu'llāh-bin-Żiyād. Imām Ḥusain forcefully rejected the proposal and ordered the Caravan to proceed ahead. Ḥurr-Riyāḥī requested to kindly adopt such a way which neither goes to Kufa nor Medina. Imām Ḥusain liked this proposal and before Caravan could proceed, addressed his companions:

> "You are aware of the changed circumstances. It seems goodness had left this world, nothing more than this remains as little water remains in the vessel even when the water moves

> away. The defeated life is similar to poisonous grass. Do you not see that Truth is not being followed and wrong is not being rejected. In such a situation the *Mūmin* (believer) desires to meet the Almighty. In my opinion if death is unavoidable to become martyr would be a reward and living in the midst of these atrocious people is suicidal." [90]

These words established the desired influence on the supporters of Imām Ḥusain. They felt the need of expressing their own views. First of all Żuhayr-Qayn stood up, but after looking at senior elder colleagues present, his attempt may appear high handedess, (to say something without their permission) he saw towards senior elder colleagues to seek their permission. All said, Yes, go on ! Then he said after prayer:

> "God may make your objective successful Oh the son of the holy Prophet! We listened to you, we are with you".[91]

Imām Ḥusain blessed him. After him Nāfa'-bin-Hilāl Jamalī Al-Murādī gave a powerful speech, only a few words of it are extracted here, he said.

> "Oh, the son of the holy Prophet! you are aware that it could not be possible for your grandfather holy Prophet also. that the love which he offered would be received by people with full devotion as he desired. Wicked people flouted the orders, even conspired against him. They promised for being loyal, but actually were traitors. He would choose such sweet honey words, but would act-ante which proved very harsh to the most exhaulted Prophet who left the world. After him your father Imām 'Alī also had to face the same situation. Some people consented to offer co-operation and fought also with his enemies, but some people also opposed to the extent that he passed away.
>
> Today the same situation is before you. Therefore, whoever breaks his promise, treads on the path of evil, he would do bad for himself and the Almighty. You kindly start your mission in the name of God, we are not at all afraid of our decision. By God, whether towards east or west we are all along with Truth and Goodness and we do not hesitate in meeting our own people we are firm on our decision and belief. We keep tolerance with everyone and hate those who are not tolerant and they are our enemies."[92]

Thereafter, Burayr-bin-Khuzayr Hamadānī addressed:

> "By God! Oh the son of the holy Prophet! God's compassion is with us that He offered us a chance that we may fight before you, for your safety, our legs and hands may be cut so, that on the day of *Qiyāmah* (Catastrophe) your grandfather may pray for our salvation, and those people would never get salvation, who would murder the grandson of the holy Prophet. Shame on them, how they would face the God, what would be their situation, when they would shout in the burning fire of the Hell".[93]

The faithful statements of the associates would have certainly obtained blessing of Imām Ḥusain. However, it also has become very clear that whoever accompanied Imām Ḥusain were not only familiar with his objectives, but also following them as aim of their life. They were even ready to sacrifice their life in the defence of Truth along with Imām Ḥusain. Firmness in their faith and certainty in action was very conspicuous. After hearing the views of companions Imām Ḥusain ordered to mount on their conveyance and return to the same path where from they came, meaning return to Medina. The followers just thought of going back, but the Yazīdī army under the Commandership of Ḥurr-Riyāḥī became the impediment on the way. Ḥurr-Riyāḥī clutched the very bridle of Imām Ḥusain's horse forcefully. Imām Ḥusain said with hrash words:

> "Be your mother mourner, tell, what's your intension?"[94]

Ḥurr-Riyāḥī shivered to hear the words. The words of Imām Ḥusain had disturbed his pride and awakened his inner-sense. Its psychological tension was clearly visible on his face. But the reply proved his nobility. He sorrowfully replied: If any other person in your present position and my position had anybody had made reference to my mother, I would had given a befitting reply in his own tone, but your mother is such a lady, whose name could not be pronounced without *Durūd-wa'l-Salām* (God's blessing).[95]

It was the first introduction of the religious wisdom of Ḥurr. Such a situation also would arise later, when his religious wisdom would display fully, but its time had not come yet. Imām Ḥusain asked, what Ḥurr wanted? Ḥurr said, I wish take you to 'Obaydu'llāh-bin-Żiyād. Imām Ḥusain replied in negative. Ḥurr said, I won't leave you! Such conversation took place in the same way twice-thrice. Ḥurr humbly said, Sir, You are choosing the path which leads to battle field and finally, you with your associates would be killed. Imām Ḥusain smiled and said, Do you wish to cowdown me with the terror of death ! He said, No Sir, and finally explained his position, I am not deputed to battle with you. I have been just ordered to be with you; to this extent that you may reach Kufa. Now, as the situation has changed, you refused to go to Kufa, so please have such a way which does not either take you to Kufa or Medina. Just this is the only justice between you and me, till then, when I have no knowledge of the view of the Governor 'Obaydu'llāh-bin-Żiyād. Imām Ḥusain accepted this proposal and ordered his Caravan to turn left from the way of Qādsıyah and 'Ažību'l Hijānāt and Ḥurr also accompanied. 'Ažību'l Hijānāt was 30 miles from there, as per historians.[96]

11. Bayzah

This place also has historical importance because Imām Ḥusain again explained his objectives before Yažīdī army and called upon them to come on the path of Truth. Imām Ḥusain said:

> "Oh People of Faith! You should know the Tradition of holy Prophet that a person who sees such a ruler who is cruel, atrocious, does not differentiate between good and bad, breaks his promise, opposes the life and conduct of the holy Prophet and promulgates the path of sin among the people, but the People tolerate the bad and do not attempt to reform, such person would be punished by the Almighty for his ideas and conduct along with the same ruler".[97]

The allusion was towards Yažīd-bin-Mu'āwiyah who possessed all these criminal qualities. He was one of those cruel leaders about whom the Qur'an says:

> "And We made them Leaders who invite unto the (Hell) fire, and on the Day of Resurrection they shall not be helped." (*Qur'an*: 28/41)

All leaders do not take their people to right path. There are some leaders who do take their followers towards advancement and prosperity, but according to the holy Qur'an there are some, who push their people into torture, fire and destruction.

12. 'Ažību'l Hijānāt

This place has been famous since ancient period, where Ḥira, an ancient king No'aman's camels were grazing. It was a fertile land. Imām Ḥusain's Caravan and Ḥurr's army were camped at a distance. In the mean time Kufa's five persons presented themselves before Imām Ḥusain mounting on their horses, a *Kotal* horse was also available with them. Ṭirimmāh-bin-'Adī was also with them as a guide. Other five persons were 'Omar-bin-Khālid Asadī Ṣaidavī, his slave Saī'd, Mujama'-bin-'Abdu'llāh 'Āyižī, his son 'Āyiž-bin-Majama' and Jinādah-bin-Ḥārith Salmānī. Ḥurr, who was strictly observing, spoke to Imām Ḥusain, these people have come from Kufa, they are not those people coming to you. He will arrest them or make them return to Kufa. Imām Ḥusain replied, that the people have reached him now and have joined his supporters, their safety is his responsibility. Ḥurr became calm after hearing the reply.

Imām Ḥusain asked these people to inform about Kufa. Mujama'-bin-'Abdu'llāh said that important people have been fully bribed with wealth and properties. All of them are unitedly against you. As far as remaining people are concerned, their heart are with you, but their swords are against you. They told about martyrdom of Qays-bin-Muṣahar Ṣaidāvī. Hearing the sad news, Imām Ḥusain's eyes began to shed tears and he recited the Qur'anic verse:

> "Of the believer are the men who are true to what they covenanted with God; of them is he who hath fulfilled his vow and of them is he who awaiteth (*its fulfilment*); and they have changed not in the least." (*Qur'an*: 33/23)

Ṭirimmāh-bin-'Adī said, when he crossed the boundaries of Kufa, he saw such a huge army which he has not seen before. He asked them for what this huge army has been deputed. They told, they were going to fight againt Imām Ḥusain. Ṭirimmāh-bin-'Adī further suggested, if Imām Ḥusain could reach the mountain of Ajā, he will be fully saved. This is the place where ancient kings Ghassān and No'aman could not be conquered. Moreover, he promised that 20,000 soldiers of his clan would be at Imām Ḥusain's service. Imām Ḥusain rejected his proposal with thanks.[98]

13. Qaṣru'l Banī Maqātil

Imām Ḥusain proceeded to rightside road avoiding Kufic highway and reached to Qaṣru'l Banī Maqātil. Ḥurr also reached there and laid his army camp at a distance. Before proceeding ahead Imām Ḥusain ordered his men to fill the utensils with water, which was carried out and the Caravan procceded further.

Imām Ḥusain proceeded a bit that he felt drowsiness on his horse, and slept, when awoke a verse of Qur'an was on his lips:

> "Verily we are God's and verily unto Him shall we return."
> (*Qur'an*: 2/ 156)

Imām Ḥusain's elder son 'Alī Akbar who was shadowing him, raising his horse presented himself in front of him and asked, Reverend father ! what happened ? Imām Ḥusain told, he was slept and heard a voice as someone was saying, he is going ahead and his death is following him. 'Alī Akbar asked, Whether they are not on the path of Truth? Imām Ḥusain smiled and said, O' My Beloved Son! How do you see the death? 'Alī Akbar replied, if it comes in the cause of Truth, then no doubt, sweeter than honey.[99]

14. Naynwān

Imām Ḥusain left Qaṣru'l Banī Maqātil and reached Naynwān, the land which was inclusive of the Wādīu'l Ṭaf, the then a part of Karbala village-group. Imām Ḥusain was just near the Naynwān, and an apparelled solider, as the messenger of Kufic Governor 'Obaydu'llāh-bin-Żiyād reached there. The letter was addressed to Ḥurr with the instruction:

> "Wherever you receive this letter, it is a must for you to stop Ḥusain from going ahead and insist him to stay at a place, where no water would be available and not any comfort to stay. I have ordered my messenger to be with you and inform me about your movements and activities. He won't leave you and would follow my orders."[100]

Ḥurr read the letter before Imām Ḥusain and stopped him from procceding ahead. Imām Ḥusain stayed there. It is clear that the behaviour of Ḥurr had been respectful with Imām Ḥusain during the journey. So 'Obaydu'llāh-bin-Żiyād had deputed a spy to observe his movement. Ḥurr placed the above letter helplessly before Imām Ḥusain. Imām Ḥusain said, let him stay in that village little ahead from here, which is called Ghazariah or in the village nearby which is called Shaffiah. Ḥurr replied politely that he has no right in this regard. Ḥusainī soldier Żuhayr-bin-Qayn suggested Imām Ḥusain that it is fairely easy now to battle them, whoever come after them for fighting, because such a big army would come and we are less in number to face them. Imām Ḥusain firmly replied, No! he doesn't like to initiate the war. Then addressing Ḥurr, Imām Ḥusain said, let him proceed ahead little. Ḥurr remained silent.

15. Karbala

Imām Ḥusain's Caravan went just a little distance turning to the left from Naynwān towards Wādīu'l Ṭaf, near the Karbala. Yażīdī army stood before again and stopped the way and asked him to get down at very place. The river was not far from there. When Imām Ḥusain asked the name of the place, all the people said that it was called Karbala. Imām Ḥusain exclaimed that it was his target place! He got down from the horse. Firstly, the Ḥusainī camps were established on the river bed, but Ḥurr's army raised the objection, then the Ḥusainī camps were removed from the bank of the river and placed at a desert place. This incident took place on 2nd Muḥarram, 61 AH /2nd October, 680 AD.[101]

Notes and References

1. An Historical Atlas of Islām: W.C. Brice.
2. Shahid-i-In sa nigat, pp. 294-320.
3. Jām'au'ṣ-Ṣaḥīḥu'l –Bukhārī, vol. 1, pp. 420-23.
4. *Amīr Mu'āwiyah's date of death is in a confused state. According to Ibn Khaldūn his death occurred during the middle of the month Rajab AH. Some say, he died in the month of Jamādīu'th Thānī, after nineteen years period of reign* (Kitābu'l-'Ibar, vol. 5, p. 52). *I have preferred 'during the middle of the month Rajab AH', i.e. 22 Rajab, 680 AH, which generally accepted.* – Author.
5. Tārīkhu'r-Rusūl wa'l-Mulūk, vol. 6, p. 180; al-Akhbāru'ṭ Ṭawāl, p. 237.
6. Kitābu'l-'Ibar, vol. 5, p. 50.
7. al-Kāmil fī' t-Tārīkh, vol. 3, p. 412, vol. 4, p. 3.
8. Tārīkhu'r-Rusūl wa'l-Mulūk, vol. 6, p. 188.
9. *This date has been fixed on the ground that Imām Ḥusain left Medina two days after meeting with the Governor of Medina.* (Tārīkhu'r-Rusūl wa'l-Mulūk, vol. 6, p. 191) *Imām Ḥusain's departure date from Medina is undisputed as 28 Rajab, 60 AH / 4 May, 680 AD. 'Abdu'llāh-bin-Żubayr*

left Medina in the night of 26 Rajab, 60 AH / 2 May, 680 AD and reached Mecca two days before the arrival of Imām Ḥusain. (al-Akhbāru'ṭ Ṭawāl, p. 230). *All these facts confirm the above date.*
The distance between Medina and Damascus is 812 miles / 1300 km. After asumming caliphate Yazīd sent his order to Medina's Governor, which reached Medina after five days. Under the 'Barīd System' the carrier runs day and night continuously. Carrier changed after a station and gets rest there. Other carrier takes charge and runs afresh. Distance of 812 miles could aprox. 5 day-night travel, with 80 miles per day +80 miles per night may be speed. –Author.

10. Tārīkhu'r-Rusūl wa'l-Mulūk, vol. 6, p. 126.
11. Tārīkhu'r-Rusūl wa'l-Mulūk, vol. 6, pp. 126, 191.
12. Kitābu'l-'Ibar, vol. 5, p. 63.
13. Tārīkhu'r-Rusūl wa'l-Mulūk, vol. 6, p. 191.
14. Bihāru'l-Anwār, vols. 1-2, p. 149; al-Maqtal: Abī Mīkhnaf, p. 15.
15. Bihāru'l-Anwār, vols. 1-2, p. 151.
16. Bihāru'l-Anwār, vols. 1-2, pp. 232-34.
17. Tārīkhu'r-Rusūl wa'l-Mulūk, vol. 6, pp. 190-215.
18. *Guessed the frame was at the rate of 40 miles (64 km) per day, which was the average speed in the deserted area caravan by a camel caravan at that time.*—Author.
19. Kitābu'l-'Ibar, vol. 3, p. 167.
20. Ḥayātu 'l-Muḥammad, p. 525.
21. The Essence of Islam, p. 137; Taqwīm Hijrī-o-Īswī, p. 1; al-Kāmil fī' t-Tārīkh, vol. 6, p. 215.
22. Bihāru'l-Anwār, vols. 1, p. 154; Tārīkhu'r-Rusūl wa'l-Mulūk, vol. 6, p. 215.
23. al-Akhbāru'ṭ Ṭawāl, p. 229.
24. al-Irshād fī Ma'rifat Ḥujjāj Allāh 'Alā 'Ibād, p. 184.
25. al-Naṣāehu'l Kāfiyah, p. 93.
26. al-Akhbāru'ṭ Ṭawāl, p. 230.
27. Bihāru'l-Anwār, vol. 1, p. 183.
28. Balāghatu'l Ḥusain, pp. 123-25.
29. al-Irshād fī Ma'rifat Ḥujjāj Allāh 'Alā 'Ibād, p. 228.
30. Bihāru'l-Anwār, vols. 1-2, p. 155.
31. al-Irshād fī Ma'rifat Ḥujjāj Allāh 'Alā 'Ibād, p. 209; Tārīkhu'r-Rusūl wa'l-Mulūk, vol. 6, p. 197.
32. Tārīkhu'r-Rusūl wa'l-Mulūk, vol. 6, p. 197.
33. *Ibid.*
34. al-Irshād fī Ma'rifat Ḥujjāj Allāh 'Alā 'Ibād, p. 210; Tārīkhu'r-Rusūl wa'l-Mulūk, vol. 6, p. 197.
35. al-Akhbāru'ṭ Ṭawāl, p. 231.
36. Tārīkhu'r-Rusūl wa'l-Mulūk, vol. 6, p. 217.
37. *Ibid.*.
38. Tārīkhu'r-Rusūl wa'l-Mulūk, vol. 6, pp. 197, 210-11.
39. al-Akhbāru'ṭ Ṭawāl, p. 232; Tārīkhu'r-Rusūl wa'l-Mulūk, vol. 6, p. 198.

40. Tārīkhu'r-Rusūl wa'l-Mulūk, vol. 6, p. 199, vol. 7, p. 58; al-Akhbāru'ṭ Ṭawāl, p. 232.
41. Tārīkhu'r-Rusūl wa'l-Mulūk, vol. 6, pp. 199-211.
42. Tārīkhu'r-Rusūl wa'l-Mulūk, vol. 6, p. 211; al-Akhbāru'ṭ Ṭawāl, p. 243.
43. Luhūf 'Alā Qatlu'l Ṭafūf: *(Urdu tr.* Usūf), p. 14.
44. al-Akhbāru'ṭ Ṭawāl, p. 234.
45. Tārīkhu'r-Rusūl wa'l-Mulūk, vol. 6, p. 201.
46. al-Akhbāru'ṭ Ṭawāl, p. 234; Tārīkhu'r-Rusūl wa'l-Mulūk, vol. 6, p. 201.
47. Tārīkhu'r-Rusūl wa'l-Mulūk, vol. 6, p. 301.
48. al-Irshād fī Ma'rifat Ḥujjāj Allāh 'Alā 'Ibād, p. 214; Tārīkhu'r-Rusūl wa'l-Mulūk, vol. 6, p. 201.
49. al-Irshād fī Ma'rifat Ḥujjāj Allāh 'Alā 'Ibād, p. 214; Tārīkhu'r-Rusūl wa'l-Mulūk, vol. 6, p. 201.
50. al-Irshād fī Ma'rifat Ḥujjāj Allāh 'Alā 'Ibād, p. 213.
51. Tanwīr-i-Majālis, p. 37.
52. al-Irshād fī Ma'rifat Ḥujjāj Allāh 'Alā 'Ibād, p. 215; Tārīkhu'r-Rusūl wa'l-Mulūk, vol. 5, p. 204.
53. al-Irshād fī Ma'rifat Ḥujjāj Allāh 'Alā 'Ibād, p. 218; Tārīkhu'r-Rusūl wa'l-Mulūk, vol. 6, p. 207.
54. al-Akhbāru'ṭ Ṭawāl, p. 240.
55. al-Irshād fī Ma'rifat Ḥujjāj Allāh 'Alā 'Ibād, p. 225; Tārīkhu'r-Rusūl wa'l-Mulūk, vol. 6, p. 212.
56. al-Irshād fī Ma'rifat Ḥujjāj Allāh 'Alā 'Ibād, pp. 225-26; Tārīkhu'r-Rusūl wa'l Mulūk, vol. 6, pp. 212-13.
57. al-Irshād fī Ma'rifat Ḥujjāj Allāh 'Alā 'Ibād p. 226; Tārīkhu'r-Rusūl wa'l-Mulūk, vol. 6, pp. 213-14.
58. al-Akhbāru'ṭ Ṭawāl, p. 142.
59. Tanwīr-i-Majālis, pp. 52-54.
60. Luhūf 'Alā Qatlu'l Ṭafūf, p. 178.
61. Usūf 'Alā Qatlu'l Ṭafūf, pp. 245-46.
62. al-Irshād fī Ma'rifat Ḥujjāj Allāh 'Alā 'Ibād, pp. 225-26; Tārīkhu'r-Rusūl wa'l Mulūk, vol. 6, pp. 212-13.
63. al-Irshād fī Ma'rifat Ḥujjāj Allāh 'Alā 'Ibād, p. 228.
64. *We should bear in mind a few basic facts of the journey:*
    Firstly, the distance between Mecca and Karbala, which is approx. 918 miles (1,470 km).
    Secondly, the mode of journey was camels' Caravan.
    Besides Imām Ḥusain and his companions, there were ladies and children. In those days dry climate, the journey could only be possible in the night.
    Thirdly, the then travel speed of the camels' Caravan was 30-40 miles per day. Imām Ḥusain's Caravan travelled 918 miles in approx. 24 days (9th September – 2nd October, 680)
    Fouthly, there may be no possibility of being stationed at 24 places, i.e. halted everywhere a day. He may had stationed at a place for more days, such as, on hearing about the killing of Muslim in Kufa, he stayed at Żabalah for more days.

Fifthly, if deduct 4 days from 24 days, the remaining 20 days' journey speed would be approx. 40 miles per day, which may be said a comfortable journey.

At a safer point, it may be said, perhaps the journey was completed with the speed of 35-40 miles per day.—Author.

65. al-Irshād fī Ma'rifat Ḥujjāj Allāh 'Alā 'Ibād, p. 225; Tārīkhu'r-Rusūl wa'l-Mulūk vol. 6, p. 212.
66. al-Irshād fī Ma'rifat Ḥujjāj Allāh 'Alā 'Ibād, p. 229.
67. al-Irshād fī Ma'rifat Ḥujjāj Allāh 'Alā 'Ibād, p. 202; Tārīkhu'r-Rusūl wa'l-Mulūk, vol. 6, p. 212.
68. al-Akhbāru'ṭ Ṭawāl, p. 245.
69. al-Irshād fī Ma'rifat Ḥujjāj Allāh 'Alā 'Ibād, p. 220; Tārīkhu'r-Rusūl wa'l-Mulūk, vol. 6, p. 218.
70. Tārīkhu'r-Rusūl wa'l Mulūk, vol. 6, p. 218; al-Irshād fī Ma'rifat Ḥujjāj Allāh 'Alā 'Ibād, p. 228.
71. al-Irshād fī Ma'rifat Ḥujjāj Allāh 'Alā 'Ibād, p. 229.
72. al-Akhbāru'ṭ Ṭawāl, p. 245.
73. al-Akhbāru'ṭ Ṭawāl, p. 247.
74. al-Irshād fī Ma'rifat Ḥujjāj Allāh 'Alā 'Ibād, p. 230.
75. al-Irshād fī Ma'rifat Ḥujjāj Allāh 'Alā 'Ibād, p. 230
76. al-Akhbāru'ṭ Ṭawāl, p. 245
77. Tārīkhu'r-Rusūl wa'l-Mulūk, vol. 6, p. 224; al-Irshād fī Ma'rifat Ḥujjāj Allāh 'Alā 'Ibād, p. 231; al-Akhbāru'ṭ Ṭawāl, p. 246.
78. Tārīkhu'r-Rusūl wa'l-Mulūk, vol. 6, p. 225; al-Irshād fī Ma'rifat Ḥujjāj Allāh 'Alā 'Ibād, p. 232.
79. Tārīkhu'r-Rusūl wa'l-Mulūk, vol. 6, p. 226; al-Irshād fī Ma'rifat Ḥujjāj Allāh 'Alā 'Ibād, pp. 231-33.
80. Luhūf 'Alā Qatlu'l Ṭafūf, p. 27.
81. Tārīkhu'r-Rusūl wa'l-Mulūk, vol. 6, p. 203.
82. al-Akhbāru'ṭ Ṭawāl, p. 247.
83. Tārīkhu'r-Rusūl wa'l-Mulūk, vol. 6, p. 246.
84. al-Irshād fī Ma'rifat Ḥujjāj Allāh 'Alā 'Ibād, p. 233.
85. Shahīd-i-Insāniyat, p. 304.
86. Tārīkhu'r-Rusūl wa'l-Mulūk, vol. 6, p. 234; al-Akhbāru'ṭ Ṭawāl, p. 247.
87. al-Irshād fī Ma'rifat Ḥujjāj Allāh 'Alā 'Ibād, p. 234; Tārīkhu'r-Rusūl wa'l-Mulūk, vol. 6, p. 227.
88. Tārīkhu'r-Rusūl wa'l-Mulūk, vol. 6, p. 228; al-Akhbāru'ṭ Ṭawāl, p. 248.
89. al-Irshād fī Ma'rifat Ḥujjāj Allāh 'Alā 'Ibād pp 235-36; Tārīkhu'r-Rusūl wa'l-Mulūk, vol. 6, p. 228.
90. al-Irshād fī Ma'rifat Ḥujjāj Allāh 'Alā 'Ibād, p. 236.
91. Tārīkhu'r-Rusūl wa'l-Mulūk, vol. 6, p. 229.
92. Tārīkhu'r-Rusūl wa'l-Mulūk, vol. 6, p. 229.
93. Tārīkhu'r-Rusūl wa'l-Mulūk, vol. 6, p. 229.
94. al-Akhbāru'ṭ Ṭawāl, p. 248.
95. al-Maqtal: Abī Mīkhnaf, p. 56; Ḥusainī Inqalāb, p. 57.

96. al-Irshād fī Ma'rifat Ḥujjāj Allāh 'Alā 'Ibād, p. 236; Tārīkhu'r-Rusūl wa'l-Mulūk, vol. 6, p. 229.
97. al-Irshād fī Ma'rifat Ḥujjāj Allāh 'Alā 'Ibād, p. 236; Tārīkhu'r-Rusūl wa'l-Mulūk, vol. 6, p. 229.
98. Tārīkhu'r-Rusūl wa'l-Mulūk, vol. 6, pp. 230-31.
99. al-Irshād fī Ma'rifat Ḥujjāj Allāh 'Alā 'Ibād, pp. 238-40.
100. al-Akhbāru'ṭ Ṭawāl, pp. 249-50.
101. Tārīkhu'r-Rusūl wa'l-Mulūk, vol. 6, p. 232.
It would be appropriate to clarify here that there was no misunderstanding about these dates; but the days are different in various calendars. As per the calendar in my use (Taqwīm Hijrī-o-Īswī: Abula'l Naṣr Muḥammad Khalidī) *2nd Muḥarram 61 AH was on Tuesday and its 10th Muḥarram was on Friday.* –Author

Chapter: Five

Attempts of Peace at Karbala

No sooner do we imagine Imām Ḥusain and Karbala, our attention is drawn to that great sacrifice, which he had laid at the altar of Karbala along with his supporters and members of his family. This sacrifice he made on 10th Muḥarram, 61 AH (10th October, 680 AD). However, he reached Karbala on 2nd Muḥarram 61 AH (2nd October, 680 AD)[1]. Imām Ḥusain's activities during this week would be discussed in the present chapter, as a preface of the great Battle of Karbala, but, not just a preface of the Battle, because Imām Ḥusain did not attempt to collect means of any type for battle in those days. He neither accumulated any war-material nor conducted any army practice. But in the mean time Imām Ḥusain clarified his objectives every now and then. Explained to the common people, who he was and what he wanted ?

Analysing the supportive basis of the important and far reaching decision of Imām Ḥusain and to ensure the Qu'ranic mandate, as an utmost duty to accept the recognised orders and to avoid the prohibited ones, besides, his personal commitment, Imām Ḥusain had dutiful responsibility towards those honest persons too, whom he had been consolling that he would do the needful at the appropriate time.

While analysing objectively the events of the life-time of Imām Ḥusain, it becomes clear that he was himself not in favour of any war. War was imposed upon him. He tried his best to avoid this imposed war. He himself initiated at a number of times to make compromise with Yażīdī Army, but the enemy side was firm in its stand. Historians and writers unanimously say that Imām Ḥusain had been attempting many times for the establishment of peace. He told Yażīdī Army repeatedly to let him go or to take him to Yażīd. He said he would convince him or he would give up the very idea of remaining in Iraq and if needed he was ready even to sacrifice 'Arab peninsula itself and would settle down some where far away. Some say that he preferred to proceed to India.

Imām Ḥusain put up three alternatives for compromise before them—

The first alternative that Imām Ḥusain would lead his life peacefully remaining again in Medina. In Medina dwelling there was no danger for the Umayyite Rule, before or after also would arise.

In the above second alternative there could not be any fear for Umayyite Rule, because Imām Ḥusain had proposed even to leave 'Arabian peninsula itself. Living in any far off place, Imām Ḥusain could not be any problem to Yażīd.

The third alternative put forward by Imām Ḥusain that he may be allowed to meet Yażīd, he would converse himself there was no danger at all for Yażīdī, all the dangers were only for Imām Ḥusain.

The learned scholars and writers like[2]: al-Majlisī, Muḥammad Bāqir (d. 1699 AD), Saiyed 'Alī Naqī Naqavī (d. 1988 AD), Saiyed Khairāt Ḥasan (d. 1989 AD) and some others have dicussed the three points of above peace proposals. They generally agree on first alternative of Imām Ḥusain peacefully remaining again in Medina. However, they did not agree with the above proposed second and third alternatives. They argue that they had found no information in any of the ancient sacred reference books that Imām Ḥusain had said to go to India. But the third alternative that Imām Ḥusain may be allowed to meet Yażīd, the scholars did not agree to the extent that they refuse the possibility of even it being happened. They declare it absolutely unbelievable because no evidence is available in the speeches, letters and discussion of Imām Ḥusain. This matter is against the policy of Imām Ḥusain too, they feel, because, it means accepting Yażīd by implication. And Imām Ḥusain would never accept Yażīd because his acceptance would be in negation of the Qu'ranic mandate, his utmost duty to accept the recognised mandate and to avoid the prohibited ones. It was against the truth and justice. In case of not accepting Yażīd's *Bay'at*. Imām Ḥusain would have been murdered, Imām Ḥusain's immaculate conduct would have been tarnished, whose counter-defence was not at all possible. The eyewitness would be enemies, who would evict the incident.

This obedient author does not agree with the distinguished scholars in these lines. As far as first alternative, Imām Ḥusain would return back to Medina, without ensuring Qu'ranic mandate, to enjoin good and prohibit evil, which is his foremost duty as the *Imām*. And also evading the promise towards those honest persons, whom he had been consolling that he would do the needful at the appropriate time. No doubt that various historians have mentioned the alternative of returning to Medina but the same historians have also recorded the third alternative of going to Damascus and appearing before Yażīd. Our learned scholars' arguments lack creditibility, because both statements are of same historians. If one part is correct other one autometically becomes incorrect. My humble opinion is both statements are correct. These were most calculated alternatives suggested by Imām Ḥusain, fully kowing its outcome.

For the second alternative of Imām Ḥusain's going in any far off place, some say, he wished to proceed to India. Some of them argue that they had not seen any ancient reference which could establish the fact. In a research, nothing is as the final verdict. On the basis of the discovery of new datas it goes on changing. Yesterday's impossible becomes possible today, it has been taking place everywhere. Previously reference-books, which were not available, are available afterwards, as has happened regarding this subject. Now-a-days authentic books are available on the subjects of issue. 'Oqbah-bin-Sama'n, who was Imām Ḥusain's wife Umm Rabāb's servant and has travelled in the Ḥusainī Caravan and eyewitness of all incidents in his *Maqtal* can be studied. Ibn Qutaybah, Abū Muḥammad 'Abdu'llāh-bin-Muslim Dīnāwarī (d. 889 AD) has written about the incident:

> "Imām Ḥusain said, if you do not agree with my going to Iraq, then leave me, I will go to Sind (Hind)."[3]

Regarding third possibility of Imām Ḥusain's visit of Damascus to meet Yażīd, our leaned scholars have argued that Imām Ḥusain was aware of all the situations, he could not have asserted to converse with Yażīd, because his going to Damascus could have been the subject to the terrific results; where in Imām Ḥusain would have been secretly martyred, there would not have been anybody, even to present his side. The historians nurtured by the Umayyite Rule could be free to describe the incident in any way as they would like. Had he not been made a Martyr, and there would a compromise with Yażīd on the basis of some matters, then what was the guarantee that Yażīd would abide by it. His father Mu'āwiyah-bin-Abū Sufyyān made a peace-agreement with Imām Ḥasan in a written manner and how vilely he broke the agreement, afterwards. How one could be assured on the agreement of Yażīd.

However, my humble view is different on the issue of Imām Ḥusain's going Damascus and proposing a chance to converse with Yażīd. In my considered opinion, it was an exemplary, unparalleled, forethought and foreseen view of Imām Ḥusain. Such a decision could only and only be taken by Imām Ḥusain and never by any ordinary person. Only that person could propose to talk directly with the other side who has a strong and firm faith and confidence in his just objectives. A person who refuses, looses his case *prima facie*. Yażīdī's refusal to agree to sit at a table and resolve the issues amounts to admit the genuineness of Ḥusainī stand. The option of direct conversation has been a successful experiment for establishing peace between two waring parties. In present age also it is a part of the Declaration of the United Nations. Why did Imām Ḥusain not use it making it as a standard for his justifiable objectives ? Raising this question with answer that there was fear of life in going to Damascus, then where was there no fear of life for Imām Ḥusain. He was always prepared to sacrifice his everything on the path of Truth, provided, it could safeguard the Islāmic accepted principles and shun the prohibited ones. Had Imām had proposed to visit Damascus, then there would have been a certain on his objectives. It is clear that Imām Ḥusain was fully apprised of the situation that Yażīdī wanted the war and not peace. Imām Ḥusain absolutely understood Yażīdī's vileness, conspiracies and atrocities, but wanted to clarify his stand keeping all his doors opened for arguments, so, that the writers and historians purchased by the Umayyites regime could not exhibit any plausibility of language. And the curtain may be taken off for ever from the cruelties. Yażīdī Governor, 'Obaydu'llāh-bin-Żiyād (Ibn-Żiyād) was not willing to accept any thing below *Bay'at* and Imām Ḥusain was not at all ready to *Bay'at* at any cost or in any form. Therefore, Imām Ḥusain put forward such a proposal, after negating it, that Yażīdī could give no argument at all. It became self-explanatory that Imām Ḥusain wanted to avoid war, but Yażīdī was not at all prepared to accept the words of Imām Ḥusain.

It is clear from the above facts that the war could be avoided in that situation only, when Imām Ḥusain could take *Bay'at* for the Ruler Yażīd-bin-Mu'āwiyah-bin-Abū Sufyyān. Yażīdī's Commander-in-Chief was not at all prepared to accept any condition less than this and Imām Ḥusain was prepared to do compromise on any other condition, but for this one. If at all there had to be compromise on this condition.

We may postpone this matter here and discuss it at an appropriate place. Let us go firstly to Karbala itself.

Karbalau'l-Mua'llah

Being Imām Ḥusain's holyland, Karbala, which was an abandoned desert became the third supreme pilgrimage centre for Muslims. On account of the Holy Ka'bah being in the *Makkah'ul-Mu'aẓẓamah* (Exalted Mecca) and *Madīnatu'l-Munawwarah* (Splendid Medina) being holy land of the Prophet Muḥammad, are held most sacred. In the same way *Karbalau'l-Mu'allah* (Sublime Karbala), because of being the place of sacrifice of Imām Ḥusain. This land has become so divine that it obtained the prestige of being *Khāku'sh-Shif'a* (Sinless Land).

At present Karbala is a famous and holy town of the middle Iraq, situated in south-west from its capital, Baghdad, at a distance of 55 miles and is linked to the capital by rails.[4] Now, whatever it was called in olden days, Karbala, it was the name of a group of villages, in the Wādīu'l Ṭaf. These villages were small in size, but they had their own special characeristics and they were named only on that basis. On the basis of separate specialities and meanings some writers have been giving them different recognitions that sometimes illusion arises. Therefore, it appears neccessary to write correct facts about the holy land of Imām Ḥusain, which is famous with different names as Karbala, Naynwān, Ghāzariya and Shaṭu'l-Furāt.[5] Let us have some primary informations about these places.

Naynwān was the very first place which has already been discussed in the previous chapter. This place was near the presently Suddau'l-Hindiya. Near by it, was a place Ghāzariya, which was named after the famous Asad clan's branch Ghāzariya tribe, who were living there. It was the biggest village. Probably this was the same land, which has now attained the glory of being called the Ḥusainīya. In this same place there was a village Shaffīya and here only, is the land of Karbala, where presently towards south-eastern side is situated the Karbala town. There was an area called 'Aqurahu'l-Bābul, which was situated in north-west of Ghāzariya. Archaeological evidences are found there. Being surrounded by the small mountains. In its middle was a land called Ḥayr, which is presently called as Ḥayār, wherein we find the holy grave of Imām Ḥusain. It is a large field surrounded by the hillocks in three directions. The hillocks starts from the north-east, where are the Bābu'l-Sadr and Minārahu'l-'Abd of the holy Mausoleum of Imām Ḥusain and passing through Bābu'l-Żainab ended in the south at Daru'l-Qiblah. It appears a segment of circle like new moon. This was that circular land wherein Imām Ḥusain was surronded and made a martyr. The way in its eastern direction leads to the Mausoleum of Abu'l-Faẓl'il-'Abbās-bin-Imām'Alī, the Ḥusainī Commander-in-Chief at Battle of Karbala.

If we closely observe the lands adjoining the Mausoleum of Imām Ḥusain, it appears to be the ancient of land in northern and western directions and in the eastern direction except the soft soil towards a hillock nothing is involve. It can be inferred from this that the ancient form of this place was such that there was plain in the east and an elevated land in a circular form in the northern and western directions.

A discussion of the River Furāt (Euphrates) appears for ever in Karbala incident. In fact, the River Euphrates has no connection at all with Karbala. Its limit touches the extenal portions of places like Kufa *via* Ḥillah, Mussayyib etc. places. From that place Karbala is 50 miles (80 kms). However, a small tributary of River Euphrates, starting from nearby Rizwāniyah was flowing into Karbala *via* deserted north-eastern valleys of today's Karbala. Passing by the Mausoleum of Abu'l-Fazl'il-'Abbās joins the original River Euphrates in Qariyau'l-Žiu'l Kafil towards north-west *via* Hindiya. This small river was famous with the name 'Alqamah and most of authors have said it to be the River Euphrates. This is not Euphrates but its tributary 'Alqamah. In the same way the 'Arabic word *Ṭaf* means, the river's shore. Specially that shore of River Euphrates towards Basra in South people call it *Furātu'l-Saghīr* (Small Euphrates). Therefore, that shore of River 'Alqamah, wherein Karbala was situated is called Ṭaf. On that basis the Battle of Karbala was also called *Waqyatu'l-Ṭaf* and Karbala is also said as *Shaṭu'l-Furāt*.

Trustee Land of Karbala

In the previous chapter a reference has already been made that Imām Ḥusain's Caravan at Qaṣru'l Banī Maqātil had collected drinking water and proceeded ahead. As soon as he reached Karbala and before establishing the camps there, he got searched land-owners of Karbala villages group. He called them and expressed his desire of purchasing their land. All the land owners unitedly told Imām Ḥusain, what was the need to purchase such a deserted land, this is not at all advantagous to us. We don't have any other big fortune except to offer you our lands unitedly, and requested to accept their gift. But Imām Ḥusain was not ready to accept their lands free of cost. He said that he wanted to purchased their lands and asked them to get the cost of their lands and he insisted that he would get their lands only with that condition. The landlords submitted that their lands were useless, just a barren ground, nothing could be sown and grown. Imām Ḥusain said that he would make a garden there. They kept quiet, because they believed that Imām could do any miracle, if he wished. Ultimately Imām Ḥusain purchased their lands. At that time people didn't feel; but today it is clear what message Imām Ḥusain gave in the name of buying lands. The graves of the family members of the holy Prophet and devoted companions are in Karbala.

Imām Ḥusain purchased from Naynwān and Ghāzariya landlords, the land 4 miles × 4 miles = 16 square miles that is 6.4 km × 6.4 km = 41 square km, on payment in cash Diraham 60,000 (sixty thousands) only and then made them its trustee![6]

Purchasing a land of Karbala by Imām Ḥusain and then donating into a trust, was an important and forethought decision, which could not be comprehended at that time. When, Karbala land became the personal property of Imām Ḥusain, and one who tried to occupy or forcefully usurp the land should always be tracepasser in the eyes of the law of any country. And any attack on the others property would be a criminal act under the law of any country. Imām Ḥusain did not attack anybody, but his personal property; his own land was attacked from outside. Imām Ḥusain always high lighted the question of security, and safety of property right. This legislation (system) was prevalent at that time, and in vogue in every age that no outsider or the force of any group can capture on anybody's property.

Intrusion by the Yażīdī Army

In the previous chapter we have already discussed about the martyrdom of Imām Ḥusain's peace-envoy Muslim and his supporters at Kufa. In the midst some other supporters also were made martyrs, specially among them were Mīṯham Tammār and Rashīd Hujarī. Yażīd in his palace at Damascus became overjoyed to get the news. He sent a letter to his Kufic Governor Ibn-Żiyād to the effect:

> "I have been informed that Ḥusain-bin-'Alī is attracted towards Iraq. Therefore, it is indispensable on your part that you may appoint tactful spies. Make the entrenchments stronger and if at all there is anything suspcious regarding anybody, arrest him immediately; making adequate arrangements."[7]

As soon as the orders were received Kufa's jails were brimful with the supporters of the Progeny of the Prophet Muḥammad. 'Obaydu'llāh-bin-Żiyād intimated to Yażīd immediately. His words were:

> "If anybody was found suspecisious of opposing the Rule, has been put inside the bars."[8]

Firm arrangements were made to arrest all those persons who could extend their help to Imām Ḥusain. Yażīdī administration was continuously scared over an abnormal regards commanded by Imām Ḥusain in Islāmic society. Everytime there was a lurking danger that if people get the information that Imām Ḥusain has entered into the battlefield for war, refusing to get into any compromise with Yažīd, then the self-prestige of Muslims in general and followers of the Progeny of the Prophet Muḥammad in particular, would get up and flourish. Masses would boil on all corners, which could not be managed. Therefore, special arrangements were made to lashout atrocities by the Yažīdī Army. The greatest fear was that the people of Basra, Madayan and their adjoining regions might assemble in support and assistance of Imām Ḥusain. So, special arrangement was made for prohibition of entry on its frontiers, because the limits of Ḥijāž, Iraq and Syria were centralised at Qādsiyah. The Kufa town *Kotwal,* Ḥiṣṣīn-bin-Numayr was appointed on the lines of frontiers along with 4000 soldiers at Qādsiyah. Army was deployed from Wāqṣah to Qaṭquṭāmah, L'aL'a and Khafān and its frontier areas and in all areas connected, where any road leading to Syria, Basra and Kufa was completely sealed off. It resulted in a situation that no person could go or come *vice versa.* Regarding Qays-bin-Muṣahar Ṣaidāvī, it has already been discussed in the above lines that only on account of the same prohibition of the frontiers he was arrested and killed by Ḥiṣṣīn-bin-Numayr at Qādsiyah.

What a huge Yažīdī Army was deputed at the frontiers has been estimated by Ṭirimmāh-bin-'Adī, who had told Imām Ḥusain that before setting out of Kufa he saw such a huge army in Kufa, as not seen before, and when he asked, he was told that all are assembled to attack Imām Ḥusain.[9]

If we study the causes of the deployment of such a huge army against such a small force of less than hundred people, said to be seventy two, including grandold men and children. It was nothing, but their psychic depressive reaction. Yažīdī Administration was extremely afraid of Imām Ḥusain's war skill and moral strength. He was the son of the great conqueror 'Alī-Ibn-Abī Ṭālib, who won each and every battle, whenever he participated and conquered the enemy. They had seen themselves the matchless valour at the Battle of Ṣiffīn. They again would see the finest war of Imām Ḥusain at the Battle of Karbala, when the time come. Keeping in view his family members' courage on several occasions during previous years it made him think that his army's strength and number of soldiers were less. As a result, Yažīdī Administration posted a very big army with 3000 soldiers in Kufic chief Ḥiṣṣīn-bin-Numayr leadership at Karbala. Afterwards proclamantion was made for general recruitment.

Yażīdī Governor 'Obaydu'llāh-bin-Żiyād himself getting away from Kufa camped at Nakhīlah village, 30 km away from Karbala.[10] He ordered Ḥajaru'l Ahajar, Shabth-bin-Raba'ī, 'Omar-bin-Ḥujjāj Żubaydī etc. that they might advance to Karbala with their Army. Everyone in their rank was equipped with a huge Army. He ordered 8000 more soldiers to accompany the Army.[11] If anybody wanted to evade on any account was not heard at all. When Shabth-bin-Raba'ī pleaded excuse for being ill, 'Obaydu'llāh-bin-Żiyād shouted that he was pretending. If he accepted subordination, then should proceed for the War. Being helpless Shabth-bin-Raba'ī started towards Karbala with his Army. There were a few people who silently returned to Kufa stealthily. On this, 'Obaydu'llāh-bin-Żiyād, when came to know ordered Swaid-bin-'Abdu'r Raḥmān Almiqrī to proceed to Kufa and arrest and present before him all those who went to Kufa not with a desire of attacking Imām Ḥusain. Swaid reached Kufa and spread the terror that one arrested person who had came to Kufa for his own personal reasons, was assasinated immediately and so terror and horror spread everywhere, all started to join battle with Imām Ḥusain.[12]

No doubt the numbers of people who were made to assemble were not against Imām Ḥusain, all were not inbued with enmity. There were some people among them, who were brought to Karbala by force. It was a life and death dilemma for them. It was a threat to their life.

There was also a group of salaried Yażīdīs who considered it as their duty to follow the orders of their officer. Their aim was to please their higher up and obtain from them options and rewards. Most of the people were such, who were having neither enmity nor friendship with Imām Ḥusain, but were going there as the soldiers. It is quite possible, they may not even be aware at all about Imām Ḥusain. In their view, they were going to fight against the rebel of the Rulers only.

The reason for not knowing anything was that the Rulers of Damascus spread very false and enviable propaganda not only against Imām 'Alī, Imām Ḥasan and Imām Ḥusain, but also against all the family members of the holy Prophet Muḥammad. There were also some old people, who were left alone, because of being medically unfit, they were cordially praying for the success of Imām Ḥusain. Yażīdī supporters were angry with them. They flag taunt on them – O' stupid people ! If you have such a goodwill towards Imām Ḥusain, why don't you sincerely fight in support of him.[13]

Upto 6th Muḥarram, 61 AH (6th October, 680 AD), four days before the day of martyrdom, the condition was that there were heads and heads only everywhere at Karbala and its adjoining places.[14]

The Strength of the Armies

There is a difference of opinion about the strength of the Yaẓīdī Army. It is said that it was in between forty thousands to four lacs. But, if we keep in mind the strength of the Yaẓīdī Army's various Commanders and their innumerable battalions, which have been mentioned by various histories, its number comes about 55,500. The least number is mentioned as four thousands by Abu'l 'Olā Maudūdī, which could not appear to be correct by any means. According to most reliable Abī Mīkhnaf, Lūṭ-bin-Yaḥyā (d. 774 AD) because the personal Army of Yaẓīdī Commander-in-Chief 'Omar-bin-Sa'd of 6000 soldiers was with him when he went to Karbala.[15] A few writers have opinion that his personal Army was 4000.[16] Besides, there were so many other Commanders under whom were big Armies ready for War. Their total could not be less than 55,500.[17]

In front of such a very huge Yaẓīdī Army the number of soldiers in Ḥusainī Army is popularly known as consisting of 72 persons only, that is 32 Foot-Soldiers and 40 Cavaliers.[18] However, the *Żiyārat-Nāḥiyah* (literally means, the Pilgrimage of Last Boundary of the Country) an edict for well-being, sanctioned by Imām Mahdī Ākhiru'ż-Żamān has included the names of the 79 martyrs, which has source of the authority of Shaykh Ṣadūq, Ibn-Bābūya, Abū Ja'far Muḥammad al-Qummī (d. 991 AD), who has been considered a great religious scholar. But 'Allāmah Ibn-Ṭāus (d. 1266 AD) has mentioned on the authority of Imām Muḥammad al-Bāqir that there were 45 Foot-Soldiers and 100 Cavaliers in Ḥusainī Army, that is, in total 145 persons.[19] According to 'Alī Naqī Naqavī 18 Hāshimites plus 92 Associates that is 110 were martyred.[20] He has mentioned 22 Associates, whose names appearer in some books, but no surity whether participated in the war of Truth, besides, he has also written the life sketches of other 46 persons, for whom he found much possibility of being with Imām Ḥusain in the battle for Truth.[21] In this way, as per his statement the total number of the martyrs of Karbala comes to 178. Thus, the maximum figure of the family members, and supporters of Imām Ḥusain may be said to be 178, who joined him in the war of Truth, against at least 55,500, well equipped Yaẓīdī Army.

First of all it is very clear that those who joined Imām Ḥusain in the war of Truth, could never be greedy or desirous of being part of Rulers, because it was well clear from the situations that they would never join hands with the enemies of Imām Ḥusain. Secondly, it was their own decision to become the martyrs alongwith Imām Ḥusain. So, it was clear that all those who joined him in the War of Truth, were well aware of his objectives and there was neither their personal advantage nor any hidden aim. They came just to sacrifice their own life, not to enjoy the comfort of the establishment. They were virtuous persons, who could never be greedy or selfish.

Besides, 18 Hāshimites, the full identity of the most reverend 92 Associates, who fought battle of Truth along with Imām Ḥusain, have been ascertained by the learned scholars by this time. That is, 10 persons came from Medina along with Imām Ḥusain, from Mecca 3 persons joined them. After starting from Mecca 10 more persons joined them, 8 persons of Basra and 58 of Kufic dwellers. In addition to those people whose dwelling places could not be ascertained, definitely there is the possibility of some Kufic dwellers, whose number is 10 only.[22]

The Creation of the Ḥusainī Army

The process of the creation of the Ḥusainī Army was neither pre-planned nor sudden. It was rather gradual in nature. Besides, a few, who being fortunate enough were offered to join the battle of Truth, there were others who have awakened themselves after hearing the call of their conscience. Some of them, who planned to join with the motive of enjoying the benefits of the Ruling cadre, which was exuberantly being distributed for last three decates, were never allowed by Imām Ḥusain to join his company and were refused politely. Despite again and again explaining the correct situation which was clearly leading to the sacrifice of life, in whom he found glimpses of Truth, were allowed to be remained with him. Such fortunate Associates, joined him from Medina, Mecca and various other places during the journey, as Abṭaḥ, near Mecca, Żarwud and Żabālah have already been narrated at the appropriate places in the previous chapter. However, without their names no list of the Associates could be visualized, so, it is being mentioned here again, without them the raising of the Ḥusainī Army could not be possible.

1. Joined from Medina

Imām Ḥusain started from Medina, the persons attached with the family of the holy Prophet, could not leave them alone at the hard time, they were —

Sa'd-bin-Ḥārith (Imām 'Alī's servant)
Jaun (Abūžar Ghaffārī's servant)
'Aun-bin-Jaun (son of Abūžar Ghaffārī's servant)

Qārib-bin-'Abdu'llāh (Imām Ḥusain's servant)
Munjiḥ-bin-Sahm (Imām Ḥusain's servant)
Salīm (Imām Ḥusain's servant)
Ḥāfiẓ Turkī (Imām Żainu'l-Ābidīn's servant)
Ḥārith-bin-Nibhān (Ḥamżah's servant)
'Oqbah-bin-Sama'n (Umm Rabāb's servant)

2. Joined from Mecca

We have discussed in the previous chapter that when Imām Ḥusain left Mecca about 60 thousand ran away raising dust by the hooves of their horses, when the dust settled down, a few persons were standing like the rock,[23] whose names are—

'Abdu'l Raḥmān-bin-'Abd Rab Anṣārī Khiżarajjī,
Jinādah-bin-K'ab-bin-Ḥārith Anṣārī Khiżarajjī,
'Omarū, 'Ābis-bin-Abī Shabīb Shākirī,
Shožab-bin-'Abdu'llāh,
Żāhir ('Omarū'l Ḥamaq's servant),
Żāhar-bin-'Omarū Aslamī Kindī,
'Ammār-bin-Ḥassān-bin-Shurayb Ṭaī, and
Ḥujjāj-bin-Masrūq Ja'fī, who came to Mecca from Kufa and joined Imām Ḥusain.

3. Joined from Abṭaḥ, near Mecca

Abṭaḥ a group of supporters met Imām Ḥusain to accompany him.[24] They were —

Żayd-bin-Thabayṭ Qaysī and his two sons
'Abdu'l Raḥmān-bin-Żayd-bin-Thabayṭ Qaysī
'Obaydu'llāh-bin-Żayd-bin-Thabayṭ Qaysī
'Āmir-bin-Muslim 'Abdī Baṣrī
Sālim ('Āmir-bin-Muslim 'Abdī Baṣrī's servants)
Shabīb-bin-'Abdu'llāh Nahashalī

4. Joined from Żarwud

This was the place, where some such associate joined who have special significance in the history of the Battle of Karbala, they include —

Ḥabīb-bin-Maẓāhir Asadī
Żuhayr-bin-Qayn-bin-Qays Numayrī Bajalī (Żuhayr-Qayn)
Burayr-bin-Khuzayr Hamadānī
Junadab-bin-Ḥajīr Kindī Khūlānī,
Yażīd-bin-Żiyād-bin-Mahāṣar
Abu'lal-Sh'athā Kindī
Ḥabāb-bin-'Āmir-bin-Ka'b Tayamī

5. Joined from Żabālah

After the alarming address of Imām Ḥusain only three people remained with him, they were —

'Ibad-bin-Muhājir-bin-Abī Muhājir Juhanī
'Oqbah-bin-Ṣulet Juhanī
Mujama'-bin-Żiyād-bin-'Omarū-Jehnī

6. Joined from 'Ażību'l Hijānāt

Depite, a mild objection raised by Ḥurr, who had created hurdle in the way of Ḥusainī Caravan, five persons from Kufa presented themselves before Imām Ḥusain and were allowed, they were —

'Omar-bin-Khālid Asadī Ṣaidavī
Saī'd ('Omar-bin-Khālid Asadī Ṣaidāvī's servant)
Mujama'-bin-'Abdu'llāh 'Āyiżī, and his son
'Āyiż-bin-Majama'-bin-'Abdu'llāh 'Āyiżī
Jinādah-bin-Ḥārith Salmānī.

7. Joined from Karbala

In spite of so many hurdles and troubles created by Yażīdī Army on all the ways to Karbala, the names of 23 daring and fervent persons, who endangering their lives were successful in reaching to Imām Ḥusain at Karbala. Their proud names were —

'Abdu'l Raḥmān-bin-'Abdu'llāh-bin-Kadan Arḥabī
'Omarū-bin-Jinādah-bin-Ka'b Khiżarajjī
'Omarū-bin-Qurẓah-bin-Ka'b Anṣārī
Abū-Thamāmah 'Omarū-bin-'Abdu'llāh Ṣāy'dī
Bish-bin-'Omarū-bin-al-Uhadūth Ḥazaramī Kindī

Ḥanẓalah-bin-Asa'd S͟hāmī
Ḥujjāj-bin-Żaid-Sa'dī Tayamī
Jiblitah-bin-'Alī S͟haybānī
Kardūs-bin-Żuhayr-bin-Ḥārit͟h Tag͟halabī
Kinānah-bin-'Atīq Tag͟hlabī
Muqsiṭ(Kurs͟h)-bin-Żuhayr-bin-Ḥārit͟h Tag͟halabī
Muslim-bin-Kat͟hīr Ṣadafī Ażdī
Nāfa'-bin-Hilāl Jamalī Al-Murādī
Naī'm-bin-'Ajalān Anṣārī
Qa'nab-bin-'Āmir Numayrī
Qāsiṭ-bin-Żuhayr-bin-Ḥārit͟h Tag͟hlabī
Rāf'a-bin-'Abdu'llāh (Muslim Ażdī's servant)
Sa'īd-bin-'Abdu'llāh Ḥasafī
Saif-bin-Mālik 'Abdī
Sālim-bin-'Omarū-bin-'Abdu'llāh (Medīnahu'l Kalbī)
S͟habīb-bin-'Abdu'llāh (Ḥārit͟h-bin-Sarī'a's servant)
Umayyah-bin-Sa'd-bin-Żaid Ṭaī
Żayd-bin-Mī'qal Ja'fī

Similarly, when Kufic Governor 'Obaydu'llāh-bin-Żiyād camped at Nak͟hīlah and started sending troops to fight against Imām Ḥusain, a family of Christian background, residing there, consisting of son, wife and mother left the place silently and joined Imām Ḥusain at Karbala. His son and wife attained the martyrdom, their names were —

Abū Wahab-Kalbī ('Abdu'llāh-bin-'Omayr Kalbī)
Umm Wahab-Kalbī-bint-'Abd

8. Ḥusainīs of Yażīdī Army

After the arrival of Imām Ḥusain at Karbala some more people came to Imām Ḥusain, leaving Yażīdī Army. For reaching Karbala, they joined Yażīdī Army, because they had no other option to escape from enemies eyes. Yażīdī Administration had made on all corners a very strong and severe prohibition of entry that catching hold off red-handed on the way their killing was very certain. They were not at all worried about their life, because they had already come forward sacrificing their own life at the alter of truth and faith in Islām, the holy Prophet and Imām Ḥusain. They were very particular to sacrifice their life at the august feet of Imām Ḥusain. Another possibility is this that some of them were in Yażīdī Army previously. But their conscience would have awakened them on the way and they would have decided to reach Karbala and join Imām Ḥusain and offer their life in the defence of the truth and justice. Whatever may be, travelling along with the enemy Force was a very risky and dangerous resolution. These warriers travelled successfully up to Karbala, whose inner-mind-status could not be understood by Yażīdī Army. Their names were —

Jābir-bin-Hujjāj Taymī ('Āmir-bin-Nahashal's servant)
Zarghamah-bin-Mālik Taghalabī
'Abdu'llāh-bin-Bishar Khith'amī
'Omarū-bin-Zab'aitah-bin-Qays-bin-Th'albah Zab'ī Taymī
Qāsim-bin-Ḥabīb-bin-Abī Bushr Ażdī

Besides them were, Masu'd-bin-Ḥujjāj Taymī and his son 'Abdu'l Raḥmān-bin-Mas'ūd-bin-Ḥujjāj Tayamī, who on the pretext of saluting Imām Ḥusain (3 days prior to the War) came out from Yażīdī Army and did not return.

Similarly, some more soldiers also came to Imām Ḥusain leaving away Yażīdī Army and become Martyrs. It would be discussed here for having the comprehensive picture of the raising of the Ḥusainī Army, though their arrival has been associated with the incidents which happened after war and will be narrated in the ensuing chapters at the appropriate places.

9. Arrival from the Yażīdī Army

There were a few such soldiers in the Yażīdī Army, who were honest and God fearing, but their moto of life was the same as people generally behave, not to indulge in any affair, keep themselves neutral and keep the personal safety and the safety of their family at top of everything. At least two of personnels of Yażīdī Army could not resist their inner call. They were thinking that ultimately there would be peace with Imām Ḥusain, everything would be settled. By joining with Imām Ḥusain they would be declared enemy, resulting different types of loss and damage. Therefore, continuing with Yażīdī Army had no harm. But when Yażīdī Army disagreed with all the attempts of peace by Imām Ḥusain, then the orduous situation emerged. They did not liked to be the part of Yażīdī Army even for a moment and immediately came to Imām Ḥusain, who pardoned them and allowed to join his small Army. The names of those soldier were —

Juvayn-bin-Mālik-bin-Qays-bin-Th'albah Tayamī-Ḥārith-bin-Imra-ul-Qays-bin-'Ābis Kindī
Sawwār-bin-Abī 'Oman Nahamī
No'mān-bin-'Omarū Ażdī

10. More from the Yażīdī Army

There were two such soldiers in the Yażīdī Army, whose conscience was not allowing to stay there any more, they took firm decision and presented themselves before Imām Ḥusain in the final night before the War. Imām Ḥusain pardoned them and they joined the Ḥusainī Army. Their name were —

Żāhayr-bin-Sulaym-bin-'Omarū Ażdī, and
Ḥallās-bin-'Omarū Ażdī Rāsbī

11. Ḥurr in the Ḥusainī Army

The name of Ḥurr-bin-Yażīd-Riyāḥī (Ḥurr) is not unfamiliar to our learned readers. He was the Yażīdī Commander of a Regiment of the Yażīdī Army, who had constrainted and brought Imām Ḥusain to Karbala. But when they reached, the soldiers quenched their thrust came in front of Imām Ḥusain, the enbodiment of compassion, who could not tolerate even his enemy to die for want of water. Not only the soldiers, but also their animals were offered water and food at least three times.[25] Its details have already been presented in the previous chapter.

Imām Ḥusain's such compassion and kindness must have been haunting Ḥurr day and night. There had been question of Heaven and Hell before him. Ḥurr followed the demand of his conscience and left the Yażīdī Army in the dawn of the day. Ḥurr has a special greatness among those who came to Imām Ḥusain's side leaving huge comforts of the Yażīdī Army for protecting the truth and justice, but this sequence commenced even before his good arrival. His great achievements are the subject of ensuing chapter.

Ḥurr did not come alone, he brought his brother, two sons and servant too along with him. We come to know that only his sons and servant were nearer, because as soon as Ḥurr left the Yażīdī Army, Ḥurr's brother Muṣa'b, two sons Sa'd and 'Alī and the servant Qurrah also driving horse met him.[26] Perhaps they also joined Imām Ḥusain along with him. Their full names were —

Ḥurr-bin-Yażīd-Riyāḥī (Ḥurr)
Muṣa'b-bin-Yażīd Riyāḥī
Sa'd-bin-Ḥurr-bin-Yażīd-Riyāḥī
'Alī-bin-Ḥurr-bin-Yażīd-Riyāḥī
Qurrah (Ḥurr-bin-Yażīd-Riyāḥī's servant)

12. Last Arrival from the Yażīdī Army

The last soldier in this order was Bakr-bin-Ḥay Tayamī, who came to Ḥusain's side during the Yażīdī Army's cowardly arrow attack. Bakr-bin-Ḥay Tayamī belonged to the Yażīdī Army's Commander-in-Chief, 'Omar-bin-Sa'd's special battalion, who came to Karbala along with him. When the War began, his inner-soul's voice made him sad. There is no information whether he submitted himself to Imām Ḥusain or not. Only this much of information is available that after the cowardly arrow attack by the Yażīdī Army, he attained peace in the Heaven.[27]

With this the total figure of the august Associates who joined comes to 82, in which 19 soldiers were those who revolted from the Yażīdī Army and joined the small Ḥusainī Army. It testifies the fact that there was confusion, frustration and sense of guilt prevailing in the Yażīdī Army and the soldiers were revolting against the Umayyites.

However, the above list cannot be claimed to be the complete and final one, because there are several other names, appear to be omitted here, but these names which are found in the list are persons who had sacrificed their lives for the cause of Truth along with Imām Ḥusain at the Battle of Karbala.

Atrocious Activities of the Yażīdī Army

No sooner did Imām Ḥusain and his companions entered Karbala, the Yażīdī Army started atrocious activities. It took possession of the land which Imām Ḥusain had purchased from Naynwān and Ghāzariya people against payment in cash and had laid their camps and tents at the bank of the river 'Alqamah. The Ḥusainī soldiers asked permission to make a crushing reply to the Yażīdī Army for its unjustified action. The facts are mentioned in above pages. There was severe reaction on behalf of the Ḥusainī soldiers over their ferrocious behaviour, when the Yażīdī Army exhibited its might and created trouble in the name of removing the camps and tents of Imām Ḥusain and their supporters from the bank of the river 'Alqamah, however, there was no justification in that, because Imām Ḥusain and his companions had reached Karbala before the Yażīdī

Army, and they had laid their tents and camps there. At the time of their camping the Yażīdī Army had not objected to that. But afterwards they wanted to fight in the same pretext. It seemed that the war would start, swords were unsheathed on either side, but Imām Ḥusain could not be influenced by war in the name of water of his objectives. He insisted his soldiers to shift their camps at a distance from the bank of the river 'Alqamah. Obedient Ḥusainī soldiers Immediatly removed their camps and the Yażīdī Army captured the river 'Alqamah. The Ḥusainī soldiers found it difficult to take water from river 'Alqamah being troubled but there was no restriction on taking water at that time.

Change of the Command

The next day on the day 3rd Muḥarram, 61 AH. (3rd October, 680 AD) 'Omar-bin-Sa'd reached Karbala as a Commandor-in-Chief of the Yażīdī Army along with 6,000 soldiers.[28] Under his leadership the Yażīdī Army fought with Imām Ḥusain and his supporters. Therefore, it would be apppropriate to contemplate on that subject.

'Omar-bin-Sa'd was the son of Sa'd-bin-Abī Waqāṣ, one of the Companions of the holy Prophet. He was considered as one of the members of *'Ashrahu'l-Mubashsharah* (Ten Evangelists) of Muslim Ummah. Amazingly, in the same way there is also another member of the *Ten Evangelists,* Mughīrah-bin-Sho'abah, on whose proposal Amīr Mu'āwiyah had appointed Yażīd as his successor. It has already been discussed at the appropriate places. Sa'd's father Abī Waqāṣ was the very brother of the Prophet Muḥammad's holy mother, Ḥazrat Āminah. But at the advent of Islām, he was was a bitter enemy of the Prophet Muḥammad. In the same way Sa'd-bin-Abī Waqāṣ's cousin 'Abbās was a cruel enemy of the holy Prophet, who wounded the holy Prophet by throwing stones on him in the famous War of Uḥad (625 AD) in which the holy Prophet lost his teeth. Sa'd's father Abī Waqāṣ entered into orbit of Islām after much retard. He attained the position, when Caliph II 'Omar (634-44 AD) appointed him the Governor of Iraq.

It is famous that once the holy Prophet said addressing him that your son would murder my son! It made serious psychological influence on him. He paid due care to the studies of his son 'Omar-bin-Sa'd and taught him rituals of an ordinary practical Muslim. No doubt, prior to Karbala, beside the greed of power on account of which he was a commander of a battalion of the Yażīdī Army, nothing is found against him.

'Omar-bin-Sa'd was not lucky to see the holy Prophet in person, however, certainly he had seen those, who had seen the holy Prophet. He would have positively received information regarding Imām Ḥasan and Imām Ḥusain and about the members of the family of the holy Prophet. Especially, his very affectionate behaviour and attitude towards the grandsons. When, Imām Ḥusain was in Kufa, during the caliphate of his beloved father Imām 'Alī-ibn-Abī Ṭālib (656-61 AD), he would have had direct and personal occasions of knowing about his noble conduct and holy life. In the midst of twenty years after the exit of Imām Ḥusain from Kufa, he might have certainly heard the incidents concerning his love of peace, tolerance, high conduct and behaviour. Perhaps this is the reason why, when he was insisted upon to fight with Imām Ḥusain, he felt delicate.

In those days when the Yażīdī Army forced Imām Ḥusain to stay in Karbala, there was hurly-burly, turmoil and revolt in Iran, Kufic Governor 'Obaydu'llāh-bin-Żiyād ordered 'Omar-bin-Sa'd to go with his Army to suppress the revolt. He also made him the Administrator of Ray (presently, Iran's capital Tehran's near by town Shāh 'Abdu'l 'Aẓīm) and its adjoining areas. As he was advancing with his Army towards Iran, in the mean time another order of 'Obaydu'llāh-bin-Żiyād reached him that first go to Karbala and find solution for the problem there, then go to Iran. 'Omar-bin-Sa'd received the orders of 'Obaydu'llāh bin Żiyād, then he was in a dilemma. It was his heartly desire to be the Administrator of Ray, but he did not want to fight with Imām Ḥusain. In this delicate situation only he consulted his close relatives and friends and well-wishers. All of them unanimously suggested him not to fight agaist Imām Ḥusain at any cost. His nephew Ḥamżah-bin-Mughīra openly advised him not to commit a sin of figuting with Imām Ḥusain, be happy to have relationship with him. Even if he would obtain the entire wealth and properties of the whole world and Ruling powers, not to enbrace the great Sin of murder of Imām Ḥusain. These suggestions made him tremble and weak for that he was not prepared. He politely prayed to be excused from being deputed at Karbala. But, 'Obaydu'llāh-bin-Żiyād firmly rejected and threaten to snatch his Administratorship of Ray.[29] At that point 'Omar-bin-Sa'd betrayed his conscience and became the object of the regular curse on him.

Attempts for the Peace

A contigent of 1,000 soldiers was already camping at Karbala, 'Omar-bin-Sa'd reached there with the contigent of 6,000 soldiers. Afterward other Commanders with their contigents reached there. Direct recruitments were also going on, resulting in a huge the Yażīdī Army of about 55,500 personel. At the beginning, 'Omar-bin-Sa'd appeared not to be eager in confrontation with Imām Ḥusain. He wished to settle the issues amicabily in a peaceful atmosphere. But the cancer of covetousness for lust of power fastened his conscience. However, 'Omar-bin-Sa'd asked his army personel Ghurrah-bin-Qays Aḥsamī to meet Imām Ḥusain and get the information regarding his going there. But due to the fact that he was one of the seven signatories of the letter sent to Imām Ḥusain inviting him Kufa, he could not dare to face him. 'Omar-bin-Sa'd discussed with others, but none could dare. Lastly, the rude and wicked Kathīr-'Abdu'llāh Sho'bī presented himself vaunting to be ready for even killing Imām Ḥusain for which he was prepared. When he reached the camp of Imām Ḥusain, the famous Ḥusainī devotee, Abū-Thamāmah 'Omarū-bin-'Abdu'llāh Ṣāy'dī stopped him and said that he may be permitted to meet the holy Imām, but he should put off his weapons. He refused. Abū-Thamāmah relaxed the condition, let keep his hand on the weapon. Kathīr could not agree. Abū-Thamāmah said, tell the message, he would bring the reply. He further refused. Then Abū-Thamāmah told him, Go and tell 'Omar-bin-Sa'd, those in service of the holy Imām would not allowed to go near him.[30]

Then, 'Omar-bin-Sa'd sent Bishr-bin-'Omarū-bin-Uḥadūth Ḥazaramī Kindī as a messenger. Ḥusainī Commander, Żuhayr-bin-Qayn Numayrī Bajalī had the some conversation with him. He agreed all connotations, came and never returned back and joined the Ḥusainī Army.[31]

Bishr-bin-'Omarū's joing the Ḥusainī Army was a great shock for 'Omar-bin-Sa'd and his colleagues. However, he sent his Cavalry Commander, Qurrah-bin-Qays Ḥanẓalī. Another Ḥusainī Commander, Ḥabīb-bin-Maẓāhir Asadī convinced him. He replied, at present he was the messenger of 'Omar-bin-Sa'd, shall consider his proposal later on. Imām Ḥusain sent a very peaceful reply through this messenger:

> "The people of your town wrote to me that I should come and guid them to the path of God. But now when they are not interested, I would go back."[32]

Being overjoyed with the reply of Imām Ḥusain, 'Omar-bin-Sa'd wrote a letter the next day to Kufic Governor 'Obaydu'llāh-bin-Żiyād:

> "Reaching here I sent my representative to Ḥusain and asked through him, why he had come over there, what he wanted, and what were his demands? He replied that the people

> of this country had written to him and sent their messengers, who met him given their invitation, but when they did not like his presence and their views were changed, then, he would go back from where he has come here."[33]

But 'Obaydu'llāh-bin-Żiyād could not appreciate the spirit of the letter. He infused confused meaning into the words. He read the letter with vindictiveness that when the grip tightened over Imām Ḥusain, he wants a solution. Never and never! Where would they go escaping. He wrote to 'Omar-bin-Sa'd:

> "Received your letter and noted the content. You should put the demand before Ḥusain that he and all his associates firstly pledge their *Bay'at* in the name of Caliph Yażīd-bin-Mu'āwiyah-bin-Abū Sufyyān, then in that situation too, he could not get any peace, when they had before done such, then I may think upon his statement."[34]

The last lines of 'Obaydu'llāh-bin-Żiyād's letter make it clear that if at all (God forbid) Imām Ḥusain could have pledged the *Bay'at* with Yażīd, in that sitnation, he could get no peace because, then the part of sentence 'I may think upon his statement' reveals that Imām Ḥusain and his associates would be on his mercy, he could punish them on the pretext why they did not pledge their *Bay'at* earlier. Moreover, what was the guarantee that 'Obaydu'llāh-bin-Żiyād would abide his words and if he did, who could assure that Yażīd would accept his proposal. If Yażīd also agreed to compromise, then how long. The result of Ḥasan-Mu'āwiyah-Treaty is on record. Everyone knows how his father Mu'āwiyah openly tarnished the written Treaty. No wise person would ever believe Umayyites. The reply of 'Obaydu'llāh-bin-Żiyād plunged 'Omar-bin-Sa'd again into darkness. He sorrowfully muttered before his colleages that he had already a suspision whether or not Amīr 'Obaydu'llāh-bin-Żiyād was desirous of amicable peace.[35] Then he sent the original-letter of 'Obaydu'llāh-bin-Żiyād itself to Imām Ḥusain. There was the same reply of Imām Ḥusain, which was required of:

> "It is not at all possible. The ultimate would be death, I am ready to welcome it."[36]

With the utter frustration 'Omar-bin-Sa'd sent the reply of Imām Ḥusain to 'Obaydu'llāh-bin-Żiyād.

Imām Ḥusain could not be disappointed, he knew the Almighty like the peace. He had never liked blood-shed among people. He himself initiated dignified decision. He sent his associate 'Omarū-bin-Qurẓah-bin-Ka'b Anṣārī to 'Omar-bin-Sa'd with this proposal that he had wished fresh discussion for achieving amicable peace. 'Omar-bin-Sa'd promptly consented and decided to resume talk during night at a place, situated in the middle of both the Armies. The next morning white carpet was spread in between both the Army. 'Omar-bin-Sa'd came with his twenty soldiers. Imām Ḥusain also reached the venue with the equal number of his associates. Reaching nearer Imām Ḥusain asked his associates to wait. 'Omar-bin-Sa'd also stopped his soldiers. Imām Ḥusain and 'Omar-bin-Sa'd met alone. Conversation continued till late night, then Imām Ḥusain returned to his camp and 'Omar-bin-Sa'd also went-back to his Army.[37] Their conversation remained confidential, but historians have recorded that Imām Ḥusain had endeavoured just to establish peace. Imām Ḥusain's statement is available on record, who told 'Omar-bin-Sa'd explaining his position:

> "I have already told you, to let me go back. If it is not possible, then take me to Yażīd, should talk to him. If it is also not possible, then I would cancel my decision of staying in Iraq and, if it was necessary, I would sacrifice the Arab country itself and would stay at any far off place."[38]

Imām Ḥusain had put up such a proposal before the enemies for giving them the last chance, on which 'Omar-bin-Sa'd became so much impressed with the proposal that informed Kufic Governor 'Obaydu'llāh-bin-Żiyād with over inthusiasm:

> "Thank God, the flame of trouble is put out and situation of continuity and integrity of Muslims has come up and the matter of Islāmic revolt has been resolved. Ḥusain has agreed that he would go to a far off place from 'Arabian peninsula. In my view now there is no reason for enmity and now this tense situation should come to a close !"[39]

It appears necessary to tell here, to the learned readers that while 'Omar-bin-Sa'd was posted as Commander-in-Chief, his staunch adversary Khiwallah-bin-Yażīd Aṣbaḥī 'Āyiżī was also posted at Karbala as a watch dog, specially for spying on the activities of 'Omar-bin-Sa'd and directly reporting to 'Obaydu'llāh-bin-Żiyād. He reported against him charging supporting the opponents.[40] Perhaps being influenced with the report of his spy, 'Obaydu'llāh-bin-Żiyād replied 'Omar-bin-Sa'd, the effects of report of Khiwallah are clear:

> "O' Son of Sa'd ! I am informed that every night you go outside your Army and you spread carpet and go on talking with Ḥusain even after mid night."[41]

After issuing above warning, 'Obaydu'llāh-bin-Żiyād became restless. If Yażīd could like Ḥusain's peace-proposal, surely, he would be punished, his reply could be approved as good political decision. Mentaly, he was unable to negate absolutely the peace-proposal of Imām Ḥusain. In his mental agony, prior to taking any decision on the proposal, he consulted his close friend and Commander of the Yażīdī Army, Shimr-bin-Žuljaushan, who was the dead enemy of Prophet Muḥammad and his family members and specially Imām Ḥusain. He suggested that those proposals should not be agreed to, because it affects your self-prestige. Imām Ḥusain should leave all his waepons without any condition, then you have every right to take any decision. 'Obaydu'llāh-bin-Żiyād remained mum. Shimr-bin-Žuljaushan further said that he has heard, he spends his night in conversation with Ḥusain.[42] His talk over provoked 'Obaydu'llāh-bin-Żiyād and he felt, 'Omar-bin-Sa'd's conversation with Imām Ḥusain was nothing, but cheating against him. 'Obaydu'llāh-bin-Żiyād in reply to 'Omar-bin-Sa'd, issued strong worded instructions:

> "I have not sent you towards Ḥusain to extend co-operation to him or you prolong talks with him or enhance his hope of life or send you for your recommendation in his favour. You see, Ḥusain and his fellow should bow before my orders and leave them at my mercy, send them to me and if they refuse then attack them, kill them, cut off their limbs, because they deserve this."[43]

In the same letter 'Obaydu'llāh-bin-Żiyād had ordered for such a heinous crime, which has ashamed the entire humanity for ever:

> "If Ḥusain is killed, then his chest and body to be crushed with the foot of horses. Because he has been the revolt causing menace and a foe and traitor. It is not my view that anybody may harm him after death. I have already told you, if murdered, behave with him only in this brutal manner. If you implement

> my these orders, then, very good on your part. You would be awarded as a dutiful person. However, if you do not agree with my orders, then hand over the charge of your post to Yażīdī Commander Shimr-bin-Žuljaushan, who has been already entrusted the details of his duties."[44]

Yażīdī Commander Shimr-bin-Žuljaushan, reached Karbala on 9th Muḥarram, 61 AH (9th October, 680 AD). And submitted the above letter to 'Omar-bin-Sa'd. Receiving the letter 'Omar-bin-Sa'd sold out his conscience. His words are safe in the pages of history:

> "Even if I have to go to Hell and burn and go even to worse place then, also neither I can give up the desire to rule Ray, nor I can see you, Shimr-bin-Žuljaushan, as the Commander-in-Chief of the Yażīdī Army."[45]

The very presence of Shimr-bin-Žuljaushan at the Yażīdī Army, had become a running sore, ill-fate and self-anguish to 'Omar-bin-Sa'd, which was in no way possible to get rid off, some thing became hard at the time.

Restraining the Water

Kufic Governor, 'Obaydu'llāh-bin-Żiyād in a letter to his Commander-in-Chief, 'Omar-bin-Sa'd, issued orders to stop water supply from the branch-river 'Alqamah to Imām Ḥusain and his Associates, in the following words:

> "As per my orders compel Ḥusain for compliance of my orders. If he does not obey my orders, stop water supply to him. I have allowed to Jews and Christians, but have strictly prohibited for the family of Ḥusain and his Associates."[46]

It was 7th Muḥarram, 61 AH (7th October, 680 AD), when as per orders of 'Omar-bin-Sa'd, heavy security force was postedon 'Alqamah river. 'Omar-bin-Sa'd posted Ḥajār-bin-Abajar and Shabth-bin-Raba'ī with 4,000 Armoury Regiments, Isḥāq-bin-Khawiyyah Ḥazramī and 'Omar-bin-Ḥujjāj Żubaydī with 500 each of their Cavalry Regiments and Ażraq Shāmī with 400 mounted soldiers for watching the bank of the river. Watchmen and security guards were posted even at far off banks of the river 'Alqamah.[47] The animals were permitted to drink water, but the

Household of the holy Prophet Muḥammad were not allowed to get even a drop of water.

It is generally believed that the water supply was stopped on 7th Muḥarram, but the circumstancial evidences reveal that the prohibition on water supply has already been imposed, just the day when Imām Ḥusain reached Karbala. It is evident that the enemies had forcefully occupied the bank of the river 'Alqamah; and camps and tent of the Ḥusainī Caravan were removed from there, under the orders of 'Obaydu'llāh-bin-Żiyād to the effect:

> "Insist on Ḥusain to remain in such a place where no water should be available."[48]

It clarifies that removal of the Ḥusainī camps was aimed to stop water supply. Even before formal stoppage of water, circumstances show that water was already finished in Ḥusainī camps and water supply was completely stopped for Imām Ḥusain and his Associates, ladies and even children. The ladies and children were more severely affected for want of water. The enemies were shamelessly ridiculing and poking:

> "Blue sky's colour, sweet water is flowing there. But till your death, you cannot take even a drop of water. O' Ḥusain! Water is available, for dogs and pigs, donkeys and even wolf drink water here, but you cannot take even a drop of water from here. We know well your relation with Muḥammad but we will not leave you to this extent that you would die suffering for want of a drop of water."[49]

In the same situation three days passed without water. Imām Ḥusain's Associates were standing like a rock of indomitable self-confidence and wish to give powerful crushing reply to the Yażīdī Army. Watchmen and security guards had no meaning for them, but how to have the consent of holy Imām, which was the most difficult question before them. In this context some historians have mentioned about bringing of water by the Ḥusainī Commander-in-Chief, Abu'l-Faẓl'il-'Abbās-bin-Imām 'Alī, which perhaps was not sufficient even for the children.[50] This incident would be in the night of 6th and 7th Muḥarram. Onwards, there was no water in the camps of Imām Ḥusain and children were impatiently longing for water.

Imām Ḥusain's Associates were highly perturbed seeing the children and babies craving for water. They were self-confident people, knowing well, even if, water could be made available, they could not take it; but they wanted water for the babies. They were capable of snatching water from the Yażīdī Army, but the orders of Imām Ḥusain were very clear, not to be aggressive to start the War. One of his associates, Nāfa'-bin-Hilāl Jamalī Al-Murādī adopted a mid-way. Why not discuss the issue with the soldiers of the Yażīdī Army. They have their children, love them, if their children were suffering like ours, could they tolerate. One of the 'Alqamah river watchmen and security personnel's Commandant, 'Omar-bin-Ḥujjāj Żubaydī was related to him. He would offer some water at his request. He came to the river and called him—I am the son of your uncle, Nāfa'-bin-Hilāl, came to request for water. The Commandant of Yażīdī Army replied—You can drink as much as you want and also quench the thirst of your cattle. The Ḥusainī soldier said—I cannot wet my lips, unless all children and Imām Ḥusain are satisfied, after taking water. 'Omar-bin-Ḥujjāj Żubaydī refused. Nāfa'-bin-Hilāl also refused to take water.[51]

Another incident has also been mentioned by the historians. After getting permission from Imām Ḥusain. Ḥusain, renowned scholar of his time, Burayr-bin-Khuzayr Hamadānī discussed with 'Omar-bin-Sa'd regarding stoppage of water; Burayr-bin-Khuzayr asked 'Omar-bin-Sa'd—What a Muslim you are, you have come to murder the family members of the Imām Ḥusain and the problem is there that water is from 'Alqamah river, which the dogs and pigs of Iraq are drinking. But he is Imām Ḥusain and his family members who have reached even to the threshold of death for want of water and are not permitted even to go near the river, 'Alqamah. 'Omar-bin-Sa'd accepting his mistake replied—If I do anything against the wishes of Governor 'Obaydu'llāh-bin-Żiyād, the very ruling of Ray would go away from my hands and this is not at all possible from me.[52]

Even at the time of non-availability of water and great hardship, when the chest of Imām Ḥusain's associates were burning to quench thirst, their unity and integrity had been unique and incomparable at all. They lived and died for Imām Ḥusain.

Cowardly Attack by the Yażīdī Army

It was the evening of Thursday of the 9th Muḥarram 61AH (9th October, 680 AD) that the Yażīdī Army, without any prior intimation suddenly attacked. It exposed 'Omar-bin-Sa'd's mental retardation and compulsion, because the very presence of Shimr-bin-Žuljaushan at the Yażīdī Army, as watchdog of his activities had terrified him at every time.

He was afraid always that any minor fault may ruin his desire of getting Ray's Administration. Therefore, to show his house in order, he attacked the camps of Imām Ḥusain.

Sunset was nearing. Spreading dark curtain of evening. Hungry and thirsty Ḥusainī soldiers had endured the hot day and for rest for the moment. Imām Ḥusain was sitting on the door of his camp, taking support of his sword; thinking something. In the mean time suddenly he heard the neighing of horses and sounds of weapons. He asked his brave brother Abu'l-Faẓl'il-'Abbās-bin-Imām 'Alī to find out the matter.

As soon as they heared the order, Ḥabīb-bin-Maẓāhir Aṣadī and Żuhayr-bin-Qayn Numayrī Bajalī joined Abu'l-Faẓl'il-'Abbās. He advanced and challenged. The Army stood there itself. 'Omar-bin-Sa'd advanced and explained the reason for the changed situation. Abu'l-Faẓl'il-'Abbās, came back to discuss with Imām Ḥusain. In the mean time Ḥabīb-bin-Maẓāhir Asadī and Żuhayr-bin-Qayn Numayrī Bajalī were talking with the enemy's soldiers and making them to be ready to surrender to Imām Ḥusain, under his leadership. Abu'l-Faẓl'il-'Abbās informed after returning that Imām Ḥusain wanted one night time. After arguments, 'Omar-bin-Sa'd agreed for one night time and said if they surrender the next morning then they would be produced before Kufic Governor 'Obaydu'llāh-bin-Żiyād. Otherwise, if he refused, then there would be a deciding War, the next day.[53]

The Last Night

The last night prior to Battle of Karbala, which is famous in the name of *Shab-i-'Āshūr* (Night of Tenth). It was a night in between 9th and 10th Muḥarram, 61 AH (9th and 10th October, 680 AD). Some historians have mentioned it as decision making night for Imām Ḥusain, but it could not be correct, because as a whole night, if we see on the basic incident's evidence it cannot be said as decision night because Imām Ḥusain has taken his decision at the time of departure from Medina itself, which is clear from his each and every activity and statements at the same this night. It can be said as the decision making night for the family members and associates of Imām Ḥusain. It cannot be said that he took his decision only in this night. But, it is quite clear that he had definitely put his signature with his blood on the martyrdom.

Historians have recorded various series of incidents that Imām Ḥusain collected all his family members and associates on this night and gave an important statement, he said in it:

"All sorts of situations are for the Almighty. We should thank Him in each and every situation of happiness or distress thank to him. O' God! You are Great, You are praiseworthy. You honoured us by creating the *Nabī* (Apostle of God) within us. Bestowed the knowledge of Qur'an. Confirmed the wisdom and spiritual ablution, provided with hearing, listening power, powerful eyes and contented heart…

Be known to all, I don't know anybody having so faithful and honest persons than that of my family-members, associates and followers, who are so dutiful and sincere. I pray God to shower on you all His blessings!

Remember that the enemy would certainly fight a war. I permit with an open mind and heart, you may go freely as you like. I remove the condition of my *Bay'at*. It is mid-night's curtain, making itself as your vehicle, start and go away. I do not ask you alone to go, while going everyone of you may take the hand of a member of my family and take that person with you. Because Yazīdī Army wants to murder me alone if they kill me, then they won't worry to get others."[54]

Imām Ḥusain put out the burning lamp after his effective speech, so that anybody may not feel hesitation in going out. It was made complete dark after putting out the burning lamp, so that, one may escape early, without facing any shame before anyone. Imām Ḥusain lit up the lamp after some time. No body even moved from his place, getting up, standing and going away was out of question at all ! At the same time there were very powerful speeches in the support of Imām Ḥusain.[55]

The speeches of Abu'l-Faẓl'il-'Abbās, Muslim-bin-'Ausajah Asadī, Sa'īd-bin-'Abdu'llāh Ḥasafī, Żuhayr-bin-Qayn Numayrī Bajalī have become the beauty and dignity of history. First of all Abu'l-Faẓl'il-'Abbās stood up and raised the question:

"Why should we do like this? Is it for the aim to live after you? Never… never, never and never. God may not show us such an unholy day."[56]

The other family members also supported him, then Imām Ḥusain pin-pointed the family of his uncle, 'Aqīl-bin-Abī Ṭālib addressing them said:

"Enough has been the martyrdom of Muslim for you, you go away, I permit you."[57]

All said in one voice:

> "No use of our being alive after yourself. It is not possible."[58]

Afterwards, the holy Prophet's old Companion Muslim-bin-'Ausajah Aṣadī stoodup. He also started questioning the issue:

> "How can we leave you? By God, it cannot be. I will fight with these enemies with my spear, which would pierce their chest and would use sword unless captured by them, and I can not leave you on any account, if I do not have any weapon to fight, then I will throw stones on them and I will support you and I would sacrifice my life at your holy feet."[59]

After him, Sa'īd-bin-'Abdu'llāh Ḥasafī said:

> "By God, we don't leave your company, unless we don't prove before God that we have not fulfilled our responsibility, indirectly on supreme Prophet Muḥammad. By God, I know that I would be murdered. If could be given life again, then again I would sacrifice my life in the path of Truth. If I could be burnt alive, my ashes sprayed into the air and it would happen 70 times with me, even then I would not leave you and ultimately I would die at your holy feet only. Here only once I would be murdered, but that eternal glory would prevail for ever."[60]

Żuhayr-bin-Qayn Numayrī Bajalī said:

> "By God, I have the desire to be murdered, then made alive and then again, killed, let this process continue for 1,000 times, but this trouble should be over forever for you and your family members."[61]

In view of brevity, all other brave Associates' speeches are not detailed here. However, the basic theme of all their speeches was, they would never never go away, leaving Imām Ḥusain alone. They had taken that decision deliberately after due thinking and understanding. They were surrendering for ever towards their objectives and text of all speeches of them are available in detail in different historic books.

Vow of Great Sacrifices

In fact Imām Ḥusain had carefully and objectively assessed the condition of the Muslim Ummah at the time, which had deviated to such extent that its reformation was not possible without such a rising and such a sacred movement in which Imām Ḥusain along with his associates may be martyred. It was necessary to save the Islām for ever from the danger of death and extinction. It would keep alive the sacred movement of Truth, and pave the path for such sacred movements in future. If look into it on the basis of historical facts, while departing from Mecca, it becomes clear that Imām Ḥusain was proceeding towards such a target, wherein he will have to give his life. Imām Ḥusain had expressed in clear terms while departring from Mecca:

> "See, those who are ready to sacrifice their life and had already prepared their mind and heart for sacrifice towards God, they may accompany me."[62]

He repeated the same again during his journey to Żabālah, which he had said addressing his Associates:

> "Now, those among you also can bear the attack of spears and swords, may come along with us, otherwise, they may part with from here itself."[63]

There are two situations for sacrificing one's own life in the view of Islām. In the first situation, one who sacrifices his own life is safe, sacrifices any animal or valuable thing, the animal which he sacrifices, it attains death. In an another situation in sacrificing he sacrifices his life by himself, but it is entirely different from suicide or attaining voluntary death. The sacrificer struggles utilising all means of self-security for attaing supreme ideal, the defence of Truth and the establishment of Justice. This struggle has been said *Jihād* in Islāmic terminology and its end commutes in the situation of *Qitāl* (fight battle) and who are killed in the battle are called Martyrs. The holy Qur'an has forbidden calling those martyrs as dead:

> "And say not of those who are slain in the path of God that they are dead; Nay, *(they are)* living, but ye perceive not."
>
> (*Qur'an*: 2/154)

The sacrifices of Imām Ḥusain and his Associates come into this category. Imām Ḥusain's influential speech and their associates dedicated speeches in the above mentioned lines draw our attention towards the fact that now a declaration has been made for offering sacrifice in a formal manner. Even when on many accessions prior to this especial event Imām Ḥusain and his Associates had resolved to sacrifice their own life, still the time had come to implement that resolution and decision.

After taking a final decision in spending the last night of his life in God's prayer, Imām Ḥusain and his associates once again established that their main objective of life was to establish God's mandate. The resonance of their prayer was making the entire atmosphere sacred and pure. Like other religious and sincere persons, they had taken a decision already that they woud give up their lives at the pious feet of Imām Ḥusain. Historians have mentioned that during this night voices of chanting the names of Allāh and verses of holy Qur'an were continuously coming from the camps of Imām Ḥusain, as if those were the insects of honey-bees producing their sounds.[64] There was an atmosphere of great satisfaction and joy among Ḥusainī soldiers. Soldiers were exchanging their greetings, fun and humour, with each other cheerfully. It seemed they were experiencing such joy and pleasure after fulfilling their desire, there was no other better joy for them. They were cleaning and polishing their swords and looking each other with great fun and enjoyment. One with joy Burayr-bin-Khuzayr Hamadānī of Ḥusainī Army made fun with 'Abdu'r Raḥmān-bin-'Abd Rab Anṣārī Khiżarajjī. Hepolitely requested him to leave it, It was no time for jokes. Burayr replied, By God, my caste and clan people know well that all along my life, from youth till this age, I had no taste for fun. But the situation now has made me indulge in the imagination of future. By God, there is only this much of distance, between me and time immemorial fate that we were attacked with anti-religious swords and my desire is, that time may come at earliest and swords may be used on us.[65]

An incident of this last night is related to the marriage of Imām Ḥasan's eldest son, Qāsim-bin-Imām Ḥasan. It is said that Imām Ḥusain himself had arranged this marriage in this last night, with a view to protect and continue his elder brother Imām Ḥasan's genealogical tree. Accordingly, he did not permit Qāsim to fight in the War, still at the end at his incessant request he was permitted to join the Army and to fight the War. So, many scholars have raised objections regarding this incident. In their opinion there was no marriage.

There were few more soldiers, besides Ḥusain's soldiers, who were with Yażīdī Army so far, especially among them was Ḥurr-bin-Yażīd-

Riyāḥī, who was an impotant Commander among the enemies. He had joined Ḥusainī Army with his two sons, brother and servent, has already been mentioned at appropriate place. Physically remaining with enemies and bearing torture of mental atomism. My pen would fail to depict the state of his sorrow, in which spent that night with so much of restlessness is known only through his breaking away in the morning from Yażīdī Army. He felt how much atrocities he had done to Imām Ḥusain, by stopping him on his way, by not providing even a drop of water and stopping water. In spite of all these could he be pardoned. Hur decided in this same dilemma that he would sacrifice his life under the leadership of Imām Ḥusain.

Imām Ḥusain was waking all the night, spending his time in prayer. Suddenly, he got up to observe his people, especially ladies of his family. What they think of the next day.[66] It has been mentioned that Imām Ḥusain, first of all went to the camp of his sister Żainab-bint-Imām 'Alī, *Sharīkatu'l Ḥusain.* He observed that she was teaching her both children 'Aun and Muḥammad, how to fight in the War and both her sons were telling her. O' Dearest Mother, you just see, tomorrow Yażīdī Army can not stand before us. Then Imām Ḥusain went to his second sister Umm Kulthūm-bint-Imām 'Alī's camp. She was not blessed with any child. He observed her praying, O' Allāh! I have no child, I had no complaint at all for this. However, when today, all the women are sacrificing their children, I feel, I have no child to sacrifice, it pricks me like anything. Imām Ḥusain went into the camp of his wife Laylā-bint-Abī Murwah Thaqafiyyah and observed that she was staring at the beautiful face of her son 'Alī-bin-Imām Ḥusain *alias* 'Alī Akbar, who had great resembleness with the Prophet Muḥammd, *Shabīhu'r-Rasūl* (Replica of the Prophet). His mother was found thinking, this whole night she would enjoy pretty face of her son and tomoow this moon like face would mix with sand.

Imām Ḥusain was happy and satisfied and started doing prayer, after returning to his camp. After a while, no idea what accrued in his mind, stood up and set out to the battlefield alone. Proceeded a few metre and heard somebody was watching behind. Asked, who was he. Imām Ḥusain's intimate associate Nāfa'-bin-Hilāl Jamalī Al-Murādī were ahead. He kept his head on the holy feet of Imām Ḥusain and imploring humbly and earnestly, My Lord, I have committed a mistake, I could not follow your orders that no one should come behind you! This slave could not control himself seeing you going alone to the battlefield. Imām Ḥusain took Nāfa'-bin-Hilāl and embraced him affectionately and said, Nāfa' do you want to see that land of earth, wherein I would be murdered? Then, in the darkness of the night he came to a lonely place and sat there itself.

Preparation for the war was going on continuing during the whole night in the Yażīdī Army. The weapons were made ready for attacking were whetted, and were being distributed among soldiers, horses were made ready, making them running for warming up. The Yażīdī Army was very busy the whole might, but there was a distinct difference between the busy nature of the Yażīdī Army and Imām Ḥusain's Army. That there was a continuous prayer in the Ḥusainī Army and there were so many entertainment programmes going in Yażīdī Army which were totally forbidden in Islām.

Observing the heavy attack of Yażīdī Army, Imām Ḥusain arranged very deep pits dug behind his camps, during this night. And set fire collecting wood, so that, enemies could not attack from behind the camp. In this way there was no chance of attacking on all the four directions by Yażīdī Army. Flames of fire was were raised above all the pits; came to know that Yażīdī Commander Shimr-bin-Žuljaushan, covering his whole body, from head to foot with iron curtains, came near the terrible fire and when he could not jump over, he glanced at his side. At his audacity, a very aged Companion of the holy Prophet, Muslim-bin-'Ausajah Asadī requested Imām Ḥusain, if he permitted, he could kill him with his arrow. Because, Shimr-bin-Žuljaushan was highly unjust and cruel, at that time, he could very easily kill him, as he was in his shooting range. But Imām Ḥusain prohibited to do like that, do not initiate war from your side!

Some scholars have mentioned that in this same night Imām Ḥusain ordered his Commander-in-Chief, Abu'l-Fażl'il-'Abbās for digging seven wells near his camps, but everytime no water was found. Digging frequently seven wells in the same place, tells the very purpose of digging the wells was some thing else. Everyone knows, in case of no availability of water at a place, the other well would be digged at a distant place. There would be no justification of his digging seven wells at the same place. It should have been digged at different places at far off, but in the same place they have been dug here. Had Imām Ḥusain wanted to have water, he would have made it digged at different places. So, many scholars say that Imām Ḥusain has already taken a decision of sacrificing his life and others. With the entire boldness and intelligence of his brave brother and Commander-in-Chief, Abu'l-Fażl'il-'Abbās, the very fate changed and converted and end of war would have been a different way altogether. Therefore, with a view to make him tired and physically weak, Imām Ḥusain made him dig seven wells. This is supported with this fact also that Imām Ḥusain did not grant permission to Abu'l-Faẓl'il-'Abbās for fighting in the War. After all, he was sent to bring water from the canal, and he was permitted to take a small club only with him for his safety.

Notes and References

1. *It is generally believed that the Gregorian date of 'Āshūrah, as 10th Muḥarram, 61 AH was on 10th October, 680 AD. I have also adopted the same. But there is a controversy in this regard. Because, these dates have been calculated through calculator. But, these calculators are not always correct. According to the book* Maqtal-i-Ḥusain, *the 9th Muḥarram 61 AH was on 12th October, 680 AD, so it appears that date of 'Āshūrah was 13th October 680 AD. Similarly, the names of days also defer. Most of scholars consider Monday as the day of 'Āshūrah but some others say Friday.*—Author
2. Bihāru'l-Anwār, vol. 1, p. 207; Shahīd-i-Insāniyat, pp. 323, 355-56; Ḥusainī Inqalāb, p. 64.
3. Kitābu'l-M 'ārif, p. 95.
4. *As per Census 1985, the total population of Karbala was 1,84,574*—Author.
5. Tārīkh-i-Karbala wa Ḥāi'r al-Ḥusain, pp. 3-7; Shahīd-i-Insāniyat, pp. 329-31.
6. Taṣwīr-i-Karbala, p. 24.
7. Tārīkhu'r-Rusūl wa'l-Mulūk, vol. 6, pp. 222-23; al-Akhbāru'ṭ Ṭawāl, p. 243.
8. al-Akhbāru'ṭ Ṭawāl, p. 243; Tārīkhu'r-Rusūl wa'l-Mulūk, vol. 6, pp. 222-23.
9. Tārīkhu'r-Rusūl wa'l-Mulūk, vol. 6, pp. 230-31; al-Akhbāru'ṭ Ṭawāl, p. 249.
10. al-Akhbāru'ṭ Ṭawāl, pp. 243-44.
11. al-Akhbāru'ṭ Ṭawāl, p. 243.
12. al-Akhbāru'ṭ Ṭawāl, p. 253.
13. Tārīkhu'r-Rusūl wa'l-Mulūk, vol. 6, p. 222.
14. al-Akhbāru'ṭ Ṭawāl, p. 244.
15. al-Maqtal, p. 65.
16. al-Akhbāru'ṭ Ṭawāl, p. 153.
17. Tārīkhu'r-Rusūl wa'l-Mulūk, vol. 6, p. 241; al-Irshād fī Ma'rifat Ḥujjāj Allāh 'Alā 'Ibād, p. 246.
18. al-Irshād fī Ma'rifat Ḥujjāj Allāh 'Alā 'Ibād, p. 246; Kitābu 'l-Buldān p. 172; Tārīkhu'r-Rusūl wa'l-Mulūk, vol. 6, p. 241; al-Akhbāru'ṭ Ṭawāl, p. 154.
19. Luhūf 'Alā Qatlu'l Ṭafūf.
20. Shahīd-i-Insāniyat, pp. 397-522.
21. Shuhdā-i-Karbala: (Part One & Two).

22. Ḥusainī Inqalab, p. 84.
23. Shahīd-i-Insāniyat, p. 293.
24. Tārīkhu'r-Rusūl wa'l Mulūk, vol. 6, p. 218; al-Irshād fī Ma'rifat Ḥujjāj Allāh 'Alā 'Ibād, p. 228.
25. Tārīkhu'r-Rusūl wa'l-Mulūk, vol. 6, p. 234; al-Akhbāru'ṭ Ṭawāl, p. 247.
26. Tārīkhu'r-Rusūl wa'l-Mulūk, vol. 6, p. 221.
27. Shahīd-i-Insāniyat, p. 445.
28. al-Maqtal: Abī Mīkhnaf, p. 65; al-Kāmil fī' t-Tārīkh, vol. 4, p. 21; Tārīkhu'r-Rusūl wa'l-Mulūk, vol. 6, p. 232.
29. Tārīkhu'r-Rusūl wa'l-Mulūk, vol. 6, p. 221.
30. al-Mukhtaṣar fī Akhbāru 'l-Bashar, vol. 1, pp. 118-19.
31. al-Kāmil fī' t-Tārīkh, vol. 4, p. 22, p. 346.
32. al-Maqtal: Abī Mīkhnaf, p. 67.
33. al-Kāmil fī't-Tārīkh, vol. 4, p. 22; Shahīd-i-Insāniyat, p. 246.
34. al-Akhbāru'ṭ Ṭawāl, p. 252.
35. al-Akhbāru'ṭ Ṭawāl, p. 251; Tārīkhu'r-Rusūl wa'l-Mulūk, vol. 6, p. 234; al-Irshād fī Ma'rifat Ḥujjāj Allāh 'Alā 'Ibād, p. 239.
36. al-Akhbāru'ṭ Ṭawāl, p. 252.
37. Tārīkhu'r-Rusūl wa'l-Mulūk, vol. 6, p. 235.
38. Tārīkhu'r-Rusūl wa'l-Mulūk, vol. 6, p. 235.
39. al-Akhbāru'ṭ Ṭawāl, pp. 253-54; Tārīkhu'r-Rusūl wa'l-Mulūk, vol. 6, p. 240; Shahīd-i-Insāniyat, p. 356.
40. al-Maqtal: Abī Mīkhnaf, p. 76.
41. al-Kāmil fī' t-Tārīkh, vol. 4, p. 22.
42. Tārīkhu'r-Rusūl wa'l-Mulūk, vol. 6, p. 236.
43. Tārīkhu'r-Rusūl wa'l-Mulūk, vol. 4, pp. 241-42; al-Akhbāru'ṭ Ṭawāl, p. 253; Shahīd-i-Insāniyat, pp. 349-58.
44. Tārīkhu'r-Rusūl wa'l-Mulūk, vol. 4, pp. 241-42; al-Akhbāru'ṭ Ṭawāl, p. 253; Shahīd-i-Insāniyat, pp. 349-58.
45. Tārīkhu'r-Rusūl wa'l-Mulūk, vol. 4, p. 242.
46. al-Maqtal: Abī Mīkhnaf, p. 76; al-Kāmil fī' t-Tārīkh, vol. 4, p. 22.
47. al-Maqtal: Abī Mīkhnaf, p. 53.
48. al-Akhbāru'ṭ Ṭawāl, pp. 249-50.
49. Tārīkhu'r-Rusūl wa'l-Mulūk, vol. 6, p. 234.
50. al-Akhbāru'ṭ Ṭawāl, p. 262; Tārīkhu'r-Rusūl wa'l-Mulūk, vol. 6, p. 244.
51. Bihāru'l-Anwār, vol. 1, p. 210.
52. Kashfu'l-Ghumma fī Ma'rifat al-Ai'mah, p. 189.
53. al-Kāmil fī' t-Tārīkh, vol. 4, 923; Tārīkhu'r-Rusūl wa'l-Mulūk, vol. 6, p. 237.
54. Ḥabīb-us-Siyar, vol. 2, p. 291; Tārīkhu'r-Rusūl wa'l-Mulūk, vol. 6, pp. 238-39.
55. Tārīkhu'r-Rusūl wa'l-Mulūk, vol. 6, pp. 238-39; al-Irshād fī Ma'rifat Ḥujjāj Allāh 'Alā 'Ibād, p. 244; Shahīd-i-Insāniyat, pp. 365-68.
56. Tārīkhu'r-Rusūl wa'l-Mulūk, vol. 6, pp. 238-39; al-Irshād fī Ma'rifat Ḥujjāj Allāh 'Alā 'Ibād, p. 244; Shahīd-i-Insāniyat, pp. 365-68.

57. Tārīkhu'r-Rusūl wa'l-Mulūk, vol. 6, pp. 238-39; al-Irshād fī Ma'rifat Ḥujjāj Allāh 'Alā 'Ibād, p. 244; Shahīd-i-Insāniyat, pp. 365-68.
58. Tārīkhu'r-Rusūl wa'l-Mulūk, vol. 6, pp. 238-39; al-Irshād fī Ma'rifat Ḥujjāj Allāh 'Alā 'Ibād, p. 244; Shahīd-i-Insāniyat, pp. 365-68.
59. Tārīkhu'r-Rusūl wa'l-Mulūk, vol. 6, pp. 238-39; al-Irshād fī Ma'rifat Ḥujjāj Allāh 'Alā 'Ibād, p. 244; Shahīd-i-Insāniyat pp. 365-68.
60. Tārīkhu'r-Rusūl wa'l-Mulūk, vol. 6, pp. 238-39; al-Irshād fī Ma'rifat Ḥujjāj Allāh 'Alā 'Ibād, p. 244; Shahīd-i-Insāniyat, pp. 365-68.
61. Tārīkhu'r-Rusūl wa'l-Mulūk, vol. 6, pp. 238-39; al-Irshād fī Ma'rifat Ḥujjāj Allāh 'Alā 'Ibād, p. 244; Shahīd-i-Insāniyat, pp. 365-68.
62. Balāghatu'l Ḥusain, pp. 123-25.
63. Tārīkhu'r-Rusūl wa'l-Mulūk, vol. 6, p. 246.
64. Tārīkhu'r-Rusūl wa'l-Mulūk, vol. 6, p. 240.
65. Tārīkhu'r-Rusūl wa'l-Mulūk, vol. 6, p. 241.
66. Tārīkhu'r-Rusūl wa'l-Mulūk, vol. 6, p. 242.

Chapter: Six

The Dawn of the Great Sacrifice

The amazing imagination of dawn always appears with ever new charming and delightful desire, wherein the vision and the dreams reflect their original form. Each day the Sun rises with a novel glory, brimming with so fresh and new maturation and inducements fore ver, never becoming old. But this dawn is related to the day of the great sacrifice of *'Āshūrah* (Tenth), 10th Muḥarram, 61 AH (10th October, 680 AD). The day there was in which such a grand war between truth and injustice would be fought at the land of Karbala. Its salient features have no synonym and equivalent in the world history. As per time schedule just about 7-8 hours, but it has circumscribed so many centuries in its jurisdiction and the effect extends to the Last Day of the Ressurecction.

The faithful believers devoted to the holy Prophet Muḥammad and his sanctified Progeny, spent the night of *'Āshūrah* in God's prayer only and as they did not sleep at all the whole night, kept awaken with redness spread arroung their eyes. They heard Imām Ḥusain's voice—Get up! It is morning prayer's time. Do the duty towards the Creater. Faithful believers stood up. No water was available to perform rituals. Imām Ḥusain's dear son 'Alī Akbar said *Ażān* (Prayer's Call), his sweet voice echoed in the atmosphere *Allāhu'-Akbar* (God is Great). Nature reciprocated no doubt 'God is Great'. For illustrating that atmosphere the great poet, Mīr Anīs's pen would be required[1]:

> The sun had run his journey o'er the night;
> Unveiled, the Dawn revealed her glorious face.
> The King who rides the heaven saw her light
> And called his brave companions to their place.
> 'The time has come at least; to God give praise;
> Arise ! In fitting prayer your voices raise.

Brave hearts ! For strife and slaughter dawns this day;
Here the blood of Muḥammad's race will flow.'
Żahra's darling, honoured, seeks the fray;
The night of parting fades 'neath union's glow.
'We are those for whom the angels weep;
To live this day we sacrificed our sleep.

This morning brings an evening ever blessed;
We who depart for Paradise will slake
Our thirst by Kau<u>th</u>ar's spring, and there find rest.
May God exalt our names for honour's sake.'
Unequalled, each of them to joy gave birth.'
Let martyrs rise in glory from the earth.'

At this faithful friends rose from their beds,
And donning glorious raiment combed their hair;
Then tying turbans on their noble heads,
They faced the peerless Lord and gathered there.
Wrapped in coloured cloaks, their fear grew less;
Rose perfume, musk and civet filled their dress.

Their dry lips sang the praise of God; and light
Shone on their faces; fear was put aside.
No grief or panic clouded o'er their sight;
They joked and laughed and shared their skills and pride.
Their charming accent gladdened ever ear;
Each word they uttered was joy a joy to hear.

There was no water for the heavenly crowd;
Before the prayer they washed in shining sand.
Their faces gleamed like sunrays through a cloud.
Sons of the Father of the Dust, this band
Became as radiant as the silver moon;
Their faces mirrors in a hazy noon.

'Make ready for your worship !', came the cry,
'The King of all Creation leaves his seat.
In ranks of light the Leader passed by;
Salvation's path bows down to touch his feet,
His radiance in the highest in the highest heaven will reign.'
The Qur'an became a prayer-mat for Husain.

After completing the morning prayer Imām Ḥusain went out of the camp and saw 'Omar-bin-Sa'd, Commander-in-Chief of Yażīdī Army mobilizing his troops to start the hostility. He stared at the intimidating army, and as large as it was Imam Husain showed no signs of compromise.

Search for the Peace

Imām Ḥusain came to the battlefield. And he raised his hands towards sky and said:

> "O' My Lord! Thou art my trust in every adversity, and my hope in every trial, and Thou art for me in every matter a trust and a support. How many adversity weakens the core and lessens the plans and in which the friend lets down and the enemy turns happy for it I would rely (for it) on Thee and complain about it to Thee for my desire to Thee among all of the others, and Thou hath made it easy for me. Thou art the Owner of every favour and the Owner of every reward and the end of every desire."[2]

Then, he asked for his camel, rode on and called upon the people with a loud voice, which eveyone heard, he said:

> "O' people, listen to my speech and don't be in a hurry until I preach for you what is your right upon me and until I apologise for my arrival to you, thus if you accept my apology and believe in my speech and give me my rights, you shall be happier with that and then you will have no reasons against me. And if, you do not accept my apology and didn't give the rights then gather up with your partners and do not let your matter be a cloudy one over you and then tell me what you do decide, and my support is God, who revealed the book and He cares for the faithful."[3]

Army Ranks Conferred

It was clear from the parade of Ḥusainī Army that Imām Ḥusain wanted to fight in an absolutely arranged manner; the number of soldiers in his army are said to be only 72, or the maximum number of soldiers assembled was only less than 200, was secondary. The important thing was that whoever joined his Army was of high conduct and behaviour and highly respectable people. It was his strength over the number. It was the least that the War would be fought within an organized manner. After prayer Imām Ḥusain organized his amall Army. Ḥabīb-bin-Maẓāhir Asadī: Commander, Left-Wing Regiment, Żuhayr-bin-Qayn Numayrī Bajalī: Commander, Right-Wing Regiment and Abu'l-Faẓl'il-'Abbās-bin-Imām 'Alī: Commander-in-Chief. He shall also had the responsibility of the Army Flag and the Central Command. Along with them were the family members and all his associates present in a queue. There was no such an Islāmic Army prior to this and afterwards, in number so less, all soldiers very brave, his family members and all his associates prepared to sacrifice their life. All the soldiers were the embodiments of simplicity, sacredness, clear and straightforward, brimming with satisfaction and peace of mind.

Compared to Ḥusainī Army Yażīdī Army's might was visible with its pomp and splendour, was like an ocean, in which the number of soldiers were minimum at 55,500 as has been said and some were of the opinion that it crossed more than 3,00,000 which has already been discussed in the previous chapter. Yażīdī Army with the leadership of the Commander-in-Chief 'Omar-bin-Sa'd, established fully equipped with different sort of weapons with the absolute preparations for the while night. Other Army leaders were—'Omar-bin-Ḥujjāj Żubaydī: Commander, Right Regiment, Shimra-bin-Žuljaushan: Commander, Left Regiment, Qurrah-bin-Qays: Commander, Cavalry Regiment, Shabth-bin-Raba'ī: Commander, Armoury Regiment, Qays-bin-Asha'th: 1st Commander, 4th Regiment, 'Abdu'llāh-bin-Żubayr Ażdī: 2nd Commander, 4th Regiment, 'Abdu'r Raḥmān Ja'fī: 3rd Commander, 4th Regiment, Ḥajaru'l Ahajar: 4th Commander, 4th Regiment, Dorayd (Żayd or Żuwayd) who represented Yażīdī Army's Flag.

Our learned reader may identify some names, in which there are 'greenery field owners', have been referred to at the appropriate places. The entire Yażīdī Army fully equipped with weapons stood in rows; battalion by battalion in front of the Ḥusainī Army.

Sermon for the Peace

Keeping in view of the situation, perhaps, it would have occurred in the mind of Imām Ḥusain even to put forward his ideas clearly before Yażīdī Army. He thanked God and praised Him and blessed the holy Prophet Muḥammad and his sanctified Progeny and said the peace over the angels and the prophets and said so many uncountable things, and no speaker before him or after him was heard with such eloquent speech:

> "Thanks to God, who created life and made it a home of vanishing and extinction, controlling its people from one situation to another, and the proud is the one who is deceived by it and the wretched is the one who got swayed with it, so do not be deceived by this life because it cuts the hopes of those who take refuge in it and disappoint the greed of those who wish for it. I see you and you've gathered for something that God became angry with you for it and turned His glorious Face away from you and revealed His wrath upon you and excluded you from His mercy. Thus, praised He is our God and evil is what bondmen are you. You've swore fealty and obedience and believed in the messenger Muḥammad and then you've crawled towards his descendants and his Household desiring their killing. Verily, the devil had taken over you and made you forget to mention the name of God the Great, so woe to you and to what you are asking for. We are to God and we shall return back to Him. These are people that disbelieved after their believing and a far removal for wrong doing folk! Then he said: and then, retrace my ancestry and see who am I, and then turn back to yourselves and blame yourselves and see why are you allowed to kill me and destroy my own property. Am I not the son of the daughter of your own prophet and the son of his successor and his cousin and (the son of) the first one who believes in the Prophet of God for what he had brought from his God, is not Ḥamżah, *the Doyen of the Martyrs* my father's uncle? Is not Jāfar Al-Ṭayyār who is in paradise with two wings my uncle? Did you not hear what the holy Prophet said about me and my brother that these are the masters of youth of paradise, so if you believe me in what I am saying and it is the truth. By God, then I didn't lie for a purpose since I knew that God hate liars, and if you do not believe in me, there are people among you whom if you ask shall tell you about this matter. Ask from Jābir-bin-'Abdu'llāh Anṣārī and Abū Saī'd Khidrī and Sahl-bin-Sa'd Sā'idī and Żayd-bin-Arqam and Anas-bin-Mālik and Borā'-bin-'Āzib, they shall tell you that they heard such speech from the holy Prophet about me and my brother. Shall not this avoid you from killing me?"[4]

Yażīdī Commander Shimra-bin-Žuljaushan tried to interupt and ridicule claiming himself a true worshipper, who understood what Imām Ḥusain was saying, and then Ḥusainī Commander Ḥabīb-bin-Maẓāhir Asadī replied back at him and said, I testify that you are saying the truth. You don't know what Imām Ḥusain is saying, because God had blackened your heart.[5] Then, Imām Ḥusain continued his speech:

> "If you are in doubt about that, do you doubt that I am the son of the daughter of your Prophet? By God, there is no son or the daughter of the holy Prophet like me in between the east and west and no one in others other than you. Woe to you, are you after me for a victim that I've killed? Or a fortune of you that I've used? Or for a revenge for some injury that I've made? But no one answered him."[6]

Then he called:

> "O' Shabth-bin-Raba'ī, O'Ḥajār-bin-Abajar, O' Qays-bin-Asha'th-bin-Qays, O' Żayd-bin-Ḥārith, didn't you all write to me that the fruit had ripened and the fields turned green, and if you come you shall find soldiers that are made for you?"[7]

They said, we did not ! Imām Ḥusain said then:

> "Sanctified is God! Yes, By God you did O people, if you hate me then let me leave to my safe place on the lands."[8]

Then Qays-bin-Asha'th said to him, Don't you come down under the rule of your cousin (Yażīd)? They will show you only what you like and never hurt you, then Imām Ḥusain said to him:

> "You are the brother of your own brother, do you want the Hāshimites to ask after more than the blood of Muslim-bin-'Aqīl-bin-Abī Ṭālib, No, By God, I shall not give you my hand like a humble man? And shall not run away like a slave. O' Bondmen of God, I have sought refuge in my Lord and your Lord lest ye stone me to death, I seek refuge in my Lord and your Lord from every scorner who believeth not in a Day of Reckoning."[9]

Then he kneeled down the camel and ordered his servant 'Oqbah-bin-Sama'n to tie it. Such an eloquent speech was inevitable, because Umayyites had been regularly propagating myths and falsething that the holy Prophet of Islām has not left any child behind him and they alone are his legal heirs. Imām Ḥusain wanted that no one should join the war against him being ignorant, all may be well aware that Imām Ḥusain is the direct relative of the Prophet Muḥammad and Yażīdī soldiers were assembled for fighting against the family members of the holy Prophet. Imām Ḥusain wanted to announce the real situation prior to the starting of the war. Therefore, he called for his horse, mounted on it, kept Qur'an before him and addressed the enemy Army.

Imām Ḥusain's true words kept the huge Yażīdī Army silent. No body was in aposition there to reply his speech. He put forward his words very boldly and in a very balanced way before the huge Yażīdī Army and got down from his horse.[10] The reference of this event says that I have not at all heard before such a chaste and beautiful flow compression fairness and wonderful use of constructive language and also not heard after this. It has been discussed in a detailed manner in various reference books.[11]

On Imām Ḥusain's speech coming to close Ḥusainī Commander, Żuhayr-bin-Qayn Numayrī Bajalī, who belonged to Umayyite clan, was struck that he came from among them, went out for them on a horse with his weapon and said:

> "O people of Kufa, this is a warning for you against the wrath of God. This is a warning that a Muslim has the right of advice over his Muslim brother, and we are with you still on one religion as long as the sword did not fall in between us, and you are deserving for the advice and when the sword falls down, thus, the bond will be cut and we shall be one nation and you shall be another nation. God had verily tested us with the sanctified Progeny of His Prophet Muḥammad to see what we and you shall do about them. We are calling you to be victorious to them, and to let down the tyrant Yażīd-bin-Mu'āwiyah and 'Obaydu'llāh-bin-Żiyād for you do not realize from the many things, except their bad rule, to take out your eyes and amputate your hands and legs and cut you into pieces and raise you up over the palms and kill people like you and the best of you pious people, who could read (Qur'an) like Ḥujr-bin-'Adī Kindī and his companions and Ḥānī-bin-'Orwah and his likes!"[12]

Then, Shimr-bin-Žuljaushan shot an arrow at him and asked to shut up, may God shut off your voice! You've bored us with your so much talking, then Żuhayr-Qayn continued his speech and loudly said:

> "O son of him, who pisses on his heels I am not talking to you, you are but a beast! By God, I don't think you are able to acknowledge two phrases from the Book of God (Qur'an) so be glad with the shame, the harsh punishment on the Judgement Day."[13]

Then a man from the Ḥusainī Army called upon him loudly, O' Abā 'Abdu'llāh (Imām Ḥusain) says to you—Come back, for by my life, if the believer man of the Pharaoh's family advised his people and prayed much, then you've advised those people.[14]

In the midst message came regarding a soldier of Ḥusainī Army, Bishr-bin-'Omarū-bin-Uḥadūth Ḥazaramī Kindī's son that 'Omarū has been arrested on the border of Ray. He said, I leave him to God, himself and also myself if it is certain that if I should be alive I won't, but like that he may remain as a prisoner. Imām Ḥusain received the message, then he told Bishr that you are free from my Oath of Allegiance. Go and try to free your son. The soldier full of truth and honesty replied, I may be eaten, by a cruel animal, if I am related to you, how can it be possible! Imām Ḥusain said, Well! Sent your another son Muḥammad. Imām Ḥusain gave five ornaments which valued more than 5000 gold coins, so that Bishr may get free his son with its value. Afterwards Bishr's son 'Omarū after being freed, reached Karbala and sacrificed himself for the cause of Truth. It is noteworthy, who ever soldiers remained the same were they who were considering death as a garland.[15]

Then Imām Ḥusain called for 'Omar-bin-Sa'd, and they called him to the meeting and he hated to come and meet him, and then he said:

> "O' 'Omar-bin-Sa'd, you will kill me and you claim that the bastard, the son of the bastard will give you the rule of al-Rayy and Jorjān? (areas presently in Iran) By God, you shall be happy with that at all, it is a covenant that was made, do whatever you want to do, you shall not be happy in this life or the Hereafter, as if I see your head being on a stick that stands in Kufa and the kids shall play with it."[16]

Then, 'Omar-bin-Sa'd turned his face away with anger and then he called his Commanders and said, what are you waiting for? Fight all together at once it is but only one bite.

With atrocious and abnormal behaviour of Yażīdī Army, one of its Commander, Ḥurr-bin-Yażīd-Riyāḥī, the man who had blocked the way of Imām Ḥusain and diverted him into Karbala, saw that the crowds insisted on fighting against Imām Ḥusain. He used to think that who would dare enough to fight with relative of the holy Prophet, ultimately there would be a compromise. With the same hope, he continued in Yażīdī Army, but now the situation was quite clear. Imām Ḥusain's words had touched his heart. Hearing the speech of Żuhayr-Qayn he lost his courage.

Ḥurr on the Path of Truth

Seeing the insistance on fighting against Imām Ḥusain, Ḥurr-bin-Yażīd-Riyāḥī said to 'Omar-bin-Sa'd, Will you really fight this man? He replied, Yes, By God, a fight in which at least the heads would fall down with the hands! Then, Ḥurr said, Are not you satisfied with what he offered? He replied, If it was in my hands, I would be satisfied, but your leader ('Obaydu'llāh-bin-Żiyād) had denied that.[17]

Then Ḥurr left him and advanced in front of the crowds with a man from his tribe called Qorrah-bin-Qays, and he said to him, O Qorrah, did you water your horse today? He replied, No I didn't, then he asked, Don't you want to water him? Qorrah said later, By God, I thought he wanted to stay from the battle and the fight, and didn't want me to see that if he did, so I said to him: I didn't water my horse and I shall go to water it, and I left that place in which he was, and By God, if he showed me what he desired then I would go out with him to Imām Ḥusain.

Yażīdī soldier Muhājir-bin-Aws Taymī asked, what do you want O son of Yażīd-Riyāḥī? Do you want to fight? But Ḥurr didn't answer and his body started to tremble, and Muhājir then said, your situation is doubtful, By God ! I've never seen you like that before and if I was asked who is the bravest among the people of Kufa, I wouldn't choose anyone but you! So, what is that I see from you? Then Ḥurr said, By Allah, verily I'm giving the options for myself to choose between Paradise and the Hell, and By God, I shall not choose anything, but the Paradise, even if, I was to be cut into pieces and burnt.

'Omar-bin-Sa'd's reply had awakened a firm faith in the mind of Ḥurr that Imām Ḥusain wants peace and Yażīdī war-mongers wanted to kill him. Now, the time has come to Ḥurr for taking a final decision. Ḥurr decided that he would proceed only on the path of Truth and give up myth. However, if he reaches Imām Ḥusain, he would be arrested immediately. Then Ḥurr began to approach towards Ḥusainī Army, little by little, towards Ḥusainī Army and put his hand over his head, showing his apologetical stand. He whipped his horse and reached the associates of Imām Ḥusain. Although Yażīdī Army sent their mounted soldiers to over take him but they could not get even the dust of his great speedy horse.

There would have been a delicacy in Ḥurr's mind that the Ḥusainī Army may stop him being in an illusion. Though he was from the Yażīdī Army, but Ḥusainī soldiers were all very good persons, they might understand that he was not coming for fighting. But how could he see face to face Imām Ḥusain. Overflowing sentiments had deluged him. He streightway surrendered at Imām's holy feet and said, O' The Son of Prophet! I sacrifice my life at your holy feet—I am the same sinner who stopped you from going back, with you on the way, and insisted you to stop at this place. By God, I had not the least suspicion that these people would refuse your peace-proposals and situation would reach this extent. I thought in my mind nothing is wrong in helping them to a certain limit and they would not know that I am away from their assiduity. I felt they would accept your peace proposal. Now, I am at your service. I am ashamed of my sin. I have come before you with folded hands, seeking permission to sacrifice my life at your holy feet! Imām Ḥusain embraced Ḥurr and said that certainly God would pardon him. I bless you, you are indeed *Ḥurr* (literally means, Independent). God will make you independent in this world also at the end.

Imām Ḥusain advised Ḥurr to get down from his horse and take rest, but he replied, I am better for you on my horse rather than on my foot, and I shall fight them over my horse for some time and then at the end I shall come down, then Imām Ḥusain said to him, Do whatever you like, may God have mercy upon you. Then Ḥurr stepped in front of Imām Ḥusain, taking permission from him, he attempted to convince those of the Yażīdī Army, with whom he was a little before, and addressed them:

> "O' people of Kufa, you did invite this faithful man and when he arrived you tried to capture him, and you claimed that you are willing to kill yourselves to protect him and then stepped with aggression towards him to kill him, and imprison him and surrounded him from all the sides to keep him away from going on the wide lands of God, so he became like the hostage between your hands and has no power for himself and

> blocked his way with his women and children and his family from the water of the 'Alqamah which flows on and Jews, Christians and the Magians drink from it, as well as, the black boars and the dogs roll in it, and here are they dying of thirst, evil is what you've done to the Progeny of the Prophet Muḥammad after him, may God never make you drink when you become thirsty."[18]

Each and every word of Ḥurr's speech was a slap at the cheek of the Yazīdī Army. They were in turmoil. But they had no reply. Leaving the Yazīdī Army and then going to the Ḥusainī Army itself was sufficient to break the will power of the Yazīdī Army. The revealing of truth by hard and harsh words of Ḥurr had its own influence. Then some men shot arrows on him so he stepped back until he stood in front of Imām Ḥusain and then said to him. If I was the first one to come out to fight you, then let me be the first one to be killed before you. May I be one of those who shall shake the hands with your grandfather Muḥammad, on the Day of Judgement. But Imām Ḥusain asked Ḥurr to return back, as no formal war was declared at the moment and he complied with.

Futile Attempt of the Yazīdī Army

'Omar-bin-Sa'd was scared that there might be a mutiny in the Yazīdī Army. It was most alarming to observe a regular trend of the squander by the soldiers leaving their army and joing hands with enemy army. Worst situation was on card, one of their bravest commanders, Ḥurr-bin-Yazīd-Riyāḥī along with his sons, brother and servant had deflected to Ḥusainī Army. Its damage control would be our first priority. He intrigued a conspiracy along with Shimr-bin-Žiljaushan. Impudent Shimr boasted of the situation and claimed, it would be like a trice for me. The Ḥusainī Army's Commander-in-Chief, Abu'l-Faẓl'il-'Abbās is son of my sister Ummu'l-Banīn, thus, he is my nephew, I would win over him. You give me written assurance for peace with him, his brothers and family members and a suitable position in our army. 'Omar-bin-Sa'd appreciated his conspiracy and issued orders accordingly.

Shimr-bin-Žiljaushan came near the Ḥusainī camps and called Abu'l-Faẓl'il-'Abbās, calling him his nephew and told that he has received written orders of 'Omar-bin-Sa'd for the safety of Abu'l-Faẓl'il-'Abbās. He does not want that 'Abbās and his other brothers may be murdered along with Imām Ḥusain. Abu'l-Faẓl'il-'Abbās firmly replied that he won't come into the fold of his words. If he wants to do some thing then arrange for the safety and security of Imām Ḥusain. <u>Sh</u>imr-bin-Žiljau<u>sh</u>an was dejected with the words of Abu'l-Faẓl'il-'Abbās. <u>Sh</u>imr repeated the same with other brothers of Abu'l-Faẓl'il-'Abbās also. All in one voice said whatever their elder brother has replied.[19] <u>Sh</u>imr-bin-Žiljau<u>sh</u>an dare not to near the Ḥusainī Army standing at the safest spot in his army. He returned ugly and awkward to 'Omar-bin-Sa'd.[20]

Commencement of Formal War

'Omar-bin-Sa'd called his slave Dorayd (Żayd or Żuwayd), who was the Bearer of Army Flag of the Yażīdī Army. Asked him to bring the flag to him, the maid handed over him the flag and was standing behind him. Yażīdī Commander-in-Chief 'Omar-bin-Sa'd aimed and sent arrows to the Ḥusainī Army and declared:

> "Be all witness before Amīr 'Obaydu'llāh-bin-Żiyād that I have shot the first arrow towards the Ḥusainī Army."[21]

The Yażīdī Army became full of joy with the words and arrow of their Commander-in-Chief. They started showering arrows on the Ḥusainī camps. Thousands of arrows were shot at the Ḥusainī camps.

The Ḥusainī soldiers were already prepared for scarifying their life, they welcomed showering arrows erecting on their chest. Imām Ḥusain asked his Army personnel to stand-up for welcoming death. God would bless you all. These are not arrows, but messengers of enemies, sent towards you. The Ḥusainī soldiers were firm at their place without being perturbed. After getting the permission of war, they all declared that they are fully ready for war. It was clear, how about 100 arrrows could make any affect on the Yażīdī Army, however, certainly in a symbolic way they retaliated.[22]

As soon as Yażīdī Army started the war, from their side two soldiers, Yasār and Sālim both slaves of Ziyād-bin-Abīh and his son Ibn-Ziyād, came to the battlefield challenging by name Ḥabīb-bin-Maẓāhir Asadī and Burayr-bin-<u>Kh</u>uzayr Hamadānī, who were emotional to proceed ahead, but Imām Ḥusain stopped them. Every Ḥusainī soldiers was eager to become first martyr and wanted to come to the war front first. Ḥurr cautiously put his claim to be first to go to the war front.[23] But the good fortune was smiling on Abū Wahab-Kalbī also known as 'Abdu'llāh-bin-'Omayr Kalbī, a courageous youth of Kufa, with Christian family background,[24] who had came with his wife and mother only with the objective of participating in the war of Justice. He submitted at the service of Imām Ḥusain and requested for permission to go to war-front. Imām Ḥusain observed him, his head to feet tall, exercised body, strong wrists, shoulders full of energy, broad back and a large forehead. Said, you seem to be very smart and brave, so if you wish.

It was the then discipline in 'Arabian Wars that two soldiers right starting against each other, at first they exchange their bio-data, heritage, braver act in a very effective style. Verses were also read to arouse the martial spirit of the soldier, resulting in opponent's will-power to be shaken. It was technically called *Rajaż* (martial songs). There was also a provision that both the soldiers should be of equal calibre, rank and status. A man of elite class fought with his counterpart and *vice versa*. Usually, both soldiers fought hand to hand. If one killed, the other came to fight against him. Unbalanced fight was avoided as far as possible. They abide by traditional pre-war verbal agreement that first skirmish between the two warring personnels would be through exchange of swords, then other weapons and at the last, when the enemies become almost defeated, then arrows would be used. But the Syrian army, as mentioned in above lines, had quickly retreated and broke the pre-war verbal agreement by using arrows and lances at the commencement of war itself. It shows their unprincipled and defeated mentality.

Wahab-Kalbī was asked about his introduction by the Yażīdī soldiers Yasār and Sālim. He told. They said, we do not know you, we want Ḥabīb-bin-Maẓāhir Asadī and Burayr-bin-Khuzayr Hamadānī for fighting, they should come. Hearing this, Abū Wahab-Kalbī became angry, with harsh words he attacked and in the first attack itself murdered Yasār. Sālim attacked him with his sword, he protected himself with his hands and his fingers were cut, but he killed Sālim also.[25] After killing both soldiers of the Yażīdī Army, Wahab-Kalbī introduced himself again enthusiastically. In the midst he addressed his wife, Umm Wahab-bint-Ma'bad – O' my beloved, I have fought only in accordance with the norms prescribed for the soldiers.[26] As soon as she heard his pleasant voice, she became emotional and readily. She rushed to the battlefield and said calling—Let my parents be sacrifice on your valour. Everyone should sacrifice towards, the family of the holy Prophet.[27] Wahab-Kalbī tried somehow to make his wife return. There was a sword in his hands and the drops of blood was dropping from it, the other hand's fingers were already cut, blood was flowing from them. He tried his best, but the brave lady removed her hand and said, I won't leave you, I also will sacrifice my life along with you. Imām Ḥusain saw them and raised his voice—God will certainly give you good fruit for this. O' true believer lady, come back, sit with the ladies of my family, because in Islām there is no permission for ladies to fight in the war-front. The believer lady became helpless, with the orders of Imām Ḥusain and returned to her camp. Wahab-Kalbī was going on fighting continuously, killed so many Yażīdīs, but ultimately Ḥānī-bin-Thobayṭ Ḥazramī and Bakīr-bin-Ha' Tayamī both from the Yażīdī Army made him martyr.[28]

After the murder of their soldiers Yasār and Sālim the Yażīdī Army became mad out of anger, 'Omar-bin-Ḥujjāj Żubaydī, Commander, Right Regiment attacked heavily with his full force and mighty battalions on Ḥusainī Army. But Ḥusainī soldiers made the attack futile. Keeping edge of spear on the earth and kneeling down, made the horses of the Yażīdī Army scared. Being helpless the soldiers had to run away from the battlefield. But they were going on showering arrows.

The war had already commenced fully, yet there was no casuality in Ḥusainī Army. It was natural for the brave warrior Ḥurr-bin-Yażīd-Riyāḥī, to think that, as he had created first hurdle on the way of Imām Ḥusain, now, he should sacrifice his life first. He appeared before Imām Ḥusain and prayed, O' Son of the holy Prophet! As I had come first to fight with you there, now, it is my wish, you may kindly permit me to offer my life at your holy feet. Imām Ḥusain graciously allowed him. Ḥurr came to the war-front and he read out some verses in his *Rajaż*: thus he attacked with his sword and made pieces of so many Yażīdī soldiers. Yażīdī Army was running away from this point to that point. During the fight Ḥurr's horse became wounded. Yażīdīs attacked on its face and head, blood was oozing. Yażīdī Commander Ḥiṣṣīn-bin-Numayr asked his soldier Yażīd-bin-Sufyyān Tamīmī, See, he is Ḥurr! You fulfil your desire of killing him. He said, Well; telling this he came outside and called Ḥurr. So, you agree to fight with me. Ḥurr replied. Yes! Certainly. Telling this, he came forward. Yażīdī Commander, Ḥiṣṣīn-bin-Numayr's own statement was that it seemed, as if his life was at the hands of Ḥurr. Ḥurr immediately attacked and made him wet in a pool of blood.[29] It was such a terrfic scene that the enemy-army lost it's self-confidence, nobody was outside its purview. Ḥurr had to return, as his horse was severely injured. Afterwards, he had to meet his martyrdom with the several attack of Yażīdī Army. It will be discussed at the appropriate place.[30]

Muslim-bin-'Ausajah Asadī, was highly reverend in the Ḥusainī Army, for being an aged Companion of the holy Prophet. His significance had perturbed thc Yażīdī Army, owing to mental defeat. The Yażīdī Army was greatly demolarised and afraid of less numbered the Ḥusainī Army, which had proved to be heavy over huge the Yażīdī Army. The defeat of the Commander of Right Regiment, 'Omar-bin-Ḥujjāj Żubaydī had turned the entire atmosphere into dcspair on all sides.

Therefore, to gain the self-confidance of his own Army 'Omar-bin-Ḥujjāj challenged the soldiers—O Stupids! Are unaware, to whom you are fighting. They are the supreme venture some of the nation, who are playing with their life, don't come anybody outside, to fight with them. They a small number of soldiers, may live for a shortwhile. Even if you all unitedly throw stones at them, you can easily kill them. This suggestion that soldiers need not fight facing each other, 'Omar-bin-Sa'd liked it, he ordered his entire Army that no one will go outside for reading the customary Recite. Then 'Omar-bin-Ḥujjāj Żubaydī went ahead and gave a speech to motivate the entire Army and said:

> "O Kufan people! Be dedicated to your master, don't be separate from your group, don't be suspicious even in the least. As far as these people who have given up the religion and are opposing presently against Imām and Caliph Yażīd..."[31]

Imām Ḥusain thought it necessary to reply to his false charges and said addressing:

> "O 'Omar-bin-Ḥujjāj! You are beckoning people against me. Did we give up religion (Justice) and you are in justice? By God, when your life will give up your body and you will go with your deeds, then you will know that who has given up Justice (Religion) and who will be flamed with the fire of Hell."[32]

Muslim-bin-'Ausajah Martyred

Being motivated by 'Omar-bin-Ḥujjāj Żubaydī the entire right command of the Yażīdī Army attacked the Ḥusainī Army again from the side of 'Alqamah river. Muslim-bin-'Ausajah Asadī with the command under him fought bravely exhibiting his full strength and intelligence and made the attack ineffective. The Ḥusainī Army fought bravely with thousands of soldiers of Yażīdī Army and stopped it from proceeding ahead. But when the atmosphere of war cleared, Muslim-bin-'Ausajah Asadī was found in a pool of blood. Imām Ḥusain immediately reached by the side of his head. Still he was alive. He blessed him. Ḥabīb-bin-Maẓāhir Asadī was with him. He went near Muslim and said to him—I am very sad for being parted from your lovely company, however, you are away to attain the Heaven! With his sinking breathing, he replied in a very week voice—You would also attain all sorts of reward vitues soon! Ḥabīb-bin-Maẓāhir said, if I could believe, that I shall remain, I would have asked to do a will, which I could fulfil. Muslim-bin-'Ausajah smiled and said, Take care of Imām Ḥusain ! Ḥabīb-bin-Maẓāhir assured firmly, Certainly! By God, no one can dare hit him and his family in my life.[33]

Muslim-bin-'Ausajah Asadī became martyr, but the Yažīdī Army being mentally defeated ran away, it was not clear to them, whether Muslim-bin-'Ausajah Asadī became martyr! The information of his becoming a martyr reached them, when the ladies of the Ḥusainī camps, his family member who came along with him, a maid-servant shouted crying—Oh Alas! my master has become martyr!! Hearing this Yažīdī Army became cheerful, people happier, but in their midst quarerel started, as who actually murdered him. Yažīdī Commander Ḥiṣṣīn-bin-Numayr himself was ashamed of it. He said, it is a matter of deep sorrow that a person like Muslim-bin-'Ausajah Asadī was murdered and you are exhibiting pleasure. By God. I have seen with my own eyes, his contributions in the service of Islām.[34] See, how truth laments and speeks from the top head of untruth and forces to praise the genuineness, this is also an example.

With the success of collective attack was restored the self-confidence of the Yažīdī Army. After the successful war, the Yažīdī Army attacked the Ḥusainī Army. There was no sign of the despair or fear in the Ḥusainī Army, rather they were most enthusiastic to become martyr first. Abū Wahab-Kalbī, who had fought earlier and was resting and restoring physical strength, asked his mother, Are you happy with my performance ? The brave lady replied, I would be happy only at that time, when defending the cause of Truth, you would sacrifice your life at the holy feet of Imām Ḥusain.

The Martyred Lady

Wahab-Kalbī took the permission from Imām Ḥusain and like a lion pounced upon Yažīdī Army, defeated its tactics of collective attack, with his wonderful tactics and bravery, killed so many Yažīdīs. His mother was immensely happy, seeing the bravery and intelligence of her son from her camp. She rushed into the battlefield with a spear and began to fight. Imām Ḥusain observed and praised her enthusiasm and convinced her that there was no permission in Islām for women to fight in the battlefield, hence, she should go back to her camp. She returned obeying the orders of Imām Ḥusain.[35]

Wahab-Kalbī had distinction of having participated in the battle of truth, with his wife and mother. After great courageous fighting, when he became martyr, his brave wife, Umm Wahab-bint-Ma'bad, who was watching the intrepid fighting of her beloved husband and when she heard the heart-rending news of his demise, she could not control herself, she ran to battlefield, reached to the dead body of her husband. Kept her beloved's head on her lap, cleaned blood from the head and said crying, Congratulation for your setting out to the Heaven! But the atrocities of the Yażīdī Army had already crossed the human limits, Shimr-bin-Žuljaushan ordered his slave Rostan to kill her, he attacked serverely on her head with a weapon and she became a martyr immediately on the spot. She is conferred with the honour of being the only female martyr of the Battle of Karbala.[36]

Prophet's Companion Burayr

The aged companion of the holy Prophet, Burayr-bin-Khuzayr Hamadānī of the Ḥusainī Army came to the war front. Challenging who is that wrectched murderer of the companions of the holy Prophet, the man should come before me. Fighting alone he killed the thirty Yażīdī soldiers.[37] Taking his name Yażīdī soldier Yażīd-bin-Ma'qal challenged him. He was familiar to Burayr Hamadānī and he used to discuss with him on religious matters. Satirically he said, Did you see how God has behaved ? Burayr Hamadānī replied, God has behaved with me very well. Yes! you say about the old man proved to be unfortunate. He said, you are telling lie, previously you never told any lie. Well, tell me about *Ahlu'l-Bayt*, the Progeny of the Prophet Muḥammad. Are you still with you're previous belief, or any change in that. Burayr Hamadānī replied, I am always staunch in my religious faith. He said, I may produce witness that you are corrupt. Burayr Hamadānī replied, If you are ready, let us pray together God may admonish and punish the lier and not whoever is with Truth, he may murder the lier. He agreed with Burayr Hamadānī. Both armies observed that both the soldiers came opposite to each other, both prayer to God raising their hands to the sky then started fighting.

It may be cleared here, that such a way or method of finding out the Truth in Islām has been called, the *Mubāhilah*. The holy Prophet of Islām himself had done the Mubāhilah, the discussion on this is available in the Holy Qur'an in Chapter III, verse 61.

Weapons were exchanged only twice between Burayr Hamadānī and his challenger. The Yażīdī soldier attacked first, but his sword slipped and went ahead, could not make any harm. Then Burayr Hamadānī attacked him with his sword on his head. He fell down on the ground from his horse, in this manner that the sword piercing his helmet reached has brain and entangled and then he was dragging it from his brain. Looking his condition, another Yażīdī soldier Razī-bin-Munqaž 'Abdī came to his rescue and started to wrestle with, Burayr defeated him and jumped on his chest. He shouted seeing his death before himself, where are our counterparts, who can save me. In the midst Yażīdī soldier Ka'b-bin-Jābir Ażdī advanced to attack. Other Yażīdīs dissuaded him not to attack on Burayr Hamadānī, saying, he was learned *Qārī* (Reciter of the Qur'an) and educates the learner in the mosque. But he did not cared all these and attacked Burayr from his back with his spear which went across his chest. Burayr fell on the ground, then he murdered him with his sword.[38]

The soldier Munjiḥ-bin-Sahm had been freed-slave of Imām Ḥusain. He is distinguished for being the pioneer among the slaves and servant in the Battle of Karbala. He exhibited his braveness at the first phase of the War itself, killed so many Yażīdī soldiers. He was deceitfully killed by the Yażīdī soldier Ḥassān-bin-Bakr Ḥanžalī.

After the commencement of the War, five Ḥusainī soldiers fought in a revolutionary manner, who thrust into Yażīdī Army. Their leader was 'Omar-bin-Khālid Asadī Ṣaidavī. His other colleagues were – his servant Saī'd, Mujama'-bin-'Abdu'llāh 'Āyižī, his son 'Āyiž-bin-Mujama' and Jinādah-bin-Ḥārith Salmānī. Our learned readers may afresh their memory, they are those persons who had met Imām Ḥusain during the journey at 'Ažību'l Hijānat and joined the Ḥusainī Caravan. Determined of sacrificing themselves on the path of God, they collectively and aggressively attacked the Yażīdī Army and killing the enemies went into the thick crowd of the forces. As the tigers pounce over the flock of sheeps, Yażīdī soldiers were hiding here and there. However, the Yażīdī Army separated them, surrounding on all sides, from the Ḥusainī Army, then, the Ḥusainī Commander-in-Chief Abu'l-Fażl'il-'Abbās rushed for their help and fighting alone he drove away the Yażīdī Army. Taking the wounded soliders, he was in way for reaching his Force. Enemies turned to chase. Keeping in view the enthuasiasm of Ḥusainī wounded soldiers, Abu'l-Fażl'il-'Abbās kept the soliders in front and for their safety himself went behind them, so, that there would be no harm for them. But as soon as the Yażīdī force advanced, the wounded soldiers became emotional and breaking the safety bond attacked the enemies. Although they were wounded, still everyone of them showed bravery. One by one all the five soldiers became martyrs. Abu'l-Fażl'il-'Abbās informed of the event to Imām Ḥusain. Imām praised their bravery and prayed God for them![39]

After them, Ḥusainī soldier, Junadab-bin-Ḥajīr Kindī Khūlānī, killed so many soliders and at last became a martyr.[40] Like him, Yażīd-bin-Żiyād-bin-Mahāṣar Abu'l al-Sh'athā Kindī also was making complain for Imām Ḥusain. He was an expert archer. He sat kneeling down before Imām Ḥusain. He had eight arrows aimed all eight and killed five. When the arrows were finished, he came to the battlefield with his sword, exhibited his skill, killed many Yażīdī key soldiers and reached the Heaven.[41]

There was no dilemma with the conduct of the Ḥusainī soldiers. On the contrary a discussion of a soldier is available, who wanted, to join this war of justice co-operating Imām Ḥusain, but at the same time wanted to save his life also. It was Zaḥāq-bin-'Abdu'llāh Mashraqī, who is also famous eyewitness author of the *Maqālātu'l Ḥusain.* He tied his horse in the camp to escape from the attack of enemies. First, he murdered two and cut ones' hand. Then he told Imām Ḥusain. The joining your Army and fighting against Evil Forces was the basis of my Oath of Allegiance. Now, I have done *Jihād,* now please remove your *Bay'at* from me. Imām Ḥusain gladly permitted him, then he mounted on his horse and ran away outside the orbit of the Yażīdī Army. Its soldiers chased him, but of no avail.[42]

Cowardly Attack by the Yażīdī Army

Most of the historians have called it as *Ḥamla-i-Oūlā* (Main Attack), but in our view, it would be more appropriate to call it as the Yażīdī Army's Cowardly Attack. Because, it was imposed without any prior notice and in an unprecedented way, in which they crossed all prescribed norms, the Syrian army quickly retreated and broke all pre-war verbal agreements, which were honoured even during pre-Islāmic era, known as *Jāhilīyah,* the Age of Ignorance.

It has already been discussed in the previous chapters, also briefly in the above lines that the arrows were used only when it was impossible to succeed with sword and other weapons. When no force was possible, they used to attacked by throwing of stone from a distance.

Right from the beginning of the War, from sunrise to afternoon, the one to one fighting was going on. With their spirited will power and enthusiasm the Ḥusainī Army was successful, on the contrary there was scare and disorder spread among the Yażīdī Army. Their continuous defeat had buried the will power. Till noon, they could not do anything other than facing losses heavily. Though the Ḥusainī Army had a meagre strength, it had proved already to be very strong and mighty over the lakhs of soldiers of the Yażīdī Army. Continuously three days' starved and thirsty disciplined Ḥusainī soldiers were very happy over their ethical victory. They were completely free of any depression.

Just on the contrary, there was more and much confusion and commotion in the Yażīdī Army. Everywhere there was disorder. They were not capable of fighting abiding any rules and regulations. They were most indisciplined. An eyewitness says, that though their number was just thousand times of the Ḥusainī Army, but at the time of the Ḥusainī soldier's powerful attack, the large Yażīdī Army's Regiments could not dare stand at the attack and turned their faces, the other side. Whatever direction Ḥusainī Army attacked forcefully, Yażīdī Army ran away from the spot.[43]

Being completely vexed and agitated with the continuous defeat of the Yażīdī Army, Qurrah-bin-Qays, Commander of Cavalry Regiment, sent a message to his Commander-in-Chief, 'Omar-bin-Sa'd, through 'Abdu'r Raḥmān-bin-Ḥaṣan. You see the worse situation of our Battalions from this morning by the hands of that small group; now please send experts of bow-arrows, so, that they can manage the war front. No doubt, the Yażīdī Army had to accept their defeat. Its commander openly addmitted his defeat in clear words. 'Omar-bin-Sa'd also was frightened. He immediately strongly ordered Shabth-bin-Raba'ī, Commander, Armoury Regiment. Why don't you go ahead? But he gave a defrauding reply. It is highly regretted that such a large cavalry regiments under great experienced commanders have failed to win over such small group of people, whom to call army would be exaggeration and for such a small job a high ranking officer has been asked for? Hearing this 'Omar-bin-Sa'd became helpless. He appointed Ḥiṣṣīn-bin-Numayr along with an Army of 500 experts of bow-arrows to go ahead very near to Ḥusainī Army and attack them with the series of arrows.[44]

In compliance, Yażīdī Army advanced very near Ḥusainī Army and attacked with thousands of rounds. But Żuhayr-bin-Qayn-bin-Qays Numayrī Bajalī, Commander, Right-Wing Regiment of the Ḥusainī Army along with just ten soldiers attacked so bravely with ten of his colleages such forcefully that Shimr-bin-Žuljaushan, Commander, Left Regiment Yażīdī Army ran away leaving his army personnels abruptly. This event was just an hour prior to noon. [45]

The severe cowardly arrows attack of the Yażīdī Army proved to be very sorrowful to the Ḥusainī Army. Ḥusaini soldiers kept their animals before them to stop the arrow-attack of the Yażīdī Army. They went ahead with their swords and began to out do the showers of arrows with their swords. They were very much worried about Imām Ḥusain and his family and to save them from any harm. They were successful in keeping Imām Ḥusain and his family members safe and nobody had any problem among them. But when the clouds of the arrows were removed, they came to know that their army, which was already very small, now became highly reduced. Besides, all the horses of the Ḥusainī Army have already been killed. The remaining mounted soldiers also were murdered. Ḥurr's injured horse was found killed. Yażīdī soldier Ayūb-bin-Masrūj, who had killed the horse of Ḥurr, was telling that he killed that horse wonderfully with an arrow. Ḥurr jumped over him like a lion and parted his head from his body.[46]

Fifty brave soldiers of the Ḥusainī Army attained the martyrdom, as a result of the cowardly arrows attack of the Yażīdī Army. Their holy names are given below in ascending order:

'Abdu'l Raḥmān-bin-'Abd Rab Anṣārī Khiżarajjī
'Abdu'l Raḥmān-bin-'Abdu'llāh-bin-Kadan Arḥabī
'Abdu'l Raḥmān-bin-Mas'ūd-bin-Ḥujjāj Tayamī
'Abdu'l Raḥmān-bin-Żayd-bin-Thabayṭ Qaysī
'Abdu'llāh-bin-Bishr Khith'amī
'Āmir-bin-Muslim 'Abdī Baṣrī
'Ammār-bin-Abū Salmah Dālāni Hamadānī
'Ammār-bin-Ḥassān-bin-Shurayb Ṭaī
'Ibad-bin-Muhājir-bin-Abī Muhājir Juhanī
'Imrān-bin-Ka'b-bin-Ḥārith Ashja'ī
'Obaydu'llāh-bin-Żayd-bin-Thabayṭ Qaysī
'Omarū-bin-Zab'aitah-bin-Qays-bin-Th'albah Zab'ī Taymī
'Oqbah-bin-Ṣulet Juhanī
Adaham-bin-Umayyah 'Abdī Baṣarī
Ḥabāb-bin-Ḥārith
Ḥabāb-bin-'Āmir-bin-Ka'b Tayamī
Ḥabshatah-bin-Qays Nahamī
Ḥallās-bin-'Omarū Ażdī Rāsbī
Ḥanẓalah-bin-'Omar Shaybānī
Ḥārith-bin-Imra-ul-Qays-bin-'Ābis Kindī
Ḥārith-bin-Nibhān (Prophet's uncle Ḥamżah's servant)
Ḥujjāj-bin-Żaid-Sa'dī Tayamī
Jābir-bin-Hujjāj Taymī 'Āmir-bin-Nahashal's servant)
Jiblitah-bin-'Alī Shaybānī
Jinādah-bin-K'ab-bin-Ḥārith Anṣārī Khiżarajjī
Juvayn-bin-Mālik-bin-Qays-bin-Th'albah Tayamī
Kardūs-bin-Żuhayr bin-Ḥārith Taghalabī

Kinānah-bin-'Atīq Taghalabī
Masu'd-bin-Ḥujjāj Taymī
Mujama'-bin-Żiyād-bin-'Omarū –Jehnī
Munī'-bin-Żiyād
Muqsiṭ Kursh)-bin-Żuhayr-bin-Ḥārith Taghalabī
Muslim-bin-Kathīr Ṣadafi Ażdī
Naī'm-bin-'Ajalān Anṣārī
Naṣar-bin-Abī Nīżar
No'mān-bin-'Omarū Ażdī
Qārib-bin-'Abdu'llāh (Imām Ḥusain's servant)
Qāsim-bin-Ḥabīb-bin-Abī Bishr Ażdī
Qāsiṭ-bin-Żuhayr-bin-Ḥārith Taghalabī
Saif-bin-Mālik 'Abdī
Sālim ('Āmir-bin-Muslim al-'Abdī's servant)
Salīm (Imām Ḥusain's servant)
Sawwār-bin-Abī 'Oman Nahamī
Shabīb-bin-'Abdu'llāh Nahashalī
Shabīb-bin-'Abdu'llāh (Ḥārith-bin-Sarī'a's servant)
Umayyah-bin-Sa'd-bin-Żaid Ṭaī
Żāhar-bin-'Omarū Aslamī Kindī
Żāhayr-bin-Bishr Khitha'mī
Żāhayr-bin-Sulaym-bin-'Omarū Ażdī
Zarghamah-bin-Mālik Taghalabī

Attack on the Ḥusainī Camps

When the Yażīdī Army faced regular failure after failure in degraded form continuously, they planned to round up the Ḥusainī soldiers from the back side of their camps, which were set-up, under the directions of Imam Ḥusain, in such a way that the camps were all mutually attached and their knots and ropes were not visible from outside, and camps were outwardly just like a strong wall or armoury and indestructible. As no direct attack was possible, 'Omar-bin-Sa'd ordered to cut the ropes of the camps and destroy them right to left direction. The Ḥusainī soldiers pondered over the situation and adopted new strategy. They went inside their camps, with the determination, if any Yażīdī soldier come inside their camps, they would chop off his head and throw away the dead-body. When Yażīdī soldiers failed in cutting the ropes, they quickly ran away and refused to go near the camps of the Ḥusainī soldiers. Being vexed and accepting his defeat and failure of battle management, 'Omar-bin-Sa'd again ordered the Yażīdī soldiers need not go into the Ḥusainī camps, but destroy them by setting them on fire.

The Ḥusainī soldiers' camps were established in such fashion that the camps of Imām Ḥusain and his family members were little away from the rows of the camps of their soldiers. By setting fire in the lines of camps of the Ḥusainī soldiers, the way of attacking from that direction automatically came to an end.

'Omar-bin-Sa'd could not visualize and realize the master mind skill of the Ḥusainī soldiers. Whereas Imām Ḥusain was well aware of Yażīdī tricks, therefore, he told his men, let them set fire. As the Ḥusainī soldiers' camps were burnt, the battlefield became more open and the visuality proved disastrous for them. 'Omar-bin-Sa'd and his commanders were so grief sticken that they could not do any thing before the bravery and intellingence of the Ḥusainī soldiers, who safeguarded themselves. Yażīdī Army felt ashamed of their failure in killing them. Shimr-bin-Žuljaushan became mad out of anger, Piercing the camps of Imām Ḥusain with his spear, he shouted—Bring the fire and I will set it in the Ḥusainī camps and burn them alive. Of course, the babies, ladies and old people of the family member of Imām Ḥusain were highly scared. Imām Ḥusain cautioned Shimr-bin-Žuljaushan and he said—If you burn out my family by setting fire in their camps, then God will certainly kill you in the fire. Hearing his words Yażīdī soldiers were afraid of other commanders also condemned Shimr. Shabth-bin-Raba'ī went near Shimr and said, I did not hear such a shameful matter, as you were telling with your tongue and I have not seen such a waste deed, as you attempted to do.[47]

In the midst, Ḥusainī Commander Żuhayr-bin-Qayn Bajalī with his ten colleagues attacked and killed many Yażīdī soldiers. His attack was so furious that Shimr and his soldiers could not stand in the battlefield. So, may Yażīdī soldiers especially Shimr's intimate friend Abū 'Omrah Žūbābī was killed.

After the attack on Ḥusainī camps there was a terrific war from both the sides. So many soldiers were killed in the Yażīdī Army. As their number was very large and long and there was no difference, if there would have been killed some hundreds even, but the number of soldiers alive in the Ḥusainī Army had reduced to the extent, if even a single person becoming a martyr, his absence was felt very much. Although their enthusiasm was going on increasing after the demise of the holy Prophet's Companion, Muslim-bin-'Ausajah Asadī, his son, (aged 12 years) took his last breath after killing 20 Yażīdī soldiers, exhibiting exemplary courage. In the same way Masu'd-bin-Ḥujjāj Taymī's son

'Abdu'l Raḥmān increased the glory of his father. Ḥurr's, sons 'Alī and Sa'd, brother Muṣa'b-bin-Yażīd Riyāḥī, his servant Qurrah and Bakr-bin-Ḥay Tayamī also achieved the glory of the martyrdom.

Grieved and composed Imām Ḥusain was sitting at the door with his remaining persons. All observed a boy coming towards them with a sword hanging at his waist. He is so young by his age that the sword was touching the ground. He came near and saluted Imām Ḥusain and requested for his permission to fight in the war. Imām Ḥusain asked the people who the boy was? He was informed that the boy 'Omarū was the son of Jinādah-bin-K'ab-bin-Ḥārith Anṣārī Khiżarajjī. Imām Ḥusain made him sit on his thigh and said your father's sacrifice is much more sufficient for your family. Don't give grief to your mother, be pleasure for her. Go and make your mother happy. The child said, this sword has been fastened on my waist by my mother herself and she has permitted me to sacrifice in the battlefield. His mother was Bahriyah-bint-Masu'd, who also said loudly from the door, My Lord, don't reject our last humble present. Imām Ḥusain accepted her request, the child came to the fore-front and fought and offered his life. A soldier of the Yażīdī Army suddenly cut the head of the child and threw it towards the Ḥusainī Army. The brave mother advanced immediately and took the head and loved and said, thank you my lad, you sacrificed your life over Imām Ḥusain and throwing the very head of her child towards Yażīdī Army, she said, We do not take back any given donation.[48]

The Prayer During War

Ṣalāt or *Namāż* (the prayer) the foremost pivot of the Religious Obligations of Islām, which occupies the central place in the elements of the Islāmic practices, affords a medium to submit spiritually to God and seek spiritual nearness to His Lordship.

The Islāmic prayer is the worshipping and submitting to God. In this form of prayer the man is drawn closer to God to the extent that rising erect from the bowing position he has got awareness that God *hast heard him who has praised His Glory*. Apart from this the *Namāż* is the most effective means to make one conform to the laws of Islām. Rushing five times daily to the call of *Allāhu'-Akbar* has a semblance in the soldiers rushing for the parade in response to the call of military siren. The purpose of the parade is to brace the soldiers to keep prepared for the war. Likewise, the daily prayer prepares the individual to combat the evil forces fighting with the virtuous forces of his conscience. Through the prayer an individual fortifies the feeling of submission to God, the consciousness of duties, the habit of obedience, the moral fear of the unseen God, the understanding of the law of Islām and the lesson of integrating with the society at large. Our reader must be familier to these things and had observed Imām Ḥusain leading the Prayer of his associates and also people of enemy group.

It was noon in the midst of the war, the time for the *Ẓuhr Namāż* (the Noon Prayer) came. Imām Ḥusain was in the battlefield with his army of a few. The Ḥusainī soldier Abū-Thamāmah 'Omarū-bin-'Abdu'llāh Ṣāy'dī reminded Imām Ḥusain, Sir ! This is the best time of the noon prayer. We are nearing to death, it would be most befitting to offer the last Prayer with you and for bowing before God. Looking up at the sky Imām Ḥusain said, certainly this is the special time of the *Ẓuhr*! Then he wished for Abū-Thamāmah Ṣāy'dī, God may count him among those who offer His prayer. Afterwards he said, Request the Yażīdī Army to stop fighting for some time, so, that we may offer the Noon Prayer. The Yażīdī Army refused permission for giving time to Imām Ḥusain for offering the Noon Prayer. But Imām Ḥusain kept the Religious Obligations of Islām, as supreme. He was ready to offer the Noon Prayer along with this brief-Army which became more consistent. Ḥusainī soldiers made lines for offering the Prayer, behind Imām Ḥusain. Imām Ḥusain was in front of all for leading the Prayer. Yażīdī Army attacked throwing arrows over the persons offering the Prayer. But how could the dedicated associates of Imām Ḥusain bear the attack over Imām while they were alive? They offered the Prayer, but extremely unprecedented altogether different of its kind in the history. Two brave Ḥusainī soldiers Żuhayr-bin-Qayn Bajalī and Sa'īd-bin-'Abdu'llāh Ḥasafī stood covering Imām Ḥusain with their swords facing towards enemies. In every Prayer lead was in such a way that others stood behind in the queue. But here two persons stood in front of the person leading the Prayer. The brave soldiers started cutting the arrows with their swords. When their attempts to cut the arrows were in vain, they went ahead emerging their chest facing the arrows. Hence, Imām Ḥusain completed his Prayer, both the bold soldiers putting their hands on one anothers shoulders, were moving completely socking in their blood, and fell down at the holy feet of Imām Ḥusain. Sa'īd-bin-'Abdu'llāh Ḥasafī was so much injured that he took his last breath quickly, bearing thirteen sharp arrows very deep in his body. Żuhayr-bin-Qayn Bajalī though highly wounded escaped alive at that time.[49]

Abū-Thamāmah 'Omarū-bin-'Abdu'llāh Ṣāy'dī, who was lucky enough to remind Imām Ḥusain for the best time of the Noon Prayer, but he could not get the opportunity of offering the last Prayer under the leadership behind Imām Ḥusain. He was ready for the Prayer, in the mean time some Yażīdī soldier fraudulently murdered him.

Prophet's Companion Ḥabīb

The Yażīdī Army not only did not give time to Imām Ḥusain for performing the Prayer, but also at his request Yażīdī Commander Ḥiṣṣīn-bin-Numayr coming outside his army shouted, Your *Namāż* would not be acceptable ! Ḥiṣṣīn's words became unbearable to Ḥusainī commander Ḥabīb-bin-Maẓāhir Asadī. He challenged and said, What did you say? Unacceptable? In your view Prophet's son's *Namāż* is not acceptable and your *Namāż* is acceptable. As soon as he heard it, Ḥiṣṣīn-bin-Numayr attacked on Ḥabīb-bin-Maẓāhir Asadī. He also came up for fighting, and attacked with his sword on the face of the horse of Ḥiṣṣīn, the horse immediately died, Ḥiṣṣīn-bin-Numayr fell on the ground, but his comrades covered him in their fold and took him away.

Now, Ḥabīb-bin-Maẓāhir Asadī has already plunged into the battlefield. With all the strength of honesty, matchless dedication towards Imām Ḥusain, anger at the sight of enemies and sorrow of their being alive challenging the enemies said, By God, if we were at least half in number, then you would have been either scattered or runaway. You are extremely worthless creature on the face of earth, both morally and in your family situation also. Ḥabīb-bin-Maẓāhir Asadī fought very boldly and killed a number of Yażīdī soldiers. When Yażīdī Army's famous wrestler Budayl-bin-Ṣoraym attacked, Ḥabīb killed him in a single attack, but some other Yażīdī soldiers attacked him from behind fraudulently and he fell on the ground. Ḥiṣṣīn-bin-Numayr, who was defeated previously, attacked him on his head with his sword and Ḥabīb-bin-Maẓāhir took his last breath. When Yażīdī soldier came to chop-off his head, Ḥiṣṣīn claimed, he should also be included in his murder. The soldier said, let me tie up his head on my horse's neck and allow it to make rounds of the army them you take him and also take the award from Governor of Kufa, 'Obaydu'llāh-bin-Żiyād. In this way Ḥiṣṣīn satisfied his anger.[50]

A detailed discussion about Ḥurr-bin-Yażīd-Riyāḥī has already been done in the previous pages on many places. Our readers are absolutely acquainted with him that after leaving the Yażīdī Army he joined the Ḥusainī Army and challenged the Yażīdī Army on many occasions. It has also been pointed out that in the Cowardly Attack of the Yażīdī Army when his horse became lightly wounded and fell down, he lost hopes and desparately fought many times. He took a vow when Ḥabīb-bin-Maẓāhir Asadī became a martyr that he would sacrifice his life, too. He came to the battlefield and began to read the battle Ricite – Be it known to all that

I cannot be murdered until I punish my enemies for their bad deeds, unless make them dead.

Żuhayr-Qayn, Ḥurr and Others

Żuhayr-bin-Qayn Bajalī joining along with Ḥurr fought in a group. Both advanced and fought and when anyone of them was fenced by enemies, then the other helped and made him free. It continued for some time. Then Yażīdī Army in the great efforts fenced Ḥurr. But still could not reach Ḥurr.[51] So many soldiers attacked Ḥurr together unitedly and wounded him with swords. Ḥurr fought ferociously until he killed around 40 men of them, and he was attacking with Żuhayr-bin-Qayn, thus, whenever one man attacked and went deep inside them, the other would attack to rescue his partner. Then the Infantry soldiers attacked Ḥurr and surrounded him in great numbers until they killed him. Imām Ḥusain carried his body to his camp, where he had put the bodies of other martyrs. While his soul still not released and his blood was gushing out, Imām Ḥusain rubbed the dust off his face and said, Congratulations O' Ḥurr, you are *Ḥurr*. Your mother has rightly named you. You are independent in this life and the Hereafter ![52]

Ultimately Żuhayr-bin-Qayn Bajalī, who had bravely fought along with Ḥurr, became alone after the martyrdom of his companion Ḥurr. He had saved and guarded Imām Ḥusain along with Sa'īd-bin-'Abdu'llāh Ḥasafī, so, that he could offer the Noon Prayer, Sa'īd Ḥasafī surrendered his soul to God but Żuhayr-Qayn was still alive. He could not bear escaping every now and then. Although he was in an extremely wounded situation still he came out with his sword to the battlefield. Emotionally said in his *Rajaż* – I am Żuhayr-Qayn, son of Qayn-bin-Qays Numayrī Bajalī. I shall finish all the enemies with my sword, whoever try to go near Imām Ḥusain. Then he fought in such a way that his enemies also accepted their defeat. Yażīdī Army attacked him in a joint way. Finally, Kat͟hīr-'Abdu'llāh S͟ho'bī and Muhājir-bin-Aws Taymī murdered him together.

After Żuhayr-Qayn, his counsin Salmān-bin-Muzārib-bin-Qays Numayrī Bajalī, who had came along with him to Karbala, fought intrepidly and joined the galaxy of martyrs.

Nāfa'-bin-Hilāl Jamalī Al-Murādī was an expert in bow-arrow play. He has inscribed his name on the tips of his arrows as he soaked them in poison. After Żuhayr-Qayn he started fighting. He murdered many soldiers of his opponent army, to this extent that his enemies surrounded him from all the four sides, his both the shoulders were wounded. Yażīdī Commander, S͟himr-bin-Żuljaus͟han with his Left Regiment arrested him.

He was brought before Commander-in-Chief 'Omar-bin-Sa'd, in the condition that blood was dropping from his beard. Mockingly, 'Omar-bin-Sa'd said, You have misbehaved with your inner soul. The brave Nāfa'-bin-Hilāl replied, God-fearer's inner soul is familiar to God. If my shoulders were not broken, you could not have arrested me. Shimr-bin-Žuljaushan murdered him.[53]

'Omarū-bin-Qurẓah-bin-Ka'b Anṣārī plugged into the battlefield with his sword, challenged the enemy forcefully and exhibiting his dedication to Imām Ḥusain, he said—All my life and family members and all things have been dedicated to Imām Ḥusain. After fighting for some time he came and stood by the side of Imām Ḥusain. Whatever arrows were showered from Yažīdī Army over Imām Ḥusain, stopping them he shattered them into pieces and he made himself as a covering of Imām Ḥusain. At last he became very much wounded and asked Imām Ḥusain, Sir, Did I not manage my duties and responsibilities? Imām said, Yes! You will reach the Heaven before myself, please make my salutations to my grandfather and say, I am also coming fast.

Prior to 'Ābis-bin-Abī Shabīb Shākirī, his servant Shožab-bin-'Abdu'llāh attained martyrdom. Then 'Ābis Shākirī himself plunged into war front for fighting, who had already some injuries on his forehead. But Yažīdī Army became scared seeing 'Ābis Shākirī, because so many people among them have already witnessed his bravery in the previous wars. Their Commander-in-Chief 'Omar-bin-Sa'd, asked his so many soliders to fight with 'Ābis Shākirī, but nobody could dare. Helpless 'Omar-bin-Sa'd suggested. If you are afraid of going near 'Ābis Shākirī then from at a distant place throw a shower of stones. 'Ābis Shākirī removed his war armour and attacked vigorously with his sword over the enemies, wherever he went all the Yažīdī soldiers began to run away scatered hither thither. Ultimately surrounding him on all sides, killed him. His head was chopped off and people shouted with joy. 'Omar-bin-Sa'd said, 'Ābis Shākirī's killer cannot be a single person, all of you unitedly killed him.

The Islāmic Prophet's one of the most reverend companion Abūžar Ghaffārī's servant's son Jaun and grandson 'Aun have some thing special in some respect. When Jaun wanted Imām Ḥusain's permission to fight with the enemies, Imām Ḥusain showed his reluctance due to his old age. Jaun felt very much and said, My complexion is black, I belong to a low caste, bad smell comes from my body, perhaps my blood cannot flow along with the blood of your high family ! Imām Ḥusain embraced him immediately and consented his jointing the battle, and prayed O' Allāh! Please change the black complexion of Jaun into white. Make his mouth colourful, his body may become fragrant. He may be accounted among the supreme *Mūminīn* (the persons perfect in Islām). Jaun successfully fought and became a martyr.

Żiyād-bin-'Arīb Hamadānī's father was also one of the companion of the holy Prophet. He fought vigorously and killed many Yażīdī soliders, finally he became a martyr.

Imām 'Alī's associate 'Orwah-bin-Ḥarrāq Ghaffārī's two sons 'Abdu'r Raḥmān and 'Abdu'llāh together fought with enemies and became martyrs. Hanẓalah-bin-Asa'd Shabāmī challenged Yażīdī Army and got into battlefield, fought, killed Yażīdīs and became martyr.

Żayd-bin-Thabayṭ u'l 'Abdī Qaysī was a resident of Basara and friend of Imām 'Alī's pupil Abu'l Aswad. He persuaded his ten sons to follow him in the fight for Truth, but his two sons 'Abdu'r Raḥmān and 'Obaydu'llāh could obey their father and became martyrs. After the martyrdom of his beloved sons, he came to battlefield, fought bravely and presented his soul to Creator.

Żayd-bin-Mī'qal Ja'fī had been among the associates of Imām 'Alī and fought in support of Imām Ḥusain against his enemies and became the martyr while fighting.

Sa'd-bin-Ḥārith was Imām 'Alī's servant. He came to the battlefield, fought and offered his life for the cause of Truth.

Saif-bin-Ḥārith-bin-Sarī' and Mālik-bin-'Abd-bin-Sarī'-bin-Jābir Hamādanī both were cousins and sons of the same mother. Their servant Shabīb-bin-'Abdu'llāh was also with them who had already become martyr in the cowardly attack of the Yażīd Army. These two brothers began crying standing near Imām Ḥusain. He inquired about the reason, they replied, We have dedicated our life for the cause of truth and would sacrifice it, but we are worried about you. We want you to be saved. We are crying over your helplessness. Imām Ḥusain praised their good intention. Both the brothers came to the battlefield, fought and killed so many soldiers and ultimately became martyrs.

Ḥāfiẓ of Turkey was the servant of Imām Ḥusain who was serving his eldest ailing son Imām Żainu'l-Ābidīn, with his permission came to the battlefield and fought matchlessly. Finally, got wounded and fell down. Imām Ḥusain came to him at the last minutes of his life and put his shoulders on his neck. He opned his eyes becoming conscious and observing Imām Ḥusain smiled and closed his eyes for ever.

Anas-bin-Kāhil-bin-Hārith Asadī was extremely old, but highly spirited more than the youths. He made himself fully decorated before of going to the battlefield. He put his turbon on his head, made his bracelet more smart, keeping his eye brows erected from his eys, tied his coverlet one his forehead. He came to the battlefield with full make up, fought and became a martyr.

Ḥujjāj-bin-Masrūq Ja'fī was so fortunate that after the arrival of Ḥurr's Army, it was time for the Noon Prayer, Imām Ḥusain asked him for performing *'Aẓān* (Formal Call to Prayer). He came to the war-front and killed many soldiers and became a martyr.

Sālim-bin-'Omarū-bin-'Abdu'llāh was Medīnahu'l Kalbī's servant. His speciality was, firstly participating in war of truth along with Muslim-bin-'Aqīl-bin-Abī Ṭālib at Kufa and after his martyrdom, he came to Karbala, joined Ḥusainī Army, fought and became martyr.

'Omarū-bin-Jinādah-bin-Ka'b Khiżarajjī also was with Muslim-bin-'Aqīl-bin-Abī Ṭālib in Kufa. After his martyrdom, somehow reached Karbala, fought against the enemies, killed many and became a martyr.

Qa'nab-bin-'Āmir Numayrī was the resident of Basara. He had met Imām Ḥusain with his colleague Ḥujjāj-bin-Żaid-Sa'dī Tayamī, who had became martyr in the cowardly attack of Yażīd Army. After him he fought with enemies and became a martyr.

Żayd-bin-Mī'qal Ja'fī had been among the associates of Imām 'Alī and fought in support of Imām Ḥusain against his enemies and became the martyr while fighting.

Rāf'a-bin-'Abdu'llāh was the servant of Muslim-bin-Kathīr Ṣadafi Ażdī, who had already attained martyrdom during the cowardly attack. After him he fought in support of Imām Ḥusain and became martyr.

Bishr-bin-'Omarū-bin-Uḥadūth Ḥazaramī Kindī has already been discussed in the previous pages, when his son 'Omarū was arrested in Raiy. His son, after his release fought for the cause of Truth and attained martyrdom. After his son, Bishr offered to sacrifice his life for Imām Ḥusain. He was among those supporters of Imām who became martyr at the last stage.

Swaid-bin-'Omar-bin-Abī Maṭa al-Khath'amī, who was very old, had already fought so, many wars previously. He came into the balttle-field after Bishr-bin-'Omarū and fought bravely, became much wounded. He was apparently considerd dead, though was alive. After the martyrdom of Imām Ḥusain, he regained consciousness. He heard the announcement of Imām Ḥusain being assassinated. It was intolerable. To his best strength, stood up. The Yażīdī Army had already looted his sword, a knife was lying thereby. He attacked the enemies with the knife. Enemies surrounded him and murdered and his head was chopped off from his body.

There may be some other martyrs, besides those Associates of Imām Ḥusain, discussed above who fought in Karbala on the path of God and attained martyrdom, who could not be discussed, because of the humble author's limited knowledge and paucity of source material for which he apologizes to his learned readers.

The community of the Ḥusainī Brahamans claims that their ancestors were martyred for the cause of truth and justice, along with Imām Ḥusain, his family, companions, kith and kin at Karbala on 10th Muḥarram, 61 AH (10th October, 680 AD). After the cruel butchery of Karbala, the family of the Ḥusainī Brahaman was driven out of 'Arab to Iran. Sir Denzil Ibbetson has mentioned in detail about them.[54] Some others also mention.[55] I have met some of the Ḥusainī Brahamans, specially famous journalist Jamuna Das Akhtar, who asserted his claim of being of the same family. In view of various facts available, it would not be advisable to reject their claim. However, further research may reveal some traces of other historical reference to it and also the possibility of the claim being true, because Hindus lived in 'Arab before the advent of Islām. Once their delegation met the holy Prophet of Islām. The holy Prophet showing affection to them had used Sanskrit word *Kushal* (safety) in wishing for their well-being.[56]

To lay one's life in defence of truth and justice has been the nature and sacrament of Indians, therefore, if some Hindus living in 'Arab had sacrificed their life in defence of truth and justice, there is nothing improbable about that. But Ḥusainī Brahaman's own Tradition is that the troop of Umayyite king Yażīd-bin-Mu'āwiyah, while on their return, after cutting off Imām Ḥusain's head, stopped in *Rahab*, their ancestor's home at Bathowal in the Sialkot district (now in Pakistan) and placed the head in his house. In the morning, finding the head to be that of the Prophet's grandson, he kept it, and gave the soldiers his own son's head instead, but they discovered that it was not the same as the one they had brought. So, Rahab cut-off all his seven sons' heads in succession and gave them to the soldiers. Since then Ḥusainī Brahamans beg from Muslims.[57]

The word *Rahab* has been used in the above event which may be the 'Arabic word *Rahib*. It is commonly used for the Christian monastic. The mention of obtaining the head of Imām Ḥusain from the Yażīdī army by *Rahib* against the temptation of money, is found in the episodes of Karbala. But there is no mention of the place Bathowal in the Sialkot district. It is just possible that the story orally narrated for over thousand years, might have changed in long course of time, which would be discussed in the ensueing chapter again. In the Saraiki language, we find poetical compositions based on the event of Karbala, which is said to be of Hindu-Shāhī period (950-1000 AD).[58]

At a safer point it may be said that they may be among the martyrs of the Battle of Karbala, because we lack full information regarding their whereabout. But it is the issue of serious research and study.

Unparallel Ḥusainī Associates

Imam Ḥusain's supporters insisted on being the first to fight. They took the brunt of the enemy attack. The battle was ferocious. Within a short time the Imam's supporters slew a large number of the enemy fighters, they were on the offensive and the enemy on the defensive. This caused apprehension and confusion in the enemy army, the 72 of Husain's against atleast 55,000 of the enemy being on the defensive.

The Battle of Karbala, if analysed, is not only torch bearer for the future of Islām, but also a Divine mirror in which both shapes of Muslims could be visualized. Whereas an ocean of rude, shameless, and infidel Muslim was striking in waves of dishonesty and selfishness against the shore of pseudo-Islām, who were paying recompense to the holy Prophet for his gracious efforts by killing his kith and kin.

It would be appropriated to refer the Words of God:

> "Say thou (*O 'Our Apostle Muḥammad !*): 'I demand not of you any recompense for it (*the toils of the apostleship*) save the love of (*my*) relatives." (*Qur'an* : 42/23)

Regarding the reasons of the Divine Revelation of the above holy verse has been mentioned by the commentators, they say that the Muslims persuaded the holy Prophet to accept some recompense *in lieu* of his gracious efforts and offered their everything at his disposal, which they own. Then the Divine revelation came.

The verse is clear in its meaning that the holy Prophet, is being commanded to ask the believers to love his kith and kin, means, the holy *Ahlu'l-Bayt* the Progeny of the Prophet Muḥammad and that love to his Progeny would be, in return of his apostolic services. This command has a very wide and extensive meaning to tell the Muslims. If they want to pay the holy Prophet, the return for his services, and be always on the right path and to be on right path you should follow my *Ahlu'l-Bayt* in words and deed and they are whom God Himself has purified. (*Qur'an*: 33/3) and they are the truthful ones and they are the custodian of original Words of God and its correct interpretation.

On the other side were such *Mūminīn*, the perfect Believer in Islām. that until even a single member of the brave soldiers of the Ḥusainī Army was alive, in spite of many efforts Yażīdī Army failed and was unable to do any harm or damage either to Imām Ḥusain or any member of his family. Just like the strong and unbreakable metalled wall, the Ḥusainī Army was extremely powerful, erecting their chest, pierceles in all respects and proved stong coercive and highly disciplined and interpreted the very words of Qu'ran were illustrated in them:

> "Verily God loveth those who fight in His way in ranks as if they were an unbreakable metalled wall." (*Qur'an*: 61/4)

The historians have gloryfying recorded that the brave Ḥusainī soldiers, till the last breath of their life, never allowed even a single arrow or sword or any weapon of enemy to touch either Imām Ḥusain or his family-members. The Ḥusainī Army was so dedicated towards them that guarded them beyond imagination. When nobody was alive from the unparalled and dedicated associates and supporters of Imām Ḥusain, then Imām Ḥusain's family-members, one by one, sons, brothers, nephews and other relatives became martyrs, which will be discussed in the ensuing lines.

The Ḥusainī Family's Sacrifice

When all the assoicates and supporters of Imām Ḥusain surrendered their soul to God, the family of Imām Ḥusain, which was actually, the family-members of the holy Prophet Muḥammad performed their duty in defence of the Truth and Justice.

'Alī Akbar-bin-Imām Ḥusain

From among the family-members of Imām Ḥusain, first of all his beloved son, 'Alī Akbar came to the battlefield. A youth of 18 years, having his great resembleness with great-grandfather, Prophet Muḥammad, so was called *Shabīh-i-Rasūl* (Prophet's Replica). Anyone who saw him turned into admirer.[59] He was a very lovely and favourite son of Imām Ḥusain. 'Alī Akbar came to Imām Ḥusain for seeking his permission for the battlefield. Imām Ḥusain advised him, first of all seek the permission from Żainab-bint-Imām 'Alī. She was important in so many ways, for being his sister, prudent lady, the next key person of the Ḥusainī Revolution, who lead the mission after the martyrdom of Imām Ḥusain, so, rightly called *Sharīkatu'l Ḥusain.* 'Alī Akbar was brought up by his aunt Żainab, who had showered upon him her entire love and affection, more than her own sons. 'Alī Akbar reached her camp smiling. Żainab asked, Has Imām Ḥusain been saved, any compromise made, what means your smiling ? 'Alī Akbar replied, the very purpose and opportunity for which you were preparing your sons, 'Aun and Muḥammad in the whole previous night, that time has come for me. He bowed on his feet and with folded hands, prayed for the permission. Imām 'Alī's valorous daughter permitted him. Then 'Alī Akbar came to Imām Ḥusain, who also allowed and made him fully equipped to get into the war-front. Then he wore his own turban on his head and prayed:

> "O' God! Whenever, I desired the pilgrimage of your Prophet, I used to see this son, now I am being deprived of having the pilgrimage of your Prophet. This son of mine reminds me your Prophet with his appearance, resemblance and noble character and conduct."[60]

'Alī Akbar came to the war-front. 'Omar-bin-Sa'd brought special soldiers from his Yażīdī Army to fight with him, but there was no effect on 'Alī Akbar. He killed them in first stroke. While fighting, 'Alī Akbar alone killed 120 strong and mighty soldiers of the Yażīdī Army.[61] It began running away out of fear and scared with his astonishing fighting. After success 'Alī Akbar returned to Imām Ḥusain. He was very thirsty and explained his position to Imām Ḥusain. He said, to put his tongue into his mouth, of course, it might give some relief. 'Alī Akbar kept his tongue into Imām's mouth, but immediately pulled it outside his mouth and said, Oh Dad! Your tongue is more dry than mine.[62] 'Alī Akbar understood that Imām Ḥusain wanted to say that being old he has been continuously bearing sadness and sorrows, he should also tolerate. 'Alī Akbar came again to war-front and started fighting. This time too he killed eighty soldiers.[63] Yażīdī soldiers Murrah-bin-Munqiż-bin-Nu'mān 'Abdī and Ḥiṣṣīn-bin-Numayr attacked from behind. Ḥiṣṣīn pierced the chest with his spear. 'Alī Akbar fell on the ground and called loudly, O' Father, Help me. Imām Ḥusain reached there. Enemies were surrounding him on all sides. He fought and removed them. Imām Ḥusain went near the dead body and tried to lift the body but could not, then called other youths of the famity, take the dead-body of your brother. All youngsters went ahead and kept the body in front of the camp, which was in the middle of the Ḥusainī Army.[64]

'Abdu'llāh-bin-Muslim-bin-'Aqīl's mother Ruqayyah was the sister of Imām Ḥusain and father Muslim-bin-'Aqīl was his cousin-brother. In this way 'Abdu'llāh was doubly nephew of Imām Ḥusain. After the martyrdom of 'Alī Akbar sadness spread in Imām Ḥusain's camp. Ladies' wailing made the atmosphere tuff, the teenagers becoming perplexed rushed outside the camp. 'Abdu'llāh, who was in his boyhood, came out. Yażīdī soldier 'Omar-bin-Ṣubaiḥ Ṣaydāvī attacked him with his arrow, which came towards his forehead. In self-defence he kept his hand on his forehead. The next arrow fell on his chest, and he became a martyr. Some people say that some merciless soldier attacked on his chest and he became a martyr.

Muḥammad and 'Aun

After the demise of 'Abdu'llāh, other youths of Muslim-bin-'Aqīl's family attacked together. Imām Ḥusain praised them and said, Yes, my cousin's sons! Be victorious over the death. First of all Muḥammad-bin-Muslim became a martyr, who was from 'Abdu'llāh's step-mother, but the son of the same father. Afterwards, Jafar-bin-'Aqīl fought and he was also killed by arrows. Then, 'Abdu'r Raḥmān-bin-'Aqīl came to war-fornt, the Yażīdī Army showered arrows on him also and made him the martyr.

'Abdu'llāh-bin-Jafar's two sons, Muḥammad and 'Aun, are always discussed together. Their father 'Abdu'llāh was the cousin of Imām Ḥusain. In this manner they were Imām's nephew, but both had equal affection from Żainab-bint-Imām 'Alī. Both the brothers came to the war-front together. They were not youth by age, they were only teen agers, but they were good in their calibre of fighting. They entered very victoriously and the Yażīdī Army became stunned to see them. They went on going even into the camp of Shimr-bin-Žuljaushan, the Commander of the Left Regiment of Yażīdī Army. Severit Shimr lost his mental balance and out of fear ran away, leaving his sword in the camp. Both brave brothers chased him together. While chasing they went far away from Ḥusainī camp and in the middle of the Yażīdī Army, where they were surrounded and murderd.

Qāsim and Other Youth

Qāsim-bin-Imām Ḥasan has already been discussed with reference to the event of Last Night in the previous chapter, whose wedding is in dispute. He was nearing the stage of youth. He was extraordinarily handsome.

The Yażīdī Army also admired is natural beauty. There was no armour on his body. He was wearing a shirt, shoes were on his legs, a buckle was broken in it.[65] 'Omar-bin-Sa'd ordered Ażraq Shāmī, a famous wrestler and watch and ward of the river to murder the boy. But he refused and said, to fight with a child, would spoil his name. Instead, he may ask one of his sons to chopp-off his head and bring it. He came for fighting, Qāsim suddenly chopped-off his head. Then his next brother came, then the third, then the fourth. Qāsim chopped-off their heads one by one, all the heads of his sons. On this Ażraq Shāmī became furious and attacked him. Qāsim was fearless, he had killed his sons in casual manner. Ażraq growling and barking attacked like wolf. Qāsim smiled and said, See, your horse's belt is broken. Ażraq bent down to see it. Qāsim attacked with his sword on his neck and pierced his chest. Then Yażīdī Army collectively attacked Qāsim and he fell down from his horse and sought Imām Ḥusain help, calling him. Imām Ḥusain rushed to the spot. Qāsim's murderer 'Omar-bin-Sa'd-bin Nufayl Ażdī was standing by his side. Imām Ḥusain attacked him with his sword, and his hand was cut, the enemy ran on all sides to save him and the murderer also was crushed and he died on the spot. Qāsim's dead-body was also crushed. Imām Ḥusain himself took the dead-body of Qāsim. His chest was attached with Qāsim's chest, going on giving marking on the ground. His dead-body was kept on the same place where the other dead-bodies were kept.

Imām Hasan's second son Abū Bakr-bin-Imām Ḥasan fought after his brother Qāsim. Yażīdī Army was unable to have any control on him, 'Abdu'llāh-bin-'Oqbah Ghanawī killed him throwing arrows on him.

Imām Ḥusain's brother Muḥammad-bin-Imām 'Alī-bin-Abī Ṭālib, who was younger than Muḥammad-bin-Ḥanafia of Imām 'Alī's children was very bravely fighting, murdered so many Yażīdī soldiers, became martyr by the arrow of Abānī Dārīmī of Yażīdī Army, who cut his head and took it to 'Omar-Sa'd.

Abu'l-Faẓl'il-'Abbās-bin-Imām 'Alī

Abu'l-Faẓl'il-'Abbās-bin-Imām 'Alī was the Commander-in-Chief of the Ḥusainī Army. He was from another mother of Imām Ḥusain, Fāṭimah-bint-Abu'l 'Ajal Kalbī. Her appellation was *Ummu'l Banīn* (Mother of Sons), because she gave birth to four unparallel brave sons, Abu'l-Faẓl'il-'Abbās, 'Abdu'llāh, 'Othmān, and Ja'far, all martyrs of the Battle of Karbala.

The Commander-in-Chief Abu'l-Faẓl'il-'Abbās sent his younger brothers one by one telling them–proceed, sacrifice your life at the holy feets of Imām Ḥusain. In the midst of time occurred that incident, which has been mentioned in the previous chapter that the Yażīdī Commander, Shimr-bin-Žuljaushan came near the Ḥusainī camps and called aloud, Where arethe sons of his sister. As their mother Ummu'l Banīn belonged the same clan, he called them, sons of his sister but they never acknowledged him as his maternal uncle, because of his enmity towards the Progeny of the Prophet Muḥammad. Shimr told them that he has obtained peace from his authorities. The sons of Ummu'l Banīn replied furiously in one voice, God's curse on you and your peace, which is not for Imām Ḥusain. We totally reject it.

'Abdu'llāh-bin-Imām 'Alī was next to Abu'l-Fazl'il 'Abbās, so, he came to battlefield, bravely fought and was killed by Yażīdī soldier Ḥānī-bin-Thobayt. Ḥazramī. Then came 'Othmān-bin-Imām 'Alī, who was killed by the arrows of Yażīdī soldier Khiwallah-bin-Yażīd Aṣbaḥī 'Āyižī and his head was cut by Abānī Dārīmī. Then came Ja'far-bin-Imām 'Alī and he was also killed by Ḥānī-bin-Thobayṭ Ḥazramī, after a tuff battle.

The Ḥusainī Army's Flag-Bearer and Commander-in-Chief, Abu'l-Faẓl'il-'Abbās-bin-Imām 'Alī was incomparable tested valourous warrior, who had proved his unique competence to the extent that once while fighting with the enemies at the Battle of Ṣiffīn (656-57 AD) against Yażīd's father Mu'āwiyah's army, in which he had put a veil on his face. His fighting had so much resemblance with the fighting of Imām 'Alī that Mu'āwiyah took advantage and propagated, Look, 'Alī himself has joined the battle.

Imām 'Alī came to the spot and thrown up the veil from the face of his son 'Abbās and said, this is *Qamaru'l Banīu'l Hāshim* (Hāshimites' Moon), which became his appellation. Historians have recorded an incident. In the morning of fateful day, the formal declaration of war was still awaited, Abu'l-Faẓl'il-'Abbās was warming his house. He passed near the Ḥabīb-bin-Maẓāhir Asadī. Ḥabīb asked, Beloved Prince, do you rememder, for what purpose you were born. 'Abbās became furious and said, you are reminding my valour, By God, let Imām Ḥusain accord the permission, the heroism would be renamed. Here it would not be pointed out afresh the memory that Imām Ḥusain had got digged wells, to get 'Abbās physically tired, the incident has been given at proper place.

The learned readers could imagine the psychological tension of the great valiant Abu'l-Faẓl'il-'Abbās, when constant challenges would be forcing to reply in its terms, self-sacrifice and sense of duty would be leading to mental torment, what a self-respected person should do, when a challenge come from enemies, 'Abbās requested Imām Ḥusain to permit him. But it appears from his attituted that he did not win the battle physically, but a victory which change the mind set of the people in general, that the war for Truth and Justice could only be won by physical strength and for Muslim Ummah in particular that the martyrdom would join them with good and prohibit from bad.

Whenever Abu'l-Faẓl'il-'Abbās requested his permission for going to the war-front, every time Imām Ḥusain made him calm telling, that he was the Commander-in-Chief. When no other person Imām Ḥusain's Army was alive, except Imām Ḥusain and 'Abbās. Imām Ḥusain again gave the same reply that you are the Commander-in-Chief. 'Abbās replied very sadly, O' Imām ! Yes, You have conferred the great honour on me, now kindly tell me where is that army, whose Commander am I? Becoming helpless Imām Ḥusain allowed him, but asked tohave the permission from his sister Żainab-bint-Imām 'Alī, *Sharīkatu'l Ḥusain.* 'Abbās entered in her camp smiling, but he was stounded to see that iron lady in serious mood. He asked the reason. She told, Once during her childhood, she was sitting in the lap of her father Imām 'Alī. Suddenly, he started kissing on her neck and shoulders. It was quite uncommon, so, she wished to know the reason. He told, a day will come when your shoulders and neck would be tied by rope. Brother 'Abbās ! hearing it, she became angry and said, Who could dare to tie the rope on her neck and shoulders. She was sister of eighteen Hāshimites' brothers. But she understood that time had come then. She accorded her permission.

Imām Ḥusain also allowed him, but conditionally, consificated his arms, allowed use of a spear in self-defence and fixed duty to bring of water for the children. 'Abbās kept his water-bag on his shoulder, the Ḥusainī Army Flag on one of his hands and spear in the other hand, came to the battlefield. There were guards of five thousand soldiers at 'Alqamah river, but no body could dare stop him. 'Abbās laid his victory-flag in the river, got into the river, soaked the dry cask for some time in side the water. Then filled in with water and put it on his shouldier.

'Abbās told his horse, drink as you wish. But when he saw that faithful horse has not touched the water, he again told, well, he was going to drink water and you also take. Telling this he took few drops of water, observed for a while and then threw it away. Neither 'Abbās nor his faithful horse made their lips wet out of the river water. The wonderful thing is even after conquenring the river 'Alqamah remembering that the children of Ḥusainī camps were suffering from horrible thirst.

Now, his task was, any how rush to Ḥusainī camps, he tried his best to make the water reach the Ḥusainī camps, so that, the children may drink water to their best, but the grateful children could not touch even the lips with never and did not drink all.

The Yażīdī Army, which was chased while making a massive attack on ‘Abbās again came united and surrounded ‘Abbās from all sides. A soldier attacked with his sowrd on his right hand and it was cut. ‘Abbās took the reign in his left hand. Then he lost his left hand too. The Ḥusainī Army’s flag was crushed on the ground. Now, ‘Abbās hid the water-bag below his chest and went very fast towards the Ḥusainī camps. Yażīdī Army started showering arrows. An arrow struck the water-bag, all the water inside drained away. As the water drained in fact the very blood of ‘Abbās flew away. Some soliders attacked on his head. ‘Abbās could not sustain and fell down from the horse. He called Imām Husain at the last moments of his life. Imām Ḥusain went to him running. Attacking, he removed the Yażīdī Army from ‘Abbās’ side. Some say that ‘Abbās took his last breath before the arrival of Imām Ḥusain. But majority of the repoters say, No ‘Abbās’ was waiting for Imām Husain. When he came, kept ‘Abbās’ head on his thigh, cleaned his face from dust, sand and blood, ‘Abbās opened his eyes and sacrificed his life seeing Imām Ḥusain. Imām Ḥusain could not bring the dead body of ‘Abbās to the camp because ‘Abbās dead body was in pieces and could not be collected and brought. ‘Abbās’ two teen aged sons Fażl, due to him he was called, Abu’l-Fażl’il-‘Abbās and his younger brother Qāsim both sad boys rushed towards the dead body of their father, they could not reach, but Yażīdī Army murdered them also.

Imām Ḥusain in the Battlefield

Imām Ḥusain formally came to the Battle field at the last. But actually speaking, he was in Battlefield since the formal declaration of the War, and even before it. He was continuously and completely experiencing the very sad murders of his people right from the morning till the last time, they came one by one all bade good bye. When all the associates and members of the family, young and old, were murdered right in front of him, even then an ocean of Yażīdī Army was striking against him. Enough is enough. There is a limit to bear the atrocities and cruelties, but the Yażīdī Army has already exceeded all limits. The ladies, young girls and children and babies were in the camps. What will happen to them after him? What to say about the sad and lamenting ladies, who could imagine the mental agony and the inner mind of Imām Ḥusain at that time. How could he rise from his torment of loneliness. It is beyond anybody’s imagination. Just a few indications are available of his great will power, tolareance and boldness and strong determination in the history books. Presenting absolutely Imām Ḥusain personality seems to be beyond human calibre. His mental, moral and spiritual power are together co-ordinated and well balanced in such a way that an ordinary mind can never be capable of perceiving it. Whatever Imām Ḥusain exhibited by his actions, if we try to visualize through our imaginations, it goes beyond our capacity. For the comprehension of such a unique nature, one may require the mind of a very great visionary. We can only present just a few events, which may be helpful in reaching to a conclusion.

Before coming to the battlefield Imām Ḥusain, visited the camps to bid good-bye to all. He asked her sister *Sharīkatu'l Ḥusain* Żainab-bint-Imām 'Alī, to bring the bundle of the clothes of his grandfather Prophet Muḥammad, chose a green decaying shirt, not usable and further tore and then put on as the inner of all his cloth. On being asked, he told, I know the Yażīdī Army will loot after me my each cloth, this decayed, not usable and torn shirt may not attract them and my dead-body may escape from remaining nude.

Then, Imām Ḥusain came with his family members to his eldest son, Imām 'Alī-Ibnu'l-Ḥusain, *Imām Żainu'l-Ābidīn,* who was in unconscious state due to being seriously ill. The *Sharīkatu'l Ḥusain* Żainab made the nephew awaken, sat in such away that her knee's could work as a support to ailing nephew. Imām Ḥusain fulfilled all the formalities and nominated him Imām of the time. Then said, Son! now you are Imām of the time, permit me to sacrifice my life also on the path of God. As Imām Żainu'l-Ābidīn was unconscious, he could not know, what has happened during the whole day. He asked, Dear Father ! why you're yourself going to fight in the war front. Better, send some of the supporters. Imām Ḥusain replied, All of them have been assassinated. Then he enquired about each of them telling the name individually. Imām Ḥusain told with full confidence about each ones' assassination. But when he asked about 'Alī Akbar, Imām Ḥusain burst into tears and replied, My dear son! You better understand, nobody is alive among gents except yourself and myself. As soon as Imām Żainu'l-Ābidīn heard this, he stood up taking support of his aunt Żainab and said, Let me also sacrifice my life. Imām Ḥusain convinced him. you have to shoulder very difficult responsibilities, you have to cross the ocean of sadness and grief, after being arrested, and would be admonished.

Yażīdī Army's clerk, Ḥamīd-bin-Muslim Ażdī says that Imām Ḥusain left his camp in such a way that the ladies were clung with the Chughah refraining him from going outside and children with his legs. All appealed to him, we all would stand in a circles and please set out from among us. He says that Imām Ḥusain left them in such a way, as if a dead-body of a youth is taken away for final ritual from his fully crowded house.

After coming out and before mounting his horse Imām Ḥusain looked with regard at all his suppprters and family members, whose dead-bodies were lying in the battlefield and asked:

> "O' my warriors! Now Ḥusain is going to the battlefield, would you not come to bid good bye to him."

Eyewitness states, I saw *Sharīkatu'l Ḥusain Żainab*, who was fully covered from the head to toe with a black blanket came out of the camp, catched hold the shoulder of Imām Ḥusain and mounted him on his horse.

As soon as Imām Ḥusain reached the war-front he challenged his enemies, no sooner than did they heard his roaring voice, then they were scacred. Nobody was daring enough to come before him. Imām Ḥusain alone was very heavy to the Yażīdī Army of several thousands. No doubt, all soldiers of the Ḥusainī Army have proved high standard of bravery and skill of warhood and had faithfully sacrificed their lives and their extraordinary personality will always inspire the generations in every age. But Imām Ḥusain attack was unique and exemplary. It seemed as if the holy Prophet Muḥammad was into the battlefield, who was present in the form of Imām Ḥusain. The enemy soliders scattered and were running on all sides out of fear. Such a situation arose, which resulted into some stampede for the Yażīdī soldier, who were standing together, began to push each other and fell down. So many soliders were crushed into death. One of the Regiments of the Yażīdi soldiers, which ran away from Karbala could only stop at Kufa reaching very fast there. With this rumour spearing in Kufa that Imām Ḥusain has reached Kufa fighting and fighting. In Kufa being dejected Yażīdī supports began to run away from their houses. Governor of Kufa, 'Obaydu'llāh-bin-Żiyād himself ran away from his official palace. Only after finding out the situation he could return to his palace.

The Yażīdī Army was in the illusion that War has come to an end, but during this last phase of the War their defeat was quite visible. Seeing the frightened state of the Yażīdī Army, its Left Regiment Commander, Shimr-bin-Žuljaushan, organized the soldiers and united them and ordered those who were experts in attack by anrrows. On frequent motivation, the Yażīdī Army attacked Imām Ḥusain from all sides with arrows. Attack by swords, knives, spears was also continuously going on. In a very outstanding manner Imām Ḥusain was bravely facing every attack. But unfortunately Imām's horse became severely wounded and therefore, he had to go on foot, even then he continued fighting forcefully and carefully also.

Six Months' Baby 'Alī Aṣghar

In the midst Imām Ḥusain heared shouting and calls from his camps. Thinking that the Yażīdī Army in frustration, perhaps, had attacked on Ḥusainī camps for terrorizing the ladies and children Imām Ḥusain rushed to his camp immediately. Asked his sister Żainab, what was the reason for their being panicky and highly sorrowful. She replied, your baby-son of six months old, 'Alī Aṣghar, 'Abdu'llāh Razī'a was highly perturbed and restless. Imām Ḥusain said, he was grief sticken for want of water, as he was very thirsty. Bring the baby and I will get water for him from the enemy Yażīdī Army. Imām Ḥusain took 'Alī Aṣghar on his hands and plunged into the war-front. Whatever may be the emenity with me, but what has done this baby. They must be kind to him. Previously, the soldiers of the Ḥusainī Army had came to the battlefield by walking on foot or riding on horse. This innocent baby-soldier came to the battlefield mounting on Imām Ḥusains' hands! Imām Ḥusain stood on a higher altititude and said dislpaying 'Alī Aṣghar at his hand:

> "O' People! If I am guilty in your view, this six months old baby cannot be guilty in anyway; see him. His mother's milk has become dry, he is about to die. Anyone of you may proceed ahead and offer him a few drops of water."

Some people started grumbling in the Yażīdī Army; Yes, this dying baby must be offered water. But none came forward. Then Imām Ḥusain laid down 'Alī Aṣghar on the burning ground of Karbala and again said:

> "It you are suspicious that I may drink water in his name; See, I have laid down this baby on the open ground, one of your may come forward and offer the baby water."

Many people in the Yażīdī Army turned into favour and shouted: The baby should be given water. But there was a big group of merciless soldiers, whose conscience could not be awaken. Then, lifting 'Alī Aṣghar on his hands, Imām Ḥusain addressed the baby himself that you yourself express your grief and hardship. Eyewitnesse says; He saw from his naked eyes, the horrible scene that 'Alī Aṣghar raised his neck and started turning his very dry tongue on the dry lips. This was such a touching scene that even the hard hearted Yažīdī soldier could not resist. People statrted shouting: The thirsty baby should be quenched immediately. Yažīdī Commander-in-Chief,'Omar-bin-Sa'd became restless, there may be mutiny within his Army, he orderd, arrow-throw expert, Ḥarmalah-bin-Kāhil Asadī; *Aqta' Kalamu'l Ḥusain*, Cut out the tongue of Ḥusain. Ḥarmalah targeted with his trident at baby 'Alī Aṣghar and his arrow pierced the neck of 'Alī Aṣghar and fished in the shoulder of Imām Ḥusain. A vomit of milk mixed blood came out of his mouth and the baby closed his eyes.

Various authors have discussed the martyrdom of Imām Ḥusain's infant son, 'Alī Aṣghar, 'Abdu'llāh Razī'a. When nobody was left in Ḥusain's camp, Imām Ḥusain. raised an immortal call for help by saying:

> "Almin Mughīthu'n Nāṣirnā (Is there anyone who can help me?)"

Hearing this call, Imām Ḥusain's infant six-month baby dropped himself from the cradle Imām Ḥusain took 'Alī Aṣghar towards the enemy camp and cried out: Is there anyone who can give some water to this thirsty child? Actuaslly speeking, Imām Ḥusain didn't literally want water for his son, but wanted to expose to the world, the cruelty that lied within the enemies of humanity. The rival army sent a best archer, Ḥarmalah, who killed 'Alī Aṣghar by shooting an arrow.

Raising up the dead body of 'Alī Aṣghar, Imām Ḥusain proceeded towards his camp and then returned. Perhaps, feeling that he brought the baby with the promise of getting quenched his thirst. In this way he went and returned from his camp thrice. Finally, after going a little distance he dug a little grave with his sword and kept the dead body of 'Alī Aṣghar into it and buried well. He had no water to make the grave wet, but there was enough tears shed by Imām Ḥusain that the grave became very wet, then covered it with a piece of cloth and again came to the battlefield.

Imām Ḥusain commenced the war again. Defeating the enemies, Imām Ḥusain reached Alqamah river. The enemies were scared that he may not drink water. Ḥiṣṣīn-bin-Numayr, Commander for guarding Alqamah river, aimed an arrow which struck his face and blood boiled out of it. Shimr-bin-Žuljaushan, Commander of Left Regiment took the Infantry Force and surrounded him from all directions but the situation was not under his control. Wherever Imām Ḥusain turned the enemy army scattered and ran away out of fear. It is mentioned that about 2,000 Yažīdī soldiers were killed by Imām Ḥusain in this attack alone. An eyewitness and officer of the Yažīdī Army 'Āmir-bin-Nahshal Tamīmī's statement has been on record that he had never seen such a person who would be seriously injured and whose all family members and associates have already been killed and even then he seemed to be satisfied and courageous like Imām Ḥusain, and fought like himself, and the situation was that the enemy soldiers surrounded him on all sides and hid him, but when he attacks on them with his sword, all the enemy soldier run away in left or right directions, as if a lion attacks on the deers.

On this occasion Imām Ḥusain gave his last Sermon to the enemies, driving them to come to the path of Truth. It is safe in the pages of history. Imām Ḥusain warned them:

> "By God, even if Ḥusain-bin-Imām ʿAlī-bin-Abī Ṭālib had possessed no other attribute on account of which the free people might have loved him, his manner of reasoning in justification of his movement and rising would have been sufficient to acknowledge him as the chief of all those persons who will rise till the Day of Judgement to support Truth and Justice and to suppress injustice...
>
> O' people of Kufa! Hear me. I have studied the state of affairs of the society carefully and I understand what the matter really is. This illegitimate son of an illegitimate, 'Obaydu'llāh-bin-Żiyād-bin-Abīh, has cornered me in such a way that I have no alternative left except to do one of the two things: Either I should unsheathe the sword and start fighting or I should accept abjectness and humiliation...But you should know that my decision is final and irrevocable. I have chosen the path of fighting, because we are not going to be humiliated. In other words the Muslim Ummah is far away from humiliation. God has made it honourable. That we should be humiliated is not liked either by God or by His Prophet or by the believers. It is not acceptable to us, who have been brought up in the pious laps of our mothers that we should open the door of objectness, humiliation, despair and despondency for ourselves or for the Ummah...
>
> The brave and dauntless persons who belong to me and who are arrayed with me would not like their own humiliation or that of the Ummah. They are not the people who would prefer submission and obedience to the nasty and mean persons, to martyrdom and self-sacrifice...
>
> Remember! God, is absolutely unhappy over my assissination. Now, I say that God will certainly honour me on

> being disregarded by your swell. Then revenge will be taken in such a way that you cannot imagine.
>
> Remember ! after killing me you will be divided amongst yourselves. There will be a civil war and ultimately you will be killed, and afterwards the last punishment, which will be very painful !"[66]

It would be appropriate to refer the Divine words, which declare last very painful punishment for those who were guilty:

> "We vengeance upon those who were guilty; and was incumbent on Us the succor of the believers." (*Qur'an*: 30/47)

Our learned readers are aware that Imām Ḥusain delivered many sermons and made many speeches on the day of *'Ās͟hūrah.* All these sermons are very eloquent and impressive. It is surprising that these sermons were delivered by an orator, who knew very well that after these speeches he would not only be called to account but would be called to account with the aid of thirty thousand spears.

These are the sermons of an orator who was thirsty and did not have even a drop of water to moist his lips. He knew that after some time his women and children were going to be made prisoners by the impudent and stone-hearted enemies. He was hungry and though he complained of thirst his self-respect prevented him from complaining of hunger. A hungry and thirsty orator delivers a speech before thirty thousand soldiers of the enemy, whose spears are ready to kill him and whose horses will trample upon his body after some time. Notwithstanding this he delivers a speech and a solid speech, too. In his speech there is eloquence and maturity. He does not betray any weakness or helplessness. As the number of his companions decreases his speech becomes more forceful and he begins speaking more clearly and more explicitly. Has the entire human history ever seen such an orator, whose manner of speech should not be affected by any development, who should not lose mental balance in any circumstances and the flow of whose speech should not undergo any change?

Afterwards, Yażīdī Army surrounded Imām Ḥusain from all sides and attacked him. Exhibitiing his maxium warriership, he fought courageously, despite of bearing the demise of his beloved associates and family-members, acute starvation for three continuous days, but he was fighting with his will power. At last there was a natural effect of bleeding from the countless wounds on his body and his condition was not stable.

It became impossible for him to stand on the foots and ultimately, he fell down on the ground. In spite of it, no enemy solider could dare enough to go near him, they were showering arrows on him or throwing stones targeting him.

Imām Ḥusain managed to sit on the ground. Then raised his hand to the sky and said:

> "O' You of the High Place, of the Mighty Power, of the Great Wisdom, not in need of the creatures, and high in His Pride, verily You are Able for whatever You desire, close in mercy, and true with the promise, and Graceful with His favours, and a Tester of goodness, close whenever You are called, and surrounding whatever You have created, and verily You accept the repenting for those who repent, and verily You are Able for what You desire, and verily You get whatever You want, Thankful if You have been praised, and You mention those who mention You, and I pray to You for my need, and ask You for my necessity, and go towards You when I am afraid and cry for my adversities, and I seek help from You when I am weak, and I depend on You when I am satisfied, judge between us and between those people for they have tricked us and let down us and betrayed us and killed us, and we are the Household of Your Prophet, and the children of Your beloved Prophet Muḥammad, the one who You have chosen him for the Message, and made him to receive the inspirations, so make for us, O'Lord, a relief from our matter O' You the most Merciful of all. Patience over what You have destined O' Lord, no other god but You, O' Helper of those who need the help."[67]

In the mean time Imām Hassan's youngst son 'Abdu'llāh rushed to the spot; Shouted at the enemies; Why are you beating my old uncle, he is not attacking you; Why should you? Imām Ḥusain advised him to go back and by the time, he embraced with the neck of Imām Ḥusain and prayed with folded hands to the soldiers; Don't harm my uncle. He is deeply wounded and also pushed Imām Ḥusain; You don't sit here. Go home. A Yażīdī soldier attacked with sword. 'Abdu'llāh raised his hands to stop him. Swords struck on his hands, which were cut like cucumber. Another soldier came forward and to cut his head. Yażīdī soldier Ḥarmalah-bin-Kāhil Asadī killed him removing from Imām Ḥusain's hands. In the midst, Imām Ḥusain's sister Żainab-bint-Imām 'Alī, *Sharīkatu'l Ḥusain* came out of camp and stood upon a raised place,

Ṭila'u'l-Żainab' and requested Yażīdī Army to be sympathetic towards the grandson of the Prophet Muḥammad. Imām Ḥusain saw Żainab had somehow convinced her to return.

Imām Ḥusain's Last Prayer and Martyrdom

Imām Ḥusain looked at the sky mid-noon, exact time for the *Namāżu'l-'Aṣr* (Afternoon Prayer) Imām Ḥusain had never missed even a single Prayer through out his life. He always prayed at the exact timings. How could he give up last Prayer of his life. This time he did not seek permission from the Yażīdī Army for time for perfoming the holy Prayer. With the profound calm he started the holy Prayer. Yażīdī Commander, Shimr-bin-Žuljaushan shouted at his soldiers, Why they delayed murdering Imām Ḥusain and what they were expecting; Kill him at once. But no soldier could dare enough to come forward to assassinate him. They were ready to come forward after so much of confusion for long time for doing that vicked act. Māliḳ-bin-Nisr Kindī came forward and attacked his head with his sword which pierced up to his forehead. Finally, Žora'h-bin-Shorayk's sword, Sinān-bin-Anas Nakha'ī's knife wounded him severely. Imām Ḥusain just kept his head on the ground, while performing the holy Prayer. Shimr-bin-Žiljaushan cut Imām Ḥusain's neck from his behind.

Not only Imām's neck was cut, the but also of Islām, Truth, Humanity! Itself was very griet sticken on 10th Muḥarram, 61 AH accordingly 10th October, 680 AD.

Imām Ḥusain's head was taken on the tip of the spear. The Yażīdī Army's announcer declared loudly; *Qad Qutlah Ḥusain Ba Karbala* (Ḥusain has been murdered on the earth of Karbala). Thereafter, absolute grief and sadness spread among the ladies and children of Imām Ḥusain's family. The nature also showed its anguish. Historians have written that a very terrific completely black storm erupted at that time, the darkness prevailed completely over the entire atmosphere of Karbala, and everywhere, there was uproar and crying, which made the Yażīdī Army despaired and kept in dismay and fear. So, many Yażīdī soldiers commited suicided by jumping into the river Alqamah, realizing their sin; What had they thought and what happened. But on the other side of the Yażīdī Army, the officers and their loyal were happy on the murder of Imām Ḥusain.

Ashamed Humanity

The clothes from the dead body of Imām Ḥusain were looted. Isḥāq-bin-Khawiyyah Ḥazramī took the shirt; and his *Żerjamah* (inner garments) were taken by Baḥr-bin-Ka'b and his turban was taken by Akhnas-bin-Murthid, and his shield was taken by 'Omar-bin-Sa'd-bin Nufayl Ażdī, and his some clothes were taken by a brother of Isḥāq-bin-Khawiyyah, and Qays-bin-Asha'th took his Qaṭīfah (Yemenic velvet), with which he was called with a bad-name of *Qays-Qaṭīfah*, and his cloak was taken by Māliḳ-bin-Nisr Kindī, and his sword was taken by Falāfis Nahashalī Dārimī, and his sandals were taken by Aswad-bin-Khālid, and his ring was taken by Bajdal-bin-Salīm Kalbī who amputated the finger with the ring.

So worried and nervous, the Yażīdī Commander-in-Chief, 'Omar-bin-Sa'd ordered his army not only to set fire to the Imam's tents (which were occupied mostly by females and children), but at the same time reinforced his fighters with more troops. Then, the Yażīdī Army attacked the camps of the families of Imām Ḥusain and looted everything. Removed the blankets from the heads of ladies to the extent that they removed mercilessly the bed of the seriously ailing unconscious Imām Żainu'l-Ābidīn, and he felldown facing his face on the ground. After the Yażīdī Army set fire in the Ḥusainī camps and all the ladies and children cried like any thing sitting on the open ground.

After these inhuman actions Yażīdī Commander-in-Chief, 'Omar-bin-Sa'd proclaimed such a contraband order that the horsemen to trample upon the supine body of Imām Ḥusain to disfigure them even further, as if the wounds, the bloodied bodies, and the headless form were not enough. On which the civil society would curse him for ever. Ten of Yażīdī soldiers could be prepared to do this nasty act. They prepared their horses. They came in line over the dead-body of Imām Ḥusain and crushed-off ruthlessly with the gallop of their horses.

'Omar-bin-Sa'd wanted to inform his master, 'Obaydu'llāh-bin-Żiyād, Governor of Kufa at the earlist and did not want to give chance to his rival Shimr-bin-Žuljaushan that he could reach Kufa and take the credit and get the reward from him. Therefore, he immediately sent his Commander Khiwallah-bin-Yażīd Aṣbaḥī 'Āyiżī with his battalion with the head of Imām Ḥusain and also with his message to Kufa. He stayed in Karbala itself with the other soldiers and planned to proceed the next day after arranging everything.

Tyrannies—No Limit

It was dark in the night. There were dead-bodies scattered everywhere in the battlefield. It was such a tense sitnation that the children were highly frightened. And it was quite natural. They sticked, themselves with their mother. Żainab-bint-Imām 'Alī, *Sharīkatu'l Ḥusain,* assembled all the ladies and children near the burning camps. Two children were found missing. The two children were; Sukayna-bint-Imām Ḥusain and 'Abdu'llāh-bin-Imām Żainu'l-Ābidīn. Żainab told her younger sister Umm Kulthūm-bint-Imām 'Alī for taking care of them, till she could search those children. Żainab proceed ahead calling the names of the children, but there was no response. A soldier was returning after making his horse drink water, Żainab enquired him about the lost childern. He replied that he saw a child with fire on his clothes, running towards that pit. Żainab went there and saw Sukayna sticking to the dead-body of his father Imām Ḥusain. Żainab took the child on her lap and returned. On the way she observed Imām Żainu'l-Ābidīn's son 'Abdu'llāh lying on ground. She went near, appeared as if child was sleeping, when tried to awaken found the child was dead. She returned to the camp with Sukayna and dead-body of 'Abdu'llāh. Further, *Sharīkatu'l Ḥusain* told all; Till yesterday my brave brother Abu'l-Faẓl'il-'Abbās -bin-Imām 'Alī had guarded our camps with whole might, today she would perform that duty in lieu of him. She took a broken sword in her hand and guarded the ladies and children the whole night. An incident is famous that durig the night the ladies of Yażīdī Army along with food-stuff and water sent Ḥurr's mother to Ḥusainī family, which was completely starving as it was the insistence of Ḥurr's mother, therefore, Żainab accepted them and offered the same to the children. In this memory *Shām-i-Gharīban* (Sad People's Evening) is celebrated in India.

Astrological Analysis

Nature has unique and independent consciousness towards Man as a personal being in the midst of this process. It reflects in the hours of sorrow and happiness. Man also realizes in his sub-consciousness. If he is happy, entire Universe appears to be cheerful and *vice versa.* Nature also reciprocates in the same manner. Astrology is the type of divination that consists in interpreting the influence of planets and stars on earthly affairs.

Nature has been cautioning human being through the medium of seasons. Chapter CV *'Al-Feel'* (The Elephant) of the Qur'an refers to memorable, miraculous event in the history of 'Arabia in which the Viceroy of the king of Abyssinia at Yemen, Abraha (570-71 AD) invaded Mecca to destroy the Holy Ka'bah. After the miraculous event Abarah's army was found lying on the groumd dead as bits of some withered and munched grass rendered useless for any purpose. In the same manner earth's terrible earthquake is mentioned in Chapter XCIX *'Aż-Żalżah'* (The Quaking). It was all in a teriffic darkness of negative and atrocious and evil powers, atrocity and the admonishing atmosphere of Karbala was made holy with the blood of Imām Ḥusain and his Associates, it was the shower of his blood which has converted the dry fields of Islām into fertile lands. There was a resonance of Islām. Islām was again established on its own religious foundation.

Emerged from the scientific traditions of the Progeny of the Prophet Muḥammad and specially under inspirations of Imām Muḥammad al-Bāqir and Imām Ja'far aṣ-Ṣādiq, the supreme Astronomist and Astrologist Al-Khawāriżmī, Abū Jā'far Muḥammad-bin-Mūsā (d. 850 AD) had calculated the astrological account of Imām Ḥusain's martyrdom at that time (10th Muḥararam, 61 AH/10 October, 680 AD) with a view what was the position of planets in the zodiac. Thus, he mentions in the following manner:

On the day of Imām Ḥusain's martyrdom the Sun was in Libra zodiac at 19.20, Moon at 20.20 in Aquarius, Saturn was in Cancer zodiac at 29.20. Similarly, Jupiter was in Capricorn zodiac at 12.40 and Venus was Virgo zodiac at 5.45 and Mucurry was in Libra at 5.45 and Rahu was in Gemini zodiac at 1.45.

It is sad that 1,200 years, rolled down, but appropriate zodiac calculations, classification and analysis have not taken place. At the request of this humble author, some eminent astrologers* have put the above zodiac result of Al-Khawāriżmī on the computer and found, despite a minor perplexity, that Sun was in Libra zodiac in the computer at 19.20, but Al-Khawāriżmī has calculated as 17.20, the remaining calculations are the same. It would be amazing to note that Al-Khawāriżmī had calculated on his fingers, 1200 years ago, computer makes the same calculations at present. The explanation and analysis are as follows:

Saturn was in Cancer zodiac with parental aptitute. Moon's position was going on. Saturn + Moon combination had full effect on the family. Therefore, the martyrdom of both sons was natural. The elder son was seriously ailing, which is a part of eight types of the death. He facing such hardship, which were more painful even than death and disease. Saturn+Moon combination reveals acute problems and deaths. Friendly effect does not work due to low-level planets. So, the Associates could not be saved.

---

* Courtsy: Pt. Ram Naresh Tripathi, Director, Bhartiya Vidya Bhavan, Allahabad.

The wheel of time of martyrdom was as under:

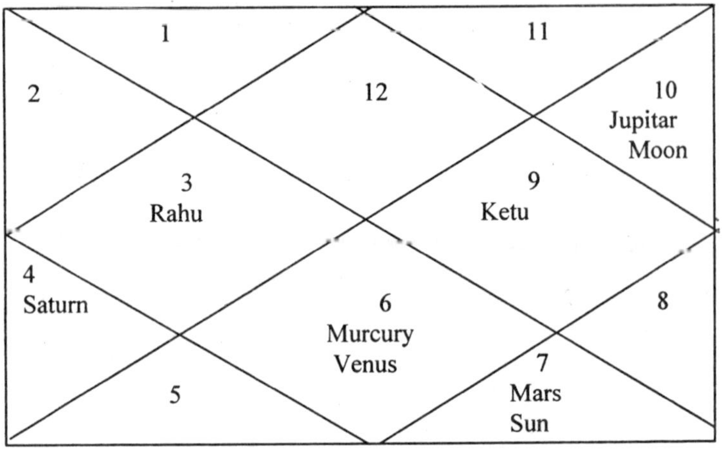

Martyrdom Timing of Imām Ḥusain @ 19.20 IST

It appears from the above horoscope that it was not favourable time when martyrdom occurred. Rahu, Gemini, Saturn, Cancer, Mercury, Venus, Virgo, Mars, Sun, Libra and Ketu were in Sagittarius zodiac.

The prevalent number of 72 is 7 + 2 = 9, which is 3, 6, 9 on the basis of the Numerology and the number 72 is not permanent one, but the division of 3, 6, 9 may be in any number. However, 9 has also connection with the numerology of Mars, which has death tendency. That's why the associates were in that number.

Moon represents water, Saturn air, Mars explosive materials. At that time all the three planets were not favourale. It was quite natural that there was a storm of wind, tempest and great affiliction in the atmosphere and explosiveness etc. It was all effect of planets.

Rahu was in the house of mother and Venus and Murcury were in wife's house. Gemini and Virgo became the cuse of prison, in other words, it was under the influence of Murcury the family would have to face hard troubles, mental and physical both.

In accordance with the present calculations, Moon was going to Capricorn zodiac, whereas Al-Khawāriżmī has considered Moon in Aquarius zodiac. There may be difference in the system of such calculations. Moon remains 2.5 days in the Aquarius zodiac. At 20.20 pm too, it was under the influence of Capricorn. It is also possible, because the present calculations are based on contemporary Calendars, which has various variations. As per our calculaton, if Moon was in the Capricorn zodiac, or in Aquarius zodiac, both situations, result remains same. But the Moon cannot be said to be good with both.

In present calculation Jupiter is in Capricorn zodiac, which is in confirmation with Al-Khawārizmī.

It was Monday on the day of martyrdom, when Moon was sitting with Saturn in 11th house and Mars in the 8th house, along with Sun. Moon and Mars became the cause of Death, then a terrific attack was done on a person. There was a blood-flow from his body. Because Mars is the authority of blood. Sun is situated in Libra zodiac, which makes full dishonour. Being disgraced give death. Moon was in Capricorn and Aquarius zodiacs, Saturn was in in the Moon zodiac in fifth phase. Jupiter was also only in Saturn zodiac. The combination of Saturn+Moon+ Jupiter was harmful. All these three planets were not favouable to him.

Lord of Ascendant Jupiter was in 11th house and Ketu in Jupiter zodiac in the 10th house and Rahu was in 4th house in Capricorn zodiac The joint combination of Rahu+Kethu and Lagnesh Guru granted him reputation. Insisted him to live for the benevolence of the society and the nation. The Mercury situated in 7th place and Venus is giving a clear indication also towards family-life. The person of such a horoscope even after his death becomes immortal and considered most respectful in the world. His followers always remember him with great honour.

In the Battle of Karbala, Imām Ḥusain and his 72 Associates became Martyrs. Imām's family and his in-laws and children were murdered. A son escaped alive, because he was very sick.

The time when Imām Ḥusain attained martyrdom, it is available in the books that a very big storm and dusty sandy wind came, the river water was jumping like anything and terrific sounds and noises spread.

Imām Ḥusain's family members (ladies and babies) were kept in Prison for a year or so after the event of Karbala.

Notes and References

1. Translated by David Matthews: The Battle of Karbala: A Marsiya of Anīs, pp. 35-42.
2. Tārīkhu'r-Rusūl wa'l-Mulūk, vol. 6, p. 241; al-Irshād fī Ma'rifat Ḥujjāj Allāh 'Alā 'Ibād, p. 246.
3. Tārīkhu'r-Rusūl wa'l-Mulūk, vol. 6, p. 241; al-Irshād fī Ma'rifat Ḥujjāj Allāh 'Alā 'Ibād, p. 246.

4. al-Maqtal: Abī Mīkhnaf, p. 278; Tārīkhu'r-Rusūl wa'l-Mulūk, vol. 6, pp. 242-43; al-Irshād fī Ma'rifat Ḥujjāj Allāh 'Alā 'Ibād, p. 248.
5. Tārīkhu'r-Rusūl wa'l-Mulūk, vol. 6, p. 242.
6. Tārīkhu'r-Rusūl wa'l-Mulūk, vol. 6, pp. 242-43; al-Irshād fī Ma'rifat Ḥujjāj Allāh 'Alā 'Ibād, p. 248.
7. al-Maqtal: Abī Mīkhnaf, p. 278; Tārīkhu'r-Rusūl wa'l-Mulūk, vol. 6, pp. 242-43; al-Irshād fī Ma'rifat Ḥujjāj Allāh 'Alā 'Ibād, p. 248.
8. Tārīkhu'r-Rusūl wa'l-Mulūk, vol. 6, pp. 242-43; al-Irshād fī Ma'rifat Ḥujjāj Allāh 'Alā 'Ibād, p. 248.
9. Tārīkhu'r-Rusūl wa'l-Mulūk, vol. 6, p. 242.
10. Maqālātu 'l Ḥusain: al-Muqrim, p. 278; Tārīkhu'r-Rusūl wa'l-Mulūk, vol. 6, p. 242.
11. al-Irshād fī Ma'rifat Ḥujjāj Allāh 'Alā 'Ibād, p. 248; Maqālātu 'l Ḥusain: a l-Muqrim, p. 278; Tārīkhu'r-Rusūl wa'l-Mulūk, vol. 6, p. 242.
12. Maqālātu 'l Ḥusain:al-Muqrim, p. 278; Tārīkhu'r-Rusūl wa'l-Mulūk, vol. 6, p. 242.
13. Tārīkhu'r-Rusūl wa'l-Mulūk, vol. 6, p. 242.
14. *The believer man of the Pharaoh's family is a story mentioned in Qur'an about a faithful man who believed in Moses and was among the Pharaoh's family and may be his minister.*—Author
15. Shahīd-i-Insāniyat, p. 366.
16. Tārīkhu'r-Rusūl wa'l-Mulūk, vol. 6, p. 243.
17. Tārīkhu'r-Rusūl wa'l-Mulūk, vol. 6, p. 244.
18. al-Irshād fī Ma'rifat Ḥujjāj Allāh 'Alā 'Ibād, p. 248; Tārīkhu'r-Rusūl wa'l-Mulūk, vol. 6, p. 242.
19. al-Irshād fī Ma'rifat Ḥujjāj Allāh 'Alā 'Ibād, p. 242; Tārīkhu'r-Rusūl wa'l-Mulūk, vol. 6, p. 237.
20. Luhūf 'Alā Qatlu'l Ṭafūf, pp. 34-35.
21. al-Irshād fī Ma'rifat Ḥujjāj Allāh 'Alā 'Ibād, p. 250; Tārīkhu'r-Rusūl wa'l-Mulūk, vol. 6, p. 245.
22. Maqālātu 'l Ḥusain: a l-Muqrim, p. 292; al-Irshād fī Ma'rifat Ḥujjāj Allāh 'Alā 'Ibād, p. 220.
23. Luhūf 'Alā Qatlu'l Ṭafūf, p. 41
24. Bihāru'l-Anwār, Vols. 1 & 2, p. 233.
25. al-Irshād fī Ma'rifat Ḥujjāj Allāh 'Alā 'Ibād, p. 250; Tārīkhu'r-Rusūl wa'l-Mulūk, vol. 6, p. 245.
26. Tārīkhu'r-Rusūl wa'l-Mulūk, vol. 6, p. 245.
27. Tārīkhu'r-Rusūl wa'l-Mulūk, vol. 6, p. 245.
28. Tārīkhu'r-Rusūl wa'l-Mulūk, vol. 6, p. 245.
29. Tārīkhu'r-Rusūl wa'l-Mulūk, vol. 6, pp. 248-49.
30. Manāqib-i-Āl-i-Abī Ṭālib, vol. 4, p. 94; Tārīkhu'r-Rusūl wa'l-Mulūk, vol. 6, p. 248.
31. Tārīkhu'r-Rusūl wa'l-Mulūk, vol. 6, p. 248.
32. Tārīkhu'r-Rusūl wa'l-Mulūk, vol. 6, p. 249; Shahīd-i-Insāniyat, p. 407.
33. Shahīd-i-Insāniyat, p. 408.

34. Tārīkhu'r-Rusūl wa'l-Mulūk, vol. 6, p. 249.
35. Luhūf 'Alā Qatlu'l Ṭafūf, p. 42; Bihāru'l-Anwār, vols. 1&2, p. 235.
36. Tārīkhu'r-Rusūl wa'l-Mulūk, vol. 6, p. 251.
37. Bihāru'l-Anwār, vols. 1&2, p. 233.
38. Tārīkhu'r-Rusūl wa'l-Mulūk, vol. 6, p. 247.
39. Tārīkhu'r-Rusūl wa'l-Mulūk, vol. 6, p. 255.
40. Shahīd-i-Insāniyat, p. 417.
41. Shahīd-i-Insāniyat, p. 418.
42. Taṣwīr-i-Karbala, pp. 84-85.
43. al-Irshād fī Ma'rifat Ḥujjāj Allāh 'Alā 'Ibād, p. 251; Tārīkhu'r-Rusūl wa'l-Mulūk, vol. 6, p. 250.
44. Tārīkhu'r-Rusūl wa'l-Mulūk, vol. 6, p. 250.
45. Maqālātu 'l Ḥusain: al-Muqrim, p. 292; al-Irshād fī Ma'rifat Ḥujjāj Allāh 'Alā 'Ibād, p. 251; Tārīkhu'r-Rusūl wa'l-Mulūk, vol. 6, p. 250.
46. al-Irshād fī Ma'rifat Ḥujjāj Allāh 'Alā 'Ibād, p. 252; Tārīkhu'r-Rusūl wa'l-Mulūk, vol. 6, p. 250.
47. Tārīkhu'r-Rusūl wa'l-Mulūk vol. 6, p. 250.
48. Shahīd-i-Insāniyat, p. 445.
49. Mushīru'l Aḥżān, p. 34; Tārīkhu'r-Rusūl wa'l-Mulūk, vol. 6, p. 252.
50. Mushīru'l Aḥżān, p. 34; Tārīkhu'r-Rusūl wa'l-Mulūk, vol. 6, p. 251.
51. Tārīkhu'r-Rusūl wa'l-Mulūk, vol. 6, p. 252.
52. al-Irshād fī Ma'rifat Ḥujjāj Allāh 'Alā 'Ibād, p. 215.
53. Tārīkhu'r-Rusūl wa'l-Mulūk, vol. 6, p. 253.
54. A Glossary of the Tribes and Castes of Punjab and North-West Frontier Povinces, vol. 2, p. 142.
55. Shahīdān-i-Karbala Ke Fidāī Hindū, p. 2.
56. Malfūzāt, p. 160.
57. A Glossary of the Tribes and Castes of Punjab and North-West Frontier Povinces, vol. 2, p. 142.
58. Durr-i-Gauhar, p. 9.
59. al-Irshād fī Ma'rifat Ḥujjāj Allāh 'Alā'Ibād, p. 237.
60. Shahīd-i-Insāniyat, p. 495.
61. Bihāru'l-Anwār, vol. 1, p. 266.
62. Bihāru'l-Anwār, vol. 1, p. 266.
63. Bihāru'l-Anwār, vol. 1, p. 266.
64. Tārīkhu'r-Rusūl wa'l-Mulūk, vol. 6, p. 256.
65. Tārīkhu'r-Rusūl wa'l-Mulūk, vol. 6, p. 256; al-Irshād fī Ma'rifat Ḥujjāj Allāh 'Alā 'Ibād, p. 254 .
66. Tārīkhu'r-Rusūl wa'l-Mulūk, vol. 6, p. 259; al-Irshād fī Ma'rifat Ḥujjāj Allāh 'Alā 'Ibād, p. 256.
67. Tārīkhu'r-Rusūl wa'l-Mulūk, vol. 6, p. 259; al-Irshād fī Ma'rifat Ḥujjāj Allāh 'Alā 'Ibād, p. 256.

Chapter: Seven

After the Great Sacrifice

Eleventh Muḥarram 61AH (11th October, 680 AD) was the first day of helpless, homeless and lonely family of holy Prophet Muḥammad, from which a new series of miseries and tyrannies were ahead. The Sun's rays of the early morning brings energy motivation, pleasure and optimism, but it was such a morning, as tied up fully with the previous night's miseries and pains. No voice of the *Ażān,* but the Nature reciprocating, echoeing in the atmosphere *Allāhu'-Akbar,* no doubt 'God is Great.'

Żainab-bint-Imām'Alī, *Sharīkatu'l Ḥusain,* grief-sticken great lady had done watch and ward through out the night. All the starving and thirsty children were lying on the sand the whole night. When it was dawn, the misery due to hunger and thirst increased very much. She was collecting all the ladies and babies at the place where the camps were burnt. The narrator says, By God, he shall never forget Żainab, while she was mourning her brother Imām Ḥusain and calling with a sad voice and a broken sad heart:

> "Alas! Muḥammad! The angels of heaven prayed upon you. This is Ḥusain covered with his blood, and his parts are amputated, and his turban and cloak are plundered and your daughters are hostages. To God shall be the complaint and to Muḥammad the Chosen, and to 'Alī al-Murtazā and to Fāṭimah aż-Żahrah and to Ḥamżah the lord of the martyrs. Alas! Muḥammad! This is Ḥusain in the desert, with his head being cut from the back."

Then, Sukayna-bint-Imām Ḥusain asked her aunt Żainab, To whom she was speaking? She answered her that to her father Ḥusain, and then she dropped down from her place to the body of her father and hugged his corpse, and made all the enemies cry, and then 'Omar-bin-Sa'd asked his soldiers to take her away from the body of her father, and then a group of nomads came and pulled her away from the body of her father, and she went away with her tears falling down.

The dead-bodies were lying on all sides. On all sides only the enemies were visible. There was no one to console. The Yażīdī soldiers were making fun of their tragic situation and were expressing joy and pleasure over their helplessness. What was the mental hazards of the remaining family-members of the holy Prophet, the very imagination itself is grief stricken.

There are a few recognized norms of humanity, which are adopted by all the people in each and every period. Each and every religion has esablished high ideals of humanity. Even at present, the cultured society has propounded so many useful rules and regulations for the safety and security of human rights. After any war, a final burial rituals of all the dead-bodies are done.

The Yażīdī Army first of all tightly bound with rope the remaining ladies and children. Seriously ailing Imām Żainu'l-Ābidīn, the only living son of Imām Ḥusain, was manacled both hands, cuf in the neck and tied with rope. No information, whether the starving and thirsty children and ladies were given food and wạter. Putting them under vigilance of some soldiers, Army officers began survey of its killed personnels. Their dead-bodies were collected and the last rituals were done with state honour.[1] But the dead-bodies of Imām Ḥusain and his family members and companions were left unburried at he places where they were lying. Open in burning heat of the sun lying on the sand. For three days the exposed bodies of the martyrs were left lying in the desert of Karbala. Whatever happened after the assassination of Imām Husain in Karbala it has ruined and blacked the entire humanity. The Yażīdī Army left the dead-bodies of Imām Ḥusain and his associates in the burning fire in the same manner.

In making the graves and burying their dead-bodies of The Yażīdī soldiers, the whole day was spent there. Then the heads of dead soldiers of the Ḥusainī Army were cut. During the process, they found one of Imām Ḥasan's son Ḥasan Mu<u>th</u>annā, who had sacrified his life along with his other family members, profoundly wounded, but still alive. His maternal uncle Asmā-bin-<u>Kh</u>ārjah Farāzī, who was of the soldiers of the Yażīdī Army, got him saved and brought him to his house. After medical treatment he became fit and retuned to Medina. Ḥasan Mu<u>th</u>annā has been also important in the genealogical history as the lineage of Imām Ḥasan is still alive through him, who are called Ḥasanī Sādāt.[2]

After cutting the heads of the martyrs, the Yažīdī Army counted the heads, who were 72 in number.[3] Then, the heads of the martyrs were picked up with the tip of spears by the soldiers of the particular clan or tribe. As such, the tribe of Kindah's 13 heads and their leader was Qays-bin-Asha'th, and the tribe of Ḥawāžin's 12 heads and their leader was Shimr-bin-Žuljaushan. And the tribe of Tamīm with 17 heads, and the tribe of Asad with 16 heads, and the tribe of Mužahab with 7 heads, and the remaining 17 heads were taken on their spear-heads by remaining soldiers.[4]

The Yažīdī Commander-in-Chief, 'Omar-bin-Sa'd had already sent Imām Ḥusain's head to Governor of Kufa, 'Obaydu'llāh-bin-Żiyād on *'Āshūrah* (the Martyr's day: 10 Muḥarram) afternoon, through Khiwallah-bin-Yažīd Asṇbahṇī 'Āyižī and Ḥamīd-bin-Muslim Ażdī. He further ordered to sever heads of other martyrs to send them to Kufa. The heads were distributed to various tribes enabling them to gain favour of 'Obaydu'llāh-bin-Żiyād. 'Omar-bin-Sa'd remained in Karbala until the next noon.[5]

The Yažīdī Army spent most of the day in the rituals of its dead soldiers. In the afternoon all the captives including the women and children tied with rope and seriously ailing Imām Żainu'l-Ābidīn, manacled both hands, cuff in the neck and tied with rope, then all were loaded onto camels with neither saddle nor shade and were moved towards Kufa. Just to terrorise, the ladies and children were taken near the dead-bodies so that they may struggle out of grief. When Żainab reached near the dead-body of Imām Ḥusain, she could not resist her grief, she made herself fallen from the horse, burst into tears and embracing the dead-body of Imām Ḥusain and she cried like anything. The Yažīdī Army mounted them again on the horses whipping severely and beating all the prisoners and asking his soldiers to take the necks of heads of dead of the Husainī soldiers on the tips of their sword, Commander-in-Chief of Yažīdī 'Omar-bin-Sa'd set out to Kufa.[6]

Martyrs Burried

As per their usual routine, the women and girls of famous Asad clan, who were living behind the Karbala, came in a flock to carry water from the 'Alqamah river. They saw the dead bodies of the family of the holy Prophet, his grandson Imām Ḥusain and his companions were lying uncared and unburried. They were moved with human passions. On return they dared enough to *per sue* the male members and expressed their strong feelings. No doubt, it was most ungraceful and against the principles of Islām, that the grandson of the Prophet with his associates was killed without any crime and none of them could stand in their support. Now, their dead bodies were lying uncared. They told their frightened condition, if they could dare to burry them, Yažīdī government would kill and finish their entire clan. The courageous ladies replied that they should remain in the houses like women but the ladies would burry the dead bodies. Being totally demoralized, the men of Asad clan went to burry the dead bodies of the great martyrs.

On the third day of Martyrdom of Imām Ḥusain (12th Muḥarram, 61AH/12th October, 680 AD) the people of Asad clan, frightful, terrified and scared, with the spades and hoes on their shoulders came to burry the dead bodies. Afraid to the extent that they turn round and looked again and again, if anyone was shadowing them. In such a mental condition, they perfomed the religious duty of burying the dead bodies.

Imām Ḥusain was buried at the same place where he became a martyr. His son 'Alī Akbar was also buried by his side only. The baby 'Alī Aṣghar was already buried by Imām Ḥusain himself. But it was taken out by Yažīdī Army, he was again buried. All these graves are near the grave of Imām Ḥusain.

Because the people of Asad clan were burying the dead bodies of the martyrs, they buried clan's leader Ḥabīb-bin-Maẓāhir Asadī in a separate grave.

They were so scared with the terror of Yažīdīs that they could not make separate graves for all. Digging a very big pit for all the other remaining martyrs buried together, all other members of the holy Prophet's family, his companions, the devotees of Imām 'Alī, famous personalities of Islām, etc. which at present are called *Ganj-i-Shahīdan* (Treasure of Martyrs), which is very near the grave of Imām Ḥusain.

The dead-body of Ḥusainī Commander-in-Chief, Abu'l-Faẓl'il-'Abbās -bin-Imām 'Alī was made into pieces, could not be taken, a separate grave was made there itself.

It is said that Ḥurr-bin-Yažīd-Riyāḥī's mother took his dead-body to her camp in the dark-night, which was available afterwards and buried separately.

Another grave of 'Aun is available, but the argument is that he is 'Aun-bin-'Abdu'llāh-bin-Ja'far Ṭayyār-bin-Abī Ṭālib or 'Aun-bin-Imām 'Alī or any other martyr.

Prisoners in Kufa

When the prisoners of Karbala reached Kufa, how long they stayed and when they were sent to Yażīd's capital Damascus from there, a reference of the definite dates is not available, just this much of information is available that the Yażīdī Army departed taking the prisoners on 11th Muḥarram, 61 AH (11th October, 680 AD) from Karbala. No idea when they reached Kufa from Karbala and how long stayed there. This stay may be of a longer period, because only after getting permission from the Caliph of the Muslim Empire, Yażīd-bin-Mu'āwiyah-bin-Abū Sufyyān, the Governor of Kufa, 'Obaydu'llāh-bin-Żiyād sent the prisoners to Damascus.

Saiyedu'l 'Ulama 'Alī Naqī Naqavī, (d. 1988 AD) has written only this much that he ordered to keep the prisoners till the messenger of 'Obaydu'llāh-bin-Żiyād did not return taking the reply.[7] Famous historian aṭ-Ṭabarī, Ibn Jarīr Abū Jā'far (d. 923 AD) has written an event in this regard that one day somebody threw a letter tying with a stone inside the prisons in which it was written that 'Obaydu'llāh-bin-Żiyād's messenger has gone to Damascus on an appointed day and would return on a specific day. If everything was normal, then they will raise the *Takbīr* (*Allāhu'-Akbar*), othere wise, the prisoners assassination shall be certain. But on the return of messenger no *Takbīr* was said, because Yażīd-bin-Mu'āwiyah had ordered to send the prisoners to Damascus. By this people were thinking that now the murder was certain.[8]

'Obaydu'llāh-bin-Żiyād's messenger's to and fro journey would have taken time. When the caravan of the Prisoners started from Kufa and reached Damascus. At what place the Prisoners were kept in Kufa and for how much period; no technical data are available regarding series of events, distance from place to place, dates on the basis of travel movement. This humble author has tried to acertain technical information on the basis of analyzing the fact scattered at various places. The findings of his research has been based on the following facts:

Reaching Kufa from Karbala

Distance from Karbala to Kufa was 33 miles (52.8 km), so the normal speed of the caravan of camels would be 30-40 miles per day. The Yażīdī Army departed from Karbala on the after-noon of 11th Muḥarram 61 AH (11th October 680 AD). Instead of going direct Kufa they went Qādsiyah, where most of their Army was concentrated and was a safe place, because after the assassination of Imām Ḥusain, general awaking has been stirred and the Yażīdī Army was afraid that people may attack and get the prisoners released. After spending the night halt at Qādsiyah they reached Kufa on 12th Muḥarram 61 AH (12th October, 680 AD).

Messenger of Damascus

As the head of Imām Ḥusain was already sent to Kufa on the Martyr's day (10th Muḥarram 61 AH) itself, probably, it reached Kufa in the same night or in the morning of 11th Muḥarram, 61AH (11th October, 680 AD). On the same day under *Barīd* system, in which 24 hours continuous service was available, the messenger would have been sent to Damascus. The distance from Kufa to Damascus was 461 miles (750 km), so by travelling 3 days and nights he could reached Damascus and after getting the orders from there, he after spending 3 days-nights, on 18 or 19 Muḥarram might have reached Kufa.

Mosque turned Prison

After reaching Kufa, the prisoners of Prophet's family-members were launched at the famous *Masjidu'l-Ḥanānah*, which was turned into prison for them. They were treated very harshly and inhumanly. A huge and heavy hand-cuff tightened on seriously ailing Imām Żainu'l-Ābidīn with a thorny chain attached with his neck and the ladies and children were tied with rope.[9]

Days in Kufa Prison

Probably the family members of the holy Prophet of Islām stayed in Kufa for a week as prisoners and on 20th Muḥarram, 61 AH (20th October, 680 AD) they were taken to Damascus from Kufa.

The Jeering off

With a view of terrorizing the atmosphere Kufa the Governor, 'Obaydu'llāh-bin-Żiyād proclaimed that on this occasion no body should come outside his house equipped with any weapon; should not be seen on road also. Watch and ward were posted on important places.

'Omar-bin-Sa'd toured with the aforementioned hostages and Yażīdī Army took the women and children as prisoners in shackles, put them on camels, and proceeded in a caravan from Karbala to Kufa. At the forefront of the procession were the heads of Imām Ḥusain and his followers on the tip of spears, under the Commanders, Shimr-bin-Żuljaushan, Qays-bin-Asha'th, and others. So, the tribe of Kindah came up with 13 heads and the tribe of Ḥawāżin came up with 12 heads and the tribe of Tamīm came up with 17 heads, and the tribe of Asad came up with 16 heads, and the tribe of Munḥaj came up with 7 heads, and the rest of the heads were taken by the people. The scene was both grotesque and pathetic. This was the leftover of the beloved family of Prophet Muḥammad, in such a deplorable unimaginable condition, all caused by people who called themselves Muslims!

Possibily, some might be aware of the situation, but public in general were in misconception and under the influence of the publicity of the government that some anti-Islāmic group has been defeated and its family-members have been brought as prisoners. When the soldiers entered Kufa along with the prisoners, taking the heads of enemies on their tip of sword, then the curiosity of people increased. Who they were, people were not aware, wanted to know about them. People were narrating in their own way. A lady was sitting on the high backyard to see the seene. She asked the prisoners themselves, who were they. She got reply, they are the prisoners from the Household of the Prophet Muḥammad.

The roads got stuck in front of the Household by the people and the people of Kufa started to mourn and cry along with the family-members of the holy Prophet of Islām. As soon as it was heard on all sides, there was a huge noise of crying.[10] All the people who were present there were very much moved seeing their pathetic situation. People were crying and shouting. Imām Ḥusain's severely sick son Imām 'Alī-Ibnu'l-Ḥusain, popularly known as *Imām Żainu'l-Ābidīn,* who was manacled both hands, cuff in the neck and tied with rope without minding his physical strain and pain spoke in his chocking voice:

> "You are those who shed our blood, now your women are crying on our situation. God only will decide about myself and yourself."[11]

Men and women began weeping and crying. Then he added:

> "You people are weeping now on our situation and who destroyed us and made us struggle ?"[12]

Bas͟hīr-bin-K͟hożaym Asadī, an eyewitness says that, then he took a look at Żainab-bint-Imām 'Alī at that day, and he had never seen a shy woman who has an eloquent speech like her, as if she was talking in the very tone of her father, the prince of the believers, Imām 'Alī-Ibn-Abī Ṭālib, and she made a sign with her hand and all the people got silent. So, then the breathes were held and the bells went silent,[13] and then she said:

"Praising shall be to God, and blessings shall be on my father, Prophet Muḥammad and his purified, chaste and kind Household. And then, Oh people of Kufa, Oh people of treachery and tricks! Do you cry? The tear shall not be dry and the weeping shall never stop, but the likes of you is like her, who unravelleth the thread, after she hath made it strong, to thin filaments, making your oaths a deceit between you.

Verily, is there anyone among you but the swaggerer and the rude? And the angry and the abominable destestable? And the adulation of maids and the trickery of the enemies, are like a pasture on the remains, or like a silver on a grave.

Verily, evil is what your souls have given to yourselves to compile the wrath of God upon you, and in the Punishment you shall remain for ever. Do you cry? Do you weep? Yes, By God, cry a lot and laugh a little, for you've done its (the life) shame and disgrace, and you shall never wash it away, and how shall you make yourselves clean from killing the descendants of the Prophet, and the core of the Message, and the lord of the youth in Paradise? The one you are (supposed to) turn to in your troubles and adversities, and your cause and the applier of your creed?

Verily, evil is what you've done, and for that you may be destroyed!

Verily, your efforts have been disappointed, and your hands are cut down, and your deal is a losing one, and you've received the wrath of God, and humiliation shall be forced upon you. Woe to you Oh people of Kufa, do you know what a level for the Prophet you have fought against? And what blood for him you have shed? And what dignified daughter of him you have exposed? And what sanctity you have violated? You've came to it (life) with its baldness and stupidity and bad shape, like the dust of the ground and the air of the sky. Are you amazed for the sky to be raining blood upon you?

Verily, the Punishment of the Judgement Day is even worse and more shameful and you shall not be nourished, so do not take the time left easy, for the revenge is surely to be taken, and your Lord is waiting for you."[14]

The narrator Saṭīr-bin-Khoraym Asadī has said swearing By God, that he had seen no better orater than her and other than 'Alī-Ibn-Abī, Ṭālib. The people at that day were puzzled and crying and they've put their hands in their mouths, and he saw an old man standing beside him and crying until his beard became wet and he said that his father and his mother might become ransom for him! Their old men were the best of the old and their youth was the best among the young and their women were best of women, and their lineage is the best of lineage, never to be ashamed.[15]

After *Sharīkatu'l Ḥusain* (Associate of Ḥusain) Żainab, from among the other ladies, Imām Ḥusain's daughter Fāṭimah, stood up and said:

> "Oh people of Kufa, Oh people of treachery and trickery and the pride! Verily we are a Household that was tested by you, and you were tested by us, and He made our test leading to goodness and made His knowledge and wisdom with us. Thus, we are the owners of His wisdom and the container of His knowledge and wisdom, and His proof in His lands for His bondmen, and verily we've been dignified with His dignity, and we've been preferred by His Prophet Muḥammad over many of His creations in an obvious way, but you've lied to us and made us like the disbelievers, and thought fighting us is allowed and our fortune is to be plundered. Your eyes were satisfied with that, and your hearts were glad with that, lying about God and for a trick that you have made, but God is the best who tricks. Verily yourselves would not get spared for the bloodshed you've made within us, and for what your hands have gotten from our fortunes, for the great adversities and troubles were destined in a book before we meet them, and that is easy for God, That ye grieve not for the sake of that which hath escaped you, nor yet exult because of that which hath been given. God loveth not all proud boasters. Woe to you! Wait for the damnation and the punishment."[16]

Then the voices raised out aloud with cries and weeping, and they requested to stop, saying Oh daughter of the purified, chaste, you have burnt our hearts and set the fire to our insides. So, she went silent. Prophet of Islām's younger granddaughter, Umm Kulthūm-bint-Imām 'Alī addressed and raised her voice with crying and she said:

> "Oh people of Kufa, evil to you, why did you let down Ḥusain and killed him, and plundered his fortunes, and imprisoned his women. Woe to you and may God destroy you!! What sin you have commited, and what burden you have taken

> over your back, and what blood did you shed, and what a dignified woman you've targeted and what children you've plundered and what fortune you have taken. You've killed the best men after the Prophet Muḥammad and the mercy was taken out from your hearts, and Verily the party of God shall be the winner, and the party of the devil shall be the loser."[17]

Then the people wept out loud and cried, and the women spread their hairs and put the dust over their heads and scratched their faces and slapped their cheeks and prayed for the woes and punishments. The men also cried, and such numbers of mourners were never seen before.

Then Imām Żainu'l-Ābidīn made a sign with his hand to make them silent and they went silent, and then he stood up, and praised God and blessed the Prophet Muḥammad and then said:

> "Oh people, who know me, verily, you know me, and who doesn't know then I shall identify myself for him, I am, 'Alī-Ibn-Imām Ḥusain-Ibn-Imām 'Alī-Ibn-Abī Ṭālib. I am the son of him whose veil was broken and his fortunes were plundered, and his money was taken and his children were imprisoned. I am the son of the one who was slain on the banks of Alqamah for no sin or crime. I am the son of him who was killed and was patient, and that is enough for my pride. Oh people, I ask you by God, do you know that you've written to my father, and then tricked him, and sworn the fealty to him and made the covenant to him and then let him down and killed him? Woe to you then for what you have done to yourselves, and evil is your thinking! By what eye (look) you shall look at the Prophet of God! When he shall say to you: you've killed my Household and broken my veils, then verily you are not from my adherent. Then the voices of the people went out loud with cries from all the directions and they said to each other: Verily you are doomed and you don't know, what Prophet Muḥammad said; May the mercy of God be upon him who accepts my advice and saved my will for the sake of God, and His Prophet, and his Household, verily we have a good example in the Prophet of God."[18]

These speeches had immense effect on the audience, extremely ashamed, unable to raise one's eyes, were shouting and telling we are all, Oh son of the Prophet of God, supporters for him and desire no one, but them, so command with his orders, God would bestow mercy, for verily they were fighters for those who fight him, and they are at peace with those who make peace with him, and they shall fight Yażīd-bin-Mu'āwiyah and make themselves free from those who wronged him and wronged them.[19] Then Imām Żainu'l-Ābidīn said:

> "God fobid! Oh you treacherous, Verily there is veil between yourselves and the lusts of yourselves, do you want to come to me like you did with my father before? No, by the God of the dancers (the planets), the wound is not yet cured, my father, may blessings of God be upon him, was killed yesterday with his Household, and I didn't forget how bereaved is the Prophet of God and my father and the children of my father, and his sadness is in my mouth and his bitterness is in my throat and his adversities are running on my chest. No wonder Imām Ḥusain was killed, for his father was even better than Ḥusain and more generous. So, Oh people of Kufa don't be happy for what happened to Ḥusain for he was more brutally slain on the banks of the river may my soul be a ransom for him may the reward of him, who killed him be the Hell."[20]

In the Court of Governor

The Kufic Governor, 'Obaydu'llāh-bin-Żiyād sat in the palace and issued a general invitation to the people for participating in the function of his Court to witness and enjoy the victory of Yażīd-bin-Mu'āwiyah over Ḥusain-Ibn-'Alī. His court was overflowing with the audience.

First of all, the head of Imām Ḥusain was brought and was put before him, so he looked at it and laughted at that head, but his laughter turned into jitters, looking at the bearer, who was shouting with over zeal that the ladder of his donkey is decked with golds and pearls, because they killed the best man on earth and he who was the son of the best man on earth. On hearing it, 'Obaydu'llāh-bin-Żiyād became furious and killed him. It was an example, how Imām Ḥusain's victory started speaking.[21]

'Obaydu'llāh-bin-Żiyād kept Imām Ḥusain's head below his seat. He had a lash in his hand, he began to hit with it the lips of Imām Ḥusain and said: "Verily he had a nice looking mouth." And further said: "Verily, the white hair came so fast to you Oh Abā 'Abdi'llāh! A day for the day of Badr, and there was in the court Anas-bin-Mālik who cried and said that he (Ḥusain) is the most like the Prophet of God and verily, he was handsome."

The holy Prophet's associate elderly person Żayd-bin-Arqam was present in the audience. He could not tolerate the scene, and when he saw that 'Obaydu'llāh-bin-Żiyād was hitting Imām Ḥusain's lips, he asked him: "Get your lash away from these lips, By God, there is no other god but Him, verily I saw the holy Prophet kiss these lips so much."[22]

Then Żayd-bin-Arqam started to weep. 'Obaydu'llāh-bin-Żiyād became furious and said to him: "May God make your eyes dry, do you cry for the relief of God? By God, if you were not an old man with senility, I would order for you to be beheaded." Żayd-bin-Arqam got up from the Court and said: "Oh people, you are the slaves now after this day, you've killed the son of Fāṭimah aż-Żahrah, *Lady of Light* and made the son of Marjānah ('Obaydu'llāh-bin-Żiyād), a ruler for you. By God, he shall kill the good of you and make slaves out of your devilish ones, who accepts the humiliation." Then Żayd-bin-Arqam said: "Oh 'Obaydu'llāh-bin-Żiyād, I shall speak to you such a talk that is harder than this, I've seen the Prophet of God made sit Ḥasan on his right thigh and Ḥusain on his left thigh and then he put his hand on their heads," and then said, "Verily I make them deposits for You and for the rest of the believers. So, how was the deposit of the Prophet of God with you Oh 'Obaydu'llāh-bin-Żiyād?"[23]

Then, the ladies of the family of Imām Ḥusain were presented with their children in the Court of 'Obaydu'llāh-bin-Żiyād, and Żainab-bint-Imām 'Alī sat in a corner in a disguise, covered under an orbit of family ladies.[24] 'Obaydu'llāh-bin-Żiyād asked the gathering arround her, "Who is she ?" After knowing that she was Żainab-bint-Imām 'Alī, *Sharīkatu'l Ḥusain,* the daughter of Fāṭimah aż-Żahrah, *Lady of Light*, the daughter of the holy Prophet Muḥammad, so 'Obaydu'llāh-bin-Żiyād came to her. The famous historian aṭ-Ṭabarī, Ibn Jarīr Abū Jā'far (d. 932 AD) has recorded the conversation[25] in between as follows:

> "Intoxicated in victory 'Obaydu'llāh-bin-Żiyād addressing Żainab said, "Praise be to God that He defamed you and killed you and showed your lies."
>
> Żainab then said, "Praise be to God, who dignified us with His Prophet Muḥammad and cleansed us, it is but the wrong-doer that shall be defamed and the lies of the unchaste shall be exposed, and we are not those."
>
> 'Obaydu'llāh-bin-Żiyād said, "How do you see the action of God against your brother and his Household?"
>
> She replied, "I didn't see anything more beautiful, these are people that death was destined upon them and to their graves

> they went. And verily God well make both of you meet each other, and the debate shall go on against you, and wait to see who shall be penalyzed then? May your mother be bereaved of you Oh son of Murjānah ('Obaydu'llāh-bin-Żiyād)!"

The narrator has written that on hearing the befitting reply of Żainab-bint-'Alī, 'Obaydu'llāh-bin-Żiyād went mad and wanted to beat her with whip but other people present in his Court prevented him from doing so. It is clear that 'Obaydu'llāh-bin-Żiyād was telling untruth, which was negating the entire Islām itself. Therefore, it was necessary for her to reply. If there was shame, least of the least in him, should have remained calm, but for initiating her for making her sad, he was going on pressing his side-view at her, continuously so that sad lady would become more sad. But 'Omar-bin-Ḥorayth calmed down him and said: She is a woman and the woman is not to be taken for what she says!

Then 'Obaydu'llāh-bin-Żiyād said, "God had cured my heart from your tyrant, Ḥusain-Ibn-'Alī-Ibn-Abī Ṭālib, and the revolutionaries of his Household."

> Żainab-bint-'Alī replied, "By my life, you've killed my old man and cut off my branch, and knocked off my roots, and if that is your cure then you had it."
>
> 'Obaydu'llāh-bin-Żiyād said, "By my life, she's a poet, and her father (Imām 'Alī) was too."
>
> Żainab said, "Oh 'Obaydu'llāh-bin-Żiyād, what a woman (like me) has to do with poetry, Verily, I have something that keeps me busy away from poetry, but it is a breath of my chest for what you have said to me."
>
> Afterwards, 'Obaydu'llāh-bin-Żiyād looked at Imām Żainu'l-Ābidīn and asked, "Who is this?" And they told him that this is 'Alī-Ibnu'l-Ḥusain!
>
> 'Obaydu'llāh-bin-Żiyād remarked, "Did not God kill 'Alī-Ibnu'l-Ḥusain?"
>
> Then Imām Żainu'l-Ābidīn answered, "I had a brother who was also called Alī-Ibnu'l-Ḥusain. He was killed by the crowds."
>
> 'Obaydu'llāh-bin-Żiyād asserted, "No, but God killed him!"
>
> Imām Żainu'l-Ābidīn replied in the words of God:
>
> "God receiveth (men's) souls at the time of their death!" (*Qur'an*: 39/42).

Then 'Obaydu'llāh-bin-Żiyād became furious and said that how he dared to reply back? And ordered his soldiers to take Imām Żainu'l-Ābidīn and behead him.

When his aunt Żainab-bint-Imām 'Alī heard that, she hugged him and said, "Oh 'Obaydu'llāh-bin-Żiyād, stop from our blood shed for you left no one of us, and if you decided to kill him, then kill me before him."

'Obaydu'llāh-bin-Żiyād looked at her and him for some time and then said, "I wonder for such tie of kinship, By God, I think she desires to be killed with him, so leave him and I shall decide later."

Then Imām Żainu'l-Ābidīn said to his aunt, "Be silent my reverend aunt, until I talk to him." And then he stood before 'Obaydu'llāh-bin-Żiyād and said, "Are you threatening me by killing Oh 'Obaydu'llāh-bin-Żiyād? Didn't you know martyrdom is a habit of ours and God favoured that for us!"[26]

And then 'Obaydu'llāh-bin-Żiyād ordered to carry 'Alī-Ibnu'l-Ḥusain to some room, beside the great mosque.

Żainab-bint-Imām 'Alī said, "No Arabian woman shall enter before us, unless she was a maid or a slave, for verily they were taken hostages like us."

Ibn-Żiyād ordered to take the head of Imām Ḥusain and tour it around in the roads of Kufa. Then, he went up the pulpit, and said in some of his speech, "Praise to God, who showed the truth and its people, and nourished the prince of the believers Yażīd-bin-Mu'āwiyah-bin-Abū Sufyyān and his party, and killed the liar, the son of the liar and his followers."

While in that situation, 'Abdu'llāh-bin-'Afīf Ażdī stood up, and he was one of the a great follower of Imām 'Alī-Ibn-Abī Ṭālib, and his left eye was gone in the Battle of Jamal (656 AD), and his right eye was gone at the Battle of Ṣiffīn (656-57 AD), which was fought between Imām 'Alī and Mu'āwiyah-bin-Abū Sufyyān, the father of Yażīd. Being physically handicapped, 'Abdu'llāh-bin-'Afīf used to remain in the great mosque and pray there until late night time, so he said, "Oh son of Murjānah ('Obaydu'llāh-bin-Żiyād)!, Verily the liar is you and your father, and the one who used you and his father, Oh Enemy of God! Do you kill the children of the holy Prophets and talk with such a speech on the pulpits of the Muslims?"

Then 'Obaydu'llāh-bin-Żiyād got mad with angry and said, "Who is that talking to me?" He replied, "I am 'Abdu'llāh-bin-

> 'Afīf Ażdī, who talks Oh enemy of God! Do you kill the purified Household which God cleansed and made clean, and claim that you are a Muslim, Alas! Any helper! Where are the sons of the Believer, they should take the revenge from you and from your tyrant, the damned the son of the damned, who was damned by the holy Prophet Muḥammad.

The narrator has stated that the anger of 'Obaydu'llāh-bin Żiyād increased until his veins blowed up and ordered to arrest him. Soldiers rushed from all directions to take him, but the nobles of the Ażdī tribe, and his cousins stood up and freed him from the soldiers, and got him out from the mosque's door and took him back to his house. And 'Obaydu'llāh-bin-Żiyād escaping the humiliation said that they should go to that blind man, the blind man of Ażdī tribe, may God make his heart blind as well, and get him for me.

So, they went to him, and when Ażdī tribe knew about that they gathered with the tribes of Yemen to protect their man, and 'Obaydu'llāh-bin-Żiyād got the tidings about that and he gathered the tribes of Modhar, under Muḥammad-bin-Asha'th, and he ordered him to fight the people, and they fought against each other severely, until a group of 'Arabs got killed, and the fellows of 'Obaydu'llāh-bin-Żiyād reached the house of 'Abdu'llāh-bin-'Afīf Ażdī, and they broke the door and got into the house.

'Abdu'llāh-bin-'Afīf's daughter shouted, "The people came from where you were afraid!"

'Abdu'llāh said, "Don't be afraid, get me the sword, and so she did and he started to defend himself."

Then his daughter said, "Oh father! how I wish that I was a man to fight before you against those wicked men, the killers of the purified Household."

The people started to rotate around him from all directions, while he was defending himself, and no one could get him, and whenever they come to him from one direction, she (his daughter) would say, "O father! they're coming from that direction, until they out-numbered him and surrounded him, and his daughter then said, "Alas! What humiliation! My father is surrounded and he has no one to nourish him, so he started to rotate his sword and said, "I swear if my eyes only can see then you would have no way to me."

And they kept on like that until they got him, and then he was carried and got into the court of 'Obaydu'llāh-bin-Żiyād, and when he saw him he said, "Praise to God who disappointed you!"

'Abdu'llāh-bin-'Afīf said then, "Oh Enemy of God, by what did He disappoint me?"

'Obaydu'llāh-bin-Żiyād replied, "By God I shall not ask you about anything else, and you shall taste death severely!"

'Abdu'llāh-bin-'Afīf said, Praise to God, the God of the creations, Verily I was asking God to make me a martyr, before your mother delivered you, and I asked God to make that by the most evil creature and the most hated one by Him, and when my eyesight was taken away, I was despaired of being a martyr, and now—praise to God—who made me have it after being despaired about it, and made me know the answer of my old prayer. So, then under the order of 'Obaydu'llāh-bin-Żiyād, his soldiers beheaded him, and so they did and he was crucified in the moorland.[27]

Way to Damascus

As mentioned in the above lines, after reaching Kufa, the prisoners of Prophet's family-members were launched at the famous Masjidu'l-Ḥanānah, which was turned into prison for them. The prisoners remained there awaiting Yażīd's order for the further action to be taken against the prisoners for which 'Obaydu'llāh-bin-Żiyād had already sent his messenger to Damascus for getting the permission from there.

After getting the orders from Yażīd, the messenger reached Kufa on 20th Muḥarram 61 AH (20th October, 680 AD) and the same day Yażīdī Army was set out to Damascus. Accordingly, the period of stay of the prisoners at Kufic Masjidu'l-Ḥanānah was 12th Muḥarram 61 AH (12th October, 680 AD) to 20th Muḥarram 61 AH (20th October, 680 AD).

Prior to departure for Damascus, 'Obaydu'llāh-bin-Żiyād orderd that Żaḥurr-bin-Qays with the head of Imām Ḥusain on the tip of his spear should tour in all the lanes and roads of Kufa.[28] Only after that Yażīdī Army should proceed to Damascus, under the command of Maḥzaṛ-bin-Tha'lbah 'Āyižī and Shimr-bin-Žuljaushan. They took the women and children as prisoners in shackles, put them on camels, and proceeded in a caravan from Karbala to Kufa. At the forefront of the procession were the heads of Imām Ḥusain and his followers on the tip of spears of various tribes, and so, Kindah with 13 heads, Ḥawāżin with 12 heads, Tamīm with 17 heads, Asad with 16 heads, Munḥaj with 7 heads, and others with the rest of the heads. Keeping the heads of dead bodies on the tip of swords and the ladies and children were mounted on camels without any safety, Imām Żainu'l-Ābidīn was hand-cuffed, and his legs were chained and his neck was tied with thorny chains. The scene was so pathetic, the spectators burst into tears.[29]

The normal distance of Kufa to Damascus is 461 miles (750 kms), but, Yażīdī Army took the family members of Imām Ḥusain, making them imprisoned, in a round about way covering the distance of about 950 miles (1,320 kms).[30] They first went from Kufa to Qādsiyah in a way to Damascus, but they took the long route of Al-Jażīrah, wherein there was no colony at all, then no place, no town, the route as under:

> Kufa→Qādsiyah→Qanāṭabar→Masakan→Sāmmarh→Takrīt→Wādī Nakhlah→Kamḥabal→Jahiniyah→Mūṣal→Tall' Āfaṛ→Sanajār→Naṣībayn→Ḥarān→Tall Abyaz→Da'wāt→Riqah→Dosaṛ→Maskanah→Aleppo→Qanasarīn→Mu'arrah→Kafaraṭāb→Shabraż→Ḥammah→Ḥamaṣ→Labwah→Ya'labak→Som'ah-Rahibah→Damascus.

A natural question arises, why such a very long route was taken, instead of a short route available. Morever, Yażīd himself was in a haste to show the world at the earliest in the assembly at Damascus for celebrating his victory, how he has taken revenge of blood from the family-members of the Prophet Muḥammad![31] It is evident from his utterings, he made at his assembly later on, which would be discussed in the ensuing lines. To ignore the ambition of Yażīd was not possible for the Governor of Kufa, 'Obaydu'llāh-bin-Żiyād. He himself was most eager to get the reward from his Caliph Yażīd. Then what was the reason to pursue this way to reach late? It has so many reasons.

Firstly, After getting the message of Imām Ḥusain's assissination, anger and hatred had spread everywhere among Muslims, against Yażīd and his rule. There were anti-waves everywhere. People became rebellions and were revolting, a stage of the mutiny was visible. The Yażīdī Army was scared, if seen with the arrested family members of Imām Ḥusain, people will attack and get the prisoners released. This fear was so deep because the Yażīdī Army, when took the prisoners to Kufa, found serious explosive situations around Kufa. So, they firstly went to Qādsiyah taking of opposite direction of Damascus, where there was an unusual concentration of the Yażīdī Army; then from there it set out to Damascus.

Secondly, in search of a safe way, such a region was easy for them, on which Amīr Mu'āwiyah's illegal and usurped state was in the east. It has already been clarified at the appropriate places that Amīr Mu'āwiyah had already spread a false propaganda regularly against Imām 'Alī-Ibn-Abī Ṭālib with bad words. Ordinary people were either not at all aware of the greatness of *Ahlu'l-Bayt* or *'Itrat,* Household or Progeny of the

Prophet Muḥammad, if at all they were aware, they considered them as anti-Islām. Therefore, taking the prisoners in this route was absolutely safe. Any well-wisher of Progeny of the Prophet Muḥammad could not make any hindrance on his way. This, as stated above happened also. It was also the reason.

Thirdly there were so many towns in this route. As Wādī-Nakhlah, Naṣībayn, Da'wāt, Aleppo (Ḥalab), Shabraż, Ḥammah, Ḥamaṣ and Ya'labak. The Yażīdī Army hoisted its victory flag pomp and splendour in its influencial areas. It made a wide publicity that its battalions fought against a person Imām Ḥusain and the Yażīdī Army murdered him along with his friends. Now, his family members would be presented before Caliph Yażīdī in Damascus, who would do justice about them. This type of vicious publicity was spread throughout the route, especially in towns where there was a larger population. Imām Żainu'l-Ābidīn was silent throughout his way, he was not at all talking to any one![32] So, many people were highly emotional knowing the pathetic situations of the holy Prophet's family members, they were expressing their reaction in different ways. Most of their reactions were symbolic, by which Yażīdī soldiers were afraid of.

Yażīdī Army took the heads of Imām Ḥusain and his associates, then in the first halt-camp there was a wonderful event. So, many scholars have written that the Yażīdī Army made their first camp near a Christian Sanctuary, thinking it was a safe place. Before going to rest they had many cups of liquor and enjoyed. They were exchanging their greetings on their victory, they saw the wall of the Sanctuary, a Divine Message written in 'Arabic language –

> Those who murdered Ḥusain can't be optimistic His grandfather will never intercede salvation at Catastroph.[33]

The Yażīdī Army asked the monk, who has written this poetry? He told that he did not know, but he was observing the same long ago, there was a terrible psychological influence of the incident. They were scared in such a way that ran away and could not stood there, leaving everything abundant. They returned only after a long time.

In the same way one more event is available in the form of the Tradition. Ibn-Lahī'ah narrates that he was busy in making third circumambulation of holy Ka'bah when he observed that somebody was crying, Oh God! begging pardon for his sins, though he knew that God would never forgive it. Ibn-Lahī'ah went near him, and convinced him telling, God is most compassionate and merciful, He forgives all for their sins. He said, but He would not forgive him. When asked about the sin he had committed, the guilty man replied that he was one among those fifty soldiers, who were carrying the very head of Imām Ḥusain to Damascus. They had the very box, in which the head was kept in the night, then they drank liqour and entertained themselves very luxuriously. One night he did not drink liquor, but the other people were highly intoxicated. He observed that once the clouds thundered and lightning flashed. He observed some great souls coming from the sky, angels were also with them. They began to beat my colleagues like anything. I wanted to go to their asylum, but they prohibited.[34]

Famous hostile historian Ibn-Jaužī (d. 1201 AD), has also recorded a similar incident that the Yażīdī Army toured with the prisoners and the head of Imām Ḥusain was with them, and whenever they would settle down in some place they would take the head out from a chest that was made for it, and put it on a spear and guard him all night until the time of moving, and then they returned it back to the chest and moved, and they settled in some places, and in one of these places there was an Abbey with an Abbess, so, they took the head from the chest as usual and put it on a spear and got it guarded, and they supported the spear with the Abbey of the Christian man, and when it was midnight, the Abbess saw a light from the place of the head to the sky, so, he went to the people and asked, Who were they? They told of being men of the government of their Caliph Yażīd-bin-Mu'āwiyah and were going to Damascus, then he asked about the head? They replied that was the head of Ḥusain bin-Imām 'Alī-bin-Abī Ṭālib, the son of Fāṭimah aż-Żahrah, the daughter of the Prophet Muḥammad. the Abbess was astounded to hear that Muslims were roaming with the head of the son of the daughter of their own Prophet! He again asked to get confirmed. They said: Yes! Then the Abbess condemned, what evil people were they! If the Messiah had a son, every Christian would make his eyes a home for him, and then he asked them to accept some deal? They wanted to know, what would it be? He said that he had 10 thousand Dirham (the then Arabian currency), they shall take it and give him the head to be with him that night and when they would want to leave, they should take it back? They agreed that there was no harm with it! So, they gave him the head and he gave them the money, and the Abbess took the head and washed it and put perfumes on it and left it with him, and put it on his thigh, and cried all night, and when the morning appeared, he said, Oh head, he has nothing but himself, and verily he testifies that there is no god but God, and your grandfather Muḥammad is His Prophet, and he testified to be one of his followers.

They said Abbey, where the Yażīdī Army stayed with the prisoners and heads was near Qansīray in nearby Iraq border Riqah and famous historical town Aleppo. In due course this place has become famous, where a stone is available, on which the Abbess gave bath.. The very head Imām Ḥusain fell on that stone which has frozen these. Even after, 1,400 years that stone is red with blood which had been carefully preserved. The prisoners who were dismounted near the Abbey, its old name was Wīr, which was situated on the bank of the river Qażīq in Jabal-Gharabī area of Mārūtu'l-Mārūsah. At present, there is a huge memorial palace, famous with the name of Mashhadu'l-Ḥusainī. A big religious institution is also available there, wherein we find schools and libraries. The miraculous stone has been preserved there very safely and carefully under a special archaelogical provision, on which there are stains of blood drops of Imām Ḥusain.[35]

The learned readers may kindly revive their memory. In the previous chapter we have already discussed that the Ḥusainī Brahamans claim that their ancestors were martyred for the cause of truth and justice, along with Imām Ḥusain. Accoding to their Tradition the Yażīdī Army, while on their return, after cutting off Imām Ḥusain's head, stopped in *Rahab*, their ancestor's home at Bathowal in the Sialkot district (now in Pakistan) and placed the head in his house. In the morning, finding the head to be of Imām Ḥusain, gave the soldiers his own son's head instead, *Rahab* cut-off all his seven sons' heads in succession and gave them to the soldiers. Sir Denzil Ibbetson has mentioned in detail about them.[36] Some others also mention.[37]

The word *Rahab* has been used in the above event which may be the 'Arabic word *Rahib*. It is commonly used for the Christian monastic. The mention of obtaining the head of Imām Ḥusain from the Yażīdī army by *Rahib* against the temptation of money, has already been mentioned in the above lines. Sir Denzil Ibbetson[38] and some others also mentioned[39] just as such without analyzing anything. It is a subject of research. Perhaps some may find out further facts during his research. Truth is hidden in this somewhere, I can tell only this much.

While taking prisoners either to any special place or popular town, Yażīdī soldiers even before reaching there would send the message of their reaching there, so, that their local administration there would make all special arrangements for them there and their victory may be celebrated among the local people. In this connection, the Yażīdī Army had sent the prior intimation of their camp at Baghlayq, therefore, to see the fun of prisoners the town people assembled there even from 6 Farsakhs (18 kms) away. In the way with some pretex or the other they were going on beating the prisoners. Imām Żainu'l-Ābidīn would say nothing to any one on being whipped, but used to take at the sky, and his feets tied with rope and still remained calm, looking the face of his aunt Żainab. In this manner, he was spending his night and days.

The Yażīdī Army was so atrocious one to disregard and to make ashamed the family members of Imām Ḥusain that they were behaving in a very indecent manner, exhibited their hatred, in an inhuman manner that Imām Ḥusain's head was made to hung on the neck of horse, when the horse galloped, the head was dashing the thigh of the horse. Seeing this inhuman and cruel behaviour holy Prophet's companion Qāsim-bin-Aṣabagh would burst into tears and shout, Oh merciless, what would they lose, if they keep the head little above.[40] The family members of Imām Ḥusain would see all their cruelties and atrocities, would keep mum tolerating everything.

Another companion of holy Prophet of Islām, Sahl-bin-S'ad has stated that when he was on a pilgrimage of the holy *Baytu'l-Muqaddas,* the Mosque of Jerusalem, which is equally a sacred place of prayer for Jews, Christian and Muslims. He reached in the evening at Damascus, where was an atmosphere of festival everywhere. He asked, Have they found out any new *Eīd*, the people told him that was the *Eīd* of Imām Ḥusain's head's arrival. Then he saw that a head was taken on the tip of a spear, which had great resemblence with the Prophet of Islām, ladies were found sitting on the naked back of camels. He went near a child and told that he was an Associate of the Prophet, when he asked the name of the child, she replied, Sukayna-bint-Imām Ḥusain. He asked, if she wishes to say something, she can say. Sukayna requested, to tell these spear holders, to let them go ahead, so people might be busy in seeing these heads and we the family-members of the Prophet may escape from becoming a fun for these people. Sahl-bin-S'ad gave 400 Dinars to the soldiers and they silently proceeded ahead.[41]

It seems from the further events that the spear holders again came near the prisoners, because 'Allāmah Ibn Ṭāūs, Saiyed Razīu'd Dīn (d.1266 AD) has written that on reaching near Damascus, Imām Ḥusain's younger sister Umm Kulthūm-bint-Imām 'Alī had requested the Yażīdī. Commander Shimr-bin-Žuljaushan, that while entering into Damascus town they should take the prisoners *via* such a way, where the visitors would be less in number and make the heads ahead of mounted soldiers, so, that they may avoid the sight of maximum number of people, but they did the exact opposite and kept the heads just in the middle of riders so that maximum number of people could look at.[42]

Entering into Damascus

Islāmic Prophets imprisoned family members entered into Damascus on 14th Safar 61 AH (13th November, 680 AD). Travelling 25 days in between from Kufa and Damascus, they could reach the capital of the Yażīdī Empire.[43]

The Caravan of prisoners entered into Damascus town, as per the orders of Yażīd. All the roads, lanes and markets were decorated like anything. Such a huge crowd of people assembled there to have the fun of seeing the prisoners that the latter were able to reach the Yażīdī Castle only late in evening, in spite of their reaching Damascus in the early morning, when the Caravan of prisoners was going in the middle of the markets, a man under the grip of Yażīdī propaganda, Ibrāhīm-bin-Ṭalḥā, looking at a side view, asked Imām Żainu'l-Ābidīn, Oh son of Ḥusain! Please tell, who achieved victory? Imām Żainu'l-Ābidīn replied politely, if he wanted to know in a practical manner who achieved victory, then he should observe during *Ażān* and *Namāż*, and listen to who achieved the victory!

In the same way when the Caravan of prisoners reached in front of the great Mosque of Damascus, an elderly person exhibiting hatred thanked God that he made Imām Ḥusain murdered and relieved the nation and society from him and offered victor over him to their Caliph Yażīd. Imām Żainu'l-Ābidīn addressing him said, Oh Shaykh ! have you read this verse of Qur'an:

> "Say thou (*O' Our Apostle Muḥammad*):' I demand not of you any compense for it (*the toils of the apostleship*) save the love of *(my)* relatives." (*Qur'an*: 42/23)

He replied in affirmative that he has read. Then Imām Żainu'l-Ābidīn asked, If he had read this verse of Qur'an too:

> "Verily God intendeth but to keep off from you *(every kind of)* uncleanness Oh ye the People of the House, and purify you *(with)* a thorough purification." (*Qur'an* 33/33).

Then Imām Żainu'l-Ābidīn told that those people, the *Ahlu'l-Bayt* or *'Itrat,* the Household or Progeny of the Prophet Muḥammad, were they themselves. That elderly man being stunned gazed at him and asked, Practically, is he himself? Imām Żainu'l-Ābidīn said, Yes, we ourselves. Hearing this that elderly man burst into tears, took off his turban and sought pardon.[44] From this incidence it can be assumed how Umayyites

Rule created illusions and ill-feelings towards the family-members of the holy Prophet and how people were confused with misconceptions.

When a group of imprisoned family members of the holy Prophet of Islām was entering Damascus, Yażīd was present on a watch-tower over Jayrūn. When those conveyances were seen and the shadow of their heads was being on the peak of Jayrūn hillock crowds began to shout *Kaun-Kaurh* (to be inauspicious sign) and he heard a crowd's sound. As soon as the heads of Imām Ḥusain and his associates were seen on the tips of swords and spears, he read out some couplets, whose meaning is as follows:

> "When those carried ones appeared and raised those suns on the hills of Jayrun. The crowd cried so I said be right or not for verily I've I have recovered my debt from the Prophet."[45]

With these couplets the very bent of mind of Yażīd can be estimated that he had equated the murder of Imām Ḥusain and his associates with the recovery of his debt from the holy Prophet of Islām. Further discussion will follow regarding this in the ensuing lines.

In the Yażīdī Court

After waiting for a very long time of entering into Damascus town, the Caravan of Prisoners could be allowed to be presented before the Castle of the Caliph Yażīd-bin-Mu'āwiyah. They were stopped near the gate, close to Central Hall. The prisoners were made to stand there for many hours, because Yażīd himself was busy in decorating his Court. Then the family members of the holy Prophet of Islām were presented in such a manner as if they were slaves. Yażīdī Commander Żaḥurr-bin-Qays submitted the victory report in a highly exaggerated fashion, dwelling on the subject itself. He prayed for reward to fill in his camels stockings with gold coins, because they had murdered a highly noble personality as per his orders. He has killed him, who read *Namāż* in his childhood facing both the Mosques, who was the greatest of the whole world. He has assaulted him, whose parents were very rightly sacred and nobble in the whole world. Although his views were against the very views of Yażīdī Rule his very soul's inner feelings were burst into, he could not control his emotions. As a result Yażīd became mad out of anger towards him. He said, if he has such feelings, why he join in murdering him? He should not hope of getting any reward from him. Telling to send him also to them, he killed him. [46]

When, the Household of the holy Prophet Muḥammad and the women were made to enter the court of Yażīd-bin-Mu'āwiyah-bin-Abū Sufyyān and they were tied with ropes, and when they all got in there, and in that situation, Imām Żainu'l-Ābidīn said:

> "By God, Oh Yażīd, what do you think the Prophet of God would say if he saw us in this situation?"

Then Yażīd ordered to cut off the ropes and he asked for a file and they started to file the cuffs that were on the neck of Imām Żainu'l-Ābidīn. When they removed the cuffs from his neck, the blood gushed out from his neck.

There was a severe reaction when the information of Imām Ḥusain becoming martyr reached the seraglio of Yażīdī palace. A lady of *Hāshimites,* the most respected clan of Quraysh, in which Prophet Muḥammad was born was present there. She began to pray shouting loudly, Oh my Master, Alas! Ḥusain!! On the information that the head of Imām Ḥusain is being hung at the main-gate of the seraglio, Yażīdī's wife Hind, who was the daughter of 'Abdu'llāh-bin-'Āmir, a highly religious sacred character and highly cultured and very well behaved lady, who had already served Imām Ḥusain, became immensely grief stricken dejected and highly sad, came out of the seraglio straight in the Court Hall. In a loud shouting asked, "Oh Yażīd ! Have you made the head of the son of the Prophet of Islām hung on her entrance. Yażīd felt very irritated when he observed his wife without face cover. Being perturbed, he ran and veiled her.

Then, Yaḥyā-bin-Ḥakam, the brother of Marwān. who was sitting there said, Verily, the head beside the river's bank is more close in relation rather than Ibn Żiyād, the slave of the dirty lineage of Sumayyah, now, it has a lineage in many numbers and today the Household of the Chosen Prophet has no lineage. Yażīd struck him on his chest and said, Shut up, may you have no mother![47]

Thereafter, Imām Ḥusain's head was presented in a golden plate before Yażīd.[48] At that time Yażīd was reciting some couplets and singing, from which his religious belief and his objective of fighting with Imām Ḥusain in Karbala become highly clear, after which there is no scope of any agility of language regarding Yażīd and his objectives. All matters are highly clear. Yażīd was highly inebriated, whose mention is available in various books.[49] The meaning of these couplets is as follows:

> Wish if my ancestors in Badr testified the fear of Khażraj
> from the swords' beats

Verily they would be glad and happy then say Oh Yażīd don't ever stop
We've killed the bravest of their masters and made, it equal to Badr's day and it was
Verily I am not from the tribe of Khondof, if I didn't take revenge from Aḥmad for what he did
Hāshim played with the throne and thus, no tidings were brought and nor inspiration.

Hearing these *Sharīkatu'l Ḥusain,* Żainab-bint-Imām 'Alī, stood. She presented her address, shaking the foundation of monarchy. Yażīd's vanity was shattered into pieces. Her words made the history. Żainab prayed first, praised the holy Prophet, then read the verse of the Qur'an:

"Then evil was the end of those who wrought evil, for belied they the signs of God, and at them they used to mock." (*Qur'an*: 30/10)

Then addressing Yażīd-bin-Mu'āwiyah, she said:

"Oh Yażīd! did you think, when you've turned the corners of the earth and the horizons of the sky over us and made hostages driven like the prisoners of war, did you think that we are hated by God and He likes you, and that was for how dangerous you are in His eyes, so, you raised your nose and looked at the tip of your cloak (with pride) in happiness, when you saw the life is assured for you and the matters are done good for you, and when our fortune and might been away from your way. Just wait, did you forget God's saying." [50]

Afterwards, Żainab read out the verse of the Qur'an again:

"It is not for God to leave the believers in the state in which ye are." (*Qur'an*: 3/179)

Then proceeding further Żainab said:

"Is it fair ? Oh son of *Ṭolaqā'* (Captives of the Battle of Badr, who were released, due to mercy by the Prophet, and Yażīd's ancestors were among them), is it fair that you put your harem behind the veils while you drive the daughters of the Prophet like prisoners, and you've broken their veils and showed their faces, and the enemies got them toured from one town to another, and people talk about them, while their faces are looked at by the near and the far, and the mean and the noble, with no man from their household, and no protector. How it is possible to look at him who chewed the liver of the faithful and his meat grown up with the blood of the martyrs? And how is it possible that he wouldn't hate us severely, the Household, who looked at us with the eyes of envy and hatred, and then you say as easy as it could be: Verily they would be glad and happy, then say Oh, Yażīd don't ever stop. While you bend on the lips of Abā 'Abdi'llāh, (Imām Ḥusain), the lord of youth of Paradise, and you hit it with your rod. How come you don't say that? And you've severed the wound and knocked off the origins by shedding the bloods of the Household of Muḥammad and the stars of earth, from the Household of 'Abdu'l-Muṭṭalib (grandfather of the Prophet), and you call your ancestors as if you were calling them, and verily you shall follow them soon, and then you will wish if you've been paralyzed and muted, and never said what you've said and never did what you've done. Take our rights, and take revenge from those who wronged us, and let your wrath befall upon those who shed our bloods and killed our protectors. By God, you've severed your skin only, and you've cut your own meat, and you shall meet the Prophet of God, with what you've put on your back, the blood of his Household and of what veils you've broken for his daughters, after God gathers them all together and take their rights. Think not of those, who are slain in the way of God, as dead. Nay, they are living. With their Lord they have provision, and God, is enough Judge, and Muḥammad is enough for an opponent, and Gabriel is enough for being a support, and he who advised you with evil and made you ruler of the Muslims' necks how evil is to be for the wrong-doers and whoever shall be in an evil place and with the weakest army. And though destiny made me talk to you, verily I see you small in my eyes and not worthy even to my rebuke, but the eyes are full of tears and the chests are full of agony. Alas! What a wonder for killing the party of God, the Chosen, by the party of Satan the free, and these are the hands, they are dropping from our bloods, and these are the mouths, they are getting from our meats, and these are the purified corpses, they are visited by the wolves and hyenas, and if you stood against us you shall find us a fierce enemy, at a time when you only see what you've done by your own hands, and verily your God is not an unjust for His bondmen. Thus, to God shall be the complaint, and He shall help. Then, trick your tricks, and walk along your path, and do your best, By God you shall never erase our mention, and never kill our inspiration, and never reach our level, and its shame shall never leave you, and what is your opinion but to doom? And what are your days but numbered? And what are your gatherings (men) but to be separated? At the day when the caller shall call and say: may the damnation of God befall upon the wrong-doers. Then praise to God, the Lord of the worlds who judged for our first with happiness and forgiveness, and to our last with martyrdom and mercy, and we shall ask God to complete their rewards and add more for them, and make it easy for us Verily, He is Merciful and Beloved, and God is our Judge and He is Dependable." [51]

The Yażīdī Court-Hall was observing spell-bound Żainab's argumentative speech. Yażīd was also spell-bound. To console himself, he addressed Imām Żainu'l-Ābidīn and said that whether the difficulty has come on you throw your hands only. Imām Żainu'l-Ābidīn read out the verse of Qur'an in reference:

> "And in the earth are signs for those who are sure in faith; And (*also*) in your own selves; will ye not then see ?" (*Qur'an*: 51/20-21)

Yażīd could smell that the argumentative speech of *Sharīkatu'l Ḥusain,* Żainab cannot be defeated on arguments, he ordered, Żainab to be whipped by his soldiers. But the old Abyssenian lady Fizzah, who was given by Prophet to his daughter Fāṭimah aż-Żahrah, as helper, was prisoner with other members of the family, she stood as rock to protect Żainab and covered her under her chest. Yażīd lost his mental balance and further ordered to whip both. Fizzah immediately challenged all those Abyssenian gaurds, and asked what had happened to their self-prestige that an elderly woman amongst them was being misbehaved. All the Abyssenian slaves, who were bodyguards became forward and rescued her.[52]

Yażīd felt disobedience among his men, so, he began attempts to repeat bad and hated conduct of provocation and dishonouring, which his

Kufic Governor 'Obaydu'llāh-bin-Żiyād had already done in his Court, with the head of Imām Ḥusain, where the holy Prophet's elderly associate Żayd-bin-Arqam had got up from his Court had opposed it. Yażīd, might had thought that who could dare enough to oppose him here, but when Yażīd attempted to keep his stick on the lips of Imām Ḥusain, the other elderly associate of the holy Prophet, Abū Barżah Aslamī stood up in the open Assembly and called upon him, "Oh Yażīd! remove your stick away from the lips of Imām Ḥusain, I have usually observed that the holy Prophet used to suck his lips. Remember now on the Day of Last Judgment 'Obaydu'llāh-bin-Żiyād only would make you free from sins!"[53]

Famous historian Ibn Athīr, 'Iżżu'd-Dīn (d. 1233 AD), has recorded an event[54] that a Syrian man, who was in the court, looked at Fāṭimah the daughter of Imām Ḥusain and requested Yażīd to give him that maid, and Fāṭimah said (later on); at that time She got shocked and thought that was allowed for them, and she took the clothes of her aunt Żainab and said, Alas! my aunt! I was made an orphan and now to be used? Then, Żainab firmly said, No, and that wicked man had no dignity. She knew that that would never happen, so she looked at the Syrian man and said, By God you've lied and been wicked, and By God that was not to be for he or for him (Yażīd). Yażīd got angry and said, By God, she had lied, He was able to do so if he wanted to! Żainab said, By God, he has not been made for him, unless he left the Islām, and then Yażīd got angry even more and said: Does she talk to him in that way? Verily, who got out from this religion, is your father and your brother, and Żainab said, By religion of God, and the religion of my father, and the religion of my brother ! Has he been guided with his grandfather and his father, if you were a Muslim!! Yażīd said that she had lied, Oh enemy of God, and she replied that Yażīd was a prince, cursed unjust and succeed with his might, then as if he was embarrased and went silent.

Then the Syrian man got back again to his request and Yażīd then asked him to stop it, May God give you a mortal fate. Then the Syrian man asked, who was that maid? Yażīd said that it was Fāṭimah, the daughter of Imām Ḥusain and that was Żainab the daughter of 'Alī-bin-Abī Ṭālib. The Syrian man then said, Ḥusain the son of Fāṭimah, the daughter of the Prophet? And 'Alī-bin-Abī Ṭālib? He replied, Yes, and then the Syrian man said, May God damn you, Oh Yażīd, do you kill the Household of your Prophet and imprison their children, By God I thought they were the Romans. Yażīd said, By God, I shall make you follow them, and then he ordered to behead him.

The same type of event happened with the Jews scholar, who was present in the Court. He asked Yażīd pointing towards Imām Żainu'l-Ābidīn, who was that young man! He replied, Ḥusain's son, 'Alī. He asked, Who was Ḥusain! Yażīd said, Prophet's daughter Fāṭimah's son. Expressing his regret that Jews scholar said, you call yourself a Muslim and you have murdered your own Prophet's family. What was their mistakes that you have murdered him so urgently. By God, had Mūsā-bin-'Imrān left any daughter among us, perhaps we would have worshipped her and your situation is this that your Prophet left the world and today you have killed his son. Your end will be very bad. Telling this be got up and went and telling that I have read in The Old Testament that a person who murders the child of his own Prophet, remains black-marked for ever, till he lives and when dies, God throws him into Hell!

In the same way, a Christian, who was a messenger from Caesar to Yażīd looked around and said that they had in some islands, the trace of the hoof of the donkey that Jesus, used to ride and they make pilgrimage there every year from all around the lands and the vows are made there, and they glorified it like Muslim glorifed their own books, and verily he testified that Yażīdī were wrong-doers. Yażīd got angry for that saying and ordered to kill him.

Yażīd being vexed, addressing again Imām Żainu'l-Ābidīn said his father did not pay any attention towards the relationship and rejected his rights and opposed giving trouble in his Kingdom, then God did the same thing with them, what they were seeing. In reply Imām Żainu'l-Ābidīn repeated the same verse (*Qur'an*: 51/20-21), which he had already read out. The idea was that in this materialistic world, it always happens somebody gets defeat and some one gets victory. But it should not be understood as the base of truth. Yażīd's were increased with this. But thinking that everyone of his Court considered himself as the criminal tried to express his cleanliness (Truth), which clarified further his conduct's black-make. He said that the people know, why that problem came to him? Only with the reason that he thought that his father 'Alī-Ibn-Abī Ṭālib was greater than his (Yażīd's) father Mu'āwiyah-bin-Abū Sufyyān, his mother was greater than my mother and his grandfather (maternal) was greater than my grandfather, and he himself was greater than Yażīd. So, he was a better candidate than himself. If Yażīd's above mentioned statement is analysed, then in telling the seniority he himself has accepted his defeat. Whatever argument he wanted to give that whom God likes, provides empire and on that basis all atrocious rulers and arrangement, against whom God sent one lakh twenty four thousand

Prophets their coming and fighting against atrocious provisions all would become meaningless and futile.

In the Yażīdī Court people were highly influenced with the talk of Imām Żainu'l-Ābidīn. They requested Yażīd to arrange for his address so, that they may enjoy the sweetness of his language. Yażīd was not unaware of the calibre of the family members of the holy Prophet of Islām. He began to say, the people do not know how knowledge has been offered to them, as if, any bird feeds grains to her children. Being helpless, at the mutual request of all the people in the Court, he ordered Imām Żainu'l-Ābidīn to address them. The *Imām* went to the pulpit, then he (Imām Żainu'l-Ābidīn) praised God and blessed the Prophet of God, and he gave a speech that made the eyes full of tears and filled the hearts with fear, and he said:

> "O people, I warn you against this life and what is in it, for it is a *vanishing* place and a moving one, that moves with its people from one situation to another. Verily, the passing old centuries have vanished, the old nations which were longer in lives more than yours and made more traces than you did; they were all destroyed by the hands of time, and conquered by the snakes and the worms, all of them were destroyed by this life as if they were not its people. The dust have eaten their flesh, and removed their beauty and wasted their organs and changed their colors, and they were grinded by the hands of time. Do you wish to live after them? God forbids!! Verily you shall follow them, so, chase after what is left of your ages with the good deeds, I can see you moving from your palaces to your graves filled with unhappiness, and how many By God there was a dead man that got his regret in complete, when there is no help for those who regret and those who wrong. They found what they did, and what they had was presented, and what they did was in front of their eyes and your Lord does not do wrong to anyone. They are verily in the homes of the adversities sleeping, and in the camps of the deads are lying, and waiting for the cry of the judgement day, and the falling of the great events day that He may reward those who do evil with evil that which they have done, and reward those who do good with goodness.
>
> Oh people, we are given six and preferred by seven: we are given the wisdom and clemency and forgiveness and eloquence and bravery and the love in the hearts of the believers. And we are preferred by: from us the Prophet of God, and from us the

Righteous (Imām 'Alī) and al-Ṭayyār (Flying Man, a title for Jā'far-Ibn-Abī Ṭālib, the brother of Imām 'Alī, because he lost his both hands in war), and from us, Ḥamżah. The lion of God and His Prophet (the Prophet's uncle), and from us the two steps of this nation (the grandsons of the Prophet).

Who knew me then he knew me, and who did not know me then I shall tell him my lineage and ancestry; Oh people, I am the son of Mecca and Minā, I am the son of Żamżam and Ṣafā (*Żamżam* is a spring in Mecca and Ṣafā is a mountain there), I am the son of him who took the Žakāt by the edges of his cloak, I am the son of the best man who wore clothes, I am the son of the best man who wore sandals and walked with bare feet, I am the son of the best man who toured and walked (in pilgrimage), I am the son of the best man who did pilgrimage, I am the son of him who was carried by al-Borāq in the air (*al-Borāq*: a creature that carried the Prophet in his ascending to Heavens), I am the son of him who was carried by night from the holy Ka'bah (Mecca) to the 'Aqṣā mosque (Jerusalem), I am the son of him, who Gabriel carried him to lote-tree of the utmost boundary, I am the son of him who drew nigh and came down till he was (distant) two bows' length or even nearer, I am the son of him who prayed with the angels of heaven, I am the son of him who got the inspiration of The Glorified, I am the so of Muḥammad the Chosen. I am the son of 'Alī al-Murtazā, I am the son of him who struck the noses of the creations until they said no other god save but God, I am the son of him who struck with two swords before the Prophet of God, and stabbed with two spears, and immigrated the two immigrations, and sworn fealty for two times, and fought in Badr and Ḥunayn, and never disbelieved in God for a blink of an eye.

I am the son of the best of the faithful men, and the heir of the Prophets, and the fighter of the disbelievers, and the bee of the believers, and the light of the *Mujāhidīn* (strugglers), and the crown of the criers and the best of the worshippers and the most patient one, and the best of prayers from the Household of *Ṭāhā* and *Yāsīn*, (both chapters of holy Qur'an) that is the Prophet of the Lord of the worlds.

I am the son of him who is supported by Gabriel, that is nourished by Michael, I am the son of him the protector of the Muslims, and the killer of the heretics and those who break the oaths and the unjust, and the fighter for those who took his rights by force, and the most honourable one who walked from the whole of Quraysh, and the first one to answer God and His Prophet from the believers, and the first one (in worshipping), and the breaker of the aggressors, and the terminator of the disbelievers, and the arrow of God against the hypocrites, and the tongue of wisdom of the worshippers, and the nourisher of the religion of God and the viceroy of the Commands of God, and the garden of wisdom of God and the holder of His sciences (wisdoms). Forgiver and with bright face, gatherer of goodness and purified, mighty and satisfied, brave with courage, patient and fasting, the cutter of the lineages and the terminator of the parties (of the disbelievers). The most brave, and with the firmest feet, and with the strongest will and with the hardest power, a brave lion, that grinds them in the war when the swords are raised and the reins are close, a grinding like the stone mill and threw them away like the winds do to the grains, the lion of Ḥijāż, and the ram of Iraq. From Mecca and Medina, fought in Badr and Oḥod, an immigrant (to Medina), from 'Arabs he is their master and in the war he is the lion, and the father of the two septs (grandsons), Al-Ḥasan and Al-Ḥusain, that is my grandfather 'Alī-Ibn-Abī Ṭālib. I am the son of Fāṭimah aż-Żahrah, *Lady of Light*, I am the son of the lady of the women, I am the son of Khadījahu'l Kubrā (the holy Prophet's wife).

I am the son of him who was killed with unjust
I am the son of him whose head was cut from its back
I am the son of him who died of thirst
I am the son of him who was laid down in Karbala
I am the son of him whose cloak and turban were stolen
I am the son of him whom the angels of heaven cried upon
I am the son of him whom the djinn cried upon on earth and the birds as well in air
I am the son of him whose head presented on the tops of spears
I am the son of him, whose *harem* are toured from Iraq to Damascus."

So, he kept saying "I am, I am," until the people went on crying and weeping and Yażīd-afraid that would lead to riot so he ordered the caller for the prayer to call. Thus, when the caller said, *Allāhu'-Akbar* (God is Great). Again it was said in Ażān *Ashhadwana Lā Ilāh Ill'allāh*, then

Imām Żainu'l-Ābidīn also said that he gives the witness that God is one and He has no partner. Again the caller said in Aźān —*As͟hhadwana Muḥammadu'r Rasūla'llāh.* then Imām Żainu'l-Ābidīn, addrerssing Yażīd asked:

> "Oh Yażīd ! Tell the truth, Muḥammad is the name of your grandfather or mine. If you say that it is your grandfather's name, then your are telling a lie and if it is the name of my grandfather, then is it justified that in each and every *Ażān* and *Namāż* my grandfathers name is taken with due regards and honour and how for is it justified to behave in such a way with his family members."[55]

Then Imām Żainu'l-Ābidīn got down from the pulpit, and all of those who were in the mosque departed and gathered around Imām Żainu'l-Ābidīn.

Imām Żainu'l-Ābidīn's has told that the day when Imām Ḥusain's head was presented before Yażīd, since then he was keeping the head of Imām Ḥusain before himself, everyday regularly, in the Court, while taking liquor and meeting different people, and he was used to insult and dishonour Imām Ḥusain. One day an Ambassador from Rome was present in the Court, he asked Yażīd, whose head was there. Yażīd asked him how are you concerned with it. He said that his emperor would require to know everything after his returning there. He wished him also to join his happiness explaining him all matters. Yażīd told that it was Ḥusain's head. He further asked, who was Ḥusain'? Yażīd replied, son of Fāṭimah the daughter of the Prophet of Islām. Hearing this, that Ambassador said regretfully that his father belonged to the genealogy of Prophet David (Dāwūd). So, many generations have already rolled down between him and his. But his Christian people in their area, give due respect and honour to him and apply the sand below his foot on their own forehead. Contrary to this, in his case, he has murdered his own Prophet's grandson, while there is just one generation-gap between him and his Prophet, then he told that in his church there was a sacred box, people say that Jesus Christ's donkeys waste is kept inside it. On this score, the whole year, there remains a huge crowd of staunch Christians, who kiss it and pray. Yażīd was immensely angry, with him and he got him murdered.[56]

Any objective assessment of facts testify the unique and unparallel wisdom of Imām Ḥusain, who had foreseen the complete events well in advance and brought his family with him who became most vocal speekers among the masses for the propagation of Truth. Suppose for the sake of argument only, if even as a measure of self-interest, they had respectfully behaved with the Household of the holy Prophet and after the martyrdom of Imām Ḥusain, if they had not prevented the burial of the martyrs and had sent the Household of the holy Prophet from Karbala to Medina direct, and if the Caliph's Court had not resorted to absurdities, and if the Household of the holy Prophet had not been able to conduct effective propaganda in their own favour, the picture of the martyrdom of Imām Ḥusain and his magnanimous companions, which has emerged in the world now, would not have taken such a shape and their enemies would not have been humiliated and disgraced in the manner they have been.

Prophet's Households in the Prison

The holy Prophet of Islām's arrested family members were put into the Prison after various types of ill-treatment and taking into the Caliph's Court. It is difficult to tell how long they were imprisoned. However, keeping in view various chains of events, if the time is calculated, then the duration into the Prison comes about a year.[57] The events during their imprisonment are also less on written record. Whichever events are known, their basis are a few *Maqātil*, which have been enlisted in the Bibliography.

'Allāmah Ibn Ṭāūs (d. 1266 AD) has written that Yażīd had ordered that the family members of Imām Ḥusain may be sent at such a place, wherein there would be no protection from heat and cold. The prisoners were brought there and as long as they stayed were crying and remembering Imām Ḥusain and his Associates. They stayed there until they were not free from the Prison.[58]

Regarding the location of the prison a definite information is available that it was near the royal palace in Damascus. Perhaps, there was a big underground cell, without any roofing only, four side walls were available, no room and no shed. There was an open sky, having dew drops, smoke and sun heat.[59]

Shaykh Mufīd, Ibn Mu'allim (d. 1022 AD) has written with reference to Fāṭimah-bint-Imām Ḥusain, who told that Yażīd had made them prisoners at such a place, wherein they were living in very pathetic conditions. Because of no shelter available, they had to live in open yard, where due to sun's horrible heat during the day and bad weather our faces were practically without skin.[60]

All types of human rights were forbiden in the jail for the prisoners. Yażīd's wife Hind-bint-'Abdu'llāh-bin-'Āmir, herself was very sad and upset with the bad deeds of her husband. She came to the prison to pay regards to the Households of the Prophet of Islām, but on seeing their extremely bad condition became highly emotional.[61] The prisoners had neither any building nor any dress. The quantity of food and water send for the prisoners was so meagre that the people were suffering from hunger. It was evident from the fact that Imām Żainu'l-Ābidīn observed that his aunt Żainab was perfoming her Namāż by sitting. He wondered, because Namāż could be perfomed by sitting only when it becomes impossible to do by standing.

Sharīkatu'l Ḥusain Żainab, who was great expert in the *Fiqh*, a theologist of Islām, how she could neglect religious orders. When Imām Żainu'l-Ābidīn asked her the reason, she replied, that very meagre quantity of food supplied from Yażīd administration which was insufficient to satisfy the hunger of the children, the remaining people were getting only half-a stomach of food. As they could not get even a small quantity of food during the last batch all of them became very weak due to hunger.

On account of facing continuous hunger and thirst, Imām Ḥusain's baby daughter, Sukaynah could not survive and she took her last breath on 5th Rabī' I 61 AH (3rd December, 682 AD) in the Prison itself.

The narrators of this sad event say that in a dream she saw a grand lady riding on a horse, keeping her hands on her head. Sukaynah asked, who was she? She told that she was her grandmother Fāṭimah aż-Żahrah, *the Lady of Light,* Prophet's daughter and your father Imām Ḥusain's mother. Sukaynah requested to take her to his father, so that she could inform him what happened after him. Fāṭimah aż-Żahrah convinced, Oh sweet daughter, don't cry her heart is broken. See this dress, it is your father's. She will take this to God.[62] After two weeks of this event Sukaynah passed away.

The very innocent girl child passed away due to daily sufferings in jail. The very water available with the food only was available to wash the dead body. Thereby the prisoners were deprived of getting water for two days. Some used family cloths were given as shroud for the dead body. Her grave is located at Damascus.

Whenever Yażīd was under the influence of liquor in his Court, he used to exhibit more bad conduct and behaviour. For dishonouring the family members of the Prophet of Islām, he would call Imām Żainu'l-Ābidīn from the Prison into the his Court and talk in insulting manner. Once, he called Imām Żainu'l-Ābidīn in the Court and said that he and Courtiers wish to enjoy the wrestling between his son Khālid (11 years) Imām's son Muḥammad (5 years). Yażīd said to Muḥammad (Imām

Muḥammad al-Bāqir) that he should start wrestling with <u>Kh</u>ālid. Muḥammad said, no wrestling give the knives to both, then he will fight with <u>Kh</u>ālid. Yażīd said why not, the snakes child is only a snake. This nature is of your tradition.[63]

The talks of the family members of the Prophet of Islām at Kufa and Damascus and in the Courts of Governor 'Obaydu'llāh-bin-Żiyād and the Caliph Yażīd-bin-Mu'āwiyah had fully explained the calamity, after the martyrdom of Imām Ḥusain. Their will-power remained invincible. With physical punishments, no sign of any sort of fattering could come to them. They seemed to be helpless, but were brimming with will-power and strong determination and bent of mind. The more Yażīd wanted to suppress them, the more they were emerging. They presented successfully the objectives of Imām Ḥusain's martyrdom and they were ever-ready to protect and defend Islām.

The Prisoners Released

Yażīd was also a stern, harsh, and coarse *Nāṣibī.* He drank and was a reprobate. He inaugurated his Rule with the killing of the martyr Imām Ḥusain and closed it with the catastrophe of al-Ḥarrah.[64] He thought that he had achieved victory after martyrdom of Imām Ḥusain but after the lapse of some time, he started getting the information that Islāmic world considered him as a criminal and he had committed a very heinous sin in murdering Imām Ḥusain, which cannot be pardoned at any cost. In between mutiny started in the empire. Hence the people despised him, he was not blessed in his life, and many took up arms against him after Imām Ḥusain such as the people of Medina—they rose for the sake of God and also established separate Rules for Traitors in Mecca. All the effects of suppression by Yażīd were in vain and futile. Afterwards he became psychologically sick. His mental tension increased day by day. He had different types of dreams every night. He saw the holy Prophet of Islām also in his drear.., who was telling him being very angry, that he had murdered his son Ḥusain for no fault of him and kept all his family members in the Prison. Yażīd was shivering with his crimes. He continued to shiver for a long time even after opening his eyes. The very crying of children in the Prison made him sleepless for so many nights and days. Without sleep in nights, he would think about his bad condition. He considered himself as victorious previously, but the real winner was Imām Ḥusain, who pushed Yażīd in his own palace in a psychological prison, Yażīd decided with his condition that the holy Prophet's family members should be made free from the Prisons.

Yażīd got afraid of the riot and the reversal of the matter, he thought to fasten the exit of the prisoners, he called Imām Żainu'l-Ābidīn and told his intention. In a false attempt to get himself acquitted from his crimes, he made Kufic Governor 'Obaydu'llāh-bin-Żiyād responsible. His words are safe with history:

> "God's Curse on Ibn Marjānā (Ibn Żiyād), if I had met your father (Imām Ḥusain), whatever he could say, I would have accepted and would not have agreed for his murder. Now, whatever, was God's will has been done. Now, go to Medina and whatever is necessary, kindly keep on advising me."[65]

Yażīd's confession of sin could not missled our learned readers, who have objectively visualized all the scenes of his Court and the Prison. We would disscuss the issue of the Responsibility of Martyrdom of Imām Husain in the ensuing chapter.

Afterwards Yażīd discussed the process of the release with Imām Żainu'l-Ābidīn. He said that he can reply only after discussing with his aunt Żainab. Imâm Żainu'l-Ābidīn informed Yażīd's message. *Sharīkatu'l Ḥusain* Żainab told him to tell Yażīd that before going home the Household of the Prophet wished to mourn the demise of their beloved ones, so that first of all a house of condolence be arranged for them in which they might remember their dear ones. Thereafter, they would like to go Medina *via* Karbala.

Yażīd asked Imām Żainu'l-Ābidīn to put up three demands, which could be fulfilled[66]. He forwarded the demands as under:

> Firstly, he asked Yażīd to give him back all of the heads to bury them in their own places, and Yażīd didn't dare to refuse, so, he gave him back the head of Imām Ḥusain with the rest of the heads of his Household and companions, and he buried them with the bodies.[67]
>
> Secondly, return our goods which have been seized away. Yażīd said that he did not know the people who have looted, He might repay its three or four times compensation in the form of gold. Imām Żainu'l-Ābidīn said that he did not want his gold, but only his things in original, such as his grandmother Fāṭimah aż-Żahrah's old cloths, veil, shirt, cloak etc. Yażīd ordered to return all belongings to him. In addition Yażīd presented 200 Dinars also, which Imām Żainu'l-Ābidīn distributed among the poor people.[68]

Thirdly, Imām Żainu'l-Ābidīn asked for a helper, who could make the family members of the Prophet of Islām reach their mother-land safely. Yażīd ordered No'mān-bin-Bashīr, former Governor of Kufa and other folks to go along with them to Medina with necessary provisions.

The Household of the holy Prophet of Islām were made free on 4th Ṣafar 62 AH (13th October, 682 AD),[69] after facing various types of punishments in the jail for about a year.

Yażīd not only accepted *Sharīkatu'l Ḥusain* Żainab's request for arranging the house of condolence in his own palace itself to mourn the demise of their beloved ones but also allowed the local family ladies to participate in mourning at Yażīdī palace. All the ladies were black dressed for mourning purpose; there was no such lady in Yażīd's palace, who had not participated in the mourning.[70] It was the first phase of *'Ażādārī* (Mouring) of the Martyrdom of Karbala, which later on formalized as a big religious institution, which is prevalent in all those countries where Muslims inhabit.

Imām Ḥusain's and others heads also were returned at that time. That moment was heart melting when the particular head was received by the person concerned. Two or three days the mourning was conducted in Yażīd's palace. Then at the proposal of Imām Zainul-Aabidin, they decided to return Medina *via* Karbala.

No'mān-bin-Bashīr, who was made officer to look after the arrangements of journey, had personally a soft corner for the *Ahlu'l-Bayt* or *'Itrat,* the Progeny of the Prophet Muḥammad. On the charges of soft attitude towards Imām Ḥusain's peace-envoy Muslim-bin-'Aqīl, he was removed and 'Obaydu'llāh-bin-Żiyād was appointed Kufic Governor in his place. No'mān-bin-Bashīr took the family members of Prophet along with 30 bodyguards with due honours from Damascus to Karbala.

It has been mentioned in the previous pages that the Progeny of the Prophet Muḥammad was brought as the Prisoners to Damascus by the Yażīdī Army in a round about way covering the long route of Al-Jażīrah, the distance of about 950 miles (1,320 kms). The reason of the same has already discussed. But now in the changed situation too, they the took the way, wherein there was no colony at all, then no place, no town. It shows they were still in the grip of fear complex that Muslim Ummah would attack on them. However, a shortest route, covering 455 miles (732 km) from Damascus to Karbala, they took, as under:

Damascus→Ruṭubah→Bādiyah-Shām→ 'Ain-Tumur →Karbala.

Again in Karbala

The Caravan of family members of the holy Prophet of Islām reached Karbala on 20th Ṣafar 62 AH (8th November, 682 AD).[71] When they reached the location, they found the famous Companion of the Prophet, Jābir-bin-'Abdu'llāh Anṣārī and some folk from the Hāshimites, and some men from the Household of the Prophet and they all came to visit the grave of Imām Ḥusain, and they all came at one time and met each other, the cries and weeping and slapping the faces and they made a mourning for some days. [72]

As reported from 'Aṭiyyahu'l-'Aufī that he went out with Jābir-bin-'Abdu'llāh Anṣārī to visit the grave of Imām Ḥusain, and when they arrived at Karbala, Jābir went to the bank of Alqmah and made a wash and then wear a cloth around his waist, and wore another cloth, and then opened a pocket with some perfume and got some of it on his body, and then he walked to the holy grave with bare feet, and didn't step one step without mentioning the name of God, and when he reached the grave he said: make me touch it, as he was a blind man. Then 'Aṭiyyah made him touch the grave, and then he fell down on the grave and went in a coma, so, he sprankled some water on him, and when he woke up, said three times, "Oh Ḥusain !" and then said, Oh beloved one that doesn't answer his lover!! Then he said, and how shall he answer? With his blood of the neck dropping down on his back, and his head was separated from his body, Verily, he was the son of the best of the Prophets, and the son of the master of Viceroys, and the son of him who is the ally to the faithful and the son of the guidance, and the fifth of the people of the cover (cloak), referring to the story in which the Prophet Muḥammad gathered his daughter, Fāṭimah aż-Żahrah, *Lady of Light,* her husband, 'Alī-ibn-Abī Ṭālib and their sons Ḥasan and Ḥusain under one cloak and he was one of them and the Prophet prayed for them. Then Jābir-bin-'Abdu'llāh looked around the grave and said, Peace upon him Oh souls that gathered around Al-Ḥusain and settled in his place.

'Aṭiyyahu'l-'Aufī says in the meantime they saw blackness on the horizon and suspected some army coming from the direction of Damascus. Jābir-bin-'Abdu'llāh looked to his slave and said to enquire what is this blackness? If they were the men of 'Obaydu'llāh-bin-Żiyād, then get back soon, so, that they may find a shelter. He retuned immediately and slapping himself told, Stand up, Oh Jābir ! and receive the *Ḥarem* of the Prophet of Islām, that was their master and lord Imām Żainu'l-Ābidīn has arrived with his aunts and his sisters. Then Jābir stood up and walked with bare feet and uncovering his head got closer to Imām

Żainu'l-Ābidīn, who asked, if he was Jābir? He replied, Yes, Oh son of the Prophet of God. Then he said, Oh Jābir, verily here his men were killed, and children were slain, and women were taken prisoners and the tents were burnt. And like they could hear *Sharīkatu'l Ḥusain* Żainab-bint-Imām 'Alī, saying:

> "Oh settlers in Karbala! do you have the tidings about our dead people and what are their banners,
>
> What is the condition of a corpse of a dead man in your lands that remained for three days with no single visitor,
>
> By God have you buried it in the ground and did its remains got into the grave?"

Then Żainab went to the grave of her brother Abā 'Abdillāhu'l Ḥusain weeping and crying, while the daughters of the Prophet were moving from the grave of Imām Ḥusain to the grave of Abu'l-Fażl'il-'Abbās-bin-Imām 'Alī. Żainab also expressed her sincere gratitude towards all the pilgrims and her salute to Jābir-bin-'Abdu'llāh.

Some ladies and gents too of neighbouring places assembled after observing them, who were going on consoling the demises, Żainab used to elaborate all the facts before all the people present, which continued for three days. It resulted into the tradition of mourning of the martyrs, which may be called the second phase of *'Ażādārī*, which has been commenced at the very palace of Yażīd at Damascus. Ḥabāb Kalbī has described that he heard every night such voices of crying rising, with which it seemed that so many people were loudly going on telling *Mithāl-Rasūlu'l-Ḥabīban* (Beloved part of holy Prophet) even after the departure of the Household of the Prophet from Karbala.[73]

Historians tell that the Household of the holy Prophet remained for 3 days in the land of Karbala, and after that they headed to Medina. But Imām Ḥusain's wife Rabāb-bint-Imarau'l Qays Kalbī, who was with Imām Ḥusain was imprisoned along with the other people of the family from Damascus, preferred not to leave the grave of her husband Imām Ḥusain alone at Karbala and she stayed there itself. For one full year she lived with the grave of her husband, Imām Ḥusain at Karbala. Nights and days she was weeping remembering Imām Ḥusain. After the full whole year, she returned to Mẹdina and joined other family member.[74]

Return to Medina

Perhaps, on 23th Ṣafar, 62 AH (11th November, 682 AD),[75] Household of the holy Prophet returned to Medina, under the supervision of Yażīdī enovy No'mān-bin-Bashīr and his 30 body guards army, in a way covering the common route of the distance of about the distance between Karbala and Medina of 1,100 miles (1,700 km) as under:

Karbala → Naynwān → Qaṭqaṭ ānah → Qaṣru'l Banī Maqātil → 'Ażību'l Hijānat → Ummu'l Qurūn → Mughīthiyah → Hamām → Masījad → Bayzah → Jabal-Żī-Ḥasam → Abū-Misk → Sharrāf → Waqṣah → 'Omiyah → Baṭnu'l 'Oqbah → Żabālah → Shaqūq → Baṭnu'l'Oqbah → Tha'labiyah → Żarwud → Khuzaymiya → Ajfar → Nūż → Sambrā' → Ḥājaż → Nuqrah → Mughīthah-Mā'wān → Rabżah → Żu'l-Qiṣṣah → Medina.

The group of remaining Houeholds of the holy Prophet of Islām, who were alive after the Battle of Karbala, reached Medina on 20th Rabī I, 62 AH (7th December, 681 AD).[76]

And when Household of the holy Prophet got closer to Medina, before entering into the town they were stopped at the orders of Imām Żainu'l-Ābidīn at the outskirts. People got down from their conveyance. they settled down there and Imām Żainu'l-Ābidīn looked at Bishr-bin-Khoṭ Hamadānī and said, May God have mercy upon his father, Verily, he was a poet, so, he would be able to say some thing? He replied in affirmative that Oh son of the Prophet, he was verily a poet. Imām Żainu'l-Ābidīn send the grief-message of Imām Ḥusain's matyrdom to Medina people and then Bishr went to Medina to mourn Imām Ḥusain and his companion martyrs. Bishr mounted on his horse, and ran until he got into Medina, and when he reached the *Masjidu'l-Nabvī* (Mosque of the Prophet) he raised his voice with weeping and said:

> "O people of Yathrib (Medina) no settling for you in it Imām Ḥusain has been killed so cry in abundance. The body is in Karbala covered with blood and his head on the spears is moved all arround."[77]

Then Bishr announced to the people of Medina, that 'Alī-Ibnu'l-Ḥusain with his aunts and sisters has reached into your vicinity and settled down in your landand he is his messenger to them to let you know his place. Hearing of my voice all the ladies came out carrying. Such a horrible and more painful day was not seen by any Muslim.[78] Bishr says that not a single noble woman stayed in her home, and all of them went out slapping their faces and praying for the punishment of the killers, and he had not seen criers as much as it was on that day. He heard a maid crying and saying:

> "Mourner mourned my master and hurt me and made me sick a moruner who mourned him and shocked me
>
> Thus, my eyes, cry a lot and pour the tears and be generous with the tears after your tears altogether
>
> Over the son of the Prophet and the son of his Viceroy though even he is far inlands that are far away from us."[79]

Bishr says that the people left him and went to meet the Houshold of the Prophet, so, he struck his horse to get back to them, and he had found the people took seats along the roads and the streets, so, he got down from his horse and passed through the necks of people until he got closer to the tent and 'Alī-ibnu'l-Ḥusain was inside, then he went out holding a kerchief wiping his tears, and behind him was his servant with a chair. So, he put it down for him, and he sat down and couldn't hold his tears, and the people raised their voices with tears and cries and gave solace from every corner, and that spot got condensed with the noise, and then he signed with his hand to let them be silent, and so, they did, then he said:

> "Praise for God, Lord of the Worlds, Master of the Day of Judgement, the Initiator of the whole creation, who got far and raised up in high Heavens, and got closer and knew the secrets, we shall praise Him for the great adversities and the troubles of time, and pains of disasters and for the bitterness of matters and the greatness of the troubles. Oh people, Verily God had—and praise to Him—tested us with great troubles, and a hole in Islām that is great, Abā 'Abdillāh was killed with his Household, and his women were imprisoned with his children, and his head was toured around the lands over the pikes, and this is the trouble that nothing is like it. Oh people, who of your men will be glad after killing him, or what heart shall not be sad for him, or what eye shall keep the tear from falling? Verily, the seven heavens cried for his death, and seas cried with its waves, and the Heavens with its corners, and the earth with its lands, and the trees with its branches, and the whales in the depth of the sea, and the closer angels, and the rest of the folks of heavens. Oh

> people, what heart wouldn't be broken for his death? Or what heart doesn't miss him, or what hearing that doesn't go deaf after hearing about such hole in Islām? Oh people, we've became banished and scattered in all lands like the children of slaves, for no crime we did, and no mistake we committed and no change in the laws of Islām we did, and we have never heard about such a thing among our ancestors, verily this is only an innovation. By God, if the Prophet of God went to fight them as much as he advised them about us, they wouldn't do much more than this. Verily, we are to God and we shall be back to Him. What a great adversity, and what painful one is it, and what a horrible one is it, and we shall depend on God for what befell us, verily He is Great and a revenge Taker."[80]

Then Imām Żainu'l-Ābidīn went to Medina and found it like ghosts town and its people mourning, and found the houses of his family empty, and mourning about its inhabitants.

As for the granddaughters of the Prophet they went to the house of Imām Ḥusain, then Umm Kul<u>th</u>ūm-bint-Imām 'Alī called and said:

> "City of our grandfather don't accept us verily we came with sadness and losses
>
> We've been out from you in numbers and came back with no men or sons."[81]

<u>Sh</u>arīkatu'l Ḥusain Żainab's husband 'Abdu'llāh-bin-Ja'far Ṭayyār heard about the martyrdom of his two sons, 'Aun and Muḥammad and he Thanked God, who had given him the honour of being part of the martyrdom of Ḥusain, when it was not physically possible for him to offer his life for Ḥusain, his both sons have successfully done that job and honoured him.[82]

Prophet's savior uncle, Abī Ṭālib family's honourable lady Umm Luqmān, who was niece of Imām Ḥusain and Kufa's martyr Muslim, along with some other ladies of the family came outside the house for welcoming them. Her head was open, she was adjusting her veil and was asking from people, What reply would they give to Prophet when he would ask them that they are among his followers and how they have behaved with his Household, when some of them were prisoners and some were wet with blood.

Imām Żainu'l-Ābidīn was alive for 33 years after the event of Karbala. He observed daily *Rożāh* (Fasting). Every evening at the ending time, food-water were brought before him. It recalled the sad memory when children were deprived of food-water etc. and had been crying, "Water, Water, Water!"

He could never relinquish that memory. He would start weeping and say that Prophet's son Ḥusain was murdered hungry and thirsty. Imām Żainu'l-Ābidīn attempted in a planned manner for making in a meaning full way of the objective of Imām Ḥusain, which would be discussed in the eensuing chapter at the appropriate places.

Notes and References

1. Tārīkhu'r-Rusūl wa'l-Mulūk, vol. 6, p. 260.
2. Taṣwīr-i-Karbala, p. 83.
3. Shahīd-i-Insāniyat, p. 524; Ḥusainī Inqalab, p. 97.
4. Luhūf 'Alā Qatlu'l Ṭafūf, p. 59.
5. Luhūf 'Alā Qatlu'l Ṭafūf, Tradition No. 222, 223.
6. al-Akhbāru'ṭ Ṭawāl, p. 256.
7. Shahīd-i-Insāniyat, p. 523.
8. Tārīkhu'r-Rusūl wa'l-Mulūk, vol. 6, p. 226.
9. Luhūf 'Alā Qatlu'l Ṭafūf, p. 71.
10. Shahīd-i-Insāniyat, p. 526.
11. Shahīd-i-Insāniyat, p. 527.
12. Shahīd-i-Insāniyat, p. 527.
13. Bihāru'l-Anwār, vol. 2, p. 12.
14. Bihāru'l-Anwār, vol. 2, p. 12; Shahīd-i-Insāniyat, p. 528.
15. Luhūf 'Alā Qatlu'l Ṭafūf, p. 61; Bihāru'l-Anwār, vol. 1, p. 12.
16. Luhūf 'Alā Qatlu'l Ṭafūf, p. 61; Bihāru'l-Anwār,vol. 1, p. 12.
17. Luhūf 'Alā Qatlu'l Ṭafūf, p. 64.
18. Luhūf 'Alā Qatlu'l Ṭafūf, p. 65.
19. Bihāru'l-Anwār, vol. 1, p. 12; Shahīd-i-Insāniyat, p. 528.
20. Luhūf 'Alā Qatlu'l Ṭafūf, p. 65.
21. Shahīd-i-Insāniyat, p. 529.
22. Bihāru'l-Anwār, vol. 1, p. 20.
23. Luhūf 'Alā Qatlu'l Ṭafūf, p. 69.
24. al-Irshād fī Ma'rifat Ḥujjāj Allāh 'Alā 'Ibād, p. 259.
25. Tārīkhu'r-Rusūl wa'l-Mulūk, vol. 6, p. 262.
26. Tārīkhu'r-Rusūl wa'l-Mulūk, vol. 6, p. 264.
27. Luhūf 'Alā Qatlu'l Ṭafūf, p. 69.
28. al-Irshād fī Ma'rifat Ḥujjāj Allāh 'Alā 'Ibād, p. 260.
29. al-Akhbāru'ṭ Ṭawāl, p. 257; al-Irshād fī Ma'rifat Ḥujjāj Allāh 'Alā 'Ibād, p. 260; Tārīkhu'r-Rusūl wa'l-Mulūk, vol. 6, p. 264.
30. *The distance has been decided, as measured in the enclosed Map.–Author.*
31. Bihāru'l-Anwār, vol. 1, p. 35.
32. Tārīkhu'r-Rusūl wa'l-Mulūk vol. 6, p. 264.

33. Luhūf 'Alā Qatlu'l Ṭafūf, p. 61; Ḥayātu'l Ḥaywan vol. 1, p. 53; Bihāru'l-Anwār, vol. 2, p. 136; Tārīkh-i-A'imah, p. 265.
34. Bihāru'l-Anwār, vol. 2, p. 28.
35. Courtesy: Āyatu'llāh Shaykh Naṣru'llāh (Aleppo).
36. A Glossary of the Tribes and Castes of Punjab and North-West Frontier Povinces, vol. 2, p. 142.
37. Shahīdān-i-Karbala Ke Fidāī Hindū, p. 2.
38. A Glossary of the Tribes and Castes of Punjab and North-West Frontier Povinces, vol. 2, p. 142.
39. Shahīdān-i-Karbala Ke Fidāī Hindū, p. 2.
40. Bihāru'l-Anwār, vol. 2, p. 138.
41. Bihāru'l-Anwār, vol. 2, p. 130
42. Luhūf 'Alā Qatlu'l Ṭafūf, p. 73.
43. *Instead of a short route of 461 miles (750 kms) in between Kufa and Damascus, Yażīdī Army took long route of 850 miles (1,350 kms) for the reasons already discussed at appropriate place. They reached Yażīdī capital Damascus on 13th November 680.*—Author.
44. Shahīd-i-Insāniyat, p. 537.
45. Shahīd-i-Insāniyat, p. 538.
46. Bihāru'l-Anwār, vol. 2, p. 130.
47. Tārīkhu'r-Rusūl wa'l-Mulūk, vol. 6, p. 265.
48. Bihāru'l-Anwār, vol. 2, p. 45.
49. Luhūf 'Alā Qatlu'l Ṭafūf, p. 75; Bihāru'l-Anwār, vol. 2, p. 35.
50. Bihāru'l-Anwār, vol. 2, p. 35.
51. al-Uṣūl-min 'al-Kāfī, vol. 1, p. 503; Bihāru'l-Anwār, vol. 2, pp. 35-36 .
52. Bihāru'l-Anwār, vol. 2, p. 38.
53. Tārīkhu'r-Rusūl wa'l-Mulūk vol. 6, p. 267.
54. al-Kāmil fī' t-Tārīkh
55. Bihāru'l-Anwār, vol. 2, p. 40.
56. Bihāru'l-Anwār, vol. 2, p. 44.
57. *The basis of our calculation has been as follows:*
   Departured from Karbala on 12th Muḥarram 61 AH (12th October, 681 AD); Reached Kufa on 14th Muḥarram 61 AH (14th October, 681 AD)
   Departured from Kufa on 20th Muḥarram 61 AH (20th October, 681 AD); Reached Damascus on 14th Ṣafar 61 AH (13th November, 681 AD)
   The Prisoners were circumambulated to various roads, lanes and markets of Damascus and then produced before the Caliph Court of Yażīd. Sukayna-bint-Imām Ḥusain died on 5th Rabī' I 61 AH (3rd December, 682 AD) in the Prison. Released on 4th Ṣafar 62 AH (13th October 682 AD) Reached again Karbala on 20th Ṣafar 62 AH (8th November, 682 AD) from Damascus. The distance between Damascus to Karbala was 455 miles (732 km). Approx. 12-13 days journey. Reached Karbala on 20th Ṣafar 62 AH (8th November, 682 AD).
   Hence, the duration at the Prison of Damascus was about a year: from 14th Ṣafar 61 AH (13th November, 681 AD) to 4th Ṣafar, 62 AH (23th October, 682 AD)—Author.

58. Luhūf 'Alā Qatlu'l Ṭafūf, p. 79.
59. Bihāru'l-Anwār, vol. 2, p. 42.
60. al-Amālī: Shaykh Mufīd, p. 72.
61. Żainab-i-Kubrā, p. 273.
62. Luhūf 'Alā Qatlu'l Ṭafūf, p. 79.
63. Bihāru'l-Anwār, vol. 2, p. 45.
64. Siyar 'Alāmu'l-Nubalā, vol. 4, pp. 37-38.
65. al-Irshād fī Ma'rifat Ḥujjāj Allāh 'Alā 'Ibād, p. 263; Tārīkhu'r-Rusūl wa'l-Mulūk, vol. 6, p. 266.
66. Bihāru'l-Anwār, vol. 2, p. 46.
67. Ḥabīb-us-Siyar.
68. Luhūf 'Alā Qatlu'l Ṭafūf, p. 82.
69. *No confirmed date is available in the history. This date is based on my conclusion, keeping in view the fact that Prophet's Household stayed for 2-3 days at Damascus after release. Then went Karbala, covering 455 miles (732 km). They would have reached there in approx 12 days: that is they reached Karbala on 20th Ṣafar 62 AH (8th November, 682 AD), which is undisputed and confirmed date. It has been mentioned by every historian. So, the date of release from the Prison at Damascus may be 4th Ṣafar 62 AH (13th October, 682 AD).* —Author
70. Tārīkhu'r-Rusūl wa'l-Mulūk, vol. 6, p. 289.
71. *This is undisputed date. Every one has mentioned as suh.* —Author
72. Luhūf 'Alā Qatlu'l Ṭafūf, p. 83.
73. al-Iṣābah fī Tamayyażu'ṣ-Ṣaḥābah, vol. 1, p. 113.
74. al-Iṣābah fī Tamayyażu'ṣ-Ṣaḥābah, vol. 1, p. 113.
75. *This date is based on my calculations.* —Author
76. *Generally, the date 8th Rabī I 62 AH (25th November, 681 AD) is prevalent, which appears to be incorrect. Perhaps, when the Mouring Period of the extended from 'Arb'īn (20th Ṣafar), it was coined at Ovadh Kingdom. I could not found any authentic reference to confirm the said date. Morever, on the basis of the period of jouney it also appears to be impossible, because of the fact that the distance between Karbala and Medina is 1,100 miles (1,700 km). The then travel speed of the camels' caravan was 30-40 miles per day. Imām Żainu'l-Ābidīn's carvan travelled 1,100 miles in approx. a month's time so, if journey commenced on 23th Ṣafar 62 AH (11th November, 682 AD), the arrival at Medina on 20th Rabī I 62 AH (7th December, 681 AD) sounds correct.* —Author
77. al-Akhbāru'ṭ Ṭawāl, p. 258.
78. Tārīkhu'r-Rusūl wa'l-Mulūk, vol. 6, p. 291.
79. Luhūf 'Alā Qatlu'l Ṭafūf, p. 86; Tārīkhu'r-Rusūl wa'l-Mulūk, vol. 6, p. 221.
80. Bihāru'l-Anwār, vol. 1, pp 49-50.
81. Bihāru'l-Anwār, vol. 2, p. 77.
82. Tārīkhu'r-Rusūl wa'l-Mulūk, vol. 6, p. 292.

Chapter: Eight

The Magnificent Living Martyrs

The social solidarity is apparent in all aspects of Prophet Muḥammad's message. The history of mankind shows that few societies have developed as strong a sense of solidarity or have co-operated as closely or acted as mercifully as have the Islāmic societies. There seems to be a feeling of social responsibility in various stages of the Ḥusainī Revolution. In fact Imām Ḥusain had assessed the condition of the Islāmic society in 60 AH (680 AD), and came to the conclusion that the Muslims had deviated so, much that their reformation and the removal of the dangerous social evils were not possible without such a rising and such a sacred movement. Imām Ḥusain was feeling that the religion of Islām and the Muslim Ummah could not survive without a rising and carnage. It was, therefore, necessary that he should be martyred and his relatives and sisters who may be called the best orators of Islām. *Sharīkatu'l Ḥusain* Żainab, Umm Kulthūm-bint-Imām 'Alī, Fāṭimah-bint-Imām Ḥusain, Imām 'Alī-ibnu'l-Imām Ḥusain, *Imām Żainu'l-Ābidīn* should be taken prisoners and be made to pass through the streets so that they might invite the attention of the Muslim Ummah to the disgraceful state of affairs of that time, and save the humanity in general and Muslims in particular from the danger of death and extinction for ever, might keep alive the sacred movement, which existed since the time prior to Imām Ḥusain, and might pave the path for such sacred movements in future.

The learned readers may now witness the farsightedness of Imām Ḥusain. The humble author endeavours to allude some basic points about the movements raised by Imām Ḥusain. It has been inferred as the causes of and the incentives to the movement of Karbala from the speeches and writings of Imām Ḥusain himself.

It is not easy to risk one's life. History has recorded many incidents where people relinquish all thought of fighing against evil. The Companions of the holy Prophet, who have been considered most reverend, the Divine verses say about them:

> "When fighting was prescribed for them, lo ! a party of them fear men as *(it shall be)* the fear of God, or even *(with)* a greater fear and say, O' Our Lord ! Why hast Thou ordained upon us fighting, Thou not grant us respite to a near end."
>
> (*Qur'an*: 4/ 77)

In the same way when the holy Prophet decided for Battle of Badr (623 AD), then fear spread on so many of his Companions that the people usually locked themselves in their own houses. Then Qur'an's verse came:

> "Fight then in God's way; it is not imposed (*on any*) except in relation to thyself; and stir up the faithful, may be God will restrain in might of those who disbelieve". (*Qur'an*: 4/84)

On this occasion it would be appropriate to discuss about the newly associates of Imām 'Alī-Ibn-Abī Ṭālib, who had joined him after his becoming the Caliph (in 656 AD), were leaving no stone unturned to declare themselves as his best supporters. Later on a group among them openly opposed Imām 'Alī and were called Khārijī (schismatics, out-casted) in history, with whom Imām 'Alī himself fought in the Battle of Nahrwān (657 AD). Besides them, there was a large section of people, addressing them Imām 'Alī himself expressed his unhappiness and used to say, When you are asked for *Jihād* you tell, this is a severe winter season and request for time, so, that cold waves could be reduced and when you are asked in summer, then you say that it is a severe summer now, please give us this much of time that summer may come down. Regretted! You are running away from summer and winter, how much more you would suffer on the tip of sword.[1] Imām Ḥasan's comrades put into risk his very life on the occasion of war.[2]

If you look upon the enemies of Imām Ḥusain at Karbala, Amīr Mu'āwiyah was none other than the very brother-in-law of the Prophet of Islām and his father Abū Sufyyān, the very father-in-law. The Commander-in-Chief of the Yażīdī Army 'Omar-bin-Sa'd in Karbala was none other than Prophet's mother Ḥazrat Āminah's close relative. The relatives are burning sticks, when they are separate, they produce smoke and when they meet start fooling jealousy!

Just opposite to these people were those, whom Imām Ḥusain-Ibn-Imām 'Alī-Ibn-Abī Ṭālib had brought in Karbala, burning forest after screening them. Whether they were elderly or youth, boys or ladies men or women, they were all faithfully loyal and true one better than the other, highly virtuous, can did and of spotless character, duty minded, obedient and dedicated to Imām Ḥusain. All people who joined the revolution along with Imām Ḥusain, whether they were associates or family members in maintaining their duties and responsibilities, seem to be the complements of each other. When at the early stage of the spread of Islām, Prophet Muḥammad's uncle Abī Ṭālib scarificed everything for his nephew Muḥammad, in saving his life and propagating his mission named Islām, Abī Ṭālib's entire heirs, grandsons-daughters, their family members, childrens, babies all of them, entire heirs sacrificed everything in preserving the standards of humanity raised by the Prophet himself. It again happened at Karbala under the successful leadership of his grandson Imām Ḥusain.

Imām Ḥusain statement regarding his matchless supporters and family members is safeguarded in pages of history, he said:

> "It should be known that I do not know anybody's friends are more grateful and better and their relatives more fortunate dutiful than mine. God may bless you all !"[3]

This statement of Imām Ḥusain proved to be cent-per-cent true at the Battle of Karbala. Islāmic revival could only be possible due to the matchless sacrifices of Imām Ḥusain and his comrades.

Besides the close relatives of Imām Ḥusain the other people also joined in the great sacrifice at Karbala, who were also no ordinary and unknown personalities. The personalities of these martyrs and their bringing at various stages, could not be possible here. Only a few specimens and highly valuable facts can be presented. Imām Ḥusain and every personality of his Associates has filed his hands on the basis of diversity in the history. There were different specialist, they were of various groups and families and races. There were gents and ladies also, there were elders, youngsters and babies too. They were with their families and also represented alone. There was uniformity on this basis only that all belonged to the highest state, standing on the highest pedestals, highly religious dedicated and highly cautious towards their duties and responsibilities.

They were truly dedicated to Imām Ḥusain and his family members. They were ever ready to sacrifice their own life for preserving and safeguarding Islām. They were resolved to the core towards truth and peace, but were just like a very strong wall against injustice and atrocities. It was also a success of Imām Ḥusain that he was able to assemble all those scattered pearls into a vault and a garland studded with jewels. If Imām Ḥusain is the rising sun on Islāmic horizon then all his associates are rays of the same sun, with whom the Ḥusainī Revolution is bright.

The Sacred Names of Martyrs

As already discussed at the appropriate places in the previous pages that the historians, writers and scholars are not unanimous in enlisting the names of the Martyrs of Karbala, but the most commonly accepted figure has been 72, which is mentioned by many writers and scholars[4] and after cutting the heads of the martyrs, when Yażīdī Army counted the heads, which were put up at the tip of spears, they were 72 in number.[5]

The other main source for ascertaining the names of the martyrs is *Żiyārat-Nāḥiyah*[6] and some of the other recognised books.[7] Because of being received from last twelver Imām Mahadī Āk͟hiru'ż-Żamān (b. 870 AD), for that reason, it is most authentic document. It is considered as the voice of Imām Āk͟hiru'ż-Żamān, in which he himself, has praised 79 martyrs and he has also admonished the murderers of some of the martyrs. There is also an appropriate review of Karbala events. But, some famous Martyr's names are also not available. It is the only *Żiyārat-Nāḥiyah* which mentions the Martyrs of Karbala by name, and in some cases it also gives the names of those who slew them and throws light upon some of the circumstances of their martyrdom.

Other sources indicate some different figures, such as 145 (45 Cavalry plus 100 Infantry),[8] 110 (18 Hās͟himite plus 92 other clans)[9], 111,[10] 147[11] and so on. As the issue has already been discussed in Chapter Five of the ensuing book, need not be repeated again.

We have reached to the figure of 135 on the basis of our exhaustive research work on the subject. But some names of other similar figures or nearer are different. Our figure comprises 126 martyrs of Karbala, deducting 9 persons, i.e. 3 survivors of Karbala, plus 5 martyrs of Kufa plus 1 martyr in the Prison of Damascus.

Why Different Figures

If pondering over the causes of difference in figure, we find the basic figure to be 72, which has had been the most popularly accepted by all.

There may be every possibility that others may have joined them later on, which has also been supported by the incidents in which people came to join with Imām Ḥusain. The figure 72 became more authentic when the Yażīdī Army picked up at the tip of spears the heads of 72 martyrs, and these 72 heads were circumambulated from Karbala to Kufa and then from Kufa to Damascus. Everywhere in markets, in roads and royal Court people saw the heads of 72 martyrs, so it became all accepted figure.

Various Groups of the Martyrs

For the purpose of the identification of the martyrs, it would be proper to simplify the process according to popular perception as under:

1. *The Basic Figure*: The Martyrs of Karbala are generally known as 72; that is, 32 Infantry and 40 Cavalry men.[12] It is classified as:

Descendants of Abū Ṭālib	=	18
Asadī	=	11
Anṣārī	=	6
Kindī and Ghaffārī	=	5
Tamīmī and Ṭaī	=	5
Bajalī and Khith'amī	=	4
Kalbī	=	4
Ja'fī	=	4
Ażdī	=	3
'Abdī	=	3
Juhanī and Tamīmī	=	3
Taghlabī	=	2
Miscellaneous	=	4

   Needless to emphesise that all the compilers of above *Basic Figures* have committed a mistake in mentioning the 'Juhni and Tamīmī' as 3. Actually it is 2, because the name of martyr 'Oqbah-bin-Ṣulet Juhanī has repeated at serial nos. 66 and 68. With a view to keep the figure 72 intact, the name of lone fimale martyr Umm Wahab-bint-Ma'bad may be added, who was also martyred with her husband 'Abdu'llāh-bin-'Omayr *alias* Wahab-Kalbī, whose name is included in the list of 72 martyrs. *The Basic Figure* is being marked as *, in the list.
2. *Żiyārat-Nāḥiyah,* (79 persons), marked as✓, in the list.

3. *Added Names* (34 persons), without whom no list may be completed, marked as +, in the list.
   (i) *Martyrs of Kufa*: 4 Persons, i.e. Muslim-bin-'Aqīl, 'Ammarah-bin-Salkhab, Ḥānī-bin-'Orwah, Ibrāhīm-bin-Muslim-bin-'Aqīl (Whereas names of 'Abdu'l 'Olā and Qays-bin-Muṣahar, who were also killed outside Karbala are included in the list.)
   (ii) *Female Martyrs*: 2 Persons, i.e. Umm Wahab-bint-Ma'bad, wife of Wahab-Kalbī, whose martyrdom has been mentioned by every historian and Sukayna-bint-Imām Ḥusain, also martyred in the Prison of Damascus.
   (iii) *Hurr's Companions:* 4 Persons, i.e. Muṣa'b-bin-Yażīd Riyāḥī (brother), 'Alī-bin-Ḥurr (son), Sa'd-bin-Ḥurr (son) and Qurrah (the servant).
   (iv) *Joined during journey:* 1 Person, i.e. 'Āyiż-bin-Mujama'-bin-'Abdu'llāh 'Āyiżī, who had joined along with his father at 'Ażību'l Hijānāt.
   (v) *Martyrs of CowardlyAttack or thereafter:* 17 Persons, i.e. Adaham-bin-Umayyah 'Abdī Baṣarī, 'Omarū-bin-Zab'aitah-bin-Qays-bin-Th'albah Zab'ī Taymī, Ḥabāb-bin-'Āmir-bin-Ka'b Tayamī, Ḥabshatah-bin-Qays Nahamī, Ḥallās-bin-'Omarū, Ḥanẓalah-bin-'Omar Shaybānī, Ḥārith-bin-Nibhān, Kardūs-bin-Żuhayr, Mujama'-bin-Żiyād-bin-'Omarū-Jehnī, Munī'-bin-Żiyād, Muslim-bin-Kathīr Ṣadafi Ażdī, Naṣar-bin-Abī Nīżar, Rāf'a-bin-'Abdu'llāh, Swaid-bin'Omar-bin-Abī Maṭaal Khath'amī, Umayyah-bin-Sa'd-bin-Żaid Ṭaī, 'Obbād-bin-Muhājir-bin-Abīu'l-Muhājir Juhanī Żiyād-bin-'Arīb Hamadānī.
   (vi) *Survivors*: 3 Persons, i.e. Ḥasan Muthannā-bin-Imām Ḥasan, 'Oqbah-bin-Sama'n Zaḥāq-bin-'Abdu'llāh Mashriqī.
4. *The largest contribution*: Abī Ṭālib's 24 grandsons and 1 grand-dauther (25 persons), sacrified their life for the cause of Truth, marked as ¤, in the list.

If we give due attention to the list of these valient Martyrs of the Ḥusainī Revolution, then we will come to know that 25 Martyrs from among them are the descendants of Ḥazrat Abū Ṭālib alone. There were 17 children of his son Imām 'Alī and his other sons has 8 children. Not only Karbala-event, but also in whole history of Islām no family had sacrificed such a large number of their own family members as this in safeguarding Islām. A discussion of wonderful sacrifice and dedication is available in the history of Islām, when there was a fear of severe attack on the life of the holy Prophet of Islām in Mecca; it was from the leadership of Abū Sufyyān (Amīr Mu'āwiyah's father and Yażīd's grandfather) that the holy Prophet of Islām could be murdered while sleeping in any night, then Prophet's uncle Abū Ṭālib-bin-'Abdu'l-Mṭṭalib waking up the holy Prophet of Islām from his sleep in night, and when required, putting in his place his sons one by one down on his bed. If at all anybody has to be murdered then any of his sons might be murdered, but his nephew Prophet Muḥammad should be alive and he should be saved at any cost. In Mecca the followers felt their duty to protect the life of their Master, Prophet of Islām. In Karbala, there was a duty of protecting the life of the Islāmic religion itself, then Abū Ṭālib's entire family had sacrificed their own life.

We have also taken minute care of the exact pronunciation of the names of the Martyrs and their Enemies and have recorded them according to internationally accepted principle of having as pronounced in its original form. Only such names have been discussed in this list whom the scholars and writers have been discussing continuously. In spite of maintaining all sorts of care, it is possible that some fault may be left in our attempt, some names would not have been included. In such a situation, we would remain seeking pardon for ever from those great personalities and sacred-souls. In our opinion, in the list of Martyrs of the Ḥusainī Revolution Kufa's martyrs should be certainly included. We have included those prominent names.

The Heads of the Ḥusainī Army

✓* ¤ 1. Imām Ḥusain: *Doyen of Martyrs, Lord of Muslims, Divine Caliph*

+ ¤ 2. Muslim-bin-'Aqīl-bin-Abī Ṭālib: *Peace-Envoy to Kufa*

✓ * ¤ 3. Abu'l-Fażl'il-'Abbās -bin-Imām 'Alī: *Commander-in-Chief*

✓ * 4. Ḥabīb-bin-Mażāhir Asadī: *Commander, Left-Wing Regiment*

✓ * 5. Żuhayr-bin-Qayn-bin-Qays Numayrī Bajalī: *Commander, Right-Wing Regiment.*

Others of the Ḥusainī Army

* 6. 'Abdu'llāh-bin-Bishr Khith'amī

✓*¤ 7. 'Abdu'llāh-bin-Imām 'Alī

✓*¤ 8. 'Abdu'llāh-bin-Imām Ḥasan

✓*¤ 9. 'Abdu'llāh-bin-Muslim-bin-'Aqīl-bin-Abī Ṭālib
✓* 10. 'Abdu'llāh-bin-'Orwah-bin-Ḥarrāq Ghaffārī
✓* 11. 'Abdu'llāh-bin-'Omayr Kalbī alias Wahab-Kalbī
* 12. 'Abdu'llāh-bin-Yaqṭar
✓ 13. 'Abdu'llāh-bin-Żayd-bin-Thabayṭ Qaysī
* 14. 'Abdu'r Raḥmān-bin-'Abd Rab Anṣarī Khiżarajjī
✓ * 15. 'Abdu'r Raḥmān-bin-'Abdu'llāh-bin-Kadan Arḥabī
*¤ 16. 'Abdu'r Raḥmān-bin-'Aqīl-bin-Abī Ṭālib.
✓ 17. 'Abdu'r Raḥmān-bin-'Orwah-bin-Ḥarrāq Ghaffārī
✓ * 18. 'Abdu'r Raḥmān-bin-Mas'ūd-bin-Ḥujjāj Tayamī
* 19. 'Abdu'l 'Olā-bin-Yażīd Kalbī
✓ * 20. 'Ābis-bin-Abī Shabīb Shākirī
+ 21. 'Alī-bin-Ḥurr-bin-Yażīd-Riyāḥī
*✓¤ 22. 'Alī-bin-Imām Ḥusain: 'Alī Aṣaghar 'Abdu'llāh Razī'a
*¤ 23. 'Alī-bin-Imām Ḥusain *alias* 'Alī Akbar
✓ * 24. 'Āmir-bin-Muslim 'Abdī Baṣrī
+ 25. 'Ammarah-bin-Salkhab Ażdī
✓ 26. 'Ammār-bin-Abū Salmah Dālānī Hamadānī
✓* 27. 'Ammār-bin-Ḥassān-bin-Shurayb Ṭaī
✓ ¤* 28. 'Aun-bin-'Abdu'llāh-bin-Ja'far Ṭayyār-bin-Abī Ṭālib
+ 29. 'Āyiž-bin-Mujama'-bin-'Abdu'llāh 'Āyižī
✓ 30. 'Imrān-bin-Ka'b-bin-Ḥārith Ashja'ī
+31. 'Obbād-bin-Muhājir-bin-Abīu'l-Muhājir Juhanī
✓ 32. 'Obaydu'llāh-bin-Żayd-bin-Thabayṭ Qaysī
* ¤ 33. 'Omar-bin-Imām 'Alī
✓ 34. 'Omar-bin-Khālid Asadī Ṣaidavī
* 35. 'Omarū-bin-Jinādah-bin-Ka'b Khiżarajjī
✓ * 36. 'Omarū-bin-'Abdu'llāh Junda'ī Hamadānī
✓ * 37. 'Omarū-bin-Qurẓah-bin-Ka'b Anṣārī
✓ 38. 'Omarū-bin-Uḥadūth Ḥazaramī Kindī
+ 39. 'Omarū-bin-Zab'aitah-bin-Qays-bin-Th'albah Zab'ī Taymī
+ 40. 'Oqbah-bin-Sama'n (Umm Rabāb's servant)
* 41. 'Oqbah-bin-Ṣulet Juhanī
✓¤ * 42. 'Othmān-bin-Imām 'Alī
✓¤ 43. Abū-'Abdu'llāh-bin-Muslim-bin-'Aqīl-bin-Abī Ṭālib
*¤ 44. Abī Bakr ('Abdu'llāh)-bin-Imām 'Alī
✓ ¤ * 45. Abī Bakr-bin-Imām Ḥasan
✓ * 46. Abū-Thamāmah 'Omarū-bin-'Abdu'llāh Ṣāy'dī
+ 47. Adaham-bin-Umayyah 'Abdī Baṣarī
✓ * 48. Anas-bin-Kāhil-bin-Ḥārith Asadī
✓ 49. Aslam-bin-Kathīr Asadī Al-'Araj

* 50. Bakr-bin-Ḥay Tayamī
✓* 51. Bishr-bin-'Omarū-bin-Uḥadūth Ḥazaramī Kindī
* 52. Burayr-bin-Khuzayr Hamadānī
+¤ 53. Fazl-bin-'Abbās -bin-Imām 'Alī
* 54. Ḥabāb-bin-Ḥārith
\+ 55. Ḥabāb-bin-'Āmir-bin-Ka'b Tayamī
\+ 56. Ḥabshatah-bin-Qays Nahamī
* 57. Ḥafiż, Tukey slave
\+ 58. Ḥallās-bin-'Omarū Ażdī Rāsbī
\+ 59. Ḥānī-bin-'Orwah
✓ * 60. Ḥanẓalah-bin-Asa'd ash-Shabāmī
+61. Ḥanẓalah-bin-'Omar Shaybānī
* 62. Ḥārith-bin-Imra-ul-Qays-bin-'Ābis Kindī
\+ 63. Ḥārith-bin-Nibhān (Prophet's uncle Ḥamżah's servant)
\+ ¤ 64. Ḥasan-bin-Imām Ḥasan (Ḥasan-Muthannā)
✓ 65. Ḥayyan-bin-Ḥārith Salmānī Ażdī.
✓ * 66. Ḥujjāj-bin-Masrūq Ja'fī
✓ 67. Ḥujjāj-bin-Żaid-Sa'dī Tayamī
✓* 68. Ḥurr-bin-Yażīd-Riyāḥī
\+ 69. Ibrāhīm-bin-Muslim-bin-'Aqīl-bin-Abī Ṭālib
✓ ¤ * 70. Ja'far-bin-'Aqīl-bin-Abī Ṭālib
✓ ¤ * 71. Ja'far-bin-Imām 'Alī
* 72. Jābir-bin-Hujjāj Tayamī ('Āmir-bin-Nahashal's servant)
✓* 73. Jaun (Abūżar Ghaffārī's servant)
* 74. Jinādah-bin-Ḥārith Salmānī
* 75. Jinādah-bin-K'ab-bin-Ḥārith Aṇsārī Khiżarajjī
✓ * 76. Jubalah-bin-'Alī Shaybānī
✓ 77. Junadab-bin-Ḥajīr Kindī Khūlānī
✓ 78. Juvayn-bin-Mālik-bin-Qays-bin-Th'albah Tayamī
\+ 79. Kardūs-bin-Żuhayr-bin-Ḥārith Taghalabī
✓ * 80. Kinānah-bin-'Atīq Taghalabī
✓ 81. Mālik-bin-'Abd-bin-Sarī'-bin-Jābir Hamādanī
✓ * 82. Masū'd-bin-Ḥujjāj Tayamī
✓¤ * 83. Muḥammad-bin-'Abdu'llāh-bin-Ja'far Ṭayyār
✓ ¤ *84. Muḥammad-bin-Abī Sa'īd-bin-'Aqīl-bin-Abī Ṭālib
✓¤ 85. Muḥammad-bin-Imām 'Alī-bin-Abī Ṭālib
*¤ 86. Muḥammad-bin-Muslim-bin-'Aqīl-bin-Abī Ṭālib
\+ 87. Mujama'-bin-Żiyād-bin-'Omarū-Jehnī
✓ * 88. Mujama'-bin-'Abdu'llāh 'Āyiżī
\+ 89. Munī'-bin-Żiyād
✓ 90. Munjiḥ-bin-Sahm (Imām Ḥusain's servant)

✓ 91. Muqsiṭ(Kursh)-bin-Żuhayr-bin-Ḥārith Taghalabī
+ 92. Muṣa'b-bin-Yažīd Riyāḥī
+ 93. Muslim-bin-Kathīr Ṣadafi Ażdī
✓ * 94. Muslim-bin-'Ausajah Asadī
✓ * 95. Nāfa'-bin-Hilāl Jamalī Al-Murādī
✓ * 96. Naī'm-bin-'Ajalān Anṣārī
+ 97. Naṣar-bin-Abī Nīżar
* 98. No'mān-bin-'Omarū Ażdī
✓* 99. Qa'nab-bin-'Omayr Numayrī
✓ 100. Qārib-bin-'Abdu'llāh (Imām Ḥusain's servant)
+ ¤ 101. Qāsim-bin-'Abbās -bin-Imām 'Alī
✓ * 102. Qāsim-bin-Ḥabīb-bin-Abī Bishr Ażdī
✓¤ *103. Qāsim-bin-Imām Ḥasan
✓ 104. Qāsiṭ-bin-Żuhayr-bin-Ḥārith Taghalabī
✓ * 105. Qays-bin-Muṣahar Ṣaidāvī
+ 106. Qurrah (Ḥurr-bin-Yažīd-Riyāḥī's servant)
+ 107. Rāf'a-bin-'Abdu'llāh (Muslim Ażdī's servant)
* 108. Sa'd-bin-Ḥārith (Imām 'Alī's servant)
+ 109. Sa'd-bin-Ḥurr-bin-Yažīd-Riyāḥī
✓ 110. Sa'īd-bin-'Abdu'llāh Ḥasafī
✓ * 111. Saī'd ('Omar-bin-Khālid Asadī Ṣaidāvī's servant)
* 112. Saif-bin-Ḥārith-bin-Sarī'
✓ * 113. Saif-bin-Mālik 'Abdī
✓ 114. Sālim ('Āmir-bin-Muslim al-'Abdī's servant)
✓* 115. Sālim-bin-'Omarū-bin-'Abdu'llāh (Medīnahu'l Kalbī's servant)
* 116. Salmān-bin-Muzārib-bin-Qays Numayrī Bajalī
✓ 117. Sawwār-bin-Abī 'Omayr Nahamī Hamādani
✓ 118. Shabīb-bin-'Abdu'llāh Nahashalī
✓ 119. Shabīb-bin-'Abdu'llāh-bin-Sarī'a
✓ 120. Shožab-bin-'Abdu'llāh ('Ābis-bin-Abī Shabīb's servant)
+ ¤ 121. Sukayna-bint-Imām Ḥusain
✓ 122. Sulayman-bin-Rakin (Imām Ḥusain Servant)
+ 123. Swaid-bin-'Omar-bin-Abī Māta' al-Khath'amī
+ 124. Umayyah-bin-Sa'd-bin-Żaid Ṭaī
+ * 125. Umm Wahab-bint-Ma'bad, wife of Wahab-Kalbī
✓ 126. Yažīd-bin-Ḥaṣṣin Hamadānī
✓* 127. Yažīd-bin-Żiyād-bin-Mahāṣar Abu'lal-Sh'athā Kindī
+ 128. Zaḥāq-bin-'Abdu'llāh Mashriqī
* 129. Žāhar ('Omarū'l Ḥamaq Aslamī Kindī's servant)
✓ 130. Żāhayr-bin-Bishr Khitha'mī

✓ * 131. Żāhayr-bin-Sulaym-bin-'Omarū Ażdī
✓* 132. Zarghamah-bin-Mālik Taghalabī
✓ 133. Żayd-bin-Mī'qal Ja'fī
✓ * 134. Żayd-bin-Thabayṭ u'l 'Abdī Qaysī
+ 135. Żiyād-bin-'Arīb Hamadānī

The Leader of the Ḥusainī Revolution

While discussing the golden chain of the Islāmic history, it becomes essential to clarify that the first phase of the period of the Ḥusainī Revolution was between the commencement of Imām Ḥusain's departure from Medina on 28th Rajab, 60 AH/4th May, 680 AD[13] and the Household of the holy Prophet's home return on 20th Rabī I, 62 AH (7th December, 681 AD),[14] being released from the Yażīdī prison. It covers a period of approx. 01 year 08 months. With a view of fecilitating the study, it may be divided into two phases:

> *First Phase*: from 28th Rajab, 60 AH/4th May, 680 AD to 10th Muḥarram, 61 AH (10th October, 680 AD), a period aprox. less than 06 months. In this duration the Ḥusainī Revolution functioned under the leadership of great visionary founder Imām Ḥusain till the date of his Martyrdom on 10th Muḥarram, 61 AH (10th October, 680 AD).
>
> *Second Phase*: from 10th Muḥarram, 61 AH (10th October, 680 AD), till the return to Medina on 20th Rabī I, 62 AH (7th December, 681 AD), a period aprox. 01 year 02 months. In this duration the Ḥusainī Revolution functioned under the leadership of his great successor Imām Żainu'l-Ābidīn.

It is also worth mentioning that during both the phases combined mentioned above, i.e. 28th Rajab, 60 AH/4th May, 680 AD and 20th Rabī I, 62 AH (7th December, 681 AD), a period of approx. 01 year 08 months, Żainab-bint-Imām 'Alī, who is well recognized as *Sharīkatu'l Ḥusain* (Associate of Imām Ḥusain) shared the leadership of the Ḥusainī Revolution. At its first phase with Imām Ḥusain, and then after his martyrdom, Associate of Imām Ḥusain provided her guidance and consultation to Imām Żainu'l-Ābidīn. She continued her leadership to the great religious revolution. With this, the group leadership of the Ḥusainī Revolution can be known and understood.

Imām Ḥusain and his successful leadership of the Ḥusainī Revolution is an identity of Islām. It would be appropriate to have a brief introduction of the main characters of the great religious revolution. The order of this discussion is that first there is the Ḥusainī Army Heads' discussion then the family members of the holy Prophet of Islām. Afterwards, Imām Ḥusain's Associates themself, their family and ladies have also been discussed. For the convenience of the learned readers, it would be apt to discuss their various categories.

Imām Ḥusain, *Saiyed-ush-Shuhadah*

Imām Ḥusain has been best known with the appellation of the *Saiyed-ush-Shuhadah (the Doyen of the Martyrs)* in the history of Islām. Imām Ḥusain's reception is presented in so many Divine Verses. There are immunable verses concerned with his and all the family members of the holy Prophet. A full chapter '*Kauthar*' (*Qur'an*:108/1) relates to Imām Ḥusain and his elder brother Imām Ḥasan.[15] Some of Qur'anic verses have already been discussed at the appropriate places. However, some other verses related to the event of Karbala could be presented here:

> "And fight (*endeavour*) ye in (*the way of*) God as it behoveth you to fight (*endeavour*) for Him" (*Qur'an*: 22/78)

Renowned scholar and exegesist, as-Suyūṭī, Jalālu'd-Dīn (d. 1505 AD) has referred Caliph II 'Omar, who had told that above verse relates to Imām Ḥusain's fight in the path of God.[16] *Vice Versa*, the following verse has been mentioned concerning the Karbala event.[17]

> "So wept on them the heavens and the eatrth not were they respited." (*Qur'an*: 44/29)

Imām Ḥusain was by nature very submissive, peace lover and patient. But at the same time, he was extremely brave, generous and fearless riser for the cause of Justice. He used to do fasting mostly and take very light and slight food daily. He used to study the Qur'an regularly. He had made 25 *Ḥajj* Pilgrimage in his life. He had special taste and interest in giving donations. He was all along highly well-behaved towards the people. He was going on pardoning the mistakes of his servant and maid-servants. He would make them free being very happy on small-small trivial things. He used to make the debtors burden free by making payment himself of various persons. He would send food to helpless persons' homes. Discussions are available in plenty in many books regarding the activities of human love. So, many instances are available regarding harmony towards people.

Numerous statements of Imām Ḥusain illustrate the very ideals of life. Refer to a few: A prestigious death is better than dishonourable life. Truth is Honour, Lie is helplessness. Faith is surity. A neighbour is a relative. Help is friendship. Deed is experience. Good Behaviour is God's Prayer. Peace is the glory of humanity. Miserliness is poverty. Generosity is richness. Whoever has faith in God, he shall certainly satisfy him etc.[18]

Imām 'Alī-Ibnu'l-Ḥusain, *Imām Żainu'l-Ābidīn*

The second leader of the Ḥusainī Revolution and fourth in the order of Imamate, Imām 'Alī-Ibnu'l-Ḥusain was the eldest son of Imām Ḥusain and Shahr Bānū, the daughter of Yezdegerd III, the last Sāsānid king of Persia,[19] and in him was perpetuated the house of the Prophet Muḥammad. He was born on Friday, the 15th of Jamādī I, 38 AH or 19th October, 658 at Medīna. Martyred by poison on Friday, 25th Muḥarram, 95 AH, or 19th October, 714 AD in Medīna and buried in al-Bāqī'h cemetery next to his uncle Imām Ḥasan and grand mother Fāṭimah aż-Żahrah.

'Alī-Ibnu'l-Ḥusain was better well-known as Imām *Żainu'l-Ābidīn* (Decor of the Pious) and *Saiyedu's-Sajidīn* (Ahead of all Prostrates). He had been known without his equal for his contentment at fate and Divine decree and for the high attitude of the worship to Lord.

He was present at the time of the tragic event of Karbala, but in extremely indisposed condition of health, nevertheless, he got up to assist his father, Imām Ḥusain, but Imām did not allow him to go to the battlefield. After the martyrdom of Imām Ḥusain he was made prisoner and taken from Karbala to Kufa, and from Kufa to Damascus (Syria). Being too weak to walk with heavy iron cuffs in hands and fetters in feet and with pointed yoke round his throat, he was being brutally dragged and flogged throughout the long passage of his miserable journey. All the same he stood firm with the hope and strength of his conviction and his absolute trust in God.

When the ailing son of Imām Ḥusain was brought before 'Obaydu'llāh, governor of Kūfa, he ordered for his killing and, thus, put an end to the progeny of Prophet Muḥammad. But he saw Żaynab, the celebrated daughter of Imām 'Alī and Fāṭimah aż-Żahrah and granddaughter of the Prophet Muḥammad, who was determined to die with her young nephew, the tyrant was struck with great fear. All women, children with young Imām 'Alī in the same condition were sent to Damascus, the then capital of Muslim empire, the soldiers of their escort carrying on the top of their lances the heads of the martyrs were produced before Yażīd-bin-Mu'āwiyah-bin-Abū Sufyyān, the then Muslim ruler. The young Imām presented the stand of his father Imām Ḥusain so effectively that Yażīd-bin-Mu'āwiyah, held his breath and the whole crowd of Yażīd-bin-Mu'āwiyah's court was simply spell bound at the confidence, force of logic and elegance of the speech of a young ailing prisoner.

If a historian could stand at the horizon of post-Karbala era, he would find that the Paganism was once more triumphant and its reaction against Islām was cruel, terrible and revolting. There was a thrill of horror throughout the spread of very essence of Islām; and sad revulsion of the feeling which eventually endangered the survival of the faith. It had resulted in the contemporary depravity, which was flowing from the Umayyite court of Damascus. Beside the butchery of Karbala, the flower of the Medīnite chivalry and the revered Companions of the Prophet Muḥammad, perished in the disastrous fight at Ḥarra, where a desperate battle took place. The holy city which had sheltered the Prophet Muḥammad, and which had been sanctified by his life and ministry, was deceitfully captured and could never recover her prosperity and glory. Its best men were either killed or fled to safe places. A few who could save their life had to acknowledge themselves the slave of Yażīd-bin-Mu'āwiyah, and the same was branded on their necks. It was the high wisdom of Imām Żainu'l-Ābidīn that he, his family and followers were spared from this ignominy. The big question was: How to re-establish the doctrine of Islām among the totally demoralized and frustrated people. This arduous task could only be accomplish by Imam Żainu'l-Ābidīn, which may be enumerated as under:

(i) To create self-confidence among demoralized people

Imām Żainu'l-Ābidīn re-established the doctrine and essence of Islām by creating self-confidence among the demoralized people in a language so simple and sweet that everyone could easily understand. It is popularly known as *aṣ-Ṣaḥīfah-al-Kāmilah-as-Sajjādia*, which contains the highest esoteric doctrines and it is through its reading that man emerges with greater courage, stronger will and purer mind. It records that the mind and spirit of morphology is an integrated part of religion. Form is not less essential than substance. The religion for national culture is the skin and the skeleton that preserves a fruit with its juice and taste. We cannot squeeze religion and hope to bottle and keep the essence of religion. The holy figures are necessary for any culture, spiritual foundation and function, as a life giving inspiration and guide.

(ii) To re-establish the institution of learning and knowledge

Imām Żainu'l-Ābidīn revived, in Medīna, the school of learning and knowledge which was established and flourished under his grandfather Imām 'Alī and continued by his father Imām Ḥusain. He equipped numberless students with knowledge and adorned them with faith in his span of life. He bought slaves from the market, educate them, until they became learned scholars, then he made them free to pursue a respectable way of life. He has the honour and credit of being the writer, next to Imām 'Alī, of the exegesis of the Qur'an. He has rightly proclaimed: what is not in Qur'an, is nowhere.

(iii) Institutionalized the message of the martyrdom of Karbala

The event of Karbala had the deepest and most painful impact on Imām Żainu'l-Ābidīn. He had made the propagation of the message of Karbala, the exclusive goal of his life. He institutionalized the message of the martyrdom of Karbala which in course of time became the guiding force in the name of *Azādārī* or *Tāziādārī* (commemoration ceremony) and became the inseparable part of Islāmic religious life, especially for Shi'īs.

(iv) To maintain and preserve the rights of Imamate

The last person among the progeny of the Prophet Muḥammad was Imām Ḥusain, who was asked by Yażīd-bin-Mu'āwiyah for his *Bai'yat* (Oath of Allegiance), resulting into the battle of Karbala. None of the Caliphs could dare to ask for pledge of allegiance from Imām Żainu'l-Ābidīn and his successors. The people, by then, had realized that the Caliphate has been usurped from the Progeny of the Prophet Muḥammad, so after the death of Yażīd-bin-Mu'āwiyah, a Hāshimite 'Abdu'llāh-bin-Żubayr, could capture Hijāz, Irāq and Khorāsān, in the name of the progeny of the Prophet Muḥammad, though he was arch enemy of them. Similarly, Mukhtār established himself in Iraq and from there hunted the murderers of Imām Ḥusain's people in the Battle of Karbala and systematically pursued and killed them like vermin. He offered the reign to Imām Żainu'l-Ābidīn, who politely declined, but expressed his pleasure when the head of Ḥarmallah, the killer of Imām Ḥusain's six month child 'Alī Aṣghar was presented to him, by the envoy of Mukhtār. Imām thanked him and ordered to celebrate the day as Eīd. No doubt, it was most successful judicial skill of Imām Żainu'l-Ābidīn that the rightful claim of the progeny of the Prophet over the Caliphate were made quite clear to stand for future.

Żainab, *the Sharīkatu'l Ḥusain*

The reason for calling the elder daughter of *Amīru'l Mūminīn* Imām 'Alī and *Lady of Light,* Fāṭimah aż-Żahrah, Żainab as *Sharīkatu'l Ḥusain* (Ḥusain's Associate) could be understood with the fact that right from Imām Ḥusain's date of departure from Medina till his martyrdom, she continued without break to remain as Associate of Imām Ḥusain. Imām Ḥusain used to take decisions only after consulting her.

Żainab is an 'Arabic word, drived from *Żaib* means glory and prestige. Word *Żainab's* other part *Ab* means Father. No doubt *Żainab* is the glory of the holy Prophet's family and a prestigious lady of Islām. There is a difference of opinion regarding her date of birth, however, it is mostly considered that she was born on Friday, the fifth day of Jamādī I, 6 AH (23rd November, 627 AD). She was named by prophet himself. She resembled her maternal grandmother *Ummu'l Mūminīn* Khadījah in her physical structure etc. and her manner of conversation resembled her father *Amīru'l Mūminīn* Imām 'Alī. She had also a sub-name as Umm-Kulthūm, which was given by the holy Prophet in the name of his mother's sister.[20]

Żainab was great devotee of her elder brother Ḥusain. Since her childhood, when she grew up, her routine was to look positively the face of her brother Ḥusain before offering the Prayer of God.[21] At the 13 years (17 AH/638 AD) of age her marriage was proposed with 'Abdu'llāh-bin-Ja'far Ṭayyār-bin-Abī Ṭālib, then she laid two conditions.

> Firstly, whenever she wished to see her brother Imām Ḥusain, she could come out of her house, and
> Secondly, if Imām Ḥusain wished to take her in his travel, then 'Abdu'llāh-bin-Ja'far would not oppose it.[22]

When Imām Ḥusain set out from Medina for sacrificing his own life, Żainab went to her husband 'Abdu'llāh-bin-Ja'far before accompanying Imām Ḥusain and obtained his permission. She had her son 'Aun from him, who became a martyr in Karbala. She had a daughter also whose name was Kulsoom, on whose basis she was called Umm-Kulthūm. (Kulthūm's mother).

There is difference of opinion on the date of the demise of Żainab. However, the scholars say that she could not servive for many days after the martyrdom of Imām Ḥusain and on 15 Rajab 62 AH (31 March, 681 AD) she surrendered her soul to God. She was accompanying her nephew Imām Żainu'l-Ābidīn on his being called by the Caliph in Damascus. In a garden near Damascus she stayed. She saw that tree at which Imām Ḥusain's head was hung. The incident became alive before her eyes, she began ambracing the tree. Some merciless person attacked her head with sickle, she died. Her mausoleum is in Damascus (Syria) itself, which is internationally famous for the pilgrimage.

Ḥusain's Associate, Żainab's personality was brimming with sympathy, pity, compassion, intimacy and self-dedication. She was glorified even after she was imprisoned in Kufa and Damascus. Her courage and bravery were praised and acknowledged by her enemies also. She had been expert in the Islāmic Jurisprudence. The ladies used to obtain solution of their social and personal problems.

Everyday during the four years tenure of the caliphate of her father Imām 'Alī in Kufa, Żainab regularly held teaching classes of the ladies, who were very fond of learning from her and therefore, they were punctual in attending her classes.[23] Żainab was an effective orator. She was addressing effectively in royal courts and markets that people felt as if Imām 'Alī himself was speaking.[24] So many incidents have already been mentioned at the appropriate places, repetition will not be relevant.

Other Households of the Holy Prophet

The great personalities of the family of the holy Prophet of Islām, who stuggled for re-establishing true Islām, under the leadership of Imām Ḥusain made a matchless contribution. Amongst them, the descendants of Ḥazrat Abū Ṭālib alone. This subject has already been discussed in the previous pages. In Abū Ṭālib's heir the very important name is Abu'l-Fażl'il-'Abbās -bin-Imām 'Alī after Imām Ḥusain, only from him the discussion of continuation can be commenced.

Abu'l-Fażl'il-'Abbās

The great Commander-in-Chief of the Ḥusainī Army at Karbala was the son of Imām Ḥusain's another mother Fāṭimah-bint-Abu'l 'Ajal Kalbī, the appellation *Ummu'l Banīn* (Mother of Sons), because she gave birth to four unparallel brave sons, Abu'l-Faẓl'il-'Abbās, 'Abdu'llāh, 'Othmān, and Ja'far, all martyrs of the Battle of Karbala. There is a special reference of the wedding of Imām 'Alī with *Ummu'l Banīn*. Imām 'Alī asked his elder brother 'Aqīl-bin-Abī Ṭālib, who was expert in the genealogy of various clans of 'Arabia, to point out a very brave clan, so that, he may marry with a woman of that clan for having unparallel brave sons.[25] As per the suggestion of 'Aqīl, Imām 'Alī married Ummu'l Banīn, who gave birth to above four sons, 'Abbās, 'Abdu'llāh, 'Othmān and Ja'far.[26] Among them Abu'l-Faẓl'il-'Abbās -bin-Imām 'Alī was the Commander-in-Chief of the Ḥusainī Army.

'Abbās-bin-Imām 'Alī was born on 17th Sha'bān 26 AH (28 May, 647 AD). He got his education and training from his father Imām 'Alī for 14 years, afterwards from Imām Ḥasan and then from Imām Ḥusain. During Karbala event he was of 34 years. He was very handsome, mighty and a great warior, called *Qamaru'l-Banī Hāshim* (moon of the Hāshimites). He was so tall that when he mounted on a horse, his feet used to touch the earth.

In previous chapter, it has been mentioned that the Yażīdī Commander, Shimr-bin-Žuljaushan had made impudent attempt to flatter 'Abbās and his brothers, who had furiously rejected it unanimously.[27] Similarly, their maternal uncle's son 'Abdu'llāh-bin-Abīu'l-Muḥal Kalbī, who was among the elites of Kufa, procured a safety decree from the Governor 'Obaydu'llāh-bin-Żiyād and arranged to send it through his servant Karnān in Karbala, but 'Abbās and his brothers, thankfully refused to accept it and said, if security has to be provided then it should be provided to Imām Ḥusain and his family members first.[28] 'Abbās's main killers were Yażīd-bin-Ruqād Ḥīthī and Ḥakīm-bin-Ṭufayl Ṭāī.

Being the Commander-in-Chief, he sent his brothers one by one to the war-front.

'Abdu'llāh-bin-Imām 'Alī

'Abdu'llāh was younger to Abu'l-Faẓl'il-'Abbās among his brothers. Sending him to the battlefield. he said—"March fast, sacrifice your life at the feet of Imām Ḥusain, so that I may see with my own eyes your being assasinated. Sorry, you have no issue." 'Abdu'llāh fought very enthursiastically, ultimately became a martyr by Ḥānī-bin-Thobayṭ Ḥazramī.

‘Othmān-bin-Imām ‘Alī

‘Abdu’llāh’s younger brother was ‘Othmān. He came to the war-front and exhibited his intrepidity. Finally, he fell down being wounded, at that time cowards, Khiwallah-bin-Yażīd Aṣbaḥī ‘Āyiżī and Abānī Dārīmī cut his head from his body.

Ja’far-bin-Imām ‘Alī

He was the youngest brother of Abu’l-Fażl’il-‘Abbās.

Addressing him he had said—“Go! I have endured the grief of both my brothers, in the same manner I will endure your sorrow also. Alas! none of you have any child. Ja’far fought and became a martyr by Ḥānī-bin-Thobayṭ Ḥazramī.

Muḥammad-bin-Imām ‘Alī

Among the sons of Imām ‘Alī he was younger than Muḥammad-bin-Ḥanafiya, and was called Muḥammadu’l-Aṣfar. His mother’s name is mentioned in two ways, Asama-bint-’Omays[29] or Laylā-bint-Mas’ūd.[30] He came to the war front fought well. The enemies could not win him. But at last he became martyr by Abānī Dārīmī.

‘Alī Akbar-bin-Imām Ḥusain

Imām Ḥusain had three sons. He named all his sons after the name of his father ‘Alī. To distinguist between the eldest son called *Akbar*, say ‘Alī Akbar; next to him *Ausaṭ*, say ‘Alī Ausaṭ and youngest son *Aṣghar*, say ‘Alī Aṣghar. Actually, Imām Żainu’l-Ābidīn has been the eldest son of Imām Ḥusain, so, naturally, he is entitled to the appellation ‘Alī Akbar. But, on the basis of being eldest martyr son of Imām Ḥusain, ‘Alī Ausaṭ has been popularly known as ‘Alī Akbar. Now, it has been accepted by all that whenever the name of ‘Alī Akbar would be referred, it would be supposed to be the name of Imām Ḥusain’s martyred eldest son and there is no confusion in this regard.

Imām Ḥusain’s martyred eldest son ‘Alī Akbar’s mother was Laylā-bint-Abī Murwah Thaqafiyyah, whose mother Maimūnah was the daughter of Abū Sufyyān, thus, she was Amīr Mu’āwiyah’s aunt and Yażīd was her nephew. On the basis of such close relationship ‘Alī Akbar commanded respects from all categories of people, including the Umayyites. Historians have narrated a story.

Once, Amīr Mu'āwiyah asked his Court people who is the supreme condidate for the post of Caliph? Sycophants replied, You Sir! Mu'āwiyah said No ! The best condidate is 'Alī, the son of Ḥusain, whose grandfather was the Prophet. All the specialities of great 'Arabian clans are inhered in him. Some poetic compositions are also available in praise of 'Alī Akbar.[31]

Analysts say that the paise of 'Alī Akbar and his Umayyite descendants side seems to be a part of any well-planned War strategy of Amīr Mu'āwiyah, because such sort of his generority was never seen towards Imām Ḥusain or Imām 'Alī, so, what even towards the holy Prophet of Islām. The objective of such praise had been an attempt to sow the seeds of dissension in the mind of 'Alī Akabr, so, that split could be made in the family of Imām Ḥusain. But 'Alī Akbar was at such a high pedestal of conduct as Imām Ḥusain adressing God sent him to the war-front, Oh God! now I am submitting at your service my most dear son, who resembles the prophet in all respects by appearance, nature and behaviour etc.

'Alī Akbar, 19 years old youth[32] attained heaven exhibiting his absolute bravery. Imām Ḥusain, reached him at the last minute of his life, wanted to take his dead body then asked the youngesters of his family, Take the dead body of your brother. All youngester went ahead bringing their brother's dead body, and placed it before the camp, which was in the middle of the Army!

'Alī Aṣghar-bin-Imām Ḥusain

Imām Ḥusain's youngest son, 'Alī Aṣghar, also called 'Abdu'llāh Razī'a. He has special significance of being youngest martyr of Karbala. 'Alī Aṣghar, 6 month old, was brought by Imām Ḥusain to the war-front asking enemies themselves for a few drops of water for the baby. They did not give water, but as per the orders of his Commander-in-Chief of the Yaẓīdī Army, Ḥarmalah-bin-Kāhil Asadī, took away his life with the attack of trident arrow. Imām Ḥusain took his dead-body to the camp, but feeling ashamed, he himself prepared a grave with his sword and put the dead body inside it.[33]

Qāsim-bin-Imām Ḥasan

Qāsim was the son of Imām Ḥusain's elder brother Imām Ḥasan. It is prevalent that Imām Ḥusain gave his daughṭer Fāṭimah Kubra in marriage to him. On this basis some Muḥarram processions are taken out in India and some other countries. But historical evidences are weak. Qāsim was very handsome and well-built. He came to the battlefield, a the Yażīdī soldier's statement is on record that it seemed as if a piece of moon had come down to the earth. He was not covered with weapons, there was no armour on his body. He was wearing just a long shirt. His slipper was broken on his foot.[34] He fought bravely. The Yażīdī Army attacked him from behind, he became a martyr. In the galloping of the horses, Qāsim's dead-body was crushed. Imām Ḥusain brought his dead body and laid it at rest along with the other dead-bodies.[35]

Abū Bakr-bin-Imām Ḥasan

He was the son of Imām Ḥasan. His mother's name was Umm-Isḥāq, who belonged to Tayamī clan. He was killed by the arrows of 'Abdu'llāh-bin-'Aqabah Ghanvī in the war.[36]

'Abdu'llāh-bin-Imām Ḥasan

'Abdu'llāh was the son.of Imām Ḥasan, who often mentioned as a baby, but it did not appear to be correct. Because Imām Ḥusain had demised in 50 AH (670 AD). 'Abdu'llāh could be above 10 years at the time. His mother was the sister of Imām Ḥusain's wife Rabāb-bint-Imarau'l Qays Kalbī. When Imām Ḥusain at the last stage of his life being highly wounded fell down, the lovely nephew 'Abdu'llāh came running and embraced him. He requested the enemies not to attack him, as his uncle was innocent and not the criminal. A merciless soldier attacked him with his sword both his hands were cut off. Ḥarmalah-bin-Kāhil Asadī killed him.

Ḥasan-bin-Imām Ḥasan

He was the son of Imām Ḥasan, who is better known as Ḥasan Muthanna generally. He joined the war. Fell down being wounded, appeared to be dead, but actually he was alive in an unconscious state. When after the war of Yażīdī Army began chopping off the heads of Ḥusainī soldiers, Ḥasan Muthanna's maternal uncle Asmā-bin-Khārjah Farāzī, who was in the Yażīdī Army, observed that Ḥasan Muthanna is breathing. He took him along with him. Ḥasan Muthanna had a new life with medical treatment and service. After regaining health, Ḥasan Muthanna returned to Medina at that time, when the family members of Imām Ḥusain, had came back tc Medina, after being released from Damascus prison. His wife Fāṭimah was the daughter of Imām Ḥusain. She was also among them. She had children from whom 'Abdu'llāhu'l Maḥaz is famous in the history of Islām. His genealogy still continue, who are called Ḥasanī Saiyed.

Muḥammad-bin-'Abdu'llāh

Muḥammad was the son of 'Abdu'llāh-bin-Ja'far-bin-Abī Ṭālib. Ja'far had been famous in the Islāmic history as Ja'far Ṭayyār. 'Abdu'llāh, was the brother-in-law (sister's husband) of Imām Ḥusain, but Muḥammad's mother's name was Khausā'-bint-Ḥafṣah, who was from Bakr-Wāil clan. Muḥammad came at the serivce of Imām Ḥusain as per the orders of his father 'Abdu'llāh-bin-Ja'far Ṭayyār, when he had already set out outside Mecca. He fought and beame a martyr at the hands of 'Āmir-bin-Nahshal Taymīmī.

'Aun-bin-'Abdu'llāh

'Aun present himself, with his brother Muḥammad, in accordance with the orders of his father 'Abdu'llāh-bin-Ja'far Ṭayyār, after setting out from Mecca at the service of Imām Ḥusain. 'Aun was the son of Ḥusain's Associate Żainab. 'Aun and Muḥammad names are taken together. Żainab was loving them as her own sons and brought them up. Both the brothers fought together. They were in boyhood, at the same time both of them were very brave and highly talented. While attacking they were surrounded by the Yażīdī Army, they piereced into the camps of Shimr-bin-Żuljaushan, Commander of Left Regiment and entered inside. They wanted to kill him, but he ran away and escaped. He killed so many the Yażīdī soldiers. But finally the Yażīdī Army surrounded him on all sides and 'Abdu'llāh-bin-Quṭayyah Nabahānī killed him.

'Abdu'llāh-bin-Muslim

He was the son of Muslim-bin-'Aqīl-bin-Abī Ṭālib, Peace-Envoy of Imām Ḥusain to Kufa. His mother Ruqayyah was the daughter of Imām 'Alī. In this way, 'Abdu'llāh was the nephew of Imām Ḥusain. He has not reached his youth. After 'Alī Akbar's becoming martyr, there was an uproar of weeping and cursing in Ḥusainī camps. Children came outside their camp out of fear, 'Abdu'llāh was among them. The Yażīdī soldier 'Omar-bin-Ṣubaiḥ Ṣaydāvī aimed with arrow which struck his forehead. He kept his hand on his forehead for protection, hand also was piered along with his fore-head. Then the other arrow struck his chest and he lost his life. The other statement is the Yażīdī soldier attacked by the lancer, having a cut in his chest, he died on the spot.[37]

Muḥammad-bin-Muslim

He was the brother of the above mentioned 'Abdu'llāh-bin-Muslim, but both the brothers had different mothers. He came to the war-front after his brother, fought, killed so many soldiers and became finally a martyr.

Ja'far-bin-'Aqīl-bin-Abī Ṭālib

He was also son of Imām Ḥusain's elder brother 'Aqīl-bin-Abī Ṭālib, who is famous in history. Jafar challenged the enemies in the battlefield, fought, killed so many soldiers and died at last.

'Abdu'r Raḥmān-bin-'Aqīl-bin-Abī Ṭālib

He was also the cousin of Imām Ḥusain. He came to the front, fought challenging the enemies and beame martyr.

Muḥammad-bin-Abī Sa'īd-bin-'Aqīl-bin-Abī Ṭālib

He was the son of the cousin-brother of the above mentioned 'Abdu'r Raḥmān. During the war, he became a martyr being attacked by Laqīṭ-bin-Nāshir Juhanī.

Fizzah, helper of Fāṭimah aż-Żahrah, *Lady of Light*

Fizzah, means silver. She was named as Maimūnah and appellation Fizzah was awarded by the holy Prophet of Islām. Though genealogically different, she is always considered as a member of the Household of the holy Prophet of Islām. She belonged to a royal Abyssenian family, whom the holy Prophet of Islām had given to his most beloved daughter Saiyedah Fāṭimah aż-Żahrah, *the Lady of Light,* for her assistance in daily routine home work. Saiyedah Fāṭimah aż-Żahrah treated her as equal in her behaviour. She made alternate working system for the entire domestic work. Accordingly, first day by Saiyedah Fāṭimah aż-Żahrah will perform every routine work. She will clean the home, wash the clothes, fetch the water, serve the food to all, etc. Fizzah shall be taking rest on that day. Next day every work will be done by Fizzah. She had brought Imām Ḥasan and Imām Ḥusain both the brothers like the mother. She was in Karbala along with other family members. She was also arrested and sent to Kufa and then Damascus and was imprisoned. After getting released from the prison she returned to Medina along with the other family members.

Ruqayyah-bint-Imām 'Alī

Imām Ḥusain's sister Ruqayyah was the daughter of mother Umm-Ḥabīb-bint-Rabī'ah. She and her brother 'Omar-bin-Imām 'Alī were twins. She was married to Muslim-bin-'Aqīl-bin-Abī Ṭālib. She was with Imām Ḥusain in Karbala. After his martyrdom she was arrested with the other family members and returned finally to Medina.

Laylā-bint-Abī Murwah Thaqafiyyah

She was the wife of Imām Ḥusain and the mother of 'Alī Akbar. She has been already dealt with while introducing 'Alī Akbar. After the martyrdom of Imām Ḥusain she was arrested along with the other family members and afterwards returned to Medina.

Rabāb-bint-Imarau'l Qays Kalbī

She was the wife of Imām Ḥusain and the mother of two babies 'Alī Aṣghar and Sukaynah, who are significant in the history. She was arrested after the assassination of Imām Ḥusain, after being released from the prison along with the other people of the family, she came to Karbala again did not return with them, but remained there as a maid servant of the grave of Imām Ḥusain for a year, which has already been discussed in the previous chapter.

Shahrbānū-bint-Yezdegerd

Shahrbānū, (means lady of the land) was the Princes of Persia, the daughter of last Sāsānid king Yezdegerd III. Her other names by which she has been referred to[38]: *Shaharbānawayh, Shahżanān, Salāmah, Salāfah, Ghażāla*, and *Ṣādirah*. She was one of the wives of Imām Ḥusain, who gave birth to Imām Żainu'l-Ābidīn. According to prevelant belief, Shahrbānū died shortly after giving birth to her son 'Alī-ibnu'l Ḥusain and was thus not present at Karbala.[39] The eighth Imām, 'Alī ar-

Reza has also been quoted as saying, that Shahrbānū died during her confinement, while she was his retainer.[40] The scholars 'Alī Sharī'atī (d. 1977 AD) and 'Āyatu'llah Murtaza Muṭahharī (d. 1979 AD) are amongst those who have declared that any narrations pertaining to Shahrbānū are weak and false. Whereas Abū Ḥanīfah Dīnāwarī (d. 896 AD),[41] aṭ-Ṭabāṭabāī, Saiyed Muḥammad Ḥusain (d. 1981 AD)[42] and many others disagree, and contend that Shahrbānū was the mother of 'Alī-ibnu'l Ḥusain, the fourth Imām Żainu'l-Ābidīn. There is a shrine named after Shahrbānū in ancient Rayy, in the southern suburbs of Tehran, Iran. But some say that she had died in Medina and was buried in the al-Bāqī cemetery alongside other members of Prophet's family.

Fāṭimah-bint-Imām Ḥusain

She was the daughter of Imām Ḥusain, her mother was Umm-Isḥāq. Imām Ḥusain had cermonised her marriage with his nephew Ḥasan Muthanna, who has already been discussed in the previous lines. While Imām Ḥusain was coming outside his camp for fighting a closed envelope and some other thing, he entruasted her in confidence, because at that time Imām Żainu'l-Ābidīn was in an unconscious state. With this it can be assumed, how much confidence and faith Imām Ḥusain had in her. Aferwards she handed over all the things to Imām Żainu'l-Ābidīn. She lived for a long time after Karbala event. She is also recognised as an important narrater of the Traditions of the holy Prophet and also interpreter of the verses of the Qur'an. Her son 'Abdu'llāhu'l-Maḥaz is also important in the history personalities.

Sukaynah-bint-Imām Ḥusain

Saiyedah Sukayna, (means, Peace) had been the appellation, her name was like her other sisters was Fāṭimah-bint-Imām Ḥusain, other appellations being Mā'ṣūmah, 'Ātikah, Kulthūm, and Żainab. She was the most beloved daughter of her father and used to sleep on the chest of her father every night. Her mother was Rabāb-bint-Imarau'l Qays Kalbī, who was also mother of'Alī Aṣghar, 'Abdu'llāh Razī'a. Both sister and brother are most significant in the history. Imām Ḥusain was often heard saying that house without Sukayna would not be worth living in.

Born on 28th Rajab 57 AH (8th June, 677 AD), Saiyedah Sukayna was just three years old during Karbala tragedy. She died at the age of five years in 61 AH (681 AD)[43] at Damascus prison itself, and is buried within the mosque of Saiyedah Ruqayyah-bint-Imām 'Alī at Damascus.

Later on after some centuries Saiyedah Sukayna's body was removed from its original burial place, dungeon of Syria, on getting information that water was pouring into the grave of Saiyedah Sukayna. Upon confirmation that ground water was actually entering the grave and ancient tomb (10′×10′) was about to collapse (1280 AH/1863 AD).[44] When shrine was opened for restoration, blessed clothed body of her was seen to be fresh and soft (never decayed or changed) as if she were still alive (although buried 1215 years before). This miracle was witnessed by the Turkish deputy governor, the supreme Judge and other personalities of rank at that time and well mentioned in history books.

Before concluding, it would be advisable to know about a figment of the Umayyite fertile imagination or, at best, a case of mistaken identity of the lady, who was a poetess and called Sakīna-bintal-Ḥusain and who died at the ripe old age of 75-80, there is no authentic evidence linking her to the tragedy of Karbala. It is most unusual in the 'Arabian culture of poetry, if that lady could be Imām Ḥusain's daughter and a poetess. Also, from all the accounts we have of Saiyedah Sukayna's piety and devotion to God and of her great sufferings it seems hardly likely that she would grow up to be a composer of non-religious poems. One is, therefore, tempted to dismiss at first place.

Look at fact, if this lady, were the daughter of Imām Ḥusain would take up residence in Damascus when her brother, the 4th Imām Żainu'l-Ābidīn was in Madina ? Why do we not get any account of a meeting between her and fifth Imām Muḥammad al-Bāqir or sixth Imām Ja'far aṣ-Ṣādiq ? Also given the affinity that Saiyedah Sukayna had with her father, it seems impossible that she would lead a life of comfort as a poetess in Damascus, the very city where she suffered so much. Even as a young girl for which ample historical evidence available.

Some Lady Associates

At the onset, it appears necceasry to mention that some lady associates' role has been greatly important in the event of Karbala, in whom Umm-Wahab-bint-'Abd have the top rank being lone woman martyr in the Battle of Karbala. Let us begin the talk on the lady associates with her good name.

Umm-Wahab-bint-'Abd

Umm-Wahab-bint-'Abd was the wife of 'Abdu'llāh-bin-'Omayr Kalbī, who has been more popularly known as Wahab Kalbī. She has been the only woman martyr in Karbala event.

She was addressed by her husband as Umm-Wahab! which literally means, mother of Wahab. Some historians also mention Umm-Wahab as the name of the mother of Wahab Kalbī. It may not be surprising in 'Arabian tradition it was quite common that the father, son and their grandfathers bear the same name. For identification they put father's name as a part of name.

She had reached Karbala along with her husband. While fighting enthusiastically, her husband became more emotional and as per 'Arabian warior's traditions, he addressed her wife, 'Oh Umm-Wahab! He would take a vow to aim spears and use swords and he fight in such a way which would be justifiable for the believers of God.[45] Needless to emphasise that such words of Wahab Kalbī are evidence that his wife was an extraordinary warrior, although she had promised her husband that she would not exploit her war-talents. After hearing the call of her husband, she became emotional and rushed to the battlefield calling, "O' my brave husband, my parents may be sacrificed for you, there should be no shortfall in sacrificing on the Household of the holy Prophet. Telling this she plunged into the battlefield. Her husband tried his best to send her back to the camp, but she was not prepared. She began to say, "I won't leave you and I also would be murdered along with you. When Imām Ḥusain saw the scène himself, he convinced her that according to the *Shari'a* (Islāmic Jurisprudence), women are not allowed to fight in the battlefield. As an obedient believer, she accompanied her victorious husband, who led her to their camp. Again her husband came and fought and became a martyr. When she observed her husband in pool of his own blood, Umm-Wahab stricken blanket, again came to the war-front now her intention was not fighting, but she wanted to offer her tears to him as final respect to her husband. She wanted to clean his face from dust-sand and she was going to tell her husband a Very Happy Journey to Heaven. A coward the Yażīdī soldier attacked her with a mace and she be came a martyr.

Wahab-Kalbī's Mother

Wahab-Kalbī's mother whom historians have mentioned as Umm-Wahab, was very pious, honest and devoted to the Household of the holy Prophet. She had dedicated life for the cause of Truh. She herself wanted to join the war of Justice, taking a rod from a camp she plunged into the war-front along with his son, however, when Imām Ḥusain advised her saying Islām does not allow ladies to fight with weapons, she returned. But when her son came to her fighting successfully and asked her whether she was happy, the brave lady replied that she would be happy only when he scarified his own life at the feet of Imām Ḥusain in safeguarding Truth.

Muslim-bin-'Ausajah's wife

She was the dedicated lady, who could not leave his husband Muslim-bin-'Ausajah alone, when the reverend Companion of the Prophet in his old age decided to sacrifice his life in the path of God, under the august leadership of Imām Ḥusain. Her name would be retained in the history for her contribution to the cause of humanity. Which shall shall be ever lasting. He came to Karbala and lived in the vicinity of the Ḥusainī camps and bore all tyrannies, injuries and injustice, along with the Ḥusainī camps.

Baḥriyah-bint-Masū'd

Baḥriyah-bint-Masū'd was the wife of Jinādah-bin-K'ab Aṇsārī. She was one of the bravesy ladies present at the Battle of Karbala. She came with her husband and a child and stayed in a camp in the vicinity of the Ḥusainī camps and bore all tyrannies, injuries and injustice, along with them. When he her husband Jinādah-bin-K'ab Aṇsārī decided to sacrifice his life, she also plunged into the battlefield. Imām Ḥusain intervened and convinced her that the Islāmic Jurisprudence did not allow a women to fight in the battlefield. So, as an obedient believer the lady returned back. But when Jinādah-bin-K'ab became martyr, she well dressed her young son 'Omarū-bin-Jinādah, with the weapens and send her son for fighting in the battlefield. Imām Ḥusain was reluctant to permit the child, but on her extraordignary pursuance allowed the child, who became martyr. The brave mother viewed the entire scene by her own eyes and felt herself proud of her son. A soldier of the Yażīdī Army cut the head of 'Omarū-bin-Jinādah and threw towards his mother. She welcomed the head of her son, kept on her chest, love and kissed and again thrown towards the Yażīdī Army, saying—We never accept back the propitiatory offerings, once given !

Dalham-bint-'Omarū

Dalham-bint-'Omarū was the wife of Żuhayr-bin-Qayn. We have discussed in detail in Chapter Four, how at Żarwud, he was aware of Imām Ḥusain's call, but he was escaping from Imām Ḥusain, because he was newly married. He wanted to avoid Imām Ḥusain at that time, he was moving far ahead. But he was chosen by Imām Ḥusain and so, he sent a letter through his son ‘Alī Akbar. Żuhayr-Qayn glanced it, kept on his head, then come to his wife and said to her; If you want I can divorce you and make you free. The wife replied. So far I was your life companion when you were an ordinary person, now you are promoted, you are separating me, Is it your justice? Żuhayr-Qayn clarified to his wife and came to Karbala with his wife. They lived in the vicinity of the Ḥusainī camps and bore all tyrannies, injuries and injustice, along with the Ḥusainī camps.

The Companions of Holy Prophet

Martyrs of Karbala who have the prestige and privilege of being the companions of Prophet Muḥammad, have special distinction of their own. In the Islāmic terminology *Ṣaḥābī* (pl. *Ṣaḥābah*), meaning companion, firmly denotes Prophet's friends, colleagues, and associates. For others any other word, other than *Ṣaḥābī* could be used. The Muslim contemporaries of the Prophet Muḥammad are considered companions, if they had any contact with him, and they were not liars or opposed him and his teachings. If they saw him, heard him, or were in his presence even for a short time, they are companions. All companions are assumed to be confirmed on *'Adl* (Divine Justice), unless they are proven otherwise. The Qur'an distinguishes between the community in honour:

> "Alike are not among you are those who spent before the victory and fought and (those who did not), they are more exalted in rank than those who spent and fought afterwards; and unto all hath promised God goodness; And verily God, of whatever ye do, is All-Aware." (*Qur'an*: 57/10)

A discussion on few of them only is possible here, because we may know little or nothing at all about them. They were the pious people, who participated in the martyrdom with Imām Ḥusain, would be seniors of the Islāmic society with plus 55-60 years, setting out for fighting in the old age cannot be based on any timely emotion. At that age, one desires to spent his time in peace with family and devoting himself in the prayer of God. But they plumged taking the sword in hand into the battlefield for the defence of religion and the Truth. Joining the *Jihād* they felt to be indispensable for him and ultimately sacrificed their own life for the sacred cause.

Muslim-bin-'Ausajah Asadī

The Islāmic Prophet's companion Muslim-bin-'Ausajah Asadī was among the elites of contemporary 'Arabia. He was the chief of his clan group Khaużaimah-Asadī Sa'dī. He was known for his chastity, purity and sage like life He used to spend the whole nights in prayer only. When he came to Karbala he was very old and highly reduced, however, he was more than the youth in his will-power. He was a Kufa dweller. He had joined with Muslim-bin-'Aqīl-bin-Abī Ṭālib, the peace-envoy of Imām Ḥusain, after his martyrdom, he came to Imām Ḥusain. Imām Ḥusain had made Muslim-bin-'Ausajah Commander of the Ḥusainī Army's Left Command. His statements and talks and details of war in support of Imām Ḥusain have already been presented in the previous pages.

Ḥabīb-bin-Maẓāhir Asadī

Ḥabīb-bin-Maẓāhir Asadī has the distinction of being simultaneously companion of the holy Prophet and boyhood friend of Imām Ḥusain. He was the chief of the clan Asadī. He was the cousin of the famous horse rider of the time Rabī'ah-bin-Khoṭah. Ḥabīb-bin-Maẓāhir was a dweller of Kufa. When the news of death of Amīr-Mu'āwiyah reached Kufa, Ḥabīb-bin-Maẓāhir was special among those people who sent a letter first to Imām Ḥusain.

Imām Ḥusain had made him the Commander of his army's Right Command. After reaching Karbala Ḥabīb-bin-Maẓāhir continuously attempted to reform the situation and find solution for the problems through dialogue. In this context so, many discussions have already been presented in the previous pages. On the insulting reply of the Yażīdī Commander Ḥiṣṣīn-bin-Numayr, when another colleague Commander of Ḥusainī Army, was requesting for time for Noon-Prayer of Imām Ḥusain, Ḥabīb-bin-Maẓāhir came for attack emotionally and actually attacked him, by which Ḥiṣṣīn-bin-Numayr fell down from his horse. The wounded Ḥiṣṣīn was scared by his friends at that time. Afterwards he and some other soldiers murdered Ḥabīb-bin-Maẓāhir jointly. Imām Ḥusain was very sad when Habib became a Martyr.

When the Yażīdī Army came to Kufa taking Karbala prisoners a Yażīdī soldier made the head of Ḥabīb-bin-Maẓāhir Asadī hanging from the neck of his horse went towards the palace of 'Obaydu'llāh-bin-Żiyād, Governor of Kufa, on the way Ḥabīb-bin-Maẓāhir's son Qāsim observed it. He submitted to him that it was the head of his father, if he might give it to him, he would bury it. He was prepared to offer anything in return. But the Yażīdī soldier refused and said that he would get reward from

Obaydu'llāh-bin-Żiyād. Qāsim, who was in an adolescent age, struggled, Afterwards in a battle Qāsim met that wicked soldier, Qāsim did not forget that sorrow, he murdered that wicked soldier!

Anas-bin-Kāhil-bin-Ḥāri<u>th</u> Asadī

Anas-bin-Kāhil-bin-Ḥāri<u>th</u> Asadī was among the companion of the Prophet of Islām. Hearing this prophecy from the Prophet himself that Imām Ḥusain would be made a Martyr in safeguarding Truth, he was awaiting, let the time come so he could sacrifice his life for the cause of Truth. He was going on anticipating it.

He was extremely old and physically weak when he came to Karbala, but as far as enthusiasm and self-confidence were concerned, he was more better than any youth. After getting permission from Imām Ḥusain to fight he tied up his waist with his turban tightly and observing his preparations for fighting. Imām Ḥusain's eyes shed tears. He became a martyr after figthing in war.

'Abdu'r Raḥmān-bin-'Abd Rab Anṣārī <u>Kh</u>iżarajjī

He was special for having a chance to join *Ḥajj* pilgrimage along with the Holy Prophet of Islām and witness the most celebrated event of *<u>Gh</u>adīru'l-<u>Kh</u>umm* in which the holy Prophet Muḥammad convened an assembly of the people accompanying him and made a long sermon to the huge gathering and then raised Imām 'Alī aloft with his arms and made the vital announcement to the effect, whomsoever he was his Lord (*Mawlā*), this 'Alī is also his Lord.[46]

Żāhir

Żāhir was distinguished companion of the Prophet on some additional grounds. He was famous among the narrators of the holy Traditions of the Prophet and he was at the service of 'Omarū'l Ḥamaq, another famous distinguished companion of the Prophet. He was very fortunate enough to submit his second Oath of Allegiance to the holy Prophet, popularly known as *Bay'atu'l Rizwān.*

He also participated in the important events of the life of the Prophet, such as Ḥudaybiyah Peace-Treaty and <u>Kh</u>aybar War (both in 628 AD). He was matchless in dedication towards the Household of the holy Prophet. 'Omarū'l Ḥamaq, his master and distinguished companion revolted against Żiyād-bin-Abīh, the then Kufa's Governor of

Mu'āwiyah Rule, and Żiyād conspired to arrest him, but he went under ground and could not be traced. On the occasion of *Ḥajj* he met Imām Ḥusain in Mecca. He became a martyr in the severe cowardly bow-arrows attack of the Yażīdī Army.

'Ammār-bin-Abū Salmah Dālāni Hamadānī

He was among the companions of the holy Prophet of Islām, who had participated in the wars for Justice, under the leadership of Imām 'Alī, in the Wars of Jamal (656 AD), Ṣiffīn (656-57 AD) and Nahrwān (657 AD), along with Imām 'Alī. He was with Imām Ḥusain in Karbala. He attained martyrdom in the severe cowardly bow-arrows attack of the Yażīdī Army.

Muslim-bin-Kat͟hīr Ṣadafi Ażdī

Prophet's noble companion Muslim-bin-Kat͟hīr Ṣadafi Ażdī was a native of Kufa. He had fought in the famous War of Jamal (656 AD) as a soldier of Islām and lost his leg. He was also killed in the severe cowardly bow-arrows attack of the Yażīdī Army.

The Associates of Imām 'Alī

After the *Ṣaḥābah*, the succeeding generation of Muslims is called as *Tāba'īn* (meaning, the Followers) in the Islāmic terminology, which has limited meaning attached with *Ṣaḥābah.* Presently, the word *Follower* has a very wide range of meaning including friends, colleagues, and associates, often used for the person accepting the leadership of another person in worldly or religious life. The term followers of Imām 'Alī has altogether a different meaning. It means a famous sect of Islām, called *S͟hi'atu'l-'Alī*, the Followers of Imām 'Alī.

But here we wish to mention about those martyrs of Karbala, who were Associates of Imām 'Alī; those of his contemporary Associates, who participated in the Wars of Jamal, Ṣiffīn and Nahrwān etc. along with him. Some among them were in his Caliphate government on various posts during the revolt period (June 655 AD-January, 661 AD). A few among them were the disciples of Imām 'Alī, who were experts in the Science and Divine Jurisprudence. Some of them had joined Kabala war along with Imām Ḥusain.

Abū-Thamāmah 'Omarū-bin-'Abdu'llāh Ṣāy'dī

Kufic resident Abū-Thamāmah 'Omarū-bin-'Abdu'llāh Ṣāy'dī is famous in the history for various distinctions. He was quite popular for his bravery in the entire 'Arabian peninsula and was highly dedicated to Imām 'Alī. He was an associate with Muslim-bin-'Aqīl-bin-Abī Ṭālib, Peace-Envoy of Imām Ḥusain, came to Kufa and acted as his Cashier. Muslim used to deposit his entire cash to him and weapons were also purchased through him, because he was an expert in this field also. When Muslim became a martyr he came in contact with Imām Ḥusain, and came out from Kufa along with the other associate Nāfa'-bin-Hilāl Jamalī Al-Murādī. When most of Ḥusainī soldiers were killed and it was the time for the *Ẓuhr Namāż* (the Noon Prayer). Abū-Thamāmah reminded him, Sir ! This is the best time of the noon prayer. Looking up at the sky Imām Ḥusain said, Certainly this is the special time of the *Ẓuhr*! Then he wished for Abū-Thamāmah Ṣāy'dī, God may count him among best one who offered His prayer. It is very difficutt to find out the appropriate time for the Noon-Prayer. Somebody asked Imām Ja'far aṣ-Ṣādiq, how could identify the first time for the Noon-Prayer? He replied, when the sun comes to the sky exactly in the middle, then a white line emerges. The inquirer said, he had tried for this several times, but could never see any white line emerged. Imām Ja'far aṣ-Ṣādiq said, that is the matter of knowledge of *Imām*. He alone can realises that line. In Karbala when Abū-Thamāmah drew the attention of Imām Ḥusain, then Imām Ḥusain after seeing towards the sky said, Certainly that is the exact time for the Noon-Prayer. With this it can be said admiring Abū-Thamāmah that although he was not Imām, but had the foresight of an Imām !

Jaun

Jaun was Abyssenian by birth. He was famous and respected being in the service of the Prophet's famous Companion, Abūżar Ghaffārī, who has the testimony of the Prophet to the effect that the Universe has seen no Truthful person better than Abūżar Ghaffārī. He had nourished Jaun in his style. Some say, he was a Christian and his actual name was John. I found no reliable source in support or denial. Possibility could not be ruled out. God knows better.

Abūżar Ghaffārī was unique and superior among the Companions of the holy Prophet of Islām. Jaun was his favourite servant, who was Abyssenian by birth. Firstly, he was the servant of Faz'l-bin-'Abbās Hāshmī. Imām 'Alī had purchased him for 150 gold coins and offered him to Abūžar <u>Gh</u>affārī. He remained with his master Abūžar <u>Gh</u>affārī throughout his life. After his demise, he served the Household of the Prophet and came to Karbala with them. He sought permission to fight and became a martyr. Imām Ḥusain showed reluctance. It hurt Jaun and he reacted sharply. Of course, I am a black man, my blood is dirty, bad smell comes from my body. It could not be mingled with the clean, pure and chaste blood! Imām Ḥusain wept, permitted him and prayed to God, Oh Almighly! Jaun's face be delighted and best smell be spread from his body. People saw the miracle after the martyrdom to be true and fact.

Shožab-bin-'Abdu'llāh

Shožab belonged to a branch of Hamādanī clan, known as <u>Sh</u>ākirī and was in the sevice of 'Ābis-bin-Abī <u>Sh</u>abīb <u>Sh</u>ākirī. He was a resident of Kufa. He attained training in religious education from Imām 'Alī. He was guiding people in religious sciences. Taking a letter from Muslim-bin-'Aqīl in Kufa, he came to Imām Ḥusain along with his master 'Ābis-bin-Abī <u>Sh</u>abīb. During war in Karbala 'Ābis asked his dutiful servant Shožab-bin-'Abdu'llāh, what he thought about sacrifice? Shožab replied, what else, except remaining with him. He would fight in support of the son of Prophet and he wished to be sacrificed. 'Ābis-bin-Abī <u>Sh</u>abīb became amicably happy and praised him ! This he expected from him. Shožab came to the war front, fought and sacrificed his life in the path of God.

Ḥujjāj-bin-Masrūq Ja'fī

Ḥujjāj-bin-Masrūq was the heir of renowned Kufic Ja'f-bin-Sa'du'l-'A<u>sh</u>īra. Getting the information that Imām Ḥusain was in Mecca, he went there for his service. Imām Ḥusain accorded him, the then one of the most high position of *Mu'ažžin* (Caller for *Ažān*) and he began to call for *Namāż* regularly and punctually, Therefore, when the then Yažīdī Commander Ḥurr-bin-Yažīd-Riyāḥī interrupted the Caravan of Imām Ḥusain, at that crutial hour too, Ḥujjāj-bin-Masrūq Ja'fī called for *Ẓuhr Namāż* and all including enemies performed the prayer under the leadership of Imām Ḥusain. In the battle of Karbala Ḥujjāj-bin-Masrūq fought in support of Imām Ḥusain and became a Martyr.

Mujama'-bin-'Abdu'llāh 'Āyižī

Mujama's father 'Abdu'llāh Sa'du'l-'A<u>sh</u>īra Ḥujjī 'Āyižī, was the

Companion of the holy Prophet of Islām and Mujama' himself was lucky enough to be the Associate of Imām 'Alī. He was one of the five people, who met Imām Ḥusain, during his journey at the camp of 'Ażību'l Hijānāt. On being enquired by Imām Ḥusain about the status of present Kufa, his words are safe with history, already discussed in the previous pages. Mujama'-bin-'Abdu'llāh 'Āyiżī fought with his team in support of Imām Ḥusain and sacrificed his life.

Shabīb-bin-'Abdu'llāh Nahashalī

When Imām Ḥusain commenced his journey from Medina, Shabīb-bin-'Abdu'llāh Nahashalī also accompanied him. He was among the Associates of Imām 'Alī and joined him in the Wars of Jamal, Ṣiffīn and Nahrwān. In Karbala he became a victim of severe cowardly bow-arrows attack of the Yażīdī Army.

Qāsiṭ-bin-Żuhayr-bin-Ḥārith Taghalabī

Qāsiṭ-bin-Żuhayr and his brothers Kardūs and Muqsit were among the famous Associates of Imām 'Alī in Kufa. Qāsit had the privilege of fighting in the Wars of Jamal, Ṣiffīn and Nahrwān. He with his brave brothers reached Imām Ḥusain in Karbala with utmost secrecy, fought and became a martyr.

Kardūs-bin-Żuhayr-bin-Ḥārith Taghalabī

Kardūs too was one of the Associates of of Imām 'Alī in Kufa. He joined Imām Ḥusain like his own brothers and became victim of cowardly bow-arrows attack of the Yażīdī Army.

Muqsiṭ (Kursh)-bin-Żuhayr-bin-Ḥārith Taghalabī

Muqsiṭ also was among the Associates of Imām 'Alī like his brothers Qāsit and Kardūs. Muqsiṭ had also been called by the histonians as Kursh He joined him in all the wars. All the three brothers reached Imām Ḥusain in a secret manner at his service and attained martyrdom in the cowardly bow-arrows attack of the Yażīdī Army.

Jinādah-bin-Ḥārith Salmānī

He was a resident of Kufa, living during the life-time of the Prophet of

Islām. He was among the supporters of Muslim-bin-'Aqīl. While fighting with enemies, he fell down on the ground and was killed. He was also among those who met Imām Ḥusain at his camp of 'Ażību'l Hijānāt.

Junadab-bin-Ḥajīr Kindī Khūlānī

He was a Kufa dweller. He had been the Associates of Imām 'Alī. He was also one of the Commanders in the Ṣiffīn-War. In Karbala he fought with the Yażīdī Army and became a martyr.

Umayyah-bin-Sa'd-bin-Żaid Ṭaī

He belonged to famous 'Arabic clan Ṭaī, and had fame for his bravery, warriorship and horse-riding. He exposed his calibre in Ṣiffīn war under Imām 'Alī. Afterwards he lived in Kufa. When Imām Ḥusain had reached Karbala, he presented himself at his service. He was also killed in the cowardly bow-arrows attack.

Jiblitah-bin-'Alī Shaybānī

He was a Kufa dweller, brave and excellent warrior. He joined Imām 'Alī in Ṣiffīn-war. He was one of the supporters of Muslim-bin-'Aqīl. After his martyrdom, somehow he reached Karbala and submitted himself to the service of Imām Ḥusain. He was killed in the cowardly bow-arrows the Yażīdī attack.

Ḥārith-bin-Nibhān

Ḥārith's father Nibhān was in the service of the holy Prophet's uncle renowned Martyr Ḥamżah-bin-'Abdu'l-Maṭṭalib. Ḥārith too lived with his father. After Ḥamżah becoming martyr in Uḥad-war (624 AD), Nibhān began to live with Imām 'Alī. Then he lived with Imām Ḥasan and then with Imām Ḥusain. When Imām Ḥusain left Medina, Ḥārith also accompanied him. He was famous as a great warrior and cavalier. In Karbala he became victim of cowardly bow-arrows the Yażīdī attack.

Ḥallās-bin-'Omarū Ażdī Rāsbī

Ḥallās was so reliable to Imām 'Alī that at the time of outbreak during his Caliphate he was a police officer of Kufa. Ḥallās had come to Karbala in 'Omar-bin-Sa'd's Army. When 'Omar-bin-Sa'd rejected the peace-proposals of Imām Ḥusain, Ḥallās could not remain in his Army. Confidentially he joined the Ḥusainī Army during night. He became a martyr in cowardly bow-arrows attack of the Yażīdī Army.

No'mān-bin-'Omarū Ażdī Rāsbī

No'mān was a resident of Kufa, who had the opportunity of being Associates of Imām 'Alī in Ṣiffīn-war. He and his brother Ḥallās came to Karbala with 'Omar-bin-Sa'd's Army. When Imām Husain's peace-proposal was rejected they left the Yażīdī Army and became martyr at the shower of cowardly bow-arrows attack of the Yażīdī Army.

Naī'm-bin-'Ajalān Anṣārī

Naī'm's father 'Ajalān-bin-No'mān Anṣārī was appointed Ruler of Baharain by Imām 'Alī. Naī'm and his other brothers Nazar and No'mān were the Associates of Imām 'Alī and had participated in the wars of Jamal, Ṣiffīn and Nahrwān with Imām 'Alī. When Imām Ḥusain reached Karbala Naī'm joined him somehow and became a martyr in the war.

Yażīd-bin-Żiyād-bin-Mahāṣar Abu'l al-Sh'athā Kindī

His father Żiyād-bin-Mahāṣar Abu'l al-Sh'athā Kindī was one of the Companions of the holy Prophet of Islām. Yażīd fought Ṣiffīn-war against Mu'āwiyah-bin-Abū Sufyyān and was deputed as a Commander by Imām 'Alī for suppressing the revolt in Ahwaz. He became a martyr while fighting in Karbala in the path of Truth.

'Omarū-bin-Uḥadūth Ḥazaramī Kindī

'Omarū-bin-Uḥadūth Ḥazaramī was a Kufan, who had fought in the wars of Jamal and Ṣiffīn under the flag of Imām 'Alī. He was one of the close colleagues of Ḥujr-bin-'Adī Kindī and his famous colleagues, Sharīk-bin-Shaddād, Zayfī-bin-Fuzayl, Qabīsah-bin-Zabī'ah, Muharaz-bin-Shahāb, Karām-bin-Jabān and 'Abdu'r-Raḥmān-bin-Ḥassān. It is one of the tragic incidents of history of Islām in which Amīr Mu'āwiyah got killed, without any crime, these pious and august Associates of Imām 'Alī. 'Omarū-bin-Uḥadūth Ḥazaramī was also under demand, but he went underground and when the wicked Governor of Kufa Żiyād-bin-Abīh died, he surfaced again and returned to Kufa. When Ḥusainī peace-envoy Muslim came to Kufa, he joined him. After Muslim's becoming a martyr, he somehow reached Imām Ḥusain, fought and became martyr.

Sa'd-bin-Ḥāri<u>th</u>

He had the honour of being at the service of Imām 'Alī. After his passing away he was at the services of Imām Hassan and then Imām Ḥusain. He came to Karbala with Imām Ḥusain from Medina. He fought with the Yażīdī Army and sacrificed his life in the path of God.

The Scholars and Scientists

All of them, who sacrificed their life for the cause of Truth in Karbala along with Imām Ḥusain, were the ardent followers of Qur'an. Some of them were famous scholars and scientists of Qur'anic knowledge and wisdom, because, to seek knowledge is a sacred duty; it is obligatory on every Muslim, male and female. The first revelation of the Qur'an was *Iqra'* (Read). Seek knowledge! Educate yourselves! Be educated. The text of the Qur'an is filled with verses inviting man to use his intellect (mind, intelligence), to ponder (think deeply), to think and to know.

The discussion on the holy Prophet's Companion 'Abdu'r Raḥmān-bin-'Abd Rab Anṣārī <u>Kh</u>iżarajjī has already been done in the previous pages. He was a renowned *Ḥāfiẓ* (literally means, a guardian or a protector, but actually he is considerd the Preserver of the Qur'an, who knows by heart each and every word of the Qur'an). He had most august position in the Islāmic history. He sacrificed his life for safeguarding the Truth.

Burayr-bin-<u>Kh</u>uzayr Hamadānī

Burayr-bin-<u>Kh</u>uzayr was the old friend of Imām 'Alī. He was *Ḥāfiẓ* and *Qāri'*. Also famous as *Saiyedu'l Qurrā'* (Leader of Qāri's) *Qāri'* (plural, *qurrā'*) the Reader, who recites the Qur'an with *Tajwīd* (the proper rules of recitation of Qur'an).

Burayr was the member of the Central Bureau, which was cteated by Imām 'Alī, intending the training of the crude 'Arabs for becoming educated and cultured persons. He was deputed for training *Qāri's* as per rules of recitation of the Qur'an, details mentioned in chapter one of the book.

Burayr was recognised as the elites of Kufa. He was considered as the expert of elucidation and application of the *Shari'a.* He was preaching the holy Qur'an and chanting and training *Qāri's* regularly in the Mosque of Kufa. Burayr was so honoured in the society that when the Yażīdī soldiers attacked him some other soldiers of the same battalion prohibited attacking him telling them that Burayr was *Ḥāfiẓ* and *Qāri'* who had been teaching people throughout his life. Still some soldiers attacked with spears from behind and it came out from his chest. Afterwards his head was chopped off with a sword.

Nāfa'-bin-Hilāl Jamalī Al-Murādī

Nāfa'-bin-Hilāl Jamalī was expert in *'Ilmu'l Qur'an* (Qur'anology) and the Islāmic jurisprudence. He was considered as most trusted narrators of *Ḥadīth* (tradition), the words of the holy Prophet Muḥammad. He was the chief of his clan and a famous warrior. He was among those Associates of Imām 'Alī, who joined him in the wars of Jamal, Ṣiffīn and Nahrwān. Being informed of the arrival of Imām Ḥusain towards Iraq, he set out from Kufa in such a hurry as his beloved horse, which he called Kāmil, somehow was left in Kufa itself. Friends arranged to get delivered it to him. Therefore, Mujama'-bin-'Abdu'llāh 'Āyiżī met Imām Ḥusain at the camp of 'Ażību'l Hijānāt on the way to Karbala. He had brought his horse also along with him. Nāfa'-bin-Hilāl was an expert in aiming an arrow. His an arrow-aiming talent has already been discussed in the previous pages. The Yażīdī Army arrested him and murdered.

Kinānah-bin-'Atīq Taghalabī

Kinānah was honoured to be an authority on the *Qur'an*. He was famous for his clean and pious life. He became a martyr being a victim of the Yażīdī Army, famous for the shower of cowardly bow-arrows attack.

Ḥanẓalah-bin-Asa'd Shabāmī

Ḥanẓalah-bin-Asa'd was a famous orator and great *Qāri'* who recited the Qur'an with the proper rules of the recitation of the Qur'an in Kufa. He perfomed the duty of peace-message of Imām Ḥusain to 'Omar-bin-Sa'd. Exhibiting his excellence oratorship on many occasions, he forcefully explained the objectives of Imām Ḥusain's rising against usurped the Islāmic Rule. He fought and became a martyr.

Wazaḥ

Wazaḥ's identity has not been by his name, but, he is better known as Turkish slave, who sacrificed his life on the path of God, as the historians mention. No doubt he was a Turkish liberated slave of Ḥārith Mashājī.

Later he served Imām Ḥusain, who offered him to Imām Żainu'l-Ābidīn. However, he had great qualities of being powerful *Qāri'* and expert of the Qur'anology. He attained martyrdom while fighting with the Yażīdī Army in the battlefield. When Imām Ḥusain reached, he was at his last breathing. Imām Ḥusain put his hands on his shoulder. He opened his eyes and saw Imām Ḥusain, smiled and closed his eyes.

Scholars, Theologists and Traditionists

In the Islāmic terminology *'Ulma* means Scholars, *Faqīh,* who deals with elucidation and application of the *Sharī'a* or Theologist and *Muḥaddith*, Expert of *Ḥadīth* or Traditionists. There are so many such persons among the Karbala martyrs through their medium, the Traditions of the holy Prophet of Islām could reach the future generations. Various Books of *Ḥadīths* are available at present of the *Ḥadīth* rendered by him. There are so many eminent personalities standing at the highest pedestals as speciality in multi-religious visions, like Muslim-bin-'Ausajah Asadī, Ḥabīb-bin-Maẓāhir Asadī, Nāfa'-bin-Hilāl Jamalī Al-Murādī, Anas-bin-Kāhil-bin-Ḥārith Asadī, Shožab-bin-'Abdu'llāh and Żāhar-bin-'Omarū Aslamī Kindī, who have already been discussed also in the above pages. Besides them, the following scholars, theologists and traditionists would be discussed as under.

Ḥabshatah-bin-Qays Nahamī

Ḥabshatah was a famous narrater of the Traditions of the holy Prophet of Islām. His grandfather Salmah-bin-Zarif Hamadani was among the companions of the Prophet. He used to refer him while narrating the Traditions of the holy Prophet. He became a martyr being a victim of the shower of cowardly bow-arrows attack of the Yażīdī Army.

Sawwār-bin-Abī 'Oman Nahamī

Sawwār-bin-Abī 'Oman Nahamī was a popular narrator of the Traditions of the holy Prophet of Islām. While fighting with the Yażīdī Army, he fell down being wounded. Soldier's took him to the Yażīdī Commander-in-Chief 'Omar-bin-Sa'd, who ordered to murder him, but the other soldiers got him saved, in view of his being the popular narrator of the Traditions of the holy Prophet. They took him with them, but he was so injured that he could not survive after, suffering for six months because of heavy wounds.

Highly Prestigious Warriors

Most of the martyrs of the Battle of Karbala were highly prestigious and honoured great warrious and were very known within Arabian peninsula. Therefore, when they came to the battlefield, though thirsty for last three days, their opponents had no courage to face them out of fear and doubt, whether to fight them or not, because they were afraid enough to face them, they themselves realized the fact. They were not mere warriors famous for their bravery, fighting skills and all that, but actually they were very popular for their devotion to God and piety and honesty etc. So, many historians have mentioned that 'Ābis-bin-Abī Shabīb Shākirī was so engrossed in the devotion of God that he use to pray the whole night for several days continuously, he was very famous for his prayers. He had obtained the title *'Ābid Shabżindādār,* such a person doing prayers for the whole nights. Muslim-bin-'Ausajah Asadī, the Companion of the Prophet of Islām has already been discussed. The remaining distinguished warriors are as mentioned below:

Ḥurr-bin-Yażīd-Riyāḥī

Ḥurr's ancestors had prestigious position in 'Arabian peninsula even prior to the advent of Islām. Hurr's grandfather 'Atab-bin-Harmī Riyāḥī was the part of the royalty of Ḥira king No'aman. After the death of 'Atab, his son Qan'ab got his post, who was the grandfather of Ḥurr. In the very family was Akhwāṣ Shā'ir, one of the Companions of the holy Prophet, also the cousin of Ḥurr's father.

Some of the facts about Ḥurr have already been discussed in detail. His speciality was, that he was the person under whose command the Yażīdī Army obstructed the jouney of Imām Ḥusain and forced him go to Karbala, then hearing the inner-voice of him, he left the post of Commander in the Yażīdī Army and fought in support of Imām Ḥusain and sacrificed his life along with his sons 'Alī and Sa'd, brother Muṣa'b and servent Qurrah.

Żuhayr-bin-Qayn-bin-Qays Numayrī Bajalī

Żuhayr-bin-Qayn was one among the elites of Kufa. He was very famous as a warrior. As he belonged to Umayyite clan, people in general thought of him being from enemy side of the Prophet, but in reality he was an ardent devotee of *Ahlu'l-Bayt* and Imām Ḥusain. Therefore, when 'Azarah of the Yażīdī Army saw him among the supporters of Imām

Ḥusain. He asked him in the wonder: Oh Żuhayr Qayn, you were not with the supporters of that family! You were of the enemy's group. Żuhayr Qayn replied, at this time by standing there, you must understand that I am the supporter of Imām 'Alī ! Żuhayr Qayn was one of the most important part of Imām Ḥusain's small army, who was bestowed the honour of Commander of the Right Wing Regiment. On many occasions, the discussion of his powerful speeches has been already done in previous pages. He fought in support of Imām Ḥusain and sacrificed his life.

Wahab-Kalbi, 'Abdu'llāh-bin-'Omayr Kalbī

The correct name of Wahab-Kalbi has come into argument easily though all are aware in the same manner right from, ancient time till the present. 'Allāmah Ibn Ṭāūs (d.1266 AD)[47] and 'Allāmah al-Majlisī, Muḥammad Bāqir (d. 1699 AD)[48] also have written his name as Wahab-bin-Habab (or Khabab) Kalabi only. But 'Allāmah 'Alī Naqī Naqavī (d. 1988 AD)[49] has written his name as 'Abdu'llāh-bin-'Omayr Kalbī besides, presenting all the same, which above noted renowned authorities have mentioned. 'Allāmah 'Alī Naqī Naqavī has given his genealogy as – Abū Wahab 'Abdu'llāh-bin-'Omayr-bin-'Abbās-bin-'Abd Qaiys-bin-'Alīm-bin-Khabāb al-Kalbī. After going through various reliable sources,[50] in my considered opinion it nothing, but a case of mistaken identity of the same person. He had the Christian family background. His brave warriorship has already been discussed in the previous pages. His mother's encouragements have also been mentioned. Wahab-Kalbi has special honour of being the husband of Umm Wahab-bint-Ma'bad, the lone lady martyr of the Battle of Karbala.

Ḥārith-bin-Imra-ul-Qays-bin-'Ābis Kindī

He was a true Believer, who had intelligently overcome the difficult situation. When he saw no way to reach Imām Ḥusain's place, he joined the Yażīdī Army and he came to Karbala from Kufa. He came out from the Yażīdī Army and joined Imām Ḥusain. He became martyr at the cowardly arrows the Yażīdī attack.

Masū'd-bin-Ḥujjāj Taymī

He was among the brave soldiers of Kufa. He reached Karbala after joining the the Yażīdī Commander-in-Chief 'Omar-bin-Sa'd's Regiment, along with his son 'Abdu'r Raḥmān. He revolted and left the Yażīdī Army, when they stopped water for Imām Ḥusain's associates, ladies and children. He came to Imām Ḥusain pretending to salute him, but did not return. He became a martyr in the cowardly arrows attack of the Yażīdī Army.

'Ābis-bin-Abī Shabīb Shākirī

He was the son of the Shākirī branch of famous Hamadanī clan, who had been matchless in support of Imām 'Alī. No person from this clan ever joined Amīr Mu'āwiyah in the wars. Imām 'Alī's poetry is available regarding them:

> Could I be gate-keeper of the Heaven,
> I would say, Hamadanī to proceed with salutation.[51]

'Ābis-bin-Abī Shabīb was known among the supporter of Imām 'Alī at Kufa. He was a famous warrior, a great leader of his community, an effective orator and was leading a simple and pure life and he was also popular for his devotion to God. He was recognised as a very courageous warrior. When Imām Ḥusain's messenger Muslim reached Kufa and read out the his letter, it was 'Ābis, who stood first in his support and said, that he dids not say about others, but as far as his personal opinion was concerned, he was determined that he should be in his company till his last breath. Firstly, 'Ābis sacrificed his attendant Shożab-bin-'Abdu'llāh and then said, If he had to sacrifice something more valuable than his life, he would certainly sacrifice it at the feet of Imām Ḥusain. Since he had just his own life remaining, he appealed to Imām Ḥusain, please allow me. He reached the war front already injured on his forehead. As soon as the war started he murdered many the Yażīdī soldiers, nobody was able to with stand before him. 'Omar-Sa'd ordered to throw stones at the brave warrior and kill him and there was actually a heavey rain of stones on the great warrior 'Ābis-bin-Abī Shabīb removed his armour and fought continuously. At last the Yażīdī s surrounded him from all sides and their crowd attacked him jointly and finally chopped off his head. Then they quarelled themselves for the credit of murdering him. 'Omar-Sa'd decided the credit should not go to any individual as, all of them have killed him.

Sa'īd-bin-'Abdu'llāh Ḥasafī

Kufan dweller and the warrior Sa'īd-bin-'Abdu'llāh Ḥasafī was remembered as deeply engrossed in prayers of God. Taking the last invitation letter of Kufa dwellers, he presented himself before Imām Ḥusain. When the Yażīdī Army refused permission to perform Namāż by Imām Ḥusain in the battlefield, but showered arrows Sa'īd-bin-'Abdu'llāh Ḥasafī stood firmly with Żuhayr-bin-Qayn-bin-Qays Numayrī Bajalī before Imām Ḥusain for gaurding him from enemies arrow showering. He was stopping the arrows with his sword, if it was not possible, then he took the arrows on his chest. Both the worriors were dancing embracing each other. Imām Ḥusain finished his Namāż, both of them fell on his feet. Żuhayr-bin-Qayn has wounds, but lived for some time, then he fought but Sa'īd-bin-'Abdu'llāh Ḥasafī went to Heavenly abode, as soon as he fell at the feet of Imām Ḥusain.

Żiyād-bin-'Arīb Hamadānī

Żiyād-bin-'Arīb's full name was Abū 'Āmir Żiyād-bin-'Omarū. His father 'Omarū-bin-'Arīb Hamadānī was among the Associates of the holy Prophet of Islām. Żiyād was not only highly pious, religious minded, simple and straightforward and dedicatd towards truth, but also was a reputed worrior of his time. He fought in Karbala supporting Imām Ḥusain and attained martydom.

'Omarū-bin-Zab'aitah-bin-Qays Zab'ī Taymī

He was a famous litigious of his time. At many times, he unfolded his flag of victory. He went to Karbala with 'Omar-Sa'd's Army and then joined Imām Ḥusain. He became victim in the cowardly arrows attack of the Yażīdī Army.

Qāsim-bin-Ḥabīb-bin-Abī Bishr Ażdī

He was among the very brave soldiers and was considered as highly reliable to Imām 'Alī. He reached Karbala with 'Omar-Sa'd's Army and joined the Ḥusainī Army. He also became victim in the cowardly arrows attack of the Yażīdī Army.

Yażīd-bin-Żiyād-bin-Mahāṣar Abu'l al-Sh'athā Kindī

He was famous among the highly brave persons of Kufa. Even prior to meeting Ḥurr, he joined Imām Ḥusain. He was an expert in aiming arrows. On the day of martyrdom, he kneeled down before Imām Ḥusain and aimed eight arrows on enemies, out of which five achieved the target and murdered the five Yażīdīs. When his arrows were exhausted, he plunged into the battlefield with his sword, fought and became a martyr.

Swaid-bin-'Omar-bin-Abī Maṭa al-Khath'amī

Swaid-bin-'Omar was one of the elderly persons of the Ḥusainī Army. He had exhibited his high talents in many battles. He was last martyr amongst the Associates of Imām Ḥusain, who came to the war front after Bishr-bin-'Omarū-bin-Uḥadūth Ḥazaramī Kindī. He fought extraordinarily and then fell down injured. People thought that he was dead. His sword and other clothes were looted. He revived from his unconsciousness, when Imām Ḥusain had already become a martyr. He became very sad. Taking a knife from near, he plunged into the battlefield and became a martyr.

Other Great Personalities

Keeping in view the convenience of the readers, we have discussed the martyrs of the different categories. We could never presume any priority among them. Their seniority could be understood on the basis that they sacrificed their own life fighting first one better than the other. Submitting of the flowers of the most heart felt homage in *Żiyarat al-Naḥiyah*, Imām al-Mahdī, it has been said, addressing them:

> "But as I have been hindered by the course of time, and (God's) decree has prevented me from helping you, and as I could not fight those who fought you, and was not able to show hostility to those who showed hostility to you, I will, therefore, lament you morning and evening, and will shed blood in place of tears, out of my anguish for you and my sorrow for all that befell you..."

Munjiḥ-bin-Sahm

Munjiḥ's name comes first among the foremost martyrs of Karbala. His mother was the attendant of Imām Ḥusain, whom he purchased from Nofil-bin-Ḥārith-bin-'Abdu'l-Maṭṭalib and married to Sahm. She was serving at Imām Żainu'l-Ābidīn's house. She came to Karbala along with Imām Ḥusain. Her son Munjiḥ also come along with her. Fought and became a martyr.

'Omar-bin-Khālid Asadī Ṣaidavī

'Omar-bin-Khālid belonged elite class of Kufa. He was dedicated to the family members of Islāmic Prophet. Offered a prominent role in support of Muslim at Kufa. After his killing, he went underground. When the enemies arrested Imām Ḥusain's other messengers Qays-bin-Muṣahar Ṣaidāvī, he declared that Imām Ḥusain has reached the Ḥājaz. Whosoever is desirous to meet him, may go there. When 'Omar-bin-Khālid received the news, he managed to meet Imām Ḥusain at his camp 'Ažību'l Hijānāt going by unknown ways along with his sevant Saī'd and three other people. On the Martyrs'day 'Omar-bin-Khālid and his friends had attacked the enemy army and entering into the army murdered so many soldiers. The Yažīdī Army took them into a strong hold. Then, immediately Imām Ḥusain set his Commander Abu'l-Fazl'il-'Abbās for his assistance. Taking him away from their cluch 'Abbās took him back. In view of security, he advanced all these five soldiers and he himself was going behind. The enemies chased, there was no limit of the wounded soldiers enthusiasm, they breaking the security armour, they attacked the enemies, they fought boldly and became martyr.

Saī'd

'Omar-bin-Khālid's servant Saī'd gave company to his master till his last breath. His brave fighting has already been discussed in the above mentioned lines.

Zaḥāq-bin-'Abdu'llāh Mashriqī

Zaḥāq Mashriqī has been unique among supporters of Imām Ḥusain in the sense that he fought for safeguarding Truth and killed enemies throwing arrows on them. When the stock of arrows exhausted, he told Imām Ḥusain that now his vow was over. He had taken an oath to struggle for Truth under your leadership, now that phase was over. And requested relieve him from his *Bay'at* from him and let him go back. Imām Ḥusain, as he was advising his Associates to return from the beginning, but no body was prepared to go back, when Zaḥāq Mashriqī wanted permission to go back, he was allowed to return with great pleasure. Mounting on his horse he struggled with the Yažīdī Army and went out. Afterwards, he was recognisied as a describer of Karbala tragedy. His book *Maqālātu'l Ḥusain* is considered as one of the main sources.

Adaham-bin-Umayyah 'Abdī Baṣarī

He belonged to 'Abd-Qays clan of Basra, where a lady Mariyah-bint-Minqad 'Abdiyah, was a special devotee of Imām 'Alī. So many other devotees used to assemble in her house. Adaham-bin-Umayyah derived motivation from them. Imām Ḥusain was only within the borders of Mecca, four persons met him, who afterward became martyrs in Karbala, Adaham-bin-Umayyah was one among them.

Jābir-bin-Hujjāj Taymī

He was residing in Kufa's famous clan Tayam, as the servant of 'Āmir-bin-Nahashal. He was known for his brave achievements. He also reached Karbala after being recruited in 'Omar-Sa'd's Army. He joined Imām Ḥusain in the night leaving the Yażīdī Army along with his other people. He became a martyr being a victim of the cowardly arrows attack of the Yażīdī Army.

Jinādah-bin-K'ab-bin-Ḥārith Anṣārī Khiżarajjī

He came to Karbala with his family from Mecca accompaning Imām Ḥusain. Became a martyr with the cowardly arrows attack of the Yażīdī Army.

Ḥabāb-bin-Ḥārith

No more information available about him except this much that he became a martyr at the cowardly arrows attack of the Yażīdī Army.

Ḥabāb-bin-'Āmir-bin-Ka'b Tayamī

He belonged to Kufa's famous clan Tayamīu'l Lat-bin-Th'albah. After Muslim's becoming of a martyr, he hid himself and when heared Imām Ḥusain heading towards Kufa, he came and joinied Imām Ḥusain in his way. He fought for Truth and became a martyr in the war.

Ḥujjāj-bin-Żaid-Sa'dī Tayamī

He was a member of Banī-Sa'd of Basra. He went to Imām Ḥusain as a bearer of the letter of Masū'd-bin-'Omarū Ażdī to whom Imām Ḥusain had written a letter at the time of his departure from Mecca. He came to Imām Ḥusain with his reply. Became a martyr at the cowardly arrows attack of the Yażīdī Army.

'Abdu'r Raḥmān-bin-'Abdu'llāh-bin-Kadan Arḥabī

He was among the veterans of Kufa. He came with the second delegation of the people of Kufa, who had brought 53 letters addressed to Imām Ḥusain expressing their faith. Thereafter, Imām Ḥusain sent his peace envoy Muslim to Kufa and 'Abdu'r Raḥmān was asked to accompany him as a guide. After the martyrdom of Muslim, 'Abdu'r Raḥmān somehow reached Karbala and became a martyr at the cowardly arrows attack of the Yażīdī Army.

Żāhayr-bin-Bishr Khitha'mī

He also became a martyr at the cowardly arrows attack of the Yażīdī Army. No further information is available.

Sālim

He was 'Āmir-bin-Muslim al-'Abdī's servant. He came to Imām Ḥusain with his master with the same group of people, in which was Żayd-bin-Thabayṭ u'l 'Abdī Qaysī from Basara.

Salīm

He was the attendant of Imām Ḥusain and scarificed his life at the cowardly arrows attack of the Yażīdī Army.

Saif-bin-Mālik 'Abdī

He was attached with a clan of Basara, 'Abd-Qays. He came to Imām Ḥusain alongwith Żayd-bin-Thabayṭ u'l 'Abdī Qaysī from Basara and attained martyrdom at the cowardly arrows attack of the Yażīdī Army.

Zarghamah-bin-Mālik Taghalabī

He was a resident of Kufa. He went underground after Muslims being murdered. He got himself recruited in the Yażīdī Army for reaching to

Karbala and attained martyrdom at the cowardly arrows attack of the Yażīdī Army.

'Āmir-bin-Muslim 'Abdī Baṣrī

He was a resident of Basara, who submitted himself before Imām Ḥusain along with Żayd-bin-Thabayṭ u'l 'Abdī Qaysī. Became a martyr at the cowardly arrows attack of the Yażīdī Army.

'Ibad-bin-Muhājir-bin-Abī Muhājir Juhanī

After the departure of Imām Ḥusain from Mecca many people had joined him. Aprising of the stitution to the people, when Imām Ḥusain at Zabālah camp, advised greedy people to leave his company, because he was not after capturing wealth, people's croud left him, but 'Ibad-bin-Muhājir did not leave him and was found standing like a rock. He came to Karbala with Imām Ḥusain and became a martyr in the war.

'Abdu'r Raḥmān-bin-Mas'ūd-bin-Ḥujjāj Tayamī

'Abdu'r Raḥmān-bin-Mas'ūd had came to the camp of Imām Ḥusain at Karbala along with his father Mas'ūd-bin-Ḥujjāj Tayamī at the pretext of paying his respect and merely saluting Imām Ḥusain. But never returned again to the Yażīdī Army. He forcefully fought for the cause of Truth and sacrificed his life at the holy feet of Imām Ḥusain.

'Abdu'llāh-bin-Bishr Khith'amī

His father Bishr Khith'amī was a great warrior of his time. He had trained his son 'Abdu'llāh in war skill. He came to Karbala along with the Yażīdī Commander-in-Chief, 'Omar-Sa'd. But serectly joined the Ḥusainī Army and attained Heavenly abode in the cowardly arrows attack of the Yażīdī Army.

'Abdu'r Raḥmān-bin-Żayd-bin-Thabayṭ Qaysī

'Abdu'r Raḥmān's father Żayd-bin-Thabayṭ Qaysī was a true believer and fully devoted to the holy Prophet and the Progeny of the Prophet Muḥammad. When he learnt the rising of Imām Ḥusain against the anti-Islāmic Umayyite rule. Żayd-bin-Thabayṭ Qaysī persuaded his ten sons to sacrifies their life at the holy feet of Imām Ḥusain, but only two of his sons supported his views. 'Abdu'r Raḥmān's was among them. He came to Karbala along with his father and became a martyr at the cowardly arrows attack of the Yażīdī Army.

'Oqbah-bin-Sama'n

He was an attendant of Umm Rabāb, the wife of Imām Ḥusain. He went to Mecca from Medina and then to Karbala with Ḥusainī caravan. On the Day of Martyrdom, he somehow escaped from death. He was also brought to Kufa as the prisoner and relieved by 'Obaydu'llāh-bin-Żiyād. He had been eyewitness of each and every incident of the Battle of Karbala. Later on he wrote the book *Maqālātu'l Ḥusain*, which is considered a reliable source.

Muṣa'b-bin-Yażīd Riyāḥī

He came to Imām Ḥusain along with his brother Ḥurr-bin-Yażīd-Riyāḥī. Fought and became a martyr.

Sa'd and 'Alī-bin-Ḥurr-bin-Yażīd-Riyāḥī

Both the sons of Ḥurr-bin-Yażīd-Riyāḥī went to Imām Ḥusain with their father Ḥurr and uncle Muṣa'b. Fought and attained Heavenly abode.

Qurrah

He was the servant of Ḥurr-bin-Yażīd-Riyāḥī. He was in the battlefield only along with his master Ḥurr. When his master rejected the Yażīdī Army and came to Imām Ḥusain, he also accompanied his master fought and and sacrificed his life.

'Oqbah-bin-Ṣulet Juhanī

He joined Imām Ḥusain on the way along with other people, but other people went away after knowing the situation. But 'Oqbah-bin-Ṣulet did not leave the path of truth, came to Karbala with Imām Ḥusain. He was a victim of cowardly arrows attack of the Yażīdī Army.

'Ammār-bin-Ḥassān-bin-Shurayb Ṭaī

'Ammār's celebrated father Ḥassān-bin-Shurayb Ṭaī was one of the

Associates of Imām 'Alī. 'Ammār came to Karbala from Mecca along with Imām Ḥusain. He became a martyr at cowardly arrows attack of the Yazīdī Army. In his heirs, 'Abdu'llāh-bin-'Āmir was a famous scholar of elucidation and application of the *Sharī'a.*

He had been medium of transmission of many Traditions through Imām Reza.

Munī'-bin-Żiyād

He was also victim of cowardly arrows attack of the Yazīdī Army. No more information available.

Naṣar-bin-Abī Nīżar

Naṣar's father Abī Nīżar belonged to a royal Abyssenian family, some say his genealogy goes to some Irani Kings. He was attracted towards Islām from his youth itself. Approached the Islāmic Prophet and followed the Islāmic religious principles and continued his training only from him. Then he continued to obtain training from Imām 'Alī. His son Naṣar's childhood and youth were associated only with Imām 'Alī and Imām Ḥasan. His remaining life was with Imām Ḥusain. He came to Karbala from Medina along with Imām Ḥusain. First his horse became a martyr, then he attained Heaven.

Bakr-bin-Ḥay Tayamī

He came to Karbala along with 'Omar-bin-Sa'd's Army, but after the commencement of the war, at the call of his inner-voice he joined the Ḥusainī Army, fought and became a martyr at the cowardly arrows attack of the Yazīdī Army.

'Omarū-bin-Qurẓah-bin-Ka'b Aṇsārī

'Omarū's father Qurẓah-bin-Ka'b Aṇsārī was one of the Companions of the holy Prophet of Islām. He joined in Uḥad-War and successive wars also. Imām 'Alī appointed him as an administrator of Kufa. Qurẓah-bin-Ka'b was with Imām 'Alī in all the wars. He had died in Kufa itself and Imām 'Alī himself performed his last prayer. 'Omarū-bin-Qurẓah was also living in Kufa. He came to Karbala, fought bravely on martyrs day, then observed that there was a shower of arrows towards Imām Ḥusain, 'Omarū-bin-Qurẓah stood before him and stopped the arrows on his chest and in this manner became a martyr. At the last moment he asked Imām

Ḥusain, Oh the son of Prophet! Did I maintain my duty and responsibility? Imām Ḥusain replied, Yes! You will reach Heaven before me. Please convey my salvation to the Prophet and say that I am also coming there soon.

Salmān-bin-Muzārib-bin-Qays Numayrī Bajalī

He was the cousin-brother of Żuhayr-bin-Qayn-bin-Qays Numayrī Bajalī, Commander of the Ḥusainī Army, he was also on way to *Ḥajj* with him. When Żuhayr-bin-Qayn took a decision of sacrificing himself under the leadership of Imām Ḥusain, then he also came along with him to Imām Ḥusain. Fought and became a martyr.

'Abdu'llāh-bin-'Orwah-bin-Ḥarrāq Ghaffārī

'Abdu'llāh's grandfather Ḥarrāq was one of the heirs of Abūżar Ghaffārī, the veteran Associates of Imām 'Alī, who had joined him in the wars of Jamal, Ṣiffīn and Naharwan. Ḥarrāq's grandson 'Abdu'llāh came to Karbala and joined Imām Husain. On martyrs' day, when trouble increased during Noon-Prayer, then after getting permission from Imām Ḥusain, he fought and became a martyr.

'Abdu'r Raḥmān-bin-'Orwah-bin-Ḥarrāq Ghaffārī

'Abdu'r Raḥmān-bin-'Orwah-bin-Ḥarrāq Ghaffārī along with his brother 'Abdu'llāh's came to Imām Ḥusain and fought with his permission and became a martyr.

Saif-bin-Ḥārith-bin-Sarī'

He joined Ḥusainī Army in Karbala. His attendant Shabīb-bin-'Abdu'llāh also was with him. He fought and sacrificed his life.

Sālim-bin-'Omarū-bin-'Abdu'llāh

He was attacked as an attendant to Medīnahu'l Kalbī. He was with Muslim in Kufa. On Muslim's expiry, he was arrested. Anyhow he reached Karbala and joined the Ḥusainī Army, fought and became a martyr.

Mālik-bin-'Abd-bin-Sarī'-bin-Jābir Hamādanī

He was the cousin-brother of Saif-bin-Ḥārith-bin-Sarī', but both were sons of the same mother. He came to Imām Ḥusain with his brother, fought and sacrificed his life.

Qa'nab-bin-'Āmir Numayrī

He was a resident of Basara. He came to Imām Ḥusain in the company of Ḥujjāj-bin-Żaid-Sa'dī Tayamī and sacrificed his life for the cause of Truth.

Żayd-bin-Thabayṭ u'l 'Abdī Qaysī

His name has been mentioned in two ways Żayd-bin-Thabayṭ and Yażīd-bin-Thabayṭ. He was among the friends of Imām 'Alī's disciple Abu'l al-Aswad. It has already been discussed that he had ten sons and desired to sacrifice all ten sons on the path of Truth. He tried his best to convince his sons. Only two of them accompanied him to Imām Ḥusain. Those obedient sons were 'Abdu'r Raḥmān-bin-Żayd-bin-Thabayṭ Qaysī and 'Obaydu'llāh-bin-Żayd-bin-Thabayt Qaysī. They joined Imām Ḥusain. After sacrificing all his sons for protecting the Truth with Imām Ḥusain ultimately he also fought and went Heavenly abode.

Rāf'a-bin-'Abdu'llāh

He was the attendant of the holy Prophet of Islām's Companion Muslim Ażdī's servant. He came to Karbala with his master and became a martyr after fighting.

Bishr-bin-'Omarū-bin-Uḥadūth Ḥazaramī Kindī

By origin, he was a native of Ḥazarmūt, but was living in Kufa of Kindī Muhallah, so Kindī. He came to Karbala and presented himself before Imām Ḥusain. He got information of his son being arrested by the Yażīdī Army. Imām Ḥusain allowed him to go and help his son. He was not prepared to leave him at that hour of crisis. He remained with Imām Ḥusain, fought and sacrificed his life for the cause of Truth.

The talk on the magnificent living martyrs ends now. Humble author salutes with greatful heart and wet eyes.

> "Verily, God loweth those who fighting His way in ranks as if they were an unbreakable metalled wall."
>
> (*Qur'an*: as-Saff 4)

Top Yażīdī Army

Yażīd-bin-Mu'āwiyah-bin-Abū Sufyyān	:	Caliph of the Muslim Empire
'Obaydu'llāh-bin-Żiyād	:	Governor of Kufa
'Omar-bin-Sa'd	:	Commander-in-Chief
'Omar-bin-Ḥujjāj Żubaydī	:	Commander, Right Regiment
Shimr-bin-Žuljaushan	:	Commander, Left Regiment
Qurrah-bin-Qays	:	Commander, Cavalry Regiment
Shabth-bin-Raba'ī	:	Commander, Infantry Regiment
Qays-bin-Asha'th	:	1st Commander, 4th Regiment
'Abdu'llāh-bin-Żubayr Ażdī	:	2nd Commander, 4th Regiment
'Abdu'r Raḥmān Ja'fī	:	3rd Commander, 4th Regiment
Ḥajaru'l Ahajar	:	4th Commander, 4th Regiment
Dorayd (Żayd or Żuwayd)	:	Bearer of Army Flag

Yażīdī Soldiers

The minimum number of the Yażīdī soldiers is said to be 40,000 and some are of the view that it was more than three lakhs; it has already been discussed in the previous chapter. It would be appropriate to list the names of important the Yażīdī soldiers among the above mentioned the Yażīdī Sergeants, who have had their place in the history on the basis of any big bad deed of their own:

'Abdu'r Raḥmān-bin-Ḥaṣan
'Abdu'llāh-bin-JaużahTyami
'Abdu'llāh Khashkārah Bajalī
'Abdu'llāh-bin-'Oqbah Ghanawī
'Abdu'llāh-bin-Hawżah Tamīmī
'Abdu'llāh-bin-Quṭayyah Nabahānī
'Abdu'llāh-bin-Žūbābī Nabahānī
'Āmir-bin-Nahshal Tamīmī
'Āmir-bin-Ṣarīmah Taymī
'Omar-bin-Khālid Juhnī Hamadānī
'Omar-bin-Sa'd-bin Nufayl Ażdī
'Omar-bin-Ṣubaiḥ Ṣaydāvī
'Orwa-bin-Qays

‘Othmān-bin-Khālid Juhnī Hamadānī
Abānī Dārīmī
Abḥar-bin-Ka’b
Abū ‘Omrah Žūbābī
Abū Juraham Ażdī
Abu’l-Ḥutūf Jo’fī
Akhnas-bin-Murthid
Asmā-bin-Khārjah Farāzī
Aswad-bin-Khālid
Ayūb-bin-Masrūj
Ażraq Shāmī
Baḥr-bin-Ka’b
Bajdal-bin-Salīm Kalbī
Bakīr-bin-Ha‘Tayamī
Bishr-bin-Khoṭ Hamadānī
Budayl-bin-Ṣoraym
Bishr-bin-Shumayṭ Fāizī
Falāfis Nahashalī Dārimī
Fīhān-bin-Żuhayr
Ghurrah-bin-Qays Aḥsami
Ḥajār-bin-Abajar
Ḥakīm-bin-Ṭufayl Ṭāī
Ḥamīd-bin-Muslim Ażdī
Ḥānī-bin-Thobayṭ Ḥazramī
Ḥarmalah-bin-Kāhil Asadī
Ḥassān-bin-Bakr Ḥanžalī
Ḥiṣṣīn-bin-Numayr
Isḥāq-bin-Khawiyyah Ḥazramī
Ka’b-bin-Jābir Ażdī
Kathīr-‘Abdu’llāh Sho’bī
Khālid-bin-Asad Juhanī
Khiwallah-bin-Yażīd Aṣbaḥī ‘Āyižī
Laqīṭ-bin-Nāshir Juhanī
Maḥzaṛ-bin-Tha’lbah ’Āyižī
Māliķ-bin-Nisr Kindī
Masrūq-bin-Wāyal Ḥazramī Taymī
Muhājir-bin-Aws Taymī
Murrah-bin-Munqiž-bin-Nu’mān ‘Abdī
Muslim ben ‘Abdillāh Zaybābī
Muslim-bin-Mālik Kindī
No’mān-bin-Bashīr

No'mān-bin-Maqātil
Rabī'-bin-Tamīm Ḥāri<u>th</u>ī
Razī-bin-Munqaž 'Abdī
Sālim (slave of Ibn-Ziyād)
Sanān-bin-Anas Na<u>kh</u>a'ī
Sinān-bin-Anas Na<u>kh</u>a'ī
Sulaymān-bin-'Awf Ḥazramī
Swaid-bin-'Abdu'r Raḥmān Almiqrī
Walīd-bin-'Oqbah
Yasār (slave of Ziyād)
Yažīd Aṣbaḥī 'Āyižī
Yažīd-bin-Sufyyān Tamīmī
Yažīd-bin-Ma'qal
Yažīd-bin-Ruqād Ḥī<u>th</u>ī
Żajar-bin-Badr Na<u>kh</u>a'ī
Żayd-bin-Ḥāri<u>th</u>
Žora'h-bin-<u>Sh</u>orayk
Żaḥurr-bin-Qays

Yažīdī Deserves Damnation

Yažīd, his father Mu'āwiyah-bin-Abū Sufyyān and the Yažīdī Aministration and Army had been responsible for the tragedy of Karbala and thereafter heinous crimes commited by them against the Household of the holy Prophet of Islām. Therefore, they deserve damnation and rejection until the Day of Resurrection. It had been unanimous finding of the Islāmic learned scholars and historians, such as, Abū Ḥanīfah Dīnāwarī (d. 896 AD), aṭ-Ṭabarī, Ibn Jarīr Abū Jā'far (d. 923 AD),[52] al-Mas'ūdī, 'Alī-bin-Ḥusain (d. 957 AD),[53] Ibn A<u>th</u>īr, 'Iżżu'd-Din, Abu'l Ḥasan (d. 1233 AD),[54] as-Suyūtī, Jalālu'd-Dīn (d. 1505 AD),[55] Dayār Bakrī Ḥusain Muḥammad Mālikī (d. 1558 AD)[56], Ibn Ḥajar, al-Hay<u>th</u>amī, al-Makkī (d. 1566 AD),[57]and a number of others, leaving a part a few people influenced by *Nāṣibīs*, (People against the Progeny of the Prophet Muḥammad).

Notes and References

1. Nahju'l-Balā<u>gh</u>ah, vol. 1, p. 77; al-Ir<u>sh</u>ād fī Ma'rifat Hujjāj Allāh 'Alā 'Ibād, p. 151; al-A<u>kh</u>bāru'ṭ Ṭawāl, p. 214.
2. Tārī<u>kh</u>u'r-Rusūl wa'l-Mulūk, vol. 6, p. 92; al-Ir<u>sh</u>ād fī Ma'rifat Hujjāj Allāh 'Alā 'Ibād, p. 194.

3. Tārīkhu'r-Rusūl wa'l-Mulūk, vol. 6, p. 238; al-Irshād fī Ma'rifat Hujjāj Allāh 'Alā 'Ibād, p. 244.
4. Ansābu 'l-Ashrāf, vol. 3, p. 105; al-Irshād fī Ma'rifat Ḥujjāj Allāh 'Alā 'Ibād, vol. 2, p. 95; al-Kāmil fī' t-Tārīkh, vol. 4, p. 10.
5. Shahīd-i-Insāniyat, p. 524; Ḥusainī Inqalab, p. 97.
6. *There are two Żiyārat-Nāḥiyah with same name, one is the shorter than other. One of the most important sources of the names of these heroes and martyrs is a Żiyārat, taught by the Twelfth Imam, known as Żiyārat-Nāḥiyah, which has been copied by all the great authorities in their reliable books. The Żiyārat-Nāḥiyah, as it has come down to us, omits certain names of martyrs, although they are well known for their participation in the holy struggle at Kerbalā. This omission may be due to some lapse in memory on the part of the reporters or inaccuracy or inadvertence of copyists.*—Author
7. *I have utilised fully the technological technical and communication Media in editing the list. A comparative study has been done with prominent books, listed with the available material on internet and learned books could be made available.*—Author
8. Luhūf 'Alā Qatlu'l Ṭafūf, p. 41.
9. Shahīd-i-Insāniyat, pp. 397-515.
10. Maqta-i-Sādāt.
11. Taṣwīr-i-Karbala, pp. 81-89.
12. *al-Irshād fī Ma'rifat Ḥujjāj Allāh 'Alā 'Ibād,* p. 246; *Kitābu 'l-Buldān,* p. 172; *Tārīkhu'r-Rusūl wa'l-Mulūk,* vol. 6, p. 241; *al-Akhbāru'ṭ Ṭawāl,* p. 154.
13. Tārīkhu'r-Rusūl wa'l-Mulūk, vol. 6, pp. 190-215.
14. *Generally 8th Rabī I 62 AH (25th November, 681 AD) is prevalent, but in view of the distance between Karbala and Medina being 1,100 miles (1,700 km) appears to be incorrect. The issue has already been dicussed at a proper place in the Chapter Seven.* —Author.
15. Tarjima-i-Kalām-i-Ilāhī, p. 958.
16. al-Durru'l-Manthūr fī'l-Tafsīr bi'l Māthūr, vol. 4, p. 371.
17. Anwāru 'l-Qur'an, p. 1147.
18. Maqālātu 'l Ḥusain: al-Yaqūbī, p. 32.
19. *Abu'l-Aswad, famous Arabic poet says:*
    Thou youth whose maternal grandfather was king of Kisrā (Yezdegerd) and grandfather was Hāshim, would be finest amongst all youth of the world. al-Uṣūl-min'al-Kāfī, p. 255.
20. al-Khaṣayaṣu'l-Żainabiyah, p. 210.
21. Żainab-i-Kubrā, p. 47.
22. Żainab-i-Kubrā, p. 65.
23. al-Khaṣayaṣu'l-Żainabiyah, p. 27.
24. Luhūf 'Alā Qatlu'l Ṭafūf, p. 146.
25. Tārīkhu'r-Rusūl wa'l-Mulūk, vol. 6, pp. 89, 236.
26. Kitābu'l-'Ibar, vol. 5, p. 95.

27. Luhūf 'Alā Qatlu'l Ṭafūf, pp. 34-35.
28. Tārīkhu'r-Rusūl wa'l-Mulūk, vol. 6, p. 236.
29. Tārīkhu'r-Rusūl wa'l-Mulūk, vol. 6, p. 256; al-Irshād fī Ma'rifat Ḥujjāj Allāh 'Alā 'Ibād, p. 254.
30. al-Akhbāru'ṭ Ṭawāl, p. 354.
31. Shahīd-i-Insāniyat, p. 492.
32. al-Irshād fī Ma'rifat Ḥujjāj Allāh 'Alā 'Ibād, p. 253.
33. Tārīkhu'r-Rusūl wa'l-Mulūk, vol. 6, p. 257; al-Irshād fī Ma'rifat Ḥujjāj Allāh 'Alā 'Ibād, p. 251.
34. Tārīkhu'r-Rusūl wa'l-Mulūk, vol. 6, p. 256; al-Irshād fī Ma'rifat Ḥujjāj Allāh 'Alā 'Ibād, pp. 253-54.
35. Tārīkhu'r-Rusūl wa'l-Mulūk, vol. 6, p. 256; al-Irshād fī Ma'rifat Ḥujjāj Allāh 'Alā 'Ibād, p. 254.
36. Tārīkhu'r-Rusūl wa'l-Mulūk, vol. 6, p. 256; al-Irshād fī Ma'rifat Ḥujjāj Allāh 'Alā 'Ibād, p. 254.
37. al-Irshād fī Ma'rifat Ḥujjāj Allāh 'Alā 'Ibād, p. 253.
38. al-Uṣūl-min 'al-Kāfī, vol. 1, p. 466; Nūru 'l-Abṣār fī Akhaž al-Thār, p. 126; The Life of Imam Zayn al-'Abidin, p. 3.
39. Ithabatu'l-Wasiya, p. 143; The Life of Imām Zayn al-'Abidin, p. 3.
40. 'Uyyun Akhbār al-Rida, p. 270.
41. al-Akhbāru'ṭ Ṭawāl, p. 201.
42. Shi'a dar Islām, p. 201.
43. Nafasul Mahmoom, pp. 388-389.
44. Summary of the Tragedy of Sayyeda Ruqayya: Booklet at Ruqayya Mosque, 2008.
45. Tārīkhu'r-Rusūl wa'l-Mulūk, vol. 6, p. 246.
46. al-Musnad: Aḥmad, vol. 4, p. 281; as-Sunan: Ibn Māja, vol. 1, p. 43.
47. Luhūf 'Alā Qatlu'l Ṭafūf, p. 42.
48. Bihāru'l-Anwār, vol. 1, p. 234.
49. Shahīd-i-Insāniyat, p. 397.
50. Maqālātu 'l Ḥusain: al-Muqrim, p. 292; al-Irshād fī Ma'rifat Ḥujjaj Allāh 'Alā 'Ibād, p. 220.
51. Murūju'ž – Žahab-wa'l-M'adinu'l-Jauhar, p. 12; Tārīkhu'r-Rusūl wa'l-Mulūk, vol. 6, p. 253.
52. Tārīkhu'r-Rusūl wa'l-Mulūk, vol. 11, p. 358.
53. Murūju'ž – Žahab-wa'l-M'adinu'l-Jauhar, vol. 8, p. 21.
54. al-Kāmil fī't-Tārīkh, vol. 4, p. 55.
55. Tārīkhu'l-Khulafah, p. 140.
56. Tārīkhu 'l-Khmīs fī Aḥwāl'u-Nafīs, p. 332.
57. aṣ-Ṣawa'qu'l-Muḥriqah fi'r-radd'alā ahli'l Rafz wa'l Zanadiqah, p. 134.

Chapter: Nine

Achievements and Effects

No revolution exists in the history of the world like the revolution of Imām Ḥusain, which shook the world, bestowed glory upon truth and created dignity for human beings, as all its parts are effulgence and all its horizons, nobility and honour. Replete with immortal lessons regarding belief that shall never be overpowered and faith that shall never be defeated and loftiness that shall never be humiliated; a revolution that began a modern age for the nations of the world and the communities of the earth, spirit of revolution and opposition to oppression and injustice, confrontation with unreasonable demands and fighting corruption are its signs.

The Ḥusainī soldiers had repeatedly told the Yażīdī Army by their action that they were not cowardly and chicken-hearted people. They were chiefs of the brave in the world. If they were killed it was not because they were weak or daunted, but it was because the time of their martyrdom had come. Imām Ḥusain was fully satisfied with the result at every stage.

Let us ponder over another point. It is possible that, from our discussion, some persons may draw the conclusion that the rising of Imām Ḥusain and his movement were the only sacred and armed campaign in Islām and there is no possibility of a similar effort being made till the Day of Judgement. However, that is not the correct position. Examples of movements similar to that of Imām Ḥusain are found before and after the holy Imām and will continue to be found in future. Yes, the sacred personality of Imām Ḥusain has been the central point of the Islāmic movements. His rising confirmed the earlier movements and set an example for future.

If someone explains the rising of Imām Ḥusain by saying that his rising has absolved the Muslim Ummah from the obligation for every movement and effort and now only in his ninth generation Imām Mahdī Ā<u>kh</u>iru'ẓ-Żamān will come one day and start such a movement and the responsibility of all other Muslims of the world on his behalf has ended, it is not correct. Such a thinking is in fact totally opposed to his aim and object.

Even before Imām Ḥusain some great personalities had been making efforts with the same object for which Imām Ḥusain rose and started their movement and these efforts continued even after Imām Ḥusain. If people do not or cannot understand the value of such efforts, it is due to their ignorance.

I have not been the formal student of the history, but had studied the history of Islām and the history of other nations to some extent. There is no doubt about the fact that not only the Muslims but the Hindus, Christians, the Jews and others, who exist on the face of the earth are alive only as a result of their efforts and dedicated movements. At the most it can be said that the Ḥusainī Revolution has arisen in the history of Islām in same special situation.

If pondered over the reasons that the tragedy of the martyrdom of Imām Ḥusain has acquired the central position among all the events, movements and armed campaigns of the history of Islām? No other rising, movement and collective martyrdom has acquired that renown and importance which has been acquired by the event of Karbala. This tragedy is the greatest among all the tragedies of the history of Islām.

The superiority of the movement and rising of Imām Ḥusain was on account of those events which took place immediately after his companions' martyrdom. On the one hand this rising became universally known by means of the prisoners belonging to the Progeny of the Prophet Muḥammad and on the other hand the killers of Imām Ḥusain played an important role in making it so known. After the martyrdom of the Imām Ḥusain and the end of the campaign the enemies showed utmost meanness. They cut the bodies of the martyrs to pieces and looted their clothes. They ransacked the tents and set them on fire. They trampled the bodies of the martyrs with the hooves of the horses and raised their heads on spears. They treated the bereaved prisoners harshly and struck their dry lips with batons. These shameful acts commenced from Karbala and continued till their arrival in Syria. And Yażīd took part in such heinous activities himself. However, wherever the prisoners belonging to the Progeny of the Prophet Muḥammad went, they talked about their own success and disgrace of the enemy with such dignity and seriousness as if nothing had happened. At the time when all the people considered them to be defeated and their enemies to be successful they made it known that, in fact it was they who had been successful and victorious and nothing except disgrace had fallen to the lot of the boastful and shameless enemy.

Three Pioneering Generations

The achievements of the Ḥusainī Revolutions could not be understood, without knowing the contributions of three generations of Imāms after Imām Ḥusain, who had remained a centre of light and learning and whose religious leadership and guidance was common for all the Muslims without any difference of cult and the way of life. All Muslims had an indisputable obsolete consent on Imām Ḥusain's eldest son 'Alī-bin-Ḥusain, who is very famous with the name of Imām Żainu'l-Ābidīn (658-713 AD), his son Imām Muḥammad al-Bāqir (677-734 AD) and his son Imām Ja'far aṣ-Ṣādiq (702-65 AD) after him, only his religious procedure was considered as true Islām only his directions and teachings all the Muslims followed without any misunderstanding. Only after Imām Ja'far aṣ-Ṣādiq various faiths and warp of procedures came into existence, which will be discussed in the ensuing pages. We desire to introduce the social good attempts of all the three Imāms here.

After the great sacrifice of Karbala Imām Ḥusain's successors scarificing their own life continuously established the Islāmic prestige and glory. In such terrific circumstances when the atrocities had already reached to such an extent that any person named as 'Alī was considered enemy and murdered, no matter, whether he was devotee of Imām 'Alī or not. In such hazard and jeopardising circumstances to safeguard the achievements of the Ḥusainī Revolution, collecting and organising the scattered like minded people, being out from the eyes of ruling power, preserving one's own rights and life, providing new horizons to Imāmate and *Sharī'a*, Sacred Law of Islām, in tight corners where there is a question of existence of Islām, providing security to the human values, giving correct consultation to the contemporary rulers, certifying pure life, sacredness and *Namāż* as the foremost pivot of religion. Such time-winning achievements, which the dust of time could not touch, Islām's face was going on gathering.

After Imām Ḥusain, Imām Żainu'l-Ābidīn for making the proper perspective and context, was successfully very active in providing its own prestigious life to the Islāmic heart drowned in despair, re-establishment of educational institutions, providing living status to all the institutions of Imām Ḥusain, and to be firm and determinant on the rights of Imāmate.

Imām Żainu'l-Ābidīn was present during Battle of Karbala He also took the reign of leadership after Imām Ḥusain's martyrdom. He was 22 years of age at that time and lived for 34 years afterwards. Discussion regarding the events from Karbala to Kufa and from Kufa to Damascus has already done at the appropriate places. He had dedicated his life for proclaiming the objectives of Imām Ḥusain. He had made celebrating the grief of Imām Ḥusain as an inseparable part of his own life. He was always keeping a small packet of *Khāk-i-Shif'ā* (Karbala's sacred sand) with him for awakening the memory of the great sacrifice of Imām Ḥusain and his Associates. He also used to teach the preaching of Imām Ḥusain to his followers. On account of an abnormal contentment and courage specially on the basis of *Saiyed-uṣ-Ṣābirīn* (leader of courageous people), *Saiyed-uṣ-Sājidīn* (leader of adorer in prayers) and *Żainu'l-Ābidīn* (glory of pious people). He was highly dedicated to God's prayer and use to spend whole nights for the same.[1] His book *Ṣaḥīfah-ul-Kāmilah-uṣ-Sajjadiya* is a compilation of prayers. He himself was reading it and used to advise other faithful people also to read it.

If we examine the dimensions of the Imām Żainu'l-Ābidīn's role, in the life of the Muslims, after his return to Medina, we find that he made use of the experience of his father, Imām Ḥusain, in reforming Muslims's social life.

Imām Żainu'l-Ābidīn, in his capacity as the Imām of the Ummah, after his father, in whom the ideological and social authority had converged, had to take the experience of his father into consideration. In its light he had to make his plans for reforms, and this he did. When the Imām Żainu'l-Ābidīn embarked on his reforms, which aimed at beginning a spiritual and cultural revolution among the Muslims, a set of objective conditions were on his side. They helped in advancing his plans futher. These conditions can be summed up in two elements:

> *First Element:* The political and social upheavals which exploded in the most important cities of the Muslim world after the tragedy of Karbala.
>
> *Second Element:* There was a warm response to the mission of the Progeny of the Prophet Muḥammad from a wide section of the Ummah and there was a sweeping feeling that the Progeny of the Prophet Muḥammad were victims of the brutal policies of the rulers. Imām Żainu'l-Ābidīn found the sympathy of the masses towards the Progeny of the Prophet helpful in his endeavour to further the Islāmic goals and bring the Islāmic historical mission to fruition.

He set certain broad guidelines according to which he acted. He broadened the popular base to the Progeny of the Prophet, sharpened peoples sentiment towards them, changing it into active and virtual loyalty. Imām Żainu'l-Ābidīn also raised the level of the Islāmic awareness of the Ummah and encouraged the masses to embrace Islām. Lastly, he created ideologically distinguished leadership which could bear the original Islāmic thought and not that thought which served the narrow interests of the Umayyite rulers.

Imām Żainu'l-Ābidīn embraced a method having special goals and aims. He firstly focused on organizing educational network. He made both the mosque of the holy Prophet and his home centres for disseminating Islāmic knowledge. Through his constructive efforts, he became a magnet attracting pioneers of the Islāmic thought at defferent levels and fields. Through his blessed efforts during a long period of time (35 years), the term of his Imamate, he graduated traditionists, jurisprudents, and leading intellectuals who emerged as leading scholars.

Imām Żainu'l-Ābidīn used to report authentic traditions from his grandfather, the Prophet of God, through a pure and reliable chain of transmitters that began with the two young Lords of Paradise, namely Imām Ḥasan and Imām Ḥusain through the Commander of the Faithful, Imām 'Alī-Ibn-Abī Ṭālib and the Prophet of God, ending with the Divine revelation itself.

With a view to strengthening his ties with Ummah, Imām Żainu'l-Ābidīn became the merciful father, the wise leader, who made a point of healing their wounds. He liked the orphans, the needy, the long-time sick, and the poor who had no supporters, to be present at his feasts. He, himself, used to distribute food among them.

Imām Ḥusain's grandson Muḥammad (Imām Muḥammad al-Bāqir) was a small four years old child and was with the Ḥusainī Caravan and he was inside the tent with the women and other children at the time of the gruesome tragedy of the wholesale massacre of his grandfather Imām Ḥusain and his companions. He also suffered with his father and the ladies of the House of the Prophet the heartless captivity and imprisonment at the hands of the devilish forces at the command of Yażīd-bin-Mu'āwiyah. He says that he still remember the killing of his grandfather Imām Ḥusain and at that moment he was inside the tent with the women and other children. The Yażīdī Army put the tents on fire. Children escaped from the tents into the desert with burning clothes and then the soldiers arrested and tied with rope taken to the Castle of Yażīd at Damascus in Syria.[2] The famous scholar, Ibn Ḥajar, al-Hayt͟hamī al-Makkī (d. 1566 AD) says:

Imām Muḥammad Bāqir passed his time peacefully in Medina praying to Allāh and guiding the people to the right path. The famous scholar, Ibn Ḥajar, al-Haythamī al-Makkī (d.1566 AD) says:

> "Imām Muḥammad al-Bāqir has disclosed the secrets of knowledge and wisdom and unfolded the principles of spiritual and religious guidance. Nobody can deny his exalted character, his God-given knowledge, his divinely-gifted wisdom and his obligation and gratitude towards spreading of knowledge. He was a sacred and highly talented spiritual leader and for this reason he was popularly titled *al-Bāqir* which means 'the expander of knowledge'. Kind of heart, spotless in character, sacred by soul and noble by nature, the Imām devoted all his time in submission to Allāh (and in advocating the teachings of the holy Prophet and his descendants). It is beyond the power of a man to count the deep impression of knowledge and guidance left by the Imam on the hearts of the faithful. His sayings in connection with devotion and abstinence, knowledge and wisdom, and religious exercise and submission to Allāh are so great in number that the volume of this book is quite insufficient to cover them all."[3]

Affirming his appellant *al-Bāqir,* he expanded the vision of knowledge. He classified various sciences and axioms, such as, *'Ilmu'l-Kimiyā* (Chemistry), *'Ilmu'l-Ajsām* (Physiology), *'Ilmu'l-Ḥaywānāt* (Zoology), *'Ilmu'l-Ḥifẓan-Ṣeḥat* (Hygiene), '*Ilmu'l-Riyāzī* (Mathematics), *'Ilmu'l-Ramal* (Geometry), *'Ilmu'l-Nabātāt* (Botany), '*Ilmu'l-Ṭabaqātu'l-Arz* (Geology) etc., which was received by Europe from Islām and developed. In the process such a confusion has prevailed that Muslim names have also been translated, for example, Imām Muḥammad al-Bāqir's famous pupil Abū Mūsā Jābir-bin-Ḥayyān, (d. 815 AD), who has been known as the father of Chemistry is known in Europe as Geber. Jābir-bin-Ḥayyān had systematized the quantitative analysis of substances as an important corpuscular theory of matter. Similar has been the case with Al-Farghānī (d. 833 AD) as Alfarganus, Ibn Sina (d.1037 AD) as Avicenna, Ibn Rushd (d. 1198 AD) as Averroës, Abū 'Abdu'llāh (d. 1525 AD) as Boadbil etc.

Imām Muḥammad al-Bāqir's expanded vision of knowledge has still not been explored. Such as '*Ilmu'l-Jafar* (Sceince of Predictions), '*Ilmu'l-Ladunnī* (Inspired Knowledge), '*Ilmu'l-Ghayb* (Occult Science), etc.

Imām Muḥammad al-Bāqir managed to collect the teachings and reforms of the holy Prophet and his *Ahlu'l-Bayt* or *'Itrat* (Household) in the form of books. His pupils compiled books on different branches of science and arts under his instructions and guidance. In the excellence of his personal purity and godly traits, he was a model of the holy Prophet and his great grandfather, 'Alī-Ibn-Abī Ṭālib. His admonitions created a spiritual sensation among the Muslims in general. He was not only hospitable even to his worst enemies, but also used to continually exhort them to follow the right path. He urged people to earn their livelihood by their own hard work.

Imām Ḥusain's great grandson Imām Ja'far aṣ-Ṣādiq specialized in the foremost object of his rising as defined:

"Enjoin Good and forbid Evil." (*Qur'an*: 22/41)

Although the *Fiqh* (Islāmic jurisprudence, elucidation and application of the *Sharī'a*) was developed by the Prophet Muḥammad and his successor Imāms, the *Fiqh*, as taught by the followers of the Household or Progeny of the Prophet, did not have the opportunity to be presented to the masses of people because of the political predicament that they suffered under the rulers for many centuries.

As the Imāms had refused to acknowledge the legitimacy of the *Umayyites* Caliphate of 89 years (661-750 AD). Later on *'Abbāsites* Caliphate of 507 years (750-1257 AD), and their governments; and thus they and their followers were exposed to tremendous harassment and persecution at the hands of the unjust Caliphs. Once the Umayyite government became weak, Imām Ja'far aṣ-Ṣādiq found a golden opportunity to formulate and spread the tradition of the Prophet Muḥammad and his family. Therefore, he was able to pass down the authentic teachings of the holy Qur'an and the Prophet Muḥammad and crystallize them in what came to be known as *Fiqhu'l-Ja'farī*, the Ja'farī Jurisprudence. His teachings were collected in 400 *Usūl* (foundations) which were written by his students and encompass Ḥadīth, the Islāmic philosophy, theology, commentary of the Qur'an, literature, and ethics.

At one time, four thousand scholars, commentators of the Qur'an, historians, and philosophers attended the classes of Imām Ja'far aṣ-Ṣādiq in the holy city of Medina. His one of the pupil, Abū Ḥanīfah No'mān-bin-Thābit-bin-Zotā (d. 767 AD), later on earned fame as the founder of the *Fiqh'l-Ḥanafī* (Ḥanafī School of Thought). Imam Abū Ḥanīfah studied under the instruction of Imām Ja'far aṣ-Ṣādiq for two years,[4] and said in regard to him that he has not seen anyone more knowledgeable than Ja'far-bin-Muḥammad, and indeed, he is the most knowledgeable one in the nation.[5]

Imām Mālik-bin-Anas Asḥabī (d. 795 AD) joined the *'Alawiyīn*, the descendants of Imām 'Alī-Ibn-Abī Ṭālib, and received his knowledge from Imām Ja'far aṣ-Ṣādiq, but thereafter, inconsistencies marked his life. At one point he was oppressed and having earned the anger of the government, he was dragged through the streets by his clothes and lashed. He wrote *al-Muwatta'*, his book of *Fiqh*, which contains the principles of the Mālikī School of Thought.

The Shāfi'ī School of Thought was headed by Imām Muḥammad-bin-Idrīs ash-Shāfi'ī (d. 819 AD), who was born in Ḥijāż and his school of thought emerged in Egypt. At the time of the Fatimid Dynasty, the Egyptians were mainly followers of *Ahlu'l-Bayt*, and the teachings of *Ahlu'l-Bayt*, were being taught in al-Aẓhar University. At a later time, Ṣalāhu'l-Dīn Ayyūbī came and waged an extensive war against the school of *Ahlu'l-Bayt* by banning the teaching of their *Mażhab* (school of thought) in al-Aẓhar and resurrecting the other schools of thought, including that of Imām Shāfi'ī, who was killed in Egypt.

The Ḥanbalī school of thought was headed by Imām Aḥmad-bin-Muḥammad Ḥanbal (d. 855 AD). He was among the severe opponent of the hypothetical principle of his teacher Imām Shāfi'ī. He only gained popularity in the region of Najd due to the ideas of Shaykh Muḥammad-Ibn-'Abdu'l Wahhāb al-Najdī (d. 1792 AD) the founder of *Wahhābīsm*. The Ḥanbalī school of thought spread in Najd, primarily due to the teachings of Aḥmad-bin-'Abdu'l-Ḥalīm al-Dimishqī, Ibn Taymiyyah (d.1328 AD) and his student Ibn al-Qayyīm al-Jawziyyah (d.1350 AD). The *Wahhābī* religious and political dominance began with the creation of the Kingdom of Saudi Arabia in 1932 AD on the 'Arabian peninsula.

A close study of the history of the schools of thought and a search into the reasons for their birth, existence, and spread, reveals that the various governments were the main factor in the birth and spread of these schools. Governmental aid took physical and financial forms by establishing schools, sponsoring books of *fiqh* (jurisprudence), adopting and sponsoring official schools of thought, and giving freedom to the founders and scholars of some of the official schools of thought. Today, the five schools of Islāmic thought accepted by all Muslims are the Ja'farī Jurisprudence, comprising 23 per cent of the Muslims; the Ḥanafī, comprising 31 per cent of the Muslims; the Mālikī, comprising 25 per cent of the Muslims; the Shāfi'ī, comprising 16 per cent of the Muslims;

and the Ḥanbalī, comprising 4 per cent of the Muslims. The remaining small percentage follow other minority schools, such as the Żaydī and the Ismā'īlī.[6]

It may be said safely, despite the fact that the *Ahlu'l-Bayt* suffered extreme oppression, tyranny, and discrimination at the hands of the *Umayyites* and *'Abbāsites*, the real spirit of Islāmic jurisprudence remains in *Fiqhu'l-Ja'farī*. The famous scholar Abu'l 'Olā Maudūdī says that all the learned Islāmic scholars are unanimous on the fact that in case of any problem related to the Islāmic jurisprudence in the Sunnī school of thought (Ḥanafī, Mālikī, Shāfi'ī, Ḥanbalī), *Fiqhu'l-Ja'farī* shall be final verdict.[7]

Is any contribution greater than that of the Ḥusainī Revolution, due to which the Islāmic jurisprudence came into existence and flourished among the Muslims, irrespective of faith, creed and nation.

The Reasons of the Revolution

Imām Ḥusain did not possess the necessary force that would enable him to win the battle in the wordly meaning; he did not even rely on those who wrote to him from Kufa. For he declared his revolution before he received their letters and delegates. The people of Ḥijāż too did not give him enough support to be able to stand against the Umayyites. Therefore, he decided to proceed to Iraq for the sole reason of preventing any bloodshed in the holy city of Mecca. Moreover, he knew that he was destined to die; yet he went there.

Why then did he insist; and why did he declare his revolution? To answer this question, one should be aware of the following facts:

Firstly, Yażīd represented a real danger to the Islāmic Ummah, for he was not a true Muslim. He was not properly educated in the teachings of Islām. And he used to drink alcohol, gamble, and commit all other sins. These findings are based on historic sources. As we have already mentioned at appropriate place, he himself had declared in his Royal Court at Damascus that actually, there was neither any message (from Allāh) nor any revelation, *Hāshimites* (The most respected clan of Quraysh, in which Prophet Muḥammad was born) staged a play to obtain the Kingdom.[8]

Such a man could not be entrusted with the affairs of the nation. Nevertheless, the faithful forces, with Imām Ḥusain as their leader, had benefited a lot from these points of weakness in the personality of such an evil ruler.

In these circumstances it might not be strange to see many Muslim dignitaries trying to convince Imām Ḥusain to avoid the confrontation with Yażīd, although they bore witness to the corruption of the Umayyites, and they also realized that it was the Imām's duty and right to face it. Thus, he was approached by Caliph II's son 'Abdu'llāh-bin-'Omar and 'Abdu'llāh-bin-Żubayr, as well as some of his family members. These are some of the manifestations of the absence of the militant spirit among most Muslim leaders.

As for the common people, this negative spirit spread among them to a terrifying extent. The people of Kufa, for example, broke all their pledges promises and oaths, once they were not only subjected to the wave of terror led by the Yażīdī Governor of Kufa 'Obaydu'llāh-bin-Żiyād, but he was also seducing them with promises of wealth and power. These factors were among the main reasons that led to the announcement of the revolution. Imām Ḥusain wanted to stir up the dead conscience of people, because he knew that there was no use of speeches and talks to galvanize and mobilize the people and solidify their morals.

Secondly, The general level of the nation as a whole was below the required moral stature to stand up to the current of sweeping deviation. A tendency to treasure the pleasures of this world began to be visible in all sections of the society, as a substitute to the spirit of sacrifice for the cause of Allah. And this enabled the opportunistic current to win and hold the positions of control, authority and domination.

Thirdly, It was necessary that the nation should learn about the true Islāmic conception of the Imamate; its true role and its dimensions. The dangerous effects of undermining the Islām, which was played by the Umayyite rule was not emerging from the grassroots level, but rather from the high levels of the leadership that monopolized all means of guidance. Therefore, in accordance with the demands of the Islāmic message, and the qualities that have to be found in a Muslim ruler, Imām Ḥusain had to explain these issues to the Muslim masses in every speech as already mentioned at appropriate places. Imām Ḥusain explained to the people that they were the members of the family of the holy Prophet Muḥammad, who were more entitled to be the rulers than those who claim what is not rightfully theirs; tthey were oppressors and tyrants.

With such roaring words Imām Ḥusain revealed that the Umayyites who have deviated from the rightful Islāmic path are not fit to be rulers, and explained to the Ummah the foundations of the course and Islāmic traits that are embodied in the Imām himself and qualify him to be *Imām*, leader, chief and guardian of the Ummah. Thus, underlining the Islāmic concept of the Imāmate and revealing the falsehood of the Umayyite claims were among the fundamental reasons that made the Imām declare his revolution.

Fourthly, The Islāmic message offers no justification for the Muslim to relieve him from performing his duties as a man he is under obligation to the message he believes in. Man in the Islāmic society is not an independent individual, but rather a person who is an integral part of his society and who should perform his duties towards the Islāmic message. But to fulfil his commitments towards *Sharī'a* (Sacred Laws of Islām, the Divine Jurisprudence) in enjoining the good and forbidding the evil, he had to follow the path of the revolution, because it was the only way that provides any hope for reform in the Islāmic Nation of the holy Prophet Muḥammad.

These are the main reasons that gave Imām Ḥusain and his companions the right to declare the much needed revolution, which immortalized Islām and inspired the coming generations to defend it and to hold fast in the Holy Wars or *Jihād*.

The Revolution's Motives

The motives of the Ḥusainī Revolution were numerous. Some were the result of direct grievances of the general people, while others were ideological. The following were the most apparent:

Firstly, There were many defects and drawbacks in the governing bodies of that time but the most dangerous one was the attempt to distort the Islāmic concepts and ideals. This aspect was of extreme importance and preoccupied the minds of responsible Muslims at the time. The fabrication of *Ḥadīth* (Traditions, the words of the holy Prophet, Muḥammad) was all too common, which had a poisonous effect on the lives of Muslims. This, was giving the Umayyites for a while a free hand to carry out their inhuman deeds and policies. The mask of religion, which they used to hide their un-Islāmic conduct, was extremely dangerous. In the long run, this could have changed Islāmic concepts and distorted social ideals. Thus, stripping off this mask and exposing the true Umayyite's picture was of the utmost necessity.

Secondly, The Governing State's structure was built on an un-Islāmic basis. Quraysh clan was born to rule, 'Arabs were second-class citizens, and non-'Arabs constituted the base of the society's pyramid. That was the general social picture of the Muslim world under the Umayyites dynasty. Freedom of thought and expression were denied, when one dared to express an opinion contrary to that of the Umayyite's, prison became his home, his property was confiscated, and even his life was at stake.

Thirdly, The Umayyites considered the Muslim world to be their own property. The alms, *Żakāt* (poor-rate, which is 2.5 per cent annual tax on the capital or total assets for the poor) and other Islāmic dues were collected, but no one knew or could question where that money went. Large gifts and donations were given to a few cruel governors and tribal chiefs in order to secure their allegiance. Large sums of money were wastefully spent on racing, gambling, wine making, and buying slave women to entertain high-class people in power. Hence, the majority of Muslims were left near starvation level while the ruling group all enjoyed the social and material privileges.

Fourthly, The Muslims had apparently got used to the un-Islāmic rule of the Umayyites as time passed by. Their resistance slackened and some people began adjusting themselves to the new conditions. Hence, the revolutionary spirit of Islām began to disappear gradually from Muslim's lives and thoughts. Therefore, a new stimulant to their souls was necessary to activate their lives and try to restore, the Islāmic conduct to the society.

The Revolution's Procedure

Imām Ḥusain made no concealment of his intentions to fight the regime of the Umayyites. The speeches he delivered at Mecca were consistent. During his jouney to Karbala, he never ceased calling people to strive for the Islāmic ideals of social justice and government, and to wage war against deviation from the Islāmic conduct. As referred in previous pages, Imām Ḥusain sent a letter through the last Kufic messengers, Ḥānī-bin-'Orwah and Sa'īd-bin-'Abdu'llāh Ḥasafī with the following content:

> "It may be clear that Imām's basic responsibility has been to see justice being implemented in letter and spirit of God's book, truth being followed and everyone to be devoted to the Almighty." [9]

During his jouney at Bayzah Imām Ḥusain again explained his objectives before the Yażīdī Army and called upon them to come on the path of Truth. Imām Ḥusain told the Tradition of the holy Prophet that a person, who sees such a ruler who is cruel, atrocious, does not differentiate between good and bad, breaks his promise, opposes the life and conduct of the holy Prophet and has taken the path of sin, but the People of Faith tolerate the bad and do not attempt to reform, such person would be punished by the Almighty for his ideas and conduct along with the same ruler.[10]

Imām Ḥusain's speeches were aiming directly at stripping the religious mask of the Umayyite's regime. He was, introducing himself to people and explaining his message to the nation. Indeed, the personality of Imām Ḥusain and his religious reputation was beyond question or doubt. Therefore, no wonder if he was carrying such agreat task while many distinguished people were not ready to raise a finger.

Multi-Dimensional Phenomenon

Any objective study of this great revolution of Imām Ḥusain will show that something unique about its multi-dimensional phenomenon. The leader predicts his own death before even setting a foot forth on the march! But, he goes on carrying out all necessary preparations for his campaign. The way Imām Ḥusain and his Companions fought was a glorious record of bravery and nobility. There were only seventy two fighting men against thousands of the Umayyite's Army. Even with this imbalance of fighting power, the Umayyite's Army used the most vicious and ignoble methods in fighting this tiny camp. The Umayyite's Army went to the extent of preventing them from drinking water and kept them for three days tortured in the burning heat of the desert. But, the firm faith of Imām Ḥusain and his followers in their cause was never shaken. Thus, they set an ever-shining torch of *Jihād* against deviation from Islāmic conduct and smashed the myth of the Umayyites of keeping allegiance to deviated regimes.

The revolution of the chief of the nobles was the first revolution in human history from the aspect that on it were built intellectual, social and political foundations. Some are the following:

The Revolution's Results

What does the Ḥusainī Revolution mean in the history? Some people, who are not familiar with its motives, innocently inquire about its results. Others have even questioned its wisdom that striking at a mighty force like the Umayyite's was fatal.

Outwardly, the Yażīdī Army had won the battlefield and Imām Ḥusain and his Associates were killed. But victory is decided on the basis of the aims and objects of the struggle, Imām Ḥusain's august aim was to restore the religion of his grandfather Muḥammad, the holy Prophet of Islām. The Yażīdī Army was virtually defeated, it could not kill the Islām and Muḥammad, the grandfather of Imām Ḥusain.

When Imām Żainu'l-Ābidīn was in the market of Damascus, in the miserable condition of a prisoner, Ibrāhīm-bin-Ṭalḥah approached him and tried to tease him, O' 'Alī-bin-al-Ḥusain! Tell me who has won? The holy Imām said in reply:

> "When it is time for prayers you pronounce call for prayer *(Ażān)* and shorter call for prayer *(Iqāmat);* This tells you, who the victor is![11]

Imām Żainu'l-Ābidīn's reply rendered him speechless, because in every *Namāż*, every time every Muslim is bound to recite the name of the holy Prophet Muḥammad, without which no *Namāż* could be possible for any Muslim:

"*Lā Ilāh Ill'allāh Muḥammadu'r Rasūla'llāh.*"
(There is no good but God, Muḥammad His Prophet.)
Marthiya

It is sufficient for the success of Imām Ḥusain that through his martyrdom he bestowed a new life to Islām and sacrificed his blood for it. Imām Ḥusain himself became successful and victorious; because he restored life and light to Islām. On the basis of this he was a reformer; perhaps it was about this aspect that the Holy Prophet had said:

"*Ḥusain Minnī w-Anā Minnal Ḥusain*".[12]
(Ḥusain is from me and I am from Ḥusain.)

Because if the sacrifice of Imām Ḥusain had not been there all the efforts of the holy Prophet of Islām and the well-being, blessings and mercy that he brought for the people would have been destroyed as Umayyite clan was bent on eradicating all the principles that this religion brought and they launced a campaign against Islām and proclaimed infidelity and apostasy, and ruled the people with a policy in which no sign of the Qur'anic command was visible.

Qāżī Nūru'llāh, ash-Shūshtarī, Mar'ashī, (d. 1610 AD), says: "If Imām Ḥusain had not borne those hardships, religion would not have become clear; because when Umayyite clan became the dominant power in the land, they indulged in corruption and tried to conceal the truth till the matter became doubtful for people and made the cursing of Imām 'Alī a part of daily prayers and filled the minds of the people with the notion that Umayyites are the Imāms of Islām. And this matter was taught to the people from childhood because teachers were ordered to impart such training to all the children under their care that Umayyites were the Imāms of religion. And opposition to them is deviation from the path of truthand when Imām Ḥusain was killed in that fashıon and his womenfolk were taken as prisoners of war, people came to their senses, that if they (Umayyites) were guides of truth they would never have committed such acts. This action of theirs had no relation to religion, faith or justice. It was not even in conformity to the oppression of oppressors."[13]

The first clear victory that Imām Ḥusain gained was to defeat the Umayyites; because his sacrifice destroyed all the pillars and foundations laid by Mu'āwiyah for strengthening the regime of Abū Sufyyān's family:

> "Whatever Mu'āwiyah had built up for his son Yażīd in years was destroyed by Imām Ḥusain in a few days. People began to look at the Caliph with disgust and apathy. Muslims were disillusioned by his policies and pointed out with contempt the blemishes that had stained him bad qualities like fraud, deception, injustice and oppression. All this was under the leadership of Imām Ḥusain, and his popularity resulted of wise policy in observing steadfastness in front of their persecution, and a well-designed programme for removing disobedience and oppression which was instrumental in this. The foresight of the Imām Ḥusain and his sincerity in his actions made all this possible."[14]

It may be recalled here, when the head of the Doyen of Martyrs Ḥusain was carried to Kufa, and the inhuman 'Obaydu'llāh-bin-Żiyād struck it on the mouth with a cane: Alas ! exclaimed the aged associate of the holy Prophet, Żayd-bin-Arqam, on these lips had he seen the lips of the holy Prophet Muḥammad. In a very distant age and climate Sir Edward Gibbon (d. 1794 AD) says:

> "The tragic scene of the death of Ḥusain will awaken the sympathy of the coldest reader."[15]

Syed Amīr 'Alī says:

> "The tragical fate of Ḥusain and his children sent a thrill of horror through Islām; and the revulsion of the feeling which it

> caused proved eventually the salvation of the Faith. It arrested the current of depravity which flowed from the Umayyite court of Damascus. It made the bulk of Muslims think of what the Master had done, and of the injuries which the children of his enemies were inflicting on Islām."[16]

By his auspicious movement, Imām Ḥusain crushed the heads that were full of pride, weighed down with arrogance and blinded by self-conceit. He initiated uprisings after uprisings that indicated his infuriated mood with Umayyite and he generously stepped forward to sacrifice his and his associates lives for the victory of these uprisings. No other effect of fear or distress remained with them till they destroyed the expressions of Umayyite arrogance and eradicated their persecution and deviation.

The Ḥusainī Revolution changed the meaning of fear and surrender that was prevalent in the community and according to the principles of revolution turned it into confronting and seeking freedom from the bonds of humiliation and slavery; because the Imām gave them a rousing power and bestowed them a revolutionary spirit to stand up and fight injustice and oppression.

Among the signs of Umayyite defeat was that their condemnation became general and people in all gatherings and assemblies openly criticized their policies and evils; so, frenzied waves of condemnation began to descend upon Yażīd – so much, so that, even his womenfolk and clansmen took up this activity, to such an extent that he was absolutely harried and began to regret the deed he had committed. Hence his relationship with Kufic Governor 'Obaydu'llāh-bin-Żiyād, according to historians, fell into gloom.

As far as the signs of Umayyite defeat after the martyrdom of Imām Ḥusain were concerned; they were as follows:

Demolition of Umayyites Caliphate

The terrible carnage of Karbala took out the Umayyites from the pale of Islām and it was proved that they still followed the barbarity and ignorance of the pre-Islāmic age. Because all the acts they committed with the Progeny of the holy Prophet proved that the Umayyites had discarted the religion of Islām and the faith of Muslims. For example, first of all they put embargo on water supply with the help of armed forces. Then after killing of Imām Ḥusain, they cut up his holy body into bits and pieces. After that they took as hostages the noble ladies of the Prophet's family and took them around towns and cities in such a way that to see them makes one hair stand on end. This was done to announce the defeat of the Prophet's family and publicize that revenge has been taken from them. Similarly, the couplets that Yażīd recited clearly indicated that it was to take revenge of the death of his disbelieving ancestors who had been killed in the Battle of Badr. Thus, all these facts clearly proved that the Umayyites were not Muslim.

The blood of Imām Ḥusain and his companions which was shed by the swords of the armed forces of Yażīd became the nucleus for change. Their pure and chaste bloods spurred up the spirit of sacrifice and devotion towards Ahlu'l-Bayt in the view of the majority of Muslims. And since that time those who were neutral to join battles for getting the power thereafter came under their flag. Those terrible tragedies that befell the beloved grandson of the holy Prophet of God were such that shocked and grieveously hurt the feelings of all those who lived at that time.

Restoring the Prestige of Ahlu'l-Bayt

The revolution of the *Doyen of the Martyrs*, Imām Ḥusain brought out the illuminated reality of Ahlu'l-Bayt and proved to the world of Islām, their powers in being steadfast on truth, their firmness in face of calamities and their sincere concerns for the future of the Islāmic community. As a result of it, the majority of Muslims began to love and regard them with respect and awe.

The tragedy of Karbala clearly showed that the Ahlu'l-Bayt were lofty examples of spiritual and practical leadership of this community and the vanguards of truth and justice on the earth. The martyrdom of Imām Ḥusain, the grandson of the holy Prophet Muḥammad was a great shock to the entire Muslim world. The way by which, he was murdered and the treatment given to his family, which was actually held in the highest esteeme and respect by all Muslims, consequently, dissociated themselves from the Umayyite's deeds and policies. Indeed, who would want to share in the curse upon those who murdered the family of the Prophet? Thus, this revolution had done the task of unveiling the Umayyite's un-Islāmic character to the general public and left no doubt in any person's heart about the Umayyite's vile substance, dark and low passions, vulgar habits and prejudices.

Therefore, the concepts, which the Umayyite's were propagating in order to distort the ideals of Islām, found no listening ear any longer. Hence, for diverting the Umayyite's mischief of changing Islāmic concepts and ideals, assumed a form of a well-defined school of thought in the life of Shi'ī people.

The unprecedented enthusiasm of Shi'ī people was misundetstood by Phillip Hitti when he says: "Shia was born on the day of 10th Muḥarram. From that day Imamate in the progeny of 'Alī became a principle of the faith of Shi'ī, just as prophethood of Muḥammad was a principle of the Islāmic faith."[17] Actually, the existence of Shi'īs has been proved during the lifetime of the holy Prophet Muḥammad, says famous anti-Shi'īs scholar of Syria, Muḥammad 'Alī Kurd.[18] However, the Ḥusainī Revolution re-established the true Doctrine of Islām, peace and justice. It led to reform in both politics and religion. It brought the people to a higher level of thought and sentiments and improved their spiritual, moral and mental life. To a great extent, it paved the way for their salvation and arrested their further downfall.

An orientalist 'Omar Abū Naṣr says: "If Ḥusain had not been killed, Shi'ī would not have come into being in Islām."[19]

The Ḥusainī Revolution bestowed unity among the Muslims in general and Shi'ī people in particular and created a spirit of co-operation among them. Before that due to the lack of motivation and loyalty in defence of their belief based on religious right of special caliphate of Ahlu'l-Bayt, they had borne grief. Those perceptions changed and they gathered the strongest manpower with which they rushed out to destroy the Umayyite regime and stood up together to take revenge for Imām Ḥusain and his companions.

The carnage of Karbala roused in the hearts of Shi'ī, feelings and sorrows and it brought them to the belief that before everything they must think of the need of unity to take revenge for the martyrdom of the great Imām who had stood up for the sake of justice and for restoring the rights of the persecuted and oppressed people. It created a terrible wave of disconcertation and deep effects on the life of Muslims and it stimulated them to undertake political action.

Continuation of the Revolution

The 'Arabian peninsula, since the martyrdom of Imām Ḥusain had burnt in the fire of war, according to famous Egyptian historian, Taqīu'l-Dīn Abu'l-'Abbās Aḥmad al-Maqrīzī (d. 1442 AD),[20] because the Islāmic communities arose as powerful oppositions and announced their anger and fury against the Umayyite regime and endeavoured to bring their downfall. Some of the uprisings were as follows:

Uprising of 'Abdu'llāh-bin-'Afīf al-Muẓāhir

The uprising of 'Abdu'llāh-bin-'Afīf al-Muẓāhir was the first uprising in

Kufa that appeared immediately after the martyrdom of the Imām and the great stalwart, 'Abdu'llāh-bin-'Afīf started it. He was the first of those who lighted the spark of revolution and changed into defeat the fake victory that 'Obaydu'llāh-bin-Żiyād, Governor of Kufa had achieved as we have already explained in detail in the foregoing pages.

Uprising of the People of Medina

The fact is that the uprising of the people of Medina was nothing, but the continuation of the Ḥusainī Revolution; because people were boiling with rage and hatred towards Yażīd-bin-Mu'āwiya as he had defiled the sanctity of the Prophet of God by killing his Progeny and by taking his children as captives. When prisoners from Ahlu'l-Bayt returned to Medina and told the people about the great tragedies and terrible hardships that they had to suffer and explained to them the calamities and captivity, which the ladies of the abode of prophethood and noble women of the family of revelation had to bear, people became deeply aggrieved and sorrowful for the beloved grandson of the holy Prophet of Islām. The granddaughter of the Prophet, Żainab-bint-Imām 'Alī, *Sharīkatu'l Ḥusain* enflamed passions for taking revenge for the killing of her brother. The Yażīdī Army ransacked Medina and gave him an army composed of at least 12000 Syrian mercenaries. For three days he made it lawful for them to do whatever they liked to the people of Medina and plunder whatever they desired from there.

Uprising of the Tawābbīn

Tawābbīn means the penitents. They had commited no crime which could necessitate any type of penitence. We have already dicussed at the appropriate place about the martyrdom of Imām Ḥusain's peace-envoy Muslim and his supporters at Kufa. Under the orders Kufic Governor, 'Obaydu'llāh-bin-Żiyād, the Kufa's jails were brimful with the supporters of the Progeny of the Prophet Muḥammad. Firm arrangements were made to arrest all those persons who could extend any help to Imām Ḥusain. Even then some reached to Imām Ḥusain and sacrificed their life on the path of Truth. These penitents were themselves ashamed, that they could not reach Karbala and sacrifice their lives.

These people of Kufa were deeply regretful that they had committed a great sin, because they could not sacrifice their live at the feet of the holy Imām. They chastised each other for the terrible inequity they had done. They unanimously decided that they must confess their sin of deserting Imām Ḥusain and it was necessary for them to take revenge of Imām Ḥusain, as expiation of their sins. One of them addressed his daughter and said: "My daughter! Your father cries to his Lord due to his sin."[21]

They held a conference at the house of Sulaymān-bin-Ṣorad Khuzā'ī, the companion of Prophet Muḥammad. He had precedence and seniority in Islām. They held discussions among themselves and concluded that this disgrace and sin cannot be washed clear without eliminating those who had martyred Imām Ḥusain.[22] In the meeting some fiery speeches were made that called for taking revenge for the blood of the great Imām and they stressed the need for unity and co-operation in this regard. Sulaymān-bin-Ṣorad Khuzā'ī was chosen as the leader of the revolt, so, that he may chalk out the political programme and make military preparations. Letters were dispatched to various localities in Iraq and outside Iraq informing and inviting them to join them in this mission.

The uprising was to take place after a gap of four years, so that, during this time volunteers could be enrolled and preparations made for war. Nukhaiylah was made the centre of revolt and the matter of uprising was be kept secret. Organs of the uprising, who according to historians, numbered one hundred, spread in the lands to start working for mobilizing help for purchase of weapons. They invited the people to cooperate with them and to join them.

In the year 686 AD, the penitents declared their impassioned revolt against the Umayyite regime. They numbered, according to historians, 4000 men. Leader of the uprising, Sulaymān-bin-Ṣorad Khuzā'ī sent Hakīm-bin-Munqiz Kindī and Walīd-bin-Athīr Kīnanī to Kufa and instructed them to raise the slogan of "Yā Thāratu'l Ḥusain!" (Rise up to take revenge of Ḥusain!").

When Hakīm and Walīd reached Kufa they raised that slogan and for the first time this effective call arose in the atmosphere of Kufa and it fell like a thunderbolt on the sinful killers, but was a medicine for the hearts of believers and Muslims. A large number of people rushed to Nukhaiylah, where Sulaymān-bin-Ṣorad delivered an effective speech among them. He explained to them that he was not in pursuit of power or booty of war. He only desired the satisfaction of God and had only the abode of Hereafter in view. He also expressed hope that the Almighty Allāh would forgive him and his brothers the sin of having deserted the beloved grandson of Prophet Muḥammad.

The penitents decided to go on a pilgrimage of the holy grave of the *Doyen of the Martyrs*, Imām Ḥusain at Karbala, so that, besides his grave they may announce their repentance in the court of the Lord of the worlds. Groups of penitents set out for Karbala and when they reached there they lamented in one voice: "Yā Ḥusain!" They wept and lamented and humbled themselves before the Almighty that He may accept their sincere repentance and forgive them. They said besides the grave of the holy Imām:

> "Oh Allāh! Have mercy on Ḥusain, the martyr and son of martyr, the guided one, son of the guided one, the truthful one, son of the truthful one. Oh Allāh! We take You as our witness that we are upon his faith and path. We are the enemies of his killers and friends of his followers. Oh Allāh! We deserted the son of the daughter of our Prophet. Thus, forgive our past and accept our repentance and have mercy on Ḥusain and his companions – the truthful martyrs. We take You as our witness that we follow their religion and that for which they laid down their lives. If You do not forgive us and not have mercy on us, we shall be of the losers."[23]

At that time they crowded on the holy grave with a crowding like that of the *Ḥajaru'l-Aswad* (the Black Stone of Ka'bah) while they were weeping and humbling before Allāh that He may forgive their sins and accept their repentance. After that they departed towards the Anbar province.

The penitents marched on till they reached 'Ainu'l-Wurdah. They camped at that place. Syrian Yażīdī Army began to attack them and furious battles took place between them. Both the sides suffered heavy losses. Leaders of the penitents, like Sulayman-bin-Ṣorad Khuzā'ī, Musayyab-bin-Najbah and 'Abdu'llāh-bin-Wā'al and others were martyred.

When the penitents saw that they were not getting help in confronting the Syrians they left the battlefield in the darkness of the night and returned to Kufa. Syrian army also did not pursue them. Both parties returned to their towns and in this way ended the war of penitents, while the Umayyites became distressed and heavy losses had been inflicted them.

Uprising of Amīr Mukhtār Thaqafī

Amīr Mukhtār-bin-Abī 'Obaydu'llāh Thaqafī has been the most famous personality of the history of Islām, because of the fact that he played an important role in the political events of that time. He was also the most outstanding politician having uncanny ability for organization and planning, and he was an expert in turning the circumstances to his advantage. He strengthened his achievements with his capabilities as a person of deep perception.

Scholars say: 'Amīr Mukhtār was very knowledgeable in psychology and well-versed in the method of propagation and communication and he spoke to the people according to their intellectual level and he did not adopt only the modes of propagation like speeches and poetry, but also employed other methods also like exhibitions, displays and propaganda. He also employed that which we call *coup d'etat* through which he took Kufa from the control of 'Abdu'llāh-bin-Żubayr.[24]

'Amīr Mukhtār was a senior personality of the Shi'ī community and a sword of the Progeny of the Prophet Muḥammad. He was intensely aggrieved and agitated in the sorrow of the purified Progeny, who were eliminated by swords of falsehood. He endeavoured to obtain rulership not because he was inclined to it but that he may avenge Ahlu'l-Bayt and take revenge from their killers.

The figments of the Umayyite fertile imagination have heaped on this great warrior serious allegations like that he was claimant of Prophethood and other false implications of which he is blameless. And for which he is absolved; because he arose to take revenge for the great Imām, he shook up the existence of Umayyite rule and destroyed the glory of their regime. He practised equity between 'Arabs and non-'Arabs, he did not accord preference to anyone over others. During his rule he tried to follow the footsteps of *Amīru'l-Mominīn* Imām 'Alī-bin-abī Ṭālib and followed his economic and social policies.

Amīr Mukhtār was extremely pious and religious. Historians say: During his brief rule, in order to thank the Almighty he fasted excessively, so that, the Almighty Lord may enable him to take revenge for the pious Progeny and to eliminate the sinful and transgressive killers. The treacherous Umayyites have made baseless allegations against this great warrior in order to decrease his status and reduce his importance. After having carefully studied his activities we have found him to be an incomparable personality of history and a famous man of the Islāmic nation. With many excellences like nobility and piety, original thinking, deep perception and good intentions, such qualities that few people of that time had possessed. We would have liked to say more on the personality of this outstanding man and explain in detail how he organized his uprising and obtained power. But due to paucity of time, it would not be possible. However, before we conclude our discussions about him we shall discuss in brief some matters related to the subject as follows:

It was fear and terror that seized the sinful murderers and killers of the beloved grandson of the Prophet Muḥammad; because they became certain that the uprising of Amīr Mukhtār has been organized to take revenge from them. Therefore, some of them fled to the wilderness and others disappeared in such a way that there was no information about them. A few of them fled to 'Abdu'l Malik to take refuge from the attack and fury of Amīr Mukhtār as one of them addressed him saying: "I come to you so that you have mercy on me and remove my hardships. But I see that you drive me away; then where can I go?"[25] 'Abdu'l Malik Taghibīn also sought his refuge saying: "I fled from Iraq to you." 'Abdu'l Malik-bin-Marwān screamed at him: "You have not fled to join me. You have fled from the reprisal of killing Ḥusain and fearing for your life you seek to take refuge with me."[26]

In the same way some of them fled to 'Abdu'llāh-bin-Żubayr and joined his army and fought on his side. It was not because they followed his faith, but it was due to the fear of Mukhtār as he had ruined their houses. and confiscated all their property. Amīr Mukhtār demolished the house of Muḥammad-bin-Asha'th, Commander of the Yażīdī Army at Karbala, took away the materials and renovated the house of the great martyr, Ḥujr-bin-'Adī Kindī that had been destroyed by Żiyād-bin-Abīh, the then Mu'āwiyah-bin-Abū Sufyyān's Kufic Governor.[27]

As for that filthy 'Omar-bin-Sa'd, Commandor-in-Chief of the Yażīdī Army at Karbala, he hid in his house, anxious and frightened; and he sent important persons to mediate for him with Amīr Mukhtār and wrote to him letters seeking pardon and safety. He gave him security on the condition that he would not take any step. However, 'Omar-bin-Sa'd in this matter spoke in a roundabout and ambiguous manner that he wasn't allowed even to go to answer the call of nature.

Amīr Mukhtār put in anguish the hearts of criminals and killers of Imām in such a way that the earth shook beneath their feet and frenzied waves of shock and terror covered them in such a way that none of them could live in peace; because the ghost of death hovered over them.

Amīr Mukhtār hastened to issue decree of death to anyone who had participated in the killing of the beloved grandson of the holy Prophet, because he endeavoured to take revenge from them and purify the earth from those filthy creatures. As such, as the renowned historian Abū Ja'far Muḥammad Jarīr Ṭabarī (d. 923 AD) says: on one day he condemned twenty of them to death and none of their commanders and leaders could escape. He killed the filthy sinner, 'Obaydu'llāh-bin-Żiyād, 'Omar-bin-Sa'd and his son Ḥafas. He executed Shimr-bin-Žuljaushan and threw his corpse to dogs. In the same way he got killed Qays-bin-Asha'th, Ḥiṣṣīn-bin-Numayr, Shabth-bin-Raba'ī and others.[28] Similar facts have also been narrated by other renowned historians.[29]

The exemplary facts are noteworthy that sinful murderers, whom in the way they had killed, made them drink the bitter cup of death and took revenge from them in the most severe manner. Almighty Allāh has truly said:

> "Such is the grasp (*of punishment*) of thy Lord when graspeth He the township while they are unjust; Verily His grasp (*punishment*) is painful, severe." (*Qur'an*: 11/102)

None of the killers of Imām Ḥusain and his companions could remain but that they were punished in the world, either by killing, getting blinded, blackening of face or downfall of power in a short time. They were punished in this world and they lie for ever in the fire of Hell in such a way that neither the punishment shall be reduced for them nor would they get any respite.

When Amīr Mukhtār had sent head of the most perfidious wretch Ḥarmalah-bin-Kāhil, the killer of Imām Ḥusain's six month child, 'Alī Aṣghar, 'Abdu'llāh Razī'a, Imām Żainu'l-Ābidīn, who had never smiled after the tragedy of Karbala, became happy and instructed the Household to celebrate the day as *Eīd*. Change the dress and spray perfume. It was the 9th of Rabī'-Awwal. Since then their followers observe the 9th of Rabī'-Awwal as *Eīdu'ż-Żahrā* every year.[30]

The date of the 9th of Rabī'-Awwal has great significance in the history of Islām. It was 9th Rabī'-Awwal, when first verse of the holy Qur'an was revealed on the holy Prophet Muḥammad:

> "Read thou ! (*O' our Apostle Muḥammad !*) In the name of thy Lord Who created (*Everything in the Universe*)." (*Qur'an*: 96/1)

Secondly, most of the learned scholar consider the 9th Rabī'-Awwal, as the date of birth of the holy Prophet.[31]

Thirdly, the auspicious date of the *Nikāḥ* (marriage) of the holy Prophet to *Ummu'l-Mūminīn* Khadījah. daughter of Khawaled of Asad clan was also the 9th Rabī'-Awwal.

Blessing and pleasure of Allāh be on Amīr Mukhtār-bin-Abī 'Obaydu'llāh Thaqafī, on the day he came in pursuit, the day he was martyred and the day he shall be raised. He was killed at the behest of 'Abdu'llāh-bin-Żubayr, but it did not weaken the revolutionary spirit of the Shi'ī.

Uprising of Imām Żayd-bin-'Alī

Uprising of Imām Żayd has great significance, because it was not merely the uprising, but commencement of the great revolution of the son of Imām Żainu'l-Ābidīn. Imām Żayd is also known as Żayd-bin-'Alī, who arose to confront injustice and oppression and after him, his son Yaḥyā enflamed the fire of his revolt. He took as their slogan the principles of Imām Ḥusain and wanted to revenge his killing.

Uprising of Imām Żayd has removed the cobweb from the mind of those, who think the Imāms had withdrawn their rightful claim of being head of Muslim state, politically as well as socially. It is futher clarified by that incident, which has been mentioned by several writers. Once Imām Mūsā al-Kāẓim (745-99 AD) was offerd to take back the Fidak (land property of the Progeny of the Prophet Muḥammad) so that, the dispute of heirship of the Prophet Muḥammad could be settled. He was asked to demarcate the boundary of the land. Imām Mūsā al-Kāẓim told the Caliph that its first limit would be Aden, second limit Samarkand, third limit Africa, and fourth limit Saifu'l Baḥr, which is situated in Arminia. In other words the then entire Muslim kingdom.[32]

Uprising of Abū Muslim Khorasanī

In this way uprisings continued till black flags appeared in the vanguards of Muslim army under the command of Abū Muslim Khorāsānīn, whose Persian name was Vehzādān Pour Vandād Hormozd (d. 755 AD) and destroyed the crown and throne of the Umayyites and crushed their oppression and arrogance.

In the last days of the Umayyites rule, their Empire was tottering and was on the verge of collapse, and a most chaotic and demoralised state of affairs prevailed throughout the Islāmic lands. The 'Abbāsites ('Abbāsī), the descendants of 'Abbās-bin-'Abdu'l-Muṭṭalib, uncle of the Prophet Muḥammad exploited such an opportunity and availing themselves of this political instability, assumed the title of *Avengers of Holy Ahlu'l Bayt*. They pretended to have stood for the cause of taking revenge on the Umayyites for shedding the innocent blood of the holy Imām Ḥusain.

The common people who were groaning under the yoke of the Umayyites, were fed up with their atrocities and were secretly yearning for the progeny of the holy Prophet to take power. They realised that if the leadership went to the holy Ahlu'l-Bayt, who were its legitimate heir, the prestige of Islām would be enhanced and the holy Prophet's misison would be genuinely propagated. They offered Imām Ja'far aṣ-Ṣādiq the throne of the Caliphate through Abū Salamā Khallāl. However, a group of 'Abbāsites secretly dedicated their lives to a campaign for seizing power from the hands of the Umayyites on the pretext that they were seizing it only to surrender it to the holy Ahlu'l Bayt. Actually, they were plotting for their own ends. Imām Ja'far aṣ-Ṣādiq was fully aware of the facts. Hence, he declined to accept the offer of the throne of the Caliphate.[33] The common people were thus deceived into supporting them and when these 'Abbāsites did succeed in snatching power from the Umayyites, they turned against the holy Ahlu'l-Bayt. Later on these 'Abbāsites killed Abū Muslim Khorāsānī.

Uprising of Muḥammad an-Nafsu'ż-Żakiyyah

Abū 'Abdu'llāh Muḥammad an-Nafsu'ż-Żakiyyah was the great grandson of Imām Ḥasan, who was assosciated with the movement against the 'Abbāsites rule. Young, energetic and brave Abū 'Abdu'llāh Muḥammad was chosen in a meeting in Medina. He declared *Jihād* against 'Abbāsites rule and fought with them with his 300 companions and was killed. This battle occurred on 7th December, 762 AD.

Imām 'Alī ar-Reza Proclaimed *'Abbāsites Heir*

The Ḥusainī Revolution threw the Umayyite regime in defeat and destroyed all its traces and made it the target of one uprising after another which were initiated by the followers of Ahlu'l-Bayt and others till finally the dark regime was destroyed by the establishment of 'Abbāsites rule. But they were no better to their predecessors. Since an extreme choking atmosphere and pressure prevailed. Even during the most chaotic periods, and it was mostly due to Imām 'Alī ar-Reza efforts that the teachings of the holy Prophet and his descendants became widespread. Imām 'Alī ar-Reza had inherited great qualities of head and heart from his ancestors. He was a versatile person and had full command over many languages. 'Abbāsites Caliph al-Ma'mūn (813-33 AD) was a very shrewd person. He made a plan to invite Imām 'Alī ar-Reza and to offer him the heirship to the throne. The Imām was summoned by a royal decree and was compelled, under the circumstances, to leave Medina—where he was living a quiet life—and present himself at the royal court of al-Ma'mūn. When he arrived on horseback at Nayshabūr, myriads of people gathered round him and all roads were overcrowded as they had come to meet and see their great Imām.

On his arrival, al-Ma'mūn showed him hospitality and great respect, then he said to him: "I want to get rid of myself of the caliphate and vest the office in you." But Imām 'Alī ar-Reza refused his offer. Then al-Ma'mūn repeated his offer in a letter saying: "If you refuse what I have offered you, then you must accept being the heir after me." In reply, Imām said: "I will agree to what you want of me as far as succession is concerned on condition that I do not command, nor order, nor give legal decisions, nor judge, nor appoint, nor dismiss, nor change anything from how it is at present." al-Ma'mūn accepted all of that. On the day when al-Ma'mūn ordered to make the pledge of allegiance to Imām 'Alī ar-Reza, a Royal decree was published saying that Imām 'Alī ar-Reza will succeed al-Ma'mūn.

To understand Imām 'Alī ar-Reza's refusal to accept the proposal of al-Ma'mūn for taking over the Caliphate and his office and then accepting his heirship, it is necessary to substract both the issues. Accepting of al-Ma'mūn's Caliphate and his office was amounting to granting legitimacy to the establishment of 'Abbāsites rule, as a true Islāmic system of governance, which could not be possible for an infallible Imām. In accepting the heirship Imām 'Alī ar-Reza would significantly restricted himself from his participation of the functioning of the then Caliphate. He would neither command, nor order, nor give legal decisions, nor judge, nor appoint, nor dismiss, nor change anything from how it is at present. Accepting the heirship by Imām 'Alī ar-Reza was a good hope that after al-Ma'mūn's, it would revert to Ahlu'l-Bayt. It is like Ḥasan-Mu'āwiyah-Treatry to compromise on the basis of the Islāmic principle of enjoining the good and forbidding the evils (*Qur'an*: 41/22). Lighting the candle of hope that Muslim Ummah would be united and the Divine system of governance would prevail, could not be possible because al-Ma'mūn matyred Imām 'Alī ar-Reza by giving him poison in the year 818 AD.

Shi'ī Caliphate of Fāṭimid Dynasty

Among the consequences of the Ḥusainī Revolution was that it bestowed a centralization to them in the limits of Shi'ī beliefs. The foundation of a strong Shi'ī Caliphate, even if Ismā'īlīs not Imāmiyyas, was just like a gland in the throat of 'Abbāsites, who had captured the Caliphate in the name of restoring it to its real claimants, the descendants of Fāṭimah-'Ali, the *Ahlu'l-Bayt.* 'Abbāsites were counterfeitly propagating to be themselves included in *Ahlu'l-Bayt.*

In 909 AD, the Fāṭimid dynasty was founded in an amazing manner. Making Imām 'Obayd'ullāhu'l-Mahdī prisoner in Tunis, by the 'Abbāsite administration gave the cause of action. This place is famous today by the name of Mahdīya seaport. The news of the arrest of Imām 'Obayd'ullāhu'l-Mahdī reached the great Ismā'īlī Abū-'Abdu'llāh Shi'ī. He attacked Kariwān, defeated Abbāsites, and got Imām 'Obayd'ullāhu'l-Mahdī released from the prison. This event is of 909 AD. Fourteen Imāms ruled, who are called *Fāṭimīnu'l-Miṣr*, Fāṭimid Dynasty:

First	Imām 'Obayd'ullāhu'l-Mahdī	(909-34 AD)
Second	Imām al-Qāim bi-amr-Illāh	(934-46 AD)
Third	Imām al-Manṣūr bi-amr-Illāh	(946-53 AD)
Fourth	Imām al-Mu'iżż li-dīn-Illāh	(953-75 AD)
Fifth	Imām al-'Ażiż b'Illāh	(975-96 AD)
Sixth	Imām al-Hākim bi-amr-Illāh	(996-1021 AD)
Seventh	Imām aẓ-Ẓāhiru'l-'Azāz-dīn-Illāh	(1021-36 AD)
Eighth	Imām al-Mustanṣir b'Illāh	(1036-94 AD)
Ninth	Imām al-Musta'lī b'Illāh	(1094-1101 AD)
Tenth	Imām al-Amr bi-Aḥkām-Illāh	(1101-30 AD)

All these ten personalities were simultaneously the Imāms, the Caliphs and the Kings. After the last Caliph of Fāṭimid dynasty, known as Imām al-Amr bi-Aḥkām-Illāh, firstly Afzalu'l-Malik, then 'Abdu'l Majīd Maimūn, who took the name *Ḥāfiz,* held the office in trust, but were not designated as Imām. Fāṭimid Caliphate remained established up to 1171 AD until Sultān Ṣalāḥu'd-Dīn Ayyūbī finished it. They were as under:

Eleventh	Caliph al-Ḥāfiẓ li-dīn-Illāh	(1130-49 AD)
Twelfth	Caliph aẓ-Ẓāfir bi-amr-Illāh	(1149-54 AD)
Thirteenth	Caliph al-Fāiż bi-naṣr-Illāh	(1154-60 AD)
Fourteenth	Caliph al-'Āzid li-dīn-Illāh	(1160-71 AD)

Here comes to conclusion our discussion about the consequences of the Imām's revolution related to the social and intellectual fields. In the same way we come to the last pages of this book and in the end, once more state the points we have mentioned before; that these pages are just some glimpses of the life of the great Imām that has conquered the feelings of the people and their sentiments and achieved a place in their hearts and minds. I am sure that whatever has been written inthis regard so far and whatever that shall be written in future would still fall short in covering all the aspects of the personality of the great Imām and would not be able to present the reality of his life in full, a life that was the continuation of the life of his grandfather, the holy Prophet and his guidance that had the benefit of humanity in view.

Socio-Political Scenario of Shi'īs Kingdoms

The Ḥusainī Revolution was effective in creating new socio-political scenario and bringing out the revolutionary spirit in people, because the community had completely changed and after remaining silent and submissive it became armed with faith and power of determination and decisiveness and it became free of all the negative notions that it had been involved in. They set out to demand their rights and made endeavour to destroy, firstly the Umayyites, then 'Abbāsites regime.

The eleventh century AD has been called *the Shi'īs century*[34], during which the Buyid were in control of Iraq and Iran, the Hamādānīs ruled over northern Syria and Fāṭimīds reigned over Egypt, southern Syria and the Ḥijāz. Despite having a freehand they never tried to impose the *Shi'īs* ideology on the persons of other Islāmic schools of thoughts and people of other faiths. However, the Shi'īs made substantial in road on the Muslim masses through emphasizing to love the Prophet Muḥammad and his pious progeny. During the Buyid era some important incidents took place, which later developed as popular religion of the Shi'īs. Mu'izzu'd-Dawla Daylamī, under the Buyid regime, instituted two great Shi'īs commemorations in 351 AH/962 AD in Baghdad: firstly, on the martyrdom day of Imām Ḥusain, the 10th day of Muḥarram, the day of the butchery of Karbala, in which the noblest spirit of time was martyred and with him perished all the members of his family, the pious companions of the Prophet Muḥammad and others, causing an atmosphere of horror throughout Islām. Secondly, the festival of *Ghadīru'l-Khumm* on 18th day of Žilḥijjah, now popularly known as *Eīdu'l-Ghadīr* among the Shi'īs, commemorating the nomination of Imām 'Alī as his successor, by the holy Prophet Muḥammad at *Ghadīru'l-Khumm* and declaration of *Islām* to be completed, perfected and chosen by the Almighty:

> "This day I have perfected for you, your religion, and have completed My favour on you, and chosen for you Islām (*to be*) the Religion." (*Qur'an*: 5/3)

We did not intend to go in detail of Shi'ī Dynasties, which ruled over the Islāmic world, but to show the effect and influence of the Ḥusainī Revolution, which was very wide in all respect: [35]

1. Buyids Dynasty: an Iranian tribe of Daylām –
   Fars (Shīrāż): 923-1062 AD
   Iraq (Baghdad): 945-1055 AD
   Other branches of family ruled in Kirmān, Hamadān, Rayy and 'Umān.
2. Hamadānid Dynasty: Taghlib tribe of 'Arabs –
   North Iraq (Mosul): 904-979 AD
   Abū Ṭāhir and Ḥusain, brother of Abū Taghlib briefly reconquered Mosul: 981-991 AD
   North Syria (Aleppo): 944-991 AD
   Aleppo eventually fell into Fāṭimid control in 1015 AD
3. 'Uqaylids Dynasty: Banū Ka'b tribe of 'Arabs –
   North Iraq (Mosul) and North Syria (Aleppo): 991-1096 AD
4. Mazyadids Dynasty: Banū Asad tribe of 'Arabs –
   South Iraq (Hilla): 1012-1150 AD
5. Mirdasids Dynasty: Banū Asad tribe of 'Arabs –
   North Syria (Aleppo): 1023-1076 AD
6. 'Ammār Dynasty: Banū 'Ammār tribe of 'Arabs –
   Tripoli: 1070-1107 AD
7. Chupanids Dynasty: Mongol tribe –
   Āżarbāyjān (Tabrīż): 1321-1355 AD
8. Jalayirid Dynasty: Mongol tribe –
   Āżarbāyjān and Baghdad: 1336-1432 AD
9. Sarbadarids Dynasty: Iranians –
   Khorāsān (*Sabżīvār*): 1337-1361 AD
10. Mar'ashī Saiyed Dynasty: 'Arabian and Iranians –
    Māżandarān (*Āmul)*: 1359-1561 AD
11. Qarā-Quyūnlū Dynasty: Turkoman tribe –
    Āżarbāyjān (Tabrīż): 1380-1469 AD
12. Ādil-Shāhī Dynasty: Iranian or Turkoman ancestry –
    Bījāpur, Deccan, India: 1489-1686 AD
13. Niẓām-Shāhī Dynasty: Indian tribe –
    Ahmadnagar, Deccan, India: 1490-1599 AD

14. Quṭb-S̲h̲āhī Dynasty: Iranian ancestry –
    Golkunda, Deccan, India: 1512-1687 AD
15. Chak Dynasty: Indian ancestry –
    Srinagar, Kashmir, India: 1561-1586 AD
16. Ṣafvīds Dynasty: Kurdish or Turkoman ancestry –
    Tabrīż, Qażvīn then Isfahān (Iran): 1501-1722 AD
17. Nawwāb/King of Awadh's Dynasty: Iranian ancestry –
    Lucknow, U.P., India: 1720-1856 AD
18. Żand Dynasty: Iranian tribe –
    South Iran (S̲h̲īraż): 1750-1794 AD
19. Qajar Dynasty: Turkoman tribe –
    Iran, Tehran: 1794-1925 AD
20. Pahlavīs Dynasty: Iranian ancestry –
    Iran, Tehran: 1925-79 AD

Here comes to conclusion our discussion about the consequences of the Ḥusainī Revolution related to the Socio-Political Scenario of S̲h̲i'īs Kingdoms, which as now a living example of Divine governance system fully based on the benefits of great sacrifice of the *Doyen of the Martyrs*, Imām Ḥusain at Karbala.

The Islāmic Republic of Iran

It may be said safely that the Islāmic Republic of Iran has been direct product of the Ḥusainī Revolution. Using the mourning days associated with 'Ās̲h̲ūrah, the 10th day of Imām Ḥusain's martyrdom at Karbala, and the commemoration ceremonies associated with these central aspects of S̲h̲i'īs belief, Ayatu'llāh Rūhu'llāh K̲h̲omeinī (d. 1989 AD) was able to transform the Iranian people's discontent into a revolutionary crisis by providing an effective channel of communication between the participant activists and the leaders of the Iranian Revolution. At the same time K̲h̲omeinī was able to provide a mechanism for the political mobilisation of the masses against the different socio-economic problems that encumbered Iranian society under Pahlavīs Dynasty regime.

The Iranian Revolution's theme slogan was *Kulli'n Yaumin 'Ās̲h̲ūrah, Kulli'n Arzin Karbala* (Everyday is 'Ās̲h̲ūrah and every earth is Karbala). This slogan shook the whole country, when raised at mid-night made the hearts of many people throb in their chest. Imām K̲h̲omeinī's role was also central in shaping the new political order that emerged from the revolution, the Islāmic Republic of Iran, came into existence, after a nationwide referendum, on March 30 and 31, 1979 AD, resulted in a massive vote in favour of the establishment of the Islāmic Republic. The Imām Khomeinī proclaimed the next day, April 1, 1979 AD, as *the first day of God's government*.[36] The institutionalization of the new order continued with the election, on August 3, 1979 AD of an Assembly of Experts (Majlis-i Khūbragan), entrusted with the task of reviewing a draft constitution that had been put forward on June 18, 1979 AD. Fifty-five of the seventy-three persons elected were religious scholars, subsequently invested with a new constitution reflecting the Shi'ī ideology of Islāmic Government. He took the *Nā'ibu'l Imām* concept to its logical conclusion by asserting the right of the *Faqīh* as the Deputy of Imām of the Time to superintend all the religious, social and political affairs in the capacity of *Vilāyat-i-Faqīh*, the concept that the government belongs by right to those who are learned in jurisprudence.

There are sharp paradoxes, the twists and turns of political developments in the Islāmic countries, but this much may be said without any hesitation that the awareness of a new system of the Islāmic democracy is on the rise, the future would decide how far successful the Islāmic democracy proves. Presently, only a few Muslim states are there, which are still under imperial rule, and the campaign for liberation is on in full swing. The scene of the imperial power to coming to an end. Muslim Imperialism has totally lost the creditability and shall die within a few years.

'Ażādārī, Lively Symbol of Sacrifice

The effect and influence of the Ḥusainī Revolution has become institutionalized in the form of *'Ażādārī*, (derived from 'Arabic *'Ażā*, means to console,[37] the Qur'an's term: *Qur'an* 70/37). It is commemorated for acknowledging the great sacrifice made by Imām Ḥusain and his Associates and regard it as a deeply tragic event and commemorate by mourning, holding public processions, organizing assemblies, beating the chest and in some cases self-flagellation. The martyrdom of Imām Ḥusain and his Associates at Karbala in 680 AD is specially commemorated during an annual 10-day period is held inevery Muḥarram by the Muslims in general and Shi'īs in particular, culminating on its tenth day, known as the *'Āshūrah*.

The *'Ażādārī*, has been a great source in spreading the message of Imām Ḥusain. It has been recognised as a religious responsibility among Muslims. Therefore, the common mass considers it as the part of his religious rituals. This responsibility will remain as *status quo* towards God and society, yes, with the dedication towards Imām Ḥusain, he will get the benefit of adoration. It's various forms remain in various countries. As a composite form it can be said that in Indian Subcontinent from Dacca to Peshawar, from Leh to Kanya Kumari *'Ażādārī* has been prevalent. After bifurcation, India has been divided into five independent countries on the world map, namely, India, Pakistan, Bangladesh, Sri Lanka and Myanmar. Among them *'Ażādārī* is specially prevalent in India, Pakistan and Bangladesh. However, it may be more appropriate that wherever there are citizens of these countries Europe, America, Latin America, Canada, Africa and Asia, *'Ażādārī* is attached with their hearts. They are ready to sacrifice everything for the propagation and development of *'Ażādārī*. In a few 'Arab countries where there is restriction on *'Ażādārī*, it is observed in their homes.

'Ażādārī has been the backbone of the Shi'ī community in educating its members about Islām. The immense sympathy which a Shi'ī feels towards the martyrs of Karbala, works as a magnet in pulling him or her to the *Majlis* and other ceremonies of *'Ażādārī*. Experience has shown that in programmes to mourn Imām Ḥusain and his Associates, the organizers do not have to go out of their way to promote it or urge the people to participate. The love which the Shi'ī have for the martyrs of Karbala pulls them to such programmes. The story is quite different when the same organizers arrange a lecture or an academic programme, even if the lecturer is of a very learned '*Ālim* or scholar.

The psychological and emotional attachment which the Shi'ī have towards the *'Ażādārī* of Imām Ḥusain is a very precious and valuable tool to implement the purpose of *'Ażādārī* outlined above. History of the Shi'ī people in different parts of the world will bear out the fact that *'Ażādārī* has been the single most important media of mass religious education. This is not to deny that some people or community might be going through the recession as far as the productivity of *'Ażādārī* is concerned, but one should not assume from his or her local circumstances that *'Ażādārī* all over the world is waste of community's time, money and energy!

Counting the value of *'Ażādārī* in dollar terms the is result of ignoring its psychological and emotional aspects. Any attempt towards eliminating the programmes of *'Ażādārī*, and diverting its time and energy to other aspects—the academic or charitable works is bound to fail and will not be as much productive. Instead of taking such a negative attitude, this writer believes that steps should be taken to improve the expansion and the quality of the institution of '*Ażādārī*. The institution of '*Ażādārī* is like a school, and if there is a problem in it then the right approach is not to eliminate the school but to reform it.

The organizers, the audience, and, above all, the speakers need to focus on the purpose of *'Ażādārī* itself; the *Majalis*, the *Nawhah* and *Marthiya*, and the *Mātam* should all be moving the people—intellectually, spiritually and emotionally—towards those two purposes. Only then will it be able to achieve the maximum out of the institution of *'Ażādārī*, and to fulfil the pledge to Imām Ḥusain; If I had been in Karbala with you, we would have sacrificed our lives also!

There are so many chapters of Multi-facet influences of the Ḥusainī Revolution. In different parts of human-life the detailed descriptions of its achievements are required, which is not possible here. However, a few symbols and indications only can be described. For an example, if we concentrate over various fine-arts in music *Sożkhwānī* cannot be ignored. Imāmbārā's construction has its own specialities in the art of construction. The army art and horse-riding art had the support of the Ḥusainī Revolution. Otherwise, these studies and Arts were almost complete in itself in Muslims. But in Muḥarram-procession it is exhibited specially, which becomes the centre of attraction of all sorts of people. Generally in celebrating the memory of the great Battle of Karbala the use of gold-silver, brass, copper, steel, wood and paper meshing handicrafts is available, by which a handicraft is specially encouraged.

Among the most prominent consequences of the Ḥusainī Revolution was that it gave rise to platforms of propagating the message of Islām, which to this day has played an important role in imparting lessons of righteousness and piety to the people and their important service was to preach the significance of sacrifice in the path of truth. These pulpits are the important factors of the progress of *'Ażādārī*, if they are utilized in a proper and organized way.

The tragedy of Abū 'Abdu'llāhu'l Ḥusain is a part not separate from the message of Islām and it shows his efforts and struggle against the transgressors and his support of the persecuted and oppressed people. The Ḥusainī pulpits are the most important contribution and the most outstanding achievements of the revolution of the *Doyen of the Martyrs*, Imām Ḥusain and it showed the natures of well-wishing in the hearts and removed the souls from the factors of corruption and deviation and guided them on the path of virtue; steadfastness and good manners, are among its distinctive qualities. In the same way these became like mobile schools for spreading faith in Allāh and teaching Islāmic values to the people.

Literature on the Ḥusainī Revolution

The world of things in which we live misses its equilibrium when its communication with the Truth is lost. Then it gives rise to terrible fights, jealousies and coercions, to a scramble for space and opportunities, for these are limited. We become painfully aware of the evils within the narrow bonds of a mutilated truth, which leads to failure. Only those people can help, who prove by their live that they have a soul, whose dwelling is the kingdom of Truth, and things lose the tyranny of fictitious price when we come to our spiritual freedom.

The theme of suffering and martyrdom occupies a central role in the history of religion from the earliest time. Sacrifices are a means for reaching higher and loftier stages of life; to give away parts of one's fortune or to sacrifice members of one's family enhances one's religious standing. Taking into account the importance of sacrifice and suffering for the development of man, literature in various languages has given a central place to the death on the battlefield reflecting the sacrifice of holy Prophet Muḥammad's grandson Imām Ḥusain-bin-'Alī, *Saiyed-ush-Shuhadah.*

Among the factors of success of the Ḥusainī Revolution has had been its stimulating the blooming of talents and capabilities and its creating an outstanding genre of literature, viz. elegy in the literary world, which is exquisite, remarkable and beautiful.

There is a very broad and wide storage on the Ḥusainī Revolution in the Literature that it is rather very difficult to discuss in a consistent and composite manner. In all the important languages of the whole world it has been written extensively: Karbala's Great-War. The Ḥusainī poetry is a true expression of the enflamed passions and its composers were neither reserved in expressing feelings nor did they borrow their ideas from others. They were themselves deeply moved by the tragedy and thus they described in the most powerful way.

These pieces of living literature are the richest examples of the literature of the world and the most outstanding cultural values in Islām. It is noteworthy that the Ḥusainī literature did not attain as much prominence and popularity in the literature of Islām, as it might have, except after a very long period of time.

'Arabic Literature

The first Marthiya on the tragedy of Karbala relates to Imām Ḥusain himself. When he reached the battlefield hearing the call of Abu'l-Fażl, found his dead-body in the pool of blood. Imām Ḥusain pounced on the Yażīdī army saying:

> He deserves mostly to console him for whom Ḥusain wept
> My beloved brother, Abu'l-Fażl, son of my father

O' cowards ! why you are running away
You have saturated the body of my brother[38].

Similarly, the Mar<u>th</u>iyas of *<u>Sh</u>arīkatu'l Ḥusain* Żainab-bint-Imām 'Alī, Umm Kul<u>th</u>ūm-bint-Imām 'Alī, Fāṭimah-bint-Imām Ḥusain and others from Ahlu'l Bayt who were eyewitness of the event of Karbala have great importance and relevence.

It has been amazing to note that during Umayyite and 'Abbāsite regimes too, the poets never restrained from composing mourning poetry on Imām Ḥusain on account of the fear of death. <u>Sh</u>ay<u>kh</u> Mufīd, Ibn Mu'allim (d. 1022 AD) and <u>Sh</u>aykhu'l-Ṭā'fah, Abū Ja'far Muḥammad, aṭ-Ṭūsī (d. 1067 AD) in their respective *al-Amālī* have mentioned the name of the first 'Arabic Mar<u>th</u>iya poet as 'Oqbah-bin-Asahamī. Others who specialized in depicting the tragedy of Karbala in their poetry had been known as Farażdaq-bin-<u>Gh</u>ālib, Sulayman-bin-Qutaybah, Ja'far-bin-'Affān, 'Abdu'llāh-bin-<u>Gh</u>ālib, Kumayt-bin-Abū 'Ammarah and Da'bal <u>Kh</u>iża'ī.

Persian Literature

The development of the whole genre of the *Mar<u>th</u>iya* poetry and *Ta'żieh* theatre in the Persian and Indo-Persian world, or in the popular Turkish tradition represents folk tradition of the time. But, if we look into the history of Persian literature, the name of Imām Ḥusain-bin-'Alī appears several times in the work of the first great Persian Ṣūfī-poet, Ḥakīm Sana'ī <u>Gh</u>ażnavī (d. 1150 AD).[39] Here, the name of the martyred hero can be found now and then in connection with bravery and selflessness, and Sanai sees him as the prototype of the martyr, higher and more important than all the other martyrs who are and have been in the world. The tendency to see Imām Ḥusain-bin-'Alī as the model of martyrdom and bravery continues in the poetry written in the *Dīvān* of Ṣūfī-poet Farīdu'd-Dīn 'Aṭṭ ār (d. 1221 AD).

When <u>Sh</u>i'ism became the official religion of Iran in the 15th century, Safavid rulers such as <u>Sh</u>āh Ṭahmāsp I (1524-76 AD), patronized poets who wrote about the tragedy of Karbala, and the genre of Mar<u>th</u>iya, but actually we see no flow in Mar<u>th</u>iya writing trend. The only most well-known fifteenth century Persian Mar<u>th</u>iya-poet had been Moḥta<u>sh</u>am Kā<u>sh</u>ānī whose *Dwāżdah-Band* (twelve stanza poem) consequently became a source of elegy emulation for Iranians.

Actually, Persian Mar<u>th</u>iya composing starts from great Mar<u>th</u>iya-poet <u>Sh</u>ay<u>kh</u> Āżarī (d. 1461 AD), who had visited India. The then Sultan

Gulbabarga ordered rupees one lakh to be presented to him. As per custom the poet was required to bow down before the Sultan. The poet refused the award saying, this head bows only before God ! Other renowned Persian Mart͟hiya-poet was Mullā Muqbal (d. 1744 AD), who had adopted Mart͟hiya writing as his profession. He had also came to India and died here, in this country itself.[40]

Azerī and Turkish Literature

Turkish tradition, especially in the later Ṣūfī's Bektashi Order, is deeply indebted to S͟hi'ism. But it seems that already in some of the earliest popular Ṣūfī songs in Turkey, those composed by Yūnus Emre in the late thirteenth or early fourteenth century, depicting the great role played by Imām Ḥusain and others from Ahlu'l Bayt.

Urdu Literature

The Ḥusainī Revolution and the great personalities of Imām Ḥusain and his martyred companions in particular and the Ahlu'l Bayt are the most favourite subjets in Urdu literature. All literary forms—prose and poetry—are brimful with the descriptions of the event of Karbala. There is a treasure of lakhs of pages. However, in Urdu a separate the Ḥusainī Revolution based literature is also available in the form of epic, which is called Mart͟hiya. Its equivalent is not availabe in Persian or 'Arabic literatures.

The first Urdu poetry on Imām Ḥusain is *Nau-Sarhār* (1503 AD) and first Urdu Prose is *Karbal-Kathā* (1732-33 AD). The most renowned Mart͟hiya poets are Mīr Anīs and Mirża Dabīr, followed by a galaxy of famous poets like Ta's͟hs͟huq, Is͟hq, Mūnis, Nafīs, Ras͟hīd etc. The legacy of Urdu Mart͟hiya has lasted to this day and many poets are still writing that kind of poetry. Both renowned poets like Muḥammad Iqbāl and Josh Malīhābādī followed the genre of six-line stanza and have produced great poetry.

Josh Malīhābādī also known as the Poet of Revolution, used the medium of Mart͟hiya as a means to propagate the view that Karbala is not only a pathos-laden event of the bygone era, but also a prototype for contemporary revolutionary struggles. Josh's writings during the late 1930s and the early 1940s, when nationalist feelings were running high in South Asia, had a momentous impact upon his generation. Josh attempted to galvanize the youth of his day by intertwining their contemporary struggle of liberation from colonization with the Battle of Karbala.

Āle Reza, Wahīd Akhtar and many others have been crucial in keeping the tradition of Urdu Marthiya dynamic in present day. Their Marthiyas rely on the images, metaphors, and traditions inherited from 19th century masters, and on the values invested in this genre by socio-religious reformers like Josh Malīhābādī. By showing a similarity between Imām Ḥusain-bin-'Alī's historic battle and the present day struggle of mankind against renewed forms of Yazīdian oppression, they deflect the interpretation of the martyrs of Karbala as mere insignia of the Islāmic history; they are instead posed as the sinews for the revival of an ideal Islāmic state affairs.

The Urdu literature connected with the Ḥusainī Revolution is not confined to its descriptive nature, but in the contemporary Urdu literature Karbala's great war is being presented as a metaphor also. In an ordinary poem, of course, the original context comes from religious, historical tradition, but the metaphor and symbol widens it. In this way a universal relevance is produced and its application is on the whole human family's vide situation and with present age can also be on the special situation of conflicts for truth and justice, striving against tyranny, oppression, dominion and exploitation.

Hindi Literature

Strangely, Hindi literature has been false short of the Islāmic literature as a creative genre. Bhartendu Harishchandra (d. 1885 AD) has been forerunner, who has written short biography of five infallibles, Muḥammad, Fāṭimah, 'Alī, Ḥasan and Ḥusain. Then Sumitranandan Pant (d. 1982 AD) and Maithili Sharan Gupt (d. 1964 AD) written poems on the Prophet Muḥammad. However, a lot of transliterations in Dev Nagri script from Urdu literature and translations mainly from English enrich Hindi literature on Islāmic theme. I have also contributed six books in Hindi, including a detailed book on the Ḥusainī Revolution.

In other Indian languages also literature related to the Battle of Karbala is available, whose total description I have already done in my Hindi book *Muslims' Contribution to Indian Literature*. However, a brief discussion could be possible. It is noteworthy that in every Indian literature on Islām and the Ḥusainī Revolution, their contributors on the subject matter of Karbala have not been confined to any particular caste, creed or religion, but the writers belongs to Hindus, Jains, Sikhs, Christians etc.

Saraiki Language

The first trace of the influence of the Battle of Karbala in Indian languages has been found in the form of traditional poetry, *Kabit* of Saraiki language,[41] which the roaming singers sung from door to door to get reward from the people in some areas of Sindh and Balochistan of Pakistan. The participation of Ḥusainī Brahamans with Amīr Mukhtār in taking successful revenge against the killers of Imām Ḥusain and his companions is also the theme of poetic composition. This poetry has been dated about thousand years back, by the experts.[42] Marthiyas of bi-lingual poet Sachal Sarmast (d.1826 AD) are also famous in Saraiki language.

Balochi Literature

Balochi literature has been rich for its traditional religious poetry. It may be divided into two parts—Islāmic principle based poetry and the poetry based on the praise of holy Prophet and his Progeny specially Imām 'Alī and Imām Ḥusain.

Sindhi Literature

As in many other fields of Sindhi poetry, Shāh 'Abdu'l Laṭīf Bhittaī of Bhitshah (d. 1752 AD) has been famous to express ideas regarding the Ḥusainī Revolution, which were later on taken up by other poets. He devoted *Sur Kedaro* in his *Shāh Jo Risālo* to the martyrdom of Imām Ḥusain the grandson of Muḥammad, and saw the event of Karbala as embedded in the whole mystical tradition of Islām.

A number of poets in Sindhi have also composed elegies on Karbala. The most famous of them is Syed Thābit 'Alī Shāh (d. 1810 AD), whose speciality was the genre of *Suwarī*. This genre, as well as the more common forms, persists in Sindhi poetry throughout the whole of the eighteenth and nineteenth centuries, and even into our own times. The devotion of Sachal Sarmast, Beydil, Mīr Ḥasan, Shāh Naser, Mirża Baddhal Beg, Mirża Kalich Beg to Imām Ḥusain-bin-'Alī is well known and deeply embedded in their Ṣūfī teachings.

Punjabi Literature

Punjabi poet Ḥāmid Shāh 'Abbāsī (d. 1805 AD) has been famous for his epic *Jang-Ḥāmid*, which relates to the Battle of Karbala. Seventeenth century poet Ḥāfiẓ Barkhurdār's *Jangnāmah Imām Ḥusain* is also very popular.

Kashmiri Literature

Some of the replicas related to the Battle of Karbala are still protected in the shrine of famous Ṣūfī saint Khwājah Mīr Saiyed 'Alī Hamādānī (d. 1385 AD), which show that *'Azādārī*, was prevalent in the valley of Kashmir since his period. During Shi'ī Chak dynasty rule (1661-86 AD) *'Azādārī* was part of Kashmir's life. Amīru'd-Dīn Kareiī's *Jang Muḥammad Hanīf Dar Inteqām Yazīd* and Pīr 'Azīzu'llāh Asad Haqqānī's *Rauza'ush-Shohadah* and *Sir'ush-Shahadataiyn* are early examples. Kashmiri Marthiya has had a very rich tradition of its own. Hundreds of people recite poems on the martyrdom of Imām Ḥusain and various aspects of the Ḥusainī Revolution.

Baltī Language

Baltī has been the language of the region which was said as Small-Tibet. As a result of partition of India, a small part of the region is being occupied by Pakistan, remaining most of the part is still in India. Baltīs were converted to Islām during thirteenth century. Presently, most of them are Shi'īs.[43] Every form of their literature denotes the influence and impact of the Ḥusainī Revolution.

Bengalī Literature

The tragedy of Karbala was firstly written in Bengalī literature in the names of *Maqtūl-Ḥusain* and *Jangnāmah*. Muḥammad Khān (d. 1686 AD) has been regarded first Marthiya poet and his *Maqtūl-Ḥusain* as first Marthiya in Bengalī literature Mīr Mosharraf Ḥusain (d. 1887 AD) wrote the novel *Bishad Shindhu* and an epic *Muḥarram Sharīf*. Qāzī Naẓaru'l Islām (d. 1974 AD) wrote many poems on the martyrdom of Imām Ḥusain. Marthiyas are still cited on the eve of *'Āshūrah* every year.

Tamil Literature

With more than fifteen Islāmic epics to its credit, this genre in Tamil has a significant place It has complete fidelity to the Tamil, even the historical Islāmic names have been translated into Tamil as per their tradition, which has given these of the Islāmic content living importance among the epics in Tamil. Among them Kaṇakavirāyar's Kaṇakāpiṣêka Mālai (1648 AD) has been a forerunner Islāmic epic. Embodying the Tamil traditions, it deals with the epic of Imām Ucaiṉṟali, in thity-six divisions (*paṭalam*).[44]

European and Other Languages

It would be no dwelling on the subject that all the most all major languages of the world have huge stock of literature relating to the Islāmic religion, philosophy, culture, history, sociology and many other aspects of study. Several billion books have been written, compiled and edited. Even if, the websites on Battle of Karbala and the Ḥusainī Revolution is counted, the figure would go in several hundreds. Due to paucity of space, it would not be possible to present here.

Salient Features of the Ḥusainī Literature

The Ḥusainī literature of various languages of the people of different regions, culture and faith has been rich with most outstanding subject matter, because it contains a rich mine most beneficial and artistic stock of the intellectual sources. Its salient features are as follows:

Firstly, It has extolled social justice and human values for whom the great Imām struggled and saved the noble message and tradition of Islām by his unsurpassed and exemplary sacrifice at Karbala.

Secondly, It has condemned oppression and fought falsehood and confronted arrogance and obstinacy.

Thirdly, It has motivated the society towards honour and lofty purpose by following Imām Ḥusain as the leader with lofty aspirations and the vanguard of human perfections.

Fourthly, It has presented the intellectual and religious attitude of the infallible Imām Ḥusain and his supreme sacrifice.

Fifthly, It has glorified the Imām Ḥusain in a way that no martyr from any walk of life, whether hero or saint had ever been exalted; because the principles of Imām Ḥusain were merged with the emotions of poets and the wave of human movement had seized that immortal revolution and they praised and glorified Imām Ḥusain in the most outstanding fashion.

Sixthly, Publicizing the decadence of Umayyites and describing their crimes in their enmity towards Islām.

Seventhly, Highlighting of the hardships and tragedies that befell the holy Ahlu'l-Bayt. Poems lamenting for the Ahlu'l-Bayt multiplied in an astounding manner, all of them arising from the depths of the hearts and the depths of souls and in this way they became a priceless treasure of the literatures of various languages.

Eighthly, Outstanding beauty and allurement in the literature of the Ḥusainī Revolution and the warmth of passion. The poetry lamenting Imām Ḥusain has been warm and fiery; because it is derived from powerful emotions and it is composed by burning and revolutionary souls. They were angry and furious because the Umayyite had snatched their rights and usurped their position. Poets have expressed their anger in poetry.

Living Example of Sacrifice

The Ḥusainī Revolution set a living example as to the duty of Muslims in such unusually challenging conditions. It had deeply penetrated people's hearts, and produced tremendous urge for doing their Islāmic duty. This feeling, which pained people all the time was transformed into repentance and then to an open revolt against the Umayyite's regime. Thus, the revolution provided the stimulant to move their spirit and set it in a dynamic movement. Indeed, the Islāmic movement was put to a new gear throughout the rest of the Islāmic history. A series of revolutions manifesting Imām Ḥusain's revolutionary spirit and reforms emerged at successive intervals. Karbala symbolizes the true face of struggle against injustice through non-violent resistance. Not taking life but sacrificing your life for Islām. In summary, it is not out of place to say in words of some known Indian poets:

> Let humanity awaken and every tribe will claim Ḥusain as their own. (Josh Malīhābādī)
>
> In the martyrdom of Imām Ḥusain, lies the death of Yażīd, for Islām resurrects after every Karbala. (Muḥammad 'Alī Jauhar)

A few comments by the men of letters are given below:

Mahatma Gandhi spoke several times regarding noble sacrifice of Imām Ḥusain, to quote a few[45]:

> "My admiration for the noble sacrifice of Imām Ḥusain as a martyr abounds, because he accepted death and the torture of

thirst for himself, for his sons, and for his whole family, but did not submit to unjust authorities."

"I learnt from Ḥusain how to achieve victory while being oppressed."

"My faith is that the progress of Islām does not depend on the use of sword by its believers, but the result of the supreme sacrifice of Imām Ḥusain."

"I have looked into the biography of Imām Ḥusain, the great martyr of Islām, and I have scrutinized the tragedy of Karbala and reached the conclusion that if India wants to be a successful country, it must follow in the footsteps of Imām Ḥusain."

"If I had an army like the 72 soldiers of Ḥusain, I would have won freedom for India in 24 hours."

Rabindranath Tagore (d. 1941 AD) said[46]:

"The world of things in which we live misses its equilibrium when its communication with the world of love is lost. Then we have to pay with our soul for objects which are immensely cheap. And this can only happen when the prison walls of things threaten us with being final in themselves. Then it gives rise to terrible fights, jealousies and coercions, to a scramble for space and opportunities, for these are limited. We become painfully aware of the evil of this and try all measures of adjustment within the narrow bonds of a mutilated truth. This leads to failure. Only he helps us who proves by his life that we have a soul whose dwelling in the kingdom of love, and things lose the tyranny of fictitious price when we come to our spiritual freedom."

"In order to keep alive justice and truth, instead of an army or weapons, success can be achieved by sacrificing lives, exactly what Imam Hussain did."

"Imām Ḥusain is the leader of humanity."

"Imām Ḥusain will warm the coldest heart."

"Ḥusain's sacrifice indicates spiritual liberation."

Pandit Jawaharlal Nehru (d. 1964 AD) said[47]:

"There is a universal appeal in his martyrdom. Ḥazrat Imām Ḥusain sacrificed his all, but he refused to submit to a tyrannical government. He never gave any weight to the fact that his material force was far less in comparison with that of an enemy; the power of faith to his greatest force, which regards all material force as nothing. This sacrifice is a beacon light of guidance for every community and every nation."

"Imām Ḥusain's sacrifice is for all groups and communities, an example of the path of righteousness."

Muḥammad 'Alī Jinnah, (d. 1948 AD) said[48]:

"The world is unable to present an example finer and brighter than the personality of Imām Ḥusain. He was the embodiment of love, valour and personification of sacrifice and devotion. Every Muslim, in particular, must learn a lesson from his life and should seek guidance from him."

Edward G. Brown said:

"...a reminder of that blood-stained field of Karbala, where the grandson of the Apostle of God fell, at length, tortured by thirst, and surround by the bodies of his murdered kinsmen, has been at anytime since then, sufficient to evoke, even in the most lukewarm and the heedless, the deepest emotion, the most frantic grief, and an exaltation of spirit before which pain, danger, and death shrink to unconsidered trifles."[49]

Sir William Muir (d. 1905 AD) said:

"The tragedy of Karbala decided not only the fate of the Caliphate, but also of Muḥammadan kingdoms long after the Caliphate had waned and disappeared."[50]

Famous Orientalist Simon Ockley (d. 1720 AD):

"Then Ḥusain mounted his horse, and took the Qur'an and laid it before him, and, coming up to the people, invited them to the performances of their duty: adding, "O God, thou art my confidence in every trouble, and my hope in all adversity!"... He next reminded them of his excellencies, the nobility of his birth, the greatness of his power, and his high descent, and said, "Consider with yourselves whether or not such a man as I am is not better than you; I who am the son of your prophet's daughter, besides whom there is no other upon the face of the earth. 'Alī was my father; Ja'far and Ḥamżah, the chief of the martyrs, were both my uncles; and the apostle of God, upon whom be peace, said both of me and my brother, that we were the chief of the youth of paradise. If you will believe me, what I say is true, for by God, I never told a lie in earnest since I had my understanding; for God hates a lie. If you do not believe me, ask the companions of the apostle of God [here he named them], and they will tell you the same. Let me go back to what I have." They asked, "What hindered him from being ruled by the rest of his relations." He answered, "God forbid that I should set my hand to the resignation of my right after a slavish manner. I have recourse to God from every tyrant that doth not believe in the day of account."[51]

Ignaz Goldziher (d. 1921 AD), Hungarian orientalist said:

"...Weeping and lamentation over the evils and persecutions suffered by the 'Alīd family, and mourning for its martyrs: these are things from which loyal supporters of the cause cannot cease. More touching than the tears of the Shi'īs has even become an Arabic proverb."[52]

Peter J. Chelkowski, Middle Eastern Studies Scholar said:

"Ḥusain accepted and set out from Mecca with his family and an entourage of about seventy followers. But on the plain of Karbala they were caught in an ambush set by the ... Caliph Yażīd-bin-Mu'āwiyah. Though defeat was certain, Ḥusain refused to pay homage to him. Surrounded by a great enemy force, Ḥusain and his company existed without water for ten days in the burning desert of Karbala. Finally Ḥusain, the adults and some male children of his family and his companions were cut to bits by the arrows and swords of Yażīd's army; his women and remaining children were taken as captives to Yażīd in Damascus. The renowned historian Abū Reyḥān al-Bīrūnī states; "... then fire was set to their camp and the bodies were trampled by the hoofs of the horses; nobody in the history of the human kind has seen such atrocities."[53]

Reynold Alleyne Nicholson (d.1945 AD) said:

> "Ḥusain fell, pierced by an arrow, and his brave followers were cut down beside him to the last man. Muḥammadan tradition, which with rare exceptions is uniformly hostile to the Umayyite dynasty, regards Ḥusain as a martyr and Yażīd as his murderer."[54]

Major Robert Durey Osborn (d.1889 AD) said:

> "Ḥusain had a child named 'Abdu'llāh Razī'a, only 6 month old. He had accompanied his father in this terrible march. Touched by its cries, he took the infant in his arms and wept. At that instant, a shaft from the hostile ranks pierced the child's ear, and it expired in his father's arms. Ḥusain placed the little corpse upon the ground. "We come from God, and we return to Him!" he cried; "O Lord, give me strength to bear these misfortunes!" ... Faint with thirst, and exhausted with wounds, he fought with desperate courage, slaying several of his antagonists. At last he was cut down from behind; at the same instance a lance was thrust through his back and bore him to the ground; as the dealer of this last blow withdrew his weapon, the ill-fated son of 'Alī rolled over a corpse. The head was severed from the trunk; the trunk was trampled under the hoofs of the victors' horses; and the next morning the women and a surviving infant son were carried away to Kufa. The bodies of Ḥusain and his followers were left unburied on the spot where they fell. For three days they remained exposed to the sun and the night dews, the vultures and the prowling animals of the waste; but then the inhabitants of a neighbouring village, struck with horror that the body of a grandson of the Prophet should be thus shamefully abandoned to the unclean beasts of the field, dared the anger of 'Obaydu'llāh-bin-Żiyād, and interred the body of the martyr and those of his heroic friends."[55]

More admiration for the noble sacrifice of Imām Ḥusain could be presented. But while concluding this chapter it may said that the men of letters are unanimous on the point that no battle in the modern and past history of mankind has earned more sympathy and admiration as well as provided more lessons than the martyrdom of Ḥusain in the battle of Karbala.

Notes and References

1. Manāqib-i-Āl-i-Abī Ṭālib, vol. 2, p. 329.
2. Maqālātu'l Ḥusain, vol. 2, p. 32.
3. aṣ-Ṣawa'qu'l-Muḥriqah fī'r-radd 'alā ahli'l Rafz wa'l Zanadiqah, p. 120.
4. Kalīlī, Min Amālī al-Imām aṣ-Ṣādiq, vol. 4, p. 157.
5. Tažkiratu'l-Ḥiffāẓ, vol. 1, p. 166; Athnau'l-Matālib, p. 55.
6. Bulletin of Affiliation: Al-Mažhab, Schools of Thought Statistic December. 1998, vol. 17-4, p. 5.
7. Khilāfat-o-Mulūkiyat, p. 289.
8. Bihāru'l-Anwār, vol. 2, p. 45.
9. Tārīkhu'r-Rusūl wa'l-Mulūk, vol. 6, pp. 197, 210-11.
10. al-Irshād fī Ma'rifat Ḥujjāj Allāh 'Alā 'Ibād, p. 236; Tārīkhu'r-Rusūl wa'l-Mulūk, vol. 6, p. 229.
11. al-Amālī: Shaykh Ṭūsī, p. 677, Tr. 143.
12. Yanābiyau'l-Muwaddah, p. 265 (Chapter 54, Tr. no. 18, p. 265).
13. Khaṣayṣu'l-Ḥusain, p. 89.
14. Raiḥānatu'r Rasūl, p. 176.
15. The Decline and Fall of the Roman Empire, vol. 5, pp. 391-92.
16. The Spirit of Islām, p. 248.
17. Tārīkhu'l 'Arab, vol. 1, p. 237.
18. Khaṭṭaṭu'sh-Shām, vol. 5, p. 25.
19. Ḥusain bin 'Alī, p. 10.
20. Až-Žahabu'l-Maslūk, p. 27.
21. Tārīkhu'r-Rusūl wa'l-Mulūk, vol. 5, p. 552.
22. Ansābu 'l-Ashrāf, vol. 6, pp. 363-365.
23. Tārīkhu'r-Rusūl wa'l-Mulūk, vol. 5, p. 589; al-Kāmil fī' t-Tārīkh, vol. 4, p. 178.
24. Al-Mukhtār, p. 43; Islām-Nāmah, pp. 356-59.
25. Ayānu'l Akhbār, vol. 1, pp. 179-180.
26. Ayānu'l Akhbār, vol. 1, pp. 179-180.
27. al-Kāmil fī' t-Tārīkh, vol. 4, p. 244.
28. Tārīkhu'r-Rusūl wa'l-Mulūk, vol. 6, p. 51.
29. al-Kāmil fī' t-Tārīkh, vol. 4, pp. 244-245; al-Akhbāru'ṭ Ṭawāl, pp. 301-302.
30. Islām-Nāmah, p. 359.
31. Sīratu'n-Nabī, vol. 1, p. 34.
32. Khawāṣu 'l-Ummat, p. 416.
33. Islām-Nāmah, p. 365.
34. An Introduction to Shi'i Islām, p. 82.
35. An Introduction to Shi 'i Islām, pp. 304-309.
36. Ṣaḥīfah-i-Nūr, vol. 5, p. 233.

37. al-Fara'idu'l-Darrutah, p. 471.
38. Nāsikhu'l Tawārīkh, vol. 6, p. 505.
39. A Millennium of Classical Persian, p. 79.
40. Dabistān-i-Ishq Ki Marsiya-Goee, p. 15.
41. Tārīkh-i-Adabiyat-i-Pakistan aur Hind, vol. 14(2), p. 264.
42. Ballochon kī Tārīkh, Qabāyal ke Ā'īne mein, vol. 1, p. 150; Durr-i-Gauhar, p. 9.
43. The Language and Races of Dardistan, p. 120.
44. The Encyclopædia of Tamil Literature, p. 360.
45. Living Thoughts on Imām Ḥusain, pp. 120-45.
46. Living Thoughts on Imām Ḥusain, p. 139.
47. Living Thoughts on Imām Ḥusain, pp. 170-72.
48. Living Thoughts on Imām Ḥusain, p. 154.
49. A Literary History of Persia, p. 227.
50. Annals of the Early Caliphate, pp. 441-442.
51. The History of the Saracens, pp. 404-5.
52. Introduction to Islāmic Theology and Law, p. 179.
53. Ta'ziyeh: Ritual and Drama in Iran, p. 2.
54. A Literary History of the Arabs, p. 197.
55. Islām Under the Arabs, pp. 126-27.

Conclusion

Martyrdom of the great Imām Ḥusain always evokes strong emotions and deep intellectual thoughts which touch and affect the whole existence of those who seek to find a path through it. But the significance of this event goes much beyond the mere unveiling of the corruption and deviations perpetrated by Umayyites. Karbala changed the course of history and continues to inspire all Truth-seeking revolutionaries.

By their martyrdom, Imām Ḥusain and his Associates achieved a victory that no revolutionary on the earth had ever obtained; because the principal aims for which he undertook the confrontation succeeded and the most important of them was the success of the Ḥusainī Revolution in his open war against the Umayyite regime, the unlawful governance, which had made the future of Islām dark and tried to uproot it, so that, no effect of it remains in the sphere of life. Imām Ḥusain took upon himself to ensure the well being and survival of Islām in future. And he martyred himself for its sake; he restored its freshness and destroyed the perils that surrounded it.

When a sensible person ponders upon the situation of that period, and how the Umayyite clan was successful in its aims and having domination over all the strata of people and the decadence of Muslims, no doubt remains that Imām Ḥusain through his martyrdom revived the religion of his grandfather and the laws of Islām; because if that event had not occurred and those true feelings had not been created stirred among the Muslims…and if the martyrdom of Imām Ḥusain hadn't taken place, Islām definitely would not have been as it is, rather it was possible that its heritage and laws would have been uprooted and destroyed; because in that period, Islām was in its initial stages.

Imām Ḥusain is who solidified the bed-rock of its sublime stature and raised its magistic and glorious edifice to empyrean heights. He irrigated the parched soil of Islām with the most sacred and noble blood and restored its freshness to its prestine glory. He gave life and light to the crying and groaning humanity, lying under the crushing heel of injustice, tyranny and violence. Imām Ḥusain and his Associates gave blood and Islām was resurrected from the throes of death. It got back it intrinsic strength to face the challenges and destroy the perils that surrounded it.

Martyrdom of the great Imām Ḥusain is the revival of heat of faith and awakening of consciousness has led to innumerable revolutions in human history, both in individual lives and in society as a whole. The message of Imām Ḥusain still resonates in the hearts of truth seekers. It inspires leaders to fulfil their obligations with respect to opposing evil and protecting goodness. It enjoins all those who heed the call of truth to rise against the unjust powers and confront evil.

The spirit of the Ḥusainī Revolution, like all teachings of Islām, require a pure heart and a sincere truth seeking soul to affect. Karbala can bring about revolution in our lives only if we observe it along with all other teachings of Islām.

The Ḥusainī Revolution has been the most strong medium of maintenance of the Islāmic Revolution; because the present Islām is dependent only on the great sacrifices. This revolution has re-established Islām on the same principles, which one lakh twentyfour thousand, Apostles, Prophets etc. have been continuing to present from the starting period until the present age. The Ḥusainī Revolution draws the attention towards the continuity and extensiveness of the basic objectives of the establishment of Islām, if God will he could have created all human beings over only one religion, but he wanted only not to do like that because He wanted that the followers of various religions might compete with one another in Good-Deeds. Therefore, the Islāmic Revolution made available a joint platform to struggle and conflict for the safety and maintenance of human rights, which is called the Ḥusainī Revolution, on which gentlemen and ladies of various and so many countries, community races and traditions can agitate unitedly as communities—on one line.

A unique elongation of metaphor and symbol of novel stage of the Ḥusainī Revolution can be presented within the manner:

Firstly, that the Ḥusainī Revolution had separated destruction from Revolution. Imām Ḥusain had not produced any fear for the life-property of innocent people. No fear was created for the life-property of people through his movement. The common people were absolutely protected and secured. However, Imām Ḥusain and his comrades scarificed their own life and properties for making the Ḥusainī Revolution successful and meaningful.

Secondly, that the objective of the Ḥusainī Revolution was not to capture ruling power for personal benefits: Whereas, mostly other revolutions are with the motive of capturing power. After the victory of the Ḥusainī Revolution, the chance of securing ruling powers came to Imām Ḥusain's son Imām Żainu'l-Ābidīn and his grandson Imām Ja'far aṣ-Ṣādiq and Imām 'Alī ar-Reza. But they refused to accept powers. Their rejection clarifies the objective of the Ḥusainī Revolution.

Thirdly, that the Ḥusainī Revolution was not made through any conspiracy. Whereas the other revolutions are the result of conspiracy of their leaders, and equally religious thinkers. On the contrary, Imām Ḥusain declared his view-point at the time of leaving Medina itself that he did not want Ruling powers and kingdom for personal benefits. Those who sacrificed their own life along with Imām Ḥusain in the Ḥusainī Revolution had the same thinking and feelings as the declaration of Imām Ḥusain and he frequently clarified also his objectives at Karbala war-front, which is safe in the pages of history.

Fourthly, that the Ḥusainī Revolution can be said to bring revolution through the medium of non-violence. The word-meaning for *Jihād* is conflict for obtaining the objectives. In the Islāmic terminology the meaning of *Jihād-Fī-Sabīl-Allāh* (struggling on the path of God) which means struggling for the Truth. It we look at it in Indian context, *Jihād* is an equivalent of *Satyagrah*. *Satya+Agrah*, that is Truth+Insistence, struggling for the attainment of truth. Mahatma Gandhi has presented *Satyagrah* in the same manner. The basic quality of Non-Violence is that the others are encouraged for the supports of one's own viewpoint through sacrifice. One's principles cannot be imposed upon others by force. Imām Ḥusain and his companions were presenting their thoughts and viewpoints quite frequently before their enemies, by which people were influenced even at that time and leaving the Yażīdī Army. They came and joined Imām Ḥusain. Did *Jihād* and became martyr without any force. They followed the principles of non-violence. The principle of non-violence propounded by Imām Ḥusain flourished in such a way that it became a guideline for the revolution itself. The famous event is that Mahatma Gandhi did *Dandi March* in the year 1930 in connection with Indian's Freedom Movement. He took 72 people along with him. In asking he replied that Imām Ḥusain took only 72 people with him on the pathway of the Truth. Afterwards, innumberable people joined, which was based on 72 people to begin with.

Fifthly, that the Ḥusainī Revolution diminished the greatness of power: Generally, it is thought that only the power can give the solutions. This power on the basis of number of persons, state and welter and greed on the basis of Army. Force gets spurred by distribution of wealth and expectations. But Imām Ḥusain changed the very definition of power, with which Ḥusainī's seaming weakness became an upper hand over the pomp and splendour of the Yażīdī Army. The Ḥusainī Revolution propounded this foundamental principle that victory cannot be achieved by external showy strength, but behind any of victory, principle and morality is very significant.

Sixthly, that the Ḥusainī Revolution was very effective and influential right from time of its commencement and also for a long period and still continues undeterred. Whereas, most of the other revolutions are tied up with their own contemporary situations and when their situations come to an end, these revolutions by whose splendour the whole world was afraid of become the prey of the revolution in which all those symbols are destroyed, which were considered for a particular period as the achievements of the revolution. The Ḥusainī Revolution provided the ideas of living to the world that an honourable death is better than a disgraceful life—without wisdom and experience, life based on exploitation. It is better that it should come to a close. But for ending it the propounders of the revolution will have to sacrifice their own life along with their followers.

Seventhly, that the Ḥusainī Revolution offers message equally to each and every community religion and country. That message is of happiness, faith, hope, peace and compromise; safety and security. Imām Ḥusain's principle of differentiating between truth and falsehood, is not limited to Muslims alone, but preaches every human being who is the claimant of the followers of Divine Religion, whether he is a Christian, or Jew, or Muslim, or Hindu, Sikh, or Bauddha, or followers of any other religion, Imām Ḥusain's message is to differentiate between truth and falsehood on the basis of your own belief and religious principles.

If we look at the Ḥusainī Revolution in the present context, then there is a need of recompilation of many sorts of political, social, cultural, religious principles and values. As a result, Islāmic directed principle – Enjoining the good and forbidding the evil! (*Qur'an*: 22/41). The need for implementing such an institution is indispensable, which can eradicate the miseries of all. Therefore, *'Ażādārī* has been developed as an institution for commemorating wonderful sacrifices of Imām Ḥusain and his Associates in Karbala.

In conclusion, the name of Imām Ḥusain is synonymous with Love, Hope, Faith, Equality, Fraternity, Dignity and Freedom. Imām Ḥusain's sacrifice exhibits the spiritual forces for liberation of mankind. The spirit of Justice and Truth should be kept alive. Success may be achieved by sacrificing life, instead of an army or weapons. The best lesson which we get from the Ḥusainī Revolution is that the numerical superiority does not count when it comes to the Truth and Falsehood. Imām Ḥusain's sacrifice has kept Islām alive or else in the world, there would be no one to take Islām's name.

Bibliography

'Aqā'idu 'sh-Shaykh Ṣadūq: Urdu tr. *Hadya-i-Ja'fariya:* Shaykh Muḥammad A'ejāz Ḥasan: Delhi, 1928.

'Aqā'idu'l-Imāmiyyau'l-Ithna 'Ashariyya: aż-Żanjānī, Ibrāhīm al-Mūsāwī, Beirut, 1973.

'Aqā'idu'sh-Shī'au'l-Ithna 'Ashariyya: al-'Āmulī, Bahāu'-Dīn, Tehran n.d.

'Ayānu'l Akhbār: Ibn Qutaybah, Abū Muḥammad 'Abdu'llāh-bin-Muslim al-Dīnāwarī (d. 889 AD): ed. C. Brockelman, Cairo, 1907.

'Ayānu'sh-Shi'a: al-'Āmulī, Muḥsin Amīn, Damascus, 1944.

'Iqdu'l-Farīd: 'Omar-bin-Aḥmad-bin Muḥammad, Cairo, 1884.

'Umdat'ul-Qārī Sharaḥu'l-Bukhārī: 'Aiynī, Badru'd-Dīn, Cairo n.d.

A Millennium of Classical Persian Poetry: Wheeler Thackston, Bethesda: Iranbooks, 1994.

A History of Western Philosophy: Bertrand Russel, London, 1948.

A Literary History of Persia: Edward G. Brown, London, 1919.

A Literary History of the Arabs: Reynold Alleyne Nicholson, Cambridge, 1930.

A Short History of the Saracens: Saiyed Amīr 'Alī, New Delhi, 1998.

A Socio-Intellectual History of the Isnā 'Asharī Shī'īs in India: Saiyid Aṭhar 'Abbās Rizvi, Canberra (Australia), 1986.

Ahsīru'l 'Ibādāt-o-Asrāru'l Shahādāt: Āqa Dar Bandī, Tabrez, 1877.

Aḥqāqu 'l-Ḥaqq: Qāżī Nūru'llāh, ash-Shūshtarī, Mar'ashī, (Urdu tr.), Lahore n.d.

Aḥyā ' u 'l-'Ulūmu'd-Dīn: al-Ghażālī, Abū Ḥāmid Muḥammad, Cairo, 1939.

al-'Iqdu'l Farīd: Ibn 'Abd Ribbo. Abū 'Omar, Aḥmad-bin-Muḥammad, Cairo, 1940.

al-Akhbāru'ṭ Ṭawāl: Abū Ḥanīfah Dīnāwarī (d. 896 AD), Cairo, 1960.

al-Amālī: Shaykh Mufīd, Ibn Mu'allim (d. 1022 AD), Tehran n.d.

al-Amālī: Shaykhu'l –Ṭā'fah, Abū Ja'far Muḥammad, aṭ-Ṭūsī (d. 1067 AD).

al-Bābu 'l-Hādī 'Ashar: al-Ḥillī, Ḥasan-bin-Yūsuf, (tr. Miller, W.W.) London, 1928.

al-Bayān fī Tafsīru'l-Qur'an: al-Khū'ī, Saiyed Abu'l Qāsim, Beirut, 1974.

al-Bidāyah w'an-Nihāyah: Ibn Kathīr, Abu'l Fidā, Ismā'īl-bin-'Omar, Cairo, 1929.

al-Durru'l-Manthūr fī'l-Tafsīr bi'l Māthūr: *as*-Suyūṭī, Jalālu'd-Dīn, Cairo, 1896.

al-Fara'idu'l-Darrutah: J.G. Hava, Delhi, 1990.

al-Farq Bayn 'ul-Firāq: al-Baghdādī, 'Abdu'l Qāhir-bin-Tāhir, (tr. Halkin, Abraham S.: *Moslem Schisms and Sects*), Tel Aviv, 1935.

al-Fārūq: Shiblī No'manī, Azamgarh, 1956.

al-Faṣl-fī 'l-Milal wa 'l-Aḥwa wa 'l-Niḥal: Ibn Ḥażm, Abū Muḥammad 'Alī-bin-Aḥmad, Cairo, 1929.

al-Firaqu 'sh-Shi'a: al-Naubakhtī, Abī Muḥammad al-Ḥasan-bin-Mūsā (tr. Hellmut Ritter, Bibiliotheca Islāmica), Instanbul, 1931.

al-Fitnatu 'l-Kubrā: Ṭāha Ḥusain, (Urdu tr. 'Abdu'l Ḥamīd No'mānī), Karachi 1978. *al-Ḥusayn: The Dead Man of The Tear:* Sheikh, 'Abdu'ż-Żahrā al-Kā'bī, Dāru'l.

al-Irshād fī Ma'rifat Ḥujjāj Allāh 'Alā 'Ibād: al-Mufīd, Ibnu 'l-Ma 'allim, Shaykh Abū 'Abdu 'llāh Muḥammad, (tr. Howard, IKA), London, 1981.

al-Irshādu 'l-Bārī fī Sharḥu 'l-Ṣaḥīḥul-Bukhārī: al-Khaṭību 'l-Qasṭalānī Aḥmad-bin-Muḥammad, Kanpur n.d.

al-Isti'āb fī Mā'rifatu'l-Aṣḥāb: 'Abdu'l-Barr 'Omar Abū Yūsuf-bin-'Abdu'llāh, Hyderabad 1900-1.

al-Istibsār fī Mukhtalifa fihi mina'l-Akhbār: Shaykhu'ṭ-Ṭā'fa, Abū Ja 'far Muḥammad-bin-Ḥasan aṭ-Ṭūsī, Lucknow, 1889-90.

al-Iṣābah fī Tamayyażu'ṣ-Ṣaḥābah: Ibn Ḥajar al-'Asqalānī, Abu'l Fazl Aḥmad, Cairo, 1939.

al-Ittaqan fī 'Ulūmu'l-Qu'an: as-Suyūtī, Jalālu'd-Dīn, Cairo, 1888.

al-Jauhar fī Sharh Waṣīyatu 'l-Imām Abū Ḥanīfa: Ḥusain, Hyderabad, 1903.

al-Kāmil fī' t-Tārīkh: Ibn Athīr, 'Iżżu'd-Din, Abu'l Ḥasan 'Alī-bin-Muḥammad (ed. C.J. Torberg & E.J. Brill), Leiden, 1868.

al-Kashshāf 'An Ḥaqāyiqu'l-Tanżīl: al-Żamakhasharī, Abu'l Qāsim Jāru'llāh Maḥmūd-bin-'Omar, Calcutta, 1859.

al-Khanāru'l Masālik: Shaykhu'l Ḥadīth Muḥammad Žakaiyā.

al-Khaṣayaṣu'l-Żainabiyah: Saiyed Nūru'llāh Jażāirī (d. 1964 AD), Tehran n.d.

al-Khaṣayṣ Murtazwī: Nasā'ī, Abū 'Abdu'r-Raḥmān-bin-Shu'ib-bin-Baḥr (Urdu tr. Abu'l Ḥasan Aḥmad), Varanasi, 1985.

al-Maqtal: Abī Mīkhnaf, Lūṭ-bin-Yaḥyā (d. 774 AD) Najaf, 1929.

al-Milal wa 'l Niḥal: ash-Shahristānī, Abu 'l-Fatḥ Muḥammad, Cairo, 1948-49.

al-Mīżān fī Tafsīr al-Qur'an: aṭ-Ṭabāṭabāī, Saiyed Muḥammad Ḥusain, Tehran, 1976.

al-Mu 'jam al-Mufhras li-Alfaẓu 'l-Qur 'ani 'l-Karīm baḥashiya al-Muṣḥafi 'l-Sharīf: Muḥammad Fawād 'Adu 'l Bāqī Miṣrī, Tehran, 1962.

al-Mua'rramīn: al-Sajastānī, Abu'l Hātim Sahl-bin-'Othmān, Cairo, 1950.

al-Mukhtaṣar fī Akhbāru 'l-Bashar: Abu'l Fidā, 'Imādu 'd-Dīn, Ismā 'īl-bin-'Alī, ash-Shāfi 'ī, Cairo, 1907.

al-Muqaddima: Ibn Khaldūn, Abū Żayd 'Abdu'r-Raḥmān (tr. R. Rosethal), New York, 1958.

al-Murtazā: an-Nadawī, Abu'l Ḥasan 'Alī Ḥasanī, Lucknow, 1988.

al-Musnad: Aḥmad-bin-Ḥanbal, Cairo, 1895.

al-Mustadrak 'Alā as-Saḥīḥayīn: an-Naysābūrī, Abū 'Abdu'llāh Muḥammad-bin-Ḥākim, Hyderabad, 1921.

al-Mustadrak: al-Hākim an-Naysābūrī, Riyādh n.d.

al-Muwaṭṭa: Mālik-bin-Anas, Cairo, 1862.
al-Naṣāehu'l Kāfiyah: Muḥammad-bin 'Aqīl al-Misrī, Cairo, 1927.
al-Nubūwwat wa 'l Khilāfat: Saiyed Najmu 'l Ḥasan (tr. L.A. Ḥaidarī) Lucknow, 1934.
al-Uṣūl-min 'al-Kāfī: al-Kulaynī, Abū Ja 'far Muḥammad-bin-Y 'āqūb, Tehran, 1972.
al-Yaqīn fī Imāra Amīru'l-Mūminīn: Ibn Ṭāwūs Raziyu'd-Din 'Alī, Qomm, 1950.
An Approach to the Understanding of Islām: 'Alī Sharī 'atī (tr. Venus Kaivantash), Tehran, 1979.
An Historical Atlas of Islām: W.C. Brice, Leiden, 1991.
An Introduction to Shi'i Islām: Moojan Momen, Oxford, 1985.
Anfāsu 'l-'Ārifīn: Shāh Walī 'ullāh Muḥaddith Dehlawī, Delhi, 1897.
Annals of the Early Caliphate: Sir William Muir, London, 1883.
Ansābu 'l-Ashrāf: al-Balāžurī, Aḥmad-bin-Yaḥyā-bin-Jābir, Cairo, 1935.
Anwāru 'l-Qur'an: (Urdu tr. & exegesis by Žīshān Ḥaider Jawādī), Lucknow, 1992.
Anwāru 't-Tanžīl: al-Bayzāwī, Abdu'llāh-bin-'Omar ash-Shāfi'ī, Cairo, 1912.
Arjaḥu 'l-Maṭālib: 'Obaydu 'llāh Amritsarī, Lahore n.d.
ar-Risālah: ash-Shāfi 'ī, Muhammad-bin-Idrīs, Cairo n.d.
ash-Shamsu 'l-Bāžighā: Mullā Maḥmūd Jaunpurī, Lucknow, 1871.
Aspects of Islām: MacDonald, D.B., New York, 1911.
as-Sunan: Abū Dāwūd Sulaymān, as-Sijistānī, Lucknow, 1900.
as-Sunan: Ibn Māja, Abū 'Alī Muḥammad-bin-Yažīd, Cairo, 1895-96.
as-Sunan: Nasā'ī, Abū 'Abdu'r-Raḥmān-bin-Shu'ib-bin-Baḥr, Kanpur, 1881-82.
as-Sunanu'l Kubrà: al-Bahīqī, Abū Fazl (d. 1086 AD) Hyderabad, 1936.
Aṣlu 'sh-Shi 'a wa Uṣūliha: al-Kāshifu 'l-Ghīta, Muḥammad Ḥusain, Najaf, 1962.
aṣ-Ṣawa 'qu'l-Muḥriqah fi'r-radd 'alā ahli'l Rafz wa'l Zanadiqah: Ibn Ḥajar, al-Haythamī, al-Makkī, Cairo, 1955.
ath-Thaqāfatu 'l-Islāmia: Rāghib at-Tabākh: (Urdu tr. Iftekhār Aḥmad Balkhī: *Tārīkh-i-Afkār-o 'Ulūm-i-Islāmī*), Delhi, 1998.
at-Tafhīmātu 'l-Ilāhiyyā: Shāh Wali'ullāh, Bijnor, 1936.
at-Tārīkh: al-Yā'qūbī, Aḥmad-bin-'Alī Yā'qūb al-Wāziḥ (ed. Houtsma), Leydon, 1883.
aṭ-Tahžību'l Tahžīb: Ibn Ḥajar al-'Asqalānī, Abu'l Fazl Aḥmad, Hyderabad, 1907.
aṭ-Ṭabaqātu'l-Kabīr: Ibn S'ad, Abū 'Abdu'llāh Muḥammad, Leiden, 1914-15.
Až-Žahabu'l-Maslūk: Taqīu'l-Dīn Abu'l-Abbās Aḥmad al-Maqrīzī (d. 1442 AD), Cairo n.d.
Balāghatu'l Ḥusain: al-Ḥa'rī, Mustafā Muḥsin al-Musāwī (Urdu tr. Muḥammad Bāqir) Khajwa (Bihar), 1953.
Ballochon kī Tārīkh, Qabāyal ke Ā'īne mein: al-Hyderī, Mīr Aḥsan, Multan n.d.
Bayānu 'l-Qur'an: Ashraf 'Alī Thānwī, Thanabhwan, 1933.
Bhartiya Islàmã Sanskriti: Saiyed Jafar Reza, Allahabad, 2011.

Bihāru'l-Anwār: al-Majlisī, Muḥammad Bāqir, Tehran 1887-88. (Urdu tr. Saiyed Ṭayyab Āg͟hā al-Mūsāwī), Lucknow, 1999-2001.

Binā-i-Karbala: Dr. Jafar S͟hahīdī.

Bustān-i-Wilāyat: Rus͟hdī, Saiyed K͟hudā Bak͟hsh, Hyderabad, 1956.

Cambridge History of Islām: (ed. P.M. Holt, *et al.*), Cambridge, 1970.

Conflict and Tensions in Islāmic Jurisprudence: Coulson, Noel J., Chicago, 1969.

Dabistān-i-Ishq Ki Marthiya-Goee: Saiyed Jafar Reza, Allahabad (4th ed) 2013.

Dabistān-i-Mažāhib: Mīržā Žulfaqār Āžar Sāsānī Mobad (author's name wrongly mentioned as Muḥsin Fānī; tr. David Shea & Anthony Troyer), London 1901, (Urdu trs. Ḥāfiẓ G͟hulām Murtazā & Ras͟hīd Aḥmad Jalandharī), Lahore, 2002.

Dīn-i-Islām aur Auwallīn Musalmānon kī do Mutazād Taṣwīren: al-Nadawī, Abu 'l Ḥasan 'Alī, Lucknow, 1984.

Dirāsatu'l Labīb: Mullā Muḥammad Mubīn, Lucknow.

Durr-i-Gauhar: Ak͟htar Waḥīd, Multan n.d.

Faizān-i-Abū Ṭālib: Saiyed Badr 'ul Ḥasan 'Ābidī, Varanasi, 1987.

Fatḥu'l-Bārī: Ibn Ḥajar al-'Asqalānī, Abu'l Fazl Aḥmad, Cairo, 1901.

Fatḥu'l-Bayān fī Maqāṣidu'l-Qur'an: Ṣiddīq Ḥasan K͟hān, Bhopal, 1883.

Fatḥu'l-Qadīr: Muḥammad-bin-'Alī, Beirut n.d.

Fuṣūlu'l-Muhimmah: Ibn al-Sabbāgh Mālikī, Najaf n.d.

Futūhul-Buldān: al-Balāžurī, Aḥmad-bin-Yaḥyā-bin-Jābir (tr. Philip K. Hitti & F.C. Murgotten – *The Origins of Islāmic State*), New York, 1916-24.

Gazetteers: Gazetteer of Alwar, Gazetteer of Bombay Presidency, Bengals District Gazetteer, Bundi State Gazetteer, Central Provinces District Gazetteers, (Seoni/Dist. Allahabad). *Indore State Gazetteer, Purnea District Gazetteer, Sindh Gazetteer.*

G͟harā 'ibu 'l-Qur 'an wa 'l-Rag͟hā 'bu 'l-Furq 'an: al-Nīs͟hāpurī, Nizāmu 'd-Dīn Ḥasan, Tehran, 1864.

Glossary of the Tribes and Castes of Punjab and North-West Frontier Province: Denzil Ibbetson, Edward Maclagan & H.A. Rose, Patiala, 1970.

Ḥabīb-us-Siyar: G͟hayāt͟h-ud-Dīn K͟hundmīr, Bombay, 1860.

Ḥayātu'l-Muḥammad: Haykal, Muḥammad Ḥusain (Urdu tr. Abū Yaḥyā Imām K͟hān), New Delhi, 1988.

Ḥayātu'l Ḥaywan: al-Damiri, Shaykh Kamalud'Din, Muhammad-bin-Isa (d. 1405 AD), Cairo, 1950.

Ḥayātu'l-Qulūb: al-Majlisī, Muḥammad Bāqir (tr. Merrick, J.L.), Boston, 1850.

History of the Fātimid K͟haliphate: O 'Lear, de Lacy, New York, 1923.

Ḥusain bin 'Alī: 'Omar Abū Naṣr, Tehran n.d.

Ḥusain Sabżwarī – *Żādu'l-'Uqba*) Lahore n.d.

Ḥusainī Inqalāb: Saiyed K͟hairāt Ḥasan, Lucknow, 2013.

Ḥusnu 'l-Muḥāzara fī Ak͟hbār Miùr wa 'l-Qāhirah: as-Suyūtī, Jalālu 'd-Dīn, Cairo, 1981-82.

Ḥayātu'l-Ḥaywānu 'l-Kubrā: ad-Damīrī, Kamālu 'd-Dīn Muḥammad, Cairo, 1950.

Inkeshāfāt-i-Qur'an: (ed. 'Abul Majīd Miṣbāḥī & Saiyed Bashārat Shikoh), Bombay, 1992.

Introduction to Islāmic Theology and Law: Ignaz Goldziher, Princeton, 1981.

Islām-Nāmah: Saiyed Khairāt Ḥasan, Lucknow, 2013.

Islām Under the Arabs: Robert Durey Osborn, Delaware, 1976.

Islām, Sidhānt aur Swarūp: Saiyed Jafar Reza, Allahabad, 2004.

Islām, the Straight Path: Morgan, Kenneth W. (ed.), New York, 1958.

Islām, A Short History: Karen Armstrong, Noida, 2008.

Islāmī 'Ulūm kā Ta'rruf: Murtazā Muṭaharī, (Urdu tr. S.M. 'Askarī), Tehran, 1996.

Islāmī Rājya banām Muslim Rājya: Saiyed Jafar Reza, Allahabad, 2004.

Islāmic Philosophy and Theology: Watt, W.M., Edinburgh, 1962.

Ithabatu'l-Wasiya: al-Mas'ūdī, 'Alī-bin-Ḥusain, Beirut, 1966

Ithnā 'Asharīya: Sell, Canon Edward (Urdu tr.), Lahore, 1925.

Iżālatu'l-Khulafā: Shāh Walīu'llāh, (Urdu tr. M. 'Abdu'r Shakūr), Karachi n.d.

Jām'au'l-Bayān fi Tafsīru 'l-Qur 'an: aṭ-Ṭabarī, Ibn Jarīr Abū Ja'far, Cairo, 1902-3.

Jam'au'l-Baynu'r-Rijālu's-Ṣaḥīḥayn: Ibnu'l-Qaysarānī, Abu'l Fazl Muḥammad-bin-Ṭāhir, Hyderabad n.d.

Jām'au't-Tawarīkh: Rashīdu 'Dīn, Lahore n.d.

Jām 'au'sh-Shawāhid fī'l Dakhūl Ghayr-Muslim fī'l-Masjid: Abu'l Kalām Āżād, Delhi, 1923.

Jām'au'ṣ-Ṣaḥīḥu'l-Bukhārī: al-Bukhārī, Abū 'Abdu'llāh Muḥammad-bin-Ismā'īl, (ed. L.K. Krehl), Leiden 1862, (Urdu tr. Mirżā Ḥairat Dehlawī), Deoband n.d.

Jām'au'ṣ-Ṣaḥīḥu'l-Muslim: al-Muslim, Abu'l Ḥusain Ibnu'l-Ḥajjāj, Cairo, 1930, (Urdu tr. 'Abdu'l-Dai'mu'l-Jalālī), Delhi, 1998.

Jām'au'ṣ-Ṣaḥīḥu'l-Mishkātu'l-Maṣābīḥ: al-Khaṭīb, Walīu'd-Dīn Muḥammad-bin-'Abdu'llāh, Amritsar 1895-96, (Urdu tr. 'Abdu'l Ḥakīm Akhtar), Delhi, 1987.

Jām'au'ṣ-Ṣaḥīḥu't-Tirmiżī: at-Tirmiżī, Abū Īsā Muḥammad, (Urdu Tr. Fazl Aḥmad), Lucknow, 1894.

Jilā 'u 'l-'Uyūn: al-Majlisī, Muḥammad Bāqir, Tehran n.d.

Kalāmī Pīr, A Treatise of Ismā 'īlī Doctrine: Ivanow W., Bombay, 1935.

Kanżu'l-Ansāb: Shāh Malik Shujāu 'l-Malik, Lahore, 1919.

Kanżu'l-'Ummāl-fī-Sunnau'l-Aqwāl-w'al-Alfāẓ: 'Alā'ud-Dīn 'Alī Muttaqī-bin-Ḥisām'ud-Dīn al-Hindī, Beirut, 1981.

Karbala se Karbala tak: Reyaz Husain Jafri, Lahore n.d.

Kashfu'l-Mahjūb: Dātāganj Bakhsh, 'Alī-bin-'Othmān al-Jalābī, (Urdu tr. Muḥammad Alṭāf), Dehli, 1992.

Kashfu'z-Zunūn: Hājī Khalīfā (tr. G. Flugel), London, 1835-58.

Kashfu'l-Ghiṭā: Shaykh Ja 'far-bin-Khizr an-Najafī.

Kashfu'l-Ghumma fī Ma'rifat al-Ai'mah: Irbīlī, Ibn al-Fakhr, Bahāu'd-Dīn 'Alī-bin-'Īsā, Tehran, 1877.

Kashifu'l Bayān fī Tafsīru 'l-Qur'an: ath-Thā 'bī, Abū Isḥāq Nīshāpūrī, Raza State Library, Rampur (Mss.)

Kāshu'n-Niqāb: Saiyed 'Alī Naqī Naqavī, (Urdu tr. *Raddu'l Wahhābīyya*), Bombay, 1986.

Khaṣayṣ'l-Ḥusain: Qāzī Nūru'llāh Shūshtarī (d. 1610 AD).

Khaṭṭaṭu'sh-Shām: Muḥammad 'Alī Kurd, Lahore, 1986.

Khawāṣu'l-Ummat: Sibṭ Ibn Jauzī, Lahore n.d.

Khilāfat-o-Mulūkiyat: Abu'l 'Olā Maudūdī, Delhi, 1981.

Khuṭabāt: Abu'l 'Olā Maudūdī, Delhi, 1993.

Kitābu 'l-Buldān: al-Yāqūbī, Ibn Wāzaḥ Aḥmad (d. 897 AD) (tr. G. Wiet) London, 1892.

Kitābu 'l-Fihrist: Ibnu 'l-Nadīm, 'Abdu 'l-Faraj Muḥammad (tr. & ed. D. Dodge), Columbia, 1970.

Kitābu 'l-Ishārāt: Ibn Sīnā, Leiden 1892 (commentary by Naṣīru'd-Dīn Ṭusī-*al Shifā*), Cairo, 1950.

Kitābu'l Wuzrā: (ed. Hans V. Mazik) Leazburg, 1926.

Kitābu'l-'Ibar: Ibn Khaldūn, Abū Żayd 'Abdu'r-Raḥmān (Urdu tr. Aḥmad Ḥusain 'Othmānī), Allahabad, 1899-1930.

Kitābu'l-Aghānī: Abu'l Farah Isfahani (tr. R.E. Brunnow) Leiden, 1888.

Kitābu'l-Ansāb: al-Sam'ānī, Abū Sa'd Abdu'l-Karīm, London, 1912.

Kitābu'l-Jihād: Nasā'ī, Abū 'Abdu'r-Raḥmān-bin-Shu'ib-bin-Baḥr, Cairo, 1888.

Kitābu'l-Kāmilu'd-Dīn: Ibn Bābūya, Abū Ja'far Muḥammad-bin-'Abdu'llāh al-Qommī, Tehran, 1959.

Kitābu'l-Khirāj: Abū Yūsuf (Urdu tr.) Hyderabad n.d.

Kitābu'l-M 'ārif: Ibn Qutaybah, Abū Muḥammad 'Abdu'llāh-bin-Muslim Dīnāwarī (d. 889 AD), Cairo, 1850.

Kitābu'l-Mabsūt: as-Sarkhasī, Abū Bakr-bin-Aḥmad, Cairo, 1906.

Kitābu'l-Maqālāt wa'l Firaq: al-Qummī, Sa 'd-bin-'Abdu'llāh, Tehran, 1963.

Kitābu'r-Rijāl: al-Najāshī, Abū 'Abbās Aḥmad, Tehran n.d.

Kitābu't-Tawḥīd: Muḥammad-bin-'Abdu'l-Wahhāb, al-Najdī (Urdu tr. 'Abdul-Mālik Mujāhid), Delhi n.d.

Lababu't-Tāwīl fī Mā 'nī-at-Tanzīl: al-Khāżin, Shaykh 'Alāu 'd-Dīn 'Alī-bin-Muḥammad 'Alāu 'd-Dīn, Lahore, 1899.

Laṭā'fu'l-Ishārāt, Tafsīr Ṣūfī Kāmilu'l-Qur'anu'l-Karīm: (ed. Bisyūnī), Cairo, 1981.

Laṭā'fu'l-Ashari: Khwājah Muḥammad Ashraf Jahangīr Ṣamnānī (d. 1405 AD) Mss. Manchester.

Lawām 'au 'l 'Tanżīl wa 's-Sawāṭ 'au 't-Tāwīl: al-Ḥā'rī, Saiyed 'Alī, Lahore n.d.

Living Thoughts on Imām Ḥusain: Mushtaq Naqvi (ed.), Lucknow, 1990.

Luhūf 'Alā Qatlu'l Ṭafūf: Ibn Ṭāūs, Saiyed Razīu'd Dīn, Abu'l Qāsim, 'Alī-bin-Mūsā-bin-Ja'far-bin-Muḥammad (d.1266 AD) (Urdu tr. *Usūf:* Baqir Husain), Lucknow, 1902.

Madārijul-Nabūwat: Shaykh 'Abdu'l Ḥaqq, (Urdu tr. Abdu 'l Majīd), Kanpur n.d.

Majālisu 'l-Mominīn: al-Majlisī, Muhammad Bāqir, Tehran n.d.

Majm'au 'l-Baḥrain: Aḥmad Ḥusain 'Aẓīmābādī, Delhi n.d.

Majm'au'l-Bayān fī 'Ulūmu'l-Qur 'an: aṭ-Ṭabarsī, Fazl Ibn Ḥasan, Tehran, 1959.

Malfūzāt: Shāh 'Abdu'l Ażīż (Urdu tr.), Karachi, 1960.

Man Lā Yahzurūhu 'l-Faqīh: Ibn Bābūyā, Abu Jā'far Muḥammad-bin-'Abdu'llāh al-Qommī, Tehran, 1972.

Manāqib-i-Āl-i-Abī Ṭālib: Ibn Shahr-i-Āshob, Abu 'Abdu'llāh Muḥammad-bin-'Alī Māżidānī (d 1192 AD), Tehran 1972.

Maqālātu'l Ḥusain: al-Balāżurī, Aḥmad-bin-Yaḥyā, Tehran n.d.

Maqālātu'l Ḥusain: al-Muqrim, Tehran n.d.

Maqālātu'l Ḥusain: Ibn 'Atham, Tehran n.d.

Maqālātu'l Ḥusain: 'Oqbah-bin-Sama'n, tr. & ed. Saiyed Mujtabā Ḥasan Kāmānpurī, Lucknow, 1951.

Maqālātu'l Ḥusain: Abu'l Fidā, 'Imādu'd-Dīn, Ismā'īl, tr. & ed. Saiyed Mujtabā Ḥasan Kāmānpurī, Lahore, 1955.

Maqālātu'l Ḥusain: Al-Khawāriżmī, Abū Jā'far Muḥammad-bin-Mūsā (d. 850 AD) Istanbul, 1930.

Maqālātu'l Ḥusain: al-Yaqūbī (d. 889 AD) tr. & ed. Saiyed Mujtabā Ḥasan Kāmānpurī, Lucknow, 1951.

Maqālātu'l Ḥusain: as-Suyūtī, Jalālu'd-Dīn & Ḥusain Dayār Bakrī, tr. & ed. Saiyed Mujtabā Ḥasan Kāmānpurī, Lashore, 1955.

Maqālātu'l Ḥusain: Ibn Ḥajar, al-Haythamī, al-Makkī.

Maqālātu'l Ḥusain: Ibn Sa'd, Tehran n.d.

Maqālātu'l Ḥusain: Zaḥāq-bin-'Abdu'llāh Mashraqī, tr. & ed. Saiyed Mujtabā Ḥasan Kāmānpurī, Rawalpindi, 1954.

Maqālātu'l-Islāmiyyīn: al-Ash'arī, Abu'l Ḥasan-bin-Ismā 'īl, (ed. H. Ritter), Istanbul, 1929-30.

Maqtal-i-Sādāt: Saiyed Munīr Ḥasan Zaidī Wasṭ ī, Lahore, 1923.

Minhāju's-Sunnau 'n-Nabawiyyā: Shaykh Ibn Taymiyya, Bulāq, 1903-5.

Modern Islām in India: Smith, Wilfred Cantwell, Lahore, 1943.

Mufātīḥu'l-Ghayb, al-mushtahir bi 'l Tafsīru 'l-Kabīr: ar-Rāzī, Fakhu 'ru 'd-Dīn Abū 'Abdu'llah Muḥammad-bin-'Omar, Cairo, 1890.

Muḥarram Nāmah: Khwājah Ḥasan Niẓāmī, (d. 1955 AD) Delhi, 1953.

Muḥammd: A Biography of the Prophet: Karen Armstrong, Noida, 2008.

Munāqīb Ahlu 'l-Bayt: Ażīżu'l Ḥaqq Nadawī, Varanasi n.d.

Munāqīb Āl Abī Ṭālib: Ibn Sharāshūb, Abu 'Abdu'llāh Muḥammad, Najaf 1956.

Munāqību'l-Imāmu'l-Āẓam Abū Ḥanīfa: al-Kurdarī, Hyderabad 1903.

Muntakhabu't-Tawārīkh: Badā 'ūnī, 'Abdu 'l Qādir, (tr. G.S.A. Ranking, W.H. Lowe & T.W. Haig) Calcutta, 1864-1925.

Muqaddima-i-Tafsīr-i-Qur 'an: Saiyed 'Alī Naqī Naqavī, Lucknow, 1976.

Murūju'ż-Żahab-wa'l-M'adinu'l-Jauhar: al-Mas'ūdī, 'Alī-bin-Ḥusain, Beirut 1966, (ed. & tr. C. Babier de Meynard) Paris, 1861-77.

Musalmānon ka 'Urūj wa Żawāl: Sa'īd Aḥmad Akbarābādī, Delhi, 1947.

Mushīru'l Aḥżān: Ja'far-bin-Muḥammad, Tehran, 1900.

Mushkilu 'l-âthār: ạt-Ṭaḥāwī, Abū Ja'far Aḥmad, Hyderabad, 1968.

Mussulman Culture: Bartold, Vassily Vladimirovitch (tr. from Russian – Shāhid Suhrawardy), Calcutta, 1934.

Mutālia-i-Qur'an: Žīshān Haider Jawādī, Lucknow, 1994.

Muwaddatu'l-Qurbā: 'Alī Ḥamedānī, Mīr Saiyed, (d. 1384 AD) (Urdu tr. Sharīf Husain), Lahore n.d.

Nafas-i-Rasūl: Saiyed 'Alī Ḥaider & Saiyed Moḥammad Bāqir, Khujwa (Bihar), 1950.

Nafasul Mahmoom: Ansariyan Publications. Qum, 2005.

Nahju'l-Balāghah: Imām 'Alī-Ibn-Abī Ṭālib (compiled by Saiyed Razī Sharīf), Urdu tr. Ja 'far Ḥusain, Lucknow 1996, Eng. tr. Saiyed Moḥammad Askarī Jafery, Karachi, 1971.

Nāsikhu'l Tawārīkh: Sipahr Ḳāshānī, Tehran n.d.

Naẓariya-i-'Adālat-i-Ṣaḥābah: Aḥmad Ḥusain Yāqūb (Urdu tr, Saiyed Žīshān Ḥaidar Jawādī) Lucknow, 1996.

Nūru 'l-Abṣār fi Akhaž al-Thār: Saiyed Muḥammad Ibrāhīm, Lucknow, n.d.

On the Sociology of Islām: 'Alī Sharī 'atī, Berkeley, 1979.

Origin and Early Development of Shi'a Islām: Jafrī, S. Ḥusain, M., Beirut, 1979.

Payām-i-'Āshūrah: Saiyed 'Aṭā Ullāh Mahājarānī, Publications and Information, Tehran, 1990.

Polemics on the Origin of the Fātimid Caliph: Mamour, Princep. H., London, 1934.

Qaul-i-Sadīd: Ziyā Aḥamd Badāyūnī, Lahore 1st. Ed. n.d.

Raiḥānatu'r Rasūl: Aḥmad Fahmī, Hyderabad, 1948.

Rawā'hu'l-Qur'an: Muḥammad 'Abbās, Lucknow, 1888.

RehlaI'lul Iraq: James Buckingham, Cairo, 1981.

Rise and Fall of the Roman Empire: Gibbon, Edward: London, 1948.

Riyāzu 'l-Munẓarah fī Fazāyilu 'l-'Ashrah: Ṭabarī, Muḥibu 'd-Dīn Aḥmad, Lahore n.d.

Rūḥu'l-Ma 'ānī fī Tafsīru 'l-Qr'anu 'l-'Aẓīm wa'l Sab'āu 'l Mathanī: Ālālūsī, Abu 'l-Fazl Shihābu 'd-Dīn Saiyed Maḥmūd, Cairo, 1883.

Ṣahīfah-i-Nūr: Imām Khomeinī, Tehran n.d.

Selected Works: Karl Marx & Frederick Encels, Moscow, 1962.

Shahīdān-i-Karbala Ke Fidāī Hindū: Shāh Naẓir Hāshmī, Al-Nāṭiq, Lucknow, 1926.

Shahīd-i-Insāniyat: Saiyed 'Alī Naqī Naqavī, Lucknow Fourt Edition.

Sharhu'l Nahju'l-Balāghah: Ibn Abī Ḥadīd, 'Iżżu'd Dīn 'Adu'l Ḥāmid, Beirut, 1950

Sharhu'l-Fiqhu 'l-Akbar: 'Alī Qārī, Delhi, 1929.

Sharḥu'l-Ṭaḥāwiyā: Ibn Abī 'Iżżā al-Ḥanafī, Cairo, 1953.

Shi'a dar Islām: aṭ-Ṭabāṭabāī, Saiyed Muḥammad Ḥusain, (tr. & ed. S. Ḥossein Naṣr), London, 1975.

Shi'ite Islām, State University of New York Press, New York, 1979.

Shuhdā-i-Karbala: (Part One & Two) Saiyed 'Alī Naqī Naqavī, Lucknow.

Sifātu 's-Shi 'a wa 'l Fazāilu's-Shi 'a: Ibn Bābūya, Abū Jā 'far Muḥammad-bin-'Abdu'llāh, al-Qommī (tr. A.A. Fyzee – *A Shi'ite Creed*), Oxford, 1942.

Sīrat Rasūlu'llāh: Ibn Hishām 'Abdu'l Malik (tr. Guillaume, Alfred: *The Life of Muḥammad*), London, 1955.

Sīratu'n-Nabī: Shiblī Nu'amānī, Āẓamgarh.

Sīratu'n-Nabī: Ibn Isḥāq, Muḥammad-bin-Isḥāq-bin-Yasār (Urdu tr. Nūr Ilāhī), New Delhi, 2000.

Sirru'l Shahādatain: Shāh 'Abdu'l Ażīż Muḥaddith Dehlawī (d. 1824 AD) (tr. Urdu: *Tanwīru'l Shahādatain,* S. Kāžim Reza) Lucknow, 1969.

Siyar 'Alāmu'l-Nubalā: al-Žahabī, Muḥammad-bin-Aḥmad.

Some Aspects of Religious Politics in India: Niẓāmī, K. A., Delhi, 1974.

Summary of the Tragedy of Sayyeda Ruqayya: Booklet at Ruqayya Mosque, 2008.

Sūratīu 'l-Ikhlaṣ wa 'l-'Alaq: Ibn Sīnā (Avicenna), Abū 'Alī al-Ḥusain-bin-'Abdu'llāh, Delhi n.d.

Ṣaḥīfahu'l-Kāmilah: 'Alī-Ibnu 'l-Ḥusain, Imām Żainu 'l-Ābidīn (Urdu tr. & exegesis by Ja'far Ḥusain), Bombay n.d.

Ṣawaṭ'au'l-Ilhām: Abū Faiz Faizī, Lucknow, 1888.

Ta'wīlu'l-Mukhtalifu 'l-ÿadīth: Ibn Qutayba, Cairo, 1908

Ta'wzīḥu'l-Majīd fī Tanqīḥ Kalāmu 'llahu'l Majīd: Saiyed 'Alī, Lucknow, 1841.

Tafsīr-i-Qur'an: Saiyed 'Alī Naqī Naqavī, Srinagar, 1983-89.

Tafsīr-i-Sàfā: Moḥsin Fayz Kashānī, Tehran, 1943.

Tafsīron mein Isrāēlī Rawāyāt: Nizāmu'd-Dīn, Deoband, 1985.

Tafsīru'l-Ḥusainī: al-Wāiẓ al-Kāshifī, Ḥusain-bin-'Alī, Lucknow, 1895.

*Tafsīru'l-Jalālayn: as-*Suyūtī, Jalālu 'd-Dīn & al-Maḥallī, Jalālu'd-Dīn, Delhi, 1864.

Tafsīru'l-Qommī: al-Qummī, Abu 'l-Ḥasan 'Alī-bin-Ibrāhim, Najaf, 1966-67.

Tafsīru'l-Qur'anu'l 'Aẓīm: Ibn Kathīr, 'Imādu'd-Dīn, Abu'l Fidā Ismā'il, Cairo, 1937.

Tafsīru'l-Qur'anu'l-Karīm: Sufyān Thūrī, Abū'Abdu'llāh (ed. Imtiāż 'Alī 'Arshī), Rampur, 1965.

Tafsīru'l-Maẓharī: Thināu'llāh 'Othmanī Pānīpatī, (Urdu tr. Abu'l Dāyam) Delhi, 1961-62.

Tahžību'l-Aḥkām: Shaykhu'ṭ-Ṭā 'fa, Abū Ja'far Muḥammad-bin-Ḥasan aṭ-Ṭusī, Najaf,1959.

Tahžību'l-Tahžīb; Ibn Hajar, Shihābu'd Dīn Aḥmad-bin-'Alī, 'Asqalānī, Hyderābād, 1907.

Tahžību'l Tahžīb; Ibn Ḥajar al-'Asqalānī, Abu'l Fazl Aḥmad (d. 1448 AD) Hyderabad, 1907.

Tajdīdu-'Aḥyāi-'Dīn: Abu'l 'Olā Mū'dīdī, Delhi, 1986.

Tanwīr-i-Majālis: ed. Jafar Reza, Utraon, Allahabad, 1958.

Taqwīm Hijrī-o-Īswī: Abula'l Naṣr Muḥammad Khalidī, Delhi, 1977.

Tārīkh-i-'Āshūrah: Dr. Ibrāhīm Āyatī, Tehran n.d.

Tārīkh-i-A'imah: Saiyed 'Alī Ḥaider, Lucknow, 1998.

Tārīkh-i-Adabiyat-i-Pakistan aur Hind: Lahore, 1969-80.

Tārīkh-i-Alfī (Vol. 1): Aḥmad-bin-Naṣru 'llāh Thattawī, University Library, Bombay (Mss.)

Tārīkh-i-Dā'wat-o-'Ażīmat: an-Nadawī, Abul Ḥasan 'Alī Ḥasanī, Lucknow, 1984.

Tārīkh-i-Fātimīn-i-Misr: Žāhid 'Alī, Hyderabad n.d.

Tārīkh-i-Guẓīda: Qażwīnī, Ḥamdu'llāh-bin-Abī Bakr, (ed. Edward G. Browne). London, 1910.

Tārīkh-i-Islām: Saiyed 'Alī Naqī Naqavi, Lucknow n.d.

Tārīkh-i-Karbala wa Ḥāi'r al-Ḥusain: al-Kilidār, 'Abdu'l-Jawād, Najaf, 1967.

Tārīkh-i-Wahhābiyat: 'Alī Aṣghar Faqīhī (Urdu tr. Iqbāl Ḥyder Ḥydery) Qomm, 2006.

Tārīkhu'l-'Arab: Phillip Hitti.

Tārīkhu'l-Baghdād: al-Khaṭību'l-Baghdādī, Cairo, 1931.

Tārīkhu'l-Khmīs fī Aḥwāl'u-Nafīs: Dayār Bakrī Ḥusain Muḥammad Mālikī, Cairo, 1866.

Tārīkhu'l-Khulafah: *as*-Suyūṭī, Jalālu'd-Dīn (tr. Jarrett, H.S.), Calcutta, 1881.

Tārīkhu'r-Rusūl wa'l-Mulūk: aṭ-Ṭabarī, Ibn Jarīr Abū Ja'far, Lucknow, 1874. (*History of the Prophets and Kings,* tr & com. I. K.A. Howard. Suny Press).

Tarjima-i-Kalām-i-Ilāhī: Saiyed Farmān 'Alī, Lucknow n.d.

Tarjimānu'l-Qur'an: Āżad, Abul Kalām, New Delhi, 1996.

Taṣwīr-i-Karbala: Saiyed Āle Muḥammad Amrohvi, Delhi, 1927.

Ta'ziyeh: Ritual and Drama in Iran: Peter J. Chelkowski, New York, 1979.

Tażkiratu'l-Ḥiffāẓ: Żahabī.

The Battle of Karbala: A Marthiya of Anīs: David Matthews, New Delhi, 2003.

The Book of Certainty: Abū Bakr Sirāju'd-Dīn, London, 1952.

The Caliphate, its Rise, Decline and Fall: Muir, Sir William, London, 1891.

The Caliphate: Arnold, Sir Thomas, Oxford, 1913.

The Decline and Fall of the Roman Empire: Sir Edward Gibbon, London, 1911.

The Deoband School and the Demand for Pakistan: Fārūqī Z.H., Bombay, 1963.

The Development of Metaphysics in Persia: Muḥammad Iqbāl, Sir, (Urdu tr. *Falsafa-i-'Ajam*: Mīr Ḥasanu'd-Dīn), Ḥyderabad, 1956.

The Encyclopædia of Tamil Literature; Chennai, 1990.

The Glory of the Shi'a World: Sykes, London, 1910.

The Heart of 'Arabia: Philby H.S.J., London, 1922.

The Hidden Truth About Karbala: Ahmed A.K., Qom, 2007.

The History of Moḥammedanism and its Sects: Taylor, W. Cooke, London, 1851.

The History of the Saracens: Simon Ockley, London, 1894.

The Holy Bible: (Containing Old and New Testaments), King James Version, The Gideons International, 1978.

The Holy Qur'an: Translated by S.V. Mīr Aḥmed 'Alī, New York, 1988.

The Indian Musalmāns: W.W. Hunter, London, 1871.

The Indian Muslims: Muḥammad Mujīb, London, 1969.

The Islāmic Dynasties: Bosworth, Clifford E., Edinburgh, 1967.

The Language and Races of Dardistan: Leitner, G.W., Lohore, 1877.

The Life of Imam Zayn al-'Abidin: Bāqir Sharīf al-Qarashī, Tehran n.d.

The Miracle Play of Ḥasan and Ḥusain: Pelly, Sir L., London, 1879.

The Muslim Community of the Indo-Pakistan Subcontinent (610-1974): Qurashī, Ishteyaq Ḥusain, (Urdu tr. *Barr-i-Āẓam-i-Hind-o-Pak kī Millat-i-Islāmia*), Karachi, 1967.

The Muslim Creed: Wensinck, A.J., Cambridge, 1932.

The Reconstruction of Religious Thought in Islām: Muḥammad Iqbal, Sir, Oxford, 1934.

The Shi'a of India: John Norman Hollister, New Delhi, 1979.

The Shi'ite Religion: Donaldson, Dwright M., London, 1933.

The Social Stucture of Islām: Levy Ruben, Cambridge 1962; tr. Urdu: *Islāmī Samāj*, Mushīru'l Ḥaq, Delhi, 1987.

The Spirit of Islām: Saiyed Amīr 'Alī, New Delhi, 1997.

The Story of Philosophy: Will Durant, New York, 1955.

The Tragedy of Karbala: by Dr. Israr Aḥmad, Al-Quran, Lahore.

Umm 'ul-Kitāb: Ivanow, Vladimir (ed. & tr.), Der'Islām, 1936.

Urdu Dāerah-i-Mu'ārif-i-Islām: Punjab University, Lahore.

Usadu'l Ghābah fī Muā'rifu'l Ṣaḥābah: Ibn Athīr 'Iẑẑu'ddīn Abu'l Ḥasan 'Alī-bin-Muḥammad Jažarī, Berut.

Uṣūl-i-Fiqh aur Shah Walīu'llah: Maẓhar Baqā, Islāmabad, 1973.

Vilāyat-i-Faqīh dar Khṣūṣ-i-Ḥukūmat-i-Islāmī: Khomeinī, Rūhu'llāh, Tehrān, 1980.

Wafiyyātu'l-'Ayān wa anbā'aż-Żamān: Ibn Khallikān, Aḥmad (tr. Baron MacGuckin de Slane) Paris, 1842-71.

War and Non-violence: Gandhi, M.K., Delhi, n.d.

Wasīyatu'n Nijāt: Mullā Mubīn Firangīmahalī (d.1810 AD) (tr. Urdu: Hādī 'Alī Khān Ḥanāfī), Lucknow, 1911.

Whither Islām: Gibb, H.A.R., London, 1932.

Žākir, Iraq Radio, Through Internet.

Yake Aż Shākh-i-Thamarbār: Saiyed Khairāt Ḥasan, Allahabad, 2011.

Yanābiyau'l-Muwaddah: Shaykh Sulaymān Ḥusainī Balkhī (Urdu tr. Malik Muḥammad Sharīf), Lucknow, 2002.

Żakhayiru'l-'Uqbā: Ṭabarī Muḥību'd-Dīn Aḥmad, Lahore n.d.

Żainab-i-Kubrā: Saiyed Abul Qāsim Dibājī, Karachi n.d.

Żiyād-bin-Abīh: K.A. Fāriq, New Delhi, 1968.

Żiyārat al-Naḥiya al-Muqaddasah (tr. Vaḥīd Majd), First Edition, 2004.

Index